TEXAS MOTIONS IN LIMINE

Julie Kay Baker, Esq.

and

David N. Finley, Esq.

Copyright © 2021 Full Court Press, an imprint of Fastcase, Inc.

All rights reserved.

No part of this book may be reproduced in any form—by microfilm, xerography, or otherwise—or incorporated into any information retrieval system without the written permission of the copyright owner. For customer support, please contact Fastcase, Inc., 711 D St. NW, Suite 200, Washington, D.C. 20004, 202.999.4777 (phone), 202.521.3462 (fax), or email customer service at support@fastcase.com.

A Full Court Press, Fastcase, Inc., Publication.

Printed and bound in the United States of America.

10 9 8 7 6 5 4 3 2 1

ISBN (print): 978-1-949884-51-7

The front cover features a map of Texas courtesy of https://freevectormaps.com/united-states/texas/US-TX-EPS-01-1001?ref=atr

Summary of Contents

Contents	vii
About the Authors	xxix
Chapter 1. Motions in Limine	1
Chapter 2. Prejudicial Evidence	19
Chapter 3. Irrelevant Evidence	65
Chapter 4. Writings and Physical Evidence	107
Chapter 5. Tests and Scientific Evidence	179
Chapter 6. Discovery Motions	223
Chapter 7. Character Evidence	275
Chapter 8. Witness Evidence	323
Chapter 9. Trial Presentation	421
Chapter 10. Personal Injury Motions	457

Contents

About the Authors xxix

Chapter 1. Motions in Limine 1

I. Motion in Limine Use and Procedure 1
    A. Description and Purpose of Motion 1
        1. Generally 1
        2. Authority for Motion 2
            a. Texas Rule of Evidence 402 2
            b. Texas Rule of Evidence 403 3
            c. Texas Rule of Evidence 103 3
            d. Texas Rule of Evidence 104 4
            e. Texas Rule of Civil Procedure 166 4
        3. Typical Use of Motion 5
            a. Limitations on Use 5
            b. Preservation of Objections 6
        4. Timing of Motion 7
        5. Scope of Motion 7
        6. Procedural Requirements 8
    B. Drafting Suggestions 8
        1. Overview 8
        2. File Motion Supported by Facts 9
        3. Be Succinct 9
        4. Consider Calling the Motion "Objections and Motion to Exclude Evidence" 9
    C. Opposition Considerations 9
        1. Preserving Error 9
        2. Offer of Proof and Bill of Exception 10
II. Sample Forms 13
    A. Sample in Limine Motion and Brief 14
    B. Sample in Limine Order 17

Chapter 2. Prejudicial Evidence — 19

I. Motion Authorities — 20
  A. Motion to Exclude Prejudicial Evidence — 20
    1. Suggested Motion Text — 20
    2. Motion Summary — 20
      a. Rule 403 Factors to Consider — 22
    3. Supporting Authorities — 24
    4. Opposing Authorities — 28
      a. Harmless Error — 32
  B. Motion to Exclude Evidence That Will Waste Court's Time — 34
    1. Suggested Motion Text — 34
    2. Motion Summary — 35
    3. Supporting Authorities — 35
    4. Opposing Authorities — 36
  C. Motion to Exclude Confusing or Misleading Evidence — 37
    1. Suggested Motion Text — 37
    2. Motion Summary — 37
    3. Supporting Authorities — 38
    4. Opposing Authorities — 40
  D. Motion to Exclude Evidence Used to Create an Emotional Bias — 40
    1. Suggested Motion Text — 40
    2. Motion Summary — 41
    3. Supporting Authorities — 41
      a. Exclusion of Evidence Intended to Inflame Jurors' Emotions — 42
    4. Opposing Authorities — 43
  E. Motion to Exclude or Limit Cumulative Evidence — 45
    1. Suggested Motion Text — 45
    2. Motion Summary — 45
    3. Supporting Authorities — 46
      a. Generally — 47
      b. Articles and Letters — 48
      c. Number of Witnesses — 49
      d. Photographs — 49
      e. Reports — 50
      f. Witness Testimony — 50
      g. Expert Testimony — 51
      h. Videotape Evidence — 51
      i. Deposition Testimony — 51

			j. Business Records	52
			k. Wills	52
		4.	Opposing Authorities	52
			a. Articles	52
			b. Letters	53
			c. Credentials	53
			d. Number of Witnesses	53
			e. Photographs	53
			f. Reports	54
			g. Expert Testimony	54
			h. Videotape Evidence	55
			i. Books and Records	55
II.	Sample Motions			56
	A.	Motion to Exclude Confusing Evidence		56
	B.	Motion to Exclude Cumulative Evidence		57
	C.	Motion to Exclude Prejudicial Evidence		59
	D.	Opposition to Motion to Exclude Prejudicial Evidence		62

Chapter 3. Irrelevant Evidence — 65

I.	Motion Authorities			66
	A.	Motion to Exclude Irrelevant Evidence		66
		1.	Suggested Motion Text	66
		2.	Motion Summary	66
		3.	Supporting Authorities	68
			a. Matters Not in Dispute	73
			b. Outside Pleadings	74
			c. Prejudicial	75
			d. Speculative Evidence	77
			e. Compromise, Offers to Compromise, and Plea Discussions	80
			f. Parties' Wealth or Poverty	81
			g. Collateral Benefits	81
			h. Out-of-Court Experiments	83
			i. Similar Claims	84
			j. Number of Friends or Family	85
			k. Real Estate Value or Appraisal	86
			l. Criminal Acquittal in Subsequent Civil Action	87
			m. Employment Policies	87

			n.	Specific Exclusions	87
		4.		Opposing Authorities	87
			a.	Evidence to Offer Additional Explanation	90
			b.	Parties' Wealth or Poverty	92
			c.	Similar Transactions, Claims, or Occurrences	92
			d.	Prior Convictions	95
			e.	Remoteness or Lapse of Time	95
			f.	Matters Not in Dispute	96
			g.	Circumstantial Evidence	96
			h.	Background Evidence	97
			i.	Real Estate Value or Appraisal	98
	B.	Motion to Exclude Evidence of Matters Not in Controversy			98
		1.		Suggested Motion Text	98
		2.		Motion Summary	99
		3.		Supporting Authorities	99
			a.	Admitted or Uncontroverted Matters	99
			b.	Collateral Issues	99
			c.	Unpleaded Issues	100
		4.		Opposing Authorities	101
			a.	Collateral Issues	101
			b.	Unpleaded Issues	101
			c.	Where Relevant to Other Issues	102
			d.	Matters Not in Dispute	102
			e.	Evidence to Provide Additional Explanation	102
			f.	Pleaded Issues	103
II.	Sample Motions				103
	A.	Motion to Exclude Irrelevant Evidence			103
	B.	Motion to Exclude Evidence of Physical Conditions Not at Issue			105

Chapter 4. Writings and Physical Evidence — 107

I.	Motion Authorities				109
	A.	Motion to Exclude Evidence Lacking Foundation			109
		1.		Suggested Motion Text	109
		2.		Motion Summary	110
		3.		Supporting Authorities, Generally	110
			a.	Determination of Admissibility Outside Presence of Jury	111
			b.	Preliminary Facts—Inadmissibility of Evidence	111

			c.	Photographs	112
			d.	Tape Recordings	113
			e.	Tests and Experiments	113
			f.	Videotapes and Motion Pictures	114
			g.	Writings	115
			h.	Public Records or Reports	116
			i.	Ancient Documents or Data Compilations	117
		4.	\multicolumn{2}{l}{Opposing Authorities, Generally}	117
			a.	Photographs	118
			b.	Physical Evidence	119
			c.	Tests and Experiments	121
			d.	Tape Recordings	121
			e.	Videotapes and Motion Pictures	122
			f.	Writings	123
			g.	Conditional Admissibility	125
	B.	\multicolumn{3}{l}{Motion to Exclude Writings, Generally}	126
		1.	\multicolumn{2}{l}{Suggested Motion Text}	126
		2.	\multicolumn{2}{l}{Motion Summary}	126
		3.	\multicolumn{2}{l}{Supporting Authorities—"Writing" Defined}	126
			a.	Exclusion, Generally	127
			b.	Unauthenticated Writings	127
				i. Public Records or Reports	128
				ii. Documents or Data Collections	128
				iii. Exclusion of Unauthenticated Writings	129
			c.	Irrelevant Evidence	129
			d.	Inadmissible Hearsay	130
				i. Examples of Inadmissible Written Hearsay	131
			e.	Inadmissible Secondary Evidence	132
		4.	\multicolumn{2}{l}{Opposing Authorities, Generally}	132
			a.	Authentication	133
			b.	Hearsay Exceptions and Nonhearsay, Generally	135
				i. Examples of Admissible Written Hearsay	137
			c.	Secondary Evidence	138
	C.	\multicolumn{3}{l}{Motion to Exclude Gruesome or Inflammatory Photographs}	139
		1.	\multicolumn{2}{l}{Suggested Motion Text}	139
		2.	\multicolumn{2}{l}{Motion Summary}	139
		3.	\multicolumn{2}{l}{Supporting Authorities, Generally}	139
			a.	Gruesome or Inflammatory Photographs	140
			b.	Purpose to Inflame Jurors' Emotions	141

			c.	Other Grounds	142
		4.	Opposing Authorities		142
			a.	Examples of Admissible Photographs	145
	D.	Motion to Exclude Prejudicial Film or Videotapes			145
		1.	Suggested Motion Text		145
		2.	Motion Summary		145
		3.	Supporting Authorities, Generally		146
			a.	Other Grounds	147
		4.	Opposing Authorities, Generally		147
			a.	Relevance	148
	E.	Motion to Exclude Published Articles			148
		1.	Suggested Motion Text		148
		2.	Motion Summary		148
		3.	Supporting Authorities		148
			a.	Prejudicial	149
			b.	Other Grounds	149
		4.	Opposing Authorities, Generally		149
			a.	Cumulative	150
			b.	No Prejudice	150
			c.	Where Relevant to Other Issues	150
			d.	Not Hearsay	150
	F.	Motion to Exclude Accident Reports			151
		1.	Suggested Motion Text		151
		2.	Motion Summary		151
		3.	Supporting Authorities		151
			a.	Generally	151
			b.	Privilege	152
			c.	Hearsay	152
			d.	Diagrams Made at the Scene and Computer Animations	152
			e.	Other Grounds	153
		4.	Opposing Authorities		153
			a.	Statements Made to Reporting Officers	153
			b.	Public Records and Reports	154
			c.	Diagrams Made at the Scene and Computer Animations	154
	G.	Motion to Exclude Letters, Emails, or Text Messages			155
		1.	Suggested Motion Text		155
		2.	Motion Summary		155
		3.	Supporting Authorities		155
			a.	Hearsay	156

			b.	Irrelevant	156
			c.	Other Grounds	157
		4.	Opposing Authorities		157
			a.	Relevancy	158
			b.	Hearsay	159
			c.	Not Hearsay	159
	H.	Motion to Exclude Maps, Models, and Charts			159
		1.	Suggested Motion Text		159
		2.	Motion Summary		160
		3.	Supporting Authorities, Generally		160
			a.	Other Grounds	160
		4.	Opposing Authorities		160
			a.	Illustrative or Demonstrative Models	161
			b.	Illustrative or Demonstrative Maps	161
			c.	Illustrative or Demonstrative Charts	161
			d.	Where Accuracy Is Not Disputed	161
	I.	Motion to Exclude Improper Medical Records, Reports, or Bills			162
		1.	Suggested Motion Text		162
		2.	Motion Summary		162
		3.	Supporting Authorities, Generally		163
			a.	Improper Hearsay Evidence	163
			b.	Medical Opinions of Others—Lack of Personal Knowledge	164
			c.	Patient Medical History	164
				i. Hearsay	165
			d.	Medical Billing—Lack of Foundation	165
			e.	Other Grounds	165
		4.	Opposing Authorities		165
			a.	Medical Opinions of Others—Opinions Used in Diagnosis or Treatment	166
			b.	Business Record Hearsay Exception	166
			c.	Patient History—Observation of Physician	167
			d.	Patient History—Pertinent to Medical Diagnosis	167
			e.	Medical Billing Records—Reasonableness of Charges	169
II.	Sample Motions				170
	A.	Motion to Exclude Gruesome Photographs			170
	B.	Motion to Exclude Written Letter			172
	C.	Motion to Exclude Improper Medical Records			175

Chapter 5. Tests and Scientific Evidence — 179

I. Motion Authorities — 180
   A. Motion to Exclude Tests, Experiments, and Related Testimony — 180
      1. Suggested Motion Text — 180
      2. Motion Summary — 180
      3. Supporting Authorities—Expert Not Qualified — 181
         a. Not Generally Accepted, Civil Cases — 183
         b. Not Generally Accepted—Kelly Decision in Criminal Cases — 185
         c. Not Made Under Substantially Similar Conditions — 185
         d. Not Reliable — 186
         e. Scientific Procedures Not Proper — 189
         f. Speculative or Conjectural — 190
         g. Too Time-Consuming/Collateral Issues/Speculative — 193
         h. Expert Testimony Not Needed — 193
         i. Not Relevant — 194
      4. Opposing Authorities — 195
         a. Court's Discretion — 196
         b. General Acceptance—Published Precedent — 197
            i. Level of Acceptance in Scientific Community — 197
            ii. Judicial Notice — 197
         c. Similar Conditions Requirement — 197
         d. Reliability — 197
         e. Cumulative — 198
         f. Weight vs. Admissibility — 199
   B. Motion to Exclude Junk Science and Related Evidence — 199
      1. Suggested Motion Text — 199
      2. Motion Summary — 199
      3. Supporting Authorities — 200
         a. Hedonic Damages Evidence — 201
         b. "Truth Serum" Evidence — 201
         c. Polygraph Evidence — 201
            i. Per Se Inadmissibility — 202
            ii. Stipulation of the Parties — 202
            iii. Refusal to Take Polygraph — 203
         d. Battered Spouse Syndrome — 203
         e. Abused Child Characteristics — 203
         f. Hypnosis Evidence — 203
         g. Psychological Profiling — 204

				h.	Accident Reconstruction Evidence	204
				i.	Biomechanic Evidence	204
				j.	Statistical Evidence—Exclusion of Confusing Evidence	205
					i. Disapproved Statistical Evidence	205
					ii. Statistical Significance Requirements	206
					iii. Statistics in Products Liability and Negligence Cases	206
					iv. Statistics in Employment Discrimination Cases	207
			4.	Opposing Authorities—Approved Tests		207
				a.	Hedonic Damages	207
				b.	Polygraph Evidence	208
					i. Stipulation of Parties	208
				c.	Battered Spouse Syndrome	209
				d.	Abused Child Characteristics	209
				e.	Hypnosis Evidence	210
				f.	Accident Reconstruction and Biomechanics	210
				g.	Statistics Evidence	211
					i. Where Relevant	211
				h.	Evidence That Is Not "Novel"	211
II.	Sample Motions					212
	A.	Motion to Exclude Evidence of Statistical Analysis				212
	B.	Motion to Exclude Evidence of Hypnosis				214
	C.	Motion to Exclude Expert Testimony				217

Chapter 6. Discovery Motions   223

I.	Motion Authorities					224
	A.	Motion for Evidentiary Sanctions				224
		1.	Suggested Motion Text			224
		2.	Motion Summary			225
		3.	Supporting Authorities			226
			a.	Misuse of Discovery Process		227
				i. Evidence Sanctions		229
				ii. Issue Sanctions		231
				iii. "Death Penalty" Sanctions (Terminating Sanctions)		231
			b.	When Prior Order Is Unnecessary		233
			c.	Monetary Sanctions		234
			d.	Depositions		234
				i. Evidentiary Sanctions		235
				ii. Monetary Sanctions		236

			iii.	"Death Penalty" Sanctions	236
		e.	Interrogatories		236
			i.	Evidentiary Sanctions	237
			ii.	Monetary Sanctions	238
			iii.	"Death Penalty" Sanctions	238
		f.	Production Requests		238
			i.	Evidentiary Sanctions	240
			ii.	Monetary Sanctions	241
			iii.	"Death Penalty" Sanctions	241
		g.	Mental and Physical Examinations		241
			i.	"Death Penalty" Cases	242
		h.	Requests for Admission		242
			i.	Deeming Matters Admitted for Lack of Response	243
			ii.	"Death Penalty" Sanctions	244
		i.	Other Grounds		244
	4.	Opposing Authorities			244
		a.	"Death Penalty" Sanctions		245
		b.	Interrogatories		247
		c.	Matters Deemed Admitted		247
		d.	Depositions		248
		e.	Production Requests		248
B.	Motion to Exclude Conclusively Established Matters				251
	1.	Suggested Motion Text			251
	2.	Motion Summary			251
	3.	Supporting Authorities			251
		a.	Purpose of Discovery		251
	4.	Opposing Authorities			252
C.	Motion to Exclude Evidence of Claims Denied in Discovery				253
	1.	Suggested Motion Text			253
	2.	Motion Summary			254
	3.	Supporting Authorities			254
		a.	Prejudicial Evidence—No Need to Show Unfair Surprise		254
			i.	Unfair Surprise	254
		b.	Where Privilege Raised in Discovery		256
		c.	Matters Not in Dispute		256
		d.	Other Grounds		256
	4.	Opposing Authorities			256
D.	Motion Regarding Expert Declarations and Expert Depositions				257
	1.	Suggested Motion Text			257

				2.	Motion Summary	257
				3.	Supporting Authorities	258
					a. Time for Disclosure of Expert Information	259
					b. Evidentiary Sanctions	260
					c. Deficient Declaration	260
					d. Undisclosed Witness	260
					e. Opinions Not Referenced in Discovery	261
				4.	Opposing Authorities	261
					a. Continuance to Depose Expert	262
					b. No Unfair Surprise	262
					c. Minor Change in Testimony	262
					d. Opportunity to Redepose Experts	263
II.	Sample Motions					263
	A.	Motion to Exclude Evidence of Claim Denied During Discovery				263
	B.	Opposition to Defendant's Motion to Limit Plaintiff's Expert's Opinions				266
	C.	Motion to Exclude Evidence of Medical Bills for Services Obtained After [Date]				270

Chapter 7. Character Evidence — 275

I.	Motion Authorities					276
	A.	Overview of Character Evidence				276
		1.	Admissible Character Evidence			276
		2.	Character Evidence Subject to Exclusion			277
		3.	Evidence Rule Limitations in Criminal Cases			277
	B.	Motion to Exclude Character Evidence Used for Impeachment				277
		1.	Suggested Motion Text			277
		2.	Motion Summary			278
		3.	Supporting Authorities			278
			a. Exclusion of Improper Impeachment Evidence			278
				i.	Alcohol Consumption	281
				ii.	Arrests or Misdemeanor Convictions	282
				iii.	Drug Use	283
				iv.	Felony Convictions	283
				v.	Fraudulent Acts	284
				vi.	Good Character of Witness	285
				vii.	Religious Belief	285
				viii.	Sexual Preference or Behavior	286
			b. Other Grounds			286

			4.	Opposing Authorities	286
				a. Witness Perceptions	288
				b. Impeachment	289
				i. Balancing Test	293
				ii. Identity	294
				iii. Rebuttal	295
				iv. Witness Veracity/Moral Turpitude	296
				v. Context Evidence	297
				vi. Clarify False Impression	298
		C.	Motion to Exclude Character Evidence Used to Prove Conduct		299
			1.	Suggested Motion Text	299
			2.	Motion Summary	299
			3.	Supporting Authorities	299
				a. Care or Skill in Negligence Cases	302
				b. Crimes Evidence	302
				c. Other grounds	303
			4.	Opposing Authorities	303
				a. Relevant to Material Issue	303
				b. Witness Impeachment	307
				c. Trait at Issue	308
				d. Permitted by Statute	309
		D.	Motion to Exclude Evidence of Prior Felony Conviction		311
			1.	Suggested Motion Text	311
			2.	Motion Summary	311
			3.	Supporting Authorities	311
				a. Balancing Prejudicial Effect of Felony Evidence	313
				b. Disposition to Commit Crime	314
				c. Must Reflect on Credibility	314
				d. Exclusion of Improper Character Evidence	314
				e. Other Grounds	315
			4.	Opposing Authorities	315
				a. Texas Code of Criminal Procedure Art. 38.37	315
				b. Moral Turpitude	316
II.	Sample Motions				316
	A.	Motion to Exclude Evidence of Alcohol Use of Witness			316
	B.	Opposition to Motion to Exclude Inflammatory Evidence			319

Chapter 8. Witness Evidence — 323

I.	Motion Authorities			325
	A.	Motion to Exclude Improper Expert Opinion		325
		1. Suggested Motion Text		325
		2. Motion Summary		326
		3. Supporting Authorities		326
			a. Not Reliable	330
			b. Hypothetical Questions	335
			c. Inadmissible Hearsay	335
			i. Opinions of Others	335
			ii. Statements of Others	335
			iii. Treatises, Documents, and Texts	336
			d. Legal Questions	336
			i. Compare: Ultimate Issues	337
			e. Matters of Common Experience	337
			f. Not Reasonably Relied on by Experts	338
			g. Not Perceived or Personally Known	338
			h. Speculation or Conjecture	339
			i. Usurping Jury Function	342
			j. Irrelevant Matters	342
			k. Conclusory Testimony	343
			l. Burden of Proof	345
			m. Other Grounds	346
		4. Opposing Authorities		347
			a. Hearsay	348
			i. Statements of Others	348
			ii. Treatises, Documents, and Texts	349
			b. Hypothetical Questions	349
			c. Legal Questions vs. Ultimate Issues	349
	B.	Motion to Exclude Testimony of Nonqualified Expert		350
		1. Suggested Motion Text		350
		2. Motion Summary		350
		3. Supporting Authorities		351
			a. Examples	354
			b. Qualification of Experts in Health Care Liability Cases	354
			i. Examples	358
			c. Other Grounds	358

		4.	Opposing Authorities	359
			a. Health Care Liability Cases	360
	C.	Motion to Exclude Opinion of Nonexpert		362
		1.	Suggested Motion Text	362
		2.	Motion Summary	362
		3.	Supporting Authorities	363
			a. Lack of Personal Knowledge	363
			b. Legal Opinions	364
			c. Not Based on Perceptions of Witness	365
			d. Not Helpful to Jury	366
			e. Speculative or Conjectural	366
			f. Other Grounds	367
		4.	Opposing Authorities	367
			a. Sanity/Mental Condition or Capacity	368
			b. Health	369
			c. Age, Size, Quality	369
			d. Damages	369
			e. Personal Knowledge	371
			f. Causation	372
			g. Hearsay	372
	D.	Motion to Exclude Testimony of Incompetent Witness		373
		1.	Suggested Motion Text	373
		2.	Motion Summary	373
		3.	Supporting Authorities	373
			a. Inability to Express or Tell Truth	374
			i. Children	374
			b. Lack of Mental Competence/Insanity	375
			c. Lack of Personal Knowledge of Subject Matter	376
			d. Other Grounds	377
		4.	Opposing Authorities	377
			a. Children	378
			b. Mental Competence/Insanity	379
			c. Dead Man's Rule	380
	E.	Motion to Exclude Testimony of Judge, Arbitrator, Mediator, or Juror		380
		1.	Suggested Motion Text	380
		2.	Motion Summary	380
		3.	Supporting Authorities—Judges	381
			a. Arbitrators	382
			b. Jurors	382

	4.	Opposing Authorities—Judges		384
		a.	Arbitrators	384
		b.	Jurors	385
F.	Motion to Exclude Witness From Courtroom Prior to Testifying			386
	1.	Suggested Motion Text		386
	2.	Motion Summary		386
	3.	Supporting Authorities		386
	4.	Opposing Authorities		388
		a.	Cannot Exclude a Party	389
		b.	Exclusion of Testimony Is Improper	390
		c.	Welfare of a Child	390
G.	Motion to Exclude Comment on Exercise of Privilege Not to Testify			391
	1.	Suggested Motion Text		391
	2.	Motion Summary		391
	3.	Supporting Authorities		391
	4.	Opposing Authorities		392
		a.	Civil Consequences of Silence	394
		b.	Harmless Error	395
H.	Motion to Exclude Evidence of Failure to Call Witness			395
	1.	Suggested Motion Text		395
	2.	Motion Summary		395
	3.	Supporting Authorities		396
		a.	Where Witness Was Equally Available to Both Parties	396
		b.	Where Comment Would Invite Speculation	396
		c.	Where Witness Was Not Available	396
		d.	Other Grounds	397
	4.	Opposing Authorities		397
		a.	Failure to Call Material Witness	398
I.	Motion to Exclude Hearsay Evidence			398
	1.	Suggested Motion Text		398
	2.	Motion Summary		399
	3.	Supporting Authorities		399
		a.	Purpose of Rule	401
		b.	Written Hearsay	401
	4.	Opposing Authorities		402
		a.	Purpose of Exceptions to the Hearsay Rule	409
		b.	Nonhearsay Evidence	409
		c.	Nonassertive Conduct	411
		d.	Multiple Hearsay	412

			e. Hearsay to Impeach Credibility or Rehabilitate Witness	412
II.	Sample Motions			413
	A.	Motion to Exclude Speculative Expert Opinion		413
	B.	Motion to Exclude Reference to Failure to Call Witness		415
	C.	Motion to Exclude Testimony and Opinions of Medical Doctor		418

Chapter 9. Trial Presentation — 421

I.	Motion Authorities				422
	A.	Motion to Exclude Improper Voir Dire			422
		1.	Suggested Motion Text		422
		2.	Motion Summary		423
		3.	Supporting Authorities		423
			a.	Preconditioning	425
				i. Preconditioning on Issue of Amount of Damages	425
			b.	Educating Jury on the Law	426
			c.	Insurance References	426
			d.	Improper Commitment to a Position	426
			e.	References to "Lawsuit Crisis"	428
			f.	Other Statutory Limitations on Voir Dire	428
		4.	Opposing Authorities		428
			a.	Constitutional Considerations	430
			b.	Court's Discretion	431
			c.	References to Insurance	432
	B.	Motion to Exclude Improper Argument in Opening Statement			432
		1.	Suggested Motion Text		432
		2.	Motion Summary		432
		3.	Supporting Authorities		432
			a.	Other Grounds	433
		4.	Opposing Authorities		433
	C.	Motion to Exclude Premature Rebuttal of Affirmative Defenses			434
		1.	Suggested Motion Text		434
		2.	Motion Summary		434
		3.	Supporting Authorities		434
		4.	Opposing Authorities		435
	D.	Motion to Exclude Reference to Lost or Destroyed Evidence			436
		1.	Suggested Motion Text		436
		2.	Motion Summary		436
		3.	Supporting Authorities		436

			a. Accidental Destruction of Evidence	437
			b. Intentional Destruction or Suppression of Evidence	440
			c. Negative Presumption	441
			d. Other Grounds	442
		4.	Opposing Authorities	442
	E.	Motion to Exclude Arbitration Evidence and Findings		444
		1.	Suggested Motion Text	444
		2.	Motion Summary	444
		3.	Supporting Authorities	444
			a. Other Grounds	445
		4.	Opposing Authorities	445
	F.	Motion to Exclude Evidence of Damages in Bifurcated Trial		447
		1.	Suggested Motion Text	447
		2.	Motion Summary	447
		3.	Supporting Authorities	447
			a. Other Grounds	448
		4.	Opposing Authorities	449
	G.	Motion to Preclude "Golden Rule" Argument		449
		1.	Suggested Motion Text	449
		2.	Motion Summary	449
		3.	Supporting Authorities	450
			a. Other Grounds	450
		4.	Opposing Authorities	450
	H.	Motion to Exclude Improper Terminology		450
		1.	Suggested Motion Text	450
		2.	Motion Summary	451
		3.	Supporting Authorities	451
			a. Exclusion of Ultimate Issue Evidence	452
			i. General Admissibility of Ultimate Issue Opinions	453
			b. Usurping Jury Function	453
		4.	Opposing Authorities	453
II.	Sample Motions			455
	A.	Motion to Exclude Reference to Lost or Destroyed Evidence		455

Chapter 10. Personal Injury Motions   457

I.	Motion Authorities		460
	A.	Motion to Exclude Evidence of Collateral Source Payments	460
		1. Suggested Motion Text	460

xxiv CONTENTS

	2.	Motion Summary		461
	3.	Supporting Authorities		461
		a.	Gratuitous Payments	462
		b.	Medical or Liability Policy Payments	463
		c.	Disability and Other Payments	463
		d.	Workers' Compensation Payments	464
		e.	Wage Payments	464
		f.	Other Grounds	464
	4.	Opposing Authorities		464
		a.	Not Wholly Independent Source	465
		b.	Relevant to Issues in Case	465
		c.	Impeachment	465
B.	Motion to Exclude Evidence of Liability Insurance			466
	1.	Suggested Motion Text		466
	2.	Motion Summary		466
	3.	Supporting Authorities		466
		a.	Evidence of Defendant's Lack of Insurance	467
		b.	Irrelevant	467
		c.	Other Grounds	467
	4.	Opposing Authorities		467
		a.	Where Relevant to Issues or Otherwise Admissible	468
		b.	Incidental Reference to Insurance	468
		c.	Nonprejudicial References to Insurance	468
		d.	Admissions	469
		e.	To Prove Ownership or Employment	469
C.	Motion to Exclude Settlement Evidence			469
	1.	Suggested Motion Text		469
	2.	Motion Summary		469
	3.	Supporting Authorities		469
		a.	Prior Settlements	470
		b.	Settlement Negotiations	470
		c.	Settlement With Codefendants	471
		d.	Where Offer Made Before Litigation	471
		e.	Other Grounds	471
	4.	Opposing Authorities		471
		a.	Bias or Prejudice	472
		b.	Impeachment	473
		c.	Settlement With Codefendant	473

			d.	State of Mind	473
D.	Motion to Exclude Evidence of Other Accidents				474
	1.	Suggested Motion Text			474
	2.	Motion Summary			474
	3.	Supporting Authorities			474
		a.	Prior Accident Evidence Used to Show Negligence		474
		b.	Lack of Similarity—Dangerous Condition/Defective Products		475
		c.	Irrelevant		476
		d.	Exclusion of Subsequent Accident Evidence		476
		e.	Other Grounds		476
	4.	Opposing Authorities			476
		a.	Similarity: Dangerous Condition/Defective Products		477
		b.	Notice		478
		c.	Evidence of Subsequent Accidents		478
E.	Motion to Exclude Evidence of Subsequent Repairs				478
	1.	Suggested Motion Text			478
	2.	Motion Summary			479
	3.	Supporting Authorities			479
		a.	Other Grounds		480
	4.	Opposing Authorities			480
		a.	Relevant to Issues		480
		b.	Strict Products Liability		481
F.	Motion to Exclude Evidence of Statute Violation				481
	1.	Suggested Motion Text			481
	2.	Motion Summary			482
	3.	Supporting Authorities			482
		a.	Not Proximate Cause		482
		b.	Not Negligence Per Se		482
		c.	Other Grounds		483
	4.	Opposing Authorities			483
		a.	Proximate Cause		483
			i.	Negligence Per Se	483
G.	Motion to Exclude Evidence of Driver's License Suspension				485
	1.	Suggested Motion Text			485
	2.	Motion Summary			485
	3.	Supporting Authorities			485
		a.	Other Grounds		486
	4.	Opposing Authorities			486

H.		Motion to Exclude Evidence of Failure to Wear Seatbelt	486
	1.	Suggested Motion Text	486
	2.	Motion Summary	486
	3.	Supporting Authorities	486
		a. Other Grounds	487
	4.	Opposing Authorities	487
		a. Where Use Would Have Reduced Injuries	487
		b. Mandatory Seatbelt Laws	487
I.		Motion to Exclude Evidence of Alcohol Consumption	489
	1.	Suggested Motion Text	489
	2.	Motion Summary	489
	3.	Supporting Authorities	489
		a. Other Grounds	489
	4.	Opposing Authorities	490
		a. Witness Perceptions	490
J.		Motion to Exclude Evidence of Prior DWI	490
	1.	Suggested Motion Text	490
	2.	Motion Summary	490
	3.	Supporting Authorities	491
		a. Exclusion of Arrests and Misdemeanor Convictions	492
		b. Exclusion of Convictions Where No Bearing on Credibility	492
		c. Where Probative Value Outweighed by Risk of Undue Prejudice	493
		d. Exclusion of DWI Evidence Where Used to Prove Improper Conduct	493
		e. Other Grounds	493
	4.	Opposing Authorities	494
		a. Use of Felony Convictions Expressly Allowed for Impeachment	494
		i. DWI as a Felony	494
		b. Relevant to Issues	495
K.		Motion to Exclude Evidence of Party's Health or Injuries Where Not at Issue	496
	1.	Suggested Motion Text	496
	2.	Motion Summary	496
	3.	Supporting Authorities	497
		a. Other Grounds	497
	4.	Opposing Authorities	497

L.	Motion to Exclude Accident Reconstruction Evidence		497
	1. Suggested Motion Text		497
	2. Motion Summary		498
	3. Supporting Authorities		498
		a. Improper Foundation or Qualification	498
		b. Vehicle Speed Determinations	499
	4. Opposing Authorities		499
		a. Competent Facts/Foundation	500
		b. Vehicle Speed	500
		c. Skid Mark Analysis	501
		d. Stopping Distances	501
		e. Point of Impact	501
		f. Reaction Time	501
		g. Safer Alternative Design	502
		h. Cases Where Biomechanics Admitted	502
M.	Motion to Exclude Evidence of Party's Financial Status		502
	1. Suggested Motion Text		502
	2. Motion Summary		502
	3. Supporting Authorities		503
		a. Punitive Damages Cases	503
		b. Other Grounds	503
	4. Opposing Authorities		504
		a. Necessary to Support Punitive Damages Claim	504
		b. Invited Error	505
N.	Motion to Exclude Tax Evidence		505
	1. Suggested Motion Text		505
	2. Motion Summary		505
	3. Supporting Authorities		505
		a. Improper Appeal to Jurors as Taxpayers	506
		b. Other Grounds	506
	4. Opposing Authorities		506
O.	Motion to Exclude Liability Evidence (Liability Not at Issue)		506
	1. Suggested Motion Text		506
	2. Motion Summary		507
	3. Supporting Authorities		507
		a. Other Grounds	507
	4. Opposing Authorities		508
P.	Motion to Exclude Improper Damage Evidence		508
	1. Suggested Motion Text		508

		2.	Motion Summary	508
		3.	Supporting Authorities	509
			a. Undisputed Matters	509
			b. Surprise Claims	509
			c. Amounts in Excess of Stated Damages	510
			d. Speculative Evidence	511
			i. Exclusion of Evidence of Speculative Damages	512
			e. Statutory Limitations on Damages	512
		4.	Opposing Authorities	514
			a. Reasonable Estimate of Damages	514
II.	Sample Motions			515
	A.	Motion to Exclude Evidence of Collateral Source Payments		515
	B.	Motion to Exclude Evidence of Defendant's Liability		517
	C.	Motion to Exclude Evidence of Computerized Valuations of Plaintiff's Business		520
	D.	Motion to Exclude Surveillance Video		523
	E.	Opposition to Motion for Destroyed or Missing Evidence Instruction		525

About the Authors

Julie Kay Baker, Esq., is an attorney licensed by the State Bar of Texas. She attended Texas Tech University School of Law, where she was an associate editor of the Texas Tech Law Review. She served as Briefing Attorney on the Court of Appeals for the Fifth District of Texas at Dallas, and practiced law in the Dallas area. She currently works as a legal consultant and author. In addition to *Texas Motions in Limine*, Ms. Baker has authored, co-authored, and/or edited a number of legal publications in Texas and throughout the United States by Thomson Reuters (West), including *Texas Summary Judgment and Related Termination Motions*, *Texas DWI Handbook* (West), and several others.

David N. Finley, Esq., is a litigation attorney and research specialist with extensive experience in motion writing and appeals. He is the creator of *Texas Motions in Limine* and has also created and contributed to multiple publications published by Thomson Reuters (West), including *Federal Motions in Limine* and *Federal Summary Judgment and Related Termination Motions*. He graduated from Hastings College of the Law, where he was a member of the Moot Court Honors Board, a brief writing award recipient, and a moot court teaching fellow. He currently writes freelance motions and appeals and teaches advanced motion drafting and pretrial practice at UCI School of Law, a top 25 nationally ranked law school.

TEXAS MOTIONS IN LIMINE

CHAPTER 1

Motions in Limine

I. Motion in Limine Use and Procedure
   A. Description and Purpose of Motion
      1. Generally
      2. Authority for Motion
         a. Texas Rule of Evidence 402
         b. Texas Rule of Evidence 403
         c. Texas Rule of Evidence 103
         d. Texas Rule of Evidence 104
         e. Texas Rule of Civil Procedure 166
      3. Typical Use of Motion
         a. Limitations on Use
         b. Preservation of Objections
      4. Timing of Motion
      5. Scope of Motion
      6. Procedural Requirements
   B. Drafting Suggestions
      1. Overview
      2. File Motion Supported by Facts
      3. Be Succinct
      4. Consider Calling the Motion "Objections and Motion to Exclude Evidence"
   C. Opposition Considerations
      1. Preserving Error
      2. Offer of Proof and Bill of Exception
II. Sample Forms
   A. Sample in Limine Motion and Brief
   B. Sample in Limine Order

I. Motion in Limine Use and Procedure

A. Description and Purpose of Motion

1. Generally

The purpose of a motion in limine is to prevent the other party from asking prejudicial questions and introducing objectionable evidence in front of the jury without first asking the court's permission. *Wackenhut Corp. v. Gutierrez*, 453 S.W.3d 917, 920 n.3 (Tex. 2016); *In re Hightower*, 580 S.W.3d 248, 254 (Tex. App.—Houston [14th Dist.]

2019, orig. proceeding); *In re BCH Development, LLC*, 525 S.W.3d 920, 925 (Tex. App.—Dallas 2017, orig. proceeding); *Vela v. Wagner & Brown, Ltd.*, 203 S.W.3d 37, 54 (Tex. App.—San Antonio 2006, no pet.); *Weidner v. Sanchez*, 14 S.W.3d 353, 363 (Tex. App.—Houston [14th Dist.] 2000, no pet.). It has been described as a "means of raising objections to a general area of inquiry prior to the matter reaching the ears of the jury through testimony, jury argument, or other means." *Taylor v. State*, 555 S.W.3d 765, 780 (Tex. App.—Amarillo 2018, pet. filed); see *Norman v. State*, 523 S.W.2d 669, 671 (Tex. Crim. App. 1975). The primary advantage of a motion in limine is to avoid the futile attempt of trying to undo the harm done when jurors have been exposed to damaging evidence, even where that evidence is later stricken by the court. By raising evidentiary issues prior to the beginning of trial, motions in limine allow for more careful consideration of evidentiary issues than would take place during the heat of battle during trial. In so doing, the motion in limine may minimize sidebar conferences and disruptions during trial and enhance the efficiency of trials and promotion of settlements by resolving potentially critical issues at the outset.

> *Note: A proceeding challenging standing in probate is sometimes referred to as an in limine proceeding, because it is a threshold or preliminary proceeding before the trial.* In re Estate of Chapman, 315 S.W.3d 162 (Tex. App.—Beaumont 2010, no pet.); Edwards v. Haynes, 690 S.W.2d 50 (Tex. App.—Houston [14th Dist.]), rev'd on other grounds, 698 S.W.2d 97 (1985).

2. *Authority for Motion*

While not expressly authorized by statute, motions in limine are commonly used trial tools that are entertained and granted within the trial court's inherent powers. *Harnett v. State*, 38 S.W.3d 650, 655 (Tex. App.—Austin 2000, pet. ref'd); *Kendrix v. S. Pac. Transp. Co.*, 907 S.W.2d 111, 113 (Tex. App.—Beaumont 1995, writ denied).

Texas case law makes a distinction between a true "motion in limine," which is preliminary in nature and broad in scope, and a pretrial ruling on the admissibility of evidence. See *Geuder v. State*, 115 S.W.3d 11, 14 (Tex. Crim. App. 2003); *In re Hightower*, 580 S.W.3d 248, 254 (Tex. App.—Houston [14th Dist.] 2019, orig. proceeding); *Huckaby v. A.G. Perry & Son, Inc.*, 20 S.W.3d 194, 203 (Tex. App.—Texarkana 2000, pet. denied). All pretrial motions seeking to exclude evidence are not motions in limine. *Huckaby v. A.G. Perry & Son, Inc.*, 20 S.W.3d 194, 203 (Tex. App.—Texarkana 2000, pet. denied). If the relief requested in the motion is the exclusion of evidence, it is not a motion in limine, but a motion to exclude evidence. *In re Hightower*, 580 S.W.3d 248, 254 (Tex. App.—Houston [14th Dist.] 2019, orig. proceeding); *Norfolk Southern Ry. Co. v. Bailey*, 92 S.W.3d 577, 583 (Tex. App.—Austin 2002, no pet.); *Huckaby v. A.G. Perry & Son, Inc.*, 20 S.W.3d 194, 203 (Tex. App.—Texarkana 2000, pet. denied).

a. *Texas Rule of Evidence 402*

Texas Rule of Evidence 402 states that "evidence which is not relevant is inadmissible." Relevant evidence is defined by Texas Rule of Evidence 401 as "having any tendency to make the existence of any fact that is of consequence to the determination of the action more probable or less probable than it would be without the evidence."

Tex. R. Evid. 401; *See Morale v. State*, 557 S.W.3d 569, 573 (Tex. 2018); *Diamond Offshore Services Ltd. v. Williams*, 542 S.W.3d 539, 549 (Tex. 2018); *Brookshire Bros. v. Aldridge*, 438 S.W.3d 9, 34 (Tex. 2014); *Rhey v. Redic*, 408 S.W.3d 440, 460 (Tex. App.—El Paso 2013, no pet.) (to be relevant, there must be some logical connection either directly or by inference between the fact offered and the fact to be proved).

b. Texas Rule of Evidence 403

Texas Rule of Evidence 403 states that relevant evidence "may be excluded if its probative value is substantially outweighed by the danger of unfair prejudice, confusion of the issues, or misleading the jury, or by considerations of undue delay, or needless presentation of cumulative evidence." *See Diamond Offshore Services Ltd. v. Williams*, 542 S.W.3d 539, 549 (Tex. 2018); *Brookshire Bros. v. Aldridge*, 438 S.W.3d 9, 34 (Tex. 2014); *Hernandez v. State*, 390 S.W.3d 310, 323 (Tex. Crim. App. 2012).

c. Texas Rule of Evidence 103

Texas Rule of Evidence 103 provides in relevant part:

> (a) Effect of Erroneous Ruling. Error may not be predicated upon a ruling which admits or excludes evidence unless a substantial right of the party is affected, and
>
> (1) Objection. In case the ruling is one admitting evidence, a timely objection or motion to strike appears of record, stating the specific ground of objection, if the specific ground was not apparent from the context. *When the court hears objections to offered evidence out of the presence of the jury and rules that such evidence be admitted, such objections shall be deemed to apply to such evidence when it is admitted before the jury without the necessity of repeating those objections.*
>
> (2) Offer of proof. In case the ruling is one excluding evidence, the substance of the evidence was made known to the court by offer, or was apparent from the context within which questions were asked.
>
> (b) Record of Offer and Ruling. The offering party shall, as soon as practicable, but before the court's charge is read to the jury, be allowed to make, in the absence of the jury, its offer of proof. The court may add any other or further statement which shows the character of the evidence, the form in which it was offered, the objection made, and the ruling thereon. The court may, or at the request of a party shall, direct the making of an offer in question and answer form.
>
> (c) Hearing of Jury. *In jury cases, proceedings shall be conducted, to the extent practicable, so as to prevent inadmissible evidence from being suggested to the jury by any means, such as making statements or offers of proof or asking questions in the hearing of the jury.* (Emphasis added.)

d. Texas Rule of Evidence 104

Texas Rule of Evidence 104(a) provides,

> Preliminary questions concerning the qualification of a person to be a witness, the existence of a privilege, or the admissibility of evidence shall be determined by the court, subject to the provisions of subdivision (b). In making its determination the court is not bound by the rules of evidence except those with respect to privileges.

Texas Rule of Evidence 104(c) further states:

> In a criminal case, a hearing on the admissibility of a confession shall be conducted out of the hearing of the jury. All other civil or criminal hearings on preliminary matters shall be conducted out of the hearing of the jury when the interests of justice so require or in a criminal case when an accused is a witness and so requests.

e. Texas Rule of Civil Procedure 166

Texas Rule of Civil Procedure 166 provides, in relevant part:

> In an appropriate action, to assist in the disposition of the case without undue expense or burden to the parties, the court may in its discretion direct the attorneys for the parties and the parties or their duly authorized agents to appear before it for a conference to consider:
> ...
> (g) The identification of legal matters to be ruled on or decided by the court;
> * * *
> (l) The marking and exchanging of all exhibits that any party may use at trial and stipulation to the authenticity and admissibility of exhibits to be used at trial;
> (m) Written trial objections to the opposite party's exhibits, stating the basis for each objection;
> * * *
> (p) Such other matters as may aid in the disposition of the action.
> * * *
> The court shall make an order that recites the action taken at the pretrial conference, the amendments allowed to the pleadings, the time within which same may be filed, and the agreements made by the parties as to any of the matters considered, and which limits the issues for trial to those not disposed of by admissions, agreements of counsel, or rulings of the court; and such order when issued shall control the subsequent course of the action, unless modified at the trial to prevent manifest injustice.

3. Typical Use of Motion

A typical in limine order excludes the category of challenged evidence and directs counsel, parties, and witnesses not to refer to the excluded matters in the presence of the jury before the trial court has ruled on admissibility. *In re Toyota Motor Sales, U.S.A., Inc.*, 407 S.W.3d 746, 760 (Tex. 2013) (orig. proceeding); *Geuder v. State*, 115 S.W.3d 11, 14-15 (Tex. Crim. App. 2003); *In re Hightower*, 580 S.W.3d 248, 254 (Tex. App.—Houston [14th Dist.] 2019, orig. proceeding); *In re V.A.G.*, 528 S.W.3d 172, 175 (Tex. App.—El Paso 2017, orig. proceeding). When a trial court issues an order granting a motion in limine, the opposing party has a duty to comply with that order and to instruct the witnesses to do the same, and noncompliance with that order may lead to contempt or other sanctions the trial court deems appropriate. *In re R.N.*, 356 S.W.3d 568, 575 (Tex. App.—Texarkana 2011, no pet.); *Dyer v. Cotton*, 333 S.W.3d 703, 715 (Tex. App.—Houston [1st Dist.] 2010, no pet.).

The violation of a motion in limine may entitle a party to relief, but any remedies available for such a violation lie with the trial court. *In re R.N.*, 356 S.W.3d 568, 575 (Tex. App.—Texarkana 2011, no pet.); *Thierry v. State*, 288 S.W.3d 80, 87 (Tex. App.—Houston [1st Dist.] 2009, pet. ref'd); *Onstad v. Wright*, 54 S.W.3d 799, 806 (Tex. App.—Texarkana 2001, pet. denied). Violating an order restricting the mention of evidence can result in contempt, sanctions, or mistrial. *In re R.N.*, 356 S.W.3d 568, 575 (Tex. App.—Texarkana 2011, no pet.); *Thierry v. State*, 288 S.W.3d 80, 87 (Tex. App.—Houston [1st Dist.] 2009, pet. ref'd); *Onstad v. Wright*, 54 S.W.3d 799, 806 (Tex. App.—Texarkana 2001, pet. denied) (monetary sanctions against counsel for violation of order and mistrial).

The trial court has discretion to determine that a curative instruction is sufficient to cure any error from a violation of an in limine order. *Gonzales v. State*, 685 S.W.2d 47, 49 (Tex. Crim. App. 1985), cert. denied, 472 U.S. 1009 (1985); *In re Wyatt Field Service Co.*, 454 S.W.3d 145, 161 (Tex. App.—Houston [14th Dist.] 2014, orig. proceeding); *In re City of Houston*, 418 S.W.3d 388, 397 (Tex. App.—Houston [1st Dist.] 2013, orig. proceeding); *Dyer v. Cotton*, 333 S.W.3d 703, 715 (Tex. App.—Houston [1st Dist.] 2010, no pet.). Violations of an order on a motion in limine are incurable if instructions to the jury would not eliminate the danger of prejudice. *BCH Development, LLC*, 525 S.W.3d 920, 925 (Tex. App.—Dallas 2017, orig. proceeding); *In re Wyatt Field Service Co.*, 454 S.W.3d 145, 161 (Tex. App.—Houston [14th Dist.] 2014, orig. proceeding); *In re City of Houston*, 418 S.W.3d 388 (Tex. App.—Houston [1st Dist.] 2013, orig. proceeding); *In re R.N.*, 356 S.W.3d 568, 575 (Tex. App.—Texarkana 2011, no pet.). When the trial court gives curative instruction to the jury to disregard the statement or evidence, on appeal the opposition must overcome the presumption that the jury followed the trial court's instruction and must show that the statement probably caused the rendition of an improper judgment. *BCH Development, LLC*, 525 S.W.3d 920, 925 (Tex. App.—Dallas 2017, orig. proceeding); *Michaelski v. Wright*, 444 S.W.3d 83, 91 (Tex. App.—Houston [1st Dist.] 2014); *In re City of Houston*, 418 S.W.3d 388, 397 (Tex. App.—Houston [1st Dist.] 2013, orig. proceeding); *Taylor v. Fabritech, Inc.*, 132 S.W.3d 613, 626 (Tex. App.—Houston [14th Dist.] 2004, pet. denied).

a. Limitations on Use

Texas case law makes a distinction between a true "motion in limine," which is preliminary in nature and broad in scope, and a ruling that is made outside the presence of the jury pursuant to Texas Rule of Evidence 103. *Geuder v. State*, 115 S.W.3d 11, 14 (Tex. Crim. App. 2003); *In re Hightower*, 580 S.W.3d 248, 254 (Tex. App.—Houston [14th Dist.] 2019, orig. proceeding); *In re R.N.*, 356 S.W.3d 568, 575 (Tex. App.—Texarkana 2011, no pet.). While pretrial rulings on objections to specific evidence may preserve the issue for review, a "motion in limine" does not. *Wackenhut Corp. v. Gutierrez*, 453 S.W.3d 917, 920 n.3 (Tex. 2016); *Fuller v. State*, 253 S.W.3d 220, 232 (Tex. Crim. App. 2008); *In re BCH Development, LLC*, 525 S.W.3d 920, 925 (Tex. App.—Dallas 2017, orig. proceeding); *Davlin v. State*, 531 S.W.3d 765, 768 (Tex. App.—Texarkana 2016, no pet.). If the relief requested in the motion is the exclusion of evidence, it is not a motion in limine, but a motion to exclude evidence. *In re Hightower*, 580 S.W.3d 248, 254 (Tex. App.—Houston [14th Dist.] 2019, orig. proceeding); *Norfolk Southern Ry. Co. v. Bailey*, 92 S.W.3d 577, 583 (Tex. App.—Austin 2002, no pet.); *Huckaby v. A.G. Perry & Son, Inc.*, 20 S.W.3d 194, 203 (Tex. App.—Texarkana 2000, pet. denied).

An order granting a motion in limine is not a ruling on the admissibility of evidence. *Fitzgerald v. Water Rock Outdoors, LLC*, 536 S.W.3d 112, 121 (Tex. App.—Amarillo 2017, pet. denied); *Southwest Country Enters., Inc. v. Lucky Lady Oil Co.*, 991 S.W.2d 490, 493 (Tex. App.—Fort Worth 1999, pet. denied). The grant of a motion in limine requires the party who wants to present the challenged evidence to approach the bench during trial and inform the court that it is about to get into the challenged evidence. The objecting party must then make the objection on the record and the judge will enter a binding, appealable ruling. *State Bar of Tex. v. Evans*, 774 S.W.2d 656, 658 n.6 (Tex. 1989); *In re Hightower*, No. 580 S.W.3d 248, 254 (Tex. App.—Houston [14th Dist.] 2019, orig. proceeding); *Fitzgerald v. Water Rock Outdoors, LLC*, 536 S.W.3d 112, 121 (Tex. App.—Amarillo 2017, pet. denied); *In re BCH Development, LLC*, 525 S.W.3d 920, 925 (Tex. App.—Dallas 2017, orig. proceeding); *Davlin v. State*, 531 S.W.3d 765, 768 (Tex. App.—Texarkana 2016, no pet.); *Thierry v. State*, 288 S.W.3d 80, 87 (Tex. App.—Houston [1st Dist.] 2009, pet. ref'd); *Weidner Sanchez*, 14 S.W.3d 353, 363 (Tex. App.—Houston [14th Dist.] 2000, no pet.).

The party against whom a motion in limine is granted and who wants to introduce the evidence in question must, in order to preserve error:

- approach the bench and ask for a ruling;
- formally offer the evidence; and
- obtain a ruling on the offer.

Fitzgerald v. Water Rock Outdoors, LLC, 536 S.W.3d 112, 121 (Tex. App.—Amarillo 2017, pet. denied); *Southwest Country Enters., Inc. v. Lucky Lady Oil Co.*, 991 S.W.2d 490, 493 (Tex. App.—Fort Worth 1999, pet. denied).

b. *Preservation of Objections*

If a motion in limine is denied, it will not be grounds for reversal, unless the objectionable evidence is offered at trial. *In re Toyota Motor Sales, U.S.A., Inc.*, 407 S.W.3d 746, 760 (Tex. 2013) (orig. proceeding); *In re Hightower*, No. 580 S.W.3d 248, 254 (Tex. App.—Houston [14th Dist.] 2019, orig. proceeding); *In re V.A.G.*, 528 S.W.3d 172, 175 (Tex. App.—El Paso 2017, orig. proceeding). If the evidence is admitted when offered at trial, the opposing party must object at trial in order to preserve the issue for appeal. *Gonzales v. State*, 685 S.W.2d 47, 50 (Tex. Crim. App. 1985), *cert. denied*, 472 U.S. 1009 (1985); *Hartford Accident & Indem. Co. v. McCardell*, 369 S.W.2d 331,

335 (Tex. 1963); *Davlin v. State*, 531 S.W.3d 765, 768 (Tex. App.—Texarkana 2016, no pet.); *Citigroup Global Mkts. Realty Corp. v. Stewart Title Guar. Co.*, 417 S.W.3d 592, 604 (Tex. App.—Houston [14th Dist.] 2013, no pet.); *Boulle v. Boulle*, 254 S.W.3d 701, 709 (Tex. App.—Dallas 2008, no pet.).

If a motion in limine is granted, but the opposing party violates that order at trial by mentioning or offering the evidence in front of the jury without first approaching the bench, the complaining party must immediately object and request the trial court to instruct the jury to disregard the evidence introduced in violation of the limine order. *State Bar of Tex. v. Evans*, 774 S.W.2d 656, 658 n.6 (Tex. 1989); *BCH Development, LLC*, 525 S.W.3d 920, 925 (Tex. App.—Dallas 2017, orig. proceeding). On appeal, if the trial court instructs the jury to disregard evidence offered in violation of a motion in limine, the appellate court will review that evidence to determine whether the instruction to disregard was adequate to cure its admission, but will presume that jurors followed the instructions they were given. *BCH Development, LLC*, 525 S.W.3d 920, 925 (Tex. App.—Dallas 2017, orig. proceeding); *In re City of Houston*, 418 S.W.3d 388, 397 (Tex. App.—Houston [1st Dist.] 2013, orig. proceeding); *Taylor v. Fabritech, Inc.*, 132 S.W.3d 613, 626 (Tex. App.—Houston [14th Dist.] 2004, pet. denied). Generally, a violation of a motion in limine order is incurable if instructions to the jury would not eliminate the danger of prejudice. *BCH Development, LLC*, 525 S.W.3d 920, 925 (Tex. App.—Dallas 2017, orig. proceeding); *Dove v. Dir., State Emps. Workers' Comp. Div.*, 857 S.W.2d 577, 580 (Tex. App.—Houston [1st Dist.] 1993, writ denied).

4. Timing of Motion

Motions in limine are typically brought at a pretrial conference or at the beginning of trial but may also be brought during trial when evidentiary issues are anticipated by the parties. *Rawlings v. State*, 874 S.W.2d 740, 742 (Tex. App.—Fort Worth 1994, no pet.). Many trial courts enter pretrial scheduling conferences that require motions in limine to be filed by a specified date.

5. Scope of Motion

A motion in limine should seek to exclude any kind of evidence that can be objected to at trial. The movant should point out any irrelevant, harmful, and overly prejudicial evidence which it believes the other party may offer. *Westview Drive Invest., LLC v. Landmark American Ins. Co.*, 522 S.W.3d 583, 600 (Tex. App.—Houston [14th Dist.] 2017, pet. denied); *In re R.N.*, 356 S.W.3d 568, 575 (Tex. App.—Texarkana 2011, no pet.); *Greenberg Traurig of New York, P.C. v. Moody*, 161 S.W.3d 56, 90 (Tex. App.—Houston [14th Dist.] 2004, no pet.). The party objecting to the motion in limine must show the factual relevance of the objectionable material. *Johnson v. Garza*, 884 S.W.2d 831, 834 (Tex. App.—Austin 1994, writ denied).

However, Texas cases have held that "a motion in limine characteristically includes: (1) an objection to a general category of evidence; and (2) a request for an instruction that the proponent of that evidence approach the bench for a hearing on its admissibility before offering it. Conspicuously absent from a motion in limine is a request for a ruling on the actual admissibility of specific evidence." *See Rawlings v. State*, 874 S.W.2d 740, 742 (Tex. App.—Fort Worth 1994, no pet.); *Fitzgerald v. Water Rock Outdoors, LLC*, 536 S.W.3d 112, 121 (Tex. App.—Amarillo 2017, pet. denied);

Southwest Country Enters., Inc. v. Lucky Lady Oil Co., 991 S.W.2d 490, 493 (Tex. App.—Fort Worth 1999, pet. denied).

6. Procedural Requirements

Motions in limine can be made orally, in writing, or both. *Lusk v. State*, 82 S.W.3d 57, 59 (Tex. App.—Amarillo 2002, pet. ref'd) (oral motion); *Kendrix v. S. Pac. Transp. Co.*, 907 S.W.2d 111, 113 (Tex. App.—Beaumont 1995, writ denied) (written motion); *Blacklock v. State*, 681 S.W.2d 155 (Tex. App.—Houston [14th Dist.] 1984, pet. ref'd) (oral motion); (written motions).

The motion asks the court to require the party who wants to offer the potentially harmful evidence to approach the bench and quietly ask the court's permission before broaching such evidence in front of the jury. Upon approach by the party, the judge has the option to excuse the jury, conduct a hearing outside their presence, and rule on the admissibility of the proposed evidence. Rule of Evidence 103c. The granting of a motion in limine does not require a written order to be enforceable. Further, the order granting a motion in limine is not a ruling on the admissibility of evidence; it simply prohibits references to specific issues without first obtaining a ruling on the admissibility of those issues outside the presence of the jury. *Fitzgerald v. Water Rock Outdoors, LLC*, 536 S.W.3d 112, 121 (Tex. App.—Amarillo 2017, pet. denied); *Southwest Country Enters., Inc. v. Lucky Lady Oil Co.*, 991 S.W.2d 490, 493 (Tex. App.—Fort Worth 1999, pet. denied).

Keep in mind that local rules may impose stricter notice and filing requirements. See, e.g., Travis County District Court Local Rule 4.2 ("Standing orders, posted online, govern the pre-trial schedule for jury trials and motions in limine. Any motion in limine requesting additional limine or a modification of the standing order will be heard by the trial judge at the time of trial. Counsel should not repeat or otherwise address the subject matter contained in the standing order except to seek a modification of the standing order."); Jefferson County District Civil Rule 4(A) ("Motions in Limine. Motions in limine and other such preliminary matters must be scheduled for hearing at a time sufficiently in advance of scheduled jury selection to allow full consideration by the Court, without causing delay in the beginning of jury selection. Thus, if jury selection is scheduled for 9:00 a.m., the motions in limine should be scheduled for hearing with the clerk sufficiently in advance, so that actual jury selection can begin at 9:00. In some cases, this will require that the motions in limine be scheduled for hearing on the preceding business day. It is the responsibility of the attorneys to have the motions heard and determined in such a fashion that jury selection is not delayed.").

To avoid any pretrial surprises, check your jurisdiction's local rules early in the proceedings and be sure to follow all procedural requirements and mark your calendar accordingly.

B. Drafting Suggestions

1. Overview

Motions in limine usually address numerous evidentiary matters, as opposed to a single-issue trial brief seeking the exclusion of evidence. It is not unusual for a trial judge to be presented with literally dozens of in limine motions—for each party—in a single case. Thus, it is not difficult to imagine the court's disdain for poorly drafted, overly verbose, or needlessly filed motions. It is also not difficult to understand why attorneys face such an uphill battle in getting motions in limine granted.

The following suggestions should enhance your chances of success.

2. File Motion Supported by Facts

By filing motions that are properly supported by facts and argument, you increase the odds of success by enhancing your credibility and reducing the total number of pages the court will be required to read.

If your motion will require the court to speculate, your chances of success are slim. Instead, a better strategy may be to preserve your motion until you anticipate that the evidence will be proffered, or other preliminary facts emerge that will give the court a factual basis to make its ruling.

3. Be Succinct

As with all motion writing, less is often more. If the court is familiar with the general facts of the case, there is no need to recite a lengthy restatement of the case history. Instead, a few introductory paragraphs refreshing the court's recollection of the pertinent facts relating to the motion issue are usually sufficient. Regarding the general authority for a motion in limine, a brief citation to a case such as *Weidner Sanchez*, 14 S.W.3d 353, 363 (Tex. App.—Houston [14th Dist.] key 2000, no pet.) will suffice. Few judges in this state will question your right to bring the motion.

If you have a specific citation supporting your argument, cite it early and then spend the balance of the motion explaining, as succinctly as possible, why the facts in your case support the requested exclusion or other in limine ruling.

4. Consider Calling the Motion "Objections and Motion to Exclude Evidence"

As discussed above, this may better preserve the error for appeal, without any need later to object at trial. *Huckaby v. A.G. Perry & Son, Inc.*, 20 S.W.3d 194, 203 (Tex. App.—Texarkana 2000, pet. denied).

Be sure to ask the trial judge for a definitive ruling on the motion and, just to be safe and ensure preservation of the issues for appeal, renew any objections at trial when the evidence is offered. *Thierry v. State*, 288 S.W.3d 80, 87 (Tex. App.—Houston [1st Dist.] 2009, pet. ref'd); *Boulle v. Boulle*, 254 S.W.3d 701, 709 (Tex. App.—Dallas 2008, no pet.); *Richmond Condos. v. Skipworth Commercial Plumbing, Inc.*, 245 S.W.3d 646, 665 (Tex. App.—Fort Worth 2008, pet. denied).

C. Opposition Considerations

1. Preserving Error

The pretrial grant of a motion in limine requires the party who wants to present the challenged evidence to approach the bench during trial and inform the court that it is about to get into the challenged evidence. The objecting party must then make the objection on the record and the judge will enter a binding, appealable ruling. *Roberts v. State*, 220 S.W.3d 521, 533 (Tex. Crim. App. 2007), *cert. denied*, 552 U.S. 920 (2007); *Thierry v. State*, 288 S.W.3d 80, 87 (Tex. App.—Houston [1st Dist.] 2009, pet. ref'd); *Boulle v. Boulle*, 254 S.W.3d 701 (Tex. App.—Dallas 2008, no pet.); *Richmond Condos. v. Skipworth Commercial Plumbing, Inc.*, 245 S.W.3d 646, 665 (Tex. App.—Fort Worth 2008, pet. denied); *Greenberg Traurig of New York, P.C. v. Moody*, 161 S.W.3d 56, 90 (Tex. App.—Houston [14th Dist.] 2004, reh'g overruled); *Schwartz v. Forest Pharm., Inc.*, 127 S.W.3d 118, 123 (Tex. App.—Houston [1st Dist.] 2003, pet. denied); *Norfolk S. Ry. Co. v. Bailey*, 92 S.W.3d 577, 583 (Tex. App.—Austin 2002, no pet.). The party against whom a motion in limine is granted and who wants to introduce the evidence in question must, in order to preserve error:

- approach the bench and ask for a ruling;
- formally offer the evidence; and
- obtain a ruling on the offer.

Kaufman v. Comm'n for Lawyer Discipline, 197 S.W.3d 867 (Tex. App.—Corpus Christi 2006, pet. denied), *cert. denied*, 552 U.S. 935 (2007); *Norfolk S. Ry. Co. v. Bailey*, 92 S.W.3d 577, 583 (Tex. App.—Austin 2002, no pet.).

2. *Offer of Proof and Bill of Exception*

Texas Rule of Evidence 103 provides in relevant part:

> (a) Effect of Erroneous Ruling. Error may not be predicated upon a ruling which admits or excludes evidence unless a substantial right of the party is affected, and
>
> (1) Objection. In case the ruling is one admitting evidence, a timely objection or motion to strike appears of record, stating the specific ground of objection, if the specific ground was not apparent from the context. When the court hears objections to offered evidence out of the presence of the jury and rules that such evidence be admitted, such objections shall be deemed to apply to such evidence when it is admitted before the jury without the necessity of repeating those objections.
>
> (2) Offer of proof. In case the ruling is one excluding evidence, the substance of the evidence was made known to the court by offer, or was apparent from the context within which questions were asked.
>
> (b) Record of Offer and Ruling. The offering party shall, as soon as practicable, but before the court's charge is read to the jury, be allowed to make, in the absence of the jury, its offer of proof. The court may add any other or further statement which shows the character of the evidence, the form in which it was offered, the objection made, and the ruling thereon. The court may, or at the request of a party shall, direct the making of an offer in question and answer form.
>
> (c) Hearing of Jury. In jury cases, proceedings shall be conducted, to the extent practicable, so as to prevent inadmissible evidence from

being suggested to the jury by any means, such as making statements or offers of proof or asking questions in the hearing of the jury.

Gunn v. McCoy, 554 S.W.3d 645, 666 (Tex. 2018) ("If a court ruling excludes evidence, a party must preserve error by filing an offer of proof informing the court of the substance of the excluded evidence.").

Wackenhut Corp. v. Gutierrez, 453 S.W.3d 917, 920 n.3 (Tex. 2016) (a pretrial motion in limine does not preserve error on evidentiary rulings at trial because it does not seek a ruling on admissibility).

Wackenhut Corp. v. Gutierrez, 453 S.W.3d 917, 920 n.3 (Tex. 2016) (the purpose of a pretrial motion in limine is to prevent the asking of prejudicial questions and the making of prejudicial statements in the presence of the jury without first seeking the trial court's permission).

Matter of Marriage of Rangel, 580 S.W.3d 675, 680 (Tex. App.—Houston [14th Dist.] 2019, no pet.) ("Once a proponent secures an exclusionary ruling, she must preserve the evidence in the record by an offer of proof to complain of the exclusion on appeal.").

Matter of Marriage of Rangel, 580 S.W.3d 675, 680 (Tex. App.—Houston [14th Dist.] 2019, no pet.) ("The rules of evidence do not mandate a 'formal' offer of proof; they require only a 'short, factual recitation of what the evidence would show' to preserve the issue for appeal.... The offer of proof nonetheless must inform the court of the substance of the evidence unless the substance is apparent from the context.... The offer must include the meat of the actual evidence' rather than a general, cursory summary, so that the appellate court can meaningfully assess whether the exclusion of the evidence was erroneous and harmful.").

Jones v. Mattress Firm Holding Corp., 558 S.W.3d 732, 738 (Tex. App.—Houston [14th Dist.] 2018, no pet.) ("A party seeking admission of evidence must inform the court of the substance of the evidence by an offer of proof, unless the substance is apparent from the context.").

Jones v. Mattress Firm Holding Corp., 558 S.W.3d 732, 738 (Tex. App.—Houston [14th Dist.] 2018, no pet.) ("Making an offer of proof enables an appellate court to determine whether the exclusion of the evidence was erroneous and harmful, and it allows the trial court to reconsider its ruling in light of the actual evidence.").

BNSF Ry. Co. v. Phillips, 434 S.W.3d 675, 699 (Tex. App.—Fort Worth 2014), rev'd on other grounds, 485 S.W.3d 908 (Tex. 2015) (if evidence subject to a motion in limine is offered at trial and the court rules the evidence inadmissible, the party must further preserve the evidence through an offer of proof; an appellate court cannot decide whether evidence was improperly excluded unless the evidence is included in the record for review).

Sturdivant v. State, 445 S.W.3d 435, 440 (Tex. App.—Houston [1st Dist.] 2014, pet. ref'd) (formal bill of exception allows the party to complain on appeal about a matter that would otherwise not appear in the record).

Sturdivant v. State, 445 S.W.3d 435, 440 (Tex. App.—Houston [1st Dist.] 2014, pet. ref'd) (formal bill of exception is a method of error preservation and is primarily used when the appellant complains on appeal about the trial court's erroneous exclusion of evidence; evidence that, because it was not admitted, would not otherwise be part of the appellate record).

Compton v. Pfannenstiel, 428 S.W.3d 881, 885 (Tex. App.—Houston [1st Dist.] 2014, no pet.) (to preserve a complaint of a trial court's exclusion of evidence for review on appeal, the complaining party must establish on the record the substance of the excluded evidence through an offer of proof or bill of exception unless the substance of the evidence is apparent from the context).

In re Commitment of Smith, 422 S.W.3d 802, 808 (Tex. App.—Beaumont 2014, pet. denied) ("[W]hen cross-examination testimony is excluded, the party need not show the answer to be expected to preserve the issue for appeal, but only need show that the substance of the evidence was apparent from the context within which the question was asked.").

Balderama v. State, 421 S.W.3d 247, 250 (Tex. App.—San Antonio 2013, no pet.) ("[I]n order to preserve error regarding a trial court's decision to exclude evidence, the complaining party must make an offer of proof which sets forth the substance of the proffered evidence.").

Balderama v. State, 421 S.W.3d 247, 250 (Tex. App.—San Antonio 2013, no pet.) (an offer of proof may be in question-and-answer format or may consist of a concise statement by counsel).

Balderama v. State, 421 S.W.3d 247, 250 (Tex. App.—San Antonio 2013, no pet.) (when an offer of proof is in the form of a statement, it "must include a reasonably specific summary of the evidence offered and must state the relevance of the evidence unless the relevance is apparent, so that the court can determine whether the evidence is relevant and admissible").

Balderama v. State, 421 S.W.3d 247, 250 (Tex. App.—San Antonio 2013, no pet.) (to preserve error when denied the opportunity to attack the credibility of a witness, an offer of proof "must merely establish what general subject matter he desired to examine the witness about during his cross-examination and, if challenged, show on the record why such should be admitted into evidence").

Linney v. State, 401 S.W.3d 764, 772 (Tex. App.—Houston [14th Dist.] 2013, pet. ref'd) ("[I]t is the appellant's burden to make a record, through a bill of exceptions, of the evidence he desires admitted.").

Linney v. State, 401 S.W.3d 764, 772 (Tex. App.—Houston [14th Dist.] 2013, pet. ref'd) ("[T]he primary purpose of an offer of proof is to enable an appellate court to determine whether the exclusion was erroneous and harmful.").

Watts v. Oliver, 396 S.W.3d 124, 129 (Tex. App.—Houston [14th Dist.] 2013, no pet.) ("[T]o adequately and effectively preserve error, an offer of proof must show the nature of the evidence specifically enough so that the reviewing court can determine its admissibility.").

Watts v. Oliver, 396 S.W.3d 124, 129 (Tex. App.—Houston [14th Dist.] 2013, no pet.) ("[T]he offer of proof may be made by counsel, who should reasonably and specifically summarize the evidence offered and state its relevance, unless already apparent.").

Watts v. Oliver, 396 S.W.3d 124, 129 (Tex. App.—Houston [14th Dist.] 2013, no pet.) (if counsel makes an offer of proof, "he must describe the actual content of the testimony and not merely comment on the reasons for it").

In re Commitment of Briggs, 350 S.W.3d 362, 368 (Tex. App.—Beaumont 2011, pet. denied) ("[W]hen a ruling excludes evidence, to preserve error the appellant must have made the substance of the evidence known to the trial court through an offer of proof, unless the substance of the evidence was apparent from the context within which the question was asked.").

Alexander Shren-Yee Cheng v. Zhaoya Wang, 315 S.W.3d 668, 673 (Tex. App.—Dallas 2010, no pet.) ("[T]o preserve error in the exclusion of evidence, a party must make an offer of proof of the excluded evidence specific enough for a reviewing court to determine its admissibility.").

Way v. House, 315 S.W.3d 216, 219 n.5 (Tex. App.—Eastland 2010, pet. denied) ("[W]ithout an offer of proof, reviewing courts cannot determine whether the exclusion of evidence was harmful.").

In re Estate of Miller, 243 S.W.3d 831, 837 (Tex. App.—Dallas 2008, no pet.) ("[T]o challenge exclusion of evidence by the trial court on appeal, the complaining party must present the excluded evidence to the trial court by offer of proof or bill of exception.").

In re Estate of Miller, 243 S.W.3d 831, 837 (Tex. App.—Dallas 2008, no pet.) ("[A]n offer of proof consists of making the substance of the evidence known to the court and shall be made as soon as practicable after the ruling excluding the evidence, but before the court's charge is read before the jury.").

In re Estate of Miller, 243 S.W.3d 831, 837 (Tex. App.—Dallas 2008, no pet.) ("[T]he offer of proof must be (1) made before the court, the court reporter, and opposing counsel, but outside the presence of the jury, and (2) preserved in the reporter's record.").

In re Estate of Miller, 243 S.W.3d 831, 837 (Tex. App.—Dallas 2008, no pet.) ("[T]he offer of proof allows a trial court to reconsider its ruling in light of the actual evidence.").

In re Estate of Miller, 243 S.W.3d 831, 837 (Tex. App.—Dallas 2008, no pet.) ("[W]hen there is no offer of proof made before the trial court, the party must introduce the excluded testimony into the record by a formal bill of exception.").

II. Sample Forms

Important Note: The samples on the following pages illustrate how the authorities cited in this text can be used to support an argument in your in limine motion briefs. The motions are examples only and should not be reproduced verbatim for filing. The facts, parties, and witnesses are fictional. The format does not necessarily comply with state or local rules. For space purposes, exhibits and declarations are not included.

Other than the samples in Chapter 1, which are included for general illustrative purposes, the samples provided throughout the balance of this text relate specifically to the subjects covered in the chapter where located.

A. Sample in Limine Motion and Brief

NO. _____

	§	
_____	§	IN THE DISTRICT COURT
	§	
v.	§	_____ JUDICIAL COURT
	§	
_____	§	_____ COUNTY, TEXAS

**PLAINTIFF'S MOTION IN LIMINE REGARDING
PRIOR ACCIDENTS**

Come now _____, Plaintiff in this cause, and files this, her Motion in Limine regarding evidence of prior accidents, and in support would show the Court the following:

I.
SUMMARY OF MOTION

By this motion, Plaintiff seeks an order from this Court excluding any and all evidence, references to evidence, testimony, or argument relating to a prior automobile accident that occurred on or about March 1, 2010, and any injury to Plaintiff arising from that accident. This motion is based upon the grounds that any injuries to Plaintiff arising from the prior accident are unrelated to the injuries for which Plaintiff is seeking reimbursement in this case and are, therefore, irrelevant. Allowing the evidence in this case would prejudice the Plaintiff and cause jury confusion.

II.
FACTUAL BACKGROUND

This action arises from a rear-end accident that occurred on September 18, 2019, whereby the Plaintiff incurred severe neck and back injuries, property damage, and lost wages.

During discovery, Defendant submitted several interrogatories regarding a prior unrelated automobile accident which occurred on March 1, 2010. In that accident, the Plaintiff broke his jaw when his face struck the steering wheel of his vehicle. Plaintiff has been completely forthcoming regarding this accident, while preserving multiple objections based on relevance and prejudice. A copy of Plaintiff's Response to Defendant's Interrogatories is attached hereto as Exhibit "A."

The prior accident occurred more than eight years before the accident in the present case. At the time of the subject accident, Plaintiff's jaw was healed, according to his prior treating physician, Dr. Mandible. Plaintiff is making no claim for the jaw injuries in this action. A copy of Dr. Mandible's Final Report is attached hereto as Exhibit "B."

Plaintiff's current treating physician, Dr. Cervical, examined the plaintiff on September 19, 2019—one day after the subject accident—and examined Plaintiff's jaw. (Plaintiff identified the jaw injury on a New Patient Questionnaire prior to being examined by Dr. Cervical.)

At that time, Dr. Cervical noted that the jaw appeared to be "completely healed" and noted that the Plaintiff had no complaints of jaw pain. A copy of Dr. Cervical's medical report dated September 19, 2019, is attached hereto as Exhibit "C."

The following section should not be included where the trial court has ordered the parties to file pretrial motions in limine.

1.
THIS COURT MAY EXCLUDE PREJUDICIAL EVIDENCE IN ADVANCE
OF TRIAL BY WAY OF AN IN LIMINE MOTION

The Court has the inherent power to grant a motion in limine to exclude evidence which could be objected to at trial, either as irrelevant or subject to exclusion as unduly prejudicial. *Wackenhut Corp. v. Gutierrez*, 453 S.W.3d 917, 920 n.3 (Tex. 2016); *In re BCH Development, LLC*, 525 S.W.3d 920, 925 (Tex. App.—Dallas 2017, orig. proceeding). Texas Rule of Evidence 403 allows the court to exclude evidence where there is a substantial danger that the probative value will be outweighed by the danger of undue prejudice. *See Diamond Offshore Services Ltd. v. Williams*, 542 S.W.3d 539, 549 (Tex. 2018); *Brookshire Bros. v. Aldridge*, 438 S.W.3d 9, 34 (Tex. 2014).

Moreover, the court may hear and determine the question of the admissibility of evidence outside the presence or hearing of the jury. *See Weidner v. Sanchez*, 14 S.W.3d 353, 363 (Tex. App.—Houston [14th Dist.] 2000, no pet.); *Kendrix v. S. Pac. Transp. Co.*, 907 S.W.2d 111, 113 (Tex. App.—Beaumont 1995, writ denied); Texas Rule of Civil Procedure 166; and Texas Rules of Evidence 103 and 104.

2.
ANY REFERENCES TO PLAINTIFF'S PRIOR INJURIES ARE IRRELEVANT
AND SHOULD BE EXCLUDED

Texas Rule of Evidence 402 states that "evidence which is not relevant is inadmissible." Relevant evidence is defined by Texas Rule of Evidence 401 as "having any tendency to make the existence of any fact that is of consequence to the determination of the action more probable or less probable than it would be without the evidence." *See Torrington v. Stutzman*, 46 S.W.3d 829, 845 n.13 (Tex. 2000). Irrelevant evidence is not admissible. *Morale v. State*, 557 S.W.3d 569, 573 (Tex. 2018); *Diamond Offshore Services Ltd. v. Williams*, 542 S.W.3d 539, 549 (Tex. 2018).

While the general rule is that evidence of a similar injury sustained in a prior accident may be relevant to the damages issue in a subsequent case [see, e.g. *Russell Stover Candies, Inc. v. Elmore*, 58 S.W.3d 154, 157 (Tex. App.—Amarillo 2001, pet. denied); *Bonham v. Baldeschwiler*, 533 S.W.2d 144, 148 (Tex. Civ. App.—Corpus Christi 1976, writ ref'd n.r.e.)], evidence of dissimilar injuries or illnesses is not relevant unless the party offering the evidence can show that it caused or contributed to the current injury. Farmers Texas County Mutual Insurance Co. v. Pagan, 453 S.W.3d 454, 462 (Tex. App.—Houston [14th Dist.] 2014, no pet.); *Houston & T.C.R. Co. v. O'Donnell*, 90 S.W. 886, 893 (Tex. Civ. App. 1905), *rev'd on other grounds*, 99 Tex. 636, 92 S.W. 409 (1906).

In the present case, Plaintiff is making no claim for injuries relating to his jaw. The pertinent medical records clearly show that the prior jaw injury is in no way similar to Plaintiff's neck and back injuries in this case. See Exhibits "B" and "C."

The Court should therefore exclude any and all evidence, including any mention of evidence, relating to the March 1, 2004, accident or any injuries arising from that accident.

3.
EVIDENCE OF PLAINTIFF'S PRIOR ACCIDENT AND INJURIES SHOULD BE EXCLUDED TO AVOID PREJUDICIAL JURY CONFUSION

Texas Rule of Evidence 403 states: "[a]lthough relevant, evidence may be excluded if its probative value is substantially outweighed by the danger of unfair prejudice, <u>confusion of the issues, or misleading the jury</u>, or by considerations of undue delay, or needless presentation of cumulative evidence." (Emphasis added.)

The Court may exclude marginally probative evidence that might easily confuse the jury. *See Brookshire Bros. v. Aldridge*, 438 S.W.3d 9, 26 (Tex. 2014) (evidence that raises a risk of prejudice and confusion of the jury should be excluded); *Farmers Texas County Mutual Insurance Co. v. Pagan*, 453 S.W.3d 454, (Tex. App.—Houston [14th Dist.] 2014, no pet.) (evidence should have been excluded where its probative value was outweighed by danger of confusion of issues and misleading jury).

In the present case, there is a substantial danger that jurors might believe that the Plaintiff's prior jaw injury somehow relates to his current neck or back injuries. As is shown in Dr. Mandible's Final Report (Exhibit "B") and Dr. Cervical's Report (Exhibit "C"), the two injuries are unrelated. Any evidence of the prior injury will only serve to confuse the jury and unfairly prejudice the Plaintiff.

The Court should therefore exclude any and all evidence, including any mention of evidence, relating to the March 1, 2004, accident or any injuries arising from that accident.

4.
CONCLUSION

Based on the foregoing, the Plaintiff respectfully requests that this Court exclude any testimony or documentary evidence, or mention of any evidence, regarding the accident dated March 1, 2004, or any injuries arising from that accident.

Dated: _____(Date)_____

By: _____

_____(Name of Counsel)_____

Attorneys for Plaintiff,

_____(Name of Plaintiff)_____

B. Sample in Limine Order

NO. _____

_____ § IN THE DISTRICT COURT
                         §
v.   § _____ JUDICIAL COURT
                         §
_____ § _____ COUNTY, TEXAS

ORDER

On this day came on to be heard Plaintiff's motion in limine regarding prior accident injuries, and the Court finds that this Motion should be GRANTED.

IT IS HEREBY ORDERED that Defendants, Defendant's counsel and Defendant's witnesses shall:

1. Not to mention, refer to, or attempt to convey to the jury in any manner, either directly or indirectly, any of the facts mentioned in this Motion, without first obtaining permission of the Court outside the presence and hearing of the jury; and
2. Not to make any reference to the fact that this motion has been filed; and
3. To warn and caution each of Defendant's witnesses to strictly follow the same instructions.

Dated: _____

_____
JUDGE OF THE DISTRICT COURT

CHAPTER 2

Prejudicial Evidence

I. Motion Authorities
   A. Motion to Exclude Prejudicial Evidence
      1. Suggested Motion Text
      2. Motion Summary
         a. Rule 403 Factors to Consider
      3. Supporting Authorities
      4. Opposing Authorities
         a. Harmless Error
   B. Motion to Exclude Evidence That Will Waste Court's Time
      1. Suggested Motion Text
      2. Motion Summary
      3. Supporting Authorities
      4. Opposing Authorities
   C. Motion to Exclude Confusing or Misleading Evidence
      1. Suggested Motion Text
      2. Motion Summary
      3. Supporting Authorities
      4. Opposing Authorities
   D. Motion to Exclude Evidence Used to Create an Emotional Bias
      1. Suggested Motion Text
      2. Motion Summary
      3. Supporting Authorities
         a. Exclusion of Evidence Intended to Inflame Jurors' Emotions
      4. Opposing Authorities
   E. Motion to Exclude or Limit Cumulative Evidence
      1. Suggested Motion Text
      2. Motion Summary
      3. Supporting Authorities
         a. Generally
         b. Articles and Letters
         c. Number of Witnesses
         d. Photographs
         e. Reports
         f. Witness Testimony
         g. Expert Testimony
         h. Videotape Evidence
         i. Deposition Testimony
         j. Business Records

k. Wills
4. Opposing Authorities
   a. Articles
   b. Letters
   c. Credentials
   d. Number of Witnesses
   e. Photographs
   f. Reports
   g. Expert Testimony
   h. Videotape Evidence
   i. Books and Records

II. Sample Motions
   A. Motion to Exclude Confusing Evidence
   B. Motion to Exclude Cumulative Evidence
   C. Motion to Exclude Prejudicial Evidence
   D. Opposition to Motion to Exclude Prejudicial Evidence

I. Motion Authorities

A. Motion to Exclude Prejudicial Evidence

1. Suggested Motion Text

(*Name of Moving Party*) hereby moves this Court for an order excluding any and all evidence, references to evidence, testimony, or argument relating to (*Describe Prejudicial Evidence*). The motion is based upon the ground that the probative value of the evidence is substantially outweighed by the danger of undue prejudice to (*Name of Moving Party*).

2. Motion Summary

This motion is used to exclude prejudicial evidence. The motion is based upon the statutory balancing test of Texas Rule of Evidence 403, the key source for excluding evidence that will create a substantial danger of unfair prejudice, result in an undue delay of trial proceedings, confuse the issues, mislead the jury, or needlessly present cumulative evidence. See *Gonzalez v. State*, 544 S.W.3d 363, 371 (Tex. Crim. App. 2018); *Diamond Offshore Services Ltd. v. Williams*, 542 S.W.3d 539, 542 (Tex. 2018); *Gigliobianco v. State*, 210 S.W.3d 637, 641 (Tex. Crim. App. 2006); *Mitchell v. State*, 377 S.W.3d 21, 28 (Tex. App.—Waco 2011, pet. dism'd, untimely filed). Note that Rule 403, as well as Rules 401 and 402, are essentially identical to Federal Rule of Evidence 403. Accordingly, Texas courts must give greater than usual deference to interpretations of the federal rules, either by federal courts or by commentary to the rules themselves. *Diamond Offshore Services Ltd. v. Williams*, 542 S.W.3d 539, 542 (Tex. 2018); *Bruton v. State*, 428 S.W.3d 865, 873 (Tex. Crim. App. 2014); *Montgomery v. State*, 810 S.W.2d 372, 387 (Tex. Crim. App. 1990); *Houston v. State*, 208 S.W.3d 585, 590 (Tex. App.—Austin 2006, no pet.). Tex. R. Evid. 403 favors the admission of relevant evidence and carries a presumption that relevant evidence will be more probative than prejudicial. *Davis v. State*, 329 S.W.3d 798, 806 (Tex. Crim. App. 2010); *Montgomery v. State*, 810 S.W.2d 372, 387 (Tex. Crim. App. 1990); *Webb v. State*, 575 S.W.3d 905 (Tex. App.—Waco 2019, pet. filed); *Lopez v. State*, 582 S.W.3d 377, 397 (Tex. App.—San Antonio 2018, pet. ref'd); *Paz v. State*, 548 S.W.3d 778, 795 (Tex. App.—Houston [1st Dist.] 2018, pet ref'd).

The trial court does not *sua sponte* engage in balancing the probative value against the prejudice, but rather does so only upon the sufficient objection by the party opposing the evidence. *In re K.C.P.*, 142 S.W.3d 574, 584 (Tex. App.—Texarkana 2004, no pet.). Once this rule is invoked by such a proper objection, the trial court has no discretion as to whether to engage in the balancing process. *In re K.C.P.*, 142 S.W.3d 574, 584 (Tex. App.—Texarkana 2004, no pet.). Unless the record shows that the trial court did not perform the balancing test, an appellate court will find no error when the trial court simply listens to the opposing party's objections to the admission of evidence and then overrules them. *In re K.C.P.*, 142 S.W.3d 574, 584 (Tex. App.—Texarkana 2004, no pet.).

When arguing that evidence is *unfairly* prejudicial, keep in mind that Rule 403 applies only to *relevant* evidence. If the evidence you are concerned with is not admissible or is irrelevant, as defined by Rule 401, then you should exclude it under Rule 402. *See Gonzalez v. State*, 544 S.W.3d 363, 371 (Tex. Crim. App. 2018); *JLG Trucking, LLC v. Garza*, 466 S.W.3d 157, 162 (Tex. 2015); *Montgomery v. State*, 810 S.W.2d 372, 387 (Tex. Crim. App. 1990).

In general, even relevant evidence may be excluded if the probative value is substantially outweighed by the risk of undue prejudice. *Gonzalez v. State*, 544 S.W.3d 363, 371 (Tex. Crim. App. 2018); *Diamond Offshore Services Ltd. v. Williams*, 542 S.W.3d 539, 542 (Tex. 2018); *Pawlak v. State*, 420 S.W.3d 807, 809 (Tex. Crim. App. 2013); *Perez v. DNT Global Star, L.L.C.*, 339 S.W.3d 692, 706 (Tex. App.—Houston [1st Dist.] 2011, no pet.).

The trial court's exclusion of prejudicial evidence under Rule 403 is *discretionary*. *See Gonzalez v. State*, 544 S.W.3d 363, 371 (Tex. Crim. App. 2018); *Diamond Offshore Services Ltd. v. Williams*, 542 S.W.3d 539, 542 (Tex. 2018); *Pawlak v. State*, 420 S.W.3d 807, 809 (Tex. Crim. App. 2013) (under the abuse of discretion standard, the ruling of the trial court must be upheld on appeal if it is within the zone of reasonable disagreement); *Bay Area Healthcare Group, Ltd. v. McShane*, 239 S.W.3d 231, 234 (Tex. 2007); *Montgomery v. State*, 810 S.W.2d 372, 387 (Tex. Crim. App. 1990); *Burke v. State*, 371 S.W.3d 252, 257 (Tex. App.—Houston [1st Dist.] 2011, pet. ref'd, untimely filed).

To overcome the presumption of admissibility for all relevant evidence and invoke the trial court's discretion under Rule 403, the probative value of the evidence must be *substantially* outweighed by the danger of unfair prejudice or from one of the other four factors listed in Rule 403. *Gonzalez v. State*, 544 S.W.3d 363, 371 (Tex. Crim. App. 2018); *Diamond Offshore Services Ltd. v. Williams*, 542 S.W.3d 539, 542 (Tex. 2018). Even then, due to Rule 403's discretionary nature, it has been suggested that Rule 403 permits the court to admit unfairly prejudicial evidence by looking to other matters. *See, e.g., Goodson v. Castellanos*, 214 S.W.3d 741, 754 (Tex. App.—Austin 2007, pet. denied) (in a suit affecting the parent-child relationship, the guiding principle is the best interest of the child, and thus the exclusion of evidence under rule providing for exclusion of relevant evidence if its probative value is substantially outweighed by the danger of unfair prejudice should be done sparingly).

When evidence is offered for limited purposes, but is prejudicial in other respects, limiting jury instructions cannot necessarily "unring the bell" or ask the jury "not to smell the skunk that's been tossed into the jury box." If evidence has a clear prejudicial effect on one issue, a limiting instruction to focus the jury's attention only on another issue may not be effective. Under such circumstances, a jury cannot be expected to parse out the ways in which the evidence can be considered and the ways it cannot. *Huynh v. R. Warehousing & Port Servs., Inc.*, 973 S.W.2d 375, 378 (Tex. App.—Tyler 1998, no writ).

If faced with trying to exclude evidence that is highly prejudicial but is also highly probative (mandating admission), consider offering to stipulate to the facts. This may decrease the probative value of the evidence offered to prove such facts down to a level where the risk of unfair prejudice mandates exclusion. *Tamez v. State*, 11 S.W.3d 198, 199 (Tex. Crim. App. 2000) ("a defendant's stipulation to a previous conviction should suffice when it carries the same evidentiary value as the judgments of prior convictions, yet substantially lessens the likelihood that the jury will improperly focus on the previous convictions or the defendant's 'bad character'"). *See Robles v. State*, 85 S.W.3d 211, 212 (Tex. Crim. App. 2002) ("evidence of the convictions' existence is not necessary if the accused stipulates to their existence because the statutory requirement has been satisfied. The admission of evidence of prior convictions is error, even though they are jurisdictional elements of the offense, because the danger of unfair prejudice from introduction of the evidence substantially outweighs its probative value.").

> *Note: The cases cited in this section support the general proposition that prejudicial evidence may be excluded under a Rule 403 balancing test. Because of the importance of this section, Rule 403 is cited throughout the remainder of this text, in addition to more specific case authorities supporting the point. While this format might appear repetitive when chapters are read sequentially, multiple references to Rule 403 are included as a reminder that it should be cited in addition to whatever other authorities may support the motion being brought. Note that a similar format has been followed for citations to Rule 402 (irrelevant evidence).*

a. Rule 403 Factors to Consider

A criminal court considers six factors when determining whether to exclude evidence as unfairly prejudicial under Rule 403: (1) the inherent probative force of the proffered item of evidence along with (2) the proponent's need for that evidence weighed against (3) any tendency of the evidence to suggest decision on an improper basis, (4) any tendency of the evidence to confuse or distract the jury from the main issues, (5) any tendency of the evidence to be given undue weight by a jury that has not been equipped to evaluate the probative force of the evidence, and (6) the likelihood that presentation of the evidence will consume an inordinate amount of time or merely repeat evidence already admitted. *See Gonzalez v. State*, 544 S.W.3d 363, 371 (Tex. Crim. App. 2018); *Gigliobianco v. State*, 210 S.W.3d 637, 641 (Tex. Crim. App. 2006); *Webb v. State*, 575 S.W.3d 905 (Tex. App.—Waco 2019, pet. filed); *Andrews v. State*, 429 S.W.3d 849, 865 (Tex. App.—Texarkana 2014, pet. ref'd); *Kirk v. State*, 421 S.W.3d 772, 782 (Tex. App.—Fort Worth 2014, pet. ref'd); *Mitchell v. State*, 377 S.W.3d 21, 28 (Tex. App.—Waco 2011, pet. dism'd, untimely filed). The balancing test set forth in the rules of evidence to determine the potentially prejudicial nature of relevant evidence carries a presumption that relevant evidence will be more probative than prejudicial. *Allen v. State*, 108 S.W.3d 281, 284 (Tex. Crim. App. 2003), cert. denied, 540 U.S. 1185, (2004); *Jones v. State*, 944 S.W.2d 642, 652 (Tex. Crim. App. 1996), cert. denied, 522 U.S. 832 (1997); *Kirk v. State*, 421 S.W.3d 772, 782 (Tex. App.—Fort Worth 2014, pet. ref'd).

Similarly, in civil cases, if the trial court determines that the proffered expert testimony is relevant and reliable, then it must determine whether to exclude the evidence because its probative value is outweighed by: the danger of unfair prejudice, confusion of the issues, or misleading the jury; by considerations of undue delay or by needless presentation of cumulative evidence. *E.I. du Pont de Nemours & Co. v. Robinson*, 923 S.W.2d 549, 557 (Tex. 1995); *Von Hohn v. Von Hohn*, 260 S.W.3d 631, 636 (Tex. App.—Tyler 2008, no pet.). As in criminal matters, the admission of relevant evidence is favored and carries the presumption that relevant evidence will be more probative than prejudicial. *Olivarez v. Doe*, 164 S.W.3d 427, 433 (Tex. App.—Tyler 2004, pet. denied); *Rogers v. Peeler*, 146 S.W.3d 765, 733 (Tex. App.—Texarkana 2004, no pet.).

The probative value of evidence is enhanced if it is critical to a party's case. *Gigliobianco v. State*, 210 S.W.3d 637, 641 (Tex. Crim. App. 2006); *Willis v. State*, 932 S.W.2d 690, 697 (Tex. App.—Houston [14th Dist.] 1996, no pet.). *See also Goodson v. Castellanos*, 214 S.W.3d 741, 754 (Tex. App.—Austin 2007, pet. denied) (in deciding whether evidence should be excluded, the court must weigh the probative value of the evidence against its potential for unfair prejudice or confusion, and must examine the necessity and probative effect of the evidence); *Cook v. Sabio Oil & Gas, Inc.*, 972 S.W.2d 106, 111 (Tex. App.—Waco 1998, pet. denied). A party opposing evidence should always consider whether the evidence is truly needed by the party offering it.

The terms "probative" and "relevant" are not synonymous. *Gigliobianco v. State*, 210 S.W.3d 637, 641 (Tex. Crim. App. 2006). Relevancy, as defined by Rule 401, "is not an inherent characteristic of any item or evidence but exists as a relation between an item of evidence and a matter properly provable in the case." *Montgomery v. State*, 810 S.W.2d 372, 387 (Tex. Crim. App. 1990) (Advisory Committee's Note to Fed. R. Evid. 401). Evidence is either relevant or it is not. The probative value of the evidence, however, relates to the strength of the relationship and can be either high or low; that is, it refers to how strongly the evidence serves to make more or less probable the existence of a fact of consequence to the litigation. *Gonzalez v. State*, 544 S.W.3d 363, 371 (Tex. Crim. App. 2018); *Gigliobianco v. State*, 210 S.W.3d 637, 641 (Tex. Crim. App. 2006); *Andrews v. State*, 429 S.W.3d 849, 865 (Tex. App.—Texarkana, 2014, pet. ref'd). Evidence is probative when it is more than a surmise or a suspicion and tends to prove the proposition. *Jessop v. State*, 368 S.W.3d 653, 694 (Tex. App.—Austin 2012, no pet.); *Manuel v. State*, 357 S.W.3d 66, 74 (Tex. App.—Tyler 2011, pet. ref'd); *Green v. Alford*, 274 S.W.3d 5, 26 (Tex. App.—Houston [14th Dist.] 2008, pet. denied).

Regarding the definition of prejudice, it should be noted that almost every piece of evidence presented at trial can be said to be prejudicial to one side or the other. *Diamond Offshore Services Ltd. v. Williams*, 542 S.W.3d 539, 542 (Tex. 2018); *Pawlak v. State*, 420 S.W.3d 807, 809 (Tex. Crim. App. 2013) (plain language of Rule 403 does not allow a trial court to exclude otherwise relevant evidence when that evidence is merely prejudicial, because all evidence against a defendant is, by its very nature, designed to be prejudicial); *Bay Area Healthcare Group, Ltd. v. McShane*, 239 S.W.3d 231, 234 (Tex. 2007). As stated by the Texas Supreme Court, testimony is not inadmissible on the sole ground that it is "prejudicial," because "in the adversarial system, much of a proponent's evidence is legitimately intended to wound the opponent."

Diamond Offshore Services Ltd. v. Williams, 542 S.W.3d 539, 542 (Tex. 2018); *Bay Area Healthcare Group, Ltd. v. McShane*, 239 S.W.3d 231, 234 (Tex. 2007). *See also Pawlak v. State*, 420 S.W.3d 807, 809 (Tex. Crim. App. 2013). Only unfairly prejudicial evidence must be excluded under Rule 403. *Diamond Offshore Services Ltd. v. Williams*, 542 S.W.3d 539, 542 (Tex. 2018). Prejudice, as contemplated by Rule 403, is that which uniquely tends to evoke an emotional bias against a party and suggests that the jury will make its decision on an improper basis. *See Gonzalez v. State*, 544 S.W.3d 363, 371 (Tex. Crim. App. 2018); *Gigliobianco v. State*, 210 S.W.3d 637, 641 (Tex. Crim. App. 2006); *Olivares v. Doe*, 164 S.W.3d 427, 433 (Tex. App.—Texarkana 2004, pet. denied). Unfair prejudice, for purposes of rule regarding unfairly prejudicial evidence, is an undue tendency to suggest a decision on an improper basis, commonly, though not necessarily, an emotional one. *Diamond Offshore Services Ltd. v. Williams*, 542 S.W.3d 539, 542 (Tex. 2018); *Pawlak v. State*, 420 S.W.3d 807, 809 (Tex. Crim. App. 2013); *Rodriguez v. State*, 345 S.W.3d 504, 508 (Tex. App.—Waco 2011, pet. ref'd).

3. Supporting Authorities

Texas Rule of Evidence 403 states:

> Although relevant, evidence may be excluded if its probative value is substantially outweighed by the danger of unfair prejudice, confusion of the issues, or misleading the jury, or by considerations of undue delay, or needless presentation of cumulative evidence.
>
> When objecting to evidence under Rule 403, show the court how the evidence is not just prejudicial, but *unfairly* prejudicial, e.g., that the primary effect of the evidence is to appeal to raw emotions or that it is inflammatory. Similarly, if opposing a Rule 403 objection, show the court how the evidence is not unfairly prejudicial, but merely prejudicial.

Old Chief v. United States, 519 U.S. 172, 180, (1997) ("unfair prejudice, as to a criminal defendant, speaks to the capacity of some concededly relevant evidence to lure the factfinder into declaring guilt on a ground different from proof specific to the offense charged").

Gonzalez v. State, 544 S.W.3d 363, 371 (Tex. Crim. App. 2018) (Rule 403 is only concerned with "undue" prejudice; "evidence is unfairly prejudicial if it has the capacity to lure the fact-finder into declaring guilt on a ground different from proof specific to the offense charged").

Diamond Offshore Services Ltd. v. Williams, 542 S.W.3d 539, 542 (Tex. 2018) ("Testimony is not inadmissible on the sole ground that it is 'prejudicial' because in our adversarial system, much of a proponent's evidence is legitimately intended to wound the opponent. Rather, unfair prejudice is the proper inquiry.").

Diamond Offshore Services Ltd. v. Williams, 542 S.W.3d 539, 542 (Tex. 2018) ("Videos of an injured plaintiff could be unfairly prejudicial ... by focusing too much on pain or graphic wounds, appealing to emotion through moving music or overly sympathetic circumstances, or depicting the plaintiff in offensive clothing or engaging in potentially objectionable activities.").

Pawlak v. State, 420 S.W.3d 807, 809 (Tex. Crim. App. 2013) ("[I]t is possible for the admission of character evidence, though not necessarily cumulative, to cross the line from prejudicial to unfairly prejudicial based on the sheer volume of character evidence admitted.").

Pawlak v. State, 420 S.W.3d 807, 809 (Tex. Crim. App. 2013) ("[T]he sheer volume of extraneous-offense evidence was unfairly prejudicial and invited the jury to convict [a defendant] of sexually assaulting or attempting to sexually assault the victims because the defendant possessed 9,900 images that included homosexual child pornography.").

Waffle House, Inc. v. Williams, 313 S.W.3d 796, 812 n.77 (Tex. 2010) (evidence of sexual behavior outside of what society deems acceptable is inherently inflammatory).

Waffle House, Inc. v. Williams, 313 S.W.3d 796, 812 (Tex. 2010) (while evidence of a plaintiff's sexually provocative speech is not always inadmissible, the trial court must carefully weigh the applicable considerations in deciding whether to admit evidence of this kind).

Bay Area Healthcare Group, Ltd. v. McShane, 239 S.W.3d 231, 234 (Tex. 2007) ("[S]tatements from pleadings, depending on their content, could potentially be excluded as evidence at trial, as irrelevant or unfairly prejudicial.").

Casey v. State, 215 S.W.3d 870, 879 (Tex. Crim. App. 2007) ("[P]robative value refers to the inherent probative force of an item of evidence—that is, how strongly it serves to make more or less probable the existence of a fact of consequence to the litigation—coupled with the proponent's need for that item of evidence.").

Prible v. State, 175 S.W.3d 724, 736 (Tex. Crim. App. 2005), *cert. denied*, 126 S. Ct. 481 (2005) ("[The] minimal probative value of autopsy photographs [of children], if any, was substantially outweighed by the danger of unfair prejudice, confusion of the issues, by unduly focusing the jury's attention upon the deaths of the children rather than the deaths of their parents for which appellant was charged, and needless presentation of cumulative evidence.").

Erazo v. State, 144 S.W.3d 487, 492 (Tex. Crim. App. 2004) (trial court erred admitting a photograph of a victim's unborn child where the photograph was unfairly prejudicial and inflammatory and not needed to prove the prosecution's case).

Salazar v. State, 90 S.W.3d 330, 338 (Tex. Crim. App. 2002) (memorial video of victim "was very lengthy, highly emotional, and barely probative of the victim's life at the time of his death" and should not have been admitted).

Proo v. State, 587 S.W.3d 789, 814 (Tex. App.—San Antonio 2019, pet. ref'd) ("Relevant evidence is evidence having any tendency to make the existence of any fact that is of consequence to the determination of the action more probable or less probable than it would be without the evidence.").

Proo v. State, No. 587 S.W.3d 789, 814 (Tex. App.—San Antonio 2019, pet. ref'd) ("To be 'material,' the evidence must relate to a fact of consequence, which includes both an elemental fact or an evidentiary fact from which an elemental fact can be inferred.").

Proo v. State, No. 587 S.W.3d 789, 814 (Tex. App.—San Antonio 2019, pet. ref'd) ("To be 'probative,' the evidence must tend to make the existence of the fact of consequence more or less probable than it would be absent the evidence.").

Proo v. State, No. 587 S.W.3d 789, 814 (Tex. App.—San Antonio 2019, pet. ref'd) ("Relevancy is not an inherent characteristic of any item of evidence but exists as a relation between an item of evidence and a matter properly provable in the case.").

Gittens v. State, 560 S.W.3d 725 (Tex. App.—San Antonio 2018, no pet.) ("Rule 403 carries with it a presumption that relevant evidence will be more probative than prejudicial.... The rule envisions exclusion of evidence only when there is a clear disparity between the degree of prejudice of the offered evidence and its probative value.").

Gittens v. State, 560 S.W.3d 725 (Tex. App.—San Antonio 2018, no pet.) ("[P]robative value refers to the inherent probative force of an item of evidence—that is, how strongly it serves to make more or less probable the existence of a fact of consequence to the litigation—coupled with the proponent's need for that item of evidence.").

Gittens v. State, 560 S.W.3d 725 (Tex. App.—San Antonio 2018, no pet.) ("Unfair prejudice refers to a tendency to suggest decision on an improper basis, commonly, though not necessarily, an emotional one.... Evidence might be unfairly prejudicial if, for example, it arouses the jury's hostility or sympathy for one side without regard to the logical probative force of the evidence.").

Majors v. State, 554 S.W.3d 802, 808 (Tex. App.—Waco 2018, no pet.) ("An analysis under Rule 403 includes, but is not limited to, the following factors: (1) the probative value of the evidence, (2) the potential to impress the jury in some irrational yet indelible way, (3) the time needed to develop the evidence, and (4) the proponent's need for the evidence.").

GB Tubulars, Inc. v. Union Gas Operating Co., 527 S.W.3d 563, 572 (Tex. App.—Houston [14th Dist.] 2017, pet. denied) ("[E]vidence of similar incidents is inadmissible if it creates undue prejudice, confusion or delay.... Prolonged proof of what happened in other accidents cannot be used to distract a jury's attention from what happened in the case at hand.").

GB Tubulars, Inc. v. Union Gas Operating Co., 527 S.W.3d 563, 572 (Tex. App.—Houston [14th Dist.] 2017, pet. denied) ("[I]n exercising their discretion regarding the admission of evidence, [trial courts should] carefully consider the bounds of similarity, prejudice, confusion, and sequence before admitting evidence of other accidents involving a product.").

Sanders v. State, 422 S.W.3d 809, 815 (Tex. App.—Fort Worth 2014, no pet.) ("Rule 403 analysis should include, but is not limited to, considering the probative value of the evidence; the potential of the evidence to impress the jury in some irrational, indelible way or to suggest a decision on an improper basis; the time the proponent needs to develop the evidence; and the proponent's need for the evidence.").

Kirk v. State, 421 S.W.3d 772, 782 (Tex. App.—Fort Worth 2014, pet. ref'd) ("Rule 403 requires that a photograph have some probative value and that its probative value not be substantially outweighed by its inflammatory nature.").

Kirk v. State, 421 S.W.3d 772, 782 (Tex. App.—Fort Worth 2014, pet. ref'd) ("[A]mong the factors a court may consider in determining whether the probative value of photographs is substantially outweighed by the danger of unfair prejudice are the number of exhibits offered, their gruesomeness, their detail, their size, whether they are in color or black-and-white, whether they are close up, the availability of other means of proof, and other circumstances unique to the individual case.").

Newland v. State, 363 S.W.3d 205, 208 (Tex. App.—Waco 2011, pet. ref'd) ("[E]vidence might be unfairly prejudicial if … it arouses the jury's hostility or sympathy for one side without regard to the logical probative force of the evidence.").

Newland v. State, 363 S.W.3d 205, 208 (Tex. App.—Waco 2011, pet. ref'd) ("probative value for bolstering [a] witness's testimony with a non-specific threat not linked to the defendant, other than generally, and gang affiliation without being able to establish that the person making the threat was in the same gang as the defendant, and which may have occurred a year before trial, was very low and the danger of unfair prejudice is high" and thus the evidence should have been excluded).

Reese v. State, 340 S.W.3d 838, 841 (Tex. App.—San Antonio 2011, no pet.) ("[W]hen determining whether to admit or exclude photographic evidence of a victim's injuries, a court may … consider: (1) the number of photographs, (2) their size, (3) whether they are black and white or color, (4) their gruesomeness, (5) whether any bodies depicted are clothed or naked, and (6) whether any bodies depicted have been altered by autopsy.").

Perez v. DNT Global Star, L.L.C., 339 S.W.3d 692, 706 (Tex. App.—Houston [1st Dist.] 2011, no pet.) ("[T]he relevancy of nonviolent crimes was slight because of their dissimilarity to the murder in question, and thus, their prejudicial value outweighed their relevance.").

Jackson v. State, 314 S.W.3d 118, 124 (Tex. App.—Houston [1st Dist.] 2010, no pet.) ("[A] court determines the probative value of evidence by determining how strongly the evidence serves to make more or less probable the existence of a fact of consequence to the litigation coupled with the proponent's need for that item of evidence … then, the trial court must assess whether the probative value is substantially outweighed by one of the countervailing considerations listed in Rule 403.").

Alexander v. State, 282 S.W.3d 143, 145 (Tex. App.—Texarkana 2009, pet. ref'd), *cert. denied*, 130 S. Ct. 1886 (2010) ("[T]rial courts have the discretion to allow displays [of symbolism] in the courtroom during a trial so long as they are not prejudicial to a litigant.").

Dickson v. State, 246 S.W.3d 733, 739 (Tex. App.—Houston [14th Dist.] 2007, pet. ref'd) ("[R]elevant evidence of an alternative perpetrator may be excluded absent proof of a sufficient nexus between the crime charged and the alleged alternative perpetrator.").

Moore v. State, 143 S.W.3d 305, 313 (Tex. App.—Waco 2004, pet. ref'd) (under Rule 403, trial court did not abuse discretion excluding evidence of witness's ten-year-old theft convictions).

Rivera v. State, 130 S.W.3d 454, 460 (Tex. App.—Corpus Christi 2004, no pet.) (police report made by victim's mother regarding alleged act of conduct by someone other than defendant properly excluded as irrelevant, unduly prejudicial, and confusing to jury).

Strauss v. Cont'l Airlines, Inc., 67 S.W.3d 428, 450 (Tex. App.—Houston [14th Dist.] 2002, no pet.) (not abuse of trial court's discretion to exclude psychiatric records as irrelevant and unduly prejudicial).

Doe v. Mobile Video Tapes Inc., 43 S.W.3d 40, 57 (Tex. App.—Corpus Christi 2001, no pet.) ("[A] trial court has wide latitude to exclude evidence if it creates undue prejudice, distracts jury from main issue or issues, or consumes undue amount of time.").

Dade v. State, 956 S.W.2d 75, 80 (Tex. App.—Tyler 1997, pet. ref'd) (in applying Rule 403 balancing test, trial court should "look to see if the evidence presented would likely impress the jury 'in some irrational but nevertheless indelible way'") (citing *Bigby v. State*, 892 S.W.2d 864 (Tex. Crim. App. 1994), *cert. denied*, 515 U.S. 1162 (1995)).

Soc'y of Mary's Stars, Inc. v. State, 748 S.W.2d 320 (Tex. App.—Fort Worth 1988, writ denied) (admission of warranty deed in condemnation proceeding properly excluded by trial court as unduly prejudicial where deed was executed two months after petition for condemnation filed and would allow party to manufacture higher purchase price).

4. *Opposing Authorities*

> *Note: The Advisory Committee Note to Federal Rule of Evidence 403 suggests that the trial court should also consider whether a limiting instruction under Federal Rule 105 (which is in effect identical to Texas Evidence Rule 105) would be effective to cure the prejudice from offered evidence, as well as whether there are other means of proof available. When opposing a Rule 403 objection to evidence, show the court how a limiting jury instruction would be effective in mitigating the prejudicial harm of the evidence, and/or show the need for the evidence by demonstrating that it is the only evidence available to offer on the material fact or is high in probative value.*

Diamond Offshore Services Ltd. v. Williams, 542 S.W.3d 539, 542 (Tex. 2018) ("Mere damage to an opponent's case does not constitute unfair prejudice.").

Diamond Offshore Services Ltd. v. Williams, 542 S.W.3d 539, 542 (Tex. 2018) ("Testimony is not inadmissible on the sole ground that it is 'prejudicial' because in our adversarial system, much of a proponent's evidence is legitimately intended to wound the opponent. Rather, unfair prejudice is the proper inquiry.").

Hernandez v. State, 390 S.W.3d 310, 323 (Tex. Crim. App. 2012) (Rule 403 "carries a presumption that relevant evidence will be more probative than prejudicial").

Hernandez v. State, 390 S.W.3d 310, 323 (Tex. Crim. App. 2012) ("[P]robative value refers to the inherent probative force of an item of evidence—that is, how strongly it serves to make more or less probable the existence of a fact of consequence to the litigation—coupled with the proponent's need for that item of evidence.").

Hernandez v. State, 390 S.W.3d 310, 323 (Tex. Crim. App. 2012) ("[U]nfair prejudice refers to the tendency to suggest that decisions may be made on an improper basis, commonly an emotional one.").

Hernandez v. State, 390 S.W.3d 310, 323 (Tex. Crim. App. 2012) ("[A]ll evidence is prejudicial to one party or the other—it is only when there is a clear disparity between the degree of prejudice of the offered evidence and its probative value that Rule 403 is applicable.").

Hammer v. State, 296 S.W.3d 555, 568 (Tex. Crim. App. 2009) ("Under Rule 403, it is presumed that the probative value of relevant evidence exceeds any danger of unfair prejudice.").

Hammer v. State, 296 S.W.3d 555, 568 (Tex. Crim. App. 2009) ("[Rule 403] envisions exclusion of evidence only when there is a 'clear disparity between the degree of prejudice of the offered evidence and its probative value.'").

Hammer v. State, 296 S.W.3d 555, 568 (Tex. Crim. App. 2009) ("Because Rule 403 permits the exclusion of admittedly probative evidence, it is a remedy that should be used sparingly, especially in 'he said, she said' sexual-molestation cases that must be resolved solely on the basis of the testimony of the complainant and the defendant.").

Bay Area Healthcare Group, Ltd. v. McShane, 239 S.W.3d 231, 234 (Tex. 2007) (testimony is not inadmissible on the sole ground that it is prejudicial because in the adversarial system, much of a proponent's evidence is legitimately intended to wound the opponent).

Newbury v. State, 135 S.W.3d 22, 41 (Tex. Crim. App. 2004), *cert. denied*, 543 U.S. 990 (2004) (trial court did not abuse discretion by admitting autopsy photographs where relevant and not unfairly prejudicial).

Rayford v. State, 125 S.W.3d 521, 529 (Tex. Crim. App. 2003) (autopsy photographs relevant and not unfairly prejudicial).

Manning v. State, 114 S.W.3d 922, 925 (Tex. Crim. App. 2003) (evidence of cocaine in defendant's system, where relevant to important issue in case, not unduly prejudicial or time-consuming).

Hayes v. State, 85 S.W.3d 809, 816 (Tex. Crim. App. 2002) (autopsy photographs were relevant and not unfairly prejudicial even though medical examiner reconstructed victim's head and had pulled skin away from wound).

Wheeler v. State, 67 S.W.3d 879, 886 (Tex. Crim. App. 2002) (trial court did not abuse discretion by admitting evidence of prior sexual assault where evidence not unfairly prejudicial and needed to assist in proving case).

Ripkowski v. State, 61 S.W.3d 378, 392 (Tex. Crim. App. 2001), *cert. denied*, 539 U.S. 916 (2003) (crime scene and victim photographs relevant and not unfairly prejudicial).

Ransom v. State, 920 S.W.2d 288, 299 (Tex. Crim. App. 1994), cert. denied, 519 U.S. 1030 (1996) (evidence of stolen car and gun, and that defendant assaulted prosecutor and own attorney after voir dire, relevant and not unfairly prejudicial).

Webb v. State, 575 S.W.3d 905, 911 (Tex. App.—Waco 2019, pet. filed) ("All testimony and physical evidence will likely be prejudicial to one party or the other.... It is only when there exists a clear disparity between the degree of prejudice of the offered evidence and its probative value that the evidence is considered unfairly prejudicial and in violation of Rule 403.").

R&M Mixed Beverage Consultants, Inc. v. Safe Harbor Benefits, Inc., 578 S.W.3d 218, 242 (Tex. App.—El Paso 2019, no pet.) ("Evidence is relevant if it has any tendency to make a fact more or less probable than it would be without the evidence and the fact is of consequence in determining the action.").

Majors v. State, 554 S.W.3d 802, 808 (Tex. App.—Waco 2018, no pet.) (video clip from social media showing the defendant saying he had been to the penitentiary and was going to buy guns was probative, and it did not take an inordinate amount of time to present, or confuse or distract the jury from the main issue, which was whether he possessed the firearm found in the center console of the vehicle he owned and was driving).

GB Tubulars, Inc. v. Union Gas Operating Co., 527 S.W.3d 563, 572 (Tex. App.—Houston [14th Dist.] 2017, pet. denied) (in a product defect case, evidence of similar "incidents may be relevant to show whether a product was defective or unreasonably dangerous or that a manufacturer was on notice of prior or continuing problems with the product").

Andrews v. State, 429 S.W.3d 849, 865 (Tex. App.—Texarkana 2014, pet. ref'd) ("[P]robative value refers to the inherent probative force of an item of evidence—that is, how strongly it serves to make more or less probable the existence of a fact of consequence to the litigation—coupled with the proponent's need for that item of evidence.").

Sanders v. State, 422 S.W.3d 809, 815 (Tex. App.—Fort Worth 2014, no pet.) ("[W]hen a trial court tests and determines that the balance is a close one, it should favor admission, in keeping with the presumption of admissibility of relevant evidence.").

Rhey v. Redic, 408 S.W.3d 440, 460 (Tex. App.—El Paso 2013, no pet.) ("[E]vidence is relevant, and therefore admissible, if it has any tendency to make the existence of any fact that is of consequence to the determination of the action more probable or less probable than it would be without the evidence.").

Rhey v. Redic, 408 S.W.3d 440, 460 (Tex. App.—El Paso 2013, no pet.) ("[T]o determine relevancy, the court must look at the purpose for offering the evidence.... There must be some logical connection either directly or by inference between the fact offered and the fact to be proved.").

Malone v. Patel, 397 S.W.3d 658, 673 (Tex. App.—Houston [1st Dist.] 2012, pet. denied) ("[A]ny evidence has probative value if it contributes to the proof of an issue.").

Ibenyenwa v. State, 367 S.W.3d 420, 425 (Tex. App.—Fort Worth 2012, pet. ref'd) (probative value of evidence of forensic interviewer's interview with child sex abuse victim was not outweighed by prejudice; "the interview was inherently probative to the issue of whether [the interviewer's] technique amounted to 'coaching' the child, and was the only evidence of whether the child equivocated in the interview").

Reese v. State, 340 S.W.3d 838, 841 (Tex. App.—San Antonio 2011, no pet.) ("[T]hat a relevant picture is gruesome does not alone require its exclusion from evidence.").

PPC Transp. v. Metcalf, 254 S.W.3d 636, 643 (Tex. App.—Tyler 2008, no pet.) ("[A]ny unfair prejudice related to evidence of [the plaintiff's] consumption of alcohol [did] not substantially outweigh its probative value.").

Young v. State, 242 S.W.3d 192, 200 (Tex. App.—Tyler 2007, no pet.) (photographs of sexual items should not have been admitted in child pornography case as none of the items had the tendency to make the existence of any fact that was of consequence to determination of the action more probable than it would be without the evidence).

Hall v. State, 137 S.W.3d 847, 854 (Tex. App.—Houston [1st Dist.] 2004, pet. ref'd) (trial court did not abuse its discretion by admitting autopsy photographs, because the photographs were relevant and not unfairly prejudicial, and did not represent mutilation caused by the autopsy itself).

Mayhew v. Dealey, 143 S.W.3d 356, 370 (Tex. App.—Dallas 2004, pet. denied) (audiotapes made three years before accident were relevant to demonstrate deceased's behavior and not unfairly prejudicial).

Apolinar v. State, 106 S.W.3d 407, 419 (Tex. App.—Houston [1st Dist.] 2003, pet. ref'd), *aff'd*, 155 S.W.3d 184 (2005) (witness's testimony regarding defendant's prior bad act relevant to identification and not unfairly prejudicial).

Jones v. State, 119 S.W.3d 412, 422 (Tex. App.—Fort Worth 2003, no pet.) (trial court did not abuse its discretion in case involving indecency with a child by determining that probative value of evidence of other acts of sexual conduct, with victim and others, outweighed prejudicial effect).

Best v. State, 118 S.W.3d 857, 864 (Tex. App.—Fort Worth 2003, no pet.) (in a case involving the possession of a controlled substance, evidence that a defendant was speeding and had an expired insurance card and inspection sticker were relevant context evidence and not unfairly prejudicial).

Booker v. State, 103 S.W.3d 521, 532 (Tex. App.—Fort Worth 2003, pet. ref'd) (evidence of prior act of kidnapping woman and her child was not "inherently inflammatory" and not unfairly prejudicial).

In re J.W., 113 S.W.3d 605, 612 (Tex. App.—Dallas 2003, pet. denied) (in a case involving termination of parental rights, evidence of parents' arrests and charges relevant and not unfairly prejudicial).

Dorsey v. State, 117 S.W.3d 332, 335 (Tex. App.—Beaumont 2003, pet. ref'd) (evidence that a defendant had rented a movie with a plot similar to the offense committed was relevant and not unfairly prejudicial).

Saxer v. State, 115 S.W.3d 765, 776 (Tex. App.—Beaumont 2003, pet. ref'd) (trial court did not abuse discretion by admitting evidence of defendant's other offenses and bad acts where evidence irrelevant and not unfairly prejudicial).

State v. Mechler, 123 S.W.3d 449, 454 (Tex. App.—Houston [14th Dist.] 2003), *aff'd*, 153 S.W.3d 435 (Tex. Crim. App. 2005) (probative value of a breathalyzer test taken an hour and a half after an offense not outweighed by the prejudicial impact of that evidence, even though the prosecution did not have a strong need for the evidence to prove its case).

Hudson v. State, 112 S.W.3d 794, 799 (Tex. App.—Houston [14th Dist.] 2003, pet. ref'd) (evidence of defendant's prior assault on victim with knife relevant and not unfairly prejudicial).

Smith v. State, 105 S.W.3d 203, 207 (Tex. App.—Houston [14th Dist.] 2003, pet. ref'd) (in prosecution for driving while intoxicated, police videotape of defendant appearing intoxicated admitting he had been incarcerated was relevant and not unfairly prejudicial).

Goldberg v. State, 95 S.W.3d 345, 375 (Tex. App.—Houston [1st Dist.] 2002, pet. ref'd), *cert. denied*, 540 U.S. 1190 (2004) (evidence of knives found in defendant's vehicle and of notebook seized three years before offense containing drawings and discussing killing women relevant and not unfairly prejudicial).

Lemmons v. State, 75 S.W.3d 513, 523 (Tex. App.—San Antonio 2002, pet. ref'd) (evidence of an offense offered to suggest that the defendant was an aggressor was relevant and not unduly prejudicial).

Moss v. State, 75 S.W.3d 132, 141 (Tex. App.—San Antonio 2002, pet. ref'd) (in prosecution for aggravated robbery, trial court did not abuse discretion by admitting numerous weapons and ammunition where evidence relevant and not unfairly prejudicial).

Ripkowski v. State, 61 S.W.3d 378, 392 (Tex. Crim. App. 2001), *cert. denied*, 539 U.S. 916 (2003) (crime scene and victim photographs relevant and not unfairly prejudicial).

Franco v. State, 25 S.W.3d 26, 28 (Tex. App.—El Paso 2000, pet. ref'd) (probative value of evidence defendant was found in a "crack house," was not outweighed by prejudicial impact of evidence).

Magee v. State, 994 S.W.2d 878, 888 (Tex. App.—Waco 1999, pet. ref'd) (trial court properly admitted the testimony of a defendant's work as a rap musician and that some people refer to the music as "gangsta rap"; the case also held that the trial court erred in admitting testimony about music labels such as "Demize," "Killer Instinct," and "Sex, Drugs and Guns, The American Way," where the inflammatory nature had potential to impress jury in an "irrational way").

Fort Worth Hotel v. Enserch Corp., 977 S.W.2d 746, 758 (Tex. App.—Fort Worth 1998, no pet.) (evidence of continued operability of hotel after explosion was prejudicial, but not unfairly prejudicial).

Draheim v. State, 916 S.W.2d 593, 601 (Tex. App.—San Antonio 1996, pet. ref'd) (videotape of a defendant sexually assaulting a child properly admitted, where the tape was extremely lengthy, in color, extremely detailed, and further cumulative of the defendant's own testimony; "the fact that the tape was 'highly inflammatory' says no more than that [the defendant's] crimes were 'highly inflammatory;' it does not establish that the tape was unfairly prejudicial.... In short, while [the] videotape was unquestionably prejudicial, it was not unfairly prejudicial").

Farr v. Wright, 833 S.W.2d 597, 602 (Tex. App.—Corpus Christi 1992, writ denied) (high probative value of evidence of a doctor's knowledge of infections in a medical malpractice case substantially outweighed prejudicial effect).

Gonzalez v. Tex. Employers Ins. Assoc., 772 S.W.2d 145, 149 (Tex. App.—Corpus Christi 1989, writ denied) ("While the evidence may have cast appellant in a negative light, we cannot say that it was so inherently prejudicial as to outweigh the jury's entitlement to know the employer's reasons for not providing him light duties and firing him instead.").

a. *Harmless Error*

Gunn v. McCoy, 554 S.W.3d 645, 666 (Tex. 2018) ("To reverse a trial court's judgment based on the exclusion of evidence, [an appeals court] must find that the trial court did in fact commit error, and that the error was harmful.").

Gonzalez v. State, 544 S.W.3d 363, 371 (Tex. Crim. App. 2018) ("If [an appeals court has] a fair assurance from an examination of the record as a whole that the error [in admission of evidence] did not influence the jury, or had but a slight effect, [the court] will not overturn the conviction.").

Gonzalez v. State, 544 S.W.3d 363, 373 Tex. Crim. App. 2018) ("In making [the] determination [of whether erroneously admitted evidence affected a defendant's substantial rights, appeals courts] consider: (1) the character of the alleged error and how it might be considered in connection with other evidence; (2) the nature of the evidence supporting the verdict; (3) the existence and degree of additional evidence indicating guilt; and (4) whether the State emphasized the complained of error.").

State v. Cent. Expressway Sign Ass'ns, 302 S.W.3d 866, 870 (Tex. 2009) (stating that if erroneously admitted or excluded evidence was crucial to a key issue, the error is likely harmful).

Prible v. State, 175 S.W.3d 724, 736 (Tex. Crim. App. 2005), *cert. denied*, 546 U.S. 962 (2005) (even though "minimal probative value of autopsy photographs [of children], if any, was substantially outweighed by the danger of unfair prejudice, confusion of the issues, by unduly focusing the jury's attention upon the deaths of the children rather than the deaths of their parents for which appellant was charged, and needless presentation of cumulative evidence", the error did not affect the appellant's substantial rights because they did "not affect the determination of appellant's guilt in this case and would not emotionally sway a factfinder until and unless he had found that appellant was the person who had caused the parents' deaths").

Equistar Chemicals, LP v. ClydeUnion DB, Ltd., 579 S.W.3d 505, 514 (Tex. App.—Houston [14th Dist.] May 16, 2019, pet. filed) ("If the excluded evidence was crucial to a key issue, the error is likely harmful.... But if the evidence was cumulative or the rest of the evidence at trial was so one-sided that the error likely made no difference in the judgment, then the error is likely harmless.... Generally, exclusion of evidence is not reversible error unless the complaining party demonstrates that the whole case turns on the particular evidence excluded.").

McMinn v. State, 558 S.W.3d 262, 271 (Tex. App.—Houston [14th Dist.] 2018, no pet.) (error in the admission of evidence is harmless if the appellate court has "fair assurance that the error did not influence the jury, or had but a slight effect").

Benson v. Chalk, 536 S.W.3d 886, 904 (Tex. App.—Houston [1st Dist.] 2017, pet. denied) ("[T]o obtain a reversal based on an error in the admission of evidence, [the appellant] must show that the trial court's ruling was erroneous and the error was calculated to cause and probably did cause the rendition of an improper judgment....The excluded evidence must be controlling on a material issue and not cumulative of other evidence.").

Kirk v. State, 421 S.W.3d 772, 782 (Tex. App.—Fort Worth 2014, pet. ref'd) (appellate court will "disregard the error in admitting evidence if the error did not affect the defendant's substantial rights"; "a substantial right is affected when the error had a substantial and injurious effect or influence in determining the jury's verdict ... an error does not affect a substantial right if the court has fair assurance that the error did not influence the jury, or had but a slight effect").

Godfrey v. Sec. Serv. Fed. Credit Union, 356 S.W.3d 720, 723 (Tex. App.—El Paso 2011, no pet.) ("[A] party complaining on appeal of the admission or exclusion of evidence must show both that the trial court's ruling was erroneous and probably caused rendition of an improper judgment.").

Puentes v. Fannie Mae, 350 S.W.3d 732, 737 (Tex. App.—El Paso 2011, pet. dism'd) ("[W]hen erroneously admitted or excluded evidence was crucial to a key issue, the error is most likely harmful.... On the other hand, the admission or exclusion of a particular exhibit is likely harmless if the evidence was cumulative of other evidence in the record, or if the balance of the evidence in the case was so one-sided that the error was not likely to have affected the judgment.").

E-Z Mart Stores, Inc. v. Ronald Holland's A-Plus Transmission & Auto., Inc., 358 S.W.3d 665, 675 (Tex. App.—San Antonio 2011, pet. denied) ("[O]n appeal, the complaining party must not only show the trial court committed error in its ruling, but also that the error probably caused the rendition of an improper judgment.... It is not necessary for the complaining party to prove that but for the exclusion of the evidence, there would have been a different outcome, but only that the exclusion of evidence probably resulted in the rendition of an improper judgment.").

E-Z Mart Stores, Inc. v. Ronald Holland's A-Plus Transmission & Auto., Inc., 358 S.W.3d 665, 675 (Tex. App.—San Antonio 2011, pet. denied) (excluded evidence concerning gas leaks from a petroleum storage system underneath a convenience store that occurred during previous owner's holding of the store property, in a case concerning contamination in a neighboring party's property, was "case-turning" in that the excluded evidence was relevant to the causation issue and to the store's defense that it did not proximately cause the contamination; exclusion of the evidence prevented the store from countering the property owner's claim that it was the store's gasoline that migrated onto the property because the store was not allowed to present evidence of leaks occurring when the previous owner owned the property).

Laird Hill Salt Water Disposal, Ltd. v. E. Tex. Salt Water Disposal, Inc., 351 S.W.3d 81, 95 (Tex. App.—Tyler 2011, pet. denied) ("[I]n determining if the excluded evidence probably resulted in the rendition of an improper judgment, a successful challenge to a trial court's evidentiary rulings requires the complaining party to demonstrate that the judgment turns on the particular evidence excluded or admitted.").

Gulf Liquids New River Project, LLC v. Gulsby Eng'g, Inc., 356 S.W.3d 54, 78 (Tex. App.—Houston [1st Dist.] 2011, no pet.) ("[E]rroneously excluded evidence constitutes reversible error if it is both controlling on a material issue and not cumulative.").

State Office of Risk Mgmt. v. Allen, 247 S.W.3d 797, 798 (Tex. App.—Dallas 2008) ("[An] error in the admission of evidence at trial is deemed harmless if the objecting party permits the same or similar evidence to be introduced without objection.").

B. Motion to Exclude Evidence That Will Waste Court's Time

1. *Suggested Motion Text*

(*Name of Moving Party*) hereby moves this Court for an order excluding any and all evidence, references to evidence, testimony, or argument relating to (*Describe Time-Wasting Evidence*). The motion is based upon the ground that there is a substantial danger that introduction of the evidence will necessitate an undue consumption of time.

2. Motion Summary

This motion is used to exclude evidence that threatens to consume an undue amount of time. It is based on Texas Rule of Evidence 403, which provides the express authority for the exclusion of such evidence. *See Alvarado v. State*, 912 S.W.2d 199, 213 (Tex. Crim. App. 1995).

3. Supporting Authorities

Texas Rule of Evidence 403 states:

> Although relevant, evidence may be excluded if its probative value is substantially outweighed by the danger of unfair prejudice, confusion of the issues, or misleading the jury, or by *considerations of undue delay*, or needless presentation of cumulative evidence. (Emphasis added.)

Prible v. State, 175 S.W.3d 724, 736 (Tex. Crim. App. 2005), *cert. denied*, 546 U.S. 962 (2005) ("[The] minimal probative value of autopsy photographs [of children], if any, was substantially outweighed by the danger of unfair prejudice, confusion of the issues, by unduly focusing the jury's attention upon the deaths of the children rather than the deaths of their parents for which appellant was charged, and needless presentation of cumulative evidence.").

Salazar v. State, 90 S.W.3d 330, 338 (Tex. Crim. App. 2002) (memorial video of victim "was very lengthy, highly emotional, and barely probative of the victim's life at the time of his death" and should not have been admitted).

Dow Chem. Co. v. Francis, 46 S.W.3d 237, 241 (Tex. 2001) ("[A] trial court may properly intervene to maintain control in the courtroom, to expedite the trial, and to prevent what it considers to be a waste of time.").

Alvarado v. State, 912 S.W.2d 199, 213 (Tex. Crim. App. 1995) ("Rule 403 authorizes exclusion of evidence due to considerations of undue delay [based on a concern] with efficiency of judicial proceedings rather than threat of inaccurate decisions.").

Matter of Marriage of Harrison, 557 S.W.3d 99, 123 (Tex. App.—Houston [14th Dist.] 2018, pet. denied) ("Trial courts have great discretion to control the disposition of cases with economy of time and effort for itself, for counsel, and for litigants.... This discretion empowers a trial court to fulfill a duty to schedule its cases in such a manner as to expeditiously dispose of them.").

Hansen v. JP Morgan Chase Bank, N.A., 346 S.W.3d 769, 777 (Tex. App.—Dallas 2011, no pet.) ("[A] trial court may properly intervene to maintain control in the courtroom, to expedite the trial, and to what it considers to be a waste of time.").

Celis v. State, 354 S.W.3d 7, 38 (Tex. App.—Corpus Christi 2011), *aff'd*, 416 S.W.3d 419 (Tex. Crim. App. 2013) ("[I]f the [excluded] evidence is generally cumulative of other evidence introduced in the case, no harm attaches.").

E-Z Mart Stores, Inc. v. Ronald Holland's A-Plus Transmission & Auto., Inc., 358 S.W.3d 665, 675 (Tex. App.—San Antonio 2011, pet. denied) ("[T]he exclusion or admission of evidence is likely harmless if the evidence was cumulative, or the rest of the evidence was so one-sided that the error likely made no difference in the judgment.").

Cleveland Reg'l Med. Ctr., L.P. v. Celtic Props., L.C., 323 S.W.3d 322, 339 (Tex. App.—Beaumont 2010, pet. denied) (evidence of email communications between landlord's prior counsel and tenant's counsel was "merely cumulative of other evidence, and appellants did not reasonably show that the exclusion of this evidence probably caused the rendition of an improper judgment").

State v. Reina, 218 S.W.3d 247, 255 (Tex. App.—Houston [14th Dist.] 2007, no pet.) (trial court is vested with great discretion over the conduct of the trial, and this discretion includes its intervention to maintain control in the courtroom, to expedite the trial, and to prevent what it considers to be a waste of time).

Doe v. Mobile Video Tapes Inc., 43 S.W.3d 40, 57 (Tex. App.—Corpus Christi 2001, no pet.) ("[A] trial court has wide latitude to exclude evidence if it creates undue prejudice, distracts jury from main issue or issues, or consumes undue amount of time.").

Castillo v. State, 939 S.W.2d 754 (Tex. App.—Houston [14th Dist.] 1997, pet. ref'd) (exclusion of evidence of overtime earned where benefit of evidence easily outweighed by potential for unnecessary delay).

Service Lloyds Ins. Co. v. Martin, 855 S.W.2d 816 (Tex. App.—Dallas 1993, no writ) (evidence of prior medical claims properly excluded where such evidence would constitute relitigation, significantly impact trial, and unduly delay resolution).

Mo., K. & T. Ry. Co. v. Bailey, 115 S.W. 601 (Tex. Civ. App.—1908, writ ref'd) (exclusion of evidence on collateral issues where it would have unduly prolonged trial).

4. Opposing Authorities

Manning v. State, 114 S.W.3d 922, 928 (Tex. Crim. App. 2003) (evidence of the presence cocaine in a defendant's system was relevant to an important issue in the case and not unduly prejudicial or time-consuming).

In re Estate of Watson, 720 S.W.2d 806, 808 (Tex. 1986) (trial court erred in excluding eighty-one letters where they were not merely cumulative but "were strongest rebuttal evidence available").

Proo v. State, 587 S.W.3d 789, 817 (Tex. App.—San Antonio 2019, pet. ref'd) ("Photographs of a victim's injuries are relevant and their relevance is not diminished merely because the jury also heard testimony about the same injuries.").

Kirk v. State, 421 S.W.3d 772, 782 (Tex. App.—Fort Worth 2014, pet. ref'd) ("[P]hotographs are neither cumulative nor lacking in significant probative value simply because they merely corroborate other kinds of evidence.").

Gulf Liquids New River Project, LLC v. Gulsby Eng'g, Inc., 356 S.W.3d 54, 78 (Tex. App.—Houston [1st Dist.] 2011, no pet.) ("[E]rroneously excluded evidence constitutes reversible error if it is both controlling on a material issue and not cumulative.").

Jaggers v. State, 125 S.W.3d 661, 670 (Tex. App.—Houston [1st Dist.] 2003, pet. ref'd) ("[A] trial court did not abuse its discretion by admitting evidence of a defendant's other acts over the defendant's Rule 403 objections where the evidence was relevant, not unfairly prejudicial or inflammatory, not unduly time-consuming, and needed by the prosecution.").

State v. Mechler, 123 S.W.3d 449, 454 (Tex. App.—Houston [14th Dist.] 2003), *aff'd*, 153 S.W.3d 435 (Tex. Crim. App. 2005) (evidence of a breathalyzer test taken an hour and a half after an offense was not unduly time-consuming).

Dewberry v. State, 979 S.W.2d 871, 876 (Tex. App.—Beaumont 1998, no pet. ref'd) (nine photographs of a murder victim were properly admitted into evidence despite considerations of undue delay where they were not repetitive, depicted the victim's wounds, and the subject of testimony at trial).

C. Motion to Exclude Confusing or Misleading Evidence

1. Suggested Motion Text

(*Name of Moving Party*) hereby moves this Court for an order excluding any and all evidence, references to evidence, testimony, or argument relating to (*Describe Confusing Evidence*). The motion is based upon the ground that there is a substantial danger that the evidence will confuse the issues or mislead the jury.

2. Motion Summary

This motion is used to exclude evidence that will create a substantial danger of confusing the issues or misleading the jury. The motion is based upon the express authority of Texas Rule of Evidence 403 and leading cases.

Confusion of the issues occurs when the introduction of contested evidence requires additional proof or other evidence that creates a side issue that unduly distracts the jury from the main issues. *See Gonzalez v. State*, 544 S.W.3d 363, 371 (Tex. Crim. App. 2018); *Casey v. State*, 215 S.W.3d 870, 879 (Tex. Crim. App. 2007); *GB Tubulars, Inc. v. Union Gas Operating Co.*, 527 S.W.3d 563, 572 (Tex. App.—Houston [14th Dist.] 2017, pet. denied); *Myuboreno v. State*, 409 S.W.3d 723, 729 (Tex. App.—Houston [1st Dist.] 2013, pet. ref'd); *Dickson v. State*, 246 S.W.3d 733, 739 (Tex. App.—Houston [14th Dist.] 2007, pet. ref'd). For example, evidence that consumes an inordinate amount of time to present or answer might tend to confuse or distract the jury from the main issues. *Casey v. State*, 215 S.W.3d 870, 879 (Tex. Crim. App. 2007); *GB Tubulars, Inc. v. Union Gas Operating Co.*, 527 S.W.3d 563, 572 (Tex. App.—Houston [14th Dist.] 2017, pet. denied); *Jackson v. State*, 314 S.W.3d 118, 124 (Tex. App.—Houston [1st Dist.] 2010, no pet.).

"Confusion of the issues" has been distinguished from "misleading the jury" in the following manner: confusion of the issues is similar to a rabbit trail or evidence that takes the jury in an incorrect direction, whereas misleading the jury refers to evidence which can cause a jury to give it more weight than it actually merits or evidence that is seductively persuasive. An example of such would the pseudo-scientific razzle-dazzle of "junk science." "Misleading the jury" refers to a tendency of an item of evidence to be given undue weight by the jury on other than emotional grounds. *Casey v. State*, 215 S.W.3d 870, 879 (Tex. Crim. App. 2007). For example, "scientific" evidence might mislead a jury that is not properly equipped to judge the probative force of the evidence. *Casey v. State*, 215 S.W.3d 870, 879 (Tex. Crim. App. 2007). In contrast, "undue delay" and "needless presentation of cumulative evidence" concern the efficiency of the trial proceeding rather than the threat of an inaccurate decision. *Casey v. State*, 215 S.W.3d 870, 879 (Tex. Crim. App. 2007).

3. Supporting Authorities

Texas Rule of Evidence 403 states:

> Although relevant, evidence may be excluded if its probative value is substantially outweighed by the danger of unfair prejudice, *confusion of the issues*, or *misleading the jury*, or by considerations of undue delay, or needless presentation of cumulative evidence. (Emphasis added.)

Henley v. State, 493 S.W.3d 77, 93 (Tex. Crim. App. 2016) (evidence that the victim had supervised visitation with her children because she lived with a husband who had been accused of assaulting children and because the husband's stepson had sexually assaulted children, was properly excluded because admission of this evidence would only have served to confuse and distract the jury from the main issues, and would have allowed them to give undue weight to this evidence for no purpose other than, possibly, jury nullification).

Layton v. State, 280 S.W.3d 235, 241 (Tex. Crim. App. 2009) ("[S]cientific evidence has the ability to mislead a jury that is not properly equipped to judge the probative force of the evidence.").

Prible v. State, 175 S.W.3d 724, 736 (Tex. Crim. App. 2005), *cert. denied*, 546 U.S. 962 (2005) ("[M]inimal probative value of autopsy photographs [of children], if any, was substantially outweighed by the danger of unfair prejudice, confusion of the issues, by unduly focusing the jury's attention upon the deaths of the children rather than the deaths of their parents for which appellant was charged, and needless presentation of cumulative evidence.").

Sells v. State, 121 S.W.3d 748, 766 (Tex. Crim. App. 2003), *cert. denied*, 540 U.S. 986 (2003) (trial court did not abuse discretion excluding videotape offered at penalty phase where confusing and distracting).

Resendiz v. State, 112 S.W.3d 541, 544 (Tex. Crim. App. 2003), *cert. denied*, 541 U.S. 1032 (2004) (trial court did not abuse discretion excluding crime scene photographs where misleading and confusing to jury and could distract them from the charges).

Salazar v. State, 90 S.W.3d 330, 338 (Tex. Crim. App. 2002) (memorial video of victim "was very lengthy, highly emotional, and barely probative of the victim's life at the time of his death" and should not have been admitted).

Owens-Corning Fiberglas Corp. v. Malone, 972 S.W.2d 35, 41 (Tex. 1998) (evidence of unpaid punitive damages awards excluded where there were risks of unfair prejudice and jury confusion).

E.I. du Pont de Nemours & Co. v. Robinson, 923 S.W.2d 549, 557 (Tex. 1995) (exclusion of expert testimony under Rule 403 is possible if there is a potential for confusing the issues and misleading the jury).

Silcott v. Oglesby, 721 S.W.2d 290, 294 (Tex. 1986) (trial court properly excluded evidence to avoid injecting "confusing collateral issues" into proceedings).

GB Tubulars, Inc. v. Union Gas Operating Co., 527 S.W.3d 563, 572 (Tex. App.—Houston [14th Dist.] 2017, pet. denied) ("[E]vidence of similar incidents is inadmissible if it creates undue prejudice, confusion or delay ... Prolonged proof of what happened in other accidents cannot be used to distract a jury's attention from what happened in the case at hand.").

GB Tubulars, Inc. v. Union Gas Operating Co., 527 S.W.3d 563, 572 (Tex. App.—Houston [14th Dist.] 2017, pet. denied) ("[I]n exercising their discretion regarding the admission of evidence, [trial courts should] 'carefully consider the bounds of similarity, prejudice, confusion, and sequence before admitting evidence of other accidents involving a product.'").

Moreno v. State, 409 S.W.3d 723, 730 (Tex. App.—Houston [1st Dist.] 2013, pet. ref'd) ("[E]vidence that consumes an inordinate amount of time to present or answer ... might tend to confuse or distract the jury from the main issues.").

Sandoval v. State, 409 S.W.3d 259, 304 (Tex. App.—Austin 2013, no pet.) ("[E]vidence showing the commission of extraneous misconduct is usually excluded because such evidence is inherently prejudicial, tends to confuse the issues of a case, and forces the accused to defend himself against charges that he had not been notified would be brought against him.").

Beckendam v. State, 398 S.W.3d 358, 366 (Tex. App.—Fort Worth 2013, no pet.) ("Scientific evidence has the ability to mislead a jury that is not properly equipped to judge the probative force of the evidence.").

Smith v. State, 352 S.W.3d 55, 68 (Tex. App.—Fort Worth 2011, no pet.) ("[The] trial court has the discretion to limit testimony that may confuse the issues or be only marginally relevant.").

McNeil v. State, 398 S.W.3d 747, 756 (Tex. App.—Houston [1st Dist.] 2011, pet. ref'd), *cert. denied*, 568 U.S. 1173 (2013) (one of the factors considered in determining whether a piece of evidence's degree of prejudice is outweighed by its probative value is to consider any tendency of the evidence to confuse or distract jury from the main issues).

Jackson v. State, 314 S.W.3d 118, 124 (Tex. App.—Houston [1st Dist.] 2010, no pet.) ("'Confusion of the issues' refers to a tendency to confuse or distract the jury from the main issues in the case.... Evidence that consumes an inordinate amount of time to present or answer, for example, might tend to confuse or distract the jury from the main issues.").

Woods v. State, 306 S.W.3d 905, 909 (Tex. App.—Beaumont 2010, no pet.) ("[T]he trial court was within its discretion to exclude the evidence on the grounds that the probative value of the evidence of [defendant's psychiatric] hospitalization three days after the incident was substantially outweighed by the danger that the evidence would confuse the issues.").

Beck v. Law Offices of Edwin J. (Ted) Terry, Jr., P.C., 284 S.W.3d 416, 444 (Tex. App.—Austin 2009, no pet.) (evidence of attorney's alcohol and drug use was properly excluded from evidence in a professional negligence action against the attorney, where there was no evidence linking the attorney's alcohol and drug use and his performance).

Goodson v. Castellanos, 214 S.W.3d 741, 754 (Tex. App.—Austin 2007, pet. denied) ("[I]n deciding whether evidence should be excluded, the court must weigh the probative value of the evidence against its potential for unfair prejudice or confusion, and must examine the necessity and probative effect of the evidence.").

Rivera v. State, 130 S.W.3d 454, 460 (Tex. App.—Corpus Christi 2004, no pet.) (evidence of police report made by victim's mother regarding alleged conduct by someone other than defendant properly excluded as irrelevant, unduly prejudicial, and confusing to jury).

Peters v. State, 93 S.W.3d 347, 351 (Tex. App.—Houston [14th Dist.] 2002, pet. denied) (unduly confusing, misleading, and cumulative to admit evidence of shotgun and marijuana in defendant's hotel room, where that evidence was offered to suggest possession of cocaine and where defendant already admitted to the elements of the charged offense).

Salazar v. State, 90 S.W.3d 330, 338 (Tex. Crim. App. 2002) (memorial video of victim "was very lengthy, highly emotional, and barely probative of the victim's life at the time of his death" and should not have been admitted).

Franco v. State, 25 S.W.3d 26, 28 (Tex. App.—El Paso 2000, pet. ref'd) (trial court improperly allowed confusing, misleading, and prejudicial blood spatter evidence by unqualified expert).

4. *Opposing Authorities*

Garcia v. State, 150 S.W.3d 598, 615 (Tex. App.—San Antonio 2004), *rev'd on other grounds*, 201 S.W.3d 695 (Tex. Crim. App. 2006), *cert. denied*, 549 U.S. 1224 (2007) (evidence of a defendant's prior "car dumping" incident ((where the defendant stopped the car, pushed his wife out of the car, and drove away)) was not probative of the defendant's motive or intent to kill his wife, nor did it rebut a defensive theory, and the trial court abused its discretion in admitting the evidence).

D. Motion to Exclude Evidence Used to Create an Emotional Bias

1. *Suggested Motion Text*

(<u>*Name of Moving Party*</u>) hereby moves this Court for an order excluding any and all evidence, references to evidence, testimony, or argument relating to (<u>*Describe Prejudicial Evidence*</u>). The motion is based upon the ground that there is a substantial danger that the evidence will unfairly inflame the passions or emotions of the jurors.

2. Motion Summary

This motion is used to exclude evidence that is being used or has the tendency to create an unfair emotional bias against a party. The motion is based upon the authority of Texas Rule of Evidence 403 and leading cases that have approved the exclusion of evidence intended principally to arouse the passions of the jury or inflame juror emotions. *See Gigliobianco v. State*, 210 S.W.3d 637, 641 (Tex. Crim. App. 2006); *Olivares v. Doe*, 164 S.W.3d 427, 433 (Tex. App.—Texarkana 2004, pet. denied); *Tex. Capital Sec. Inc. v. Sandefur*, 58 S.W.3d 760, 780 (Tex. App.—Houston [1st Dist.] 2001, pet. denied).

3. Supporting Authorities

Texas Rule of Evidence 403 states that relevant evidence "may be excluded if its probative value is substantially outweighed by the danger of unfair prejudice, confusion of the issues, or misleading the jury, or by considerations of undue delay, or needless presentation of cumulative evidence." When objecting to evidence under Rule 403, show the court how the evidence is not just prejudicial, but *unfairly* prejudicial, e.g., that the primary effect of the evidence is to appeal to raw emotions or that it is inflammatory. Consider offering to stipulate to the facts so that the probative value of the evidence offered to prove such facts is minimized, and the risk of unfair prejudice mandates exclusion. Alternatively, if opposing a Rule 403 objection, show the court how the evidence is not unfairly prejudicial, but merely prejudicial, as well as highly probative, thereby mandating admission.

Old Chief v. United States, 519 U.S. 172, 180 (1997) ("unfair prejudice as to a criminal defendant, speaks to the capacity of some concededly relevant evidence to lure the factfinder into declaring guilt on a ground different from proof specific to the offense charged").

Render v. State, 347 S.W.3d 905, 921 (Tex. App.—Eastland 2011, pet. ref'd) ("[E]vidence is unfairly prejudicial when it has an undue tendency to suggest an improper basis for reaching a decision.").

Newland v. State, 363 S.W.3d 205, 208 (Tex. App.—Waco 2011, pet. ref'd) ("[E]vidence might be unfairly prejudicial if ... it arouses the jury's hostility or sympathy for one side without regard to the logical probative force of the evidence.").

Peters v. State, 93 S.W.3d 347, 351 (Tex. App.—Houston [14th Dist.] 2002, pet. denied) (unduly confusing, misleading, and cumulative to admit evidence of a shotgun and marijuana in defendant's hotel room, where that evidence was offered to suggest possession of cocaine and where defendant already admitted to the elements of the charged offense).

Doe v. Mobile Video Tapes Inc., 43 S.W.3d 40, 57 (Tex. App.—Corpus Christi 2001, no pet.) ("[A] trial court has wide latitude to exclude evidence if it creates undue prejudice, distracts jury from main issue or issues, or consumes undue amount of time.").

Dade v. State, 956 S.W.2d 75, 80 (Tex. App.—Tyler 1997, pet. ref'd) (in applying Rule 403 balancing test, trial court should "look to see if the evidence presented would likely impress the jury 'in some irrational but nevertheless indelible way'") (citing

Bigby v. State, 892 S.W.2d 864 (Tex. Crim. App. 1994), *cert. denied*, 515 U.S. 1162 (1995)).

a. Exclusion of Evidence Intended to Inflame Jurors' Emotions

Pawlak v. State, 420 S.W.3d 807, 809 (Tex. Crim. App. 2013) ("[S]exually related bad acts and misconduct involving children are inherently inflammatory.").

Waffle House, Inc. v. Williams, 313 S.W.3d 796, 812 n.77 (Tex. 2010) (evidence of sexual behavior outside of what society deems acceptable is inherently inflammatory).

Waffle House, Inc. v. Williams, 313 S.W.3d 796, 812 (Tex. 2010) (while evidence of a plaintiff's sexually provocative speech is not always inadmissible, the trial court must carefully weigh the applicable considerations in deciding whether to admit evidence of this kind).

Prible v. State, 175 S.W.3d 724, 736 (Tex. Crim. App. 2005), *cert. denied*, 546 U.S. 962 (2005) ("[M]inimal probative value of autopsy photographs [of children], if any, was substantially outweighed by the danger of unfair prejudice, confusion of the issues, by unduly focusing the jury's attention upon the deaths of the children rather than the deaths of their parents for which appellant was charged, and needless presentation of cumulative evidence.").

Erazo v. State, 144 S.W.3d 487, 492 (Tex. Crim. App. 2004) (trial court erred admitting a photograph of a victim's unborn child where the photograph was unfairly prejudicial and inflammatory and not needed to prove the prosecution's case).

Barrientos v. State, 539 S.W.3d 482, 492 (Tex. App.—Houston [1st Dist.] 2017, no pet.) ("Gang membership is highly inflammatory character evidence likely to cause an individual to be convicted for being a bad person apart from sufficient indicia of guilt regarding this particular crime.").

Kirk v. State, 421 S.W.3d 772, 782 (Tex. App.—Fort Worth 2014, pet. ref'd) ("Rule 403 requires that a photograph have some probative value and that its probative value not be substantially outweighed by its inflammatory nature.").

Moreno v. State, 409 S.W.3d 723, 730 (Tex. App.—Houston [1st Dist.] 2013, pet. ref'd) (unfair prejudice refers to an undue tendency to suggest a decision on an improper basis, commonly an emotional one).

Rodriguez v. State, 345 S.W.3d 504, 508 (Tex. App.—Waco 2011, pet. ref'd) ("'Unfair prejudice' does not, of course, mean that the evidence injures the opponent's case—the central point of offering evidence. Rather it refers to an undue tendency to suggest decision on an improper basis, commonly, though not necessarily, an emotional one.").

Bradshaw v. State, 244 S.W.3d 490, 500 (Tex. App.—Texarkana 2007, pet. stricken), 2008 WL 1930683 (Tex. Crim. App. 2008) ("evidence is unfairly prejudicial when it has an undue tendency to suggest that a decision be made on an improper basis, commonly, but not necessarily, an emotional one").

Castro v. Cammerino, 186 S.W.3d 671, 681 (Tex. App.—Dallas 2006, pet. denied) ("[P]hotographs that are merely calculated to arouse the sympathy, prejudice, or passion of the jury and do not serve to illustrate disputed issues or aid the jury in its understanding of the case should not be admitted.").

Jones v. State, 111 S.W.3d 600, 608 (Tex. App.—Dallas 2003, pet. ref'd) ("[T]he danger of unfair prejudice caused by the gruesomeness of the photographs substantially outweighed their slight probative value because the photographs had the potential to irrationally focus the jury on defendant's murder conviction instead of his two aggravated assault convictions.").

Erazo v. State, 144 S.W.3d 487, 492 (Tex. Crim. App. 2004) (trial court erred admitting a photograph of a victim's unborn child where the photograph was unfairly prejudicial and inflammatory and not needed to prove the prosecution's case).

Peters v. State, 93 S.W.3d 347, 351 (Tex. App.—Houston [14th Dist.] 2002, pet. denied) (unduly confusing, misleading, and cumulative to admit evidence of a shotgun and marijuana in defendant's hotel room, where that evidence was offered to suggest possession of cocaine and where the defendant already admitted to the elements of the charged offense.).

Taylor v. State, 93 S.W.3d 487, 506 (Tex. App.—Texarkana 2002, pet. ref'd) (error to admit evidence of pornographic story on defendant's computer hard drive where such evidence was prejudicial and inflammatory).

Gonzales v. State, 929 S.W.2d 546 (Tex. App.—Austin 1996, pet. ref'd) (in assault of officer, trial court did not abuse its discretion by excluding officer's alleged racially inflammatory statement where confusing, misleading, and unduly prejudicial).

Tidrow v. State, 916 S.W.2d 623, 631 (Tex. App.—Fort Worth 1996, no pet.) ("[A] photograph should be excluded if so horrifying or appalling that a juror of normal sensitivity would necessarily encounter difficulty rationally deciding critical issues after viewing it.").

Magee v. State, 994 S.W.2d 878, 888 (Tex. App.—Waco 1999, pet. ref'd) (trial court erred in admitting testimony about music labels such as "Demize," "Killer Instinct," and "Sex, Drugs and Guns, The American Way," where the inflammatory nature had the potential to impress the jury in an "irrational way").

4. Opposing Authorities

> *Note: The Advisory Committee Note to Federal Rule of Evidence 403 suggests that the trial court should also consider whether a limiting instruction under Federal Rule 105 (which is in effect identical to Texas Evidence Rule 105) would be effective to cure the prejudice from offered evidence, as well as whether there are other means of proof available. When opposing a Rule 403 objection to evidence, show the court how a limiting jury instruction would be effective in mitigating the prejudicial harm of the evidence, and/or show the need for the evidence by demonstrating that it is the only evidence available to offer on the material fact or is high in probative value.*

Rayford v. State, 125 S.W.3d 521, 529 (Tex. Crim. App. 2003) (autopsy photographs relevant and not unfairly prejudicial).

Wheeler v. State, 67 S.W.3d 879, 886 (Tex. Crim. App. 2002) (trial court did not abuse discretion by admitting evidence of prior sexual assault where evidence not unfairly prejudicial and needed to assist in proving case).

Proo v. State, 587 S.W.3d 789, 817 Tex. App.—San Antonio 2019, pet. ref'd) ("Photographs showing a victim's bruises may be admitted to clarify and support observations and conclusions about the victim's injuries, so long as they are not admitted solely to inflame the minds of the jurors.").

Proo v. State, 587 S.W.3d 789, 817 Tex. App.—San Antonio 2019, pet. ref'd) ("The mere fact that a photo or video depicts a child's badly bruised body and is hard to view does not automatically render it too inflammatory or unfairly prejudicial to be admitted.").

Proo v. State, 587 S.W.3d 789, 817 Tex. App.—San Antonio 2019, pet. ref'd) ("The trial court does not err in admitting photographs merely because they are gruesome.").

Barrientos v. State, 539 S.W.3d 482, 492 (Tex. App.—Houston [1st Dist.] 2017, no pet.) ("[E]vidence of gang membership is admissible during the guilt-innocence phase to show bias, motive, or intent, or to refute a defensive theory").

Jett v. State, 319 S.W.3d 846, 856 (Tex. App.—San Antonio 2010, no pet.) (autopsy photographs of victim showing stabbing and cutting injuries, were not prejudicially inflammatory because the photographs did not show the mutilation caused by the autopsy, the photographs were a visual representation of the medical examiner's testimony, and the wounds were described in an autopsy report admitted without objection).

Bradshaw v. State, 244 S.W.3d 490, 500 (Tex. App.—Texarkana 2007, pet. stricken), 2008 WL 1930683 (Tex. Crim. App. 2008) ("The concern that jurors might irrationally favor or disfavor a defendant due to his choice to seek help from a Christian counselor was much too weak to 'substantially outweigh' probative value of the testimony.").

Jaggers v. State, 125 S.W.3d 661, 670 (Tex. App.—Houston [1st Dist.] 2003, pet. ref'd) (a trial court did not abuse its discretion by admitting evidence of a defendant's other acts over the defendant's Rule 403 objections where the evidence was relevant, not unfairly prejudicial or inflammatory, not unduly time-consuming, and needed by the prosecution).

Jones v. State, 119 S.W.3d 412, 422 (Tex. App.—Fort Worth 2003, no pet.) (in case involving indecency with a child, trial court did not abuse discretion by determining probative value of evidence of other acts of sexual conduct with victim and others outweighed prejudicial effect).

In re J.W., 113 S.W.3d 605, 612 (Tex. App.—Dallas 2003, pet. denied) (in termination of parental rights case, evidence of parents' arrests and charges was relevant and not unfairly prejudicial).

State v. Mechler, 123 S.W.3d 449, 454 (Tex. App.—Houston [14th Dist.] 2003), *aff'd*, 153 S.W.3d 435 (Tex. Crim. App. 2005) (evidence of a breathalyzer test taken an hour and a half after an offense held not likely to unfairly inflame jury).

Rayford v. State, 125 S.W.3d 521, 529 (Tex. Crim. App. 2003) (autopsy photographs relevant and not unfairly prejudicial).

Goldberg v. State, 95 S.W.3d 345, 375 (Tex. App.—Houston [1st Dist.] 2002, pet. ref'd), *cert. denied*, 540 U.S. 1190 (2004) (evidence of notebook containing drawings and discussing killing women seized three years before offense relevant and not unfairly prejudicial).

Moss v. State, 75 S.W.3d 132, 141 (Tex. App.—San Antonio 2002, pet. ref'd) (trial court did not abuse discretion in prosecution for aggravated robbery by admitting numerous weapons and ammunition where relevant and not unfairly prejudicial).

Wheeler v. State, 67 S.W.3d 879, 886 (Tex. Crim. App. 2002) (trial court did not abuse discretion by admitting evidence of prior sexual assault where evidence not unfairly prejudicial and needed to assist in proving case).

Franco v. State, 25 S.W.3d 26, 28 (Tex. App.—El Paso 2000, pet. ref'd) (probative value of evidence that defendant was found in "crack house" was not outweighed by prejudicial impact).

Draheim v. State, 916 S.W.2d 593, 601 (Tex. App.—San Antonio 1996, pet. ref'd) (videotape of a defendant sexually assaulting a child properly admitted, where the tape was extremely lengthy, in color, extremely detailed, and further cumulative of the defendant's own testimony; "the fact that the tape was 'highly inflammatory' says no more than that [the defendant's] crimes were 'highly inflammatory;' it does not establish that the tape was unfairly prejudicial.... In short, while [the] videotape was unquestionably prejudicial, it was not unfairly prejudicial").

Ventroy v. State, 917 S.W.2d 419, 423 (Tex. App.—San Antonio 1996, pet. ref'd) ("[G]ruesomeness by itself does not make picture more prejudicial than probative.").

E. Motion to Exclude or Limit Cumulative Evidence

1. Suggested Motion Text

(*Name of Moving Party*) hereby moves this Court for an order excluding or limiting the introduction of any and all evidence, references to evidence, testimony, or argument relating to (*Describe Cumulative Evidence*). The motion is based upon the ground that the evidence is cumulative and will therefore necessitate an undue consumption of time and will create a substantial danger of undue prejudice to (*Name of Moving Party*).

2. Motion Summary

This motion is used to exclude cumulative evidence. It is based upon the court's discretionary powers under Texas Rule of Evidence 403 to exclude prejudicial and time-consuming evidence, as well as a long line of supporting cases. *See Jones v. Mattress Firm Holding Corp.*, 558 S.W.3d 732, 737 (Tex. App.—Houston [14th Dist.] 2018, no pet.); *Benavides v. Cushman*, 189 S.W.3d 875, 883 (Tex. App.—Houston [1st Dist.] 2006, no pet.). This factor is concerned with the efficiency of judicial proceedings rather than the threat of inaccurate decisions. *See Casey v. State*, 215 S.W.3d 870, 879 (Tex. Crim. App. 2007); *Alvarado v. State*, 912 S.W.2d 199, 213 (Tex. Crim. App. 1995); Montgomery v. State, 810 S.W.2d 372, 391 (Tex. Crim. App. 1991).

The test for whether the evidence is inadmissible as cumulative is not merely whether the evidence to be adduced from the two witnesses is similar, but also whether the excluded testimony would have added substantial weight to the offering parties' case. *Hooper v. Chittaluru,* 222 S.W.3d 103, 110 (Tex. App.—Houston [14th Dist.] 2006, pet. denied); *Benavides v. Cushman,* 189 S.W.3d 875, 883 (Tex. App.—Houston [1st Dist.] 2006, no pet.); *Sims v. Brackett,* 885 S.W.2d 450, 454 (Tex. App.—Corpus Christi 1994, writ denied).

> *Note: It might appear to be an uphill battle to prevail on a motion to exclude cumulative evidence prior to the commencement of trial, where no other evidence has yet been introduced. However, fact patterns may present themselves to justify an argument that anticipated cumulative evidence will prejudice your client. For example, where your opponent lists numerous experts with similar qualifications to render similar opinions, this would appear to be at least arguably cumulative and subject to exclusion under a Rule 403 objection. See Cruz v. Hinojosa, 12 S.W.3d 545, 550 (Tex. App.—San Antonio 1999, pet. denied). Other evidence that may raise a red flag includes photographs, newspaper clippings, or letters, which may be unduly prejudicial compared to other means of proving the same point. Even if a motion in limine is denied, the citations referenced in this section provide a helpful basis for objecting to and striking cumulative evidence during trial.*

3. Supporting Authorities

Texas Rule of Evidence 403 states:

> Although relevant, evidence may be excluded if its probative value is substantially outweighed by the danger of unfair prejudice, confusion of the issues, or misleading the jury, *or by considerations of undue delay, or needless presentation of cumulative evidence.* (Emphasis added.)

Dow Chem. Co. v. Francis, 46 S.W.3d 237, 241 (Tex. 2001) ("[A] trial court may properly intervene to maintain control in the courtroom, to expedite the trial, and to prevent what it considers to be a waste of time.").

Jones v. Mattress Firm Holding Corp., 558 S.W.3d 732, 737 (Tex. App.—Houston [14th Dist.] 2018, no pet.) ("[A] trial court may exclude relevant evidence ... if the probative value is substantially outweighed by unfair prejudice, confusion of the issues, the potential to mislead the jury or cause undue delay, or needless presentation of cumulative evidence.").

McNeil v. State, 398 S.W.3d 747, 756 (Tex. App.—Houston [1st Dist.] 2011, pet. ref'd), *cert. denied,* 568 U.S. 1173 (2013) (one of the factors considered in determining whether a piece of evidence's degree of prejudice is outweighed by its probative value is the likelihood that presentation of the evidence will consume inordinate amount of time or merely repeat evidence already admitted).

Doe v. Mobile Video Tapes Inc., 43 S.W.3d 40, 57 (Tex. App.—Corpus Christi 2001, no pet.) ("[A] trial court has wide latitude to exclude evidence if it creates undue prejudice, distracts jury from main issue or issues, or consumes undue amount of time.").

Cecil v. T.M.E. Invs., 893 S.W.2d 38, 46 (Tex. App.—Corpus Christi 1994, no writ) (in the interest of expedience, a trial court may properly exclude cumulative evidence).

Food Source Inc. v. Zurich Ins. Co., 751 S.W.2d 596, 600 (Tex. App.—Dallas 1988, writ denied) ("[T]he general conduct of trial is the judge's responsibility and the judge may properly intervene to promote expedition and prevent unnecessary waste of time.").

a. *Generally*

Texas Rule of Evidence 403 states:

> Although relevant, evidence may be excluded if its probative value is substantially outweighed by the danger of unfair prejudice, confusion of the issues, or misleading the jury, or by considerations of undue delay, *or needless presentation of cumulative evidence*. (Emphasis added.)

Pawlak v. State, 420 S.W.3d 807, 809 (Tex. Crim. App. 2013) ("[I]t is possible for the admission of character evidence, though not necessarily cumulative, to cross the line from prejudicial to unfairly prejudicial based on the sheer volume of character evidence admitted.").

Pawlak v. State, 420 S.W.3d 807, 809 (Tex. Crim. App. 2013) ("[T]he sheer volume of extraneous-offense evidence was unfairly prejudicial and invited the jury to convict [a defendant] of sexually assaulting or attempting to sexually assault the victims because the defendant possessed 9,900 images that included homosexual child pornography.").

Valle v. State, 109 S.W.3d 500, 506 (Tex. Crim. App. 2003) (where videotaped evidence was held unnecessary after an expert stated he relied on the videotaped evidence to form his opinion, the lack of need for the evidence provided a reason for excluding the videotape under Rule 403; note: videotaped evidence actually excluded under Texas Rule of Evidence 705).

Alvarado v. State, 912 S.W.2d 199, 213 (Tex. Crim. App. 1995) ("'cumulative' suggests other evidence on same point already received").

McNeil v. State, 398 S.W.3d 747, 756 (Tex. App.—Houston [1st Dist.] 2011, pet. ref'd), *cert. denied*, 568 U.S. 1173 (2013) (One factor considered in determining whether a piece of evidence's degree of prejudice is outweighed by its probative value is the likelihood that presentation of the evidence will consume inordinate amount of time or merely repeat evidence already admitted.).

Puentes v. Fannie Mae, 350 S.W.3d 732, 737 (Tex. App.—El Paso 2011, pet. dism'd) ("[T]he admission or exclusion of a particular exhibit is likely harmless if the evidence was cumulative of other evidence in the record, or if the balance of the evidence in the case was so one-sided that the error was not likely to have affected the judgment.").

Welch v. McLean, 191 S.W.3d 147, 164 (Tex. App.—Fort Worth 2005, no pet.) (a trial court has the authority to exclude evidence if its probative value is substantially outweighed by the danger of needless presentation of cumulative evidence).

Jones v. State, 111 S.W.3d 600, 608 (Tex. App.—Dallas 2003, pet. ref'd) ("[T]he danger of unfair prejudice caused by the gruesomeness of the photographs substantially outweighed their slight probative value because the photographs had the potential to irrationally focus the jury on defendant's murder conviction instead of his two aggravated assault convictions.").

Valle v. State, 109 S.W.3d 500, 506 (Tex. Crim. App. 2003) (where videotaped evidence was held unnecessary after an expert stated he relied on the videotaped evidence to form his opinion, the lack of need for the evidence provided a reason for excluding the videotape under Rule 403; note: videotaped evidence actually excluded under Texas Rule of Evidence 705).

Peters v. State, 93 S.W.3d 347, 351 (Tex. App.—Houston [14th Dist.] 2002, pet. denied) (unduly confusing, misleading, and cumulative to admit evidence of a shotgun and marijuana in defendant's hotel room, where that evidence was offered to suggest possession of cocaine and where the defendant already admitted to the elements of the charged offense).

Boswell v. Brazos Elec. Power Co-op., Inc., 910 S.W.2d 593, 604 (Tex. App.—Fort Worth 1995, writ denied) (cumulative evidence "may be excluded if its probative value is substantially outweighed by its cumulative nature").

Alvarado v. State, 912 S.W.2d 199, 213 (Tex. Crim. App. 1995) ("'cumulative'" suggests other evidence on same point already received").

Sims v. Brackett, 885 S.W.2d 450, 454 (Tex. App.—Corpus Christi 1994, writ denied) (court has authority to exclude testimony to avoid needless presentation of cumulative evidence).

Gen. Chem. Corp. v. De La Lastra, 815 S.W.2d 750, 761 (Tex. App.—Corpus Christi 1991), *aff'd in part, rev'd in part on other grounds*, 852 S.W.2d 916 (Tex. 1993), *cert. dismissed*, 510 U.S. 985 (1993) ("a trial court may, in its discretion, limit the amount of evidence on a particular issue").

Linthicum v. Richardson, 245 S.W. 713, 715 (Tex. Civ. App.—Beaumont 1922, no writ) ("Cumulative evidence is additional evidence of the same kind, to the same point.").

b. Articles and Letters

Petty v. State, 346 S.W.3d 200, 206 (Tex. App.—Amarillo 2011, no pet.) (the admission of a picture drawn by an eyewitness to a shooting was error where the picture did not "contribute anything of consequence toward proof of any of the elements of the offense.... At best, the picture was simply cumulative of the testimony of the witness).

Minnesota Mining & Mfg. Co. v. Nisika Ltd., 885 S.W.2d 603, 631 (Tex. App.—Beaumont 1994), *rev'd on other grounds*, 953 S.W.2d 733 (Tex. 1997) (exclusion of complaint letters was proper where they were merely cumulative of other admitted evidence).

Mottu v. Navistar Int'l Transp. Corp., 804 S.W.2d 144, 147 (Tex. App.—Houston [14th Dist.] 1990, writ denied) (trial court properly excluded letters where they were cumulative of evidence already received by the court).

Peat Marwick Main v. Haass, 775 S.W.2d 698, 705 (Tex. App.—San Antonio 1989), *rev'd on other grounds*, 818 S.W.2d 381 (Tex. 1991) (the exclusion of approximately 200 letters was proper because they were cumulative of trial testimony).

Mollinedo v. Tex. Employment Comm'n, 662 S.W.2d 732, 739 (Tex. App.—Houston [1st Dist.] 1983, writ ref'd n.r.e.) (no error in excluding a letter from a doctor describing a plaintiff's handicap where the court had previously admitted similar evidence through another witness).

c. Number of Witnesses

Signature Mgmt. Team, LLC v. Quixtar, Inc., 281 S.W.3d 666, 673 (Tex. App.—Dallas 2009, no pet.), *rev'd on other grounds*, 315 S.W.3d 28 (Tex. 2010) (a trial court acted within its discretion by striking six affidavits as cumulative of the live testimony that was presented; "two of the affiants, plus one other [witness], testified live at the hearing to the same or similar facts").

Gainsco County Mut. Ins. Co. v. Martinez, 27 S.W.3d 97, 107 (Tex. App.—San Antonio 2000, pet. dism'd by agr.) (there was no error in excluding the cumulative testimony of a personal injury plaintiff's biomechanical expert when an expert neurologist proffered substantially similar evidence).

d. Photographs

Young v. State, 283 S.W.3d 854, 874 (Tex. Crim. App. 2009), *cert. denied*, 130 S. Ct. 1015, 175 L. Ed. 2d 622 (2000) ("When determining whether the trial court erred in admitting relevant photographs into evidence, [appellate] review is limited to determining whether the probative value of the photos is substantially outweighed by the danger of unfair prejudice, confusion of the issues, or misleading the jury, or by considerations of undue delay or needless presentation of cumulative evidence.").

Alvarado v. State, 912 S.W.2d 199, 213 (Tex. Crim. App. 1995) ("trial court must balance probative value of ... photographs against potential for unfair prejudice").

Jones v. Mattress Firm Holding Corp., 558 S.W.3d 732, 737 (Tex. App.—Houston [14th Dist.] 2018, no pet.) ("Photographs taken at or around the same time from the same angle are generally cumulative and excluding them is not an abuse of discretion.").

Kirk v. State, 421 S.W.3d 772, 782 (Tex. App.—Fort Worth 2014, pet. ref'd) ("[A]mong the many factors a court may consider in determining whether the probative value of photographs is substantially outweighed by the danger of unfair prejudice are the number of exhibits offered, their gruesomeness, their detail, their size, whether they are in color or black-and-white, whether they are close up, the availability of other means of proof, and other circumstances unique to the individual case.").

Petty v. State, 346 S.W.3d 200, 206 (Tex. App.—Amarillo 2011, no pet.) (the admission of a picture drawn by an eyewitness to a shooting was error where the picture did not "contribute[] anything of consequence toward proof of any of the elements of the offense.... At best, the picture was simply cumulative of the testimony of the witness.").

Bartosh v. Gulf Health Care Ctr.–Galveston, 178 S.W.3d 434, 443 (Tex. App.—Houston [14th Dist.] 2005, no pet.) (photographs taken of nursing home resident after a fire ant attack, offered to show number of the ant bites and resulting pain suffered by resident, were properly excluded as cumulative of photographs admitted into evidence in action brought against home by resident's daughter after resident's death).

Jones v. State, 111 S.W.3d 600, 608 (Tex. App.—Dallas 2003, pet. ref'd) ("[T]he danger of unfair prejudice caused by the gruesomeness of the photographs substantially outweighed their slight probative value because the photographs had the potential to irrationally focus the jury on defendant's murder conviction instead of his two aggravated assault convictions.").

Huckaby v. A.G. Perry & Son, Inc., 20 S.W.3d 194, 209 (Tex. App.—Texarkana 2000, pet. denied) (the exclusion of fifteen photographs of the deceased was held to be proper where the proponent failed to show they proved any element not already proved by the one admitted photograph).

Tidrow v. State, 916 S.W.2d 623, 631 (Tex. App.—Fort Worth 1996, no pet.) (photographs may be excluded based on considerations of undue delay or needless presentation of cumulative evidence).

Alvarado v. State, 912 S.W.2d 199, 213 (Tex. Crim. App. 1995) ("[T]rial court must balance the probative value of ... photographs against potential for unfair prejudice.").

Cecil v. T.M.E. Invs., 893 S.W.2d 38, 46 (Tex. App.—Corpus Christi 1994, no writ) (the exclusion of two photographs was proper when they merely duplicated two admitted photographs).

e. Reports

United Servs. Auto. Ass'n v. Gordon, 103 S.W.3d 436, 442 (Tex. App.—San Antonio 2002, no pet.) (no reversible error in admitting an expert's report where it was cumulative of another expert's testimony, and it was not controlling on a material issue or dispositive of the case).

Hill v. Heritage Res., Inc., 964 S.W.2d 89, 136 (Tex. App.—El Paso 1997, pet. ref'd) (no error in excluding a report as cumulative where the subject matter of the report was the basis of testimony by more than one witness at the trial).

Bagley v. Scott, 582 S.W.2d 511, 512 (Tex. Civ. App—Beaumont 1979, no writ) (no error in excluding three reports when the authors of the reports already testified to the substance of each report).

Minor v. Commercial Ins. Co. of Newark, N. J., 557 S.W.2d 608, 609 (Tex. Civ. App.—Texarkana 1977, no writ) (exclusion of a medical record notation regarding a plaintiff's pain was harmless "because the issue of his pain was not disputed, and in fact was well established by other proof adduced by [the party]").

f. Witness Testimony

Diamond Offshore Mgmt. Co. v. Guidry, 84 S.W.3d 256, 265 (Tex. App.—Beaumont 2002), *rev'd on other grounds*, 171 S.W.3d 840 (Tex. 2005) ("If the evidence is cumulative and not controlling on a material issue dispositive to the case, [appeals courts] do not reverse the trial court's judgment.").

Sims v. Brackett, 885 S.W.2d 450, 454 (Tex. App.—Corpus Christi 1994, writ denied) (court has authority to exclude testimony to avoid needless presentation of cumulative evidence and undue delay).

Hooper v. Torres, 790 S.W.2d 757, 761 (Tex. App.—El Paso 1990, writ denied) (no error excluding report and testimony of accident investigation police officers where "essential aspects of the officer's testimony was already before the jury").

g. *Expert Testimony*

Welch v. McLean, 191 S.W.3d 147, 164 (Tex. App.—Fort Worth 2005, no pet.) (the record demonstrated "a legitimate basis—the similarity in opinions and credentials—for the trial court's exclusion of [an expert's] testimony as needlessly cumulative of [another expert's] testimony").

Cruz v. Hinojosa, 12 S.W.3d 545, 550 (Tex. App.—San Antonio 1999, pet. denied) (exclusion of portions of a video-taped expert witness's deposition testimony was not error where it was merely cumulative of other evidence already presented in plaintiff's case-in-chief).

h. *Videotape Evidence*

Ford Motor Co. v. Miles, 967 S.W.2d 377, 388 (Tex. 1998) (videos that would inflame jurors' emotions were properly excluded where other, non-inflammatory sources of impeachment evidence were available).

Valle v. State, 109 S.W.3d 500, 506 (Tex. Crim. App. 2003) (where videotaped evidence was held unnecessary after an expert stated he relied on the videotaped evidence to form his opinion, the lack of need for the evidence provided a reason for excluding the videotape under Rule 403; note: videotaped evidence actually excluded under Texas Rule of Evidence 705).

Cruz v. Hinojosa, 12 S.W.3d 545, 550 (Tex. App.—San Antonio 1999, pet. denied) (videotaped deposition testimony was properly excluded where it was cumulative of other admitted evidence).

Padgett v. Burt Ogden Motor's, Inc., 869 S.W.2d 532, 537 (Tex. App.—Corpus Christi 1993, writ denied) (there was no error excluding a videotaped exhibit to a video deposition where it was cumulative and added nothing to the deponent's video testimony played before the jury).

Mottu v. Navistar Int'l Transp. Corp., 804 S.W.2d 144, 147 (Tex. App.—Houston [14th Dist.] 1991, writ denied) (exclusion of videotapes in a products liability action was where they were merely cumulative of other evidence).

i. *Deposition Testimony*

Reina v. Gen. Accid. Fire & Life Assurance Corp. Ltd., 611 S.W.2d 415, 417 (Tex. 1981) (no error in excluding deposition testimony as cumulative where substantially all of the excluded testimony was elicited from other witnesses).

Davis v. Snider Indus., 604 S.W.2d 341, 345 (Tex. Civ. App.—Texarkana 1980, writ ref'd n.r.e.) (no reversible error in excluding deposition testimony that duplicated already-entered extensive testimony on the same issue).

j. Business Records

Nat'l Bugmobiles, Inc. v. Jobi Props., 773 S.W.2d 616, 618 (Tex. App.—Corpus Christi 1989, writ denied) (no error excluding business record where merely cumulative of other admitted testimony).

Sharp v. Sinton Indep. Sch. Dist., 696 S.W.2d 592, 598 (Tex. App.—Corpus Christi 1985, no writ ref'd n.r.e.) (not reversible error to exclude three business documents where the summary testimony of the content had already been introduced).

k. Wills

Boswell v. Brazos Elec. Power Co-op., Inc., 910 S.W.2d 593, 604 (Tex. App.—Fort Worth 1995, writ denied) (trial court properly excluded a will where it duplicated prior testimony as to its contents).

4. Opposing Authorities

Hill v. Heritage Res., Inc., 964 S.W.2d 89, 136 (Tex. App.—El Paso 1997, pet. ref'd) (where other competent evidence of a fact in question appears in the record, the improper admission of cumulative evidence will not constitute reversible error).

Boswell v. Brazos Elec. Power Co-op., Inc., 910 S.W.2d 593, 604 (Tex. App.—Fort Worth 1995, writ denied) ("[C]umulative evidence can be admitted when it adds substantial weight to the offering parties' case.").

Sims v. Brackett, 885 S.W.2d 450, 454 (Tex. App.—Corpus Christi 1994, writ denied) ("[T]o exclude evidence under Rule 403, the trial court must conduct a balancing test and only where the balance weighs significantly on the side of judicial efficiency may relevant evidence be excluded as cumulative.").

Linthicum v. Richardson, 245 S.W. 713, 715 (Tex. Civ. App.—Beaumont 1922, no writ) ("[A]lthough evidence tends to prove the same proposition as that previously introduced, yet it is not cumulative when it is of a different character, and merely tends to prove the former proposition by proof of a new and distinct fact.").

a. Articles

Pittsburgh Corning Corp. v. Walters, 1 S.W.3d 759, 777 (Tex. App.—Corpus Christi 1999, pet. denied) (a trial court properly admitted two excerpts from the *Federal Register* supporting the underlying basis of an expert's already admitted testimony).

City of Austin v. Houston Lighting & Power Co., 844 S.W.2d 773, 791 (Tex. App.—Dallas 1992, writ denied) (the admission of articles harmless error where the articles merely cumulative of other evidence).

b. Letters

In re Estate of Watson, 720 S.W.2d 806, 808 (Tex. 1986) (eighty-one letters introduced to show love and affection should have been admitted where the letters were not cumulative and were the strongest rebuttal evidence available).

Beneficial Pers. Servs. of Tex. v. Rey, 927 S.W.2d 157, 175 (Tex. App.—El Paso 1996), *vacated and remanded pursuant to settlement agreement*, 938 S.W.2d 717 (Tex. 1997) (a trial court properly admitted a letter even though it was cumulative of other testimony of witnesses).

c. Credentials

Olin Corp. v. Smith, 990 S.W.2d 789, 791 (Tex. App.—Austin 1999, pet. denied) (a trial court properly heard extensive testimony regarding experts' qualifications).

d. Number of Witnesses

Van Heerden v. Van Heerden, 321 S.W.3d 869, 877 (Tex. App.—Houston [14th Dist.] 2010, no pet.) ("[A]lthough Texas courts often correctly exclude evidence because it is cumulative, the fact that another witness may have given substantially the same testimony is not the decisive factor. Rather, [the appellate] court considers whether the stricken testimony would have added substantial weight to the case.").

Roberts v. Williamson, 52 S.W.3d 343, 348 (Tex. App.—Texarkana 2001), *aff'd in part, rev'd in part on other grounds*, 111 S.W.3d 113 (Tex. 2003) (no harm allowing a second medical expert to testify where the testimony was cumulative of a previous expert's testimony).

Sims v. Brackett, 885 S.W.2d 450, 454 (Tex. App.—Corpus Christi 1994, writ denied) (the test for excluding cumulative evidence "is not merely whether the evidence to be adduced is similar, but also whether excluded testimony would add substantial weight to the offering parties' case. If so, it is error to exclude it").

e. Photographs

Ladd v. State, 3 S.W.3d 547, 569 (Tex. Crim. App. 1999), *cert. denied*, 529 U.S. 1070 (2000) (photographs were properly admitted, even though they cumulative of other evidence, where they were probative of the manner of death and were not particularly horrible).

Alvarado v. State, 912 S.W.2d 199, 213 (Tex. Crim. App. 1995) (even cumulative evidence may enhance effectiveness and heighten rather than reduce probative force).

Matamoros v. State, 901 S.W.2d 470, 476 (Tex. Crim. App. 1995) (a still photograph is not cumulative of videotape evidence).

Proo v. State, 587 S.W.3d 789, 817 Tex. App.—San Antonio 2019, pet. ref'd) ("Photographs of a victim's injuries are relevant and their relevance is not diminished merely because the jury also heard testimony about the same injuries.").

Kirk v. State, 421 S.W.3d 772, 782 (Tex. App.—Fort Worth 2014, pet. ref'd) ("[P]hotographs are neither cumulative nor lacking in significant probative value simply because they merely corroborate other kinds of evidence.").

Kirk v. State, 421 S.W.3d 772, 782 (Tex. App.—Fort Worth 2014, pet. ref'd) ("[A]mong the many factors a court may consider in determining whether the probative value of photographs is substantially outweighed by the danger of unfair prejudice are the number of exhibits offered, their gruesomeness, their detail, their size, whether they are in color or black-and-white, whether they are close up, the availability of other means of proof, and other circumstances unique to the individual case.").

Reese v. State, 340 S.W.3d 838, 841 (Tex. App.—San Antonio 2011, no pet.) ("[V]isual evidence accompanying oral testimony is not cumulative or of insignificant probative value.").

Alami v. State, 333 S.W.3d 881, 889 (Tex. App.—Fort Worth 2011, no pet.) ("[P]hotographs are neither cumulative nor lacking in significant probative value simply because they merely corroborate other kinds of evidence.").

Jett v. State, 319 S.W.3d 846, 856 (Tex. App.—San Antonio 2010, no pet.) (autopsy photographs of victim showing stabbing and cutting injuries, were not prejudicially inflammatory because they photographs did not show the mutilation caused by the autopsy, the photographs were a visual representation of the medical examiner's testimony, and the wounds were described in an autopsy report admitted without objection).

f. Reports

United Servs. Auto. Ass'n v. Gordon, 103 S.W.3d 436, 442 (Tex. App.—San Antonio 2002, no pet.) (no reversible error in admitting an expert's report that was cumulative of another expert's testimony and was not controlling on a material issue or dispositive of the case).

Second Injury Fund of Tex. v. Avon, 985 S.W.2d 93, 94 (Tex. App.—Eastland 1998, pet. denied) (not error to admit doctor's report even though it was cumulative of testimony already offered by another plaintiff expert).

g. Expert Testimony

In re Commitment of Winkle, 434 S.W.3d 300, 308 (Tex. App.—Beaumont 2014, pet. denied) (expert testimony of psychologist concerning expert's primary research studying recidivism risks in sexually violent predators, which addressed the quality of actuarial predictions compared to predictions that are based on clinical judgment and the defendant's test result on the Static-99 that placed the defendant in a group with a low risk of reoffending, was not cumulative of testimony of defendant's other psychiatrist expert).

Hooper v. Chittaluru, 222 S.W.3d 103, 110 (Tex. App.—Houston [14th Dist.] 2006, pet. denied) ("[While] a trial court has authority to prevent the needless presentation of cumulative evidence under Texas Rule of Evidence 403 ... the mere fact that another witness may have given the same or substantially the same testimony is not the decisive factor.... [The court can] consider whether the excluded testimony would have added substantial weight to the [party's] case.").

Benavides v. Cushman, 189 S.W.3d 875, 883 (Tex. App.—Houston [1st Dist.] 2006, no pet.) ("Under Rule 403, the test is not merely whether the evidence to be adduced from the two witnesses is similar, but also whether the excluded testimony would have added substantial weight to the offering parties' case.").

Sims v. Brackett, 885 S.W.2d 450, 454 (Tex. App.—Corpus Christi 1994, writ denied) (it was error for expert witness testimony to be excluded where the testimony related to a hotly contested issue even though it was cumulative of other testimony).

Ponder v. Texarkana Mem'l Hosp., Inc., 840 S.W.2d 476, 479 (Tex. App.—Houston [14th Dist.] 1991, writ denied) (testimony by the only expert on brain function and the causes of brain damage was not merely cumulative).

h. Videotape Evidence

Pittsburgh Corning Corp. v. Walters, 1 S.W.3d 759, 777 (Tex. App.—Corpus Christi 1999, pet. denied) (sufficient probative value existed to admit a videotape where, even though parts of the video were cumulative of other testimony, it was a deceased plaintiff's only opportunity to inform the jury about his condition).

Yates v. State, 941 S.W.2d 357, 368 (Tex. App.—Waco 1997, pet. ref'd) ("[V]ideotape evidence is generally not cumulative of still photographs because it presents a three-dimensional perspective.").

Owens-Corning Fiberglas Corp. v. Wasiak, 917 S.W.2d 883, 894 (Tex. App.—Austin 1996, no writ), *aff'd*, 972 S.W.2d 35 (Tex. 1998) (a "video scrapbook" showing scenes from a deceased's life was properly admitted although it was cumulative of other photographs and the testimony by the plaintiff).

Draheim v. State, 916 S.W.2d 593, 601 (Tex. App.—San Antonio 1996, pet. ref'd) (videotape of a defendant sexually assaulting a child properly admitted, where the tape was extremely lengthy, in color, extremely detailed, and further cumulative of the defendant's own testimony; "the fact that the tape was 'highly inflammatory' says no more than that [the defendant's] crimes were 'highly inflammatory;' it does not establish that the tape was unfairly prejudicial.... In short, while [the] videotape was unquestionably prejudicial, it was not unfairly prejudicial.").

i. Books and Records

Kan v. State, 4 S.W.3d 38, 45 (Tex. App.—San Antonio 1999, pet. ref'd) (victim's medical records admitted even though cumulative of other evidence presented to jury in victim's testimony).

II. Sample Motions

A. Motion to Exclude Confusing Evidence

NO. _____

_____	§	IN THE DISTRICT COURT
	§	
v.	§	_____ JUDICIAL COURT
	§	
_____	§	_____ COUNTY, TEXAS

PLAINTIFF'S MOTION TO EXCLUDE CONFUSING EVIDENCE

Comes now _____, Plaintiff in this cause, and files this, her Motion to Exclude Confusing Evidence, and in support thereof, Plaintiff would show the Court the following:

1.
FACTUAL BACKGROUND

This is a personal injury action arising out of a snorkeling accident that occurred on May 29, 2019. The Defendant retained medical doctors to dispute the nature and extent of the Plaintiff's injuries and damages. In correspondence, discovery, and prior hearings, the Defendant has described the defense medical doctors as "independent." This motion seeks to preclude the Defendant from using the term "independent," or any related terminology, to describe said witnesses at the time of trial.

2.
THIS COURT MAY PRECLUDE EVIDENCE THAT IS CONFUSING

Texas Rule of Evidence 403 states "[a]lthough relevant, evidence may be excluded if its probative value is substantially outweighed by the danger of unfair prejudice, <u>confusion of the issues</u>, or <u>misleading the jury</u>, or by considerations of undue delay, or needless presentation of cumulative evidence." (Emphasis added.) *Brookshire Bros. v. Aldridge*, 438 S.W.3d 9, 26 (Tex. 2014) (evidence that raises a risk of prejudice and confusion of the jury should be excluded); *Farmers Texas County Mutual Insurance Co. v. Pagan*, 453 S.W.3d 454, (Tex. App.—Houston [14th Dist.] 2014, no pet.) (evidence should have been excluded where its probative value was outweighed by danger of confusion of issues and misleading jury).

In this case, the probative value of referring to defense medical witnesses as "independent" is nonexistent and would only cause undue confusion and give improper weight and credibility to the defense witnesses. Admission of such evidence will necessitate undue consumption of time to present rebuttal and cross-examination about the lack of independence of the defense witnesses. The jury will be misled, and other relevant issues will be confused by the admission of such evidence.

As such, any references to Defendant's physicians as "independent" should be forbidden.

3.
CONCLUSION

Based upon all of the above, exclusion or reference to the defense medical witnesses as "independent" is proper.

Dated: _____(Date)_____

By: _____

_____(Name of Counsel)_____

Attorneys for Plaintiff,

_____(Name of Plaintiff)_____

B. Motion to Exclude Cumulative Evidence

NO. _____

_____ § IN THE DISTRICT COURT
                                    §
v.   § _____ JUDICIAL COURT
                                    §
_____ § _____ COUNTY, TEXAS

PLAINTIFF'S MOTION TO EXCLUDE CUMULATIVE EVIDENCE

Comes now _____, Defendant in this cause, and files this Motion to Exclude Cumulative Evidence, and in support thereof would show the Court as follows:

1.
FACTUAL BACKGROUND

This case arises from an alleged excessive use of force by an El Paso County Sheriff's Deputy. The Plaintiff was injured when her vehicle lost control during a high-speed police pursuit. The Plaintiff claims to have incurred a broken ankle, broken ribs, a bruised kidney, and soft tissue neck and back injuries.

In her witness designation list, the Plaintiff identified the following medical witnesses: 1) Dr. Cervical [Orthopedic Surgeon]; 2) Dr. Bones [Chiropractor]; 3) Dr. Fixit [General M.D.]; 4) Dr. Organs [Internal Medicine]; 5) Dr. Superfluous [Orthopedic Surgeon]; 6) Dr. Needless [General M.D.]; and 7) Dr. Overkill [Internal Medicine]. The Plaintiff indicated that the experts' proposed testimonies would encompass "the nature and extent of Plaintiff's injuries."

By this motion, the Defendant seeks to exclude the testimony of Dr. Superfluous, Dr. Needless, and Dr. Overkill, based upon the clearly cumulative nature of the expected testimony of these witnesses.

2.
THE COURT MAY LIMIT THE NUMBER OF EXPERT WITNESSES CALLED TO TESTIFY

The Court may limit the number of witnesses called to testify on a single question. *See McInnes v. Yamaha Motor Corp. U.S.A.*, 673 S.W.2d 185, 188 (Tex. 1984) (exclusion of additional plaintiff's witness testimony not reversible error where substance of excluded testimony already in record from testimony of other witnesses); *Welch v. McLean*, 191 S.W.3d 147, 164 (Tex. App.—Fort Worth 2005, no pet.) (the similarity in opinions and credentials of two defense expert witnesses provided a legitimate basis for the trial court's exclusion of the testimony of one expert as needlessly cumulative of the other expert's testimony); *Sims v. Brackett*, 885 S.W.2d 450, 454 (Tex. App.—Corpus Christi 1994, writ denied) (court has authority to exclude testimony to avoid needless presentation of cumulative evidence and undue delay).

Expert testimony that is merely cumulative of prior testimony may be excluded. *Welch v. McLean*, 191 S.W.3d 147, 164 (Tex. App.—Fort Worth 2005, no pet.); *Gainsco County Mut. Ins. Co. v. Martinez*, 27 S.W.3d 97, 107 (Tex. App.—San Antonio 2000, pet. dism'd by agr.) (no error in excluding cumulative testimony of personal injury plaintiff's biomechanical expert where neurologist proffered substantially similar evidence); *Cruz v. Hinojosa*, 12 S.W.3d 545, 550 (Tex. App.—San Antonio 1999, pet. denied) (deposition testimony by expert witness excluded where cumulative of other evidence already presented in plaintiff's case-in-chief); *Keene Corp. v. Rogers*, 863 S.W.2d 168 (Tex. App.—Texarkana 1993, writ dism'd) (expert witness's videotape testimony excluded where cumulative of other testimony). *See also Sinko v. City of San Antonio*, 702 S.W.2d 201 (Tex. App.—San Antonio 1985, writ ref'd n.r.e.).

In the present case, the Plaintiff has listed two orthopedic surgeons, two general medical doctors, and two internal medicine specialists. It is unclear how the testimony of these duplicate specialists will differ. What is clear is that Dr. Superfluous, Dr. Needless, and Dr. Overkill were not treating physicians and would not be expected to offer testimony as reliable or material as their treating counterparts.

Allowing the testimony of these witnesses will add hours, if not days, of needless duplicate testimony. Clearly, under the above-described case law, this Court has the authority to limit the number of Plaintiff's experts, as requested herein.

3.
THIS COURT MAY PRECLUDE EVIDENCE THAT WILL WASTE TIME

Texas Rule of Evidence 403 states "[a]lthough relevant, evidence may be excluded if its probative value is substantially outweighed by the danger of unfair prejudice, confusion of the issues, or misleading the jury, or by <u>considerations of undue delay</u>, or needless presentation of cumulative evidence." (Emphasis added.) In addition, case law supports the fact that this Court can preclude evidence that will waste time. *See Dow Chem. Co. v. Francis*, 46 S.W.3d 237, 241 (Tex. 2001) ("a trial court may properly intervene to maintain control in the courtroom, to expedite the trial, and to prevent what it considers to be a waste of time").

As indicated above, three of the Plaintiff's seven designated experts are duplicative and clearly unnecessary. Allowing the testimony will prolong this trial significantly, wasting the valuable time and resources of the Court and all other participants, while adding absolutely nothing new to the evidence.

4.
CONCLUSION

Based upon the above Points and Authorities, the Defendant respectfully requests that this Court limit the Plaintiff's medical experts as requested herein.

Dated: _____ *(Date)* _____

By: _____

_____ *(Name of Counsel)* _____

Attorneys for Defendant,

_____ *(Name of Defendant)* _____

C. Motion to Exclude Prejudicial Evidence

NO. _____

_____	§	IN THE DISTRICT COURT
	§	
v.	§	_____ JUDICIAL COURT
	§	
_____	§	_____ COUNTY, TEXAS

PLAINTIFF'S MOTION TO EXCLUDE PREJUDICIAL FIREWORKS EVIDENCE

Comes now _____, Defendant in this cause, and files this Motion to Exclude Prejudicial Evidence and in support thereof would show the Court as follows:

1.
FACTUAL BACKGROUND

Plaintiff filed this suit alleging that Defendant committed assault against Plaintiff. On July 4, 2019, Defendant was celebrating the Fourth of July at his home by setting off fireworks. Plaintiff, who is Defendant's neighbor, objected to the use of the fireworks and an argument ensued. The two parties engaged in a fistfight and Plaintiff suffered a broken nose and other injuries.

Plaintiff intends to introduce evidence that Defendant's use of the fireworks at his home was unlawful. By this motion, Defendant seeks an order precluding the introduction of any evidence, or any mention of evidence, relating to the unlawful use of fireworks. This motion is based upon the grounds that the evidence is unduly prejudicial, irrelevant, and clearly inadmissible under the laws of this state.

2.
THIS COURT MAY EXCLUDE EVIDENCE IN ADVANCE OF TRIAL BY WAY OF AN IN LIMINE MOTION

The Court has the inherent power to grant a motion in limine to exclude evidence which could be objected to at trial, either as irrelevant or subject to exclusion as unduly prejudicial. *Wackenhut Corp. v. Gutierrez,* 453 S.W.3d 917, 920 n.3 (Tex. 2016); *In re BCH Development, LLC,* 525 S.W.3d 920, 925 (Tex. App.—Dallas 2017, orig. proceeding). Texas Rule of Evidence 403 allows the court to exclude evidence where there is a substantial danger that the probative value will be outweighed by the danger of undue prejudice. *See Diamond Offshore Services Ltd. v. Williams,* 542 S.W.3d 539, 549 (Tex. 2018); *Brookshire Bros. v. Aldridge,* 438 S.W.3d 9, 34 (Tex. 2014).

Moreover, the court may hear and determine the question of the admissibility of evidence outside the presence or hearing of the jury. *See Weidner v. Sanchez,* 14 S.W.3d 353, 363 (Tex. App.—Houston [14th Dist.] 2000, no pet.); *Kendrix v. S. Pac. Transp. Co.,* 907 S.W.2d 111, 113 (Tex. App.—Beaumont 1995, writ denied); Tex. R. Civ. P. 166; Tex. R. Evid. 103, 104.

3.
THIS COURT MAY EXCLUDE PREJUDICIAL EVIDENCE PURSUANT TO TEXAS RULE OF EVIDENCE 403

Texas Rule of Evidence 403 states "[a]lthough relevant, evidence may be excluded if its probative value is substantially outweighed by the danger of unfair prejudice, confusion of the issues, or misleading the jury, or by considerations of undue delay, or needless presentation of cumulative evidence."

In *Waffle House, Inc. v. Williams,* 313 S.W.3d 796, 812 (Tex. 2010), evidence that an employee had made statements that she had an open marriage, had had extramarital relations, and had made "overtures" to a female coworker, outweighed that evidence's probative value in the employee's action for sexual harassment. The Court reasoned that, even if the alleged harasser had been aware of the employee's statements, the employee's interest, if any, in other men or women bore little relevance to whether she welcomed the alleged harasser's advances.

In the present matter, any evidence of the unlawful use of fireworks is not probative to the action. Texas Rule of Evidence 403 justifies the preclusion of the requested evidence in this case. The fact that the Defendant was using fireworks in a neighborhood will likely confuse and mislead the jury into thinking that the issue is whether the Defendant was breaking the law instead of whether Defendant committed an assault against Plaintiff. Consequently, such evidence will unduly prejudice the Defendant.

4.
EVIDENCE OF THE UNLAWFUL USE OF FIREWORKS IS IRRELEVANT TO THIS COURT ACTION AND IS THEREFORE INADMISSIBLE

Texas Rule of Evidence 402 states that "evidence which is not relevant is inadmissible." Relevant evidence is defined by Texas Rule of Evidence 401 as "having any tendency to make the existence of any fact that is of consequence to the determination of the action more probable or less probable than it would be without the evidence." *See Torrington Co. v. Stutzman*, 46 S.W.3d 829, 845 n.13 (Tex. 2000). Irrelevant evidence is not admissible. *Morale v. State*, 557 S.W.3d 569, 573 (Tex. 2018); *Diamond Offshore Services Ltd. v. Williams*, 542 S.W.3d 539, 549 (Tex. 2018).

Any evidence of the unlawful use of fireworks is not relevant in this case. Evidence of the Defendant's prior activities on the night of the altercation between the parties does not tend to make the existence of any fact more or less probable. Accordingly, the evidence is not relevant to the claims at issue, and the evidence should be excluded.

5.
CONCLUSION

Based on the foregoing, Defendant respectfully requests that this Court enter an order excluding any and all evidence pertaining to the unlawful use of fireworks.

Dated: _____*(Date of Motion)*_____

By: _____

_____*(Name of Counsel)*_____

Attorneys for Defendant,

_____*(Name of Defendant)*_____

D. Opposition to Motion to Exclude Prejudicial Evidence

NO. _____

	§	IN THE DISTRICT COURT
_____	§	
v.	§	_____ JUDICIAL COURT
	§	
_____	§	_____ COUNTY, TEXAS

DEFENDANT'S OPPOSITION TO PLAINTIFF'S MOTION TO EXCLUDE PREJUDICIAL VIDEO EVIDENCE

Comes now _____, Defendant in this cause, and files this Opposition to Plaintiff's Motion to Exclude Prejudicial Evidence and in support thereof would show the Court as follows:

1.
FACTUAL BACKGROUND

This is an assault case arising out of an incident that occurred when Defendant physically removed Plaintiff from her store. On December 17, 2019, Plaintiff was shopping at a store owned by the Defendant. When Plaintiff became unruly and disruptive, she was asked to leave the store. Upon her refusal to leave, the Defendant called security and had Plaintiff physically removed. Throughout the incident, Plaintiff hurled profanity at everyone around her.

Defendant intends to introduce the security video of the incident. In her motion to exclude prejudicial evidence, Plaintiff has asked the court to exclude evidence of the specific words she used on grounds that such evidence is unduly prejudicial.

By this opposition to Plaintiff's motion, Defendant requests that the court deny Plaintiff's motion upon the grounds that the evidence is not prejudicial or irrelevant, and clearly admissible under the laws of this state.

2.
THE EVIDENCE IS NOT UNDULY PREJUDICIAL PURSUANT TO RULE 403

Texas Rule of Evidence 403 states that the court may only exclude relevant evidence "if its probative value is substantially outweighed by the danger of undue prejudice, confusion of the issues, or misleading the jury, or by considerations of undue delay, or needless presentation of cumulative evidence."

As noted by the Texas Supreme Court, "testimony is not inadmissible on the sole ground that it is 'prejudicial' because in our adversarial system, much of a proponent's evidence is legitimately intended to wound the opponent." *Diamond Offshore Services Ltd. v. Williams,* 542 S.W.3d 539, 542 (Tex. 2018); *Bay Area Healthcare Group, Ltd. v. McShane,* 239 S.W.3d 231, 234 (Tex. 2007). The party moving for exclusion of "prejudicial" evidence must show that the evidence is unduly prejudicial. *Bay Area Healthcare Group, Ltd. v. McShane*, 239 S.W.3d 231, 234 (Tex. 2007).

In the present matter, the Plaintiff's use of profanity, while prejudicial to her, does not outweigh the probative value of her specific words to the consequential facts of the case. Texas Rule of Evidence 403 does not justify the preclusion of the requested evidence in this case. The evidence of Plaintiff's use of profanity should not be excluded.

3.
THE EVIDENCE IS RELEVANT TO THIS COURT ACTION AND IS THEREFORE ADMISSIBLE

Texas Rule of Evidence 402 states that "evidence which is not relevant is inadmissible." See Relevant evidence is defined by Texas Rule of Evidence 401 as "having any tendency to make the existence of any fact that is of consequence to the determination of the action more probable or less probable than it would be without the evidence." *See Torrington Co. v. Stutzman*, 46 S.W.3d 829, 845 n.13 (Tex. 2000). Irrelevant evidence is not admissible. *Morale v. State*, 557 S.W.3d 569, 573 (Tex. 2018); *Diamond Offshore Services Ltd. v. Williams*, 542 S.W.3d 539, 549 (Tex. 2018).

In this case, merely stating that Plaintiff used profanity does not give a complete picture of the incident. Evidence of the specific words Plaintiff used throughout her disruptive and unruly behavior during the incident is clearly relevant to whether Defendant's subsequent actions were necessary. Accordingly, the evidence is relevant to the claims at issue and should not be excluded.

4.
CONCLUSION

Based on the foregoing, Defendant respectfully requests that this Court enter an order denying Plaintiff's motion to exclude prejudicial evidence.

Dated: _____*(Date of Motion)*_____

By: _____

_____*(Name of Counsel)*_____

Attorneys for Defendant,

_____*(Name of Defendant)*_____

CHAPTER 3

Irrelevant Evidence

I. Motion Authorities
   A. Motion to Exclude Irrelevant Evidence
      1. Suggested Motion Text
      2. Motion Summary
      3. Supporting Authorities
         a. Matters Not in Dispute
         b. Outside Pleadings
         c. Prejudicial
         d. Speculative Evidence
         e. Compromise, Offers to Compromise, Plea Discussions
         f. Parties' Wealth or Poverty
         g. Collateral Benefits
         h. Out-of-Court Experiments
         i. Similar Claims
         j. Number of Friends or Family
         k. Real Estate Value or Appraisal
         l. Criminal Acquittal in Subsequent Civil Action
         m. Employment Policies
         n. Specific Exclusions
      4. Opposing Authorities
         a. Evidence to Offer Additional Explanation
         b. Parties' Wealth or Poverty
         c. Similar Transactions, Claims, or Occurrences
         d. Prior Convictions
         e. Remoteness or Lapse of Time
         f. Matters Not in Dispute
         g. Circumstantial Evidence
         h. Background Evidence
         i. Real Estate Value or Appraisal
   B. Motion to Exclude Evidence of Matters Not in Controversy
      1. Suggested Motion Text
      2. Motion Summary
      3. Supporting Authorities
         a. Admitted or Uncontroverted Matters
         b. Collateral Issues
         c. Unpleaded Issues
      4. Opposing Authorities
         a. Collateral Issues

  b. Unpleaded Issues
  c. Where Relevant to Other Issues
  d. Matters Not in Dispute
  e. Evidence to Provide Additional Explanation
  f. Pleaded Issues
II. Sample Motions
 A. Motion to Exclude Irrelevant Evidence
 B. Motion to Exclude Evidence of Physical Conditions Not at Issue

I. Motion Authorities

A. Motion to Exclude Irrelevant Evidence

1. *Suggested Motion Text*

 (*Name of Moving Party*) hereby moves this Court for an order excluding any and all evidence, references to evidence, testimony or argument relating to (*Describe Irrelevant Evidence*). The motion is based upon the ground that the evidence is irrelevant and immaterial to the issues in this action and therefore inadmissible.

2. *Motion Summary*

This motion is used to exclude irrelevant evidence, i.e., evidence that neither proves or disproves any of the facts in issue or that is unable to support any reasonable inference or presumption regarding the matters in dispute pursuant to the authority of Texas Rule of Evidence 402. See *Gonzalez v. State*, 544 S.W.3d 363, 371 (Tex. Crim. App. 2018); *JLG Trucking, LLC v. Garza*, 466 S.W.3d 157, 162 (Tex. 2015); *Jones v. Red Arrow Heavy Hauling, Inc.*, 816 S.W.2d 134, 135 (Tex. App.—Beaumont 1991, writ denied). Irrelevant evidence may be excluded by in limine motion. *Estate of Finney*, 424 S.W.3d 608, 614 (Tex. App.—Dallas 2013, no pet.); *Gravis v. Parke-Davis & Co.*, 502 S.W.2d 863, 871 (Tex. Civ. App.—Corpus Christi 1973, reh'g denied, writ ref'd n.r.e.). Other evidence that may be excluded under the authority of Rule 402 includes that which is speculative [*In the Matter of V.M.D.*, 974 S.W.2d 332, 350 (Tex. App.—San Antonio 1998, no writ)], outside the pleadings [*Benavides v. Cushman, Inc.*, 189 S.W.3d 875, 883 (Tex. App.—Houston [1st Dist.] 2006, no pet.); *Benson v. Weaver*, 250 S.W.2d 770, 772 (Tex. Civ. App.—Austin 1952), *aff'd*, 150 Tex. 50, 254 S.W.2d 95 (1952)], or undisputed [*Blackburn v. State*, 820 S.W.2d 824, 826 (Tex. App.—Waco 1991, pet. ref'd)].

 Relevance, probative value, and materiality are not the same. Texas Rule of Evidence 401 defines "relevant evidence" in terms of the degree to which it is probative or material. Relevancy, as defined by Rule 401, "is not an inherent characteristic of any item or evidence but exists as a relation between an item of evidence and a matter properly provable in the case." *Montgomery v. State*, 810 S.W.2d 372, 387 (Tex. Crim. App. 1990). For evidence to be "material," it must be shown to be addressed to the proof of a material proposition. A material proposition is any fact that is of consequence to the determination of the action. If the evidence is offered to help prove a proposition that is not a matter in issue, the evidence is immaterial. *Henley v. State*, 493 S.W.3d 77, 83 (Tex. Crim. App. 2016); *Jones v. State*, 531 S.W.3d 309, 323 (Tex. App.—Houston [14th

Dist.] 2017, pet. ref'd). "Materiality" means that the proposition for which the evidence is offered must be of consequence to the determination of the action, as set out by the pleadings and the relevant substantive law. If the evidence is offered to prove a proposition that is not a material issue in the case, the evidence is said to be "immaterial." The probative value of the evidence relates to the strength of the relationship and can be either high or low; that is, it refers to how strongly the evidence serves to make more or less probable the existence of a fact of consequence to the litigation. *Gonzalez v. State*, 544 S.W.3d 363, 371 (Tex. Crim. App. 2018); *Gigliobianco v. State*, 210 S.W.3d 637, 641 (Tex. Crim. App. 2006); *Andrews v. State*, 429 S.W.3d 849, 865 (Tex. App.—Texarkana, 2014, pet. ref'd). Evidence is probative when it is more than a surmise or a suspicion and tends to prove the proposition. *Jessop v. State*, 368 S.W.3d 653, 694 (Tex. App.—Austin 2012, no pet.); *Manuel v. State*, 357 S.W.3d 66, 74 (Tex. App.—Tyler 2011, pet. ref'd).

If your motion in limine has been denied, remember that any error in the admission of the evidence is not preserved by the ruling denying your motion in limine. You must object when the evidence is offered at trial to preserve error. *Wackenhut Corp. v. Gutierrez*, 453 S.W.3d 917, 920 n.3 (Tex. 2016); *Fuller v. State*, 253 S.W.3d 220, 232 (Tex. Crim. App. 2008). Similarly, even if your motion in limine is granted, you will still need to make a proper objection at trial to preserve error with regard to questions that are claimed to violate the motion. See, e.g., *Pool v. Ford Motor Co.*, 715 S.W.2d 629, 637 (Tex. 1986); *Rhey v. Redic*, 408 S.W.3d 440, 460 (Tex. App.—El Paso 2013, no pet.); *Martinez v. State*, 345 S.W.3d 703, 705 (Tex. App.—Amarillo 2010, no pet.); *Boulle v. Boulle*, 254 S.W.3d 701, 709 (Tex. App.—Dallas 2008, no pet.). Thus, if a point in a motion in limine is granted, it does not exclude the evidence. Rather, the ruling requires the party who wants to present the challenged evidence to approach the bench during trial and inform the court that it is about to get into the challenged evidence. The objecting party must then make the objection on the record and the judge will enter a binding, appealable ruling. *Roberts v. State*, 220 S.W.3d 521, 533 (Tex. Crim. App. 2007); *State Bar of Tex. v. Evans*, 774 S.W.2d 656, 658 n.6 (Tex. 1989); *Fitzgerald v. Water Rock Outdoors, LLC*, 536 S.W.3d 112, 121 (Tex. App.—Amarillo 2017, pet. denied); *In re BCH Development, LLC*, 525 S.W.3d 920, 925 (Tex. App.—Dallas 2017, orig. proceeding); *Davlin v. State*, 531 S.W.3d 765, 768 (Tex. App.—Texarkana 2016, no pet.).

If the other side has had a motion in limine granted against evidence you want to introduce, remember that to preserve error you must make an offer of proof under Texas Rule of Evidence 103(a)(2). See, e.g., *Gunn v. McCoy*, 554 S.W.3d 645, 666 (Tex. 2018); *Jones v. Mattress Firm Holding Corp.*, 558 S.W.3d 732, 738 (Tex. App.—Houston [14th Dist.] 2018, no pet.); *BNSF Ry. Co. v. Phillips*, 434 S.W.3d 675, 699 (Tex. App.—Fort Worth 2014), rev'd on other grounds, 485 S.W.3d 908 (Tex. 2015). The reason for this is to enable an appellate court to determine whether the exclusion of the evidence was erroneous and harmful. *Jones v. Mattress Firm Holding Corp.*, 558 S.W.3d 732, 738 (Tex. App.—Houston [14th Dist.] 2018, no pet.); *Linney v. State*, 401 S.W.3d 764, 772 (Tex. App.—Houston [14th Dist.] 2013, pet. ref'd); *Ludlow v. DeBerry*, 959 S.W.2d 265, 270 (Tex. App.—Houston [14th Dist.] 1997, no pet.).

In order to preserve error, you must:

(1) approach the bench and ask for a ruling;
(2) formally offer the evidence; and
(3) obtain a ruling on the offer.

Fitzgerald v. Water Rock Outdoors, LLC, 536 S.W.3d 112, 121 (Tex. App.—Amarillo 2017, pet. denied); *Southwest Country Enters., Inc. v. Lucky Lady Oil Co.*, 991 S.W.2d 490, 493 (Tex. App.—Fort Worth 1999, pet. denied).

3. Supporting Authorities

Texas Rule of Evidence 402 states that "evidence which is not relevant is inadmissible." Relevant evidence is defined by Texas Rule of Evidence 401 as "having any tendency to make the existence of any fact that is of consequence to the determination of the action more probable or less probable than it would be without the evidence." *See Morale v. State*, 557 S.W.3d 569, 573 (Tex. 2018); *Diamond Offshore Services Ltd. v. Williams*, 542 S.W.3d 539, 549 (Tex. 2018); *Brookshire Bros. v. Aldridge*, 438 S.W.3d 9, 34 (Tex. 2014).

Morale v. State, 557 S.W.3d 569, 573 (Tex. 2018) ("Irrelevant evidence is not admissible...." Evidence is relevant if it has any tendency to make a fact more or less probable than it would be without the evidence" and "the fact is of consequence in determining the action.").

Enbridge Pipelines (East Texas) L.P. v. Avinger Timber, LLC, 386 S.W.3d 256, 262 (Tex. 2012) (trial court must act as evidentiary gatekeeper to exclude irrelevant and unreliable expert evidence).

Enbridge Pipelines (East Texas) L.P. v. Avinger Timber, LLC, 386 S.W.3d 256, 262 (Tex. 2012) (expert testimony must be relevant to the issues and based upon a reliable foundation).

Blasdell v. State, 384 S.W.3d 824, 830 (Tex. Crim. App. 2012) ("[I]f a hypothetical question fails to echo any particular 'event' that occurred in that particular case, it would result in expert testimony that is not relevant for purposes of Rule 702 because it does not 'fit' the facts of the case and therefore cannot help the jury.").

Devoe v. State, 354 S.W.3d 457, 469 (Tex. Crim. App. 2011) ("[S]ame-transaction contextual evidence is admissible only when the offense would make little or no sense without also bringing in that evidence, and it is admissible only to the extent that it is necessary to the jury's understanding of the offense.").

Tillman v. State, 354 S.W.3d 425, 438 (Tex. Crim. App. 2011) ("[T]he relevance inquiry is whether the evidence 'will assist the trier of fact' and is sufficiently tied to the facts of the case.... To be relevant, the expert must make an effort to tie pertinent facts of the case to the scientific principles that are the subject of his or her testimony.").

TXI Transp. Co. v. Hughes, 306 S.W.3d 230, 234 (Tex. 2010) (to be admissible, expert testimony must be relevant and based on a reliable foundation).

TXI Transp. Co. v. Hughes, 306 S.W.3d 230, 234 (Tex. 2010) (expert testimony based on an unreliable foundation or flawed methodology is unreliable and does not satisfy relevancy requirement).

State v. Cent. Expressway Sign Assocs., 302 S.W.3d 866, 870 (Tex. 2009) (to be relevant, the expert's opinion must be based on the facts; to be reliable, the expert's opinion must be based on sound reasoning and methodology).

Layton v. State, 280 S.W.3d 235, 241 (Tex. Crim. App. 2009) (when determining whether evidence is relevant, courts examine the purpose for which the evidence is being introduced).

Layton v. State, 280 S.W.3d 235, 241 (Tex. Crim. App. 2009) (for evidence to be relevant, there must be some direct or logical connection between the actual evidence and the proposition sought to be proved).

City of San Antonio v. Pollack, 284 S.W.3d 809, 817 (Tex. 2009) (opinion testimony that is conclusory or speculative is not relevant because it does not tend to make the existence of a material fact more probable or less probable).

Sells v. State, 121 S.W.3d 748, 766 (Tex. Crim. App. 2003), *cert. denied*, 540 U.S. 986 (2003) (trial court did not err excluding videotape offered by the defendant where irrelevant).

E.I. du Pont de Nemours & Co. v. Robinson, 923 S.W.2d 549, 557 (Tex. 1995) ("Evidence that has no relationship to any of the issues in the case is irrelevant and does not satisfy [Texas Rule of Evidence] 702's requirement that the testimony be of assistance to the jury. It is thus inadmissible under 702 as well as under 401 and 402.").

Pittman v. Baladez, 158 Tex. 372, 381, 312 S.W.2d 210, 216 (Tex. 1958) (evidence probative if some logical connection either directly or by inference between fact offered and fact to be proved).

O'Hern v. Mughrab, 579 S.W.3d 594, 604 (Tex. App.—Houston [14th Dist.] 2019, no pet.) ("conclusory statements are not probative evidence and accordingly will not suffice to establish a prima facie case").

R&M Mixed Beverage Consultants, Inc. v. Safe Harbor Benefits, Inc., 578 S.W.3d 218 (Tex. App.—El Paso 2019) ("Irrelevant evidence is not admissible.... Evidence is relevant if it has any tendency to make a fact more or less probable than it would be without the evidence and the fact is of consequence in determining the action.").

Proo v. State, 587 S.W.3d 789, 814 (Tex. App.—San Antonio 2019, pet. ref'd) ("[R]elevant evidence is evidence having any tendency to make the existence of any fact that is of consequence to the determination of the action more probable or less probable than it would be without the evidence.").

Proo v. State, 587 S.W.3d 789, 814 (Tex. App.—San Antonio 2019, pet. ref'd) ("To be 'material,' the evidence must relate to a fact of consequence, which includes both an elemental fact or an evidentiary fact from which an elemental fact can be inferred.").

Proo v. State, 587 S.W.3d 789, 814 (Tex. App.—San Antonio 2019, pet. ref'd) ("To be 'probative,' the evidence must tend to make the existence of the fact of consequence more or less probable than it would be absent the evidence.").

Proo v. State, 587 S.W.3d 789, 814 (Tex. App.—San Antonio 2019, pet. ref'd) ("Relevancy is not an inherent characteristic of any item of evidence but exists as a relation between an item of evidence and a matter properly provable in the case.").

Loera v. Fuentes, 511 S.W.3d 761, 771 (Tex. App.—El Paso 2016, no pet.) ("[I]rrelevant evidence is of no assistance to the jury.").

Loera v. Fuentes, 511 S.W.3d 761, 771 (Tex. App.—El Paso 2016, no pet.) ("Conclusory or speculative opinion testimony is not relevant because it does not tend to make the existence of a material fact more probable or less probable.").

Benson v. Chalk, 536 S.W.3d 886, 904 (Tex. App.—Houston [1st Dist.] 2017, pet. denied) ("For an expert's testimony to be admissible, the expert witness must be qualified to testify about scientific, technical, or other specialized knowledge, and the testimony must be relevant and based upon a reliable foundation.").

Benson v. Chalk, 536 S.W.3d 886, 904 (Tex. App.—Houston [1st Dist.] 2017, pet. denied) ("[E]xpert testimony based on an unreliable foundation or flawed methodology is unreliable and does not satisfy the relevancy requirement.").

Ashby v. State, 527 S.W.3d 356, 362 (Tex. App.—Houston [1st Dist.] 2017, pet. ref'd) ("In determining relevance, courts must examine the purpose for which particular evidence is being introduced.... It is critical that there is a direct or logical connection between the actual evidence and the proposition sought to be proved.").

PNP Petroleum I, LP v. Taylor, 438 S.W.3d 723, 735 (Tex. App.—San Antonio 2014, pet. denied) (relevant evidence is evidence having the tendency to make the existence of any fact that is of consequence to the determination of the action more probable or less probable than it would be without the evidence).

PNP Petroleum I, LP v. Taylor, 438 S.W.3d 723, 735 (Tex. App.—San Antonio 2014, pet. denied) (the test for relevancy is satisfied only when there is some logical connection between the fact offered and the fact to be proven).

Andrews v. State, 429 S.W.3d 849, 865 (Tex. App.—Texarkana 2014, pet. ref'd) ("[P]robative value refers to the inherent probative force of an item of evidence—that is, how strongly it serves to make more or less probable the existence of a fact of consequence to the litigation—coupled with the proponent's need for that item of evidence.").

Rhey v. Redic, 408 S.W.3d 440, 460 (Tex. App.—El Paso 2013, no pet.) ("[T]o determine relevancy, the court must look at the purpose for offering the evidence.... There must be some logical connection either directly or by inference between the fact offered and the fact to be proved.").

Russell Equestrian Ctr., Inc. v. Miller, 406 S.W.3d 243, 247 (Tex. App.—San Antonio 2013, no pet.) (opinion testimony that is conclusory or speculative is not relevant evidence because it does not tend to make the existence of a material fact more probable or less probable).

Sennett v. State, 406 S.W.3d 661, 668 (Tex. App.—Eastland 2013, no pet.) ("[R]elevance is the broader concept of whether the evidence will assist the trier of fact and is sufficiently tied to the facts of the case.").

Haley v. State, 396 S.W.3d 756, 763 (Tex. App.—Houston [14th Dist.] 2013, no pet.) (to be relevant, an expert's testimony must assist the trier of fact to understand the evidence or to determine a fact in issue).

Young v. State, 358 S.W.3d 790, 803 (Tex. App.—Houston [14th Dist.] 2012, pet. ref'd) (to be relevant, expert testimony must tie pertinent facts of the case to the scientific principles that are the subjects of the testimony).

Madrigal v. State, 347 S.W.3d 809, 813 (Tex. App.—Corpus Christi 2011, pet. ref'd) ("[T]estimony that is based solely on speculation and conjecture necessarily lacks probative value, and therefore fails to meet the relevancy requirements of the rules of evidence.").

Manuel v. State, 357 S.W.3d 66, 74 (Tex. App.—Tyler 2011, pet. ref'd) (to be relevant, evidence must be material and probative).

Manuel v. State, 357 S.W.3d 66, 74 (Tex. App.—Tyler 2011, pet. ref'd) (for evidence to be material and thus relevant, it must be shown to be addressed to the proof of a material proposition, i.e., any fact that is of consequence to the determination of the action).

S. Plains Lamesa R.R., Ltd. v. Heinrich, 280 S.W.3d 357, 363 (Tex. App.—Amarillo 2008, no pet.) (for evidence to be relevant, it must logically tend to make a particular proposition more or less likely; additionally, the proposition to be proved must be of consequence to some issue in the trial).

Gentry v. State, 259 S.W.3d 272, 279 (Tex. App.—Waco 2008, pet. ref'd) ("[F]irst step in a trial court's determination of whether evidence should be admitted before the jury is finding the evidence to be relevant.").

Stephenson v. State, 255 S.W.3d 652, 661 (Tex. App.—Fort Worth 2008, no pet.) (evidence is relevant if it has any tendency to make the existence of any fact that is of consequence to the determination of the action more probable or less probable than it would be without the evidence).

Bradshaw v. State, 244 S.W.3d 490, 500 (Tex. App.—Texarkana 2007, pet. stricken), No. PD-017-08, 2008 WL 1930683 (Tex. Crim. App. 2008) (to determine whether evidence is relevant, courts look to the purpose for offering the evidence and whether there is a direct or logical connection between the offered evidence and the proposition sought to be proved).

Bradshaw v. State, 244 S.W.3d 490, 500 (Tex. App.—Texarkana 2007, pet. stricken), No. PD-017-08, 2008 WL 1930683 (Tex. Crim. App. 2008) (balancing test set forth in the rules of evidence as to a determination of the potentially prejudicial nature of relevant evidence carries a presumption that relevant evidence will be more probative than prejudicial).

PPC Transp. v. Metcalf, 254 S.W.3d 636, 643 (Tex. App.—Tyler 2008, no pet.) (if there is some logical connection either directly or by inference between the evidence and a fact to be proved, the evidence is relevant).

Richmond Condos. v. Skipworth Commercial Plumbing, Inc., 245 S.W.3d 646, 665 (Tex. App.—Fort Worth 2008, pet. denied) (testimony of individual partners in joint venture for redevelopment of building as condominium project, that they had no personal desire to recover from plumbing contractor, was not relevant in action by builder's risk insurer, as subrogee of joint venture, against contractor for negligence, relating to fire during redevelopment; such testimony was not related to whether contractor was liable for the fire).

Dickson v. State, 246 S.W.3d 733, 739 (Tex. App.—Houston [14th Dist.] 2007, pet. ref'd) (under evidentiary rules, a trial court follows a two-step process in determining whether evidence is admissible; first, trial court must decide whether evidence is relevant and, second, the trial court must determine if evidence should be excluded because of some other provision, whether constitutional, statutory, or evidentiary).

Dickson v. State, 246 S.W.3d 733, 739 (Tex. App.—Houston [14th Dist.] 2007, pet. ref'd) ("relevant evidence" is evidence having any tendency to make the existence of any fact that is of consequence to the determination of the action more probable or less probable than it would be without the evidence).

Dickson v. State, 246 S.W.3d 733, 739 (Tex. App.—Houston [14th Dist.] 2007, pet. ref'd) (evidentiary rule pertaining to exclusion of relevant evidence on special grounds favors admission of relevant evidence and carries a presumption that relevant evidence will be more probative than prejudicial).

Dickson v. State, 246 S.W.3d 733, 739 (Tex. App.—Houston [14th Dist.] 2007, pet. ref'd) ("[R]elevant evidence of an alternative perpetrator may be excluded absent proof of a sufficient nexus between crime charged and alleged alternative perpetrator.").

City of Houston v. Jackson, 135 S.W.3d 891, 904 (Tex. App.—Houston [1st Dist.] 2004), *rev'd on other grounds*, 192 S.W.3d 764 (Tex. 2006) (letter written by aggrieved party asking for job transfer and high sum of money irrelevant to demonstrate motive).

Hale v. State, 140 S.W.3d 381, 395 (Tex. App.—Fort Worth 2004, pet. ref'd) (evidence of other sexual acts by victims irrelevant and properly barred by rape shield statute in case involving sexual offenses).

Moore v. State, 143 S.W.3d 305, 313 (Tex. App.—Waco 2004, pet. ref'd) (evidence regarding victim's prior DUI conviction irrelevant to issue of his truthfulness and properly excluded where offered as impeachment).

Rivera v. State, 130 S.W.3d 454, 460 (Tex. App.—Corpus Christi 2004, no pet.) (result of police report made by victim's mother regarding alleged conduct by someone other than defendant properly excluded as irrelevant, unduly prejudicial, and confusing to jury).

Ellis v. State, 99 S.W.3d 783, 789 (Tex. App.—Houston [1st Dist.] 2003, pet. ref'd) (trial court did not abuse discretion excluding irrelevant testimony by defendant's father where offered to suggest bias by police against defendant when defendant's father had no knowledge of circumstances surrounding charged offenses).

Bellaire v. State, 110 S.W.3d 664, 670 (Tex. App.—Houston [14th Dist.] 2003, pet ref'd) (photograph of defendant's genital area properly excluded as irrelevant in sexual assault case).

Goodwin v. State, 91 S.W.3d 912, 917 (Tex. App.—Fort Worth 2002, no pet.) (evidence of victim's mental health history properly excluded as irrelevant).

Alexander v. State, 88 S.W.3d 772, 777 (Tex. App.—Corpus Christi 2002, pet. ref'd) (evidence of weapon seized at defendant's arrest irrelevant and prejudicial and should not have been admitted, even where offered as "context evidence").

Potter v. State, 74 S.W.3d 105, 113 (Tex. App.—Waco 2002, no pet.) ("[T]he graphic picture of [a victim's] bloody face at the morgue more inflammatory than probative of [the defendant] as a ringleader of the crimes committed.... Thus, [it was] an abuse of discretion in admitting the photo because the probative value of the photograph is small and its inflammatory potential great.").

Strauss v. Cont'l Airlines, Inc., 67 S.W.3d 428, 450 (Tex. App.—Houston [14th Dist.] 2002, no pet.) (trial court did not abuse its discretion by excluding psychiatric records of a party as irrelevant and unduly prejudicial).

Associated Carriages, Inc. v. Int'l Bank of Commerce, 37 S.W.3d 69, 74 (Tex. App.—San Antonio 2000, pet. denied) (expert's proposed deposition testimony on corporate law properly excluded as irrelevant).

Williams v. State, 27 S.W.3d 599, 602 (Tex. App.—Waco 2000, pet. ref'd) (evidence of another inmate's misconduct was irrelevant and should have been excluded where it was improper background evidence).

King v. State, 17 S.W.3d 7, 19 (Tex. App.—Houston [14th Dist.] 2000, pet. ref'd) (in theft case, evidence of victim's alleged misrepresentation in contract with defendant properly excluded as irrelevant).

Contreras v. State, 915 S.W.2d 510, 518 (Tex. App.—El Paso 1995, pet. ref'd) (other individual's fingerprints submitted for comparison not relevant and properly excluded).

Hawkins v. State, 871 S.W.2d 539, 541 (Tex. App.—Fort Worth 1994, no pet.) ("Relevancy is not an inherent characteristic, it arises from the evidence's relation to a matter properly provable in the case.").

Ladner v. State, 868 S.W.2d 417, 425 (Tex. App.—Tyler 1993, pet. ref'd) (evidence regarding victim's prior bad acts in a murder case irrelevant).

Perez v. State, 830 S.W.2d 684, 687 (Tex. App.—Corpus Christi 1992, no pet.) (evidence of members of defendant's gang irrelevant and should not have been admitted).

Jones v. Red Arrow Heavy Hauling, Inc., 816 S.W.2d 134, 135 (Tex. App.—Beaumont 1991, writ denied) (evidence that is not relevant is inadmissible).

Blackburn v. State, 820 S.W.2d 824, 826 (Tex. App.—Waco 1991, pet. ref'd) (photograph irrelevant and should have been excluded).

Montelongo v. Goodall, 788 S.W.2d 717, 720 (Tex. App.—Austin 1990, no pet.) (evidence of safety standards shown to not apply to condition at issue properly excluded as irrelevant).

Buchanan v. Am. Nat'l Ins. Co., 446 S.W.2d 384, 387 (Tex. Civ. App.—El Paso 1969, writ ref'd n.r.e.) (circumstances offered must have probative value sufficient to maintain basis of legal inference of fact sought to be proved).

a. Matters Not in Dispute

Exxon Pipeline Co. v. Zwahr, 88 S.W.3d 623, 629 (Tex. 2002) (evidence that has no relationship to any issue in the case is not admissible as it is irrelevant).

Gammill v. Jack Williams Chevrolet, Inc., 972 S.W.2d 713, 720 (Tex. 1998) (scientific evidence having no relationship to issues in case irrelevant).

Brown v. State, 757 S.W.2d 739, 741 (Tex. Crim. App. 1988) (evidence of victim's emotional trauma following rape irrelevant where only disputed issue was identity of rapist, not fact of rape).

PNP Petroleum I, LP v. Taylor, 438 S.W.3d 723, 735 (Tex. App.—San Antonio 2014, pet. denied) (relevant evidence is evidence having the tendency to make the existence of any fact of consequence to the determination of the action more probable or less probable than it would be without the evidence).

PNP Petroleum I, LP v. Taylor, 438 S.W.3d 723, 735 (Tex. App.—San Antonio 2014, pet. denied) (the test for relevancy is satisfied only when there is some logical connection between the fact offered and the fact to be proven).

Berryman's South Fork, Inc. v. J. Baxter Brinkmann Int'l Corp., 418 S.W.3d 172, 185 (Tex. App.—Dallas 2013, pet. denied) (where damages evidence does not relate to the amount of damages sustained under the proper measure of damages, that evidence is both irrelevant and legally insufficient to support a judgment).

Hernandez v. State, 327 S.W.3d 200, 205 (Tex. App.—San Antonio 2010, pet. ref'd) (in deciding whether evidence is relevant, trial court should ask whether a reasonable person, with some experience in the real world, would believe the evidence is helpful in determining the truth or falsity of any fact that is of consequence to the lawsuit).

S. Plains Lamesa R.R., Ltd. v. Heinrich, 280 S.W.3d 357, 363 (Tex. App.—Amarillo 2008, no pet.) (for evidence to be relevant, the proposition to be proved must be of consequence to some issue in the trial).

Petras v. Criswell, 248 S.W.3d 471, 478 (Tex. App.—Corpus Christi 2008, no pet.) (two-part test governs the admissibility of expert evidence: (1) the expert must be qualified; and (2) the testimony must be relevant and based on a reliable foundation).

Goss v. Kellogg Brown & Root, Inc., 232 S.W.3d 816, 818 (Tex. App.—Houston [14th Dist.] 2007, pet. denied) (to be relevant, expert testimony must be so sufficiently tied to the facts of the case that it will aid the jury in resolving a factual dispute).

Harris County Appraisal Dist. v. Kempwood Plaza Ltd., 186 S.W.3d 155, 158 (Tex. App.—Houston [1st Dist.] 2006, no pet.) (evidence that has no relationship to the issues in the case is irrelevant).

Huynh v. R. Warehousing & Port Servs., Inc., 973 S.W.2d 375, 377 (Tex. App.—Tyler 1998, no writ) (evidence of failure to take drug test irrelevant to negligent entrustment claim).

Palomo v. State, 925 S.W.2d 329, 336 (Tex. App.—Corpus Christi 1996, no pet.) (evidence that defendant had tattoo suggesting gang membership irrelevant where defendant did not contest issue of gang membership).

Brown v. State, 757 S.W.2d 739, 741 (Tex. Crim. App. 1988) (evidence of victim's emotional trauma following rape irrelevant where only disputed issue was identity of rapist, not fact of rape).

b. Outside Pleadings

Erisman v. Thompson, 140 Tex. 361, 365, 167 S.W.2d 731, 733 (Tex. 1943) ("[P]leadings determine the issues upon which parties go to trial, and it is not even proper to admit evidence unless it is addressed to or bears upon some issue raised by the pleadings.").

Benavides v. Cushman, Inc., 189 S.W.3d 875, 883 (Tex. App.—Houston [1st Dist.] 2006, no pet.) (improper to admit evidence unless it is addressed to or bears upon some issue raised by the pleadings).

Benavides v. Cushman, Inc., 189 S.W.3d 875, 883 (Tex. App.—Houston [1st Dist.] 2006, no pet.) (because a golf course groundskeeper did not plead either a marketing defect or a failure to warn and did not request a trial amendment to add such a cause of action, marketing defect was not one of groundskeeper's theories of recovery in his product liability action and therefore groundskeeper's expert's testimony, which was directed at proving the elements of a marketing defect cause of action, was not admissible).

Benson v. Weaver, 250 S.W.2d 770, 772 (Tex. Civ. App.—Austin 1952), *aff'd*, 152 Tex. 50, 254 S.W.2d 95 (1952) (admissibility of evidence depends on whether relevant to issues made by pleadings).

Mo., K. & T. Ry. Co. v. Keaveney, 80 S.W. 387, 389 (Tex. Civ. App. 1904) (evidence must correspond to allegations in the pleadings).

c. Prejudicial

Gonzalez v. State, 544 S.W.3d 363, 371 (Tex. Crim. App. 2018) (Rule 403 is only concerned with "undue" prejudice; "evidence is unfairly prejudicial if it has the capacity to lure the fact-finder into declaring guilt on a ground different from proof specific to the offense charged").

Diamond Offshore Services Ltd. v. Williams, 542 S.W.3d 539, 542 (Tex. 2018) ("Testimony is not inadmissible on the sole ground that it is 'prejudicial' because in our adversarial system, much of a proponent's evidence is legitimately intended to wound the opponent. Rather, unfair prejudice is the proper inquiry.").

Pawlak v. State, 420 S.W.3d 807, 809 (Tex. Crim. App. 2013) ("[I]t is possible for the admission of character evidence, though not necessarily cumulative, to cross the line from prejudicial to unfairly prejudicial based on the sheer volume of character evidence admitted.").

Waffle House, Inc. v. Williams, 313 S.W.3d 796, 812 (Tex. 2010) (evidence of sexual behavior outside of what society deems acceptable is inherently inflammatory).

Proo v. State, 587 S.W.3d 789, 817 (Tex. App.—San Antonio 2019, pet. ref'd) ("Rule 403 permits the exclusion of relevant evidence when its probative value is substantially outweighed by the danger of unfair prejudice, or, in other words when the evidence has 'an undue tendency to suggest that a decision be made on an improper basis.'").

Proo v. State, 587 S.W.3d 789, 817 (Tex. App.—San Antonio 2019, pet. ref'd) ("In evaluating whether the probative value of photographs or video is outweighed by the danger of unfair prejudice, the court considers several factors, including the number of exhibits offered, their gruesomeness, their detail, their size, whether they are black and white or color, whether they are close-up, and whether the body depicted is naked or clothed.... The court must also consider the availability of other means of proof and the unique circumstances of the individual case.").

Webb v. State, 575 S.W.3d 905 (Tex. App.—Waco 2019, pet. filed) ("When considering a Rule 403 objection, the trial court must balance (1) the inherent probative force of the proffered item of evidence along with (2) the proponent's need for that evidence against (3) any tendency of the evidence to suggest a decision on an improper basis, (4) any tendency of the evidence to confuse or distract the jury from the main issues, (5) any tendency of the evidence to be given undue weight by a jury that has not been equipped to evaluate the probative force of the evidence, and (6) the likelihood that presentation of the evidence will consume an inordinate amount of time or merely repeat evidence already admitted.").

Williams v. State, 531 S.W.3d 902, 918 (Tex. App.—Houston [14th Dist.] 2017, pet. granted) ("[E]xtraneous offense evidence that does not have relevance apart from character conformity is inadmissible during the guilt/innocence phase of trial.").

Newland v. State, 363 S.W.3d 205, 208 (Tex. App.—Waco 2011, pet. ref'd) ("[P]robative value for bolstering [a] witness's testimony with a non-specific threat not linked to the defendant, other than generally, and gang affiliation without being able to establish that the person making the threat was in the same gang as the defendant, and which may have occurred a year before trial, was very low and the danger of unfair prejudice is high" and thus the evidence should have been excluded.).

Republic Waste Servs., Ltd. v. Martinez, 335 S.W.3d 401, 409 (Tex. App.—Houston [1st Dist.] 2011, no pet.) ("The probative value of evidence showing only that the plaintiff is an illegal immigrant, who could possibly be deported, is slight because of the highly speculative nature of such evidence.... Without a showing that a plaintiff will likely be deported in his working lifetime, the jury is invited to engage in conjecture and speculation regarding whether he will be deported, when he will be deported, and, if deported, whether he will return to the United States to work. As a result, the probative value of evidence concerning a plaintiff's illegal immigrant status is low, while the prejudicial effect of this evidence is high.").

Young v. State, 242 S.W.3d 192, 200 (Tex. App.—Tyler 2007, no pet.) (photographs of sexual items should not have been admitted in child pornography case as none of the items had the tendency to make the existence of any fact that was of consequence to determination of the action more probably than it would be without the evidence).

Alexander v. State, 88 S.W.3d 772, 777 (Tex. App.—Corpus Christi 2002, pet. ref'd) (evidence of weapon seized at defendant's arrest irrelevant and prejudicial and should not have been admitted).

Williams v. State, 27 S.W.3d 599, 602 (Tex. App.—Waco 2000, pet. ref'd) (evidence of another person's misconduct was irrelevant and should have been excluded).

Huynh v. R. Warehousing & Port Servs., Inc., 973 S.W.2d 375, 377 (Tex. App.—Tyler 1998, no writ) (exclusion of evidence where irrelevant or unfairly prejudicial).

In Interest of Martin, 881 S.W.2d 531, 534 (Tex. App.—Texarkana 1994, pet. denied) ("Although cross-examination is a valuable right and an effective tool for producing evidence, it does not extend so far as to include irrelevant evidence.... The only relevant issue in this case is whether Burleson is the father of the child. The mother's sexual activity outside the time period during which the child could have been conceived is not relevant to a determination of paternity.").

IRRELEVANT EVIDENCE 77

Eoff v. Hal & Charlie Peterson Found., 811 S.W.2d 187, 193 (Tex. App.—San Antonio 1991, no writ) (portion of letter criticizing amount of fee should have been excluded as irrelevant and prejudicial).

Dudley v. Humana Hosp. Corp., 817 S.W.2d 124, 127 (Tex. App.—Houston [14th Dist.] 1991, no writ) (expert testimony not admissible if irrelevant, prejudicial, or confusing).

d. *Speculative Evidence*

Bostic v. Georgia-Pacific Corp., 439 S.W.3d 332, 348 (Tex. 2013) (scientific evidence that is not grounded in the methods and procedures of science is no more than subjective belief or unsupported speculation and is inadmissible).

Natural Gas Pipeline Co. of America v. Justiss, 397 S.W.3d 150, 155 (Tex. 2012) ("[T]he owner of real property "can testify to its market value, even if he could not qualify to testify about the value of like property belonging to someone else... [but] a property owner's testimony must be based on market value, rather than intrinsic or some other speculative value of the property.").

Natural Gas Pipeline Co. of America v. Justiss, 397 S.W.3d 150, 155 (Tex. 2012) (testimony is speculative if it is based on guesswork or conjecture).

Natural Gas Pipeline Co. of America v. Justiss, 397 S.W.3d 150, 155 (Tex. 2012) (opinion testimony that is conclusory or speculative is not relevant evidence because it does not tend to make the existence of a material fact more probable or less probable).

Natural Gas Pipeline Co. of America v. Justiss, 397 S.W.3d 150, 155 (Tex. 2012) (if a property owner's estimate is speculative, "the owner's testimony may be of such minimal probative force to warrant a judge's refusal even to submit the issue to the jury").

Serv. Corp. Int'l v. Guerra, 348 S.W.3d 221, 229 (Tex. 2011) (findings based on evidence that allow for no more than speculation, a guess, are based on legally insufficient evidence).

Coastal Transp. Co. v. Crown Ctr. Petroleum Corp., 136 S.W.3d 227, 231 (Tex. 2004) (conclusory and speculative expert testimony is irrelevant and insufficient to overcome a directed verdict motion by the opposing party).

City of Pearland v. Alexander, 483 S.W.2d 244, 247 (Tex. 1972) ("[E]vidence based on possibilities rather than reasonable probabilities [is] incompetent.").

Ochoa-Bunsow v. Soto, 587 S.W.3d 431, 440 (Tex. App.—El Paso 2019, pet. denied) ("Expert opinions that are conclusory or speculative lack probative value and constitute no evidence, even if they are not objected to.").

Shultz on Behalf of Shultz v. Lone Star Road Construction, Ltd., 593 S.W.3d 750, 758 (Tex. App.—Houston [14th Dist.] 2019, no pet.) ("Expert opinions must be supported by facts in evidence, not conjecture.... When an expert's opinion is based on an assumed fact that varies materially from the actual facts, the opinion lacks probative value and cannot raise a genuine fact issue.... If the record contains no evidence supporting an expert's material factual assumptions, or if such assumptions are contrary to conclusively proven facts, opinion testimony founded on those assumptions is not competent evidence.").

Tuttle v. Builes, 572 S.W.3d 344 (Tex. App.—Eastland 2019, no pet.) ("An owner's valuation testimony is not relevant if it is conclusory or speculative.... As with expert testimony, property valuations may not be based solely on a property owner's ipse dixit.").

Van Duren v. Chife, 569 S.W.3d 176 (Tex. App.—Houston [1st Dist.] 2018, no pet.) (a property owner's testimony as to the value of his property "cannot be speculative or conclusory.... The owner must substantiate his opinion of market value with the factual basis on which his opinion rests, which may include evidence of facts such as the price he paid, nearby sales, tax valuations, appraisals, and online resources.... If the owner's testimony does not satisfy these requirements, it is not evidence.").

Van Der Linden v. Khan, 535 S.W.3d 179, 193 (Tex. App.—Fort Worth 2017, pet. denied) ("[A] witness's testimony regarding what another person was thinking is inadmissible speculation and should not be considered.").

Loera v. Fuentes, 511 S.W.3d 761, 771 (Tex. App.—El Paso 2016, no pet.) ("Conclusory or speculative opinion testimony is not relevant because it does not tend to make the existence of a material fact more probable or less probable.").

Integrated of Amarillo, Inc. v. Kirkland, 424 S.W.3d 131, 135 (Tex. App.—Amarillo 2014, no pet.) (opinion testimony that is conclusory or speculative is objectionable and inadmissible as lacking relevance because it does not tend to make the existence of a material fact more probable or less probable).

iLight Techs. Inc. v. Clutch City Sports & Entertainment, L.P., 414 S.W.3d 842, 848 (Tex. App.—Houston [1st Dist.] 2013, pet. denied) ("[E]xpert opinions must be supported by facts in evidence, not conjecture").

Russell Equestrian Ctr., Inc. v. Miller, 406 S.W.3d 243, 247 (Tex. App.—San Antonio 2013, no pet.) (opinion testimony that is conclusory or speculative is not relevant evidence because it does not tend to make the existence of a material fact more probable or less probable).

Nzewi v. State, 359 S.W.3d 829, 832 (Tex. App.—Houston [14th Dist.] 2012, pet. ref'd) ("[A] conclusion reached by speculation may not be completely unreasonable, but it is not sufficiently based on facts or evidence to support a finding beyond a reasonable doubt.").

Methodist Hosp. v. German, 369 S.W.3d 333, 348 (Tex. App.—Houston [1st Dist.] 2011, pet. denied) ("[P]roximate cause cannot be satisfied by mere conjecture, guess, or speculation").

Caldwell v. State, 356 S.W.3d 42, 46 (Tex. App.—Texarkana 2011, no pet.) ("[A] criminal defendant is entitled to present evidence that another party is responsible for the crime alleged against the defendant; but the defendant must show that his proffered evidence regarding the alleged alternative perpetrator is sufficient, on its own or in combination with other evidence in the record, to show a nexus between the crime charged and the alleged 'alternative perpetrator.'... A defendant must do more than offering unsupported speculation of another, alternative perpetrator of defendant's charged offense.")

Chesser v. LifeCare Mgmt. Servs., L.L.C., 356 S.W.3d 613, 622 n.5 (Tex. App.—Fort Worth 2011, pet. denied) ("[E]xpert opinion testimony that is conclusory or speculative is not relevant evidence, because it does not tend to make the existence of a material fact more probable or less probable.").

Madrigal v. State, 347 S.W.3d 809, 813 (Tex. App.—Corpus Christi 2011, pet. ref'd) ("[T]estimony that is based solely on speculation and conjecture necessarily lacks probative value, and therefore fails to meet the relevancy requirements of the rules of evidence.").

State Office of Risk Mgmt. v. Adkins, 347 S.W.3d 394, 403 (Tex. App.—Dallas 2011, no pet.) ("[I]n the medical context, expert testimony that is not based on reasonable medical probability, but relies instead on possibility, speculation, or surmise, does not assist the jury and cannot support a judgment.").

Republic Waste Servs., Ltd. v. Martinez, 335 S.W.3d 401, 409 (Tex. App.—Houston [1st Dist.] 2011, no pet.) ("The probative value of evidence showing only that the plaintiff is an illegal immigrant, who could possibly be deported, is slight because of the highly speculative nature of such evidence.... Without a showing that a plaintiff will likely be deported in his working lifetime, the jury is invited to engage in conjecture and speculation regarding whether he will be deported, when he will be deported, and, if deported, whether he will return to the United States to work. As a result, the probative value of evidence concerning a plaintiff's illegal immigrant status is low, while the prejudicial effect of this evidence is high.").

Paradigm Oil, Inc. v. Retamco Operating, Inc., 242 S.W.3d 67, 74 (Tex. App.—San Antonio 2007, pet. denied) ("[F]or an expert's opinion testimony on an ultimate issue to be competent, it must not be speculative or conclusory.").

Paradigm Oil, Inc. v. Retamco Operating, Inc., 242 S.W.3d 67, 74 (Tex. App.—San Antonio 2007, pet. denied) ("[E]xpert opinion that has no factual substantiation in the record is speculative or conclusory.").

Paradigm Oil, Inc. v. Retamco Operating, Inc., 242 S.W.3d 67, 74 (Tex. App.—San Antonio 2007, pet. denied) ("[E]xpert opinion testimony on damages must be supported by objective facts, figures, or data from which the amount may be ascertained with reasonable certainty; if it is not, it is speculative and conclusory and will not support a judgment.").

Price v. Davita, 224 S.W.3d 331, 337 (Tex. App.—Houston [1st Dist.] 2006, pet. denied) (conclusory or speculative expert opinion is neither relevant nor competent in a medical malpractice action).

Garza v. State, 18 S.W.3d 813, 822 (Tex. App.—Fort Worth 2000, pet. ref'd) (evidence of person originally suspected to be offender was speculative and properly excluded as irrelevant).

In the Matter of V.M.D., 974 S.W.2d 332, 350 (Tex. App.—San Antonio 1998, no writ) (speculative and inconclusive nature of proffered evidence supported decision to exclude).

Jaramillo v. State, 817 S.W.2d 842, 845 (Tex. App.—Fort Worth 1991, pet. ref'd) (cross-examination that asked officer to speculate about meaning of victim's actions properly excluded).

Southwestern Pub. Serv. Co. v. Vanderburg, 526 S.W.2d 692, 695 (Tex. Civ. App.—Amarillo 1975, no writ) (speculative evidence of value in condemnation case should be excluded).

e. *Compromise, Offers to Compromise, and Plea Discussions*

Bowley v. State, 310 S.W.3d 431, 435 (Tex. Crim. App. 2010) ("[E]vidence of plea negotiations is generally not relevant to proving the elements of an offense, and it might be prejudicial to a defendant.").

Bowie v. State, 135 S.W.3d 55, 62 (Tex. Crim. App. 2004) (statements made in plea discussions held in other states are to be excluded under Rule 410).

Bowie v. State, 135 S.W.3d 55, 62 (Tex. Crim. App. 2004) ("Rule 410(3) does not protect only the entry of the plea or written stipulations," it also protects statements made under oath and subject to cross-examination).

Lerma v. Border Demolition & Environmental, Inc., 459 S.W.3d 695, 700 (Tex. App.—El Paso 2015, pet. denied [mand. denied]) (Settlement offers are inadmissible "to prove liability for or invalidity of the claim or its amount.... However, a settlement offer may be offered for other purposes.").

Certain Underwriters at Lloyd's, London v. Chicago Bridge & Iron Co., 406 S.W.3d 326, 339 (Tex. App.—Beaumont 2013, pet. denied) ("[E]vidence of settlement negotiations is inadmissible to prove liability for or invalidity of a claim or its amount.").

Certain Underwriters at Lloyd's, London v. Chicago Bridge & Iron Co., 406 S.W.3d 326, 339 (Tex. App.—Beaumont 2013, pet. denied) ("[W]hether documents constitute an offer of settlement depends on whether something is given up by one of the parties to avoid litigation where some concession is made by one or both of the parties.").

Certain Underwriters at Lloyd's, London v. Chicago Bridge & Iron Co., 406 S.W.3d 326, 339 (Tex. App.—Beaumont 2013, pet. denied) ("[E]xclusion of settlement offer evidence is not required when the evidence is offered for another purpose, such as proving bias, prejudice, or interest of a witness or party, negating a contention of undue delay, or proving an effort to obstruct a criminal investigation or prosecution.").

In re Am. Nat. County Mut. Ins. Co., 384 S.W.3d 429, 435 (Tex. App.—Austin 2012, orig. proceeding) ("[E]xclusion of settlement offers promotes the settlement of claims and recognizes that such evidence does not represent a party's actual position, but is an amount he is willing to give or take to avoid the expense and annoyance of litigation.").

Vinson Minerals, Ltd. v. XTO Energy, Inc., 335 S.W.3d 344, 353 (Tex. App.—Fort Worth 2010, pet. denied) ("The purpose of Rule 408 (excluding evidence of offers to compromise a claim) is to encourage settlement.").

Vinson Minerals, Ltd. v. XTO Energy, Inc., 335 S.W.3d 344, 353 (Tex. App.—Fort Worth 2010, pet. denied) ("[O]ffers of settlement are not admissible to prove liability or invalidity of a claim or its amount.").

Vinson Minerals, Ltd. v. XTO Energy, Inc., 335 S.W.3d 344, 353 (Tex. App.—Fort Worth 2010, pet. denied) ("[I]n an offer of settlement or compromise, a party concedes some right to which that party believes he or she is entitled in order to bring about a mutual settlement.").

Abdygapparova v. State, 243 S.W.3d 191, 206 (Tex. App.—San Antonio 2007, pet. ref'd) ("[B]ecause the plea bargaining process is recognized as an important and necessary integral aspect of the criminal justice system, Rule 410 protects statements made during plea negotiations.")

Abdygapparova v. State, 243 S.W.3d 191, 206 (Tex. App.—San Antonio 2007, pet. ref'd) ("[A] defendant, in the course of plea negotiations must be free to negotiate settlements without fear that his statements will later be used against him.").

Abdygapparova v. State, 243 S.W.3d 191, 206 (Tex. App.—San Antonio 2007, pet. ref'd) ("Rule 410 should bar the use of pleas and plea-related statements for impeachment.... Thus the trial court erred in allowing the State to proceed with questions relating to statements made during plea negotiations.").

Jones v. Red Arrow Heavy Hauling, Inc., 816 S.W.2d 134, 135 (Tex. App.—Beaumont 1991, writ denied) (evidence of settlement of claim against insurance company on unrelated contract irrelevant).

f. *Parties' Wealth or Poverty*

Southwestern Elec. Power Co. v. Burlington Northern R. Co., 966 S.W.2d 467, 472 (Tex. 1998) ("[A] party's financial condition is not relevant to the question of whether one party suffers a gross inequity.").

Knox v. Taylor, 992 S.W.2d 40, 65 (Tex. App.—Houston [14th Dist.] 1999, no pet.) ("[T]he net worth of a party is not admissible during the liability phase of a bifurcated trial.").

Wal-Mart Stores, Inc. v. Cordova, 856 S.W.2d 768, 774 (Tex. App.—El Paso 1993, pet. denied) (error to admit irrelevant testimony of defendant's net worth without first determining prima facie case of gross negligence).

Carter v. Exxon Corp., 842 S.W.2d 393, 399 (Tex. App.—Eastland 1992, writ denied) ("Testimony concerning the wealth or poverty of a party is ordinarily inadmissible in a civil case.... This type of evidence is inadmissible because it is irrelevant and often prejudicial.").

Block v. Waters, 564 S.W.2d 113, 115 (Tex. Civ. App.—Beaumont 1978, no writ) ("Testimony as to the wealth or poverty of a party is ordinarily inadmissible upon the trial of a civil case. Not only is such testimony immaterial, its receipt may very well prove to be prejudicial.").

g. *Collateral Benefits*

Haygood v. De Escabedo, 356 S.W.3d 390, 395 (Tex. 2011) (collateral source rule "precludes any reduction in a tortfeasor's liability because of benefits received by the plaintiff from someone else—a collateral source").

Haygood v. De Escabedo, 356 S.W.3d 390, 395 (Tex. 2011) ("evidence of a claim of damages that are not compensable" is inadmissible).

Huston v. United Parcel Service, Inc., 434 S.W.3d 630, 639 (Tex. App.—Houston [1st Dist.] 2014, pet. denied) (damages statute, Tex. Civ. Prac. & Rem. Code § 41.0105, "limits recovery, and consequently the evidence at trial, to expenses that the medical provider has a legal right to be paid … Because a claimant is not allowed to recover medical expenses that the provider is not entitled to be paid, 'evidence of such charges is irrelevant to the issue of damages and is inadmissible.'").

Big Bird Tree Services v. Gallegos, 365 S.W.3d 173, 176 (Tex. App.—Dallas 2012, pet. denied) ("[T]he collateral source rule reflects the position of the law that a benefit that is directed to the injured party should not be shifted so as to become a windfall to the tortfeasor.").

Henderson v. Spann, 367 S.W.3d 301, 303 (Tex. App.—Amarillo 2012, pet. denied) ("Since a claimant is not entitled to recover medical charges that a provider is not entitled to be paid, evidence of such charges is irrelevant to the issue of damages… [A]ny relevance of such evidence is substantially outweighed by the confusion it is likely to generate, and therefore the evidence of unadjusted medical bills must be excluded.").

Henderson v. Spann, 367 S.W.3d 301, 303 (Tex. App.—Amarillo 2012, pet. denied) (the collateral source rule applies to adjusted medical expenses; the jury cannot know if plaintiff or another entity paid the adjusted, recoverable amounts).

Tate v. Henderson, 280 S.W.3d 534, 538 (Tex. App.—Amarillo 2009, no pet.) ("[D]ischarge of medical expenses through bankruptcy is akin to the discharge of an obligation by a collateral source.").

Tate v. Henderson, 280 S.W.3d 534, 538 (Tex. App.—Amarillo 2009, no pet.) (in a negligence case, "a plaintiff is permitted to recover damages for past and future medical expenses as compensation for the debt incurred. How that debt is ultimately settled, either through payment, gratuity, insurance, write-down, write-off, or bankruptcy is of no consequence to the issue of whether the plaintiff has been damaged by the wrongdoer.").

LMC Complete Auto., Inc. v. Burke, 229 S.W.3d 469, 480 (Tex. App.—Houston [1st Dist.] 2007, pet. denied) ("[T]he collateral source rule precludes a tortfeasor from obtaining the benefit of, or even mentioning, payments to the injured party from sources other than the tortfeasor.").

LMC Complete Auto., Inc. v. Burke, 229 S.W.3d 469, 480 (Tex. App.—Houston [1st Dist.] 2007, pet. denied) (under the collateral source rule, a defendant is not entitled to present evidence of, or obtain an offset for, funds received by the plaintiff from a collateral source).

Triumph Trucking, Inc. v. S. Corporate Ins. Mgrs., Inc., 226 S.W.3d 466, 471 (Tex. App.—Houston [1st Dist.] 2006, pet. denied) (under the "collateral source rule," a "defendant may not offer evidence of payment from a collateral source and may not take an offset for such payments"; the rule is an exception to the one-satisfaction rule).

Taylor v. Am. Fabritech, Inc., 132 S.W.3d 613, 626 (Tex. App.—Houston [14th Dist.] 2004, pet. denied) ("[T]he collateral source rule is both a rule of evidence and a rule of damages.").

Jones v. Red Arrow Heavy Hauling, Inc., 816 S.W.2d 134, 135 (Tex. App.—Beaumont 1991, writ denied) (evidence of injured party receiving benefits from collateral source inadmissible under rules of relevancy).

h. *Out-of-Court Experiments*

Merck & Co. v. Garza, 347 S.W.3d 256, 263 (Tex. 2011) ("[W]hile the controlled, experimental, and prospective nature of clinical trials undoubtedly make them more reliable than retroactive, observational studies, both must show a statistically significant doubling of the risk in order to be some evidence that a drug more likely than not caused a particular injury.").

Merck & Co. v. Garza, 347 S.W.3d 256, 263 (Tex. 2011) (clinical trials and epidemiological studies "must show a statistically significant doubling of the risk in order to be some evidence that a drug more likely than not caused a particular injury").

Fort Worth & Denver Ry. Co. v. Williams, 375 S.W.2d 279, 281 (Tex. 1964) ("In order to render evidence of an experiment made out of court and without the presence of the opposing party admissible, it is generally held that there must be a substantial similarity between conditions existing at the time of the occurrence which gives rise to the litigation and those in existence at the time the experiment is conducted for demonstration purposes.").

Benson v. Chalk, 536 S.W.3d 886, 904 (Tex. App.—Houston [1st Dist.] 2017, pet. denied) ("When an experiment is conducted out-of-court and in the absence of opposing counsel, there must be a substantial similarity between the conditions existing at the time of the experiment and the actual event that is the subject of litigation… However, the conditions need not be identical.").

Lewis v. State, 402 S.W.3d 852, 864 (Tex. App.—Amarillo 2013), *aff'd*, 428 S.W.3d 860 (Tex. Crim. App. 2014) ("[A] computer animation is merely a series of images generated by a computer that serves as demonstrative evidence… [and] may be authenticated by the witness's testimony that the computer animation presents a fair and accurate depiction of what it purports to represent; if it does not represent what it purports to represent, it will not be admissible.").

Lewis v. State, 402 S.W.3d 852, 864 (Tex. App.—Amarillo 2013), *aff'd*, 428 S.W.3d 860 (Tex. Crim. App. 2014) ("[A]ny staged, re-enacted criminal acts or defensive issues involving human beings are impossible to duplicate in every minute detail and are therefore inherently dangerous, offer little in substance, and the impact of re-enactments is too highly prejudicial to insure the State or the defendant a fair trial.").

Lewis v. State, 402 S.W.3d 852, 864 (Tex. App.—Amarillo 2013), *aff'd*, 428 S.W.3d 860 (Tex. Crim. App. 2014) ("[T]he artificial re-creation of an event may unduly accentuate certain phases of the happening, and because of the forceful impression made on the minds of the jurors by this kind of evidence, it should be received with caution.… This is especially true where the event sought to be depicted is simple, the testimony adequate, and the animation adds nothing more than a one-sided, manipulated visual image to the mental picture already produced in the mind of the jurors by the oral testimony of an eyewitness who has been subjected to the crucible of cross-examination.").

Lincoln v. Clark Freight Lines, Inc., 285 S.W.3d 79, 84 (Tex. App.—Houston [1st Dist.] 2009, no pet.) ("[W]hen an experiment is conducted out of court and in the absence of opposing counsel, there must be a substantial similarity between the conditions existing at the time of the experiment and the actual event that is the subject of litigation. However, the conditions do not need to be identical.").

i. Similar Claims

Colone v. State, 573 S.W.3d 249 (Tex. Crim. App. 2019) (evidence of an extraneous offense is impermissible show bad character; "It is the general rule that a defendant may be tried only for the offense charged and not for any other crimes or for being a criminal generally.").

Dallas Ry. & Terminal Co. v. Farnsworth, 227 S.W.2d 1017, 1020 (Tex. 1950) ("It has been said that evidence of similar transactions or conduct on other occasions is not competent to prove the commission of a particular act charged 'unless the acts are connected in some special way, indicating a relevancy beyond mere similarity in certain particulars.'").

Gittens v. State, 560 S.W.3d 725 (Tex. App.—San Antonio 2018, no pet.) ("An accused may not be tried for being a criminal generally.... Evidence of extraneous offenses is not admissible at the guilt phase of a trial to prove that a defendant committed the charged offense in conformity with a bad character.").

GB Tubulars, Inc. v. Union Gas Operating Co., 527 S.W.3d 563, 572 (Tex. App.—Houston [14th Dist.] 2017, pet. denied) (in a product defect case, evidence of similar "incidents may be relevant to show whether a product was defective or unreasonably dangerous or that a manufacturer was on notice of prior or continuing problems with the product").

GB Tubulars, Inc. v. Union Gas Operating Co., 527 S.W.3d 563, 572 (Tex. App.—Houston [14th Dist.] 2017, pet. denied) ("[E]vidence of similar incidents is inadmissible if it creates undue prejudice, confusion or delay.... Prolonged proof of what happened in other accidents cannot be used to distract a jury's attention from what happened in the case at hand.").

GB Tubulars, Inc. v. Union Gas Operating Co., 527 S.W.3d 563, 572 (Tex. App.—Houston [14th Dist.] 2017, pet. denied) ("[I]n exercising their discretion regarding the admission of evidence, [trial courts should] carefully consider the bounds of similarity, prejudice, confusion, and sequence before admitting evidence of other accidents involving a product.").

Griffis v. State, 441 S.W.3d 599, 609 (Tex. App.—San Antonio 2014, pet. ref'd), cert. denied, 136 S.Ct. 58, 193 L.Ed.2d 60 (2015) (evidence of extraneous offenses is not admissible at the guilt phase of a trial to prove that a defendant committed the charged offense in conformity with a bad character).

Griffis v. State, 441 S.W.3d 599, 609 (Tex. App.—San Antonio 2014, pet. ref'd), cert. denied, 136 S.Ct. 58, 193 L.Ed.2d 60 (2015) (contextual or same-transaction evidence is admissible only when the offense would make little or no sense without also bringing in that evidence, and it is admissible only to the extent that it is necessary to the jury's understanding of the offense).

Sandoval v. State, 409 S.W.3d 259, 304 (Tex. App.—Austin 2013, no pet.) ("[E]vidence showing the commission of extraneous misconduct is usually excluded because such evidence is inherently prejudicial, tends to confuse the issues of a case, and forces the accused to defend himself against charges that he had not been notified would be brought against him.").

Burke v. State, 371 S.W.3d 252, 257 (Tex. App.—Houston [1st Dist.] 2011, pet. ref'd, untimely filed) ("[R]elevant factors in determining whether the prejudice of an extraneous offense substantially outweighs its probative value include: (1) how compellingly the extraneous-offense evidence serves to make a fact of consequence more or less probable—a factor that is related to the strength of the evidence presented by the proponent to show the defendant in fact committed the extraneous offense; (2) the potential the other offense evidence has to impress the jury in some irrational but nevertheless indelible way; (3) the time the proponent will need to develop the evidence, during which the jury will be distracted from consideration of the indicted offense; and (4) the force of the proponent's need for this evidence to prove a fact of consequence, i.e., the proponent has other probative evidence available to help establish this fact, and whether this fact is related to an issue in dispute.").

Haagensen v. State, 346 S.W.3d 758, 766 (Tex. App.—Texarkana 2011, no pet.) ("[The] accused must be tried only for the offense charged; the accused may not be tried for a collateral crime or for being a criminal generally.").

Martinez v. State, 304 S.W.3d 642, 657 (Tex. App.—Amarillo 2010, pet. ref'd) (generally, to prevent an accused from being prosecuted for some collateral crime or misconduct, the State may not introduce evidence of bad acts similar to the offense charged).

Huckaby v. A.G. Perry & Son, Inc., 20 S.W.3d 194, 209 (Tex. App.—Texarkana 2000, pet. denied) ("Before the evidence of previous accidents at this intersection could be admitted into evidence, the proponent would have had to show a predicate of similar or reasonably similar conditions, a connection of the conditions in some special way, or that the incidents occurred by means of the same instrumentality.... Opinions that are stated in conclusory terms by witnesses do not give the court an opportunity to evaluate whether the prior accidents were similar in causation to the extent that they should be considered relevant in the case on trial.").

j. Number of Friends or Family

Miller v. Harrison, 446 S.W.2d 372, 376 (Tex. Civ. App.—Houston [1st Dist.] 1969, no writ) (evidence of being married or single, that others depend upon one for support, or of matters relative to social standing, rank, or condition in life generally inadmissible in evidence upon the trial, unless such facts have some legitimate bearing upon the issues involved.

Applegate v. McFadin, 20 S.W.2d 396, 398 (Tex. Civ. App.—Austin 1929, no writ) ("Nor was it competent to show whether Mr. Breeden's friends were many or few. Such matters would throw no light upon the issue submitted, and a showing of lack of friends might tend to prejudice the jury against him.").

k. Real Estate Value or Appraisal

City of Harlingen v. Estate of Sharboneau, 48 S.W.3d 177, 182 (Tex. 2001) ("Patterson's subdivision development analysis determined only what a developer could hypothetically afford to pay to profitably subdivide the property, not what a developer would pay in the competitive, risk-filled marketplace of the real world. Because the appraisal did not account for these forces, it was not relevant to establishing the market value of Mrs. Sharboneau's property.").

Blackwell v. Coleman County, 94 Tex. 216, 220, 59 S.W. 530, 530 (Tex. 1900) (testimony of surveyor as to what he intended to include not admissible to aid second survey; "[i]n determining the location of land in such cases, the courts seek to ascertain the true intentions of the parties concerned in the survey. But the intention referred to is not in the mind of the surveyor").

Tuttle v. Builes, 572 S.W.3d 344 (Tex. App.—Eastland 2019, no pet.) ("An owner's valuation testimony is not relevant if it is conclusory or speculative.... As with expert testimony, property valuations may not be based solely on a property owner's ipse dixit.").

Williams v. State, 406 S.W.3d 273, 283 (Tex. App.—San Antonio 2013, pet. denied) ("[C]ourts will hold an appraiser's testimony to be unreliable if the appraiser violated well-established legal rules of valuation.").

Williams v. State, 406 S.W.3d 273, 283 (Tex. App.—San Antonio 2013, pet. denied) ("[A]ll appraisal opinion is at best something of a speculation, and the question of market value is peculiarly one for the fact-finding body.").

Williams v. State, 406 S.W.3d 273, 283 (Tex. App.—San Antonio 2013, pet. denied) (if the comparable sales evidence is "so attenuated that the appraiser and the fact-finder cannot make valid adjustments for these differences, a court should not admit the sale as comparable").

Williams v. State, 406 S.W.3d 273, 283 (Tex. App.—San Antonio 2013, pet. denied) (when the condemned property is raw acreage, it is improper to admit evidence of hypothetical nonexistent subdivisions).

Dallas County v. Crestview Corners Car Wash, 370 S.W.3d 25, 36 (Tex. App.—Dallas 2012, pet. denied) ("[E]xpert's 'bald assurance' that he used a widely accepted appraisal method is not sufficient to demonstrate that his opinion is reliable.").

Collin County v. Hixon Family P'ship, Ltd., 365 S.W.3d 860, 870 (Tex. App.—Dallas 2012, pet. denied) (if the comparable sales method for appraising is used, and "the comparison is so attenuated that the appraiser and the fact finder cannot make adjustments for differences, a court should refuse to admit evidence of a 'comparable' sale").

Royce Homes, L.P. v. Humphrey, 244 S.W.3d 570, 579 (Tex. App.—Beaumont 2008, pet. denied) ("[T]o be admitted into evidence, a real estate appraiser's expert opinion must be relevant and reliable.").

Royce Homes, L.P. v. Humphrey, 244 S.W.3d 570, 579 (Tex. App.—Beaumont 2008, pet. denied) ("[W]hen real estate appraiser's expert testimony is based on a comparable sales analysis ... the sales must be comparable to the property in question.").

Taiwan Shrimp Farm Vill. Ass'n, Inc. v. U.S.A. Shrimp Farm Dev., Inc., 915 S.W.2d 61, 71 (Tex. App.—Corpus Christi 1996, writ denied) (purchase price "is generally not admissible to show fair market value at a particular later time").

Boswell v. Brazos Elec. Power Co-op., Inc., 910 S.W.2d 593, 604 (Tex. App.—Fort Worth 1995, writ denied) ("The general rule in condemnation cases, however, is that when the property condemned is raw acreage ... it is improper to admit evidence of hypothetical, nonexistent subdivisions.").

l. *Criminal Acquittal in Subsequent Civil Action*

Am. Gen. Fire & Cas. Co. v. McInnis Book Store, Inc., 860 S.W.2d 484, 487 (Tex. App.—Corpus Christi 1993, no writ) ("An acquittal in a criminal action is not ordinarily admissible evidence in a subsequent civil prosecution involving common fact issues.").

m. *Employment Policies*

In re H.E. Butt Grocery Co., 17 S.W.3d 360, 371 (Tex. App.—Houston [14th Dist.] 2000, orig. proceeding) ("In support of his argument of procedural unconscionability, Swinton relies on the affidavits of three other HEB employees, who stated that they were required to sign the benefit agreement as a condition of employment. According to Swinton, these affidavits were offered to impeach Roberson's testimony that HEB does not force employees to sign the benefit agreement. Because unconscionability is determined on an individual case-by-case basis, HEB's policy and the circumstances of other HEB employees are irrelevant.").

n. *Specific Exclusions*

For the exclusion of specific types of evidence to prove a particular point or in a particular case, see generally, Texas Rules of Evidence, Rule 404 [character evidence not admissible to prove conduct]; Rule 407 [evidence of subsequent remedial measures not admissible to prove negligence or culpable conduct]; Rule 408 [exclusion of evidence of compromise and offers to compromise]; Rule 409 [exclusion of evidence of payment of medical and similar expenses]; Rule 410 [inadmissibility of pleas]; Rule 411 [exclusion of evidence of liability insurance]; and Rule 412 [exclusion of evidence of previous sexual conduct by victim].

4. *Opposing Authorities*

Gonzalez v. State, 544 S.W.3d 363, 371 (Tex. Crim. App. 2018) ("Evidence does not need to prove or disprove a particular fact by itself to be relevant; it is sufficient if the evidence provides a small nudge toward proving or disproving a fact of consequence.").

Pawlak v. State, 420 S.W.3d 807, 809 (Tex. Crim. App. 2013) ("[P]lain language of Rule 403 does not allow a trial court to exclude otherwise relevant evidence when that evidence is merely prejudicial, because all evidence against a defendant is, by its very nature, designed to be prejudicial").

Blasdell v. State, 384 S.W.3d 824, 830 (Tex. Crim. App. 2012) ("[F]or the testimony of an eyewitness identification expert to be relevant for purposes of Rule 702, it is enough that he is able to say that a particular identification procedure, or the facts or circumstances attending a particular eyewitness event, has been empirically demonstrated to be fraught with the potential to cause a mistaken identification.").

Ex parte Smith, 309 S.W.3d 53, 61 (Tex. Crim. App. 2010) (evidence "need not by itself prove or disprove a particular fact to be relevant; it is sufficient if the evidence provides a small nudge toward proving or disproving some fact of consequence").

Allen v. State, 108 S.W.3d 281, 284 (Tex. Crim. App. 2003) (that victim in murder case had been sexually assaulted relevant and not unduly prejudicial).

Resendiz v. State, 112 S.W.3d 541, 544 (Tex. Crim. App. 2003), *cert. denied*, 541 U.S. 1032 (2004) (crime scene photographs depicting other offenses committed by defendant relevant to issue of defendant's sanity; note that trial judge properly excluded photographs under Rule 403 due to potential to confuse jury).

Hayes v. State, 85 S.W.3d 809, 816 (Tex. Crim. App. 2002) (autopsy photographs relevant and not unfairly prejudicial, even though medical examiner had reconstructed victim's head and pulled skin away from wound).

Ripkowski v. State, 61 S.W.3d 378, 392 (Tex. Crim. App. 2001), *cert. denied*, 539 U.S. 916 (2003) (crime scene and victim photographs relevant and not unfairly prejudicial).

Ransom v. State, 920 S.W.2d 288, 299 (Tex. Crim. App. 1994) (evidence that defendant assaulted prosecutor and his attorney was relevant and not unfairly prejudicial).

Davis v. State, 581 S.W.3d 885, 892 (Tex. App.—Dallas 2019, pet. ref'd) ("Evidence of a crime other than the one charged ... may be admissible ... for a purpose other than character conformity, such as proof of a defendant's plan or intent.... Evidence of extraneous misconduct may also be admitted to rebut a defensive issue that negates one of the elements of a charged offense.").

Proo v. State, 587 S.W.3d 789, 817 (Tex. App.—San Antonio 2019, pet. ref'd) ("Rule 403 favors the admission of relevant evidence and carries a presumption that relevant evidence is more probative than prejudicial.").

Lamarand v. State, 540 S.W.3d 252, 260 (Tex. App.—Houston [1st Dist.] 2018 pet. ref'd) ("Rule 403 favors admissibility of relevant evidence, and the presumption is that relevant evidence will be more probative than prejudicial.").

Jones v. Mattress Firm Holding Corp., 558 S.W.3d 732, 738 (Tex. App.—Houston [14th Dist.] 2018, no pet.) ("When a photograph is relevant to an issue in a case, it is admissible if it is authenticated by a witness as an accurate portrayal.").

Benson v. Chalk, 536 S.W.3d 886, 904 (Tex. App.—Houston [1st Dist.] 2017, pet. denied) ("An expert's testimony is relevant when it assists the jury in determining an issue or in understanding other evidence.").

Esparza v. State, 513 S.W.3d 643, 646 (Tex. App.—Houston [14th Dist.] 2016, no pet.) ("A defendant has a fundamental right to present evidence of a defense as long as the evidence is relevant and is not excluded by an established evidentiary rule.").

Nabors Well Services, Ltd v. Romero, 508 S.W.3d 512, 529 (Tex. App.—El Paso 2016, pet. denied) ("Expert opinion testimony is relevant when it is sufficiently tied to the facts of the case so that it will aid the jury in resolving a factual dispute.")

Coutta v. State, 385 S.W.3d 641, 664 (Tex. App.—El Paso 2012, no pet.) ("[T]o be relevant in proving a fact, evidence need not prove the fact, but it is sufficient if the evidence provides a small nudge toward proving or disproving some fact of consequence.").

Young v. State, 358 S.W.3d 790, 803 (Tex. App.—Houston [14th Dist.] 2012, pet. ref'd) ("[R]elevance is a looser notion than reliability, and is a simpler, more straightforward matter to establish.").

Young v. State, 358 S.W.3d 790, 803 (Tex. App.—Houston [14th Dist.] 2012, pet. ref'd) ("[R]elevance inquiry is whether the evidence will assist the trier of fact and is sufficiently tied to the facts of the case.").

In re Beeson, 378 S.W.3d 8, 11 (Tex. App.—Houston [1st Dist.] 2011, orig. proceeding) ("[I]nformation is relevant if it tends to make the evidence of a fact that is of consequence to the determination of the action more or less probable than it would be without the information.").

In re Estate of Denman, 362 S.W.3d 134, 141 (Tex. App.—San Antonio 2011, no pet.) ("[R]elevant evidence is evidence having the tendency to make the existence of any fact that is of consequence to the determination of the action more probable or less probable than it would be without the evidence.... The test for relevancy is satisfied only when there is some logical connection between the fact offered and the fact to be proven.").

Mitchell v. State, 377 S.W.3d 21, 28 (Tex. App.—Waco 2011, pet. dism'd, untimely filed) ("[E]vidence need not by itself prove or disprove a particular fact to be relevant; it is sufficient if the evidence provides a small nudge toward proving or disproving some fact of consequence.").

Republic Waste Servs., Ltd. v. Martinez, 335 S.W.3d 401, 409 (Tex. App.—Houston [1st Dist.] 2011, no pet.) (test for relevancy is satisfied if there is directly, or by inference, some logical conclusion between the fact offered and the fact to be proven).

Clark v. Randalls Foods, Inc., 317 S.W.3d 351, 357 (Tex. App.—Houston [1st Dist.] 2010, pet. denied) (if there is some logical connection either directly or by inference between the evidence and a fact to be proved, the evidence is relevant).

Woods v. State, 306 S.W.3d 905, 909 (Tex. App.—Beaumont 2010, no pet.) ("[T]estimony of a mental disease or defect that directly rebuts the particular *mens rea* necessary for a charged offense is relevant and admissible unless excluded under a specific evidentiary rule.").

PPC Transp. v. Metcalf, 254 S.W.3d 636, 643 (Tex. App.—Tyler 2008, no pet.) (if there is some logical connection either directly or by inference between the evidence and a fact to be proved, the evidence is relevant).

Maranda v. State, 253 S.W.3d 762, 767 (Tex. App.—Amarillo 2007), *pet. stricken*, No. PD-0010-08, 2008 WL 974786 (Tex. Crim. App. Apr. 9, 2008) (relevant evidence is presumed admissible).

Sessums v. State, 129 S.W.3d 242, 249 (Tex. App.—Texarkana 2004, pet. ref'd) (evidence of victim's prognosis, treatment, and injuries relevant as it "logically increased the possibility that [the defendant] abused [the victim], and the court's ruling admitting the evidence was not outside the zone of reasonable disagreement").

Bain v. State, 115 S.W.3d 47, 49 (Tex. App.—Texarkana 2003, pet. ref'd) ("The test for relevancy is much broader during the punishment phase, because it allows a jury to consider more evidence in exercising its discretion to assess punishment within the appropriate range.").

Allen v. State, 108 S.W.3d 281, 284 (Tex. Crim. App. 2003) (that victim in murder case had been sexually assaulted relevant and not unduly prejudicial).

Goldberg v. State, 95 S.W.3d 345, 375 (Tex. App.—Houston [1st Dist.] 2002, pet ref'd), *cert. denied*, 540 U.S. 1190 (2004) (notebook seized three years before offense that had drawings and discussed killing women relevant and not unfairly prejudicial).

Hayes v. State, 85 S.W.3d 809, 816 (Tex. Crim. App. 2002) (autopsy photographs were relevant and not unfairly prejudicial even though medical examiner reconstructed victim's head and had pulled skin away from wound).

Ripkowski v. State, 61 S.W.3d 378, 392 (Tex. Crim. App. 2001), *cert. denied*, 539 U.S. 916 (2003) (crime scene and victim photographs relevant and not unfairly prejudicial).

Levario v. State, 964 S.W.2d 290, 297 (Tex. App.—El Paso 1997, no pet.) (gun found near hidden narcotics relevant to defendant's state of mind).

Yates v. State, 941 S.W.2d 357, 368 (Tex. App.—Waco 1997, pet. ref'd) (defendant's taking and disposing of victim's vehicle after murder relevant to issues of intent and consciousness of guilt).

Palomo v. State, 925 S.W.2d 329, 336 (Tex. App.—Corpus Christi 1996, no pet.) (defendant's tattoo suggesting gang membership irrelevant when defendant did not contest gang membership and should not have been admitted).

Ransom v. State, 920 S.W.2d 288, 299 (Tex. Crim. App. 1994, reh'g overruled) (evidence that defendant assaulted prosecutor and his attorney after voir dire relevant and not unfairly prejudicial).

a. Evidence to Offer Additional Explanation

Proo v. State, 587 S.W.3d 789, 817 (Tex. App.—San Antonio 2019, pet. ref'd) ("Photographs of a victim's injuries are relevant and their relevance is not diminished merely because the jury also heard testimony about the same injuries.").

Lamarand v. State, 540 S.W.3d 252, 260 (Tex. App.—Houston [1st Dist.] 2018 pet. ref'd) ("[E]vidence [in criminal case] that a defendant attempted suicide after the offense is relevant to show the defendant's consciousness of guilt.... And evidence of a consciousness of guilt, in turn, is relevant to show that the defendant committed the offense.").

Williams v. State, 531 S.W.3d 902, 918 (Tex. App.—Houston [14th Dist.] 2017, pet. granted) (extraneous offense "evidence is admissible when the extraneous act is: (1) relevant to a fact of consequence in the case aside from its tendency to show action in conformity with character, and (2) its probative value is not substantially outweighed by the danger of unfair prejudice").

Hernandez v. Moss, 538 S.W.3d 160, 168 (Tex. App.—El Paso 2017, no pet.) ("[C]ollateral sources are relevant for impeachment purposes when a witness gives testimony inconsistent with the receipt of benefits.").

Rhey v. Redic, 408 S.W.3d 440, 460 (Tex. App.—El Paso 2013, no pet.) (computer presentation was properly admitted because it assisted the jury to understand the nature of one of the parties' business operation, and because it tended to rebut the assertions made by counsel for the opposition).

In re Am. Nat. County Mut. Ins. Co., 384 S.W.3d 429, 435 (Tex. App.—Austin 2012, orig. proceeding) ("[S]ettlement offers are not admissible to prove liability for, or invalidity of, the claim or its amount, but may be admissible for another purpose.").

Keith v. State, 384 S.W.3d 452, 460 (Tex. App.—Eastland 2012, pet. ref'd) (evidence of threats had "relevance apart from the tendency to show conduct in conformity with character. Acts designed to reduce the likelihood of prosecution, conviction, or incarceration for the offense at issue are admissible under Rule 404(b) to show the defendant's 'consciousness of guilt'").

In re Tex. Farm Bureau Underwriters, 374 S.W.3d 651, 657 (Tex. App.—Tyler 2012, orig. proceeding) ("[A] settlement offer ordinarily is inadmissible in the trial of a disputed breach of contract claim, but may be admissible on the extracontractual claims to rebut evidence that the insurer acted in bad faith.").

WPS, Inc. v. Expro Americas, LLC, 369 S.W.3d 384, 407 (Tex. App.—Houston [1st Dist.] 2012, pet. denied) (the rule excluding settlements or offers to settle "does not require exclusion when the evidence is offered for another purpose, such as proving bias or prejudice or interest of a witness or a party, negativing a contention of undue delay, or proving an effort to obstruct a criminal investigation or prosecution").

Ibenyenwa v. State, 367 S.W.3d 420, 425 (Tex. App.—Fort Worth 2012, pet. ref'd) (probative value of evidence of forensic interviewer's interview with child sex abuse victim was not outweighed by prejudice; "the interview was inherently probative to the issue of whether [the interviewer's] technique amounted to 'coaching' the child, and was the only evidence of whether the child equivocated in the interview").

Render v. State, 347 S.W.3d 905, 921 (Tex. App.—Eastland 2011, pet. ref'd) (when an accused raises a self-defense theory, the State may introduce evidence of prior violent acts where the accused was an aggressor in order to show intent and to rebut the defense).

Vinson Minerals, Ltd. v. XTO Energy, Inc., 335 S.W.3d 344, 353 (Tex. App.—Fort Worth 2010, pet. denied) ("[A]n offer or demand for settlement may be admissible for another purpose, such as to demonstrate bias or prejudice.").

Sessums v. State, 129 S.W.3d 242, 249 (Tex. App.—Texarkana 2004, pet. ref'd) (victim's prognosis, treatment, and injuries were relevant as it "logically increased the possibility that [the defendant] abused [the victim], and the court's ruling admitting the evidence was not outside the zone of reasonable disagreement").

Tennison v. State, 969 S.W.2d 578, 580 (Tex. App.—Texarkana 1998, no pet.) ("[E]vidence by a doctor that child sexual abuse victims do not always show physical signs of abuse and that the victim ... could have been sexually abused is probative to the material issue of whether she was sexually abused.").

Callaway v. State, 818 S.W.2d 816, 826 (Tex. App.—Amarillo 1991, pet. ref'd) (evidence can be relevant as context evidence or to fully explain another matter already introduced).

b. Parties' Wealth or Poverty

Lunsford v. Morris, 746 S.W.2d 471, 474 (Tex. 1988), disapproved of on other grounds by *Walker v. Packer*, 827 S.W.2d 833 (Tex. 1992) (defendant's net worth relevant in cases where punitive damages may be awarded).

In re Islamorada Fish Co. Tex., L.L.C., 319 S.W.3d 908, 912 (Tex. App.—Dallas 2010, orig. proceeding) ("[N]et worth is relevant and discoverable when punitive damages may be awarded.").

c. Similar Transactions, Claims, or Occurrences

Devoe v. State, 354 S.W.3d 457, 469 (Tex. Crim. App. 2011) ("[E]xtraneous offense evidence may be admissible when it has relevance apart from character conformity.... For example, it may be admissible to show proof of motive, opportunity, intent, preparation, plan, knowledge, identity, or absence of mistake or accident.").

Serv. Corp. Int'l v. Guerra, 348 S.W.3d 221, 235 (Tex. 2011) (evidence of other wrongs or acts is "admissible to show a party's intent, if material, provided the prior acts are so connected with the transaction at issue that they may all be parts of a system, scheme, or plan.... This can be shown through evidence of similar acts temporally relevant and of the same substantive basis").

Wheeler v. State, 67 S.W.3d 879, 886 (Tex. Crim. App. 2002) (trial court did not abuse discretion admitting evidence of prior sexual assault where evidence not unfairly prejudicial and needed to assist in proving case).

Powell v. State, 63 S.W.3d 435, 440 (Tex. Crim. App. 2001) (evidence of defendant's other sexual offenses relevant to rebut defendant's claim he lacked opportunity to commit charged offenses).

Uniroyal Goodrich Tire Co. v. Martinez, 977 S.W.2d 328, 341 (Tex. 1998), *cert. denied*, 526 U.S. 1040 (199) (evidence of other lawsuits or claims occurring under reasonable similar circumstances admissible).

Missouri-Kansas-Texas R.R. Co. v. May, 600 S.W.2d 755, 756 (Tex. 1980) ("Evidence of earlier accidents which occurred under reasonably similar but not necessarily identical circumstances [is] admissible.").

Davis v. State, 581 S.W.3d 885, 892 (Tex. App.—Dallas 2019, pet. ref'd) ("Extraneous-offense evidence need not be completely identical to the charged offense in order to be probative.").

Gittens v. State, 560 S.W.3d 725 (Tex. App.—San Antonio 2018, no pet.) ("To be admissible, extraneous offense evidence must pass the two-prong test imposed by Texas Rules of Evidence 404(b) and 403: (1) the extraneous offense evidence must be relevant to a fact of consequence in the case apart from its tendency to prove conduct in conformity with character; and (2) the probative value of the evidence [must not be] substantially outweighed by unfair prejudice.").

Gittens v. State, 560 S.W.3d 725 (Tex. App.—San Antonio 2018, no pet.) (extraneous offense evidence may be "offered to show proof of motive, opportunity, intent, preparation, plan, knowledge, identity, or absence of mistake or accident.... Additionally, extraneous evidence may be relevant and admissible to rebut a defensive theory").

Barrientos v. State, 539 S.W.3d 482, 492 (Tex. App.—Houston [1st Dist.] 2017, no pet.) ("[E]vidence of gang membership is admissible during the guilt-innocence phase to show bias, motive, or intent, or to refute a defensive theory").

GB Tubulars, Inc. v. Union Gas Operating Co., 527 S.W.3d 563, 572 (Tex. App.—Houston [14th Dist.] 2017, pet. denied) (in a product defect case, evidence of similar "incidents may be relevant to show whether a product was defective or unreasonably dangerous or that a manufacturer was on notice of prior or continuing problems with the product").

Griffis v. State, 441 S.W.3d 599, 609 (Tex. App.—San Antonio 2014, pet. ref'd), cert. denied, 136 S.Ct. 58, 193 L.Ed.2d 60 (2015) (because the jury is entitled to hear relevant surrounding facts and the circumstances of the charged offense, some extraneous misconduct evidence is admissible).

Almaguer v. State, 492 S.W.3d 338, 354 (Tex. App.—Corpus Christi 2014, pet. ref'd) (criminal acts that are designed to reduce the likelihood of prosecution, conviction, or incarceration for the offense on trial are admissible under Rule of Evidence 404(b) as showing consciousness of guilt).

Hernandez v. State, 426 S.W.3d 820, 825 (Tex. App.—Eastland 2014, pet. ref'd) ("[R]ebuttal of a defensive theory is one of the permissible purposes for which extraneous offense evidence may be admitted.").

Hernandez v. State, 426 S.W.3d 820, 825 (Tex. App.—Eastland 2014, pet. ref'd) ("[E]xtraneous offenses are admissible to rebut theories raised by the testimony of a defense witness during direct examination or a State's witness during cross-examination.").

Mason v. State, 416 S.W.3d 720, 739 (Tex. App.—Houston [14th Dist.] 2013, pet. ref'd) ("[E]xtraneous offense evidence may be admissible for other purposes, such as proof of motive, opportunity, intent, preparation, plan, knowledge, identity, or absence of mistake or accident.... This list is illustrative, rather than exhaustive, and extraneous-offense evidence may be admissible when a defendant raises a defensive issue that negates one of the elements of the offense.").

Mason v. State, 416 S.W.3d 720, 739 (Tex. App.—Houston [14th Dist.] 2013, pet. ref'd) ("[E]xtraneous offense evidence is admissible under both Rules of Evidence 404(b) and 403 if that evidence satisfies a two-prong test: whether the evidence is relevant to a fact of consequence in the case apart from its tendency to prove conduct in conformity with character and whether the probative value of the evidence is substantially outweighed by unfair prejudice.").

Morales v. State, 389 S.W.3d 915, 919 (Tex. App.—Houston [14th Dist.] 2013, no pet.) ("[The] purpose of admitting extraneous evidence as same-transaction contextual evidence is to place the instant offense in context.").

Morales v. State, 389 S.W.3d 915, 919 (Tex. App.—Houston [14th Dist.] 2013, no pet.) ("[S]ame-transaction contextual evidence is admissible as an exception under Rule 404(b) only when the offense would make little or no sense without also bringing in that evidence, and only to the extent that it is necessary to the jury's understanding of the offense.").

Dana v. State, 420 S.W.3d 158, 166 (Tex. App.—Beaumont 2012, pet. ref'd) ("[T]he Rule 404(b) list of permissible uses of 'other crimes, wrongs or acts' evidence is not exhaustive.... The evidence may be used to rebut a defense.... The defendant may 'open the door' to the evidence.... And a witness may be cross-examined about an extraneous offense "if the extraneous offense would tend to correct the false impression left by the witness' direct examination testimony.").

Gomez v. State, 380 S.W.3d 830, 835 (Tex. App.—Houston [14th Dist.] 2012, pet. ref'd) ("[P]rior acts of violence between the victim and the accused may be offered to illustrate the nature of their relationship as long as they also meet the requirements of Rule of Evidence 404(b).").

Desormeaux v. State, 362 S.W.3d 233, 238 (Tex. App.—Beaumont 2012, no pet.) ("[S]ame transaction contextual evidence is evidence that imparts to the trier of fact information essential to understanding the context and circumstances of events which, although legally separate offenses, are blended or interwoven.").

Martinez v. State, 304 S.W.3d 642, 657 (Tex. App.—Amarillo 2010, pet. ref'd) (evidence of similar acts may be admissible as "proof of motive, opportunity, intent, preparation, plan, knowledge, identity, or absence of mistake or accident").

Martinez v. State, 304 S.W.3d 642, 657 (Tex. App.—Amarillo 2010, pet. ref'd) ("[A] party may introduce evidence of similar or other crimes, wrongs, or acts if such evidence logically serves to make more or less probable an elemental fact, or defensive evidence that undermines an elemental fact.").

Columbia Med. Ctr. Subsidiary, L.P. v. Meier, 198 S.W.3d 408, 412 (Tex. App.—Dallas 2006, pet. denied) ("[U]nrelated incident may be relevant and admissible if it and the incident involved in the lawsuit occurred under reasonably similar circumstances, the two incidents are connected in a special way, or the incidents occurred by means of the same instrumentality.... The burden to show the incidents are reasonably similar, but not necessarily identical, is on the proponent of the evidence.").

Jaggers v. State, 125 S.W.3d 661, 670 (Tex. App.—Houston [1st Dist.] 2003, pet. ref'd) (trial court did not abuse discretion admitting evidence of defendant's other acts over defendant's Rule 403 objections where evidence relevant, not unfairly prejudicial or inflammatory, not unduly time-consuming, and needed by prosecution).

Apolinar v. State, 106 S.W.3d 407, 419 (Tex. App.—Houston [1st Dist.] 2003, pet. ref'd), *aff'd*, 155 S.W.3d 184 (2005) (witness's testimony regarding defendant's prior bad act relevant to issue of identification and not unfairly prejudicial).

Jones v. State, 119 S.W.3d 412, 422 (Tex. App.—Fort Worth 2003, no pet.) (evidence of defendant's similar offenses relevant to demonstrate defendant's state of mind and to rebut character testimony).

Ex parte Twine, 111 S.W.3d 664, 666 (Tex. App.—Fort Worth 2003, pet. ref'd) (in habeas corpus hearing alleging prosecutorial misconduct as cause of mistrial, evidence that same prosecutor had asked similar improper question in prior case and had caused mistrial was relevant and should not have been excluded).

Saxer v. State, 115 S.W.3d 765, 776 (Tex. App.—Beaumont 2003, pet. ref'd) (trial court did not abuse discretion admitting evidence of defendant's other offenses and bad acts where relevant and not unfairly prejudicial).

Hudson v. State, 112 S.W.3d 794, 799 (Tex. App.—Houston [14th Dist.] 2003, pet. ref'd) (evidence of defendant's prior assault on victim with knife relevant and not unfairly prejudicial).

Lemmons v. State, 75 S.W.3d 513, 523 (Tex. App.—San Antonio 2002, pet. ref'd) (evidence of prior offense offered to suggest defendant was aggressor relevant and not unduly prejudicial).

Taylor v. State, 93 S.W.3d 487, 506 (Tex. App.—Texarkana 2002, pet. ref'd) (evidence of pornographic materials found on defendant's computer hard drive relevant to issue of defendant's state of mind).

Wheeler v. State, 67 S.W.3d 879, 886 (Tex. Crim. App. 2002) (trial court did not abuse discretion admitting evidence of prior sexual assault where evidence not unfairly prejudicial and needed to assist in proving case).

Suarez v. State, 901 S.W.2d 712, 720 (Tex. App.—Corpus Christi 1995, pet. ref'd) (evidence of other bad acts relevant to prove knowledge and intent).

Flukinger v. Straughan, 795 S.W.2d 779, 790 (Tex. App.—Houston [14th Dist.] 1990, writ denied) (evidence of recent sales of similar property admissible to prove market value).

Magic Chef, Inc. v. Sibley, 546 S.W.2d 851, 855 (Tex. Civ. App.—San Antonio 1977, writ ref'd n.r.e.) (evidence of other accidents involving same product admissible in product liability case).

> *See also Texas Rule of Evidence 406, which specifically provides for the admissibility of evidence of the habit or routine practice of a person or organization. Such evidence is relevant to prove conformity with the particular habit or routine practice.*

d. Prior Convictions

Landry v. Travelers Ins. Co., 458 S.W.2d 649, 651 (Tex. 1970) ("But in a case such as this one, in which the remoteness or immediacy of the conviction falls somewhere between those two extremes, the matter is left to the trial court's discretion.... In exercising such discretion, the trial judge should have the power and the duty to consider all pertinent factors in deciding whether to admit or exclude the evidence.").

e. Remoteness or Lapse of Time

Mayhew v. Dealey, 143 S.W.3d 356, 370 (Tex. App.—Dallas 2004, pet. denied) (audiotapes made three years before accident relevant to demonstrate deceased's behavior and not unfairly prejudicial).

Palmer v. Miller Brewing Co., 852 S.W.2d 57, 62 (Tex. App.—Fort Worth 1993, pet. denied) ("[A]lthough evidence can be excluded when it is too remote to be material, the question of remoteness is within the trial court's discretion.... Where the evidence is directly related to the main subject in controversy, it need not relate to the exact time in question.").

f. Matters Not in Dispute

Mayes v. State, 816 S.W.2d 79, 87 (Tex. Crim. App. 1991, pet. denied) (relevant evidence need not pertain only to facts in dispute but includes any evidence that influences consequential facts).

g. Circumstantial Evidence

Johnson v. State, 560 S.W.3d 224 (Tex. Crim. App. 2018) ("[T]he law requires no particular type of evidence. Direct and circumstantial evidence are equally probative, and "circumstantial evidence alone can be sufficient to establish guilt.").

In re Lipsky, 460 S.W.3d 579, 589 (Tex. 2015) (orig. proceeding) ("Circumstantial evidence is indirect evidence that creates an inference to establish a central fact.").

Dobbs v. State, 434 S.W.3d 166, 170 (Tex. Crim. App. 2014) ("[C]ircumstantial evidence is as probative as direct evidence in establishing the guilt of the actor, and circumstantial evidence alone may be sufficient to establish guilt.").

Bush v. State, 628 S.W.2d 441, 444 (Tex. Crim. App. 1982) (although not essential element of crime, "evidence of motive is always admissible where relevant as circumstance tending to prove commission of crime").

Lone Star Gas Co. v. State, 137 Tex. 279, 313, 153 S.W.2d 681, 700 (Tex. 1941) (evidence of circumstances and events surrounding administrative order admissible on validity of order).

Young v. State, 591 S.W.3d 579, 587 (Tex. App.—Austin 2019, no pet.) ("[D]irect and circumstantial evidence are treated equally and ... circumstantial evidence is as probative as direct evidence in establishing the guilt of an actor and can be sufficient on its own to establish guilt.").

O'Hern v. Mughrab, 579 S.W.3d 594, 604 (Tex. App.—Houston [14th Dist.] 2019, no pet.) ("A prima facie case may be established through circumstantial evidence.").

Bell Helicopter Textron, Inc. v. Burnett, 552 S.W.3d 901, 913 (Tex. App.—Fort Worth 2018, pet. filed) ("Any ultimate fact may be proved by circumstantial evidence.... A fact is established by circumstantial evidence when the fact may be fairly and reasonably inferred from other facts proved in the case.").

In Interest of R.H.W. III, 542 S.W.3d 724, 734 (Tex. App.—Houston [14th Dist.] 2018, no pet.) ("[C]ircumstantial evidence is simply indirect evidence that creates an inference to establish a central fact.... All evidentiary standards, including clear and convincing evidence, recognize the relevance of circumstantial evidence.").

Juarez v. State, 409 S.W.3d 156, 162 (Tex. App.—Houston [1st Dist.] 2013, pet. ref'd) ("[C]ircumstantial evidence is as probative as direct evidence in establishing the guilt of an actor, and circumstantial evidence alone can be sufficient to establish guilt.").

Russell Equestrian Ctr., Inc. v. Miller, 406 S.W.3d 243, 247 (Tex. App.—San Antonio 2013, no pet.) ("[B]oth negligence and proximate cause may be inferred from the circumstances surrounding an event, so that it is not necessary to prove these elements of a cause of action by direct and positive testimony.").

Lewis v. State, 402 S.W.3d 852, 864 (Tex. App.—Amarillo 2013), *aff'd*, 428 S.W.3d 860 (Tex. Crim. App. 2014) (since direct evidence of intent is rarely available, the existence of a conspiracy can be proven through circumstantial evidence).

Soon Phat, L.P. v. Alvarado, 396 S.W.3d 78, 110 (Tex. App.—Houston [14th Dist.] 2013, pet. denied) ("[M]alice may be proven by direct or circumstantial evidence.").

Brown v. State, 334 S.W.3d 789, 796 (Tex. App.—Tyler 2010, pet. ref'd) ("[C]ircumstantial evidence is as probative as direct evidence in establishing the guilt of an actor, and circumstantial evidence alone can be sufficient to establish guilt.").

Brown v. State, 334 S.W.3d 789, 796 (Tex. App.—Tyler 2010, pet. ref'd) (in a circumstantial evidence case, it is unnecessary for every fact to point directly and independently to the defendant's guilt; rather, it is sufficient if the finding of guilt is supported by the cumulative force of all the incriminating evidence).

JSC Neftegas-Impex v. Citibank, N.A., 365 S.W.3d 387, 396 (Tex. App.—Houston [1st Dist.] 2011, pet. denied) ("[C]ircumstantial evidence is not legally insufficient merely because more than one reasonable inference may be drawn from it; if circumstantial evidence will support more than one reasonable inference, it is for the jury to decide which is more reasonable.").

Lincoln v. State, 307 S.W.3d 921, 924 (Tex. App.—Dallas 2010, no pet.) ("[P]roof of mental state will almost always depend on circumstantial evidence.").

In re J.P., 296 S.W.3d 830, 834 (Tex. App.—Fort Worth 2009, no pet.) (any ultimate fact may be proved by circumstantial evidence).

Dorsey v. State, 117 S.W.3d 332, 335 (Tex. App.—Beaumont 2003, no pet. ref'd), *cert. denied*, 554 U.S. 920 (2008) (evidence that defendant rented movie with plot similar to offense relevant and not unfairly prejudicial).

Yates v. State, 941 S.W.2d 357, 368 (Tex. App.—Waco 1997, pet. ref'd) (evidence that defendant took and disposed of victim's vehicle after murder relevant to intent and consciousness of guilt).

Darby v. State, 922 S.W.2d 614, 619 (Tex. App.—Fort Worth 1996, pet. ref'd) (evidence of sexually explicit magazine found in defendant's closet relevant as circumstantial evidence of intent).

Jones v. State, 825 S.W.2d 470, 471 (Tex. App.—Corpus Christi 1991, pet. ref'd) (DWI videotape relevant circumstantial evidence of degree of intoxication).

h. Background Evidence

Colone v. State, 573 S.W.3d 249, 266 (Tex. Crim. App. 2019) ("Rule 404(b) allows the admission of evidence of extraneous offenses for purposes other than character conformity ... Rule 404(b) expressly allows evidence of extraneous offenses to show 'motive.'").

Lone Star Gas Co. v. State, 137 Tex. 279, 313, 153 S.W.2d 681, 700 (Tex. 1941) (background evidence, although rarely involving disputed matters, admissible to help jury's understanding).

Best v. State, 118 S.W.3d 857, 864 (Tex. App.—Fort Worth 2003, no pet.) (evidence that defendant had been speeding and had expired insurance card and inspection sticker relevant context evidence and not unfairly prejudicial in case involving possession of controlled substance).

Yates v. State, 941 S.W.2d 357, 368 (Tex. App.—Waco 1997, pet. ref'd) (evidence of circumstances surrounding offense relevant as context evidence).

Callaway v. State, 818 S.W.2d 816, 826 (Tex. App.—Amarillo 1991, pet. ref'd) (evidence can be relevant as context evidence or to fully explain another matter already introduced).

i. *Real Estate Value or Appraisal*

Williams v. State, 406 S.W.3d 273, 284 (Tex. App.—San Antonio 2013, pet. denied) (courts give "appraisers a wide degree of latitude based on their experience when determining admissibility").

Williams v. State, 406 S.W.3d 273, 284 (Tex. App.—San Antonio 2013, pet. denied) ("[A]n expert's opinion testimony of real estate value is not legally insufficient because it lacks market data to support the opinion.").

Williams v. State, 406 S.W.3d 273, 284 (Tex. App.—San Antonio 2013, pet. denied) ("[E]vidence of comparable sales need not be in the immediate vicinity of the subject land so long as they meet the test of similarity.").

Williams v. State, 406 S.W.3d 273, 284 (Tex. App.—San Antonio 2013, pet. denied) (evidence of "comparable sales [is] generally admissible unless it appears that reasonable minds cannot differ from the conclusion that the evidence of the other sales lack probative force because of their dissimilarity to the condemned property").

Williams v. State, 406 S.W.3d 273, 284 (Tex. App.—San Antonio 2013, pet. denied) (a court's discretion is "very broad in determining whether a sale is sufficiently similar to be admissible as a circumstance influencing an expert witness in arriving at his opinion of value").

Williams v. State, 406 S.W.3d 273, 284 (Tex. App.—San Antonio 2013, pet. denied) (alleged "gaps between the comparable sales data and the conclusions drawn from it may go to the weight of an appraiser's testimony but not to its admissibility").

B. Motion to Exclude Evidence of Matters Not in Controversy

1. Suggested Motion Text

(*Name of Moving Party*) hereby moves this Court for an order excluding any and all evidence, references to evidence, testimony, or argument relating to (*Describe Matter Not in Controversy*). The motion is based upon the ground that the evidence relates to a matter that is not in controversy in this action and is therefore irrelevant, immaterial, and inadmissible.

2. Motion Summary

This motion is based on leading cases and statutory authority prohibiting the introduction of evidence of matters not in controversy.

3. Supporting Authorities

Texas Rule of Evidence 402 states that "evidence which is not relevant is inadmissible." Relevant evidence is defined by Texas Rule of Evidence 401 as "having any tendency to make the existence of any fact that is of consequence to the determination of the action more probable or less probable than it would be without the evidence." *Hawkins v. State*, 871 S.W.2d 539, 541 (Tex. App.—Fort Worth 1994, no pet.) (relevancy arises from evidence's relation to matter properly provable); *Jones v. Red Arrow Heavy Hauling, Inc.*, 816 S.W.2d 134, 135 (Tex. App.—Beaumont 1991, writ denied) (evidence not relevant is inadmissible).

a. Admitted or Uncontroverted Matters

Bryant v. Levy, 196 S.W.3d 166, 170 (Tex. App.—Amarillo 2006, pet. dism'd) ("[I]f an expert's opinion in a medical negligence action is based upon assumed facts that vary materially from the actual, undisputed facts, the opinion is without probative value and cannot support a verdict or judgment.").

Palomo v. State, 925 S.W.2d 329, 336 (Tex. App.—Corpus Christi 1996, no pet.) (that defendant had tattoo suggesting gang membership irrelevant and should not have been admitted where defendant did not contest issue of gang membership).

Blackburn v. State, 820 S.W.2d 824, 826 (Tex. App.—Waco 1991, pet. ref'd) (photograph should have been excluded as irrelevant where defendant did not contest possession of controlled substance).

b. Collateral Issues

Pierson v. State, 426 S.W.3d 763, 722 (Tex. Crim. App. 2014), *cert. denied*, 574 U.S. 885 (2014) (general rule is that impeachment on a collateral matter is impermissible).

TXI Transp. Co. v. Hughes, 306 S.W.3d 230, 234 (Tex. 2010) (statements concerning a party's immigration status were inadmissible because "it was a collateral matter, that is, not relevant to proving a material issue in the case").

Colone v. State, 573 S.W.3d 249 (Tex. Crim. App. 2019) (evidence of an extraneous offense is impermissible to show bad character; "It is the general rule that a defendant may be tried only for the offense charged and not for any other crimes or for being a criminal generally.").

Kulow v. State, 524 S.W.3d 383, 387 (Tex. App.—Houston [14th Dist.] 2017, pet. ref'd) ("A party cannot impeach a witness with extrinsic evidence on a collateral issue ... 'An issue is collateral if, beyond its impeachment value, a party would not be entitled to prove it as a part of his case tending to establish his plea.'").

Harris County Appraisal Dist. v. Kempwood Plaza Ltd., 186 S.W.3d 155, 158 (Tex. App.—Houston [1st Dist.] 2006, no pet.) (evidence that has no relationship to the issues in the case is irrelevant).

Hale v. State, 140 S.W.3d 381, 395 (Tex. App.—Fort Worth 2004, pet. ref'd) (in case involving sexual offenses, evidence of victims' other sexual acts irrelevant and properly barred by rape shield statute).

Moore v. State, 143 S.W.3d 305, 313 (Tex. App.—Waco 2004, pet. ref'd) (evidence of victim's DWI conviction irrelevant to truthfulness and evidence properly excluded where offered as impeachment).

Alexander v. State, 88 S.W.3d 772, 777 (Tex. App.—Corpus Christi 2002, pet. ref'd) (evidence of weapon seized at defendant's arrest irrelevant and prejudicial and should not have been admitted).

Williams v. State, 27 S.W.3d 599, 602 (Tex. App.—Waco 2000, pet. ref'd) (evidence of another person's misconduct irrelevant and should have been excluded).

Benson v. Weaver, 250 S.W.2d 770, 772 (Tex. Civ. App.—Austin 1952, no writ.), *aff'd*, 152 Tex. 50, 254 S.W.2d 95 (1952) (not error to exclude evidence on collateral issues).

Mo., K. & T. Ry. Co. v. Keaveney, 80 S.W. 387, 389 (Tex. Civ. App. 1904) (rules of evidence exclude all evidence of collateral facts or those incapable of affording any reasonable presumption or inference as to principal fact or matter in dispute).

c. Unpleaded Issues

Bos v. Smith, 556 S.W.3d 293, 307 (Tex. 2018) ("The doctrine of trial by consent does not apply when the evidence of an unpleaded matter is relevant to the pleaded issues because it would not be calculated to elicit an objection.").

Erisman v. Thompson, 140 Tex. 361, 365, 167 S.W.2d 731, 733 (Tex. 1943) ("[P]leadings determine the issues upon which parties go to trial, and it is not even proper to admit evidence unless it is addressed to or bears upon some issue raised by the pleadings").

Armstrong v. Armstrong, 570 S.W.3d 783 (Tex. App.—El Paso 2018, pet. denied) ("[T]rial by consent applies only where it appears from the record that the issue was actually tried, although not pleaded.... To determine whether the issue was tried by consent, we must examine the record not for evidence of the issue, but rather for evidence of trial of the issue.").

RR Maloan Invs., Inc. v. New HGE, Inc., 428 S.W.3d 355, 363 (Tex. App.—Houston [14th Dist.] 2014, no pet.) ("[T]o determine whether an issue was tried by consent, the court must examine the record not merely for evidence of the issue, but for evidence of trial of the issue.").

Benavides v. Cushman, 189 S.W.3d 875, 883 (Tex. App.—Houston [1st Dist.] 2006, no pet.) (not proper to admit evidence unless it is addressed to or bears upon some issue raised by the pleadings).

Marsh v. Marsh, 949 S.W.2d 734, 745 (Tex. App.—Houston [14th Dist.] 1997, no writ) ("[A]ny mutual mistake by the parties concerning the potential tax consequences of the premarital agreement was properly excluded in the absence of a pleading to that effect.").

Benson v. Weaver, 250 S.W.2d 770, 772 (Tex. Civ. App.—Austin 1952), *aff'd*, 152 Tex. 50, 254 S.W.2d 95 (1952) (admissibility of evidence depends on whether it is relevant to issues made by the pleadings).

Mo., K. & T. Ry. Co. v. Keaveney, 80 S.W. 387, 389 (Tex. Civ. App. 1904) (evidence must correspond to allegations in pleadings).

4. Opposing Authorities

Jones v. State, 119 S.W.3d 412, 422 (Tex. App.—Fort Worth 2003, no pet.) (evidence regarding similar offenses committed by the defendant relevant to demonstrate the defendant's state of mind and to rebut his character testimony).

Yates v. State, 941 S.W.2d 357, 368 (Tex. App.—Waco 1997, pet. ref'd) (evidence regarding the circumstances surrounding the offense relevant as context evidence).

Mayes v. State, 816 S.W.2d 79, 87 (Tex. Crim. App. 1991, pet. denied) ("relevant evidence" need not pertain only to facts in dispute but includes any evidence that influences consequential facts).

a. Collateral Issues

Maranda v. State, 253 S.W.3d 762, 767 (Tex. App.—Amarillo 2007), *pet. stricken*, No. PD-0010-08, 2008 WL 974786 (Tex. Crim. App. Apr. 9, 2008) ("[E]xtraneous offenses may be admissible as same transaction contextual evidence when several crimes are intermixed, or blended with one another, or connected so that they form an indivisible criminal transaction.").

Maranda v. State, 253 S.W.3d 762, 767 (Tex. App.—Amarillo 2007), *pet. stricken*, No. PD-0010-08, 2008 WL 974786 (Tex. Crim. App. Apr. 9, 2008) ("[A]dmissible extraneous offense evidence results when an extraneous matter is so intertwined with the State's proof of the charged crime that avoiding reference to it would make the State's case difficult to understand or incomplete ... Under such circumstances, the jury is entitled to know all relevant surrounding facts and circumstances of the charged offense, as an offense is not tried in a vacuum.").

Moreno v. State, 821 S.W.2d 344, 353 (Tex. App.—Waco 1991, pet. ref'd) (defendants' other offenses relevant as context evidence why police stopped defendants for charged offense).

b. Unpleaded Issues

Bos v. Smith, 556 S.W.3d 293, 307 (Tex. 2018) (Trial by consent can cure lack of pleading).

RR Maloan Invs., Inc. v. New HGE, Inc., 428 S.W.3d 355, 363 (Tex. App.—Houston [14th Dist.] 2014, no pet.) ("[A]n unpleaded issue may be considered tried by consent when evidence on the issue is developed under circumstances indicating that both parties understood the issue was in the case, and the other party failed to make an appropriate complaint.").

Eun Bok Lee v. Ho Chang Lee, 411 S.W.3d 95, 106 (Tex. App.—Houston [1st Dist.] 2013, no pet.) (an issue is tried by consent when both parties present evidence on an issue and the issue is developed during trial without objection).

Maytag Southwestern Co. v. Moore, 74 S.W.2d 183, 184 (Tex. Civ. App.—Amarillo 1934, writ dism'd) (in absence of affirmative showing to contrary, it is duty of court to presume that pleadings are sufficient to warrant issues charged to jury and admitted testimony).

c. Where Relevant to Other Issues

Jones v. State, 119 S.W.3d 412, 422 (Tex. App.—Fort Worth 2003, no pet.) (defendant's similar offenses relevant to demonstrate defendant's state of mind and to rebut character testimony).

Palomo v. State, 925 S.W.2d 329, 336 (Tex. App.—Corpus Christi 1996, no pet.) (evidence of defendant's gang initiation activities relevant to whether defendants acted together to commit offense).

CNA Ins. Co. v. Scheffey, 828 S.W.2d 785, 788 (Tex. App.—Texarkana 1992, writ denied) (evidence of events before incident the occurred relevant to the cause of plaintiff's damages).

Martin v. State, 823 S.W.2d 726, 728 (Tex. App.—Waco 1992, pet. ref'd) (value of drug has relevance and materiality in cases involving possession of drugs where evidence allows jury to understand amount of contraband in question).

Moreno v. State, 821 S.W.2d 344, 353 (Tex. App.—Waco 1991, pet. ref'd) (evidence of defendants' other offenses relevant as context evidence to demonstrate why police stopped defendants for charged offense).

d. Matters Not in Dispute

Mayes v. State, 816 S.W.2d 79, 87 (Tex. Crim. App. 1991, pet. denied) ("relevant evidence" need not pertain only to facts in dispute but includes any evidence that influences consequential facts).

e. Evidence to Provide Additional Explanation

Yates v. State, 941 S.W.2d 357, 368 (Tex. App.—Waco 1997, pet. ref'd) (evidence of circumstances surrounding offense relevant as context evidence).

Callaway v. State, 818 S.W.2d 816, 826 (Tex. App.—Amarillo 1991, pet. ref'd) (evidence can be relevant as context evidence or to fully explain another matter already introduced).

Moreno v. State, 821 S.W.2d 344, 353 (Tex. App.—Waco 1991, pet. ref'd) (evidence of defendants' other offenses relevant as context evidence to demonstrate why police stopped defendants for charged offense).

f. Pleaded Issues

Belew v. Rector, 202 S.W.3d 849, 854 (Tex. App.—Eastland 2006, no pet.) ("[An] affirmative defense allows the defendant to introduce evidence to establish an independent reason why the plaintiff should not prevail; it does not rebut the factual proposition of the plaintiff's pleading.").

Buls v. Fuselier, 55 S.W.3d 204, 211 (Tex. App.—Texarkana 2001, no pet.) ("[E]vidence supporting an inferential rebuttal is admissible under a general denial, since its purpose is to rebut an element of the plaintiff's cause of action.").

II. Sample Motions

A. Motion to Exclude Irrelevant Evidence

NO. _____

_____	§	IN THE DISTRICT COURT
	§	
v.	§	_____ JUDICIAL COURT
	§	
_____	§	_____ COUNTY, TEXAS

Motion to Exclude Irrelevant Evidence

Comes now _____, Plaintiff in this cause, and file this, his Motion to Exclude Irrelevant Evidence, and in support thereof, Plaintiff would show the Court the following:

1.
FACTUAL BACKGROUND

This is a personal injury action arising out of an automobile versus bicycle accident that occurred on January 15, 2019, in which the Plaintiff incurred a broken left clavicle and two broken ribs. Plaintiff has indicated that he will not be making a claim for recovery of past or future lost earnings. This motion seeks to preclude the Defendant from attempting to present prejudicial and irrelevant evidence relating to the Plaintiff's immigration status at the time of trial.

2.
PLAINTIFF'S IMMIGRATION STATUS IS NOT RELEVANT
TO ANY MATERIAL ISSUE IN THIS CASE

Texas Rule of Evidence 402 states that "evidence which is not relevant is inadmissible." Relevant evidence is defined by Texas Rule of Evidence 401 as "having any tendency to make the existence of any fact that is of consequence to the determination of the action more probable or less probable than it would be without the evidence." *See Torrington v. Stutzman*, 46 S.W.3d 829, 845 (Tex. 2000). Irrelevant evidence is not admissible. *Morale v. State*, 557 S.W.3d 569, 573 (Tex. 2018); *Diamond Offshore Services Ltd. v. Williams*, 542 S.W.3d 539, 549 (Tex. 2018).

Evidence may be properly excluded where not relevant to matters at issue. *See Morale v. State,* 557 S.W.3d 569, 573 (Tex. 2018). Plaintiff's immigration or residence status is not relevant to the issues in the case. *See TXI Transp. Co. v. Hughes,* 306 S.W.3d 230, 234 (Tex. 2010); *Zamarron v. Adame,* 864 S.W.2d 173, 175 (Tex. App.—El Paso 1993, reh'g overruled, writ denied) (plaintiff's immigration status irrelevant). Since the Plaintiff is making no claim for past or future loss of earnings, Plaintiff's immigration or residence status is not relevant to the determination of any damages at issue in this case and should clearly be excluded.

3.
ADMISSION OF PLAINTIFF'S IMMIGRATION STATUS WOULD CREATE UNDUE PREJUDICE TO PLAINTIFF

Texas Rule of Evidence 403 states: "[a]lthough relevant, evidence may be excluded if its probative value is substantially outweighed by the danger of unfair prejudice, confusion of the issues, or misleading the jury, or by considerations of undue delay, or needless presentation of cumulative evidence." *Brookshire Bros. v. Aldridge,* 438 S.W.3d 9, 26 (Tex. 2014) (evidence that raises a risk of prejudice and confusion of the jury should be excluded); *Farmers Texas County Mutual Insurance Co. v. Pagan,* 453 S.W.3d 454, (Tex. App.—Houston [14th Dist.] 2014, no pet.) (evidence should have been excluded where its probative value was outweighed by danger of confusion of issues and misleading jury).

Texas Rule of Evidence 403 justifies the preclusion of the requested evidence in this case. Given the clear lack of relevance, Defendant's intention by admitting such evidence can only be to prejudice the Plaintiff and cause the jury to look negatively or with ill feelings toward the Plaintiff. Certainly, the issues will be confused, and the jury will be misled by the admission of such evidence. And clearly the probative value of the evidence is nonexistent, given the Plaintiff's lack of any claim for lost earnings.

4.
CONCLUSION

Based upon all of the above, exclusion of any reference to the Plaintiff's immigration or residence status is proper.

Dated: _____*(Date)*_____

By: _____

_____*(Name of Counsel)*_____

Attorneys for Plaintiff,

_____*(Name of Plaintiff)*_____

B. Motion to Exclude Evidence of Physical Conditions Not at Issue

NO. _____

	§	IN THE DISTRICT COURT
_____	§	
	§	
v.	§	_____ JUDICIAL COURT
	§	
_____	§	_____ COUNTY, TEXAS

Plaintiff's Motion to Exclude Evidence of Certain Physical Conditions

Comes now _____, Plaintiff in this cause, and file this, his Motion to Exclude Evidence of Certain Physical Conditions, and in support thereof, Plaintiff would show the Court the following:

1.
FACTUAL BACKGROUND

The incident giving rise to this lawsuit for professional negligence occurred on about June 30, 2019, when the Plaintiff underwent multiple surgeries by the Defendant. Plaintiff alleges and will prove at trial that during the surgeries, the Defendant fell below the standard of care in the community.

In his proposed witness list, the Defendant has included health care practitioners who have treated plaintiff for conditions or injuries in areas of the body other than those alleged to have been injured in the within action. By this motion, the Plaintiff seeks to exclude the testimony of any witness on such matters.

2.
PREJUDICIAL EVIDENCE MAY BE EXCLUDED

Texas Rule of Evidence 403 states: "[a]lthough relevant, evidence may be excluded if its probative value is substantially outweighed by the danger of unfair prejudice, confusion of the issues, or misleading the jury, or by considerations of undue delay, or needless presentation of cumulative evidence." *See Brookshire Bros. v. Aldridge*, 438 S.W.3d 9, 26 (Tex. 2014) (evidence that raises a risk of prejudice and confusion of the jury should be excluded); *Farmers Texas County Mutual Insurance Co. v. Pagan*, 453 S.W.3d 454, (Tex. App.—Houston [14th Dist.] 2014, no pet.) (evidence should have been excluded where its probative value was outweighed by danger of confusion of issues and misleading jury).

3.
ONLY RELEVANT EVIDENCE IS ADMISSIBLE

Texas Rule of Evidence 402 states that "evidence which is not relevant is inadmissible." Relevant evidence is defined by Texas Rule of Evidence 401 as "having any tendency to make the existence of any fact that is of consequence to the determination of the action more probable or less probable than it would be without the evidence." *See Torrington v. Stutzman*, 46 S.W.3d 829, 845 (Tex. 2000). Irrelevant evidence is inadmissible. *Morale v. State*, 557 S.W.3d 569, 573 (Tex. 2018); *Diamond Offshore Services Ltd. v. Williams*, 542 S.W.3d 539, 549 (Tex. 2018).

4.
EVIDENCE OF PHYSICAL CONDITIONS THAT ARE NOT AT ISSUE ARE PROPERLY EXCLUDED

In *Monk v. Cooper*, 454 S.W.2d 244, 247 (Tex. Civ. App.—Texarkana 1970, writ ref'd n.r.e.), the trial court properly excluded evidence related to physical conditions that were not shown to be related to the incident at issue. Similarly, in *New York Underwriters Ins. Co. v. Upshaw*, 560 S.W.2d 433, 434 (Tex. Civ. App.—Beaumont 1977, no writ), the court found that it was proper to exclude evidence of unrelated prior injuries in a workers' compensation suit.

5.
DISCUSSION

In the present case, any evidence of a physical condition not alleged to have been caused by the subject incident is completely irrelevant. Allowing the jury to hear this evidence creates a very real danger that the Plaintiff will be prejudiced, since the evidence will create a perception that the Plaintiff seeks to recover more than he is entitled to by law. This prejudice significantly outweighs any marginal probative value of admitting such irrelevant and inflammatory evidence.

6.
CONCLUSION

Based on the aforementioned authorities and facts, it is respectfully requested that this Court grant this motion and that all witnesses be precluded from testifying regarding injuries other than those at issue in this case.

Dated: _____ *(Date)* _____

            Respectfully submitted,

            By: _____

               _____ *(Name of Counsel)* _____

            Attorneys for Plaintiff,

               _____ *(Name of Plaintiff)* _____

CHAPTER 4

Writings and Physical Evidence

I. Motion Authorities
   A. Motion to Exclude Evidence Lacking Foundation
      1. Suggested Motion Text
      2. Motion Summary
      3. Supporting Authorities, Generally
         a. Determination of Admissibility Outside Presence of Jury
         b. Preliminary Fact—Inadmissibility of Evidence
         c. Photographs
         d. Tape Recordings
         e. Tests and Experiments
         f. Videotapes and Motion Pictures
         g. Writings
         h. Public Records or Reports
         i. Ancient Documents or Data Compilations
      4. Opposing Authorities, Generally
         a. Photographs
         b. Physical Evidence
         c. Tests and Experiments
         d. Tape Recordings
         e. Videotapes and Motion Pictures
         f. Writings
         g. Conditional Admissibility
   B. Motion to Exclude Writings, Generally
      1. Suggested Motion Text
      2. Motion Summary
      3. Supporting Authorities—"Writing" Defined
         a. Exclusion, Generally
         b. Unauthenticated Writings
            i. Public Records or Reports
            ii. Documents or Data Collections
            iii. Exclusion of Unauthenticated Writings
         c. Irrelevant Evidence
         d. Inadmissible Hearsay
            i. Examples of Inadmissible Written Hearsay
         e. Inadmissible Secondary Evidence
      4. Opposing Authorities, Generally
         a. Authentication
         b. Hearsay Exceptions and Nonhearsay, Generally

            i. Examples of Admissible Written Hearsay
        c. Secondary Evidence
    C. Motion to Exclude Gruesome or Inflammatory Photographs
        1. Suggested Motion Text
        2. Motion Summary
        3. Supporting Authorities, Generally
            a. Gruesome or Inflammatory Photographs
            b. Purpose to Inflame Jurors' Emotions
            c. Other Grounds
        4. Opposing Authorities
            a. Examples of Admissible Photographs
    D. Motion to Exclude Prejudicial Film or Videotapes
        1. Suggested Motion Text
        2. Motion Summary
        3. Supporting Authorities, Generally
            a. Other Grounds
        4. Opposing Authorities, Generally
            a. Relevance
    E. Motion to Exclude Published Articles
        1. Suggested Motion Text
        2. Motion Summary
        3. Supporting Authorities
            a. Prejudicial
            b. Other Grounds
        4. Opposing Authorities, Generally
            a. Cumulative
            b. No Prejudice
            c. Where Relevant to Other Issues
            d. Not Hearsay
    F. Motion to Exclude Accident Reports
        1. Suggested Motion Text
        2. Motion Summary
        3. Supporting Authorities
            a. Generally
            b. Privilege
            c. Hearsay
            d. Diagrams Made at the Scene and Computer Animations
            e. Other Grounds
        4. Opposing Authorities
            a. Statements Made to Reporting Officer
            b. Public Records and Reports
            c. Diagrams Made at the Scene and Computer Animations
    G. Motion to Exclude Letters, Emails, or Text Messages
        1. Suggested Motion Text
        2. Motion Summary
        3. Supporting Authorities
            a. Hearsay
            b. Irrelevant
            c. Other Grounds

4. Opposing Authorities
   a. Relevancy
   b. Hearsay
   c. Not Hearsay
H. Motion to Exclude Maps, Models, and Charts
   1. Suggested Motion Text
   2. Motion Summary
   3. Supporting Authorities, Generally
      a. Other Grounds
   4. Opposing Authorities
      a. Illustrative or Demonstrative Models
      b. Illustrative or Demonstrative Maps
      c. Illustrative or Demonstrative Charts
      d. Where Accuracy Is Not Disputed
I. Motion to Exclude Improper Medical Records, Reports, or Bills
   1. Suggested Motion Text
   2. Motion Summary
   3. Supporting Authorities, Generally
      a. Improper Hearsay Evidence
      b. Opinions of Others—Lack of Personal Knowledge
      c. Patient Medical History
         i. Hearsay
      d. Billing Records—Lack of Foundation
      e. Other Grounds
   4. Opposing Authorities
      a. Medical Opinions of Others—Opinions Used in Diagnosis or Treatment
      b. Business Record Hearsay Exception
      c. Patient History—Observation of Physician
      d. Patient History—Pertinent to Medical Diagnosis
      e. Medical Billing Records—Reasonableness of Charges
II. Sample Motions
   A. Motion to Exclude Gruesome Photographs
   B. Motion to Exclude Written Letter
   C. Motion to Exclude Improper Medical Records

I. Motion Authorities

A. Motion to Exclude Evidence Lacking Foundation

1. Suggested Motion Text

(*Name of Moving Party*) hereby moves this Court for an order excluding any and all evidence, references to evidence, testimony, or argument relating to (*Describe Evidence Lacking Foundation*). The motion is based upon the ground that the evidence lacks a necessary foundation for admission and therefore should be excluded pursuant to Texas Rule of Evidence 104.

2. Motion Summary

This motion is used to exclude evidence that lacks a required foundation for admission. The motion is based upon Texas Rule of Evidence 104(a), which gives the court the discretion to exclude evidence lacking a necessary preliminary fact. Counsel should be prepared to demonstrate, where possible, the lack of actual foundational facts and the prejudice that will occur if the evidence is presented to the jury. See Texas Rule of Evidence 403. This balancing is an important element to the motion, since the court has the power to admit evidence conditionally under Texas Rule of Evidence 104(b).

The sections that follow provide a number of representative cases where general foundational deficiencies were identified. Not all possible evidence types are included in this text. For a discussion of preliminary facts relating to a variety of different types of evidence, see Notes of Decisions, Texas Rule of Evidence 104.

3. Supporting Authorities, Generally

Texas Rule of Evidence 103 provides in relevant part:

> (a) Effect of Erroneous Ruling. Error may not be predicated upon a ruling which admits or excludes evidence unless a substantial right of the party is affected, and
>
> (1) Objection. In case the ruling is one admitting evidence, a timely objection or motion to strike appears of record, stating the specific ground of objection, if the specific ground was not apparent from the context. *When the court hears objections to offered evidence out of the presence of the jury and rules that such evidence be admitted, such objections shall be deemed to apply to such evidence when it is admitted before the jury without the necessity of repeating those objections.*
>
> (2) Offer of proof. In case the ruling is one excluding evidence, the substance of the evidence was made known to the court by offer or was apparent from the context within which questions were asked.
>
> (b) Record of Offer and Ruling. The offering party shall, as soon as practicable, but before the court's charge is read to the jury, be allowed to make, in the absence of the jury, its offer of proof. The court may add any other or further statement which shows the character of the evidence, the form in which it was offered, the objection made, and the ruling thereon. The court may, or at the request of a party shall, direct the making of an offer in question and answer form.
>
> (c) Hearing of Jury. *In jury cases, proceedings shall be conducted, to the extent practicable, so as to prevent inadmissible evidence from being suggested to the jury by any means, such as making statements or offers of proof or asking questions in the hearing of the jury.* (Emphasis added).

Texas Rule of Evidence 104(c) states:

> In a criminal case, a hearing on the admissibility of a confession shall be conducted out of the hearing of the jury. All other civil or criminal hearings on preliminary matters shall be conducted out of the hearing of the jury when the interests of justice so require or in a criminal case when an accused is a witness and so requests.

a. *Determination of Admissibility Outside Presence of Jury*

Holmes v. State, 248 S.W.3d 194 (Tex. Crim. App. 2008) (defendant in criminal case may challenge the admissibility of evidence in either of two ways: (1) defendant may object to the admission of the evidence at the time it is offered at trial and request a hearing outside the presence of the jury, or (2) defendant may file a pretrial motion to suppress evidence and have it heard and ruled upon before trial).

Nelson v. State, 765 S.W.2d 401 (Tex. Crim. App. 1989) (court may conduct preliminary hearing outside presence of jury during trial's guilt/innocence phase).

Walter v. State, 581 S.W.3d 957, 982 (Tex. App.—Eastland 2019, pet. ref'd) ("It is within the jury's purview to 'determine whether an item of evidence is indeed what its proponent claims; the trial court need only make the preliminary determination that the proponent of the item has supplied facts sufficient to support a reasonable jury determination that the proffered evidence is authentic.'").

In re Estate of Miller, 243 S.W.3d 831 (Tex. App.—Dallas 2008, no pet.) (to challenge exclusion of evidence by the trial court on appeal, the complaining party must present the excluded evidence to the trial court by offer of proof or bill of exception).

b. *Preliminary Facts—Inadmissibility of Evidence*

Texas Rule of Evidence 104(a) states:

> Preliminary questions concerning the qualification of a person to be a witness, the existence of a privilege, or the admissibility of evidence shall be determined by the court, subject to the provisions of subdivision (b). In making its determination the court is not bound by the rules of evidence except those with respect to privileges.

Druery v. State, 225 S.W.3d 491 (Tex. Crim. App. 2007), *cert. denied*, 552 U.S. 1028 (2007) (preliminary questions of admissibility are determined by the court).

Walter v. State, 581 S.W.3d 957, 982 (Tex. App.—Eastland 2019, pet. ref'd) ("To properly authenticate a piece of evidence, the proponent must produce evidence sufficient to support a finding that the item is what the proponent claims it is.").

Gentry v. State, 259 S.W.3d 272 (Tex. App.—Waco 2008, pet. ref'd) (first step in a trial court's determination of whether evidence should be admitted before the jury is finding the evidence relevant).

Sierad v. Barnett, 164 S.W.3d 471 (Tex. App.—Dallas 2005, no pet.) (when authenticity of evidence is challenged, a trial court must determine preliminary questions of admissibility; this determination will not be overturned absent an abuse of discretion).

St. Paul Med. Ctr. v. Cecil, 842 S.W.2d 808 (Tex. App.—Dallas 1992, no writ.) (qualification of expert witness is matter for preliminary determination by trial court).

c. *Photographs*

Fowler v. State, 544 S.W.3d 844, 849 (Tex. Crim. App. 2018) ("video recordings without audio are treated as photographs and are properly authenticated when it can be proved that the images accurately represent the scene in question and are relevant to a disputed issue").

Jones v. Mattress Firm Holding Corp., 558 S.W.3d 732, 737 (Tex. App.—Houston [14th Dist.] 2018, no pet.) ("When a photograph is relevant to an issue in a case, it is admissible if it is authenticated by a witness as an accurate portrayal.... The verifying witness must be familiar with the objects involved in the photograph and be able to state the photograph correctly represents them.").

Watson v. State, 421 S.W.3d 186, 190 (Tex. App.—San Antonio 2013, pet. ref'd) ("the predicate for introduction of a photograph and a silent videotape not accompanied by sound requires proof of (1) its accuracy as a correct representation of the subject at a given time, and (2) its material relevance to a dispute issue").

Watson v. State, 421 S.W.3d 186 (Tex. App.—San Antonio 2013, pet. ref'd) (the predicate for introduction of a photograph and a silent videotape not accompanied by sound need not be laid by the photographer, the individual being photographed, or even a person present in the photograph in question; any witness observing the scene depicted in the photograph may lay the predicate so long as the witness can provide testimony based on personal knowledge, sufficient to support a finding that the matter in question is what its proponent claims).

Delacerda v. State, 425 S.W.3d 367 (Tex. App.—Houston [1st Dist.] 2011, pet. ref'd) (before being admitted into evidence, a photograph must ordinarily be shown to be a correct representation of the subject at a given time; and the only identification or authentication required is that the offered evidence properly represents the person, object, or scene in question).

Rankin v. Union Pac. R. Co., 319 S.W.3d 58 (Tex. App.—San Antonio 2010, no pet.) (photographs of heavy brush, vegetation, and trees alongside railroad tracks near railroad crossing, taken on date on which train struck motorist's vehicle, standing alone, were not probative evidence of an extra-hazardous condition that would give rise to duty on part of railroad to provide extraordinary warning devices at crossing, or to instruct its crew to travel through crossing at a reduced speed; trees, vegetation, trailers, and buildings appeared in photographs, but only at unknown distances from crossing and tracks, no train appeared in photographs, and photographs did not establish that motorist would have been unable to get out of the way of a train traveling at 59 miles per hour before being hit).

Kelly v. State, 22 S.W.3d 642 (Tex. App.—Waco 2000, pet. ref'd) (photographs authenticated by testimony of any witness with personal knowledge that particular item accurately represents scene or event it purports to portray). *See also Davidson v. Great Nat'l Life Ins. Co.*, 737 S.W.2d 312 (Tex. 1987); *Reichhold Chems. v. Puremco Mfg.*, 854 S.W.2d 240 (Tex. App.—Waco 1999, writ denied).

d. Tape Recordings

Seymour v. Gillespie, 608 S.W.2d 897 (Tex. 1980) (sound recording may be authenticated by one or more witnesses' testimony that: recording device was capable of taking testimony; operator of device was competent; recording is true and accurate portrayal; no changes, additions, or deletions; recording has been preserved and accuracy maintained; speakers are who claim to be; and testimony was voluntary).

Miller v. State, 208 S.W.3d 554 (Tex. App.—Austin 2006, pet. ref'd) (voice mail recording was not properly authenticated in capital murder prosecution; exhibit was admitted in evidence at close of State's evidence, after victim's daughter was recalled and asked if she could identify voice in the recording, she said that she recognized voice as defendant's as he had called her earlier, neither victim's daughter nor any other witness, however, identified recording or explained circumstances in which it was made, and it was learned only from statements made by counsel outside jury's presence that this was voicemail message left on defendant's step-father's phone).

e. Tests and Experiments

Ex parte Coty, 418 S.W.3d 597 (Tex. Crim. App. 2014) (a defendant can establish that a laboratory technician's sole possession of a substance and testing results derived from that possession are unreliable, and the court will infer that the evidence in question is false, if the defendant shows that: (1) the technician in question is a state actor, (2) the technician has committed multiple instances of intentional misconduct in another case or cases, (3) the technician is the same technician who worked on the applicant's case, (4) the misconduct is the type of misconduct that would have affected the evidence in the applicant's case, and (5) the technician handled and processed the evidence in the applicant's case within roughly the same period of time as the other misconduct; once the defendant satisfies this initial burden by establishing the identified factors, the defendant has proven that the technician in question has engaged in a pattern of misconduct sufficiently egregious in other cases that the errors could have resulted in false evidence being used in the defendant's case).

Ex parte Coty, 418 S.W.3d 597 (Tex. Crim. App. 2014) (if a defendant can establish the necessary predicate facts regarding a technician's pattern of misconduct, then the burden shifts to the State to offer evidence demonstrating that the laboratory technician committed no such intentional misconduct in the defendant's case).

Fort Worth & Denver Ry. Co. v. Williams, 375 S.W.2d 279 (Tex. 1964) (must be evidence of substantial similarity between conditions existing at time of occurrence and conditions created at time of experiment).

Lewis v. State, 402 S.W.3d 852 (Tex. App.—Amarillo 2013), *aff'd*, 428 S.W.3d 860 (Tex. Crim. App. 2014) (a computer animation is merely a series of images generated by a computer that serves as demonstrative evidence, and may be authenticated by the witness's testimony that the computer animation presents a fair and accurate depiction of what it purports to represent; if it does not represent what it purports to represent, it will not be admissible).

Lewis v. State, 402 S.W.3d 852 (Tex. App.—Amarillo 2013), *aff'd*, 428 S.W.3d 860 (Tex. Crim. App. 2014) (any staged, re-enacted criminal acts or defensive issues involving human beings are impossible to duplicate in every minute detail and are therefore inherently dangerous, offer little in substance, and the impact of re-enactments is too highly prejudicial to insure the State or the defendant a fair trial).

Lewis v. State, 402 S.W.3d 852 (Tex. App.—Amarillo 2013), *aff'd*, 428 S.W.3d 860 (Tex. Crim. App. 2014) (the artificial re-creation of an event may unduly accentuate certain phases of the happening, and because of the forceful impression made on the minds of the jurors by this kind of evidence, it should be received with caution, particularly where the event sought to be depicted is simple, the testimony adequate, and the animation adds nothing more than a one-sided, manipulated visual image to the mental picture already produced in the mind of the jurors by the oral testimony of an eyewitness who has been subjected to the crucible of cross-examination).

Kia Motors Corp. v. Ruiz, 348 S.W.3d 465 (Tex. App.—Dallas 2011), *rev'd on other grounds*, 432 S.W.3d 865 (Tex. 2014) (video of crash test was properly excluded where the vehicles in the crash test were similar to the vehicles involved the accident at issue, and both the crash test and the accident at issue involved offset frontal crashes, but where the crash test video depicted a sports utility vehicle crashing into a sedan at a nearly 45-degree angle, whereas in the accident at issue, a pick-up truck crashed into a small sedan head-on).

Lincoln v. Clark Freight Lines, Inc., 285 S.W.3d 79 (Tex. App.—Houston [1st Dist.] 2009, no pet.) (when an experiment is conducted out of court and in the absence of opposing counsel, there must be a substantial similarity between the conditions existing at the time of the experiment and the actual event that is the subject of litigation; however, the conditions do not need to be identical).

Hutton v. AER Mfg. II, Inc., 224 S.W.3d 459 (Tex. App.—Dallas 2007, pet. denied) (trial court did not abuse its discretion when it allowed jury to view videotape for the limited purpose of demonstrating the general scientific principles of gravitational, centrifugal, and linear forces on a vehicle occupant during a rollover, in product liability trial, although the vehicle in the tape was not similar to the vehicle involved in the accident at issue; defendants noted the differences between the rollover tests and the rollover involved in the case; witnesses specifically informed the jury that the videotape was not a re-creation of the rollover; and the videotape did not go into the jury room and was marked for record purposes only).

Cont'l Bus Sys., Inc. v. Biggers, 322 S.W.2d 1 (Tex. Civ. App.—Houston 1959, writ ref'd n.r.e.) (party offering evidence of out-of-court experiments must lay proper foundation by showing similarity of circumstances and conditions).

f. *Videotapes and Motion Pictures*

Diamond Offshore Services Ltd. v. Williams, 542 S.W.3d 539, 547 (Tex. 2018) ("as a general rule, a trial court should view video evidence before ruling on admissibility when the contents of the video are at issue").

Diamond Offshore Services Ltd. v. Williams, 542 S.W.3d 539, 547 n.26 (Tex. 2018) ("Video can be authenticated by anyone with knowledge of the information recorded, including the party against whom it is offered."). *Watson v. State*, 421 S.W.3d 186 (Tex. App.—San Antonio 2013, pet. ref'd) (the predicate for introduction of a photograph and a silent videotape not accompanied by sound requires proof of (1) its accuracy as a correct representation of the subject at a given time, and (2) its material relevance to a dispute issue).

Watson v. State, 421 S.W.3d 186 (Tex. App.—San Antonio 2013, pet. ref'd) (the predicate for introduction of a photograph and a silent videotape not accompanied by sound need not be laid by the photographer, the individual being photographed, or even a person present in the photograph in question; any witness observing the scene depicted in the photograph may lay the predicate so long as the witness can provide testimony based on personal knowledge, sufficient to support a finding that the matter in question is what its proponent claims).

S.D.G. v. State, 936 S.W.2d 371 (Tex. App.—Houston [14th Dist.] 1996, writ denied) (predicate for introduction of silent videotape requires proof of accuracy as correct representation of subject at given time and relevance to material issue). *See also Huffman v. State*, 746 S.W.2d 212 (Tex. Crim. App. 1988).

Apache Ready Mix Co., Inc. v. Creed, 653 S.W.2d 79 (Tex. App.—San Antonio 1983, writ dism'd) (when motion picture is proper representation of important fact in issue, admission or rejection is matter of trial court's discretion). See also Texas Rules of Evidence 901 to 902 and 1001, et seq.

g. *Writings*

Texas Rule of Evidence 901(a) states that:

> [t]he requirement of authentication or identification as a condition precedent to admissibility is satisfied by evidence sufficient to support a finding that the matter in question is what its proponent claims.

Tienda v. State, 358 S.W.3d 633 (Tex. Crim. App. 2012) (evidence has no relevance if it is not authentically what its proponent claims it to be).

Rogers v. RREF II CB Acquisitions, LLC, 533 S.W.3d 419, 432 (Tex. App.—Corpus Christi 2016, no pet.) ("special concerns may arise if the subject of the business records affidavit is a document which originated from a third-party... documents received from another entity are not admissible under rule 803(6), if the witness is not qualified to testify about the entity's record keeping").

Gunville v. Gonzales, 508 S.W.3d 547, 559 (Tex. App.—El Paso 2016, no pet.) ("Simply attaching a document to a pleading neither makes the document admissible as evidence, dispenses with proper foundational evidentiary requirements, or relieves a litigant of complying with other admissibility requirements.").

Gunville v. Gonzales, 508 S.W.3d 547, 559 (Tex. App.—El Paso 2016, no pet.) ("A document may only be considered authentic if a sponsoring witness vouches for its authenticity or if the document otherwise meets the requirements of authentication as set out in the rules of evidence.").

Lissiak v. SW Loan OO, L.P., 499 S.W.3d 481, (Tex. App.—Tyler 2016, no pet.) ("A Rule 93(7) verified denial challenges the authenticity of the document and addresses the document's admissibility as an evidentiary issue.").

Ortega v. Cach, LLC, 396 S.W.3d 622 (Tex. App.—Houston [14th Dist.] 2013, no pet.) (if the source of information or the method or circumstances of preparation indicate lack of trustworthiness, even a properly authenticated record may be inadmissible).

Sohail v. State, 264 S.W.3d 251 (Tex. App.—Houston [1st Dist.] 2008, pet. ref'd) (letter allegedly found by defendant that was written by victim stating that defendant never hit or pushed her, certified affidavit by victim requesting dismissal of protective order so she could reunite with defendant, and tape-recorded statement by victim contained inadmissible hearsay and extraneous information, and thus, were inadmissible in prosecution for domestic violence assault).

Abdygapparova v. State, 243 S.W.3d 191 (Tex. App.—San Antonio 2007, pet. ref'd) (letter sent by individual to defendant, outlining individual's sexual desires and fantasies with defendant and other women, was not relevant in capital murder prosecution; although State contended that defendant's sexual orientation was relevant to sexual assault of victim, letter sent to defendant by individual, living in another state and whom she had never met, did not tend to make anything as to defendant, much less her sexual orientation or whether she committed sexual assault, any more or less probable).

Miller v. State, 208 S.W.3d 554 (Tex. App.—Austin 2006, pet. ref'd) (cell phone bill was inadmissible hearsay in capital murder prosecution; victim's daughter's testimony identifying two of 166 phone calls bill documented was not sufficient to establish accuracy of process by which bill was generated).

Nat'l Mut. Acc. Ins. Co. v. Davis, 46 S.W.2d 351 (Tex. Civ. App.—Amarillo 1932, no writ) (evidence of letter received in reply to letter sent through mail may be satisfactory proof of authenticity). See also Texas Rules of Evidence 901 to 902 and 1001, et seq.

h. Public Records or Reports

Rule 901(b)(7) provides for the authentication of public records or reports:

> Evidence that a writing authorized by law to be recorded or filed and in fact recorded or filed in a public office, or a purported public record, statement, or data compilation, in any form, is from the public office where times of this nature are kept.

In re Cullar, 320 S.W.3d 560 (Tex. App.—Dallas 2010, orig. proceeding) (photocopies of pages from a website, purported to be voting records and other documents purporting to address residency, were not properly sworn or certified and not admissible as public records or reports).

Mega Child Care, Inc. v. Tex. Dep't of Protective & Regulatory Servs., 29 S.W.3d 303 (Tex. App.—Houston [14th Dist.] 2000, no pet.) (investigator could not authenticate copy of administrative judge's opinion where investigator was not author of opinion and did not purport to have personal knowledge of opinion).

i. Ancient Documents or Data Compilations

Rule 901(b)(8) provides for the authentication of ancient documents or data compilations:

> Evidence that a document or data compilation, in any form, (A) is in such condition as to create no suspicion concerning its authenticity, (B) was in a place where it, if authentic, would likely be, and (C) has been in existence twenty years or more at the time it is offered.

4. Opposing Authorities, Generally

Fowler v. State, 544 S.W.3d 844, 849 (Tex. Crim. App. 2018) ("Authenticity may be established with evidence of distinctive characteristics and the like, which include the appearance, contents, substance, internal patterns, or other distinctive characteristics of the item, taken together with all the circumstances.").

Fowler v. State, 544 S.W.3d 844, 849 (Tex. Crim. App. 2018) ("Conclusive proof of authenticity before allowing admission of disputed evidence is not required.").

Ryder v. State, 581 S.W.3d 439, 454 (Tex. App.—Houston [14th Dist.] 2019, no pet.) ("To properly authenticate an item of evidence, 'the proponent must produce evidence sufficient to support a finding that the item is what the proponent claims it is.'").

Ryder v. State, 581 S.W.3d 439, 454 (Tex. App.—Houston [14th Dist.] 2019, no pet.) ("Evidence is properly authenticated if the proponent supplies 'facts that are sufficient to support a reasonable jury determination that the evidence he had proffered is authentic.'").

Ryder v. State, 581 S.W.3d 439, 454 (Tex. App.—Houston [14th Dist.] 2019, no pet.) ("The proponent of the evidence does not need 'to rule out all possibilities inconsistent with authenticity, or prove beyond any doubt that the evidence is what it purports to be.'").

Hunter v. State, 513 S.W.3d 638, 640 (Tex. App.—Texarkana 2016) ("The trial court need not be persuaded beyond all doubt that the proffered evidence is authentic; rather, the key question for admissibility is whether the proponent has supplied facts sufficient to support a reasonable jury determination that the evidence is authentic.").

Haas v. State, 494 S.W.3d 819, 823 (Tex. App.—Houston [14th Dist.] 2016, no pet.) ("A document may be authenticated under either Texas Rule of Evidence 901 or 902 and need not be authenticated under both.... The requirement of authentication or identification as a condition precedent to admissibility is satisfied by evidence sufficient to support a finding that the matter in question is what its proponent claims.").

Taylor v. Tex. Dep't of Protective & Regulatory Servs., 160 S.W.3d 641 (Tex. App.—Austin 2005, pet. denied) (sufficient foundation to establish witness qualified to testify as expert social worker).

Sharp v. State, 210 S.W.3d 835 (Tex. App.—Amarillo 2006, no pet.) (penitentiary packet showing prior conviction for involuntary manslaughter was adequately authenticated, in trial for indecency with child, in that it was certified by custodian representing that contents were correct copies of originals).

Carone v. Retamco Operating, Inc., 138 S.W.3d 1 (Tex. App.—San Antonio 2004, pet. denied) (letters sufficiently authenticated by party's admission that he signed them).

Pittsburgh Corning Corp. v. Walters, 1 S.W.3d 759 (Tex. App.—Corpus Christi 1999, pet. denied) (sufficient foundation to establish certain experts qualified to testify).

Stroud v. State, 46 S.W.2d 689 (Tex. Crim. App. 1931, no pet.) (sufficient predicate laid for introduction of dying declaration).

a. Photographs

Fowler v. State, 544 S.W.3d 844, 849 (Tex. Crim. App. 2018) ("video recordings without audio are treated as photographs and are properly authenticated when it can be proved that the images accurately represent the scene in question and are relevant to a disputed issue").

Davis v. State, 313 S.W.3d 317 (Tex. Crim. App. 2010) (admissibility of photographs over an objection is within the sound discretion of the trial court). *Proo v. State*, 587 S.W.3d 789, 817 (Tex. App.—San Antonio 2019, pet. ref'd) ("In evaluating whether the probative value of photographs or video is outweighed by the danger of unfair prejudice, the court considers several factors, including 'the number of exhibits offered, their gruesomeness, their detail, their size, whether they are black and white or color, whether they are close-up, and whether the body depicted is naked or clothed.'... The court must also consider the availability of other means of proof and the unique circumstances of the individual case.").

Proo v. State, 587 S.W.3d 789, 817 (Tex. App.—San Antonio 2019, pet. ref'd) ("Generally, a photograph is admissible if verbal testimony as to matters depicted in the photograph is also admissible.;").

Proo v. State, 587 S.W.3d 789, 817 (Tex. App.—San Antonio 2019, pet. ref'd) ("'If verbal testimony is relevant, photographs of the same are also relevant.'").

Jones v. Mattress Firm Holding Corp., 558 S.W.3d 732, 737 (Tex. App.—Houston [14th Dist.] 2018, no pet.) ("Photographs are admissible if they are relevant to any issue in a case.").

Jones v. Mattress Firm Holding Corp., 558 S.W.3d 732, 737 (Tex. App.—Houston [14th Dist.] 2018, no pet.) ("When a photograph is relevant to an issue in a case, it is admissible if it is authenticated by a witness as an accurate portrayal.").

Jones v. Mattress Firm Holding Corp., 558 S.W.3d 732, 737 (Tex. App.—Houston [14th Dist.] 2018, no pet.) ("Conditions in a photograph do not need to be identical to the conditions at the time of the event in question if the changes are explained in such a manner that the photograph ... will help the jury in understanding the nature of the condition at the time of the event at issue.").

Haq v. State, 2013 Tex. App. LEXIS 5565 (Tex. App.—Houston [1st Dist.] May 7, 2013, pet. ref'd) (photo arrays were properly authenticated by witnesses, who testified that their signatures were next to the picture they had selected).

Jett v. State, 319 S.W.3d 846 (Tex. App.—San Antonio 2010, no pet.) (photograph is generally admissible in a criminal prosecution if verbal testimony about the matters depicted in the photograph is also admissible).

In re K.Y., 273 S.W.3d 703 (Tex. App.—Houston [14th Dist.] 2008, no pet.) (photographs are admissible if oral testimony as to the matters depicted in the photographs is also admissible).

In re K.Y., 273 S.W.3d 703 (Tex. App.—Houston [14th Dist.] 2008, no pet.) (probative value of autopsy photographs of child was not substantially outweighed by danger of unfair prejudice in parental rights termination proceeding; pictures were important to assisting jury in understanding medical examiner's testimony, and visual evidence had significant probative value apart from testimonial evidence on same subject, and probative value of photographs to demonstrate child's physical condition at time of her death outweighed small risk that jury may have been improperly influenced by incorrectly concluding that father, rather than someone else, inflicted other injuries as well).

Kirwan v. City of Waco, 249 S.W.3d 544 (Tex. App.—Waco 2008), *rev'd on other grounds*, 298 S.W.3d 618 (Tex. 2009) (admissibility of a photograph is conditioned upon its identification by a witness as an accurate portrayal of the facts, and on verification by that witness or a person with knowledge that the photograph is a correct representation of such facts).

Kirwan v. City of Waco, 249 S.W.3d 544 (Tex. App.—Waco 2008), *rev'd on other grounds*, 298 S.W.3d 618 (Tex. 2009) (affidavit of city park's recreational director, to which five photographs of park were attached, served to properly authenticate photographs, in context of wrongful death lawsuit brought by mother, individually, and as representative of son's estate, against city, after son fell from cliff located in park and died, as affidavit stated that director had personal knowledge of facts therein, identified date on which photographs were taken, and stated that photographs accurately represented scenes depicted therein as he had observed them prior to son's death, and it was not required that director made photographs, observed their making, or knew when they were taken).

Dunklin v. State, 194 S.W.3d 14 (Tex. App.—Tyler 2006, no pet.) (photograph admitted as evidence should add something that is relevant, legitimate, and logical to the testimony that accompanies it and assists the jury in its decision; if there are elements of a photograph that are genuinely helpful to the jury in making its decision, the photograph is inadmissible only if the emotional and prejudicial aspects substantially outweigh the helpful aspects).

Kelly v. State, 22 S.W.3d 642 (Tex. App.—Waco 2000, pet. ref'd) (photographs properly authenticated).

Farrell v. State, 837 S.W.2d 395 (Tex. App.—Dallas 1992), *aff'd*, 864 S.W.2d 501 (Tex. Crim. App. 1993) (photograph admissible where testimony that photo taken at time of incident and person in photo identified as appellant).

Cheek v. Zalta, 693 S.W.2d 632 (Tex. App.—Houston [14th Dist.] 1985, no writ) (dispute of photograph's accuracy goes to weight and not admissibility).

b. *Physical Evidence*

Druery v. State, 225 S.W.3d 491 (Tex. Crim. App. 2007), *cert. denied*, 552 U.S. 1028 (2007) (absent evidence of tampering or other fraud, problems in the chain of custody of evidence do not affect the admissibility of the evidence; instead, such problems affect the weight that the factfinder should give the evidence, which may be brought out and argued by the parties).

Garza v. State, 213 S.W.3d 338 (Tex. Crim. App. 2007) (trial court did not abuse its discretion by requiring defendant to display to jury his tattoos that showed his affiliation with criminal street gang, in prosecution for capital murder and engaging in organized criminal activity; tattoos established "criminal street gang" element of engaging in organized criminal activity charge).

Lagrone v. State, 942 S.W.2d 602 (Tex. Crim. App. 1997), *cert. denied*, 522 U.S. 917 (1997) (without evidence of tampering, most questions concerning the care and custody of an item go to the weight attached, not the admissibility, of the evidence).

Maranda v. State, 253 S.W.3d 762 (Tex. App.—Amarillo 2007), *pet. stricken*, No. PD0010-08, 2008 WL 974786 (Tex. Crim. App. Apr. 9, 2008) (Rule 901 requires only a showing satisfying the trial court that the matter in question is what its proponent claims).

Maranda v. State, 253 S.W.3d 762 (Tex. App.—Amarillo 2007), *pet. stricken*, No. PD-0010-08, 2008 WL 974786 (Tex. Crim. App. Apr. 9, 2008) (physical evidence should be admitted if the trial court finds that a reasonable juror could find that the evidence was authenticated).

Maranda v. State, 253 S.W.3d 762 (Tex. App.—Amarillo 2007), *pet. stricken*, No. PD-0010-08, 2008 WL 974786 (Tex. Crim. App. Apr. 9, 2008) (proof of the beginning and end of the chain of custody will support admission of an object, barring any evidence of tampering or alteration).

Maranda v. State, 253 S.W.3d 762 (Tex. App.—Amarillo 2007), *pet. stricken*, No. PD-0010-08, 2008 WL 974786 (Tex. Crim. App. Apr. 9, 2008) (once the proponent of the physical evidence meets the threshold requirement of presenting testimony that the evidence is what the proponent says it is, the weight given to the evidence and related testimony is within the province of the trier-of-fact).

Maranda v. State, 253 S.W.3d 762 (Tex. App.—Amarillo 2007), *pet. stricken*, No. PD-0010-08, 2008 WL 974786 (Tex. Crim. App. Apr. 9, 2008) (knife that State offered at aggravated robbery trial was properly authenticated as the knife used for commission of the offense and thus was admissible, where direct testimony established that police officer returned to store with the knife another officer found in defendant's possession, store employee positively identified the knife as the weapon with which defendant threatened him, police officer testified on cross-examination that employee was the only person able to identify the knife when he returned the knife to the store, and officer maintained custody of the knife until later that day when he tagged it and booked it into the evidence room where it remained in an envelope until the morning of trial).

Ingram v. State, 213 S.W.3d 515 (Tex. App.—Texarkana 2007) (State provided proper chain of custody for contraband; testimony showed that defendant delivered drugs to officer, that officer placed them in plastic bag, took them to his office, and delivered them to individual, who secured them in evidence locker; later, another officer took drugs from locker to crime laboratory, where they were kept in secure vault, and supervising forensic scientist at State laboratory retrieved them from vault and delivered them to court in sealed envelope).

c. Tests and Experiments

Lincoln v. Clark Freight Lines, Inc., 285 S.W.3d 79 (Tex. App.—Houston [1st Dist.] 2009, no pet.) (when there is dissimilarity in the conditions existing at the time of an accident and the conditions existing at the time of an out-of-court experiment conducted for litigation concerning the accident, the admission of the experiment is within the trial court's discretion if the differences are minor or are explained to the jury).

Augillard v. Madura, 257 S.W.3d 494 (Tex. App.—Austin 2008, no pet.) (showing of the possibility of tampering or commingling of results in a DNA test is not sufficient to bar admission of the evidence and goes only to the weight of the evidence).

Whirlpool Corp. v. Camacho, 251 S.W.3d 88 (Tex. App.—Corpus Christi 2008), *rev'd on other grounds*, 298 S.W.3d 631 (Tex. 2009) (Consumer Product Safety Commission (CPSC) Report on Lint Fires was relevant and not unduly prejudicial and therefore was admissible in products liability design defect action against clothes dryer manufacturer arising from fatal home fire, despite claim that testing performed therein was highly technical and did not focus on real-world function; CPSC report contained diagrams of how air flowed through a dryer model similar to the incident dryer, how lint accumulated on various parts of the dryer, and how lint could start on fire while passing over the heating element).

Tex. Dep't of Pub. Safety v. Durand, 994 S.W.2d 352 (Tex. App.—Austin 1999, no writ) (testimony by technical supervisor provided sufficient foundation to establish reliability of breath alcohol testing machine).

Lopez v. State, 731 S.W.2d 682 (Tex. App.—Houston [1st Dist.] 1987), *rev'd on other grounds*, 779 S.W.2d 411 (Tex. Crim. App. 1989) (proper predicate for admitting blood test results).

d. Tape Recordings

Estrada v. State, 313 S.W.3d 274 (Tex. Crim. App. 2010) (recording from 911 call when murder victim's family discovered her body was admissible in guilt phase of capital murder trial, although it was seven minutes, family members could be heard screaming and crying uncontrollably about the victim's bloody body, and most of recording related to administration of first aid; recording provided framework within which particulars of State's evidence could be developed, even though evidence did not of itself establish any material fact not otherwise proven in the balance of the State's case).

Hines v. State, 383 S.W.3d 615 (Tex. App.—San Antonio 2012, pet. ref'd) (witness is not required to be the maker of the recording or have otherwise participated in the conversation in order for his testimony that the recording is what it is claimed to be to sufficiently authenticate it).

Source v. State, 736 S.W.2d 851 (Tex. App.—Houston [14th Dist.] 1987, pet. ref'd) (determination of proper predicate for tape recording within trial court's discretion).

e. *Videotapes and Motion Pictures*

Proo v. State, 587 S.W.3d 789, 817 (Tex. App.—San Antonio 2019, pet. ref'd) ("In evaluating whether the probative value of photographs or video is outweighed by the danger of unfair prejudice, the court considers several factors, including 'the number of exhibits offered, their gruesomeness, their detail, their size, whether they are black and white or color, whether they are close-up, and whether the body depicted is naked or clothed.'... The court must also consider the availability of other means of proof and the unique circumstances of the individual case.").

Hines v. State, 383 S.W.3d 615 (Tex. App.—San Antonio 2012, pet. ref'd) (witness is not required to be the maker of the recording or have otherwise participated in the conversation in order for his testimony that the recording is what it is claimed to be to sufficiently authenticate it).

Hines v. State, 383 S.W.3d 615 (Tex. App.—San Antonio 2012, pet. ref'd) (although portions of a video were choppy and the incident was not recorded in its entirety, a police officer identified those portions that did purport to represent the incident as being accurate depictions, and testified that the portions of the evening that the dashboard camera recorded depicted exactly what happened the night defendant was arrested for DWI, and this was sufficient for the trial court to find the videotape was what the witness and the State claimed it to be).

Thierry v. State, 288 S.W.3d 80 (Tex. App.—Houston [1st Dist.] 2009, pet. ref'd) (store's videotape of defendant was sufficiently authenticated to be admitted into evidence at trial for fraudulent use or possession of identifying information, even though loss prevention officer who testified to accuracy of tape was not present at time of incident; officer described intricacies of store's recording system and its computer systems, he detailed how he was able to link encoding on receipts to time and date that account was opened, to transactions in question, to cashier, to terminal, and finally to video camera that recorded transactions, and he testified that he had personally copied relevant recordings from multiplex to videotape).

Varkonyi v. State, 276 S.W.3d 27 (Tex. App.—El Paso 2008, pet. ref'd) (trial court did not abuse its discretion when it determined that email and video offered by State in obscenity trial were authenticated, under the reply letter doctrine; defendant showed the video to undercover officers in his home, one of the officers, in an email sent to defendant's email address, stated that he had been searching for the video "you showed us" and asked whether defendant would either tell him where he found it or send him the file, and in direct response to the email, defendant replied, "I attached one clip" of the video).

Ballard v. State, 23 S.W.3d 178 (Tex. App.—Waco 2000, no pet.) (duplicate of videotaped recording properly authenticated where accurate depiction and not altered).

Farrell v. State, 837 S.W.2d 395 (Tex. App.—Dallas 1992), *aff'd*, 864 S.W.2d 501 (Tex. Crim. App. 1993) (proper predicate for admissibility of videotape where true and accurate representation of what purported to be).

Ford Motor Co. v. Durrill, 714 S.W.2d 329 (Tex. App.—Corpus Christi 1986), *vacated by agreement*, 754 S.W.2d 646 (Tex. 1988) (videotape admitted although no proper foundation laid).

f. Writings

Tienda v. State, 358 S.W.3d 633 (Tex. Crim. App. 2012) (the internal content of Myspace postings, including photographs, comments, and music, was sufficient circumstantial evidence to establish a prima facie case such that a reasonable juror could have found that the content was created by the defendant, and was therefore admissible).

Druery v. State, 225 S.W.3d 491 (Tex. Crim. App. 2007), *cert. denied*, 552 U.S. 1028 (2007) (evidence was sufficient to support a finding that defendant wrote letter that contained incriminating statements, and thus letter, letter's envelope, and copy of letter and envelope were sufficiently authenticated at capital murder trial, even though return address on envelope, which contained letter and was mailed from a jail, identified an inmate other than defendant; defendant was in custody at jail from earliest possible date that letter could have been mailed, letter writer identified himself as defendant by using nickname by which defendant was known, and letter, *inter alia*, was written to defendant's cousin and discussed facts known to defendant about his case).

Walter v. State, 581 S.W.3d 957, 982 (Tex. App.—Eastland 2019, pet. ref'd) ("Authentication of text messages may 'be accomplished in myriad ways,' including through the testimony of a witness with knowledge.").

Maree v. Zuniga, 577 S.W.3d 595 (Tex. App.—Houston [14th Dist.] 2019, no pet.) ("Some documents are self-authenticating, such as certified copies of public records or public documents that are sealed and signed.").

Rogers v. RREF II CB Acquisitions, LLC, 533 S.W.3d 419, 432 (Tex. App.—Corpus Christi 2016, no pet.) ("verification of accuracy is [not] the sole means of admitting third-party documents under the business records exception.... A document authored or created by a third party may be admissible as business records of a different business if: (1) the document is incorporated and kept in the course of the testifying witness's business, (2) that business typically relies upon the accuracy of the document's content, and (3) the circumstances otherwise indicate the document's trustworthiness.").

Rogers v. RREF II CB Acquisitions, LLC, 533 S.W.3d 419, 432 (Tex. App.—Corpus Christi 2016, no pet.) ("if the proponent of the business record verifies the facts underlying the document using a reliable means, based on personal knowledge, this may resolve a third-party record problem").

Gunville v. Gonzales, 508 S.W.3d 547, 559 (Tex. App.—El Paso 2016, no pet.) ("The authentication requirement is satisfied by evidence sufficient to support a finding that the matter in question is what its proponent claims.... The predicate for admissibility under rule 901 may be proven by circumstantial evidence.... One example of such proof is that the item can be authenticated by its appearance, contents, substance, internal patterns, or other distinctive characteristics of the item, taken together with all the circumstances.").

Lissiak v. SW Loan OO, L.P., 499 S.W.3d 481, (Tex. App.—Tyler 2016, no pet.) ("A Rule 93(7) verified denial challenges the authenticity of the document and addresses the document's admissibility as an evidentiary issue.... Absent a verified denial, the document is received into evidence as fully proved.").

Haas v. State, 494 S.W.3d 819, 823 (Tex. App.—Houston [14th Dist.] 2016, no pet.) ("Public records or reports may be authenticated by evidence that a writing authorized by law to be recorded or filed and in fact recorded or filed in a public office, or a purported public record, report, statement, or data compilation, in any form, is from the public office where items of this nature are kept.... Thus, a public record may be authenticated by showing that the document is from a public office authorized to keep such a record.").

Sennett v. State, 406 S.W.3d 661 (Tex. App.—Eastland 2013, no pet.) (email may be properly authenticated if its appearance, contents, substance, or other distinctive characteristics, taken in conjunction with the circumstances, support a finding that the document is what the proponent claims it to be).

Manuel v. State, 357 S.W.3d 66 (Tex. App.—Tyler 2011, pet. ref'd) (under the "reply letter doctrine," a letter received in the due course of mail purportedly in answer to another letter is prima facie genuine and admissible without further proof of authenticity; this doctrine also applies to emails).

Manuel v. State, 357 S.W.3d 66 (Tex. App.—Tyler 2011, pet. ref'd) (email is properly authenticated if its appearance, contents, substance, or other distinctive characteristics, taken in conjunction with circumstances, support a finding that the document is what its proponent claims; text messages can be authenticated by applying the same factors).

Manuel v. State, 357 S.W.3d 66 (Tex. App.—Tyler 2011, pet. ref'd) (characteristics to consider in determining whether email evidence has been properly authenticated include: (1) consistency with the email address in another email sent by the alleged author; (2) the author's awareness, shown through the email, of the details of the alleged author's conduct; (3) the email's inclusion of similar requests that the alleged author had made by phone during the time period; and (4) the email's reference to the author by the alleged author's nickname).

Manuel v. State, 357 S.W.3d 66 (Tex. App.—Tyler 2011, pet. ref'd) (photographs and printouts of text messages received from a defendant on a victim's phone, as well as MySpace emails, included information that sufficiently identified the defendant, and thus were admissible in a stalking prosecution).

Flores v. State, 299 S.W.3d 843 (Tex. App.—El Paso 2009, pet. ref'd) (recording from 911 call when murder victim's family discovered her body was admissible in guilt phase of capital murder trial, although it was seven minutes, family members could be heard screaming and crying uncontrollably about the victim's bloody body, and most of recording related to administration of first aid; recording provided framework within which particulars of State's evidence could be developed, even though evidence did not of itself establish any material fact not otherwise proven in the balance of the State's case).

Varkonyi v. State, 276 S.W.3d 27 (Tex. App.—El Paso 2008, pet. ref'd) (trial court did not abuse its discretion when it determined that email and video offered by State in obscenity trial were authenticated, under the reply letter doctrine; defendant showed the video to undercover officers in his home, one of the officers, in an email sent to defendant's email address, stated that he had been searching for the video "you showed us" and asked whether defendant would either tell him where he found it or send him the file, and in direct response to the email, defendant replied, "I attached one clip" of the video).

Reese v. State, 273 S.W.3d 344 (Tex. App.—Texarkana 2008, no pet.) (exhibit containing defendant's prior driving while intoxicated (DWI) judgment was admissible as a self-authenticating document in prosecution for felony DWI, where exhibit bore a seal purporting to be that of county district clerk).

Pardue v. State, 252 S.W.3d 690 (Tex. App.—Texarkana 2008, no pet.) (admission of advisory letter issued by county district attorney's office to defendant who operated a gaming establishment, advising defendant that cash payouts for gambling activities constituted a criminal offense, did not violate due process in prosecution for engaging in organized criminal activities, even though letter contained a statement of law made by someone other than the trial court; letter was relevant and admissible to prove defendant's intent, State implied on only two occasions that letter was a correct statement of law, State did not expressly represent the letter as a correct statement of the law until after trial court had instructed jury on the applicable law, and letter's interpretation of the law was substantially correct).

Rios v. State, 230 S.W.3d 252 (Tex. App.—Waco 2007, pet. ref'd) (post-offense letters written by defendant to alleged victim were admissible in prosecution for aggravated kidnapping; defendant did not merely refer to letters, but raised subject of letters and inquired into specific portions of content; in doing so, he entitled State to introduce those portions of letters addressing same subject, namely relationship between defendant and victim following offense; taken out of context, letters could have misled jury and left false impression as to subsequent relationship between parties, magnitude of allegations, and effect of offense on victim).

Avila v. State, 252 S.W.3d 632 (Tex. App.—Tyler 2008, no pet.) (evidence consisting of summary of the more than 2,180 G-28 forms submitted by or on behalf of respondents' clients for purpose of seeking immigration benefits was admissible under business records exception to hearsay rule, in action brought by State under Deceptive Trade Practices-Consumer Protection Act to enjoin respondents from operating immigration services business, as government agent, who acted as custodian of records, laid the necessary predicate by describing the purpose of the documents and the manner in which they were processed).

Johnson v. State, 208 S.W.3d 478 (Tex. App.—Austin 2006, pet. ref'd) (evidence was sufficient to support finding that capital murder defendant wrote anonymous letter found on computer and addressed to newspaper reporter involved in the coverage of shooting of her husband, such that letter was properly authenticated and admissible at murder trial; letter contained numerous intimate details of defendant's life, including her previous marriages, the suicide of her second husband, meeting her accomplice while both were receiving psychiatric treatment, and her upcoming trip to Europe).

g. *Conditional Admissibility*

Texas Rule of Evidence 104(b) states:

> When the relevancy of evidence depends upon the fulfillment of a condition of fact, the court shall admit it upon, or subject to the introduction of evidence sufficient to support a finding of the fulfillment of the condition.

Harrell v. State, 884 S.W.2d 154 (Tex. Crim. App. 1994) (evidence that defendant selling television raised question of conditional relevance).

Druery v. State, 225 S.W.3d 491 (Tex. Crim. App. 2007), *cert. denied*, 552 U.S. 1028 (2007) (whether a conditional fact has been proven to show the relevancy of evidence is a question for a jury, and a trial judge's role is limited to determining whether there is sufficient evidence to support such a finding; in other words, the trial judge should admit evidence that is relevant based upon a conditional fact only if there is sufficient evidence to support a jury finding that the conditional fact is true).

Perez v. State, 21 S.W.3d 628 (Tex. App.—Houston [14th Dist.] 2000, no pet.) ("Evidence should not be excluded merely because its relevance may depend upon the production of additional evidence at a later point in the trial or because its probative strength is alone insufficient to prove a significant fact." (Citations omitted.). *See also Rosales v. State*, 867 S.W.2d 70 (Tex. App.—El Paso 1993, no pet.).

Owens-Corning Fiberglas v. Keeton, 922 S.W.2d 658 (Tex. App.—Austin 1996, writ denied) (court may admit evidence subject to fulfillment of condition).

Howard v. State, 896 S.W.2d 401 (Tex. App.—Amarillo 1995, pet. ref'd) (conditional relevance of prior conviction).

Wal-Mart Stores, Inc. v. Cordova, 856 S.W.2d 768 (Tex. App.—El Paso 1993, pet. denied) (if evidence prejudicial, should not come in under conditional relevance or any other theory).

B. Motion to Exclude Writings, Generally

1. Suggested Motion Text

(*Name of Moving Party*) hereby moves this Court for an order excluding any and all evidence, references to evidence, testimony, or argument relating to (*Describe Nature of Writing or Other Document to Be Excluded*). The motion is based upon the ground that the document (*Describe Basis for Exclusion, e.g., Lacks Proper Authentication, is Inadmissible Hearsay, etc.*).

2. Motion Summary

This motion generally challenges the introduction of writings where the evidence is deficient for one of several commonly encountered reasons, including authenticity, hearsay, or insufficient secondary evidence. The motion is based upon the following statutory authority: Texas Rule of Evidence 901 [authenticity]; Texas Rule of Evidence 802 [hearsay]; Texas Rules of Evidence 1002 to 1004 [secondary evidence].

3. Supporting Authorities—"Writing" Defined

Texas Rule of Evidence 1001 defines a "writing" as:

> "Writings" consist of letters, words, or numbers or their equivalent, set down by handwriting, typewriting, printing, photostatting, photographing, magnetic impulse, mechanical or electronic recording, or other form of data compilation

a. Exclusion, Generally

Taylor v. State, 93 S.W.3d 487 (Tex. App.—Texarkana 2002, pet. ref'd) (evidence of pornographic story on defendant's computer hard drive prejudicial and inflammatory and should not have been admitted).

Strauss v. Cont'l Airlines, Inc., 67 S.W.3d 428 (Tex. App.—Houston [14th Dist.] 2002, no pet.) (trial court did not abuse discretion by excluding party's psychiatric records where irrelevant and unduly prejudicial).

Reynolds v. Warthan, 896 S.W.2d 823 (Tex. App.—Tyler 1995, no writ) (exclusion of incident reports where marginal relevance outweighed by danger of confusing and misleading jury).

Montelongo v. Goodall, 788 S.W.2d 717 (Tex. App.—Austin 1990, no pet.) (evidence of safety standards not shown to apply to condition at issue irrelevant and properly excluded).

Soc'y of Mary's Stars, Inc. v. State, 748 S.W.2d 320 (Tex. App.—Fort Worth 1988, writ denied) (admission of warranty deed in condemnation proceeding properly excluded by trial court as unduly prejudicial where deed executed two months after petition for condemnation filed and would allow party to manufacture higher purchase price).

b. Unauthenticated Writings

Texas Rule of Evidence 901(a) states:

> The requirement of authentication or identification as a condition precedent to admissibility is satisfied by evidence sufficient to support a finding that the matter in question is what its proponent claims.

Tienda v. State, 358 S.W.3d 633 (Tex. Crim. App. 2012) (evidence has no relevance if it is not authentically what its proponent claims it to be).

Ryder v. State, 581 S.W.3d 439, 454 (Tex. App.—Houston [14th Dist.] 2019, no pet.) ("To properly authenticate an item of evidence, 'the proponent must produce evidence sufficient to support a finding that the item is what the proponent claims it is.'").

Ryder v. State, 581 S.W.3d 439, 454 (Tex. App.—Houston [14th Dist.] 2019, no pet.) ("Evidence is properly authenticated if the proponent supplies 'facts that are sufficient to support a reasonable jury determination that the evidence he had proffered is authentic.'").

Ryder v. State, 581 S.W.3d 439, 454 (Tex. App.—Houston [14th Dist.] 2019, no pet.) ("The proponent of the evidence does not need 'to rule out all possibilities inconsistent with authenticity, or prove beyond any doubt that the evidence is what it purports to be.'").

Rogers v. RREF II CB Acquisitions, LLC, 533 S.W.3d 419, 432 (Tex. App.—Corpus Christi 2016, no pet.) ("special concerns may arise if the subject of the business records affidavit is a document which originated from a third-party ... documents received from another entity are not admissible under rule 803(6), if the witness is not qualified to testify about the entity's record keeping").

Gunville v. Gonzales, 508 S.W.3d 547, 559 (Tex. App.—El Paso 2016, no pet.) ("Simply attaching a document to a pleading neither makes the document admissible as evidence, dispenses with proper foundational evidentiary requirements, or relieves a litigant of complying with other admissibility requirements.").

Gunville v. Gonzales, 508 S.W.3d 547, 559 (Tex. App.—El Paso 2016, no pet.) ("A document may only be considered authentic if a sponsoring witness vouches for its authenticity or if the document otherwise meets the requirements of authentication as set out in the rules of evidence.").

Lissiak v. SW Loan OO, L.P., 499 S.W.3d 481, (Tex. App.—Tyler 2016, no pet.) ("A Rule 93(7) verified denial challenges the authenticity of the document and addresses the document's admissibility as an evidentiary issue.").

Soeffe v. Jones, 270 S.W.3d 617 (Tex. App.—San Antonio 2008, no pet.) (general rule is that trial court may not take judicial notice of testimony from a previous proceeding unless the testimony is properly authenticated and admitted into evidence).

i. Public Records or Reports

Rule 901(b)(7) provides for the authentication of public records or reports:

> Evidence that a writing authorized by law to be recorded or filed and in fact recorded or filed in a public office, or a purported public record, statement, or data compilation, in any form, is from the public office where times of this nature are kept.

Mega Child Care, Inc. v. Tex. Dep't of Protective & Regulatory Servs., 29 S.W.3d 303 (Tex. App.—Houston [14th Dist.] 2000, no pet.) (investigator could not authenticate copy of administrative judge's opinion where investigator not author of opinion and did not purport to have personal knowledge of opinion).

Maree v. Zuniga, 577 S.W.3d 595 (Tex. App.—Houston [14th Dist.] 2019, no pet.) (copies of documents from court clerk's records were not authenticated; the offering party "submitted no affidavit, testimony, or other evidence to authenticate any of these documents.... [They were] not sealed and signed in accordance with Texas Rule of Evidence 902.... [They bore] watermarks stating each document is an "Unofficial Copy.").

Harris Co. v. Allwaste Tank Cleaning, Inc., 808 S.W.2d 149 (Tex. App.—Houston [1st Dist.] 1992, writ dism'd w.o.j.) (must show public records were regularly made and preserved).

ii. Documents or Data Collections

Rule 901(b)(8) provides for the authentication of ancient documents or data compilations:

> Evidence that a document or data compilation, in any form, (A) is in such condition as to create no suspicion concerning its authenticity,

(B) was in a place where it, if authentic, would likely be, and (C) has been in existence twenty years or more at the time it is offered.

Aguillera v. John G. and Marie Stella Kenedy Memorial Foundation, 162 S.W.3d 689 (Tex. App.—Corpus Christi 2005, pet. denied) (recitals in an ancient document are admissible as evidence of the facts recited, provided that the instrument: (1) is over twenty years old, (2) comes from proper custody, and (3) is not suspicious in appearance).

See Texas Rule of Evidence 901, et seq., for a number of pre-approved methods for authenticating writings.

iii. Exclusion of Unauthenticated Writings

Gunville v. Gonzales, 508 S.W.3d 547, 559 (Tex. App.—El Paso 2016, no pet.) ("Simply attaching a document to a pleading neither makes the document admissible as evidence, dispenses with proper foundational evidentiary requirements, or relieves a litigant of complying with other admissibility requirements.").

Gunville v. Gonzales, 508 S.W.3d 547, 559 (Tex. App.—El Paso 2016, no pet.) ("A document may only be considered authentic if a sponsoring witness vouches for its authenticity or if the document otherwise meets the requirements of authentication as set out in the rules of evidence.").

Black v. State, 358 S.W.3d 823 (Tex. App.—Fort Worth 2012, pet. ref'd) (text messages purporting to be expressions of a desire to engage in a drug transaction inadmissible hearsay in a drug case).

Miller v. State, 208 S.W.3d 554 (Tex. App.—Austin 2006, pet. ref'd) (cell phone bill inadmissible hearsay in capital murder prosecution; victim's daughter's testimony identifying two of 166 phone calls bill documented insufficient to establish accuracy of process by which bill was generated).

Reynolds v. Warthan, 896 S.W.2d 823 (Tex. App.—Tyler 1995, no writ) (unauthenticated package inserts excluded where no showing inserts were authoritative or reliable).

Durkay v. Madco Oil Co., 862 S.W.2d 14 (Tex. App.—Corpus Christi 1993, writ denied) (failure to authenticate document renders it inadmissible; report estimating value of oil and gas lease not properly authenticated where no testimony as to completeness, accuracy, and basis of calculation).

c. *Irrelevant Evidence*

Gentry v. State, 259 S.W.3d 272 (Tex. App.—Waco 2008, pet. ref'd) (medical records, allegedly indicating victim and another couple had sexually transmitted disease "herpes," were not sufficiently relevant to establish motive for third party to murder victim, and thus, were inadmissible in murder prosecution; although defendant claimed that medical records supported allegation of marital infidelity as possible motive for third party to murder victim, her husband, evidence standing alone was highly speculative).

d. Inadmissible Hearsay

Texas Rule of Evidence 802 states:

> Hearsay is not admissible except as provided by statute or these rules or by other rules prescribed pursuant to statutory authority. Inadmissible hearsay admitted without objection shall not be denied probative value merely because it is hearsay.

Texas Rule of Evidence 801(a) defines what constitutes a statement:

> A "statement" is (1) an oral or written verbal expression or (2) non-verbal conduct of a person, if it is intended by the person as a substitute for verbal expression.

Benson v. Chalk, 536 S.W.3d 886, 894 (Tex. App.—Houston [1st Dist.] 2017, pet. denied) ("Hearsay is defined as a statement, other than one made by the declarant while testifying at the trial or hearing, offered in evidence to prove the truth of the matter asserted.... Hearsay is not admissible except as provided by the rules of evidence or some other statute.... The proponent of hearsay has the burden of showing that the testimony fits within an exception to the general rule prohibiting the admission of hearsay evidence.").

Benson v. Chalk, 536 S.W.3d 886, 895 (Tex. App.—Houston [1st Dist.] 2017, pet. denied) ("Hearsay within hearsay is not admissible unless each part of the combined statements conforms with an exception to the general rule excluding hearsay.").

Benson v. Chalk, 536 S.W.3d 886, 895 (Tex. App.—Houston [1st Dist.] 2017, pet. denied) ("When a police report contains a hearsay statement, the statement must fall under some hearsay exception of its own because neither the public records and reports exception, nor the records of regularly conducted activities exception, protects hearsay within hearsay.").

Rogers v. RREF II CB Acquisitions, LLC, 533 S.W.3d 419, 432 (Tex. App.—Corpus Christi 2016, no pet.) ("special concerns may arise if the subject of the business records affidavit is a document which originated from a third-party ... documents received from another entity are not admissible under rule 803(6), if the witness is not qualified to testify about the entity's record keeping").

Black v. State, 358 S.W.3d 823 (Tex. App.—Fort Worth 2012, pet. ref'd) (text messages purporting to be expressions of a desire to engage in a drug transaction inadmissible hearsay in a drug case).

Kacz v. State, 287 S.W.3d 497 (Tex. App.—Houston [14th Dist.] 2009, no pet.) (while a declarant's admissions may also implicate someone else's interest, such as a third party or co-actor, unless the statement against that other person's interest is also sufficiently against declarant's own interest, it cannot be considered reliable under hearsay exception for statements against penal interest; a statement that incriminates another but not the declarant himself does not merit an exception to the hearsay rule).

Teague v. State, 268 S.W.3d 664 (Tex. App.—Fort Worth 2008, pet. ref'd) (sheriff's hearsay statement, that he guessed he had been lied to, made after listening to a copy of 911 tape at issue in a dispute between a police officer and defendant's coworker in dispatch office, was not admissible as a present sense impression, as evidence of then existing mental or emotional state, or as an excited utterance in aggravated perjury prosecution arising from defendant's grand jury testimony that she did not make or assist in making edited version of tape).

Smith v. State, 236 S.W.3d 282 (Tex. App.—Houston [1st Dist.] 2007, pet. ref'd) (law enforcement officer's indirect testimony that a second officer had agreed with his conclusion that a latent print found at scene belonged to defendant was inadmissible hearsay at trial for burglary of a habitation).

Trevino v. State, 218 S.W.3d 234 (Tex. App.—Houston [14th Dist.] 2007, no pet.) (admission against a codefendant declarant's penal interest may be admissible against defendant so long as it is sufficiently against declarant's interest to be reliable and is sufficiently corroborated by other evidence).

Clark v. State, 947 S.W.2d 650 (Tex. App.—Fort Worth 1997, pet. ref'd) (testimony excluded where not against codefendant's interest and did not satisfy hearsay exception for statements against interest).

Kratz v. Exxon Corp., 890 S.W.2d 899 (Tex. App.—El Paso 1994, no writ) (statements not within public records exception to the hearsay rule properly excluded).

Delhi Gas Pipeline Co. v. Newman, 512 S.W.2d 741 (Tex. Civ. App.—Tyler 1974, no writ) (testimony about what was read in newspapers inadmissible hearsay).

i. Examples of Inadmissible Written Hearsay

Black v. State, 358 S.W.3d 823, 832 (Tex. App.—Fort Worth 2012, pet. ref'd) (text messages from a cell phone not admissible as a statement against penal interest because there was no showing that the defendant "wrote or ratified any of the messages ... and no showing that the messages were written while the cell phone was in [defendant's] possession").

In re Estate of Vackar, 345 S.W.3d 588, 594 (Tex. App.—San Antonio 2011, no pet.) (medical record listing of medications inadmissible because treating physician did not lay the predicate for the introduction of the list as a business record).

Kennedy v. State, 193 S.W.3d 645 (Tex. App.—Fort Worth 2006, pet. ref'd) (documents that are inadmissible under the exception to the hearsay rule for public records, which excludes from its scope in criminal cases "matters observed by police officers and other law enforcement personnel," may not be admitted under the hearsay exception for business records).

Lacy v. Lacy, 922 S.W.2d 195 (Tex. App.—Tyler 1995, writ denied) (investigator's report properly excluded as hearsay).

Tex. Dep't of Pub. Safety v. Nesmith, 559 S.W.2d 443 (Tex. Civ. App.—Corpus Christi, 1977, no writ) (writing must fall within some exception to hearsay rule to be admissible, even if authentic).

Simms v. Sw. Tex. Methodist Hosp., 535 S.W.2d 192 (Tex. Civ. App.—San Antonio 1976, writ ref'd n.r.e.) (statements contained in treatises, books, etc. inadmissible hearsay; excerpts from writings excluded as hearsay).

Sherril v. Estate of Plumley, 514 S.W.2d 286 (Tex. Civ. App.—Houston [1st Dist.] 1974, writ ref'd n.r.e.) (newspaper obituary inadmissible hearsay).

e. Inadmissible Secondary Evidence

Texas Rule of Evidence 1002 states:

> To prove the content of a writing, recording, or photograph, the original writing, recording or photograph is required except as otherwise provided in these rules or by law.

Danby v. State, 530 S.W.3d 213, 229 (Tex. App.—Tyler 2017, pet. ref'd) ("Under the best evidence rule, an original writing, recording, or photograph is required to prove its content unless the rules or another law provides otherwise.").

Ellis v. State, 517 S.W.3d 922, 930 (Tex. App.—Fort Worth 2017, no pet.) ("For electronically stored information, rule of evidence 1001(d) defines an 'original' as any print-out—or other output readable by sight—if it accurately reflects the information.... When a "print-out" or "other output" is not obtainable, rule of evidence 1004(b) allows the content of the original to be proven through "other evidence" of its content.").

Block v. Tarrant Wholesale Drug. Co., 138 S.W.2d 874 (Tex. Civ. App.—Galveston 1940, no writ) (secondary evidence of contents of books of account inadmissible).

Barnes v. State, 95 S.W.2d 112 (Tex. Crim. App. 1936, no writ) (admission of secondary evidence erroneous where proper predicate not laid).

S. Sur. Co. v. Eoff, 22 S.W.2d 964 (Tex. Civ. App.—Beaumont 1929, no writ.) (insufficient predicate for admission of secondary evidence).

> *Note that Rule 1001 and related Rules 1002 (original writing), 1003 (admissibility of duplicates) and 1004 (admissibility of other evidence of contents), replaced the common law Best Evidence Rule. For expanded discussion and instructive cases interpreting the former law, see Comments, Texas Rules of Evidence 1001 et seq. (Vernon 1999); see also* Texas Rules of Evidence Handbook, *30 Houston L. Rev. 1096 (1993).*

4. Opposing Authorities, Generally

Black v. State, 358 S.W.3d 823 (Tex. App.—Fort Worth 2012, pet. ref'd) (screensaver picture of what appeared to be methamphetamine, present on cell phone found in defendant's possession, was not hearsay evidence because it was a statement).

Johnson v. State, 425 S.W.3d 344 (Tex. App.—Houston [1st Dist.] 2011, pet. ref'd) (affidavit of nonprosecution was not inadmissible hearsay because it was offered to show that the defendant attempted to induce a witness not to testify; attempt to tamper with a witness is evidence of "consciousness of guilt").

Stafford v. State, 248 S.W.3d 400 (Tex. App.—Beaumont 2008, pet. ref'd) (divorce forms that were recovered from the back-seat area of a vehicle operated primarily by defendant were not hearsay in prosecution for murdering wife; they were offered as circumstantial evidence of the deteriorated condition of the marriage at the time of the murder).

Stafford v. State, 248 S.W.3d 400 (Tex. App.—Beaumont 2008, pet. ref'd) (will form that was found on a scanner during the dismantling of a computer located in defendant's personal computer room was not hearsay in prosecution for murdering wife; it was not offered to prove truth of matters asserted).

Goldberg v. State, 95 S.W.3d 345 (Tex. App.—Houston [1st Dist.] 2002, pet ref'd), *cert. denied*, 540 U.S. 1190 (2004) (evidence of notebook seized three years before offense containing drawings and discussing the killing of women relevant and not unfairly prejudicial).

a. Authentication

Tienda v. State, 358 S.W.3d 633 (Tex. Crim. App. 2012) (evidence may be authenticated in a number of ways, including by direct testimony from a witness with personal knowledge, by comparison with other authenticated evidence, or by circumstantial evidence).

Druery v. State, 225 S.W.3d 491 (Tex. Crim. App. 2007), *cert. denied*, 552 U.S. 1028 (2007) (letter, letter's envelope, and copy of letter and envelope were sufficiently authenticated at capital murder trial).

Angleton v. State, 971 S.W.2d 65 (Tex. Crim. App. 1998) (testimony of one person sufficient to authenticate unique objects or documents).

Alvarado v. State, 912 S.W.2d 199 (Tex. Crim. App. 1995) (testimony of serial number on dollar bill found at crime scene sufficient to authenticate it).

Walter v. State, 581 S.W.3d 957, 982 (Tex. App.—Eastland 2019, pet. ref'd) ("To properly authenticate a piece of evidence, the proponent must produce evidence sufficient to support a finding that the item is what the proponent claims it is.").

Walter v. State, 581 S.W.3d 957, 982 (Tex. App.—Eastland 2019, pet. ref'd) ("Authentication of text messages may be accomplished in myriad ways, including rough the testimony of a witness with knowledge.").

Ryder v. State, 581 S.W.3d 439, 454 (Tex. App.—Houston [14th Dist.] 2019, no pet.) ("To properly authenticate an item of evidence, 'the proponent must produce evidence sufficient to support a finding that the item is what the proponent claims it is.'").

Ryder v. State, 581 S.W.3d 439, 454 (Tex. App.—Houston [14th Dist.] 2019, no pet.) ("Evidence is properly authenticated if the proponent supplies 'facts that are sufficient to support a reasonable jury determination that the evidence he had proffered is authentic.'").

Ryder v. State, 581 S.W.3d 439, 454 (Tex. App.—Houston [14th Dist.] 2019, no pet.) ("The proponent of the evidence does not need 'to rule out all possibilities inconsistent with authenticity, or prove beyond any doubt that the evidence is what it purports to be.'").

Maree v. Zuniga, 577 S.W.3d 595 (Tex. App.—Houston [14th Dist.] 2019, no pet.) ("Some documents are self-authenticating, such as certified copies of public records or public documents that are sealed and signed.").

Haas v. State, 494 S.W.3d 819, 823 (Tex. App.—Houston [14th Dist.] 2016, no pet.) ("Public records or reports may be authenticated by evidence that a writing authorized by law to be recorded or filed and in fact recorded or filed in a public office, or a purported public record, report, statement, or data compilation, in any form, is from the public office where items of this nature are kept.... Thus, a public record may be authenticated by showing that the document is from a public office authorized to keep such a record.").

Dominguez v. State, 441 S.W.3d 652 (Tex. App.—Houston [1st Dist.] 2014, no pet.) (the requirement of authentication or identification as a condition precedent to admissibility is satisfied by evidence sufficient to support a finding that the matter in question is what its proponent claims; this rule does not require the State to prove anything).

Dominguez v. State, 441 S.W.3d 652 (Tex. App.—Houston [1st Dist.] 2014, no pet.) (evidence may be authenticated or identified by different methods, including testimony from a witness with knowledge that an item is what it is claimed to be).

Williams Farms Produce Sales, Inc. v. R & G Produce Co., 443 S.W.3d 250 (Tex. App.—Corpus Christi 2014, no pet.) (printouts from government websites were self-authenticating under Texas Rule of Evidence 902(5)).

Concept Gen. Contracting, Inc. v. Asbestos Maint. Servs., Inc., 346 S.W.3d 172 (Tex. App.—Amarillo 2011, pet. denied) (evidence is authenticated by proof that the challenged evidence is what its proponent claims it to be).

F-Star Socorro, L.P. v. City of El Paso, 281 S.W.3d 103 (Tex. App.—El Paso 2008, no pet.) (delinquent tax records may be admitted as evidence even if they are prepared solely for the purpose of litigation, as long as they are properly authenticated).

F-Star Socorro, L.P. v. City of El Paso, 281 S.W.3d 103 (Tex. App.—El Paso 2008, no pet.) (certified tax statement supplied by city in delinquent tax collection action was self-authenticating document; even though seal was not visible on photocopies, original document submitted by city carried seal which was visible and tactile, and first page of statement bore signature of the tax assessor-collector and certification that assessor-collector who signed statement was custodian of the city's tax records).

Reese v. State, 273 S.W.3d 344 (Tex. App.—Texarkana 2008, no pet.) (exhibit containing defendant's prior driving while intoxicated (DWI) judgment was admissible as a self-authenticating document in prosecution for felony DWI, where exhibit bore a seal purporting to be that of county district clerk).

McCoy v. Knobler, 260 S.W.3d 179 (Tex. App.—Dallas 2008, no pet.) (authentication of foreign judgment in compliance with evidence rule governing self-authenticating documents satisfied authentication requirements of the full faith and credit clause).

In re M.M.S., 256 S.W.3d 470 (Tex. App.—Dallas 2008, no pet.) (mother sufficiently authenticated documents for trial court to admit them into evidence in proceeding to enforce child support obligations of divorce decree; mother testified that the documents were true and correct copies of the medical bills, receipts, and explanations of benefits she received, kept the documents in the ordinary course of obtaining medical treatment for the children, and had sent copies of all the documents being offered into evidence to father within ten days of receiving them, as required by the divorce decree).

Stafford v. State, 248 S.W.3d 400 (Tex. App.—Beaumont 2008, pet. ref'd) (testimony of victim's daughter that handwriting on three letters was that of her mother authenticated the letters in murder prosecution of victim's husband).

Johnson v. State, 208 S.W.3d 478 (Tex. App.—Austin 2006, pet. ref'd) (evidence sufficient to support finding that capital murder defendant wrote anonymous letter found on computer and addressed to newspaper reporter involved in the coverage of shooting of her husband, such that letter was properly authenticated and admissible at murder trial; letter contained numerous intimate details of defendant's life, including her previous marriages, the suicide of her second husband, meeting her accomplice while both were receiving psychiatric treatment, and her upcoming trip to Europe).

Carone v. Retamco Operating, Inc., 138 S.W.3d 1 (Tex. App.—San Antonio 2004, pet. denied) (letters sufficiently authenticated by party's admission that he signed them).

McMillen Feed, Inc. v. Harlow, 405 S.W.2d 123 (Tex. Civ. App.—Austin 1966, writ ref'd n.r.e.) (sufficient predicate laid for admission of charts).

Barrerra v. Duval County Ranch Co., 135 S.W.2d 518 (Tex. Civ. App.—San Antonio 1939, writ ref'd) (conflicting evidence on genuineness goes to weight, not admissibility).

b. Hearsay Exceptions and Nonhearsay, Generally

Benson v. Chalk, 536 S.W.3d 886, 895 (Tex. App.—Houston [1st Dist.] 2017, pet. denied) ("A present sense impression is 'a statement describing or explaining an event or condition made while the declarant was perceiving the event or condition, or immediately thereafter.'... Present sense impressions possess the following safeguards which make them likely to be true and thus admissible: (1) the report at the moment of the thing then heard, seen, etc. is safe from any error from defect of memory of the declarant; (2) there is little or no time for calculated misstatement; and (3) the statement will usually be made to another—the witness who reports it—who would have equal opportunity to observe and check a misstatement.").

Benson v. Chalk, 536 S.W.3d 886, 895 (Tex. App.—Houston [1st Dist.] 2017, pet. denied) ("prior inconsistent statements made under the penalty of perjury at a trial, hearing, or other proceeding, or in a deposition, are considered non-hearsay and may be used").

Wilkinson v. State, 523 S.W.3d 818, 829 (Tex. App.—Houston [14th Dist.] 2017, pet. ref'd) ("A prior consistent statement is not considered hearsay when the statement is offered to rebut an express or implied charge against the declarant of recent fabrication or improper influence or motive and the declarant made the statement before the alleged improper influence or motive arose.").

Wilkinson v. State, 523 S.W.3d 818, 829 (Tex. App.—Houston [14th Dist.] 2017, pet. ref'd) ("An excited utterance is defined as a statement relating to a startling event or condition, made while the declarant was under the stress of excitement that it caused.... The reasoning behind the excited utterance exception is psychological: when a person is in the instant grip of violent emotion, excitement, or pain, that person ordinarily loses capacity for the reflection necessary for fabrication, and the truth will come out.").

Wilkinson v. State, 523 S.W.3d 818, 829 (Tex. App.—Houston [14th Dist.] 2017, pet. ref'd) ("In determining whether a hearsay statement is admissible as an excited utterance, the court may consider as factors the time elapsed and whether the statement was in response to a question.... The focus, however, must remain on whether the declarant was still dominated by the emotions, excitement, fear, or pain of the event at the time of the statement.").

Nat'l Health Res. Corp. v. TBF Fin., LLC, 429 S.W.3d 125 (Tex. App.—Dallas 2014, no pet.) (a document created by one business may become a record of a second business if the second business determines the accuracy of the information generated by the first business).

Puentes v. Fannie Mae, 350 S.W.3d 732 (Tex. App.—El Paso 2011, pet. dism'd) (to be admissible under the business records hearsay exception, the proponent of the evidence must demonstrate: (1) the records were made and kept in the course of a regularly conducted business activity, (2) it was the regular practice of the business activity to create such records, (3) the records were created at or near the time of the event recorded, and (4) the records were created by a person with knowledge who was acting in the regular course of business).

Puentes v. Fannie Mae, 350 S.W.3d 732 (Tex. App.—El Paso 2011, pet. dism'd) (admissibility under business records hearsay exception may be provided in the form of an affidavit by the custodian of records or other qualified witness who has personal knowledge of the information contained therein).

Concept Gen. Contracting, Inc. v. Asbestos Maint. Servs., Inc., 346 S.W.3d 172 (Tex. App.—Amarillo 2011, pet. denied) (for a witness to establish the business record exception to hearsay rule, the witness need not have been the record's creator or have any personal knowledge of the contents of the record; rather, the witness need only have personal knowledge of the manner in which the records were prepared).

Simien v. Unifund CCR Partners, 321 S.W.3d 235 (Tex. App.—Houston [1st Dist.] 2010, no pet.) (pursuant to hearsay exception for business records, a document authored or created by a third party may be admissible as a business record of a different business if: (1) the document is incorporated and kept in the course of the testifying witness's business; (2) that business typically relies upon the accuracy of the contents of the document; and (3) the circumstances otherwise indicate the trustworthiness of the document).

Simien v. Unifund CCR Partners, 321 S.W.3d 235 (Tex. App.—Houston [1st Dist.] 2010, no pet.) (although a business's confirmation of the accuracy of another business's records is one way to support admissibility under hearsay rule, another way is to show that the business reasonably relied on the accuracy of the other business's records).

Riddle v. Unifund CCR Partners, 298 S.W.3d 780 (Tex. App.—El Paso 2009, no pet.) (business records that have been created by one entity, but that have become another entity's primary record of the underlying transaction, may be admissible pursuant to business records exception to the hearsay rule).

Clark v. State, 282 S.W.3d 924 (Tex. App.—Beaumont 2009, no pet.) ("excited utterance" exception to the rule excluding hearsay is a statement relating to a startling event or condition made while the declarant was under the stress of excitement caused by the event or condition).

Clark v. State, 282 S.W.3d 924 (Tex. App.—Beaumont 2009, no pet.) (in determining whether a hearsay statement is admissible as an excited utterance, the court may consider the length of time between the occurrence and the statement, the declarant's demeanor, whether the statement is made in response to a question, and whether the statement is self-serving; the critical determination is whether the declarant was still dominated by the emotions, excitement, fear, or pain of the event or condition at the time of the statement).

Ltd. Logistics Servs., Inc. v. Villegas, 268 S.W.3d 141 (Tex. App.—Corpus Christi 2008, no pet.) (signed instrument, such as a contract, that creates legal rights is not hearsay because it has legal effect independent of the truth of any statement contained in it).

Morris v. State, 214 S.W.3d 159 (Tex. App.—Beaumont 2007), *aff'd*, 301 S.W.3d 281 (Tex. Crim. App. 2009) (court acted within its discretion at second trial for intoxication manslaughter in concluding that a witness's testimony that he was told by a person on defendant's watercraft that the person was operating it at time of fatal collision was not sufficiently trustworthy to be admissible under exception to hearsay rule for statements against penal interest).

Vinson v. State, 221 S.W.3d 256 (Tex. App.—Houston [1st Dist.] 2006), *aff'd in part, rev'd on other grounds in part*, 252 S.W.3d 336 (Tex. Crim. App. 2008) (victim's statements to deputy when he investigated 911 calls were admissible in assault trial under exception to hearsay rule for excited utterances).

Bee v. State, 974 S.W.2d 184 (Tex. App.—San Antonio 1998, no pet.) (witness's testimony at prior trial admissible under former testimony exception to hearsay rule).

White v. State, 982 S.W.2d 642 (Tex. App.—Texarkana 1998, pet. ref'd) (accomplice's out-of-court statements admissible under hearsay exception for statements against interest).

McCrory v. State, 627 S.W.2d 762 (Tex. App.—Houston [1st Dist.] 1981, no writ) (hearsay evidence admissible in theft cases as proof of market value).

i. Examples of Admissible Written Hearsay

Tienda v. State, 358 S.W.3d 633 (Tex. Crim. App. 2012) (the internal content of MySpace postings, including photographs, comments, and music, was sufficient circumstantial evidence to establish a prima facie case such that a reasonable juror could have found that the content was created by the defendant, and was therefore admissible).

In re Estate of Denman, 362 S.W.3d 134 (Tex. App.—San Antonio 2011, no pet.) (letters sent by devisee who received ranch property under testator's will to trustee for testator's residual estate regarding devisee's demand that residual estate pay for taxes imposed on devisee's property were not hearsay, where letters were offered to show when controversy arose between the parties concerning testator's intent rather than to prove truth of matters asserted in letters).

Manuel v. State, 357 S.W.3d 66 (Tex. App.—Tyler 2011, pet. ref'd) (photographs and printouts of text messages received from a defendant on a victim's phone, as well as

MySpace emails, included information that sufficiently identified the defendant, and thus were admissible in a stalking prosecution).

Concept Gen. Contracting, Inc. v. Asbestos Maint. Servs., Inc., 346 S.W.3d 172 (Tex. App.—Amarillo 2011, pet. denied) (records relating to work performed on apartment complex construction project and photographs portraying various stages of the work were admissible under business-records exception to hearsay rule, regardless of whether custodian of records and photographs had personal knowledge of the contents of the records and photographs, because the owner had personal knowledge of the manner in which the records were prepared).

Avila v. State, 252 S.W.3d 632 (Tex. App.—Tyler 2008, no pet.) (Evidence consisting of summary of the more than 2,180 G-28 forms submitted by or on behalf of respondents' clients for purpose of seeking immigration benefits was admissible under business records exception to hearsay rule, in action brought by State under Deceptive Trade Practices-Consumer Protection Act to enjoin respondents from operating immigration services business, as government agent, who acted as custodian of records, laid the necessary predicate by describing the purpose of the documents and the manner in which they were processed.).

Sullivan v. State, 248 S.W.3d 746 (Tex. App.—Houston [1st Dist.] 2008, no pet.) (notes of substance abuse counselor, taken during a substance abuse consult with defendant approximately three months before motor vehicle accident, were admissible under the business records exception to the hearsay rule in trial for intoxication manslaughter; during the consult, defendant answered questions that were routine for a patient with a history of substance abuse problems checking into a hospital, observations in the report memorialized counselor's impressions of defendant's medical condition at that time, and it was normal for hospital workers to memorialize their notes in that fashion).

Shaffer v. State, 184 S.W.3d 353 (Tex. App.—Fort Worth 2006, *pet. struck*) (in prosecution for possession of pseudoephedrine with intent to manufacture methamphetamine, labels on packages of cold medicine were admissible under market reports and commercial publications exception to hearsay rule as proof that contents contained pseudoephedrine; fact that cold medicine was contained in bottles that remained unopened indicated that the contents had not been changed since the manufacturer bottled them).

Gilmore v. State, 666 S.W.2d 136 (Tex. App.—Amarillo 1983, writ ref'd) (admission of newspaper articles did not violate hearsay rule).

McMillen Feed, Inc. v. Harlow, 405 S.W.2d 123 (Tex. Civ. App.—Austin 1966, writ ref'd n.r.e.) (charts contained in magazine admissible as exceptions to hearsay rule).

c. *Secondary Evidence*

Gibson v. State, 121 S.W.2d 361 (Tex. Crim. App. 1938) (introduction of secondary evidence in sound discretion of trial court).

Lindsay v. Woods, 27 S.W.2d 263 (Tex. Civ. App.—Amarillo 1930, no writ) (admitting secondary evidence of written instruments that were beyond the court's jurisdiction).

Tex., Gulf & N. Ry. Co. v. Berlin, 165 S.W. 62 (Tex. Civ. App.—El Paso 1914, writ dism'd w.o.j.) ("where letters and telegrams are beyond the jurisdiction or process of the trial court it is no error to admit secondary evidence of their contents").

C. Motion to Exclude Gruesome or Inflammatory Photographs

1. Suggested Motion Text

(*Name of Moving Party*) hereby moves this Court for an order excluding any and all evidence, references to evidence, testimony, or argument relating to photographs depicting (*Describe Photographic Evidence*). The motion is based upon the ground that the evidence is (*State Grounds, e.g., Unduly Gruesome, Intended Solely to Inflame the Jurors' Emotions, etc.*) and will therefore create a substantial danger of undue prejudice to (*Name of Moving Party*).

2. Motion Summary

This motion is used to exclude photographs that are unduly gruesome or inflammatory. The motion is based upon the balancing test of Texas Rule of Evidence 403, as well as case law that has held such photographs may be excluded where the principal effect is to arouse the jury's passion. See, e.g., *Erazo v. State*, 144 S.W.3d 487 (Tex. Crim. App. 2004). Gruesome photographs may also be excluded where they are cumulative of other, less inflammatory evidence. *Tidrow v. State*, 916 S.W.2d 623 (Tex. App.—Fort Worth 1996, no pet.). Issues to be considered include the number of photographs, the size of the photograph, whether photograph is in color or black and white, the detail shown in the photograph, whether the photograph is gruesome, whether the body is naked or clothed, and whether the body has been altered since the crime in some way that might enhance the gruesomeness of the photograph to defendant's detriment. *Shuffield v. State*, 189 S.W.3d 782 (Tex. Crim. App.), *cert. denied*, 549 U.S. 1056 (2006).

Relevant evidence is not excluded simply on the ground that it would create prejudice if admitted. *Huckaby v. A.G. Perry & Sons, Inc.*, 20 S.W.3d 194 (Tex. App.—Texarkana 2000, pet. denied). The fact that photographs are gruesome does not render them inadmissible. *Castro v. Cammerino*, 186 S.W.3d 671 (Tex. App.—Dallas 2006, pet. denied); *Huckaby v. A.G. Perry & Sons, Inc.*, 20 S.W.3d 194 (Tex. App.—Texarkana 2000, pet. denied). Nevertheless, photographs that are merely calculated to arouse the sympathy, prejudice, or passion of the jury and do not serve to illustrate disputed issues or aid the jury in its understanding of the case should not be admitted. *Castro v. Cammerino*, 186 S.W.3d 671 (Tex. App.—Dallas 2006, pet. denied).

3. Supporting Authorities, Generally

Texas Rule of Evidence 402 states that "evidence which is not relevant is inadmissible." Relevant evidence is defined by Texas Rule of Evidence 401 as "having any tendency to make the existence of any fact that is of consequence to the determination of the action more probable or less probable than it would be without the evidence."

See Torrington v. Stutzman, 46 S.W.3d 829 (Tex. 2000); *Ellis v. State*, 99 S.W.3d 783 (Tex. App.—Houston [1st Dist.] 2003, pet. ref'd) (trial court did not abuse discretion excluding evidence as irrelevant); *Alexander v. State*, 88 S.W.3d 772 (Tex. App.—Corpus Christi 2002, pet. ref'd) (trial court erred admitting irrelevant evidence); *Williams v. State*, 27 S.W.3d 599 (Tex. App.—Waco 2000, pet. ref'd) (irrelevant evidence should have been excluded). As a general rule, photographs relevant to any issue in the case are admissible. *Castro v. Cammerino*, 186 S.W.3d 671 (Tex. App.—Dallas 2006, pet. denied); *Huckaby v. Perry & Sons, Inc.*, 20 S.W.3d 194 (Tex. App.—Texarkana 2000, pet. denied).

To be admissible, photographs must illustrate disputed fact issues and portray facts relevant to an issue. *Heddin v. Delhi Gas Pipeline Co.*, 522 S.W.2d 886 (Tex.1975); *Castro v. Cammerino*, 186 S.W.3d 671 (Tex. App.—Dallas 2006, pet. denied); *Fibreboard Corp. v. Pool*, 813 S.W.2d 658 (Tex. App.—Texarkana 1991, writ denied), *overruled on other grounds by Owens-Corning Fiberglas Corp. v. Malone*, 972 S.W.2d 35 (Tex. 1998).

a. Gruesome or Inflammatory Photographs

Erazo v. State, 144 S.W.3d 487 (Tex. Crim. App. 2004) (trial court erred admitting photograph of victim's unborn child where photograph unfairly prejudicial and inflammatory and not needed to prove prosecution's case).

Resendiz v. State, 112 S.W.3d 541 (Tex. Crim. App. 2003), *cert. denied*, 541 U.S. 1032 (2004) (trial court did not abuse discretion excluding crime scene photographs where misleading and confusing to jury).

Alvarado v. State, 912 S.W.2d 199 (Tex. Crim. App. 1995) (trial court must balance photographs' probative value against potential for unfair prejudice).

Reyes v. State, 491 S.W.3d 36, 49 (Tex. App.—Houston [14th Dist.] 2016, no pet.) ("A court may consider many factors in determining whether the probative value of photographs is substantially outweighed by the danger of unfair prejudice, including: the number of photographs offered, their gruesomeness, their detail, their size, whether they are in color or black-and-white, whether they are close up, whether the body depicted is clothed or naked, the availability of other means of proof, and other circumstances unique to the individual case.").

Kirk v. State, 421 S.W.3d 772 (Tex. App.—Fort Worth 2014, pet. ref'd) (Rule 403 requires that a photograph have some probative value and that its probative value not be substantially outweighed by its inflammatory nature).

Kirk v. State, 421 S.W.3d 772 (Tex. App.—Fort Worth 2014, pet. ref'd) (among the factors a court may consider in determining whether the probative value of photographs is substantially outweighed by the danger of unfair prejudice are the number of exhibits offered, their gruesomeness, their detail, their size, whether they are in color or black-and-white, whether they are close up, the availability of other means of proof, and other circumstances unique to the individual case).

Estrada v. State, 352 S.W.3d 762 (Tex. App.—San Antonio 2011, pet. ref'd) (determining whether the probative value of photographs is substantially outweighed by the danger of unfair prejudice, the court may consider a variety of factors, including: "the number of exhibits offered, their gruesomeness, their detail, their size, whether they are in color or black-and-white, whether they are close-up, whether the body depicted is clothed or naked, the availability of other means of proof, and other circumstances unique to the individual case").

Nadal v. State, 348 S.W.3d 304, 317 (Tex. App.—Houston [14th Dist.] 2011, no pet.) (to be admissible, a photograph must have probative value, and its probative value must not be substantially outweighed by its inflammatory nature).

Thrift v. State, 134 S.W.3d 475, 477 (Tex. App.—Waco 2004), *aff'd*, 176 S.W.3d 221 (Tex. Crim. App. 2005) (trial court abused discretion in indecency-with-child case by admitting photographs of other naked and aroused teenagers found at defendant's house where evidence unduly prejudicial and inflammatory).

Jones v. State, 111 S.W.3d 600 (Tex. App.—Dallas 2003, pet. ref'd) (harmless error to admit gruesome, prejudicial, and cumulative photographs at sentencing phase).

Alexander v. State, 88 S.W.3d 772 (Tex. App.—Corpus Christi 2002, pet. ref'd) (defendant's mug shot prejudicial and should not have been admitted).

Huckaby v. A.G. Perry & Sons, Inc., 20 S.W.3d 194 (Tex. App.—Texarkana 2000, pet. denied) (exclusion of fifteen photographs proper where proponent failed to show they proved any element not already shown by one admitted photograph).

Tidrow v. State, 916 S.W.2d 623 (Tex. App.—Fort Worth 1996, no pet.) (photographs may be excluded based on considerations of undue delay or needless presentation of cumulative evidence).

Alvarado v. State, 912 S.W.2d 199 (Tex. Crim. App. 1995) (trial court must balance photographs' probative value against potential for unfair prejudice).

Cecil v. T.M.E. Invs., 893 S.W.2d 38 (Tex. App.—Corpus Christi 1994, no writ) (exclusion of two of four photographs proper where they merely duplicated what was in two admitted photographs).

Franco v. Graham, 470 S.W.2d 429 (Tex. Civ. App.—Corpus Christi 1971), *aff'd as reformed*, 488 S.W.2d 390 (Tex. 1972) (no error refusing to admit photographs of damaged vehicle where cumulative of evidence already presented).

b. *Purpose to Inflame Jurors' Emotions*

Pawlak v. State, 420 S.W.3d 807 (Tex. Crim. App. 2013) (the sheer volume of extraneous-offense evidence was unfairly prejudicial and invited the jury to convict a defendant of sexually assaulting or attempting to sexually assault the victims because the defendant possessed 9,900 images that included homosexual child pornography).

Erazo v. State, 144 S.W.3d 487 (Tex. Crim. App. 2004) (trial court erred admitting photograph of victim's unborn child where photograph unfairly prejudicial and inflammatory and not needed to prove prosecution's case).

Reyes v. State, 491 S.W.3d 36, 49 (Tex. App.—Houston [14th Dist.] 2016, no pet.) ("With regard to photographs and other visual depictions such as videos, the images are inadmissible under Rule 403 when they have an undue tendency to suggest a decision on an emotional basis and the probative value of the photograph or video image is substantially outweighed by such unfair prejudice.").

Thrift v. State, 134 S.W.3d 475, 477 (Tex. App.—Waco 2004), *aff'd*, 176 S.W.3d 221 (Tex. Crim. App. 2005) (trial court abused discretion in indecency-with-child case by admitting photographs of other naked and aroused teenagers found at defendant's house where evidence unduly prejudicial and inflammatory).

Tidrow v. State, 916 S.W.2d 623 (Tex. App.—Fort Worth 1996, no pet.) (photograph should be excluded if so horrifying or appalling that juror of normal sensitivity would necessarily encounter difficulty rationally deciding critical issues after viewing it).

c. Other Grounds

Other potential grounds for excluding photographs include:

- Confusing or misleading;
- Solely intended to create an emotional bias;
- Cumulative;
- Improper foundation.

4. Opposing Authorities

Davis v. State, 313 S.W.3d 317 (Tex. Crim. App. 2010) (autopsy photographs are generally admissible unless they depict mutilation of the victim caused by the autopsy itself).

Davis v. State, 313 S.W.3d 317 (Tex. Crim. App. 2010) (court may consider many factors in determining whether the probative value of photographs is substantially outweighed by the danger of unfair prejudice, including availability of other means of proof, number of exhibits offered, their gruesomeness, their detail and size, and whether they are in color or black and white, close up or not, depicting clothed or naked body, and other circumstances unique to the individual case).

Gallo v. State, 239 S.W.3d 757 (Tex. Crim. App. 2007) (admissibility of a photograph is within the sound discretion of the trial judge).

Gallo v. State, 239 S.W.3d 757 (Tex. Crim. App. 2007) (generally, a photograph is admissible if verbal testimony as to matters depicted in the photographs is also admissible; in other words, if verbal testimony is relevant, photographs of the same are also relevant).

Newbury v. State, 135 S.W.3d 22 (Tex. Crim. App. 2004), *cert. denied*, 543 U.S. 990 (2004) (trial court did not abuse discretion admitting autopsy photographs where relevant and not unfairly prejudicial).

Escamilla v. State, 143 S.W.3d 814 (Tex. Crim. App. 2004), *cert. denied*, 544 U.S. 950 (2005) (autopsy photographs relevant and admissible).

Rayford v. State, 125 S.W.3d 521 (Tex. Crim. App. 2003, reh'g denied) (trial court did not abuse discretion admitting autopsy photographs where relevant and not unfairly prejudicial).

Ripkowski v. State, 61 S.W.3d 378 (Tex. Crim. App. 2001), *cert. denied*, 539 U.S. 916 (2003) (crime scene and victim photographs relevant and not unfairly prejudicial).

Proo v. State, 587 S.W.3d 789, 817 (Tex. App.—San Antonio 2019, pet. ref'd) ("Photographs of a victim's injuries are relevant and their relevance is not diminished merely because the jury also heard testimony about the same injuries.").

Proo v. State, 587 S.W.3d 789, 817 (Tex. App.—San Antonio 2019, pet. ref'd) ("The mere fact that a photo or video depicts a child's badly bruised body and is hard to view does not automatically render it too inflammatory or unfairly prejudicial to be admitted.").

Proo v. State, 587 S.W.3d 789, 817 (Tex. App.—San Antonio 2019, pet. ref'd) ("'Photographs showing a victim's bruises may be admitted to clarify and support observations and conclusions about the victim's injuries, so long as they are not admitted solely to inflame the minds of the jurors.'").

Paz v. State, 548 S.W.3d 778, 795 (Tex. App.—Houston [1st Dist.] 2018, pet. ref'd) ("changes rendered by the autopsy process are of minor significance if the disturbing nature of the photograph is primarily due to the injuries caused by the appellant").

Dawkins v. State, 557 S.W.3d 592, 605 (Tex. App.—El Paso 2016, no pet.) ("A photograph should add something that is relevant, legitimate, and logical to the testimony that accompanies it and that assists the jury in its decision-making duties. Sometimes this will, incidentally, include elements that are emotional and prejudicial.... If there are elements of a photograph that are genuinely helpful to the jury in making its decision, the photograph is inadmissible only if the emotional and prejudicial aspects substantially outweigh the helpful aspects.").

Reyes v. State, 491 S.W.3d 36, 49 (Tex. App.—Houston [14th Dist.] 2016, no pet.) ("Autopsy photographs will generally be admissible under Rule 403 unless they depict mutilation caused by the autopsy itself.").

Reyes v. State, 491 S.W.3d 36, 49 (Tex. App.—Houston [14th Dist.] 2016, no pet.) ("the fact that the photographs are gruesome does not, without more, render the probative value of the exhibits outweighed by any unfair prejudice").

Reyes v. State, 491 S.W.3d 36, 49 (Tex. App.—Houston [14th Dist.] 2016, no pet.) ("the autopsy photographs, although gruesome, were highly probative to show the full extent of the injuries appellant inflicted on [the victim] and to prove that she was still alive, at least initially, when appellant committed the aggravated sexual assault").

Sanchez v. State, 418 S.W.3d 302 (Tex. App.—Fort Worth 2013, pet. ref'd) (autopsy photographs are generally admissible unless they depict mutilation of the victim caused by the autopsy itself).

Sanchez v. State, 418 S.W.3d 302 (Tex. App.—Fort Worth 2013, pet. ref'd) (photographs that depict the nature, location, and extent of a wound are generally probative enough to outweigh any prejudicial effect).

Hill v. State, 392 S.W.3d 850 (Tex. App.—Amarillo 2013, pet. ref'd) (generally, a photograph is admissible if verbal testimony as to matters depicted in the photograph is admissible).

Hill v. State, 392 S.W.3d 850 (Tex. App.—Amarillo 2013, pet. ref'd) (if verbal testimony is relevant, photographs of the same also are relevant).

Hill v. State, 392 S.W.3d 850 (Tex. App.—Amarillo 2013, pet. ref'd) (a court may consider several factors in determining whether the probative value of photographs is substantially outweighed by the danger of unfair prejudice, including: the number of exhibits offered; their gruesomeness; their detail; their size; whether they are black-and-white or color; whether they are close-up; whether the body is depicted naked or clothed; the availability of other means of proof; and the circumstances unique to each individual case).

Hill v. State, 392 S.W.3d 850 (Tex. App.—Amarillo 2013, pet. ref'd) (photographs that depict the nature, location, and extent of a wound have been found sufficiently probative to outweigh prejudicial effect).

Estrada v. State, 352 S.W.3d 762 (Tex. App.—San Antonio 2011, pet. ref'd) (autopsy photographs are generally admissible unless they depict mutilation of the victim caused by the autopsy itself; a photograph is also generally admissible if verbal testimony about the matters depicted in the photograph is also admissible).

In re K.Y., 273 S.W.3d 703 (Tex. App.—Houston [14th Dist.] 2008, no pet.) (photographs are admissible if oral testimony as to the matters depicted in the photographs is also admissible).

In re J.B.C., 233 S.W.3d 88 (Tex. App.—Fort Worth 2007, pet. denied) (court may consider the following factors in determining whether the probative value of photographs is substantially outweighed by the danger of unfair prejudice: the number of exhibits offered; their gruesomeness; their detail; their size; whether they are offered in color or in black and white; whether they are close-up; and whether the body depicted is clothed or naked).

In re J.B.C., 233 S.W.3d 88 (Tex. App.—Fort Worth 2007, pet. denied) (autopsy photographs are generally admissible unless they depict mutilation caused by the autopsy itself; changes rendered by the autopsy process are of minor significance if the disturbing nature of the photograph is primarily due to the injuries caused by the defendant).

Castro v. Cammerino, 186 S.W.3d 671 (Tex. App.—Dallas 2006, pet. denied) (even when a defendant stipulates to actual and gross negligence, photographs depicting a person's injuries can help the jury to assess the full extent of the impact of the defendant's conduct).

Hall v. State, 137 S.W.3d 847 (Tex. App.—Houston [1st Dist.] 2004, pet. ref'd) (trial court did not abuse discretion admitting autopsy photographs where relevant, not unfairly prejudicial, and did not represent mutilation caused by autopsy itself).

Drew v. State, 76 S.W.3d 436 (Tex. App.—Houston [14th Dist.] 2002, pet. ref'd), *cert. denied*, 537 U.S. 1047 (2002) (trial court did not abuse discretion admitting autopsy photographs).

> Note: *Gruesome photographs are more difficult to exclude in criminal cases where they tend to be relevant to issues arising in murder, mayhem, and similar prosecutions. See generally,* Hall v. State, *137 S.W.3d 847 (Tex. App.—Houston [1st Dist.] 2004, pet. ref'd);* Ripkowski v. State, *61 S.W.3d 378 (Tex. Crim. App. 2001), cert. denied, 539 U.S. 916 (2003).*

a. Examples of Admissible Photographs

Davis v. State, 313 S.W.3d 317 (Tex. Crim. App. 2010) (trial court did not abuse its discretion in admission of autopsy photograph of a cross-section of a victim's tongue, which showed hemorrhaging within the tongue because cross-sectioning was necessary to show hemorrhaging).

Hayes v. State, 85 S.W.3d 809 (Tex. Crim. App. 2002) (autopsy photographs were relevant and not unfairly prejudicial where medical examiner reconstructed victim's head and pulled skin away from wound).

Ripkowski v. State, 61 S.W.3d 378 (Tex. Crim. App. 2001), *cert. denied*, 539 U.S. 916, (2003) (crime scene and victim photographs relevant and not unfairly prejudicial).

Sanchez v. State, 418 S.W.3d 302 (Tex. App.—Fort Worth 2013, pet. ref'd) (autopsy photograph's probative value outweighed any prejudice, because it portrayed the extent and location of the victim's injuries and aided the jury in identifying which wound was the primary cause of death).

Nadal v. State, 348 S.W.3d 304, 317 (Tex. App.—Houston [14th Dist.] 2011, no pet.) (photographs of an unclothed child, representing the child's injury, were relevant to a key issue in the case—"whether the injuries were caused by a small dog or by a sharp instrument in the hands of another person. The photographs were particularly important for the jury in understanding the testimony offered by [the medical expert] and for forming their own conclusions regarding the cause of the injury. Although the photographs depict a gruesome injury, they 'portray no more than the gruesomeness of the injuries inflicted on the child.'").

Andrade v. State, 246 S.W.3d 217 (Tex. App.—Houston [14th Dist.] 2007, pet. ref'd) (photograph of defendant holding the murder weapon had a tendency to make the existence of a fact of consequence to the determination of the action, i.e. the person who committed the murder, more probable than it would be without the evidence, and therefore, photograph was relevant and admissible).

D. Motion to Exclude Prejudicial Film or Videotapes

1. Suggested Motion Text

(*Name of Moving Party*) hereby moves this Court for an order excluding any and all evidence, references to evidence, testimony, or argument relating to a videotape [or film] made on or about (*Date*) depicting (*Describe Nature of Contents of Videotape Evidence*). The motion is based upon the ground that the evidence is (*State Grounds, e.g., Confusing, Cumulative, Inflammatory, etc.*) and will therefore create a substantial danger of undue prejudice to (*Name of Moving Party*).

2. Motion Summary

This motion is used to exclude videotape or related evidence that creates a risk of undue prejudice to the moving party. The motion is based upon a Rule 403 balancing, as well as case law that supports the exclusion of prejudicial evidence. *See Salazar v.*

State, 90 S.W.3d 330 (Tex. Crim. App. 2002); *Ford Motor Co. v. Miles*, 967 S.W.2d 377 (Tex. 1998).

3. Supporting Authorities, Generally

Fowler v. State, 544 S.W.3d 844, 849 (Tex. Crim. App. 2018) ("video recordings without audio are treated as photographs and are properly authenticated when it can be proved that the images accurately represent the scene in question and are relevant to a disputed issue").

Volkswagen of Am., Inc. v. Ramirez, 159 S.W.3d 897 (Tex. 2004) (unidentified eyewitness's videotaped statement of accident taken by television reporter at site of accident in which he claimed he saw vehicle's rear tire blow up, and that vehicle then crossed median before colliding with other car, did not fall within excited utterance exception to rule against hearsay, and was inadmissible in action against vehicle manufacturer brought by administrator of estate of other car's driver and passenger's next friend).

Sells v. State, 121 S.W.3d 748 (Tex. Crim. App. 2003), *cert. denied*, 540 U.S. 986 (2003) (trial court did not abuse discretion excluding videotape offered at penalty phase where confusing and distracting).

Salazar v. State, 90 S.W.3d 330 (Tex. Crim. App. 2002) (trial court erred admitting lengthy video depicting victim's life during penalty phase where video unfairly prejudicial, inflammatory, time-consuming, confusing, and prosecution did not have great need for videotape).

Ford Motor Co. v. Miles, 967 S.W.2d 377 (Tex. 1998) (exclusion of videos proper where would inflame juror's emotions and other sources of impeachment evidence available).

Watson v. State, 421 S.W.3d 186 (Tex. App.—San Antonio 2013, pet. ref'd) (the predicate for introduction of a photograph and a silent videotape not accompanied by sound requires proof of (1) its accuracy as a correct representation of the subject at a given time, and (2) its material relevance to a dispute issue).

Watson v. State, 421 S.W.3d 186 (Tex. App.—San Antonio 2013, pet. ref'd) (the predicate for introduction of a photograph and a silent videotape not accompanied by sound need not be laid by the photographer, the individual being photographed, or even a person present in the photograph in question; any witness observing the scene depicted in the photograph may lay the predicate so long as the witness can provide testimony based on personal knowledge, sufficient to support a finding that the matter in question is what its proponent claims).

Hankey v. State, 231 S.W.3d 54 (Tex. App.—Texarkana 2007, no pet.) (video recording of interview of child victim nearly three years after victim initially reported sexual assault was inadmissible hearsay at trial for aggravated sexual assault).

Petruccelli v. State, 174 S.W.3d 761 (Tex. App.—Waco 2005, pet. ref'd), *cert. denied*, 127 S. Ct. 106 (2006) ("day in the life" videotape unduly prejudicial and should have been excluded in guilt/innocence phase of trial).

Rodriguez v. Universal Fastenings Corp., 777 S.W.2d 513 (Tex. App.—Corpus Christi 1989, no writ) (video deposition testimony excluded where potential for confusing and prejudicing jury).

a. Other Grounds

Other grounds for exclusion of videotape evidence:

- Confusing or misleading (Chapter 2);
- Solely intended to create an emotional bias (Chapter 2);
- Cumulative (Chapter 2);
- Irrelevant (Chapter 3);
- Improper foundation;
- Gruesome or inflammatory photographs.

4. Opposing Authorities, Generally

Hines v. State, 383 S.W.3d 615 (Tex. App.—San Antonio 2012, pet. ref'd) (witness is not required to be the maker of the recording or have otherwise participated in the conversation in order for his testimony that the recording is what it is claimed to be to sufficiently authenticate it).

Hines v. State, 383 S.W.3d 615, 625 (Tex. App.—San Antonio 2012, pet. ref'd) ("although portions of a video are choppy and the incident was not recorded in its entirety, [a police officer] identified those portions which do not purport to represent the incident as being accurate depictions, and testified that the portions of the evening that the dashboard camera recorded depicted exactly what happened the night [defendant] was arrested for DWI," and this was sufficient for the trial court to find the videotape was what the witness and the State claimed it to be).

Varkonyi v. State, 276 S.W.3d 27 (Tex. App.—El Paso 2008, pet. ref'd) (email and video offered by the State in an obscenity trial were authenticated, under the reply letter doctrine. "Under this doctrine, a letter received in the due course of mail purportedly in answer to another letter is prima facie genuine and admissible without further proof of authenticity. A reply letter needs no further authentication because it is unlikely that anyone other than the purported writer would know of and respond to the contents of the earlier letter addressed to him.").

Hutton v. AER Mfg. II, Inc., 224 S.W.3d 459, 464 (Tex. App.—Dallas 2007, pet. denied) (videotape of rollover tests was proper even though the vehicle in the tape was not similar to the vehicle involved in the accident at issue).

Smith v. State, 105 S.W.3d 203 (Tex. App.—Houston [14th Dist.] 2003, pet. ref'd) (in prosecution for driving while intoxicated, police videotape of defendant appearing intoxicated and admitting he had been incarcerated held relevant and not unfairly prejudicial).

Wal-Mart Stores, Inc. v. Hoke, No. 14-99-00503-CV, 2001 WL 931658 (Tex. App.—Houston [14th Dist.] Aug. 16, 2001, no pet.) (not designated for publication) (no abuse of discretion admitting "day in the life" videotape).

Draheim v. State, 916 S.W.2d 593 (Tex. App.—San Antonio 1996, writ ref'd) (videotape of defendant sexually assaulting child which was extremely lengthy, in color, extremely detailed, and cumulative of defendant's own testimony, properly admitted: "[T]he fact that the tape was 'highly inflammatory' says no more than that Draheim's crimes were 'highly inflammatory;' it does not establish that the tape was unfairly prejudicial.... In short, while Draheim's videotape was unquestionably prejudicial, it was not unfairly prejudicial.").

Jones v. Colley, 820 S.W.2d 863 (Tex. App.—Texarkana 1991, writ denied) (videotaped testimony may be more convincing and revealing than oral or written testimony where more stimulating and conveys nonverbal messages that may be helpful to jury).

Apache Ready Mix Co., Inc. v. Creed, 653 S.W.2d 79 (Tex. App.—San Antonio 1983, writ dism'd) (not abuse of discretion admitting "day in the life" videotape).

a. Relevance

Amador v. State, 242 S.W.3d 95 (Tex. App.—Beaumont 2007), *rev'd on other grounds*, 275 S.W.3d 872 (Tex. Crim. App. 2009) (videotape of a stop involving a charge for driving while intoxicated that depicts the driver's impairment would be relevant to the issue of intoxication).

Smith v. State, 105 S.W.3d 203 (Tex. App.—Houston [14th Dist.] 2003, pet. ref'd) (in prosecution for driving while intoxicated, police videotape of defendant appearing intoxicated and admitting he had been incarcerated held relevant and not unfairly prejudicial).

E. Motion to Exclude Published Articles

1. Suggested Motion Text

(*Name of Moving Party*) hereby moves this Court for an order excluding any and all evidence, references to evidence, testimony, or argument relating to an article from the (*Date*) issue of (*Describe Name of Publication*). The motion is based upon the ground that the evidence is (*State Ground, e.g., Cumulative, Hearsay, etc.*) and will create a substantial danger of unfair prejudice to (*Name of Moving Party*).

2. Motion Summary

This motion is used to exclude newspaper or magazine articles and related evidence where the prejudicial nature of such evidence outweighs the probative value. *See Shadowens v. Shadowens*, 271 S.W.2d 165 (Tex. Civ. App.—Waco 1954, no writ) (newspaper article). See also Texas Rule of Evidence 403. Newspaper and magazine articles have been excluded where they were prejudicial [*Lewis v. State*, 676 S.W.2d 136 (Tex. Crim. App. 1984, no writ) (magazines)], or where they contained inadmissible hearsay [*Elder v. State*, 614 S.W.2d 136 (Tex. Crim. App. 1981) (newspaper article)].

3. Supporting Authorities

Deramus v. Thornton, 333 S.W.2d 824 (Tex. 1960) (copies of newspaper articles hearsay and could not be considered in mandamus proceeding).

Envtl. Procedures, Inc. v. Guidry, 282 S.W.3d 602 (Tex. App.—Houston [14th Dist.] 2009, pet. denied) (trade publications on financial instability of liability insurer and criminal investigation of parent corporation's founder could be excluded as hearsay in insureds' fraud suit against broker; the issues were offered to show that broker should have known the truth of the statements at the time the issues were published, and insureds contended that broker should have known that insurer was financially unsound or should have conducted independent investigation).

Elder v. State, 614 S.W.2d 136 (Tex. Crim. App. 1981) (newspaper article found at appellant's house inadmissible hearsay).

Duncan v. State, 146 S.W.2d 749 (Tex. Crim. App. 1940) (newspaper report on murder victim inadmissible hearsay).

Mauzey v. Sutliff, 125 S.W.3d 71 (Tex. App.—Austin 2003, pet. denied) (trial court, in medical malpractice action brought by parents of minor child against physician after child was born with a respiratory disorder, did not abuse its discretion in not allowing jury, by means of overhead display, to view two tables taken from learned treatises that displayed the incidence rate of respiratory distress syndrome infants born at various gestational ages, where rule of evidence governing hearsay exception for information found in learned treatises provided that such treatises could not be received as exhibits).

Atchison, T. & S. F. Ry. Co. v. Ham, 454 S.W.2d 451 (Tex. Civ. App.—Austin 1970, writ ref'd n.r.e.) (newspaper article properly excluded as hearsay).

Houston Packing Co. v. Griffith, 164 S.W. 431 (Tex. Civ. App.—San Antonio 1914, no writ) (newspaper market quotes offered as evidence of market value should have been rejected as hearsay).

Poling v. San Antonio & A.P. Ry. Co., 75 S.W. 69 (Tex. Civ. App.—San Antonio 1903, writ ref'd) (newspaper account of proceedings of Board of Medical Examiners inadmissible hearsay).

a. Prejudicial

Price v. State, 579 S.W.2d 492 (Tex. Crim. App. 1979, no pet.) (prejudicial effect of admission of magazines required reversal).

Shadowens v. Shadowens, 271 S.W.2d 165 (Tex. Civ. App.—Waco 1954, no writ) (court assumed prejudice in introduction of newspaper clippings in will contest action).

b. Other Grounds

Other grounds for exclusion of articles are:

- Confusing or misleading;
- Solely intended to create an emotional bias;
- Irrelevant;
- Improper foundation;
- Inadmissible writings.

4. Opposing Authorities, Generally

Pittsburgh Corning Corp. v. Walters, 1 S.W.3d 759 (Tex. App.—Corpus Christi 1999, pet. denied) (two excerpts from *Federal Register* properly admitted where supported underlying basis of expert's already admitted testimony).

Miller v. Lone Star Tavern, Inc., 593 S.W.2d 341 (Tex. Civ. App.—Waco 1979, no writ) (harmless error to allow magazine to be exhibited in court).

a. Cumulative

City of Austin v. Houston Lighting & Power Co., 844 S.W.2d 773 (Tex. App.—Dallas 1992, writ denied) (admission of articles harmless error where merely cumulative of other evidence).

Manhattan Fire & Marine Ins. Co. v. Melton, 329 S.W.2d 338 (Tex. Civ. App.—Texarkana 1959, writ ref'd n.r.e.) (newspaper giving account of windstorm not admitted in error where merely cumulative of other evidence).

b. No Prejudice

Nenno v. State, 970 S.W.2d 549 (Tex. Crim. App. 1998), *overruled on other grounds*, *State v. Terrazas*, 4 S.W.3d 720 (Tex. Crim. App. 1999) (sexually explicit magazines relevant and not unduly prejudicial during punishment phase of capital murder trial).

Paz v. State, 749 S.W.2d 626 (Tex. App.—Corpus Christi 1988, pet. ref'd) (newspaper found in car defendant was driving when arrested admissible and not prejudicial).

San Antonio River Auth. v. Garrett Bros., 528 S.W.2d 266 (Tex. Civ. App.—San Antonio 1975, writ ref'd n.r.e.) (admission of hearsay newspaper article did not require reversal where no showing of prejudice).

Murphy v. Murphy, 237 S.W. 640 (Tex. Civ. App.—Dallas 1922, writ dism'd w.o.j.) (admission of newspaper write-up harmless absent showing of prejudice).

c. Where Relevant to Other Issues

Gilmore v. State, 666 S.W.2d 136 (Tex. App.—Amarillo 1983, writ ref'd) (newspaper articles found in defendant's motel room did not violate hearsay rule where they evidenced defendant's knowledge and interest in murder story).

City of Austin v. Davis, 615 S.W.2d 316 (Tex. Civ. App.—Austin 1981, no writ), *aff'd*, 632 S.W.2d 331 (Tex. 1982) (admitting newspaper advertisements over hearsay objection for limited purpose of showing that they were published and made public knowledge).

Murphy v. Murphy, 237 S.W. 640 (Tex. Civ. App.—Dallas 1922, writ dism'd w.o.j.) (newspaper articles admitted as part of *res gestae* of oral conversation although articles would be hearsay independently).

Cox v. State, 234 S.W. 72 (Tex. Crim. App. 1921) (newspaper articles denouncing accused admitted where relevant to question of prejudice, requiring change of venue).

d. Not Hearsay

Patel v. Kuciemba, 82 S.W.3d 589 (Tex. App.—Corpus Christi 2002, pet. denied) (where it is proven that publications of market prices or statistical compilations are generally recognized as reliable and regularly used in a trade or specialized activity by persons so engaged, such publications are admissible for the truth of the matter published).

City of Austin v. Houston Lighting & Power Co., 844 S.W.2d 773 (Tex. App.—Dallas 1992, writ denied) (newspaper articles not hearsay where used to show notice or public perception).

Tejas Gas Corp. v. Herrin, 705 S.W.2d 177 (Tex. App.—Texarkana 1985), *rev'd on other grounds*, 716 S.W.2d 45 (Tex. 1986) (newspaper accounts not offered for the truth of matter asserted not inadmissible hearsay).

Richardson v. State, 690 S.W.2d 22 (Tex. App.—Beaumont 1985, pet. ref'd) (admission of newspaper articles on suicide did not violate hearsay rule where not offered for truth of statements contained in articles).

F. Motion to Exclude Accident Reports

1. Suggested Motion Text

(*Name of Moving Party*) hereby moves this Court for an order excluding any and all evidence, references to evidence, testimony, or argument relating to an accident report prepared on (*Date*) by (*Name of Reporting Officer*) pertaining to the underlying automobile accident in this case.

2. Motion Summary

This motion is used to prevent the introduction of accident reports into evidence in actions arising out of automobile collisions. The motion is based upon the express statutory authority of Transportation Code Section 550.066 and leading cases.

3. Supporting Authorities

Texas Transportation Code § 550.066 states:

> An individual's response to the information requested on an accident report form as provided by Section 550.064(b)(4) is not admissible evidence in a civil trial.

a. Generally

Benson v. Chalk, 536 S.W.3d 886, 895 (Tex. App.—Houston [1st Dist.] 2017, pet. denied) ("When a police report contains a hearsay statement, the statement must fall under some hearsay exception of its own because neither the public records and reports exception, nor the records of regularly conducted activities exception, protects hearsay within hearsay.").

Huckaby v. A.G. Perry & Sons, Inc., 20 S.W.3d 194 (Tex. App.—Texarkana 2000, pet. denied) (trial court's denial of motion to exclude written accident reports harmful error, warranting new trial).

Mosquera v. State, 877 S.W.2d 40 (Tex. App.—Corpus Christi 1994, no writ) (portion of plea agreement packet containing police reports inadmissible hearsay and should not have been used to impeach witness).

Hooper v. Torres, 790 S.W.2d 757 (Tex. App.—El Paso 1990, writ denied) (trial court did not abuse discretion excluding officer's report regarding whether there was negligent driving by either party where officer did not qualify as expert in accident reconstruction).

City of Denton v. Mathes, 528 S.W.2d 625 (Tex. Civ. App.—Fort Worth 1975, writ ref'd n.r.e.) (portion of police report containing officer's hearsay statements excluded).

McClesky v. Smades, 245 S.W.2d 269 (Tex. Civ. App.—Fort Worth 1952, no writ) (accident reports made by State highway patrolmen hearsay and should be excluded unless used to impeach officers' testimony).

b. Privilege

Martin v. Jenkins, 381 S.W.2d 115 (Tex. Civ. App.—Amarillo 1964, writ ref'd n.r.e.) (peace officer's accident reports are privileged communications).

c. Hearsay

> Note: Texas Rule of Evidence 803(8)(B) specifically excludes those matters in criminal cases "observed by police officers and other law enforcement personnel" from the public records exception to the hearsay rule.

Pilgrim's Pride Corp. v. Smoak, 134 S.W.3d 880, 892 (Tex. App.—Texarkana 2004, pet. denied) (investigating officer's conclusions on the causation of an accident contained in the officer's official police report were not admissible).

Mosquera v. State, 877 S.W.2d 40 (Tex. App.—Corpus Christi 1994, no writ) (portion of plea agreement packet containing police reports inadmissible hearsay and should not have been used to impeach witness).

Kuczaj v. State, 848 S.W.2d 284 (Tex. App.—Fort Worth 1993, no writ) (harmless error to admit testimony that serial numbers matched numbers reported to be stolen in police report where report was hearsay).

City of Denton v. Mathes, 528 S.W.2d 625 (Tex. Civ. App.—Fort Worth 1975, writ ref'd n.r.e.) (portion of police report containing officer's hearsay statements excluded).

McClesky v. Smades, 245 S.W.2d 269 (Tex. Civ. App.—Fort Worth 1952, no writ) (accident reports made by State highway patrolmen are hearsay and should be excluded unless used to impeach officers' testimony).

d. Diagrams Made at the Scene and Computer Animations

Miller v. State, 741 S.W.2d 382, 388 (Tex. Crim. App. 1987) ("With respect to animations involving animate objects, … any staged, re-enacted criminal acts or defensive issues involving human beings are impossible to duplicate in every minute detail and are therefore inherently dangerous, offer little in substance and the impact of re-enactments is too highly prejudicial to insure the State or the defendant a fair trial").

Venegas v. State, 560 S.W.3d 337 (Tex. App.—San Antonio 2018, no pet.) ("When a staged, re-enactment involves human beings, it is impossible to duplicate every minute detail and is therefore inherently dangerous and offers little in substance and the impact of re-enactments is too highly prejudicial to insure the State or the defendant a fair trial").

Lewis v. State, 402 S.W.3d 852, (Tex. App.—Amarillo 2013), *aff'd*, 428 S.W.3d 860 (Tex. Crim. App. 2014), cert. denied sub. nom., *Nolley v. State*, 574 U.S. 901 (2014) (animation based on speculation and not supported by the evidence should not have been admitted).

Richter's Bakery, Inc. v. Verden, 394 S.W.2d 230 (Tex. Civ. App.—Waco 1965, writ ref'd n.r.e.) (diagram of accident showing positioning of vehicles excluded where facts diagram could establish already admitted).

e. Other Grounds

Other grounds for excluding accident reports include:

- Cumulative;
- Improper foundation;
- Inadmissible writings;
- Improper impeachment evidence;
- Inadmissible hearsay;
- Improper evidence of statute violation.

4. Opposing Authorities

Spearman v. State, 307 S.W.3d 463 (Tex. App.—Beaumont 2010, pet. ref'd) (four prerequisites must be shown for the admission of a recorded recollection: the witness must have insufficient recollection to enable the witness to testify fully and accurately about the event; the memorandum or record must be one made or adopted by the witness; the recollection must have been recorded when the matter was fresh in the witness's memory; and the recorded recollection must reflect the witness's prior knowledge correctly).

Brown v. State, 333 S.W.3d 606 (Tex. App.—Dallas 2009, no pet.) (for a statement to be admissible under recorded recollection exception to hearsay rule, the witness must have had firsthand knowledge of the event; the statement must be an original memorandum made at or near the time of the event while the witness had a clear and accurate memory of it; the witness must lack a present recollection of the event; and the witness must vouch for the accuracy of the written memorandum).

Hines v. Nelson, 547 S.W.2d 378 (Tex. Civ. App.—Tyler 1977, no writ) (police officer allowed to use accident report to refresh memory before testifying).

Avnet v. Hull, 265 S.W.2d 906 (Tex. Civ. App.—Dallas 1954, writ ref'd n.r.e.) (investigating officer allowed to refresh recollection from copy of accident report)

a. Statements Made to Reporting Officers

Corrales v. Dep't of Family & Protective Servs., 155 S.W.3d 478 (Tex. App.—El Paso 2004, no writ) (police reports containing statements of witnesses not present and available for cross-examination admissible in termination of parental rights case).

Kratz v. Exxon Corp., 890 S.W.2d 899 (Tex. App.—El Paso 1994, no writ) (accident reports admitted at pre-trial hearing with witness statements omitted).

Almaraz v. Burke, 827 S.W.2d 80 (Tex. App.—Fort Worth 1992, writ denied) (witness statements contained in police officer's report admissible under excited utterance exception to hearsay rule).

Spradling v. State, 628 S.W.2d 123 (Tex. App.—Beaumont 1981, writ ref'd) (oral statements contained in accident reports filed with Department of Public Safety may be admissible).

b. Public Records and Reports

Avila v. State, 252 S.W.3d 632 (Tex. App.—Tyler 2008, no pet.) (evidence consisting of summary of the more than 2,180 G-28 forms submitted by or on behalf of respondents' clients for purpose of seeking immigration benefits was admissible under business records exception to hearsay rule, in action brought by State under Deceptive Trade Practices-Consumer Protection Act to enjoin respondents from operating immigration services business, as government agent, who acted as custodian of records, laid the necessary predicate by describing the purpose of the documents and the manner in which they were processed).

TXI Transp. Co. v. Hughes, 224 S.W.3d 870 (Tex. App.—Fort Worth 2007), *rev'd on other grounds*, 306 S.W.3d 230 (Tex. 2010) (generally, accident reports prepared by investigating officers, possessing sufficient training in accident reconstruction, are admissible as an exception to the hearsay rule).

Corrales v. Dep't of Family & Protective Servs., 155 S.W.3d 478 (Tex. App.—El Paso 2004, no writ) (police reports admissible as public records in termination of parental rights case).

Carter v. Steere Tank Lines, Inc., 835 S.W.2d 176 (Tex. App.—Amarillo 1992, writ denied) (accident report admissible under public records exception to hearsay rule).

c. Diagrams Made at the Scene and Computer Animations

Holding v. State, 460 S.W.2d 133 (Tex. Crim. App. 1970) (no error admitting diagram made at scene).

Venegas v. State, 560 S.W.3d 337 (Tex. App.—San Antonio 2018, no pet.) ("A computer animation is merely a series of images generated by a computer that serves as demonstrative evidence. It may, for example, illustrate what a witness saw, demonstrate for the jury the general principles that underlie an expert opinion, or depict an expert's theory of how an accident occurred. In each such instance, the evidence may be authenticated by the witness's testimony that the computer animation presents a fair and accurate depiction ... [of] what they purport to represent. If they do not, they will not be admissible.").

Venegas v. State, 560 S.W.3d 337 (Tex. App.—San Antonio 2018, no pet.) ("when an animation is based on inanimate objects and quantifiable measurements, the factual discrepancies depicted do not cause the probative value of the evidence to be substantially outweighed by any unfair prejudice from its admission").

Venegas v. State, 560 S.W.3d 337 (Tex. App.—San Antonio 2018, no pet.) (computer-animated recreation of a crime scene was properly admitted because it was based on calculations derived from inanimate objects and quantifiable measurements).

Lewis v. State, 402 S.W.3d 852, (Tex. App.—Amarillo 2013), *aff'd*, 428 S.W.3d 860 (Tex. Crim. App. 2014), cert. denied sub. nom., *Nolley v. State*, 574 U.S. 901 (2014) ("The use of animations to depict a crime scene has been approved by Texas courts.").

Hurd v. State, No. 07-01-0140-CR, 2002 WL 737296 (Tex. App.—Amarillo Apr. 26, 2002, no pet.) (not designated for publication) (diagram of the scene made by an unidentified officer was properly admitted into evidence based upon the testimony of other witnesses who had viewed the scene).

Holding v. State, 460 S.W.2d 133 (Tex. Crim. App. 1970) (no error admitting diagram made at scene).

G. Motion to Exclude Letters, Emails, or Text Messages

1. Suggested Motion Text

(*Name of Moving Party*) hereby moves this Court for an order excluding any and all evidence, references to evidence, testimony, or argument relating to a letter [email or text message] written by (*Name of Author item*) pertaining to (*Describe Nature of Content of item*). The motion is based upon the ground that the evidence is (*State Ground, e.g., Cumulative, Irrelevant, Collateral, etc.*) and will create a substantial danger of undue prejudice to (*Name of Moving Party*).

2. Motion Summary

This motion is used to exclude letters, emails, or text messages containing irrelevant, collateral, or other inappropriate matter likely to prejudice the party seeking exclusion. The motion is based upon the authority of Texas Rule of Evidence 403 and leading cases that have approved of the exclusion of such evidence. *See Rische v. State*, 834 S.W.2d 942 (Tex. App.—Houston [1st Dist.] 1992, writ ref'd) (exclusion of irrelevant letters); *Leverett v. State*, 455 S.W.2d 312 (Tex. Crim. App. 1970, no pet.) (letters immaterial, collateral, and prejudicial).

3. Supporting Authorities

Jones v. State, 479 S.W.2d 307 (Tex. Crim. App. 1972, no writ) (letters calculated to prejudice appellant's rights before jury should have been excluded).

Mata v. State, 517 S.W.3d 257, 266 (Tex. App.—Corpus Christi 2017, pet. ref'd) ("evidence that merely shows the association of a phone number with a purported sender [of a text]—alone—might be too tenuous" for the evidence to be admissible).

City of Houston v. Jackson, 135 S.W.3d 891 (Tex. App.—Houston [1st Dist.] 2004), *rev'd on other grounds*, 192 S.W.3d 764 (Tex. 2006) (letter written by aggrieved party asking for job transfer and high sum of money not relevant to demonstrate motive in case involving grievance matter).

Minnesota Min. & Mfg. Co. v. Nishika Ltd., 885 S.W.2d 603 (Tex. App.—Beaumont 1994), *rev'd on other grounds*, 953 S.W.2d 733 (Tex. 1997) (exclusion of complaint letters where merely cumulative of other evidence).

Mottu v. Navistar Int'l Transp. Corp., 804 S.W.2d 144 (Tex. App.—Houston [14th Dist.] 1990, writ denied) (trial court properly excluded letters where cumulative of evidence already received).

Peat Marwick Main v. Haass, 775 S.W.2d 698 (Tex. App.—San Antonio 1989), *rev'd on other grounds*, 818 S.W.2d 381 (Tex. 1991) (exclusion of approximately 200 letters where cumulative of trial testimony).

Contact Prods. Inc. v. Dixico, Inc., 672 S.W.2d 607 (Tex. App.—Dallas 1984, no writ) (trial court properly excluded two letters where cumulative of oral testimony from both letters' authors).

Mollinedo v. Tex. Employment Comm'n, 662 S.W.2d 732 (Tex. App.—Houston [1st Dist.] 1983, writ ref'd n.r.e.) (no error excluding letter from doctor describing plaintiff's handicap where court previously admitted similar evidence through another witness).

Bobbie Brooks, Inc. v. Goldstein, 567 S.W.2d 902 (Tex. Civ. App.—Eastland 1978, writ refused n.r.e.) (exclusion of letter where would not have added anything to material issues).

City of Houston v. Hamons, 496 S.W.2d 662 (Tex. Civ. App.—Houston [14th Dist.] 1973, writ refused n.r.e.) (no reversible error excluding letters where substance stated by numerous other evidence items).

Jones v. State, 479 S.W.2d 307 (Tex. Crim. App. 1972, no pet.) (letters calculated to prejudice appellant's rights before jury should have been excluded).

Sewell v. Lake Charles Planing Mill Co., 253 S.W. 892 (Tex. Civ. App.—San Antonio 1923, no writ) (letters should have been excluded as prejudicial).

a. Hearsay

Washington Nat'l Ins. Co. v. Curry, 97 S.W.2d 525 (Tex. Civ. App.—Dallas 1936, no writ) (letters written by insured's attorney to insurer prejudicial and should have been excluded as hearsay).

b. Irrelevant

City of Houston v. Jackson, 135 S.W.3d 891 (Tex. App.—Houston [1st Dist.] 2004), *rev'd on other grounds*, 192 S.W.3d 764 (Tex. 2006) (letter written by aggrieved party asking for job transfer and high sum of money not relevant to demonstrate motive in case involving grievance matter).

Bobbie Brooks, Inc. v. Goldstein, 567 S.W.2d 902 (Tex. Civ. App.—Eastland 1978, writ ref'd n.r.e.) (exclusion of letter where would not have added anything to material issues).

c. Other Grounds

Other grounds for excluding letters include:

- Collateral to issues in case;
- Cumulative;
- Irrelevant;
- Improper foundation;
- Inadmissible writings.

4. Opposing Authorities

Butler v. State, 459 S.W.3d 595, (Tex. Crim. App. 2015) ("text messages may be authenticated by evidence sufficient to support a finding that the matter is what its proponent claims").

Butler v. State, 459 S.W.3d 595, (Tex. Crim. App. 2015) ("A witness might have 'knowledge' of the authorship of a text message for a number of reasons. One reason might be that the witness is the actual author of the text message. Another reason might be that the witness personally observed the purported author actually type and/or send the message. A witness might also claim to have knowledge that a text message came from a phone number known to be associated with the purported sender. The association of a cell-phone number with a particular individual might suggest that the owner or user of that number may be the sender of a text message. Indeed, the suggestion may be quite strong. Unlike so-called 'land lines,' commonly utilized by an entire household, cell phones tend to be personal and user-specific.").

Butler v. State, 459 S.W.3d 595, (Tex. Crim. App. 2015) ("When considering the admissibility of text messages, just as when considering the admissibility of letters, emails, instant messages, and other similar written forms of communications, courts must be especially cognizant that such matters may sometimes be authenticated by distinctive characteristics found within the writings themselves and by comparative reference from those characteristics to other circumstances shown to exist by the evidence presented at trial. Conversations and events that precede or follow the communications at issue, when identified or referred to within the written communication, can provide contextual evidence demonstrating the authenticity of such communications.").

In re Estate of Watson, 720 S.W.2d 806 (Tex. 1986) (trial court erred excluding eighty-one letters where strongest rebuttal evidence available and not merely cumulative).

Mata v. State, 517 S.W.3d 257, 266 (Tex. App.—Corpus Christi 2017, pet. ref'd) ("As with other types of evidence, the proponent may authenticate text messages by evidence sufficient to support a finding that the matter is what its proponent claims.... He can accomplish this in a myriad of ways, depending on the unique facts and circumstances of the case, including through the testimony of a witness with knowledge or through evidence showing distinctive characteristics.").

Manuel v. State, 357 S.W.3d 66 (Tex. App.—Tyler 2011, pet. ref'd) (under the "reply letter doctrine," a letter received in the due course of mail purportedly in answer to another letter is prima facie genuine and admissible without further proof of authenticity; this doctrine also applies to emails).

Manuel v. State, 357 S.W.3d 66 (Tex. App.—Tyler 2011, pet. ref'd) (email is properly authenticated if its appearance, contents, substance, or other distinctive characteristics, taken in conjunction with circumstances, support a finding that the document is what its proponent claims; text messages can be authenticated by applying the same factors).

Manuel v. State, 357 S.W.3d 66 (Tex. App.—Tyler 2011, pet. ref'd) (characteristics to consider in determining whether email evidence has been properly authenticated include: consistency with the email address in another email sent by the alleged author; the author's awareness, shown through the email, of the details of the alleged author's conduct; the email's inclusion of similar requests that the alleged author had made by phone during the time period; and the email's reference to the author by the alleged author's nickname).

Stafford v. State, 248 S.W.3d 400 (Tex. App.—Beaumont 2008, pet. ref'd) (handwriting may be authenticated by way of nonexpert opinion testimony as to its genuineness based upon the nonexpert's familiarity of the handwriting acquired independently of the litigation).

Stafford v. State, 248 S.W.3d 400 (Tex. App.—Beaumont 2008, pet. ref'd) (testimony of victim's daughter that handwriting on three letters was that of her mother authenticated the letters in murder prosecution of victim's husband).

Ins. Co. of N. Am. v. Morris, 928 S.W.2d 133 (Tex. App.—Houston [14th Dist.] 1996), *aff'd in part, rev'd in part on other grounds*, 981 S.W.2d 667 (Tex. 1998) (letters to insurance agent admitted where merely cumulative of other evidence and to show background and structure of sureties).

Fibreboard Corp. v. Pool, 813 S.W.2d 658 (Tex. App.—Texarkana 1991, writ denied) (danger of unfair prejudice did not outweigh probative value of letters showing manufacturers' knowledge of asbestos).

Stanton v. State, 747 S.W.2d 914 (Tex. App.—Dallas 1988, pet. ref'd), *overruled on other grounds by Owens-Corning Fiberglas Corp. v. Malone*, 972 S.W.2d 35 (Tex. 1998) (probative value of letter outweighed potential prejudice).

a. Relevancy

Kappel v. State, 402 S.W.3d 490 (Tex. App.—Houston [14th Dist.] 2013, no pet.) (letters were properly admitted into evidence where they were highly probative and the State's need for them was substantial, the time required to present the letters into evidence did not greatly extend the trial, and they were not cumulative of other evidence; the letters could be interpreted as apologies for the defendant's assault of the victim).

NETCO, Inc. v. Montemayor, 352 S.W.3d 733 (Tex. App.—Houston [1st Dist.] 2011, no pet.) (letter from escrow agent's employee was admissible because it demonstrated that a lien at issue had not been released, and that one of the parties did not discover a bank error until after settlement; this evidence was relevant to the accrual date of the cause of action).

State Bar of Tex. v. Dolenz, 3 S.W.3d 260 (Tex. App.—Dallas 1999, no pet.) (trust letters written by defendant relevant in disciplinary action).

Price v. State, 627 S.W.2d 253 (Tex. App.—Fort Worth 1982, no writ) (exclusion of letters written by defendant warranted reversal where relevant to insanity defense).

Mendiola v. Garza Bros., 185 S.W. 391 (Tex. Civ. App.—San Antonio 1916, no writ) (letters written between defendant and mill relevant and material to amount of wheat shipped and results of grinding). *See also Messner v. State*, 182 S.W. 329 (Tex. Crim. App. 1916, no writ) (letters directly relevant to transaction would be admissible if properly proven-up).

b. Hearsay

Marin v. IESI TX Corp., 317 S.W.3d 314 (Tex. App.—Houston [1st Dist.] 2010, pet. denied) (forged letters that contradicted previous letters, which were offered because they triggered an investigation, were not hearsay because they were not offered to prove the truth of their contents).

Sohail v. State, 264 S.W.3d 251 (Tex. App.—Houston [1st Dist.] 2008, pet. ref'd) (letter allegedly found by defendant that was written by victim stating that defendant never hit or pushed her, certified affidavit by victim requesting dismissal of protective order so she could reunite with defendant, and tape-recorded statement by victim contained inadmissible hearsay and extraneous information, and thus, were inadmissible in prosecution for domestic violence assault).

Stafford v. State, 248 S.W.3d 400 (Tex. App.—Beaumont 2008, pet. ref'd) (murder victim's written correspondence was admissible hearsay as relating to victim's then existing state of mind, emotion, sensation, or physical condition before murder by her husband).

First Equitable Title Co., Inc. v. Prods. Diversified, Inc., 678 S.W.2d 524 (Tex. App.—Houston [14th Dist.] 1984, writ ref'd n.r.e.) (copies of letters admitted over hearsay objection where presumption of receipt of originals).

O'Connor v. Nat'l Motor Club of Tex., 385 S.W.2d 558 (Tex. Civ. App.—Houston 1964, no writ) (complaint letters admitted over hearsay objection for limited purpose of showing complaints were made).

c. Not Hearsay

Southwest Indus. Inv. Co. v. Scalf, 604 S.W.2d 233 (Tex. Civ. App.—Dallas 1980, no writ) (letters may be authenticated and received in evidence where not hearsay and otherwise relevant).

H. Motion to Exclude Maps, Models, and Charts

1. Suggested Motion Text

(*Name of Moving Party*) hereby moves this Court for an order excluding any and all evidence, references to evidence, testimony, or argument relating to (*Describe Map, Model, or Chart*). The motion is based upon the ground that the evidence is (*State Ground, e.g., It is*

Unreliable, Not Authentic, Confusing, etc.) and will create a substantial danger of undue prejudice to (*Name of Moving Party*).

2. Motion Summary

This motion is made under Texas Rule of Evidence 403 and is used to exclude maps, models, and charts where the accuracy or reliability of the evidence is in doubt and may cause jury confusion or other prejudice. *See Schenck v. Ebby Halliday Real Estate, Inc.*, 803 S.W.2d 361 (Tex. App.—Fort Worth 1990, no writ) (charts); *Taylor v. McLennan County*, 120 S.W.2d 134 (Tex. Civ. App.—Waco 1938, no writ) (maps).

3. Supporting Authorities, Generally

Schenck v. Ebby Halliday Real Estate, Inc., 803 S.W.2d 361 (Tex. App.—Fort Worth 1990, no writ) (exclusion of charts that did not contain any additional evidence).

Ramos v. Champlin Petroleum Co., 750 S.W.2d 873 (Tex. App.—Corpus Christi 1988, writ denied), *abrogated on other grounds by Reagan v. Vaughn*, 804 S.W.2d 463 (Tex. 1990) (exclusion of replicated model of welding lead).

Steelman v. Rosenfeld, 408 S.W.2d 330 (Tex. Civ. App.—Dallas 1966, no writ) (exclusion of maps not in error where doubts as to accuracy).

Falls County v. Young, 77 S.W.2d 912 (Tex. Civ. App.—Fort Worth 1934, writ dism'd) (exclusion of sketches of maps harmless error where copies of maps already in evidence).

Howard v. State, 242 S.W. 739 (Tex. Crim. App. 1922, no pet.) (material error in admission of maps that were added hearsay).

a. Other Grounds

Other grounds for excluding evidence

- Collateral to issues in case;
- Confusing or misleading;
- Cumulative;
- Improper foundation;
- Inadmissible writings;
- Inadmissible hearsay.

4. Opposing Authorities

Houston Lighting & Power Co. v. Klein Indep. Sch. Dist., 739 S.W.2d 508 (Tex. App.—Houston [14th Dist.] 1987, writ denied) (no error admitting charts even though hearsay and cumulative of other evidence).

Settegast v. Meyer, 257 S.W. 343 (Tex. Civ. App.—Galveston 1923, no writ) (improper admission of maps did not require reversal where cumulative of other evidence).

a. Illustrative or Demonstrative Models

Vollbaum v. State, 833 S.W.2d 652 (Tex. App.—Waco 1992, writ ref'd) (Styrofoam model properly admitted where would assist jury in understanding expert's testimony).

Coastal Indus. Water Auth. v. Trinity Portland Cement Div., 523 S.W.2d 462 (Tex. Civ. App.—Houston [1st Dist.] 1975, writ ref'd n.r.e.) (three-dimensional model of condemned property admissible to show future uses of property).

Davis v. Callen, 250 S.W. 305 (Tex. Civ. App.—Beaumont 1923, no writ) (mechanical model properly admitted to illustrate mechanical principle).

b. Illustrative or Demonstrative Maps

Falls County v. Young, 77 S.W.2d 912 (Tex. Civ. App.—Fort Worth 1934, writ dism'd) (copies of maps admitted to show relative location of land surveys).

Seaway Co. v. Attorney General, 375 S.W.2d 923 (Tex. Civ. App.—Houston 1964, writ ref'd n.r.e.) (hearsay evidence of ancient maps admitted to show use and history of stage lines).

c. Illustrative or Demonstrative Charts

Hartsock v. State, 322 S.W.3d 775 (Tex. App.—Fort Worth 2010, no pet.) (it is within the trial court's discretion to permit the use of visual aids, charts, and video recordings during trial).

Hartsock v. State, 322 S.W.3d 775 (Tex. App.—Fort Worth 2010, no pet.) (demonstrative evidence has no independent relevance to the case but is offered to help explain or summarize the witness's testimony or to put events and conditions into a better perspective).

Hartsock v. State, 322 S.W.3d 775 (Tex. App.—Fort Worth 2010, no pet.) (demonstrative evidence is evidence admitted to serve as a visual aid or illustration that meets the tests of relevancy and materiality, as well as the limitations imposed by evidence rule under which otherwise admissible evidence may be excluded if its probative value is substantially outweighed by danger of unfair prejudice).

First Heights Bank, FSB v. Gutierrez, 852 S.W.2d 596 (Tex. App.—Corpus Christi 1993, writ denied) (hand-drawn charts made by attorneys at trial admissible for demonstrative purposes).

Barnes v. State, 797 S.W.2d 353 (Tex. App.—Tyler 1990, no writ) (allowing use of charts for demonstrative purposes).

Buzzard v. Mapco, Inc., 499 S.W.2d 352 (Tex. Civ. App.—Amarillo 1973, writ ref'd n.r.e.) (admitting charts for illustrative purposes).

d. Where Accuracy Is Not Disputed

Atl. Refining Co. v. Gulf Land Co., 122 S.W.2d 197 (Tex. Civ. App.—Austin 1938), *aff'd*, 131 S.W.2d 73 (Tex. 1939) (admitting maps shown to be substantially same in number and location as larger maps already admitted).

I. Motion to Exclude Improper Medical Records, Reports, or Bills

1. Suggested Motion Text

Alternative One (General):

>(*Name of Moving Party*) hereby moves this Court for an order excluding any and all evidence, references to evidence, testimony, or argument relating to (*Describe Nature of Medical Report or Related Document to Be Excluded*). The motion is based upon the ground that the document (*Describe Basis for Exclusion, e.g., Lacks Proper Authentication, is Inadmissible Hearsay, etc.*).

Alternative Two (Exclusion of Medical History):

>(*Name of Moving Party*) hereby moves this Court for an order excluding any and all evidence, references to evidence, testimony, or argument relating to Plaintiff's [or Decedent's] medical history and especially any evidence relating to (*Describe Inflammatory and Irrelevant Matter in History, e.g., "Plaintiff's prior treatment for addiction to alcohol"*). The motion is based upon the ground that the information is irrelevant and intended solely to inflame the jurors' emotions and that any probative value is outweighed by the prejudicial impact of such evidence.

Alternative Three (Billing Records):

>(*Name of Moving Party*) hereby moves this Court for an order excluding any and all evidence, references to evidence, testimony, or argument relating to billing records from (*Name of Medical Provider(s)*) for treatment of Plaintiff occurring from (*List Treatment Dates*). The motion is based upon the ground that the Plaintiff and Plaintiff's experts have failed to establish in any pretrial discovery that the billings were reasonable and necessary for treatment arising from the subject incident and therefore a proper foundation cannot be established and jurors would be misled and confused by the introduction of any such evidence, to the prejudice of the Defendant.

2. Motion Summary

This motion is used to exclude improper medical reports, medical history, opinions, or billing records. The motion may be used to exclude improper hearsay, character evidence, or otherwise inadmissible matter contained in the reports, or, where appropriate, the entire report, record, or bill. The motion is based upon the general exclusion of prejudicial evidence [Texas Rule of Evidence 403] as well as specific challenges to a report's foundation [*Cornelison v. Aggregate Haulers, Inc.*, 777 S.W.2d 542 (Tex. App.—Fort Worth 1989, writ denied)], hearsay [*Hooper v. Torres*, 790 S.W.2d 757 (Tex. App.—El Paso 1990, writ denied)], improper history [*Cornelison v.*

Aggregate Haulers, Inc., 777 S.W.2d 542 (Tex. App.—Fort Worth 1989, writ denied)], or the reasonableness of billings [*Six Flags Over Tex., Inc. v. Parker*, 759 S.W.2d 758 (Tex. App.—Fort Worth 1988, no writ)].

3. Supporting Authorities, Generally

Texas Rule of Evidence 901(a) provides:

> The requirement of authentication or identification as a condition precedent to admissibility is satisfied by evidence sufficient to support a finding that the matter in question is what its proponent claims.

Texas Rule of Evidence 104(a) states:

> Preliminary questions concerning the qualification of a person to be a witness, the existence of a privilege, or the admissibility of evidence shall be determined by the court, subject to the provisions of subdivision (b). In making its determination the court is not bound by the rules of evidence except those with respect to privileges.

Hurtado v. Tex. Employment Ins. Ass'n, 574 S.W.2d 536 (Tex. 1978) (trial court erred admitting large volume of medical records over opposing party's objection as to relevance, as opposing party should not be required to sort through such large amount of evidence and cite to court which items are relevant and which are not).

Hooper v. Torres, 790 S.W.2d 757 (Tex. App.—El Paso 1990, writ denied) (portion of medical report representing summaries of findings by other physicians inadmissible).

Cornelison v. Aggregate Haulers, Inc., 777 S.W.2d 542 (Tex. App.—Fort Worth 1989, writ denied) (improper foundation for medical records containing statement regarding causation and should not have been admitted).

Sec. Southwest Life Ins. Co. v. Gomez, 768 S.W.2d 505 (Tex. App.—El Paso 1989) (insufficient foundation for physician's letters and reports regarding diagnosis and prognosis).

Hurtado v. Tex. Employment Ins. Ass'n, 574 S.W.2d 536 (Tex. 1978) (trial court erred admitting large volume of medical records over opposing party's objection as to relevance, as opposing party should not be required to sort through such large amount of evidence and cite to court which items are relevant and which are not).

a. Improper Hearsay Evidence

Rodgers v. Dallas Area Rapid Transit, No. 11-02-00127-CV, 2003 WL 1571571 (Tex. App.—Eastland Mar. 27, 2003, no pet.) (not designated for publication) (insufficient foundation for admission of medical records under business records exception to hearsay rule).

Blaylock v. State, No. 12-01-00295-CR, 2003 WL 60533 (Tex. App.—Tyler June 11, 2003, pet. ref'd) (not designated for publication) (insufficient foundation for defendant's blood test results where no evidence regarding who performed blood draw or whether results were recorded by person with personal knowledge of results).

Hooper v. Torres, 790 S.W.2d 757 (Tex. App.—El Paso 1990, writ denied) (portion of medical report representing summaries of findings by other physicians inadmissible).

Cornelison v. Aggregate Haulers, Inc., 777 S.W.2d 542 (Tex. App.—Fort Worth 1989, writ denied) (harmless error admitting statement from medical records regarding cause of incident where record did not establish who made statement and if had personal knowledge of events); but see Texas Rule of Evidence 803(6) (business records exception to hearsay rule).

b. Medical Opinions of Others—Lack of Personal Knowledge

Texas Rule of Evidence 602 states:

> A witness may not testify to a matter *unless evidence is introduced sufficient to support a finding that the witness has personal knowledge of the matter.* Evidence to prove personal knowledge may, but need not, consist of the testimony of the witness. This rule is subject to the provision of Rule 703, relating to opinion testimony by expert witnesses. (Emphasis added.)

Hooper v. Torres, 790 S.W.2d 757 (Tex. App.—El Paso 1990, writ denied) (portion of medical report representing summaries of findings by other physicians inadmissible).

Cornelison v. Aggregate Haulers, Inc., 777 S.W.2d 542 (Tex. App.—Fort Worth 1989, writ denied) ("Statements contained in a medical record as to how an accident happened or where it happened, age, medical history, etc. are not admissible as a business-record exception to the hearsay rule, because the party making the entry in the record does not have personal knowledge as to these matters, and the statements do not become trustworthy just because it is hospital routine to record them.") (Citations omitted.)

c. Patient Medical History

Strauss v. Cont'l Airlines, Inc., 67 S.W.3d 428 (Tex. App.—Houston [14th Dist.] 2002, no pet.) (trial court did not abuse discretion excluding party's psychiatric records where irrelevant and unduly prejudicial).

Hooper v. Torres, 790 S.W.2d 757 (Tex. App.—El Paso 1990, writ denied) (portion of medical report representing summaries of findings by other physicians inadmissible).

Cornelison v. Aggregate Haulers, Inc., 777 S.W.2d 542 (Tex. App.—Fort Worth 1989, writ denied) ("Statements contained in a medical record as to how an accident happened or where it happened, age, medical history, etc. are not admissible as a business-record exception to the hearsay rule, because the party making the entry in the record does not have personal knowledge as to these matters, and the statements do not become trustworthy just because it is hospital routine to record them.") (Citations omitted.)

i. Hearsay

In re Estate of Vackar, 345 S.W.3d 588 (Tex. App.—San Antonio 2011, no pet.) (medical record listing of medications was inadmissible because treating physician did not lay the predicate for the introduction of the list as a business record).

Power v. Kelly, 70 S.W.3d 137 (Tex. App.—San Antonio 2001, pet. denied) (statement regarding past treatment that is made for purposes of medical diagnosis or treatment is not admissible under Rule 803(4)).

Hooper v. Torres, 790 S.W.2d 757 (Tex. App.—El Paso 1990, writ denied) (portion of medical report representing summaries of findings by other physicians inadmissible).

Cornelison v. Aggregate Haulers, Inc., 777 S.W.2d 542 (Tex. App.—Fort Worth 1989, writ denied) (trial court erred admitting statement from medical records regarding cause of incident where record did not establish who made statement and if had personal knowledge of events).

d. Medical Billing—Lack of Foundation

Six Flags Over Tex., Inc. v. Parker, 759 S.W.2d 758 (Tex. App.—Fort Worth 1988, no writ) ("Proof of amounts charged or paid is not proof of reasonableness, and recovery of such expenses will be denied in the absence of evidence showing the charges were reasonable and necessary." (Citations omitted.)).

e. Other Grounds

Other grounds for excluding medical record and billing evidence include:

- Collateral to issues in case;
- Confusing or misleading;
- Cumulative;
- Improper foundation;
- Inadmissible writings;
- Inadmissible hearsay.

4. Opposing Authorities

Reyes v. State, 48 S.W.3d 917 (Tex. App.—Fort Worth 2001, no pet.) (medical records properly authenticated by custodian of records). *See also Glenn v. C & G Elec., Inc.*, 977 S.W.2d 686 (Tex. App.—Fort Worth 1998, pet. denied).

Corpus v. State, 931 S.W.2d 30 (Tex. App.—Austin 1996, pet. dism'd) (defendant's medical records properly authenticated).

Oil Country Haulers, Inc. v. Griffin, 668 S.W.2d 903 (Tex. App.—Houston [14th Dist.] 1984, no writ) (medical bills may be authenticated by individual who received bills).

Home Indem. Co. v. Eason, 635 S.W.2d 593 (Tex. App.—Houston [14th Dist.] 1982, no writ) (medical bills properly authenticated by patient who received them).

a. Medical Opinions of Others—Opinions Used in Diagnosis or Treatment

Burroughs Wellcome Co. v. Crye, 907 S.W.2d 497 (Tex. 1995) (diagnosis contained in medical records admissible as business record).

Castaneda v. State, 28 S.W.3d 685 (Tex. App.—Corpus Christi 2000, pet. ref'd) (medical records of victim, including victim's description of incident, admissible as business records).

Moyer v. State, 948 S.W.2d 525 (Tex. App.—Fort Worth 1997, pet. ref'd) (subjective statements of patient to paramedic admissible where statements made for purposes of diagnosis).

Brooks v. State, 901 S.W.2d 742 (Tex. App.—Fort Worth 1995, writ ref'd) (handwritten notes contained in medical records regarding defendant's statement that his leg was broken and could not walk, admissible as business records).

b. Business Record Hearsay Exception

Texas Rule of Evidence 803 provides, in relevant part, as follows:

> The following are not excluded by the hearsay rule, even though the declarant is available as a witness:
>
> ...
>
> **(6) Records of Regularly Conducted Activity**. A memorandum, report, record, or data compilation, in any form, of acts, events, conditions, opinions, or diagnoses, made at or near the time by, or from information transmitted by, a person with knowledge, if kept in the course of a regularly conducted business activity, and if it was the regular practice of that business activity to make the memorandum, report, record, or data compilation, all as shown by the testimony of the custodian or other qualified witness, or by affidavit that complies with Rule 902(10), unless the source of information or the method or circumstances of preparation indicate lack of trustworthiness. "Business" as used in this paragraph includes any and every kind of regular organized activity whether conducted for profit or not.

Williams v. State, 176 S.W.3d 476 (Tex. App.—Houston [1st Dist.] 2004, no pet.) (medical records properly admitted as business records where foundation provided by registered nurse who recognized them and had participated in patient's treatment).

Reyes v. State, 48 S.W.3d 917 (Tex. App.—Fort Worth 2001, no pet.) (medical records properly admitted as business records).

Castaneda v. State, 28 S.W.3d 685 (Tex. App.—Corpus Christi 2000, pet. ref'd) (medical records of victim admissible as business records). *See also Kan v. State*, 4 S.W.3d 38 (Tex. App.—San Antonio 1999, pet. ref'd).

Glenn v. C & G Elec., Inc., 977 S.W.2d 686 (Tex. App.—Fort Worth 1998, pet. denied) (medical records properly admitted as business records).

Moyer v. State, 948 S.W.2d 525 (Tex. App.—Fort Worth 1997, pet. ref'd) (sufficient foundation provided by paramedic for admission of incident report as business record).

Corpus v. State, 931 S.W.2d 30 (Tex. App.—Austin 1996, pet. dism'd) (defendant's medical records properly admitted as business records).

Brooks v. State, 901 S.W.2d 742 (Tex. App.—Fort Worth 1995, writ ref'd) (handwritten notes in medical records regarding defendant's statement that leg was broken and could not walk admissible as business records, even though custodian of records could not identify handwriting).

Taylor v. State, 755 S.W.2d 548 (Tex. App.—Houston [1st Dist.] 1988, writ ref'd) (sufficient foundation provided by custodian of records for admission of victim's medical records as business records).

c. *Patient History—Observation of Physician*

Glenn v. C & G Elec., Inc., 977 S.W.2d 686 (Tex. App.—Fort Worth 1998, pet. denied) (medical records containing opinions and diagnosis of physicians properly admitted as business records).

d. *Patient History—Pertinent to Medical Diagnosis*

Texas Rule of Evidence 803, states in relevant part:

> The following are not excluded by the hearsay rule, even though the declarant is available as a witness:
>
> (1) Present Sense Impression. A statement describing or explaining an event or condition made while the declarant was perceiving the event or condition, or immediately thereafter.
>
> (2) Excited Utterance. A statement relating to a startling event or condition made while the declarant was under the stress of excitement caused by the event or condition.
>
> (3) Then Existing Mental, Emotional, or Physical Condition. A statement of the declarant's then existing state of mind, emotion, sensation, or physical condition (such as intent, plan, motive, design, mental feeling, pain, or bodily health), but not including a statement of memory or belief to prove the fact remembered or believed unless it relates to the execution, revocation, identification, or terms of declarant's will.
>
> (4) Statements for Purposes of Medical Diagnosis or Treatment. Statements made for purposes of medical diagnosis or treatment and describing medical history, or past or present symptoms, pain, or sensations, or the inception or general character of the cause or external source thereof insofar as reasonably pertinent to diagnosis or treatment.
>
> ...

(24) Statement Against Interest. A statement which was at the time of its making so far contrary to the declarant's pecuniary or proprietary interest, or so far tended to subject the declarant to civil or criminal liability, or to render invalid a claim by the declarant against another, or to make the declarant an object of hatred, ridicule, or disgrace, that a reasonable person in declarant's position would not have made the statement unless believing it to be true. In criminal cases, a statement tending to expose the declarant to criminal liability is not admissible unless corroborating circumstances clearly indicate the trustworthiness of the statement.

Burroughs Wellcome Co. v. Crye, 907 S.W.2d 497 (Tex. 1995) (diagnosis contained in medical records admissible as business record).

Taylor v. State, 268 S.W.3d 571, 591 (Tex. Crim. App. 2008); *Munoz v. State*, 288 S.W.3d 55 (Tex. App.—Houston [1st Dist.] 2009, no pet.) ("in the context of long-term, on-going, after-the-fact mental-health treatment, that the proponent should make it readily apparent on the record 1) that it was important to the efficacy of the treatment (if, in fact, it was important) for the child-declarant to disclose the true identity of the perpetrator and 2) that the child, prior to the disclosure, understood that importance").

Taylor v. State, 268 S.W.3d 571 (Tex. Crim. App. 2008); *Munoz v. State*, 288 S.W.3d 55 (Tex. App.—Houston [1st Dist.] 2009, no pet.) (In the context of statements made by a child to a therapist, "it is incumbent upon the proponent of the hearsay exception for statements for purposes of medical diagnosis or treatment to make the record reflect both (1) that truth-telling was a vital component of the particular course of therapy or treatment involved, and (2) that it is readily apparent that the child-declarant was aware that this was the case.").

Mbugua v. State, 312 S.W.3d 657 (Tex. App.—Houston [1st Dist.] 2009, pet. ref'd) (For statements to be admitted under the exception to the hearsay rule for statements made for purposes of medical diagnosis or treatment, the proponent of the evidence must show that (1) the declarant was aware that the statements were made for the purposes of medical diagnosis or treatment and that proper diagnosis or treatment depended on the veracity of the statement, and (2) the particular statement offered is also pertinent to treatment, that is, it was reasonable for the health care provider to rely on the particular information in treating the declarant.).

Munoz v. State, 288 S.W.3d 55 (Tex. App.—Houston [1st Dist.] 2009, no pet.) (hearsay exception for statements for purposes of medical diagnosis or treatment is premised on the declarant's desire to receive an appropriate medical diagnosis or treatment, and the assumption that the declarant appreciates that the effectiveness of the diagnosis or treatment may depend on the accuracy of the information provided; thus, the declarant's motive in making the statement must be consistent with the purpose of promoting treatment).

Munoz v. State, 288 S.W.3d 55 (Tex. App.—Houston [1st Dist.] 2009, no pet.) (witness need not expressly state that the hearsay declarant recognized the need to be truthful in her statements for the medical treatment hearsay exception to apply; instead, the reviewing court must look to the record to determine if it supports a conclusion that the declarant understood the importance of honesty in the context of medical diagnosis and treatment).

Munoz v. State, 288 S.W.3d 55 (Tex. App.—Houston [1st Dist.] 2009, no pet.) (evidence supported finding that it was important for sexual assault victim to tell her therapist the truth about alleged abuse and that she knew that it was important to tell the truth so as to admit therapist's testimony under medical treatment hearsay exception; therapist impressed on victim that it was important for her to tell therapist truth about her sexual abuse, including identity of perpetrator, in order to facilitate therapist in treating her depression and other manifestations of abuse, and although victim had difficulty telling truth and often lied to escape consequences of her actions, she was aware of need to be truthful with her therapist, and she always acknowledged to her therapist when she had been untruthful).

State Off. Of Risk Mgmt. v. Escalante, 162 S.W.3d 619 (Tex. App.—El Paso 2005, pet. dism'd) (reports of workers' compensation claimant's treating physician properly were admitted under business records hearsay exception; State Office of Risk Management (SORM) did not contend that any of the objectionable documents contained entries which were not made by physician, nor did it suggest that the reports were written solely in response to a request by the insurance carrier or that the evaluation would not have been done otherwise).

Sessums v. State, 129 S.W.3d 242 (Tex. App.—Texarkana 2004, pet. ref'd) (letter written by psychologist who evaluated alleged child victim was admissible in prosecution for indecency with a child under hearsay exception for records of medical diagnosis; psychologist was licensed and had master's degree in counseling psychology, and psychologist treated child).

Reyes v. State, 48 S.W.3d 917 (Tex. App.—Fort Worth 2001, no pet.) (hearsay statements in medical records made for purposes of seeking treatment properly admitted).

Cameron v. State, 988 S.W.2d 835 (Tex. App.—San Antonio 1999, pet. ref'd) (rule 803(4) does not require that the statement be made to a physician, so long as the statement is made for the purpose of medical diagnosis of treatment).

Glenn v. C & G Elec., Inc., 977 S.W.2d 686 (Tex. App.—Fort Worth 1998, pet. denied) (medical records containing opinions and diagnosis of physicians properly admitted as business records).

Moyer v. State, 948 S.W.2d 525 (Tex. App.—Fort Worth 1997, pet. ref'd) (subjective statements of patient to paramedic where statements made for purposes of diagnosis).

Brooks v. State, 901 S.W.2d 742 (Tex. App.—Fort Worth 1995, writ ref'd) (handwritten notes in medical records regarding defendant's statement that leg was broken and could not walk admissible as business records, even though custodian of records could not identify handwriting).

e. *Medical Billing Records—Reasonableness of Charges*

Oil Country Haulers, Inc. v. Griffin, 668 S.W.2d 903 (Tex. App.—Houston [14th Dist.] 1984, no writ) (sufficient foundation that patient's medical bills reasonable and necessary).

Home Indem. Co. v. Eason, 635 S.W.2d 593 (Tex. App.—Houston [14th Dist.] 1982, no writ) (sufficient foundation through testimony of patient and doctor that medical bills reasonable and necessary).

II. Sample Motions

A. Motion to Exclude Gruesome Photographs

NO. _____

_____	§	IN THE DISTRICT COURT
	§	
v.	§	_____ JUDICIAL COURT
	§	
_____	§	_____ COUNTY, TEXAS

Motion to Exclude Gruesome Photographs

Comes now _____, Plaintiff in this cause, and file this, his Motion to Exclude Gruesome Photographs, and in support thereof, Plaintiff would show the Court the following:

1.
FACTUAL BACKGROUND

This is a personal injury action arising out of an automobile versus pedestrian accident that occurred on January 15, 2019. At the time of the incident, the Plaintiff incurred certain injuries to his left knee and kneecap. Discovery in this action revealed that a bystander by the name of Peter Snapshot took fourteen photographs of the accident scene and eight photographs of Plaintiff's injured knee shortly after the incident occurred.

The subject of this motion relates to three close-up photographs taken of the Plaintiff's injured knee by Mr. Snapshot. Copies of the three photographs are attached hereto as Exhibits "A," "B," and "C" respectively. The Defendant does not object to any other photographs identified by Plaintiff in his list of proposed exhibits, including several other shots of Plaintiff's knee taken at the scene and several post-operation photographs. Note too, that for purposes of this motion, Defendant does not challenge the authenticity of the three disputed photographs but reserves the right to raise this objection at trial.

The Defendant seeks to preclude each of the three photographs, based upon the clearly prejudicial and cumulative nature of this evidence.

2.
THIS COURT MAY PRECLUDE PREJUDICIAL OR CUMULATIVE
EVIDENCE PURSUANT TO TEXAS RULE OF EVIDENCE 403

Texas Rule of Evidence 403 states: "[a]lthough relevant, evidence may be excluded if its probative value is substantially outweighed by the danger of unfair prejudice, confusion of the issues, or misleading the jury, or by considerations of undue delay, or needless presentation of cumulative evidence." *Brookshire Bros., Ltd. v. Aldridge*, 438 S.W.3d 9, 26 (Tex. 2014) (evidence that raises a risk of prejudice and confusion of the jury should be excluded); *Farmers Texas County Mutual Insurance Co. v. Pagan*, 453 S.W.3d 454, (Tex. App.—Houston [14th Dist.] 2014, no pet.) (evidence should have been excluded where its probative value was outweighed by danger of confusion of issues and misleading jury).

3.
GRUESOME PHOTOGRAPHS MAY BE EXCLUDED UNDER A RULE 403 BALANCING

A number of courts have held that gruesome photographs may be excluded where offered for no other purpose but to inflame the emotions of the jury. *See Erazo v. State*, 144 S.W.3d 487 (Tex. Crim. App. 2004); *Thrift v. State*, 134 S.W.3d 475, 477 (Tex. App.—Waco 2004), *aff'd*, 176 S.W.3d 221 (Tex. Crim. App. 2005) (trial court abused discretion in indecency with child case by admitting photographs of other naked and aroused teenagers found at defendant's house where evidence unduly prejudicial and inflammatory); *Tidrow v. State*, 916 S.W.2d 623 (Tex. App.—Fort Worth 1996, no pet.) (photograph should be excluded if so horrifying or appalling that juror of normal sensitivity would necessarily encounter difficulty rationally deciding critical issues after viewing it).

In the present case, the three disputed photographs show various angles of extreme close-ups of Plaintiff's injured knee. All three photographs are extremely graphic and add nothing of relevance to Plaintiff's case that could not, and presumably will not, be presented by Plaintiff's medical witnesses and other nonobjectionable photographs of Plaintiff's knee.

The only logical purpose for the introduction of this evidence is to inflame the jury's passions in favor of the Plaintiff and against the Defendant. Avoiding such a result is the very purpose underlying the above-described decisions. As such, the Defendant respectfully requests that the evidence be excluded.

4.
THE PHOTOGRAPHS SHOULD BE EXCLUDED AS CUMULATIVE OF OTHER EVIDENCE

Cumulative photographs may be excluded where the proponent cannot show how the photographs differ from other evidence. *Jones v. State*, 111 S.W.3d 600 (Tex. App.—Dallas 2003, pet. ref'd) (gruesome, prejudicial, and cumulative photographs should not have been admitted at sentencing phase); *Huckaby v. A.G. Perry & Sons, Inc.*, 20 S.W.3d 194 (Tex. App.—Texarkana 2000, pet. denied) (exclusion of fifteen photographs proper where proponent failed to show proved any element not already shown by one admitted photograph); *Tidrow v. State*, 916 S.W.2d 623 (Tex. App.—Fort Worth 1996, no pet.) (photographs may be excluded based on considerations of undue delay or needless presentation of cumulative evidence); *Cecil v. T.M.E. Invs.*, 893 S.W.2d 38 (Tex. App.—Corpus Christi 1994, no writ) (exclusion of two of four photographs proper where merely duplicating two admitted photographs); *Franco v. Graham*, 470 S.W.2d 429 (Tex. Civ. App.—Corpus Christi 1971), *aff'd as reformed*, 488 S.W.2d 390 (Tex. 1972) (no error refusing to admit damaged vehicle photographs where cumulative of evidence already presented).

In the present case, the Plaintiff has identified more than a dozen additional photographs of his injured knee. Clearly, the Plaintiff will have an opportunity to prove his case for damages with ample photographic evidence that objectively shows the nature and extent of his injuries.

The three disputed photographs add nothing to Plaintiff's case that is not presented in the other photographs. What these photographs do add, however, is an extremely bloody close-up view of the inside of Plaintiff's injured knee.

Clearly this evidence is cumulative and intended solely to inflame the jury against the Defendant. As such, the Defendant requests that the evidence be excluded.

Dated: _____ *(Date)* _____

By: _____

_____ *(Name of Counsel)* _____

Attorneys for Defendant,

_____ *(Name of Defendant)* _____

B. Motion to Exclude Written Letter

NO. _____

	§	IN THE DISTRICT COURT
_____	§	
	§	_____ JUDICIAL COURT
v.	§	
_____	§	_____ COUNTY, TEXAS

Motion to Exclude Written Letter

Comes now _____, Plaintiff in this cause, and file this, his Motion to Exclude a Written Letter, and in support thereof, Plaintiff would show the Court the following:

1.
FACTUAL BACKGROUND

This is a personal injury action arising out of a slip-and-fall accident within Defendant's privately owned store. Plaintiff sued Defendant for failure to maintain and failure to properly train its employees. Defendant owns and operates a small grocery store, which Plaintiff frequents. On December 12, 2018, Plaintiff was shopping when she slipped and fell in a puddle of water on the floor. Plaintiff contends Defendant was negligent in the operation of the store and in maintaining a safe environment. Plaintiff has sustained injuries to her hip from the fall.

After the fall, "Smith" created a report relating to the incident. Subsequent to creating the report, "Smith" wrote a private email to several other store employees commenting about the female Plaintiff's physique and provocative clothing.

The manager, who is familiar with the recordkeeping of the store, will testify as to the extent of his duties within the store at the time of the accident. Defendant is informed and believes that Plaintiff will attempt to admit evidence of the email letters written by Smith after the incident. It is noteworthy that Smith was not present at the time of the accident. Plaintiff contends the purpose of the evidence of the letter is to impeach the manager by specific acts of misconduct.

By this motion, Defendant seeks an order precluding the introduction of any evidence, or any mention of evidence, relating to the email letters written by Smith in this matter. This motion is based upon the grounds that the evidence is unduly prejudicial, irrelevant, inadmissible hearsay, and clearly inadmissible under the laws of this state.

2.
THIS COURT MAY EXCLUDE PREJUDICIAL EVIDENCE IN ADVANCE OF TRIAL BY WAY OF AN IN LIMINE MOTION

The Court has the inherent power to grant a motion in limine to exclude evidence which could be objected to at trial, either as irrelevant or subject to exclusion as unduly prejudicial. *Wackenhut Corp. v. Gutierrez*, 453 S.W.3d 917, 920 n.3 (Tex. 2016); *In re BCH Development, LLC*, 525 S.W.3d 920, 925 (Tex. App.—Dallas 2017, orig. proceeding). Texas Rule of Evidence 403 allows the court to exclude evidence where there is a substantial danger that the probative value will be outweighed by the danger of undue prejudice. *See Diamond Offshore Services Ltd. v. Williams*, 542 S.W.3d 539, 549 (Tex. 2018); *Brookshire Bros., Ltd. v. Aldridge*, 438 S.W.3d 9, 34 (Tex. 2014).

Moreover, the court may hear and determine the question of the admissibility of evidence outside the presence or hearing of the jury. *See Weidner v. Sanchez*, 14 S.W.3d 353, 363 (Tex. App.—Houston [14th Dist.] 2000, no pet.); *Kendrix v. S. Pac. Transp. Co.*, 907 S.W.2d 111, 113 (Tex. App.—Beaumont 1995, writ denied); Texas Rule of Civil Procedure 166; and Texas Rules of Evidence 103 and 104.

In the present matter, evidence of manager's allegedly prurient letters is not probative as to show any bias or corruption of the manager. Whether the manager wrote a sexually explicit letter does not shed light on the manager's duties. Moreover, such evidence would be much more prejudicial to the Defendant than probative because of the substantial danger that the jury may confuse the issue as to the Defendant's liabilities. The manager's letters are not probative as to whether the Defendant adequately trained the manager, and therefore would unduly disadvantage the Defendant if such evidence were introduced.

3.
THE MANAGER'S LETTER TO ANOTHER EMPLOYEE CONSTITUTES INADMISSIBLE HEARSAY

Texas Rule of Evidence 802 states "[h]earsay is not admissible except as provided by statute or these rules or by other rules prescribed pursuant to statutory authority." Texas Rule of Evidence 801(d) defines hearsay as "a statement, other than one made by the declarant while testifying at the trial or hearing, offered in evidence to prove the truth of the matter asserted."

In the present case, Plaintiff intends to introduce the letters to prove the manager's specific act of misconduct, namely the sexually explicit contents of the letter. This is hearsay in its purest form; the Plaintiff is offering the letter to prove the truth of the contents of the letter. Thus, the letters are inadmissible hearsay and should be excluded.

4.
EVIDENCE OF DEFENDANT'S LETTER IS IRRELEVANT AND SHOULD THEREFORE BE EXCLUDED

Texas Rule of Evidence 402 states that "evidence which is not relevant is inadmissible." Relevant evidence is defined by Texas Rule of Evidence 401 as "having any tendency to make the existence of any fact that is of consequence to the determination of the action more probable or less probable than it would be without the evidence." See *Torrington v. Stutzman*, 46 S.W.3d 829 (Tex. 2000) (evidence not relevant is inadmissible).

The fact that the manager had written this letter containing sexually explicit stories would have no bearing on the manager's ability to adequately manage the store, nor have any bearing on the Defendant's ability to adequately maintain the store or train employees.

In *Abdygapparova v. State,* 243 S.W.3d 191 (Tex. App.—San Antonio 2007, pet. ref'd), a letter sent by an individual to the defendant, outlining the individual's sexual desires and fantasies with the defendant and other women, was not relevant in a capital murder prosecution. Although the State contended that the defendant's sexual orientation was relevant to the sexual assault of the victim, the letter was sent to the defendant by an individual, living in another state and whom she had never met, did not tend to make anything as to the defendant, much less her sexual orientation or whether she committed a sexual assault, any more or less probable.

5.
EVIDENCE OF THE LETTERS IS IMPROPER IMPEACHMENT UNDER THE TEXAS RULES OF EVIDENCE

There are public policy limitations of examination concerning a witness's credibility. In the present case, the manager's letters to another employee may be likened to an immoral act but may not be equated with a specific act of misconduct, namely one that results in a conviction. It is for these reasons that any inquiry into the manager's letters for the purpose of impeachment by specific acts is improper and therefore inadmissible under the Texas Rules of Evidence.

6.
CONCLUSION

Based on the foregoing, Defendant respectfully requests that this Court enter an order excluding any and all evidence pertaining to Defendant's email letters.

Dated: _____(Date of Motion)_____

By: _____

_____(Name of Counsel)_____

Attorneys for Plaintiff,

_____(Name of Plaintiff)_____

C. Motion to Exclude Improper Medical Records

NO. _____

	§	IN THE DISTRICT COURT
_____	§	
	§	_____ JUDICIAL COURT
v.	§	
	§	
_____	§	_____ COUNTY, TEXAS

Motion to Exclude Medical Records

Comes now _____, Plaintiff in this cause, and file this, his Motion to Exclude Medical Records, and in support thereof, Plaintiff would show the Court the following:

1.
FACTUAL BACKGROUND

This is a personal injury action arising out of an all-terrain vehicle (ATV) accident involving a pedestrian Plaintiff that occurred on the night of December 23, 2018, when the Plaintiff suffered a broken leg, two cracked ribs, a fractured ankle, and a deep cut above the left eye requiring 34 stitches. Plaintiff seeks recovery of medical expenses and recovery for future lost earnings. This motion seeks to preclude the Defendant from attempting to present irrelevant, prejudicial, and hearsay evidence relating to the Plaintiff's medical history at the time of trial. Plaintiff's medical history includes two separate references to prior treatment for the use of nonprescription drugs, Plaintiff's participation in an alcohol rehabilitation program in 2002, and a statement Plaintiff made to a treating physician that Plaintiff experienced "symptoms of withdrawal" a few hours prior to sustaining injuries caused by his collision with an ATV. Plaintiff was not impaired at the time of the accident.

2.
PLAINTIFF'S MEDICAL HISTORY IS NOT RELEVANT TO ANY MATERIAL ISSUE IN THIS CASE

Texas Rule of Evidence 402 states that "evidence which is not relevant is inadmissible." Relevant evidence is defined by Texas Rule of Evidence 401 as "having any tendency to make the existence of any fact that is of consequence to the determination of the action more probable or less probable than it would be without the evidence." *See Torrington v. Stutzman*, 46 S.W.3d 829, 845 (Tex. 2000). Irrelevant evidence is not admissible. *Morale v. State*, 557 S.W.3d 569, 573 (Tex. 2018); *Diamond Offshore Services Ltd. v. Williams*, 542 S.W.3d 539, 549 (Tex. 2018).

Plaintiff's medical history referencing prior drug and alcohol use is not relevant to the determination of liability in this case. In *Engelman Irrigation Dist. v. Shields Bros., Inc.*, 960 S.W.2d 343 (Tex. App.—Corpus Christi 1997), *pet. denied per curiam*, 989 S.W.2d 360 (Tex. 1998), the court of appeals determined that the trial court did not abuse its discretion by excluding evidence of a prior conviction of a farmer for a drug offense and a resulting forfeiture of $37,000, offered to impeach the farmer's testimony on the reason why a bank loan was denied to a farming enterprise. There was little, if any relevance of the denied bank loan to the main issue in the case of whether an irrigation district breached a contract to deliver water to the farming enterprise within a reasonable time.

Here, because no evidence exists of Plaintiff's impairment at the time of the accident, Plaintiff's medical history (including Plaintiff's participation in rehabilitation eight years ago) is irrelevant to the determination of any damages at issue in this case and should be excluded.

3.
ADMISSION OF PLAINTIFF'S MEDICAL RECORDS WOULD CREATE UNDUE PREJUDICE TO PLAINTIFF

Texas Rule of Evidence 403 states that "[a]lthough relevant, evidence may be excluded if its probative value is substantially outweighed by the danger of unfair prejudice, confusion of the issues, or misleading the jury, or by considerations of undue delay, or needless presentation of cumulative evidence." *See E.I. du Pont de Nemours & Co. v. Robinson*, 923 S.W.2d 549 (Tex. 1995) (exclusion of expert testimony under Rule 403 where potential for confusing issues and misleading jury); *Sells v. State*, 121 S.W.3d 748 (Tex. Crim. App. 2003), *cert. denied*, 540 U.S. 986 (2003) (confusing videotape); *Rivera v. State*, 130 S.W.3d 454 (Tex. App.—Corpus Christi 2004, no pet.) (confusing evidence regarding results of police report); and *Franco v. State*, 25 S.W.3d 26 (Tex. App.—El Paso 2000, pet. ref'd) (confusing scientific evidence by an unqualified expert).

Rule 403 justifies the preclusion of the requested evidence in this case. Plaintiff's medical history is irrelevant because of the sensitive nature and negative associations people carry and ultimately project on to drug and alcohol users. Therefore, the Defendant's admission of this evidence would certainly prejudice the Plaintiff because it would allow for the characterization of Plaintiff as an addict or, at best, a former addict. Because the sobriety of the Plaintiff is not at issue in this case, Plaintiff's prior drug use, if admitted, may only serve the purpose of inflaming the jury or creating a prejudicial bias against the moving party. In the present case, Plaintiff's veracity is not under attack and any attempts Defendant makes to derail Plaintiff's credibility by exploiting Plaintiff's previous drug and alcohol use is unfair and does not serve the interests of justice. Therefore, the evidence concerning Plaintiff's medical history and past drug use is misleading and has next to no probative value. In order to keep the jury from confusing the issues or harboring ill feelings for the Plaintiff, the medical history should be kept out.

4.
CONCLUSION

Based upon all of the above, and the highly sensitive nature of Plaintiff's medical history involving prior drug use, alcohol rehabilitation, and statement to his doctor about withdrawal symptoms, exclusion of reference to the Plaintiff's medical history is proper in this case especially since Plaintiff was sober when struck by Defendant's ATV.

Dated: _____ *(Date of Motion)* _____

By: _____

_____ *(Name of Counsel)* _____

Attorneys for Plaintiff,

_____ *(Name of Plaintiff)* _____

CHAPTER 5

Tests and Scientific Evidence

I. Motion Authorities
   A. Motion to Exclude Tests, Experiments, and Related Testimony
      1. Suggested Motion Text
      2. Motion Summary
      3. Supporting Authorities—Expert Not Qualified
         a. Not Generally Accepted, Civil Cases
         b. Not Generally Accepted—*Kelly* Decision in Criminal Cases
         c. Not Made Under Substantially Similar Conditions
         d. Not Reliable
         e. Scientific Procedures Not Proper
         f. Speculative or Conjectural
         g. Too Time-Consuming/Collateral Issues/Speculative
         h. Expert Testimony Not Needed
         i. Not Relevant
      4. Opposing Authorities
         a. Court's Discretion
         b. General Acceptance—Published Precedent
            i. Level of Acceptance in Scientific Community
            ii. Judicial Notice
         c. Similar Conditions Requirement
         d. Reliability
         e. Cumulative
         f. Weight vs. Admissibility
   B. Motion to Exclude Junk Science and Related Evidence
      1. Suggested Motion Text
      2. Motion Summary
      3. Supporting Authorities
         a. Hedonic Damages Evidence
         b. "Truth Serum" Evidence
         c. Polygraph Evidence
            i. Per se Inadmissibility
            ii. Stipulation of the Parties
            iii. Refusal to Take Polygraph
         d. Battered Spouse Syndrome
         e. Abused Child Characteristics
         f. Hypnosis Evidence
         g. Psychological Profiling
         h. Accident Reconstruction Evidence

i. Biomechanic Evidence
j. Statistical Evidence—Exclusion of Confusing Evidence
   i. Disapproved Statistics Evidence
   ii. Statistical Significance Requirements
   iii. Statistics in Products Liability or Negligence Cases
   iv. Statistics in Employment Discrimination Cases
4. Opposing Authorities—Approved Tests
   a. Hedonic Damages
   b. Polygraph Evidence
      i. Stipulation of Parties
   c. Battered Spouse Syndrome
   d. Abused Child Characteristics
   e. Hypnosis Evidence
   f. Accident Reconstruction and Biomechanic
   g. Statistics Evidence
      i. Where Relevant
   h. Evidence That Is Not "Novel"

II. Sample Motions
   A. Motion to Exclude Evidence of Statistical Analysis
   B. Motion to Exclude Evidence of Hypnosis
   C. Motion to Exclude Expert Testimony

I. Motion Authorities

A. Motion to Exclude Tests, Experiments, and Related Testimony

1. Suggested Motion Text

(*Name of Moving Party*) hereby moves this Court for an order excluding any and all evidence, references to evidence, testimony, or argument relating to (*Describe Nature of Test or Experiment*) conducted by (*Name of Witness That Conducted Test or Experiment*). The motion is based upon the ground that the evidence is (*Describe Challenges to Evidence, e.g., "not generally accepted in the scientific community," "not made under substantially identical conditions to subject incident," "not reliable," etc.*) and is therefore inadmissible.

2. Motion Summary

This motion is used to exclude evidence of tests and experiments that do not meet established requirements for admissibility. In general, to determine whether scientific evidence is admissible, the court must consider: 1) the extent to which the theory has been or can be tested; 2) the extent to which the technique relies upon the subjective interpretation of the expert; 3) whether the theory has been subjected to peer review and/or publication; 4) the technique's potential rate of error; 5) whether the underlying theory or technique has been generally accepted as valid by the relevant scientific community; 6) the nonjudicial uses which have been made of the theory or technique; 7) any other factor which is helpful to determine the reliability of scientific evidence. *Transcontinental Ins. Co. v. Crump*, 330 S.W.3d 211, 215 (Tex. 2010); *Mack Trucks, Inc. v. Tamez*, 206 S.W.3d 572, 578 (Tex. 2006); *E.I. du Pont de Nemours & Co. v. Robinson*, 923 S.W.2d 549, 557 (Tex. 1995).

Test evidence may be challenged for a variety of reasons, including: lack of proper expert qualifications; dissimilar conditions; not grounded in science; speculative; unreliable; and too time-consuming. See generally *Sears, Roebuck & Co. v. Kunze*, 996 S.W.2d 416, 424 (Tex. App.—Beaumont 1999, pet. denied).

This motion is typically presented at what is referred to as a *Robinson* hearing, named after the leading case of *E.I. du Pont de Nemours & Co. v. Robinson*, 923 S.W.2d 549, 557 (Tex. 1995).

3. Supporting Authorities—Expert Not Qualified

Texas Rule of Evidence 702 sets out the basic requirements for expert qualification:

> If scientific, technical, or other specialized knowledge will assist the trier-of-fact to understand the evidence or to determine a fact in issue, a witness qualified as an expert by knowledge, skill, experience, training, or education may testify thereto in the form of an opinion or otherwise.

Gunn v. McCoy, 554 S.W.3d 645, 662 (Tex. Crim. App. 2018) ("To testify as an expert, a witness must be qualified, and the proposed testimony must be relevant to the issues in the case and based upon a reliable foundation.").

Gunn v. McCoy, 554 S.W.3d 645, 662 (Tex. Crim. App. 2018) ("An expert's opinion may be considered unreliable if it is based on assumed facts that vary materially from the actual facts, or if it is based on tests or data that do not support the conclusions reached.").

Gunn v. McCoy, 554 S.W.3d 645, 662 (Tex. Crim. App. 2018) ("Expert testimony may also be unreliable if there is simply too great an analytical gap between the data [relied upon] and the opinion proffered.... [Courts] are not required to ignore fatal gaps in an expert's analysis or assertions that are simply incorrect, and such a flaw in an expert's reasoning renders the scientific testimony unreliable and, legally, no evidence.").

In re Commitment of Bohannan, 388 S.W.3d 296, 304 (Tex. 2012), *cert. denied*, 133 S. Ct. 2747 (May 28, 2013) (experts must be qualified by knowledge, skill, experience, training, or education to assist the trier of fact to understand the evidence or to determine a fact in issue).

In re Commitment of Bohannan, 388 S.W.3d 296, 304 (Tex. 2012), *cert. denied*, 133 S. Ct. 2747 (May 28, 2013) (that a witness has knowledge, skill, expertise, or training does not necessarily mean that the witness can assist the trier of fact).

In re Commitment of Bohannan, 388 S.W.3d 296, 304 (Tex. 2012), *cert. denied*, 133 S. Ct. 2747 (May 28, 2013) (credentials alone do not qualify an expert to testify).

In re Commitment of Bohannan, 388 S.W.3d 296, 304 (Tex. 2012), *cert. denied*, 133 S. Ct. 2747 (May 28, 2013) (the test is whether the offering party has established that the expert has knowledge, skill, experience, training, or education regarding the specific issue before the court, which would qualify the expert to give an opinion on that particular subject).

In re Mem'l Med. Ctr., Inc., 275 S.W.3d 458, 463 (Tex. 2008) (orig. proceeding) ("[T]here is no validity ... to the notion that every licensed medical doctor should be automatically qualified to testify as an expert on every medical question.").

Gen. Motors Corp. v. Iracheta, 161 S.W.3d 462, 470 (Tex. 2006) (expert testimony inadmissible because the expert not qualified).

Gammill v. Jack Williams Chevrolet, Inc., 972 S.W.2d 713, 719 (Tex. 1998) (no error in determining one of the mechanical engineers was not qualified to testify as an expert on the subject matter at issue).

Schultz on Behalf of Schultz v. Lone Star Road Construction, Ltd., 593 S.W.3d 750, 758 (Tex. App.—Houston [14th Dist.] 2019, no pet.) ("When an expert's opinion is based on an assumed fact that varies materially from the actual facts, the opinion lacks probative value and cannot raise a genuine fact issue.").

Schultz on Behalf of Schultz v. Lone Star Road Construction, Ltd., 593 S.W.3d 750, 758 (Tex. App.—Houston [14th Dist.] 2019, no pet.) ("If the record contains no evidence supporting an expert's material factual assumptions, or if such assumptions are contrary to conclusively proven facts, opinion testimony founded on those assumptions is not competent evidence.").

Equistar Chemicals, LP v. ClydeUnion DB, Ltd., 579 S.W.3d 505, 511 (Tex. App.—Houston [14th Dist.] 2019, pet. denied) ("Expert testimony is not reliable if there is too great an analytical gap between the data on which the expert relies and the opinion offered.... Whether an analytical gap exists is largely determined by comparing the facts the expert relied on, the facts in the record, and the expert's ultimate opinion ... An analytical gap exists if the expert's opinion is based on assumed facts that vary materially from the facts in the record.").

Padilla v. Loweree, 354 S.W.3d 856, 863 (Tex. App.—El Paso 2011, pet. denied) ("In deciding whether an expert is qualified to testify, the trial court must ensure those who purport to be experts truly have expertise concerning the 'actual subject about which they are offering an opinion.'").

Pediatrix Med. Group, Inc. v. Robinson, 352 S.W.3d 879, 884 (Tex. App.—Dallas 2011, no pet.) ("Under the requirements set out in section 74.401, the proper inquiry concerning whether a physician is qualified to testify as a medical expert in a medical malpractice action is not the physician's area of practice, but the stated familiarity with the issues involved in the claim before the court.").

Champion v. Great Dane Ltd. P'ship, 286 S.W.3d 533, 544 (Tex. App.—Houston [14th Dist.] 2009, no pet.) ("[I]f the expert is not qualified to offer a particular opinion in a particular case, then the expert's testimony is not admissible because it does not rise above mere speculation, and, accordingly, does not offer genuine assistance to the jury.").

MCI Sales & Serv., Inc. v. Hinton, 272 S.W.3d 17, 30 (Tex. App.—Waco 2008), *aff'd*, 329 S.W.3d 475 (Tex. 2010), *cert. denied*, 131 S. Ct. 2903 (2011) ("[T]o establish a witness's expert qualifications, the party calling the witness must show that the expert has knowledge, skill, experience, training, or education regarding the specific issue before the court which would qualify the expert to give an opinion on that particular subject.").

Page v. State Farm Lloyds, 259 S.W.3d 257, 267 (Tex. App.—Waco 2008), *rev'd on other grounds*, 315 S.W.3d 525 (Tex. 2010) (in deciding if an expert is qualified, trial courts must ensure that those who purport to be experts truly have expertise concerning the actual subject about which they are offering an opinion).

Bryan v. Watamull, 230 S.W.3d 503, 518 (Tex. App.—Dallas 2007, pet. denied) ("[I]n order to demonstrate the expert is qualified, the offering party must establish the expert has knowledge, skill, experience, training, or education regarding the specific issue before the trial court which would qualify the expert to given an opinion on that particular subject.").

Quiroz v. Covenant Health Sys., 234 S.W.3d 74, 88 (Tex. App.—El Paso 2007, pet. denied) (physician's expert opinion regarding the link between a child's permanent brain injury and cerebral palsy was not admissible where the doctor testified not only to the complexity of this issue but also about his lack of professional experience with similar injuries).

Praytor v. Ford Motor Co., 97 S.W.3d 237, 245 (Tex. App.—Houston [14th Dist.] 2002, no pet.) (trial court properly determined insufficient foundation to qualify certain witnesses as expert witnesses).

a. Not Generally Accepted, Civil Cases

Merck & Co. v. Garza, 347 S.W.3d 256, 263 (Tex. 2011) ("[W]hile the controlled, experimental, and prospective nature of clinical trials undoubtedly make them more reliable than retroactive, observational studies, both must show a statistically significant doubling of the risk in order to be some evidence that a drug more likely than not caused a particular injury.").

Nabors Well Services, Ltd v. Romero, 508 S.W.3d 512, 531 (Tex. App.—El Paso 2016, pet. denied) ("A single study by itself would not suffice to establish legal causation.... The study must show other indicia of scientific validity, such an adequate sample size, an accounting for confounding variables, and a proper confidence interval.... Courts should be skeptical of scientific evidence which is neither published nor peer reviewed.... A related factor ... is whether the study was prepared only for litigation.... And once the study showing general causation is accepted, the party must show that their circumstances are similar to the group analyzed in the study.").

In re Allied Chem. Corp., 227 S.W.3d 652, 656 (Tex. 2007) (orig. proceeding) (claimants in a mass toxic tort action must have an expert who can answer "why [an epidemiological] study is reliable, and how the plaintiffs' exposure is similar to that of the study's subjects. An expert must also exclude other causes with reasonable certainty.").

Cooper Tire & Rubber Co. v. Mendez, 204 S.W.3d 797, 805 (Tex. 2006) (expert's testimony regarding "wax contamination theory amounted to no more than subjective belief or unsupported speculation.... His explanation for the tire failure was a naked hypothesis untested and unconfirmed by the methods of science and was legally insufficient to establish a manufacturing defect that caused the failure" of a tire).

E.I. du Pont de Nemours & Co. v. Robinson, 923 S.W.2d 549, 557 (Tex. 1995) (scientific evidence not grounded "in the methods and procedures of science" is no more than "subjective belief or unsupported speculation").

Dallas County v. Crestview Corners Car Wash, 370 S.W.3d 25, 37 (Tex. App.—Dallas 2012, pet. denied) (expert's "bald assurance" that he used a widely accepted appraisal method is not sufficient to demonstrate that his opinion is reliable).

Lockett v. HB Zachry Co., 285 S.W.3d 63, 68 (Tex. App.—Houston [1st Dist.] 2009, no pet.) (use of epidemiological studies to demonstrate increased risk of injury caused by exposure to a toxic substance, requires "a plaintiff to show that he is similar to the individuals in the study.... This showing includes proof that the injured person was exposed to the same substance, that the exposure or dose levels were comparable to or greater to those in the studies, that the exposure occurred before the onset of injury, and that the timing of the onset of injury was consistent with that experienced by those in the study.").

Lincoln v. Clark Freight Lines, Inc., 285 S.W.3d 79, 83 (Tex. App.—Houston [1st Dist.] 2009, no pet.) (scientific evidence that is not grounded in the methods and procedures of science is no more than subjective belief or unsupported speculation and is therefore inadmissible).

Whirlpool Corp. v. Camacho, 251 S.W.3d 88, 97 (Tex. App.—Corpus Christi 2008), *rev'd on other grounds*, 298 S.W.3d 631 (Tex. 2009) (scientific expert testimony is reliable, rather than mere subjective belief or unsupported speculation, if it is grounded in the methods and procedures of science).

Hernandez v. State, 127 S.W.3d 206, 220 (Tex. App.—Houston [1st Dist.] 2003, pet. ref'd) (trial court did not abuse discretion excluding proposed expert testimony where the doctor "generated no written report, and, other than briefly mentioning that he had applied the DSM–IV, he did not explain on what other 'mainstream psychiatry' studies or techniques he relied, how he had applied those studies or techniques to appellant. Likewise, the doctor did not identify the 'historical data' on which he based his opinion concerning appellant's mental state.").

Green v. State, 55 S.W.3d 633, 639 (Tex. App.—Tyler 2001, pet. ref'd), *aff'd*, 116 S.W.3d 26 (Tex. 2003), *cert. denied*, 535 U.S. 958 (2002) (defendant failed to show proposed expert reliable where expert failed to show what authorities in field he relied upon for opinions).

> *Note: Texas no longer follows the* Frye *"general acceptance" test. See* Frye v. United States, *293 F. 1013 (D.C. Cir. 1923). Instead, whether an underlying technique or theory has been generally accepted is just one factor to consider in determining the admissibility of scientific evidence. See* E.I. du Pont de Nemours & Co. v. Robinson, *923 S.W.2d 549, 557 (Tex. 1995) (listing seven factors to consider in determining admissibility of expert testimony);* Merck & Co., Inc. v. Ernst, *296 S.W.3d 81, 263 (Tex. App.—Houston [14th Dist.] 2009, pet. denied), cert. denied, 132 S. Ct. 1980 (2012);* Sears, Roebuck & Co. v. Kunze, *996 S.W.2d 416, 424 (Tex. App.—Beaumont 1999, pet. denied) (applying seven factors to test evidence).*

b. Not Generally Accepted—Kelly *Decision in Criminal Cases*

Wolfe v. State, 509 S.W.3d 325, 335 (Tex. Crim. App. 2017) ("For expert testimony to be admissible under [the Rules of Evidence], the proponent of the expert scientific evidence must demonstrate by clear and convincing evidence that the testimony is sufficiently reliable and relevant to help the jury in reaching accurate results.").

Wolfe v. State, 509 S.W.3d 325, 335 (Tex. Crim. App. 2017) ("[T]he proponent [of expert scientific evidence] must prove two prongs: (1) the testimony is based on a reliable scientific foundation, and (2) it is relevant to the issues in the case.").

Wolfe v. State, 509 S.W.3d 325, 335 (Tex. Crim. App. 2017) (citing *Kelly*, "[T]he proponent of scientific evidence must prove: (1) the underlying scientific theory must be valid; (2) the technique applying the theory must be valid; and (3) the technique must have been properly applied on the occasion in question" and the court must consider the seven factors of reliability).

Wolfe v. State, 509 S.W.3d 325, 335 (Tex. Crim. App. 2017) ("In weighing [the] factors as a means of assessing reliability [of expert scientific evidence], 'the focus is to determine whether the evidence has its basis in sound scientific methodology such that testimony about "junk science" is weeded out.'").

Bigon v. State, 252 S.W.3d 360, 367 (Tex. Crim. App. 2008) (proponent of scientific evidence must show the court, by clear and convincing evidence, that the evidence is reliable, and to show reliability, three criteria must be met: (1) the underlying theory is valid; (2) the technique applying said theory is valid; and (3) the technique was properly applied on the occasion in question).

Vela v. State, 209 S.W.3d 128, 133 (Tex. Crim. App. 2006) ("[R]eliability [of expert testimony] depends upon whether the evidence has its basis in sound scientific methodology. This demands a certain technical showing that gives a trial judge the opportunity to weed out testimony pertaining to so-called 'junk science.'").

Kelly v. State, 824 S.W.2d 568, 572 (Tex. Crim. App. 1992) (evidence must be relevant and reliable to be admissible; DNA evidence should have been admitted).

Haley v. State, 396 S.W.3d 756, 766 n.2 (Tex. App.—Houston [14th Dist.] 2013, no pet.) ("[T]he fact another trial court has previously allowed scientific testimony by a particular witness does not mean the witness's testimony is *ipso facto* scientifically reliable in the present case.").

c. Not Made Under Substantially Similar Conditions

Kainer v. Walker, 377 S.W.2d 613, 616 (Tex. 1964), *rev'd on other grounds, Burk Royalty Co. v. Walls*, 616 S.W.2d 911 (Tex. 1981) (evidence of out-of-court experiment should be admitted by trial court only when there is also evidence that experiments were conducted "under conditions substantially similar to those in existence at the time of the accident" at issue).

Fort Worth & Denver Ry. Co. v. Williams, 375 S.W.2d 279, 282 (Tex. 1964) ("In order to render evidence of an experiment made out of court and without the presence of the opposing party admissible, it is generally held that there must be a substantial similarity between conditions existing at the time of the occurrence which gives rise to the litigation and those in existence at the time the experiment is conducted for demonstration purposes.").

Benson v. Chalk, 536 S.W.3d 886, 904 (Tex. App.—Houston [1st Dist.] 2017, pet. denied) ("When an experiment is conducted out-of-court and in the absence of opposing counsel, there must be a substantial similarity between the conditions existing at the time of the experiment and the actual event that is the subject of litigation.").

Benson v. Chalk, 536 S.W.3d 886, 904 (Tex. App.—Houston [1st Dist.] 2017, pet. denied) ("Where there exists a dissimilarity in the conditions, if the differences are minor or are explained to the jury, the admission of the experiment is within the trial court's discretion to determine whether the dissimilarity would cause the evidence to confuse rather than aid the jury and, thus, whether the evidence should be excluded.").

Cont'l Bus Sys., Inc. v. Biggers, 322 S.W.2d 1, 11 (Tex. Civ. App.—Houston 1959, writ ref'd n.r.e.) ("[T]he party offering evidence of out-of-court experiments must lay proper foundation by showing a similarity of circumstances and conditions.").

Hill v. Hanan & Son, 62 Tex. Civ. App. 191, 193, 131 S.W. 245, 246 (Tex. Civ. App. 1910, no writ) ("Experiments, comparisons, other instances, and occurrences are at best very unsatisfactory evidence, and before the same are admitted it should be made to appear that the conditions or circumstances were identical, or at least so similar as that the proposed evidence will reasonably tend to establish the truth as to the subject of inquiry.").

d. Not Reliable

Gunn v. McCoy, 554 S.W.3d 645, 661 (Tex. Crim. App. 2018) ("[E]xamination of an expert's underlying methodology is a task for the trial court in its role as gatekeeper.").

Rogers v. Zanetti, 518 S.W.3d 394, 405 (Tex. 2017) (expert's "assurance of familiarity and credibility is not a demonstrable and reasoned basis upon which to evaluate his opinion.... An ipse dixit is still an ipse dixit even if offered by the most trustworthy of sources.").

Rogers v. Zanetti, 518 S.W.3d 394, 405 (Tex. 2017) ("An expert's familiarity with the facts is not alone a satisfactory basis for his or her opinion.").

Wolfe v. State, 509 S.W.3d 325, 335 (Tex. Crim. App. 2017) ("Unreliable scientific evidence is inadmissible because it simply will not assist the jury to understand the evidence or accurately determine a fact in issue; such evidence obfuscates rather than leads to an intelligent evaluation of the facts.").

Southwestern Energy Production Company v. Berry–Helfand, 491 S.W.3d 699, 717 (Tex. 2016) ("Courts must 'rigorously examine the validity of the facts and assumptions on which expert testimony is based.' If an expert's opinion is unreliable because it is based on assumed facts that vary from the actual facts, the opinion is not probative evidence.").

Kumho Tire Co. Ltd. v. Carmichael, 526 U.S. 137, 147 (1999) (*Daubert* standard for determining reliability of testimony stating scientific conclusions may apply to both scientists and nonscientists).

Gharda USA, Inc. v. Control Solutions, Inc., 464 S.W.3d 338, 349 (Tex. 2015) ("Reliable expert testimony must be based on a probability standard, rather than on mere possibility.").

Gharda USA, Inc. v. Control Solutions, Inc., 464 S.W.3d 338, 349 (Tex. 2015) ("Expert testimony is unreliable if there is too great an analytical gap between the data on which the expert relies and the opinion offered.... Whether an analytical gap exists is largely determined by comparing the facts the expert relied on, the facts in the record, and the expert's ultimate opinion.").

Gharda USA, Inc. v. Control Solutions, Inc., 464 S.W.3d 338, 349 (Tex. 2015) ("Analytical gaps may include circumstances in which the expert unreliably applies otherwise sound principles and methodologies, ... the expert's opinion is based on assumed facts that vary materially from the facts in the record, ... or the expert's opinion is based on tests or data that do not support the conclusions reached.").

Bostic v. Georgia-Pacific Corp., 439 S.W.3d 332, 349 (Tex. 2013) (if an expert's scientific testimony is not reliable, it is not evidence).

Bostic v. Georgia-Pacific Corp., 439 S.W.3d 332, 349 (Tex. 2013) (in a product liability case, proof that a defendant's product more than doubled the plaintiff's risk of injury must be shown through reliable expert testimony that is based on epidemiological studies or similarly reliable scientific testimony).

Merck & Co. v. Garza, 347 S.W.3d 256, 263 (Tex. 2011) (clinical trials and epidemiological studies must show a statistically significant doubling of the risk in order to be some evidence that a drug more likely than not caused a particular injury).

Merck & Co. v. Garza, 347 S.W.3d 256, 263 (Tex. 2011) (the use of scientifically reliable epidemiological studies and the requirement of more than a doubling of the risk strikes a balance between the needs of our legal system and the limits of science).

Merck & Co. v. Garza, 347 S.W.3d 256, 263 (Tex. 2011) (for testimony concerning clinical trials to be admitted, the evidence must "first pass the primary reliability inquiry by meeting *Havner*'s threshold requirements of general causation; then, courts must conduct the secondary reliability inquiry that examines the soundness of a study's findings using the totality of the evidence test").

Whirlpool Corp. v. Camacho, 298 S.W.3d 631, 642 (Tex. 2009) ("[T]esting is not always required to support an expert's opinion, but lack of relevant testing to the extent it was possible, either by the expert or others, is one factor that points toward a determination that an expert opinion is unreliable and inadmissible.").

Ford Motor Co. v. Ledesma, 242 S.W.3d 32, 38 (Tex. 2007) ("[E]xpert's testimony, to be admissible, must possess a reliable foundation.").

Ford Motor Co. v. Ledesma, 242 S.W.3d 32, 38 (Tex. 2007) (expert testimony is unreliable, and therefore inadmissible, if it is based on unreliable data, or if the expert draws conclusions from his underlying data based on flawed methodology).

Cooper Tire & Rubber Co. v. Mendez, 204 S.W.3d 797, 805 (Tex. 2006) (expert's testimony regarding "wax contamination theory amounted to no more than subjective belief or unsupported speculation.... His explanation for the tire failure was a naked hypothesis untested and unconfirmed by the methods of science and was legally insufficient to establish a manufacturing defect that caused the [tire's] failure.").

Mack Trucks, Inc. v. Tamez, 206 S.W.3d 572, 578 (Tex. 2006) (in determining the reliability of an expert's testimony, the trial court should undertake a rigorous examination of the facts on which the expert relies, the method by which the expert draws an opinion from those facts, and how the expert applies the facts and methods to the case at hand).

Schultz on Behalf of Schultz v. Lone Star Road Construction, Ltd., 593 S.W.3d 750, 758 (Tex. App.—Houston [14th Dist.] 2019, no pet.) ("If an expert's opinion is based on an assumption about the facts, courts cannot disregard evidence showing that assumption to be unfounded.").

Equistar Chemicals, LP v. ClydeUnion DB, Ltd, 579 S.W.3d 505, 511 (Tex. App.—Houston [14th Dist.] 2019, pet. denied) ("To be admissible, an expert's opinion testimony must have a reliable foundation.").

Equistar Chemicals, LP v. ClydeUnion DB, Ltd, 579 S.W.3d 505, 511 (Tex. App.—Houston [14th Dist.] 2019, pet. denied) ("Expert testimony is not reliable if there is too great an analytical gap between the data on which the expert relies and the opinion offered.... Whether an analytical gap exists is largely determined by comparing the facts the expert relied on, the facts in the record, and the expert's ultimate opinion.... An analytical gap exists if the expert's opinion is based on assumed facts that vary materially from the facts in the record.").

Discovery Operating, Inc. v. BP Am. Prod. Co., 311 S.W.3d 140, 173 (Tex. App.—Eastland 2010, pet. denied) ("[T]rial courts may consider several factors when determining whether expert testimony is reliable.... One such factor is whether the expert conducted testing to exclude other possible causes of the damage.").

Lincoln v. Clark Freight Lines, Inc., 285 S.W.3d 79, 83 (Tex. App.—Houston [1st Dist.] 2009, no pet.) (expert testimony must be shown to be reliable before it is admitted).

Lincoln v. Clark Freight Lines, Inc., 285 S.W.3d 79, 83 (Tex. App.—Houston [1st Dist.] 2009, no pet.) (unreliable scientific or technical evidence is of no assistance to the jury and is therefore inadmissible).

Lincoln v. Clark Freight Lines, Inc., 285 S.W.3d 79, 83 (Tex. App.—Houston [1st Dist.] 2009, no pet.) (if an expert relies on unreliable foundational data, any opinion drawn from that data is likewise unreliable, and therefore inadmissible).

Trejos v. State, 243 S.W.3d 30, 52 (Tex. App.—Houston [1st Dist.] 2007, pet. ref'd) ("[F]actors that [a court] must examine to determine a cadaver dog's qualifications and reliability are whether the dog (1) is a breed or type that typically works well off-lead, (2) has been trained to discriminate between human scents and animal scents, and (3) has been found by experience to be reliable; these factors are not exclusive, and other factors may be considered in an appropriate case.").

Hernandez v. State, 127 S.W.3d 206, 220 (Tex. App.—Houston [1st Dist.] 2003, pet. ref'd) (trial court did not abuse discretion by excluding proposed expert testimony where defendant failed to demonstrate it to be sufficiently reliable).

Green v. State, 55 S.W.3d 633, 639 (Tex. App.—Tyler 2001, pet. ref'd), *aff'd*, 116 S.W.3d 26 (Tex. 2003), *cert. denied*, 535 U.S. 958 (2002) (defendant failed to show proposed expert reliable where expert failed to show what authorities in field were relied upon for opinions).

Franco v. State, 25 S.W.3d 26, 29 (Tex. App.—El Paso 2000, pet. ref'd) ("[S]cientific testimony must meet the proper tests for scientific reliability, and the testimony must reflect information outside the general knowledge of lay persons").

e. Scientific Procedures Not Proper

Gunn v. McCoy, 554 S.W.3d 645, 661 (Tex. Crim. App. 2018) ("[E]xamination of an expert's underlying methodology is a task for the trial court in its role as gatekeeper.").

Gunn v. McCoy, 554 S.W.3d 645, 662 (Tex. Crim. App. 2018) ("Expert testimony may also be unreliable if there is simply too great an analytical gap between the data [relied upon] and the opinion proffered.... [Courts] are not required to ignore fatal gaps in an expert's analysis or assertions that are simply incorrect, and such a flaw in an expert's reasoning renders the scientific testimony unreliable and, legally, no evidence.").

TXI Transp. Co. v. Hughes, 306 S.W.3d 230, 234 (Tex. 2010) ("[E]xpert testimony based on an unreliable foundation or flawed methodology is unreliable and does not satisfy relevancy requirement.").

Ford Motor Co. v. Ledesma, 242 S.W.3d 32, 38 (Tex. 2007) (expert testimony is unreliable, and therefore inadmissible, if there is simply too great an analytical gap between the data and the opinion proffered).

Gammill v. Jack Williams Chevrolet, Inc., 972 S.W.2d 713, 719 (Tex. 1998) (where analytical gap between an expert's theories and conclusions too great, held not reliable).

Equistar Chemicals, LP v. ClydeUnion DB, Ltd., 579 S.W.3d 505, 511 (Tex. App.—Houston [14th Dist.] 2019, pet. denied) ("Expert testimony is not reliable if there is too great an analytical gap between the data on which the expert relies and the opinion offered.... Whether an analytical gap exists is largely determined by comparing the facts the expert relied on, the facts in the record, and the expert's ultimate opinion.... An analytical gap exists if the expert's opinion is based on assumed facts that vary materially from the facts in the record.").

Key Energy Servs., LLC v. Shelby Cnty. Appraisal Dist., 428 S.W.3d 133, 142 (Tex. App.—Tyler 2014, pet. denied) ("[E]xpert testimony is unreliable if it is based on unreliable data, or if the expert draws conclusions from his underlying data based on flawed methodology.").

Sennett v. State, 406 S.W.3d 661, 668 (Tex. App.—Eastland 2013, no pet.) ("[E]xpert did not provide the court any scientific methodology that could be verified and replicated in evaluating his opinions" so the testimony was inadmissible.).

Bhatia v. Woodlands N. Houston Heart Ctr, PLLC, 396 S.W.3d 658, 668 (Tex. App.—Houston [14th Dist.] 2013, pet. denied) ("[T]he determination on reliability [of an expert's testimony] must focus on the expert's methodology, foundational data, and whether too great an analytical gap exists between the data and methodology, on the one hand, and the expert's opinions, on the other.").

U.S. Renal Care, Inc. v. Jaafar, 345 S.W.3d 600, 609 (Tex. App.—San Antonio 2011, pet. denied) ("an impermissible analytical gap between the data and the opinion proffered by an expert witness] exists if an expert has offered nothing to suggest that what he or she believes could have happened actually did happen, because, in that case, his or her opinions are little more than subjective belief or unsupported speculation.... It is not so simply because an expert says it is so.").

Taber v. Roush, 316 S.W.3d 139, 148 (Tex. App.—Houston [14th Dist.] 2010, no pet.) ("[E]xpert testimony is unreliable if there is simply too great an analytical gap between the data and the opinion proffered.").

Taber v. Roush, 316 S.W.3d 139, 148 (Tex. App.—Houston [14th Dist.] 2010, no pet.) ("A reviewing court is not required to ignore gaps in an expert's analysis or assertions that are simply incorrect, and a trial court is not required to admit evidence connected to existing data only by the expert's *ipse dixit*.").

Lincoln v. Clark Freight Lines, Inc., 285 S.W.3d 79, 83 (Tex. App.—Houston [1st Dist.] 2009, no pet.) (expert testimony unreliable and inadmissible even when underlying data is sound if expert's methodology is flawed).

Merrell v. Wal-Mart Stores, Inc., 276 S.W.3d 117, 126 n.11 (Tex. App.—Texarkana 2008), *rev'd on other grounds*, 313 S.W.3d 837 (Tex. 2010) (to be reliable, scientific techniques or principles underlying expert testimony must be well grounded in the methods and procedures of science).

Purina Mills, Inc. v. Odell, 948 S.W.2d 927, 934 (Tex. App.—Texarkana 1997, pet. denied) ("To be reliable, the underlying scientific technique must be grounded in the methods and procedures of science.").

f. *Speculative or Conjectural*

Bustamante v. Ponte, 529 S.W.3d 447, 462 (Tex. Crim. App. 2017) ("An expert's testimony is conclusory if the witness simply states a conclusion without an explanation or factual substantiation.... If no basis for the opinion is offered, or the basis offered provides no support, the opinion is merely a conclusory statement and cannot be considered probative evidence, regardless of whether there is no objection.").

Bustamante v. Ponte, 529 S.W.3d 447, 462 (Tex. Crim. App. 2017) ("[A]n expert's simple ipse dixit is insufficient to establish a matter; rather, the expert must explain the basis of the statements to link the conclusions to the facts.").

Rogers v. Zanetti, 518 S.W.3d 394, 405 (Tex. 2017) ("When an expert's opinion is based on assumed facts that vary materially from the actual, undisputed facts, the opinion is without probative value and cannot support a verdict or judgment ... even when some basis is offered for an opinion, if that basis does not, on its face, support the opinion, the opinion is still conclusory.").

Bostic v. Georgia-Pacific Corp., 439 S.W.3d 332, 349 (Tex. 2013) (scientific evidence that is not grounded in the methods and procedures of science is no more than subjective belief or unsupported speculation).

In re Commitment of Bohannan, 388 S.W.3d 296, 304 (Tex. 2012), *cert. denied*, 569 U.S. 1009 (2013) (opinions too dependent upon an expert's subjective guesswork must be excluded).

Wal-Mart Stores, Inc. v. Merrell, 313 S.W.3d 837, 840 (Tex. 2010) (expert's failure to explain or adequately disprove alternative theories of causation makes his or her own theory speculative and conclusory).

Ford Motor Co. v. Ledesma, 242 S.W.3d 32, 38 (Tex. 2007) (expert's opinion is unreliable, and therefore inadmissible, if based solely upon his subjective interpretation of the facts).

Cooper Tire & Rubber Co. v. Mendez, 204 S.W.3d 797, 805 (Tex. 2006) (scientific testimony is unreliable if it is not grounded in the methods and procedures of science and amounts to no more than a subjective belief or unsupported speculation).

Coastal Transp. Co., Inc. v. Crown Cent. Petroleum Corp., 136 S.W.3d 227, 232 (Tex. 2004) (conclusory and speculative expert testimony is irrelevant and insufficient to overcome directed verdict motion by opposing party).

Gammill v. Jack Williams Chevrolet, Inc., 972 S.W.2d 713, 719 (Tex. 1998) (expert's opinions speculative and unreliable).

Schultz on Behalf of Schultz v. Lone Star Road Construction, Ltd., 593 S.W.3d 750, 758 (Tex. App.—Houston [14th Dist.] 2019, no pet.) ("If an expert's opinion is based on an assumption about the facts, courts cannot disregard evidence showing that assumption to be unfounded.").

Schultz on Behalf of Schultz v. Lone Star Road Construction, Ltd., 593 S.W.3d 750, 758 (Tex. App.—Houston [14th Dist.] 2019, no pet.) ("Expert opinions must be supported by facts in evidence, not conjecture.").

Equistar Chemicals, LP v. ClydeUnion DB, Ltd., 579 S.W.3d 505, 511 (Tex. App.—Houston [14th Dist.] 2019, pet. denied) ("[I]f an expert's opinion is conclusory, the testimony is incompetent and cannot support a judgment.").

Equistar Chemicals, LP v. ClydeUnion DB, Ltd., 579 S.W.3d 505, 511 (Tex. App.—Houston [14th Dist.] 2019, pet. denied) ("[T]o be competent evidence, an expert's opinion must have a demonstrable and reasoned basis on which to evaluate the opinion.").

Integrated of Amarillo, Inc. v. Kirkland, 424 S.W.3d 131, 135 (Tex. App.—Amarillo 2014, no pet.) (opinion testimony that is conclusory or speculative is objectionable and inadmissible as lacking relevance because it does not tend to make the existence of a material fact more probable or less probable).

Russell Equestrian Ctr., Inc. v. Miller, 406 S.W.3d 243, 247 (Tex. App.—San Antonio 2013, no pet.) ("[O]pinion testimony that is conclusory or speculative is not relevant evidence, because it does not tend to make the existence of a material fact more probable or less probable.").

Hamilton v. State, 399 S.W.3d 673, 684 (Tex. App.—Amarillo 2013, pet. ref'd) (computer generated animation should not have been admitted where nothing in the record supported many of the details contained in the animation, and those details were provided by nothing more than pure speculation on the part of the experts).

Brogan v. Brownlee, 358 S.W.3d 369, 371 (Tex. App.—Amarillo 2011, no pet.) (conclusory statements made by experts are not probative evidence).

Chesser v. LifeCare Mgmt. Servs., L.L.C., 356 S.W.3d 613, 622 n.5 (Tex. App.—Fort Worth 2011, pet. denied) (expert opinion testimony that is conclusory or speculative is not relevant evidence, because it does not tend to make the existence of a material fact more probable or less probable).

Damian v. Bell Helicopter Textron, Inc., 352 S.W.3d 124, 148 (Tex. App.—Fort Worth 2011, pet. denied) ("[I]f no basis for expert opinion is offered, or the basis offered provides no support, the opinion is merely a conclusory statement and cannot be considered probative evidence.").

State Office of Risk Mgmt. v. Adkins, 347 S.W.3d 394, 403 (Tex. App.—Dallas 2011, no pet.) (in the medical context, "expert testimony that is not based on reasonable medical probability, but relies instead on possibility, speculation, or surmise, does not assist the jury and cannot support a judgment").

THI of Tex. at Lubbock I, LLC v. Perea, 329 S.W.3d 548, 563 n.25 (Tex. App.—Amarillo 2010, pet. denied) ("perhaps" and "possibly" in a medical expert's testimony indicate conjecture, speculation, or mere possibility, rather than qualified opinions based on reasonable medical probability).

DMC Valley Ranch, L.L.C. v. HPSC, Inc., 315 S.W.3d 898, 905 (Tex. App.—Dallas 2010, no pet.) (expert testimony is considered conclusory or speculative when it has no factual substantiation in the record).

Duncan-Hubert v. Mitchell, 310 S.W.3d 92, 102 (Tex. App.—Dallas 2010, pet. denied) (scientific evidence that is not grounded in methods and procedures of science is no more than subjective belief or unsupported speculation and is unreliable).

Plunkett v. Conn. Gen. Life Ins. Co., 285 S.W.3d 106, 118 (Tex. App.—Dallas 2009, pet. denied) ("[C]ompetent expert medical causation evidence, whether expressed in testimony or in medical records, must be grounded in reasonable medical probability, not speculation or conjecture.").

Merrell v. Wal-Mart Stores, Inc., 276 S.W.3d 117, 127 (Tex. App.—Texarkana 2008), *rev'd on other grounds*, 313 S.W.3d 837 (Tex. 2010) (naked and unsupported opinion of expert witness is incompetent evidence).

Merrell v. Wal-Mart Stores, Inc., 276 S.W.3d 117, 127 (Tex. App.—Texarkana 2008), *rev'd on other grounds*, 313 S.W.3d 837 (Tex. 2010) (expert opinion is conclusory when it offers an opinion with no factual substantiation; the expert must explain how he reached his conclusion).

Merrell v. Wal-Mart Stores, Inc., 276 S.W.3d 117, 127 (Tex. App.—Texarkana 2008), *rev'd on other grounds*, 313 S.W.3d 837 (Tex. 2010) (conclusory expert evidence lacks probative value due to insufficient factual substantiation, not from differing conclusions as to the underlying factual situation).

Quiroz v. Covenant Health Sys., 234 S.W.3d 74, 88 (Tex. App.—El Paso 2007, pet. denied) (opinion based on unreliable scientific data is inadmissible as it is nothing more than the expert's subjective belief or speculation).

Durham Transp. Co., Inc. v. Beettner, 201 S.W.3d 859, 868 n.5 (Tex. App.—Waco 2006, pet. denied) (expert testimony is considered conclusory or speculative when it has no factual substantiation in the record).

Naegeli Transp. v. Gulf Electroquip, Inc., 853 S.W.2d 737, 741 (Tex. App.—Houston [14th Dist.] 1993, writ denied) ("[E]xpert testimony cannot be based on mere guess or speculation, but must have a proper factual basis.").

g. Too Time-Consuming/Collateral Issues/Speculative

State v. Esparza, 353 S.W.3d 276, 282 n.9 (Tex. App.—El Paso 2011), *aff'd*, 413 S.W.3d 81 (Tex. Crim. App. 2013) (even if breath tests are shown to be reliable, the opponent of the evidence "can still object, and attempt to show, that the evidence is inadmissible under Rule 702 because the probative value of the evidence is substantially outweighed by the danger of unfair prejudice, confusion of the issues, or misleading the jury, or by considerations of undue delay, or needless presentation of cumulative evidence").

Von Hohn v. Von Hohn, 260 S.W.3d 631, 636 (Tex. App.—Tyler 2008, no pet.) ("[I]f the trial court determines that the proffered expert testimony is relevant and reliable, it must then determine whether to exclude the evidence because its probative value is outweighed by the danger of unfair prejudice, confusion of the issues, or misleading the jury, or by considerations of undue delay, or needless presentation of cumulative evidence.").

h. Expert Testimony Not Needed

Wolfe v. State, 509 S.W.3d 325, 335 (Tex. Crim. App. 2017) ("For expert testimony to be admissible under [the Rules of Evidence], the proponent of the expert scientific evidence must demonstrate by clear and convincing evidence that the testimony is sufficiently reliable and relevant to help the jury in reaching accurate results.").

K-Mart Corp. v. Honeycutt, 24 S.W.3d 357, 360 (Tex. 2000) (expert testimony assists the trier-of-fact when the expert's knowledge and experience on a relevant issue are beyond that of the average juror and the testimony helps the trier-of-fact understand the evidence or determine a fact issue; "When the jury is equally competent to form an opinion about the ultimate fact issues or the expert's testimony is within the common knowledge of the jury, the trial court should exclude the expert's testimony.").

GTE Sw. v. Bruce, 998 S.W.2d 605, 619 (Tex. 1999) ("Where ... the issue involves only general knowledge and experience rather than expertise, it is within the province of the jury to decide, and admission of expert testimony on the issue is error.").

Fire Ins. Co. v. Lynd Co., 399 S.W.3d 206, 217 (Tex. App.—San Antonio 2012, pet. denied) (when the jury is equally competent to form an opinion on the ultimate fact issues, or the expert's testimony is within the jury's common knowledge, then the expert testimony is not necessary or helpful and should be excluded).

Great W. Drilling, Ltd. v. Alexander, 305 S.W.3d 688, 696 (Tex. App.—Eastland 2009, no pet.) ("[I]n instances in which the jury is equally competent to form an opinion about the ultimate fact issues or the expert's testimony is within the common knowledge of the jury, the trial court should exclude the expert's testimony.").

Burns v. Baylor Health Sys., 125 S.W.3d 589, 594 (Tex. App.—El Paso 2003, no pet.) (when a jury is equally competent to form an opinion about the ultimate fact issues or the expert's testimony is within the common knowledge of the jury, the trial court should exclude the expert's testimony).

Fire Ins. Co. v. Lynd Co., 399 S.W.3d 206, 217 (Tex. App.—San Antonio 2012, pet. denied) ("[W]hen the jury is equally competent to form an opinion on the ultimate fact issues, or the expert's testimony is within the jury's common knowledge, then the expert testimony is not necessary or helpful and should be excluded.").

Great W. Drilling, Ltd. v. Alexander, 305 S.W.3d 688, 696 (Tex. App.—Eastland 2009, no pet.) ("[I]n instances in which the jury is equally competent to form an opinion about the ultimate fact issues or the expert's testimony is within the common knowledge of the jury, the trial court should exclude the expert's testimony.").

Burns v. Baylor Health Sys., 125 S.W.3d 589, 594 (Tex. App.—El Paso 2003, no pet.) (when a jury is equally competent to form an opinion about the ultimate fact issues or the expert's testimony is within the common knowledge of the jury, the trial court should exclude the expert's testimony).

i. Not Relevant

Gunn v. McCoy, 554 S.W.3d 645, 661 (Tex. Crim. App. 2018) ("[E]xamination of an expert's underlying methodology is a task for the trial court in its role as gatekeeper.").

Enbridge Pipelines (East Texas) L.P. v. Avinger Timber, LLC, 386 S.W.3d 256, 262 (Tex. 2012) (a trial court must act as an evidentiary gatekeeper to exclude irrelevant and unreliable expert evidence).

Enbridge Pipelines (East Texas) L.P. v. Avinger Timber, LLC, 386 S.W.3d 256, 262 (Tex. 2012) (an expert's testimony must be relevant to the issues and based upon a reliable foundation).

State v. Cent. Expressway Sign Assocs., 302 S.W.3d 866, 870 (Tex. 2009) (to be relevant, the expert's opinion must be based on the facts; to be reliable, the expert's opinion must be based on sound reasoning and methodology).

Fleming v. Kinney ex rel. Shelton, 395 S.W.3d 917, 928 (Tex. App.—Houston [14th Dist.] 2013, pet. denied) (an expert may state an opinion on a mixed question of law and fact if the opinion is limited to the relevant issues and is based on proper legal concepts).

Integrated of Amarillo, Inc. v. Kirkland, 424 S.W.3d 131, 135 (Tex. App.—Amarillo 2014, no pet.) (opinion testimony that is conclusory or speculative is not relevant evidence because it does not tend to make the existence of a material fact more probable or less probable).

Schronk v. Laerdal Med. Corp., 440 S.W.3d 250, 257 (Tex. App.—Waco 2013, pet. denied) (to be relevant, the expert's opinion must be based on the facts).

Chesser v. LifeCare Mgmt. Servs., L.L.C., 356 S.W.3d 613, 622 n.5 (Tex. App.—Fort Worth 2011, pet. denied) (expert opinion testimony that is conclusory or speculative is not relevant evidence, because it does not tend to make the existence of a material fact more probable or less probable).

Discovery Operating, Inc. v. BP Am. Prod. Co., 311 S.W.3d 140, 165 (Tex. App.—Eastland 2010, pet. denied) (to be relevant, an expert's opinion must be based on the facts; to be reliable, the opinion must be based on sound reasoning and methodology).

Baldree v. State, 248 S.W.3d 224, 228 (Tex. App.—Houston [1st Dist.] 2007, pet. ref'd) (in the field of "soft sciences," which include nonscientific disciplines that rely principally upon technical or specialized knowledge, skill, or experience, such as psychology, the proponent of the scientific evidence must show that: (1) the field of expertise involved is legitimate; (2) the subject matter of the expert's testimony is within the scope of that field; and (3) the expert's testimony properly relies upon or utilizes the principles involved in that field).

Baldree v. State, 248 S.W.3d 224, 228 (Tex. App.—Houston [1st Dist.] 2007, pet. ref'd) ("[E]xpert [offering scientific testimony] must make an effort to tie pertinent facts of the case to the scientific principles that are the subject of his testimony.").

Baldree v. State, 248 S.W.3d 224, 228 (Tex. App.—Houston [1st Dist.] 2007, pet. ref'd) ("[T]he standard for relevance of scientific testimony by an expert is whether the scientific principles 'will assist the trier-of-fact' and are 'sufficiently tied' to the pertinent facts of the case"; the inquiry is not whether there are some facts that the expert failed to take into account, but whether the expert took into account enough pertinent facts to be of assistance to the trier-of-fact.).

Wyndam Inter., Inc. v. Ace Am. Ins. Co., 186 S.W.3d 682, 689 (Tex. App.—Dallas 2006, no pet.) (consultant's expert opinion about hotel owner's business income losses in months after terrorist attacks of September 11, 2001, was not based upon a reliable foundation and was irrelevant).

Nguyen v. State, 21 S.W.3d 609, 611 (Tex. App.—Houston [1st Dist.] 2000, pet. ref'd) (insufficient factual foundation existed to make an expert's testimony relevant).

4. Opposing Authorities

In re National Lloyds Insurance Company, 532 S.W.3d 794, 815 (Tex. 2017) ("[W]hen a witness is properly disclosed and designated as an expert and the main substance of the witness's testimony is based on specialized knowledge, skill, experience, training, and education, the testimony will generally be expert testimony within the scope of Rule 702.").

Gharda USA, Inc. v. Control Solutions, Inc., 464 S.W.3d 338, 349 (Tex. 2015) (courts "do not decide whether the expert's opinions are correct; rather, [they] determine whether the analysis used to form those opinions is reliable").

Transcontinental Ins. Co. v. Crump, 330 S.W.3d 211, 215 (Tex. 2010); *TXI Transp. Co. v. Hughes*, 306 S.W.3d 230, 234 (Tex. 2010); *E.I. du Pont de Nemours & Co. v. Robinson*, 923 S.W.2d 549, 557 (Tex. 1995) (to determine admissibility of scientific evidence, court must consider: (1) extent to which theory has been or can be tested; (2) extent to which technique relies upon subjective interpretation of expert; (3) whether theory has been subjected to peer review and/or publication; (4) technique's potential rate of error; (5) whether underlying theory or technique generally accepted as valid by relevant scientific community; (6) nonjudicial uses which have been made of theory or technique; and (7) any other factor helpful to determine reliability of scientific evidence).

Custom Transit, L.P. v. Flatrolled Steel, Inc., 375 S.W.3d 337, 357 (Tex. App.—Houston [14th Dist.] 2012, no pet.) ("[W]hile an expert should address evidence that contradicts his conclusions, it is not required that an expert categorically exclude each and every possible alternative cause in order to render the proffered testimony admissible.").

IHS Acquisition No. 131, Inc. v. Crowson, 351 S.W.3d 368, 372 (Tex. App.—El Paso 2010, no pet.) (fact that an expert is not a specialist in the particular area at issue does not necessarily disqualify the expert from providing an expert opinion).

Krause v. State, 243 S.W.3d 95, 109 (Tex. App.—Houston [1st Dist.] 2007, pet. ref'd) ("[T]he party seeking to introduce evidence of a scientific principle need not always present expert testimony, treatises, or other scientific material to satisfy the *Kelly* test.").

Taylor v. Tex. Dep't of Protective & Regulatory Servs., 160 S.W.3d 641, 650 (Tex. App.—Austin 2005, pet. denied) (sufficient foundation to establish a witness was qualified to testify as expert social worker).

Pittsburgh Corning Corp. v. Walters, 1 S.W.3d 759, 774 (Tex. App.—Corpus Christi 1999, pet. denied) (sufficient foundation existed to establish that certain experts were qualified to testify).

Tennison v. State, 969 S.W.2d 578, 580 (Tex. App.—Texarkana 1998, no pet.) (expert testimony that many victims do not show signs of sexual abuse relevant to explain why victim may not have shown signs of abuse in charged offense).

a. Court's Discretion

Enbridge Pipelines (East Texas) L.P. v. Avinger Timber, LLC, 386 S.W.3d 256, 262 (Tex. 2012) (a trial court must act as an evidentiary gatekeeper to exclude irrelevant and unreliable expert evidence; it has broad discretion with respect to this function).

Mack Trucks, Inc. v. Tamez, 206 S.W.3d 572, 578 (Tex. 2006) (when an expert's processes or methodologies are obscured or concealed by testimony that is excessively internally contradictory, nonresponsive, or evasive, a trial court will not have abused its discretion in determining that the expert's testimony is not admissible).

Hernandez v. State, 127 S.W.3d 206, 220 (Tex. App.—Houston [1st Dist.] 2003, pet. ref'd) (appellate court reviews trial judge's decision regarding whether to allow expert testimony for an abuse of discretion).

McAllister v. Magnolia Petroleum Co., 319 S.W.2d 411, 414 (Tex. Civ. App.—Dallas 1958, writ ref'd n.r.e.) ("[T]he trial court has considerable latitude in determining whether the conditions are sufficiently similar to permit testimony about the tests.").

Ervay-Canton Apartments, Inc. v. Hatterick, 239 S.W.2d 150, 152 (Tex. Civ. App.—Fort Worth 1951, writ ref'd n.r.e.) (within court's discretion to admit out-of-court experiments if made under substantially same circumstances).

b. General Acceptance—Published Precedent

Scott's Marina at Lake Grapevine Ltd. v. Brown, 365 S.W.3d 146, 155 (Tex. App.—Amarillo 2012, pet. denied) (there was published support for an expert's opinion as to a scientifically significant link between the plaintiff's exposure and his development of illness).

Pittsburgh Corning Corp. v. Walters, 1 S.W.3d 759, 774 (Tex. App.—Corpus Christi 1999, pet. denied) (sufficient foundation to establish reliability of opinions where there was universal acceptance of methods and sufficient literature to support opinions).

i. Level of Acceptance in Scientific Community

Pittsburgh Corning Corp. v. Walters, 1 S.W.3d 759, 774 (Tex. App.—Corpus Christi 1999, pet. denied) (sufficient foundation to establish reliability of opinions where there was universal acceptance of methods and sufficient literature to support opinions).

ii. Judicial Notice

Hernandez v. State, 116 S.W.3d 26, 29 (Tex. Crim. App. 2003) (courts can sometimes take judicial notice of relevance of a widely accepted methodology; note that court refused to take judicial notice of reliability of methodology where not done in trial court).

Emerson v. State, 880 S.W.2d 759, 764 (Tex. Crim. App. 1994) (appellate court could take judicial notice of reliability of theory and methodology of scientific evidence even if publications consulted by appellate court not considered by trial court or raised by parties).

c. Similar Conditions Requirement

McAllister v. Magnolia Petroleum Co., 319 S.W.2d 411, 414 (Tex. Civ. App.—Dallas 1958, writ ref'd n.r.e.) ("[T]the trial court has considerable latitude in determining whether the conditions are sufficiently similar to permit testimony about the tests.").

Ervay-Canton Apartments, Inc. v. Hatterick, 239 S.W.2d 150, 152 (Tex. Civ. App.—Fort Worth 1951, writ ref'd n.r.e.) (it is within a court's discretion to admit out-of-court experiments if they are made under substantially same circumstances).

Fort Worth & D.C. Ry. Co. v. Yantis, 185 S.W. 969, 974 (Tex. Civ. App.—Fort Worth 1916, writ ref'd) (testimony regarding experiments is admissible where the same conditions are shown, and the testimony is not collateral).

d. Reliability

Campbell v. State, 910 S.W.2d 475, 478 (Tex. Crim. App. 1995) ("[T]o be considered reliable, evidence of a scientific theory must satisfy the following three criteria: (a) the underlying theory must be valid; (b) the technique applying the theory must be valid; and (c) the technique must have been properly applied on the occasion in question.").

Kelly v. State, 824 S.W.2d 568, 569 (Tex. Crim. App. 1992) (novel evidence must be relevant and reliable to be admissible).

Schronk v. Laerdal Med. Corp., 440 S.W.3d 250, 257 (Tex. App.—Waco 2013, pet. denied) (the approach to assessing reliability must be flexible depending on the nature of the evidence).

City of Sugar Land v. Home & Hearth Sugarland, L.P., 215 S.W.3d 503, 511 (Tex. App.—Eastland 2007, pet. denied) (analysis used by condemnee's appraisal expert, to determine that restaurant was highest and best use for 1.7709-acre parcel taken by city, was sufficiently reliable).

Formosa Plastics Corp. v. Kajima Intern., Inc., 216 S.W.3d 436, 452 (Tex. App.—Corpus Christi 2006, pet. denied) (testimony of contractor's expert witness regarding calculation of reasonable value of work performed by contractor was reliable).

e. Cumulative

In re Commitment of Winkle, 434 S.W.3d 300, 309 (Tex. App.—Beaumont 2014, pet. denied) (expert testimony of psychologist concerning expert's primary research studying recidivism risks in sexually violent predators, which addressed the quality of actuarial predictions compared to predictions that are based on clinical judgment and the defendant's test result on the Static–99 that placed the defendant in a group with a low risk of reoffending, was not cumulative of testimony of defendant's other psychiatrist expert).

Eldred v. State, 431 S.W.3d 177, 187 (Tex. App.—Texarkana 2014, no pet.) (state's expert's testimony concerning "grooming" of child victims was not needlessly cumulative).

United Servs. Auto. Ass'n v. Gordon, 103 S.W.3d 436, 442 (Tex. App.—San Antonio 2002, no pet.) (it was harmless error to allow a report by another expert where the admitted report was cumulative of the other expert's testimony and not controlling on a material issue).

Roberts v. Williamson, 52 S.W.3d 343, 348 (Tex. App.—Texarkana 2001), *aff'd in part, rev'd in part on other grounds*, 111 S.W.3d 113 (Tex. 2003) (no harm allowing second medical expert to testify where testimony was cumulative of previous expert's testimony).

Garza v. Guerrero, 993 S.W.2d 137, 141 (Tex. App.—San Antonio 1999, no pet.) (no error in admitting report from doctor which was cumulative of testimony already offered by another plaintiff's expert).

Pittsburgh Corning Corp. v. Walters, 1 S.W.3d 759, 774 (Tex. App.—Corpus Christi 1999, pet. denied) (trial court properly admitted two excerpts from *Federal Register* supporting underlying basis of expert's already admitted testimony).

Second Injury Fund of Tex. v. Avon, 985 S.W.2d 93, 94 (Tex. App.—Eastland 1998, pet. denied) (no error admitting report from doctor cumulative of testimony already offered by another plaintiff expert).

f. Weight vs. Admissibility

Gunn v. McCoy, 554 S.W.3d 645, 661 (Tex. Crim. App. 2018) ("[A]n expert's factual assumptions must [not] be uncontested or established as a matter of law—if the evidence conflicts, it is normally the province of the jury to determine which evidence to credit.").

Jordan v. State, 928 S.W.2d 550, 556 (Tex. Crim. App. 1996) (the fact that an expert did not consider all the relevant factors affected the weight and not the admissibility of the expert's opinion).

Spence v. State, 795 S.W.2d 743, 750 (Tex. Crim. App. 1990), *cert. denied*, 499 U.S. 932 (1991) (lack of agreement about exact methodology to use for bite mark identification affected weight and not admissibility of evidence).

Autry v. State, 143 Tex. Crim. 252, 269, 157 S.W.2d 924, 933 (Tex. Crim. App. 1941, no pet.) (objection that evidence on experiments speculative went to weight and not admissibility).

Jones v. Pesak Bros. Constr., Inc., 416 S.W.3d 618, 632 (Tex. App.—Houston [1st Dist.] 2013, no pet.) (expert was qualified to testify on foundation issues, and his failure to address certain issues went to the weight of his testimony, not the admissibility).

In re D.J.R., 319 S.W.3d 759, 771 (Tex. App.—El Paso 2010, pet. denied) (credibility of expert witness goes to the weight rather than the admissibility of expert's proffered testimony).

Augillard v. Madura, 257 S.W.3d 494, 502 n.13 (Tex. App.—Austin 2008, no pet.) ("[S]howing of the possibility of tampering or commingling [of results in a DNA test] is not sufficient to bar admission of the evidence, and goes only to the weight of the evidence.").

B. Motion to Exclude Junk Science and Related Evidence

1. Suggested Motion Text

(*Name of Moving Party*) hereby moves this Court for an order excluding any and all evidence, references to evidence, testimony, or argument relating to (*Insert Description of Test or Evidence, e.g., Polygraph Tests; or, a Party's or Witness's Refusal or Willingness to Take a Polygraph Test; or, the Results of Polygraph Tests, etc.*). The motion is based upon the grounds that such evidence is unreliable and inadmissible pursuant to established laws of this state and will create a substantial danger of undue prejudice to (*Name of Moving Party*).

2. Motion Summary

This section provides a number of citations supporting the exclusion of evidence relating to new scientific techniques or disapproved existing techniques based upon a failure to satisfy reliability requirements for admissibility. See generally *Jordan v. State*, 928 S.W.2d 550, 556 (Tex. Crim. App. 1996); *Kelly v. State*, 824 S.W.2d 568, 569 (Tex. Crim. App. 1992). Where the matter has not been tested by the appellate courts of this State, citations from other jurisdictions may be helpful. *See Emerson v. State*, 880 S.W.2d 759, 764 (Tex. Crim. App. 1994). Texas courts have recognized that "professional expert witnesses are available to render an opinion on almost any theory, regardless of its merit." *E.I. du Pont de Nemours & Co. v. Robinson*, 923 S.W.2d 549, 557 (Tex. 1995). The motion seeks to exclude the testimony of experts who "are more than willing to proffer opinions of dubious value for the proper fee."

As is the case where seeking to exclude expert testimony, the court, in considering whether to exclude "junk" or "novel" science must consider: 1) the extent to which the theory has been or can be tested; 2) the extent to which the technique relies upon the subjective interpretation of the expert; 3) whether the theory has been subjected to peer review and/or publication; 4) the technique's potential rate of error; 5) whether the underlying theory or technique has been generally accepted as valid by the relevant scientific community; 6) the non-judicial uses which have been made of the theory or technique; and 7) any other factor which is helpful to determine the reliability of scientific evidence. *Transcontinental Ins. Co. v. Crump*, 330 S.W.3d 211, 215 (Tex. 2010); *Mack Trucks, Inc. v. Tamez*, 206 S.W.3d 572, 578 (Tex. 2006); *E.I. du Pont de Nemours & Co. v. Robinson*, 923 S.W.2d 549, 557 (Tex. 1995).

3. Supporting Authorities

Wolfe v. State, 509 S.W.3d 325, 335 (Tex. Crim. App. 2017) (in weighing the factors as a means of assessing reliability [of expert scientific evidence], the focus is to determine whether the evidence has its basis in sound scientific methodology such that testimony about 'junk science' is weeded out").

In re M.P.A., 364 S.W.3d 277, 286 n.16 (Tex. 2012) (reliable evidence should be admitted in both the civil and criminal context, and unreliable evidence or "junk science" should be kept out of court in either context).

In re M.P.A., 364 S.W.3d 277, 286 (Tex. 2012) (*Kelly v. State* applies to all scientific evidence, regardless of whether it is novel).

E.I. du Pont de Nemours & Co. v. Robinson, 923 S.W.2d 549, 557 (Tex. 1995) (it is especially important that trial judges scrutinize proffered evidence for scientific reliability when it is based upon novel scientific theories, sometimes referred to as "junk science").

Coronado v. State, 384 S.W.3d 919, 923 (Tex. App.—Dallas 2012, no pet.) (focus of the reliability analysis is to determine whether the evidence has its basis in sound scientific methodology such that testimony about "junk science" is weeded out).

Five Star Intern. Holdings Inc. v. Thomson, 324 S.W.3d 160, 168 (Tex. App.—El Paso 2010, pet. denied) (when measuring the reliability of an expert's opinion in nonscientific fields, courts should consider whether: (1) the field of expertise is a legitimate one; (2) the subject matter of the expert's testimony is within the scope of that field; and (3) the expert's testimony properly relies upon the principles involved in that field).

In re E.C.L., 278 S.W.3d 510, 519 (Tex. App.—Houston [14th Dist.] 2009, pet. denied) ("[I]n determining the admissibility of novel scientific evidence, the threshold question asked is whether that testimony will help the trier-of-fact understand the evidence or determine a fact in issue.").

In re E.C.L., 278 S.W.3d 510, 519 (Tex. App.—Houston [14th Dist.] 2009, pet. denied) ("[W]hen soft sciences, such as psychology, are at issue, the trial court deciding whether to admit expert testimony on the subject should inquire: (1) whether the field of expertise is legitimate; (2) whether the subject matter of the expert's testimony is within the scope of that field; and (3) whether the expert's testimony properly relies upon or uses the principles involved in that field.").

Green v. State, 55 S.W.3d 633, 639 (Tex. App.—Tyler 2001, pet. ref'd), *aff'd*, 116 S.W.3d 26 (Tex. 2003), *cert. denied*, 535 U.S. 958 (2002) (defendant failed to show proposed expert regarding false confessions was reliable where expert failed to show what authorities in field were relied upon for opinions).

Hernandez v. State, 55 S.W.3d 701, 705 (Tex. App.—Corpus Christi 2001), *aff'd*, 116 S.W.3d 26 (Tex. Crim. App. 2003) (insufficient evidence supported reliability of State's proposed scientific evidence where there was no showing of the validity of the underlying scientific theory and the validity of the technique applying the theory).

a. Hedonic Damages Evidence

Golden Eagle Archery, Inc. v. Jackson, 116 S.W.3d 757, 764 (Tex. 2003) (a jury can award hedonic damages, but care must be taken to ensure there is no double recovery).

Wal-Mart Stores Texas, LLC v. Bishop, 553 S.W.3d 648 (Tex. App.—Dallas 2018, pet. granted) ("The process of awarding damages for amorphous, discretionary injuries such as mental anguish or pain and suffering is inherently difficult because the alleged injury is a subjective, unliquidated, nonpecuniary loss.... The amount of damages awarded for pain and suffering is necessarily speculative and each case must be judged on its own facts.").

Patlyek v. Brittain, 149 S.W.3d 781, 785 (Tex. App.—Austin 2004, pet. denied) ("[T]o prevent the risk of double recovery ... plaintiff [seeking hedonic damages must] prove that effect of physical impairment extends beyond any impediment to earning capacity and beyond any pain and suffering and mental anguish to the extent that it produces a separate and distinct loss that is substantial and for which plaintiff should be compensated.").

b. "Truth Serum" Evidence

Cain v. State, 549 S.W.2d 707, 712 (Tex. Crim. App. 1977) (results of "truth serum" tests inadmissible where technique has not gained scientific acceptance).

Dean v. State, 636 S.W.2d 8, 9 (Tex. App.—Corpus Christi 1982, no pet.) (results of "truth serum" interview of defendant properly excluded).

c. Polygraph Evidence

Ex parte Mayhugh, 512 S.W.3d 285, 302 (Tex. Crim. App. 2016) ("[P]olygraph results themselves are inadmissible because they are unreliable.").

Ex parte Mayhugh, 512 S.W.3d 285, 302 (Tex. Crim. App. 2016) ("Rule 703 allows an expert to base his or her opinion on otherwise inadmissible evidence, [but Texas courts have] specifically declined to allow this rule to be used to admit polygraph results by claiming that the results themselves were necessary to support the expert's opinion.... Rule 703 cannot be used a conduit for admitting opinions based on scientific, technical, or other specialized knowledge that would not meet Rule 702's reliability requirement.").

Leonard v. State, 385 S.W.3d 570, 581 (Tex. Crim. App. 2012) (results of polygraph tests should not be received into evidence, over objection, even if there had been a prior agreement or stipulation by the parties to admit the results).

Leonard v. State, 385 S.W.3d 570, 581 (Tex. Crim. App. 2012) ("[T]total reliance on inadmissible and untrustworthy facts, [including polygraph evidence,] is not reasonable [and does not] achieve the minimum level of reliability necessary for admission under Rule 702.").

Nesbit v. State, 227 S.W.3d 64, 66 n.4 (Tex. Crim. App. 2007) (results of a polygraph test, and the "fact" of failing a polygraph test, are not admissible in a Texas criminal proceeding).

Martines v. State, 371 S.W.3d 232, 250 (Tex. App.—Houston [1st Dist.] 2011, no pet.) ("[D]ue to their inherent unreliability and tendency to be unduly persuasive, the existence and results of polygraph examinations are inadmissible for any purpose in a criminal proceeding on proper objection.").

Woods v. State, 301 S.W.3d 327, 333 (Tex. App.—Houston [14th Dist.] 2009, no pet.) (trial court properly excluded evidence that a defendant had taken a polygraph examination).

i. Per Se Inadmissibility

Ex parte Mayhugh, 512 S.W.3d 285, 302 (Tex. Crim. App. 2016) ("[P]olygraph results themselves are inadmissible because they are unreliable.").

Tennard v. State, 802 S.W.2d 678, 684 (Tex. Crim. App. 1990), *cert. denied*, 501 U.S. 1259 (2001) ("[E]xistence and results of polygraph examination are inadmissible for all purposes.").

Martines v. State, 371 S.W.3d 232, 250 (Tex. App.—Houston [1st Dist.] 2011, no pet.) ("[D]ue to their inherent unreliability and tendency to be unduly persuasive, the existence and results of polygraph examinations are inadmissible for any purpose in a criminal proceeding on proper objection.").

Hernandez v. State, 10 S.W.3d 812, 818(Tex. App.—Beaumont 2000, pet. ref'd) (polygraph evidence is not admissible for any purpose).

ii. Stipulation of the Parties

Leonard v. State, 385 S.W.3d 570, 581 (Tex. Crim. App. 2012) (results of polygraph tests should not be received into evidence, over objection, even if there had been a prior agreement or stipulation by the parties to admit the results).

Landrum v. State, 977 S.W.2d 586, 587 (Tex. Crim. App. 1998) (rules of evidence exclude polygraphs even where parties stipulate to them).

Robinson v. State, 550 S.W.2d 54, 60 (Tex. Crim. App. 1977) (court cannot affirm unreliability of lie detector tests and then admit results of stipulated test).

iii. Refusal to Take Polygraph

Tennard v. State, 802 S.W.2d 678, 684 (Tex. Crim. App. 1990), *cert. denied*, 501 U.S. 1259 (2001) ("[E]xistence and results of polygraph examination are inadmissible for all purposes.").

Leach v. State, 548 S.W.2d 383, 385 (Tex. Crim. App. 1977) (improper to question accused whether he or she refused to take polygraph test).

Renesto v. State, 452 S.W.2d 498, 500 (Tex. Crim. App. 1970) (proof may not be made that accused or witness refused to take polygraph test).

d. Battered Spouse Syndrome

Cox v. State, 843 S.W.2d 750, 755 (Tex. App.—El Paso 1992, pet. ref'd) (trial court did not abuse discretion excluding evidence regarding "battered spouse syndrome" as irrelevant).

e. Abused Child Characteristics

Reyes v. State, 274 S.W.3d 724, 730 (Tex. App.—San Antonio 2008, pet. ref'd) (expert may testify in a criminal case involving a child victim that the child witness exhibits symptoms consistent with sexual abuse, but not that a witness is truthful).

Perez v. State, 25 S.W.3d 830, 832 (Tex. App.—Houston [1st Dist.] 2000, no pet.) (witness not properly qualified to testify as expert on "child abuse accommodation syndrome" and trial court abused discretion allowing testimony).

f. Hypnosis Evidence

State v. Medrano, 127 S.W.3d 781, 786 (Tex. Crim. App. 2004) (trial court's exclusion of hypnotically enhanced testimony was correctly excluded, based on *Zani* standard).

Zani v. State, 758 S.W.2d 233, 244 (Tex. Crim. App. 1988) (established the *Zani* standard: admission of hypnotically enhanced testimony is allowed "if, after consideration of the totality of the circumstances, the trial court should find by clear and convincing evidence that hypnosis neither rendered the witness's posthypnotic memory untrustworthy nor substantially impaired the ability of the opponent fairly to test the witness's recall by cross-examination").

Soliz v. State, 961 S.W.2d 545, 547 (Tex. App.—San Antonio 1997, pet. ref'd) ("The trial court must be alert to the four-prong dangers of hypnosis: hypersuggestibility, confabulation, loss of critical judgment, and memory cementing.") Note: in this case, victim's hypnotically refreshed testimony not sufficiently trustworthy, based upon qualifications of person who conducted hypnosis and manner in which conducted, and therefore, trial court should not have admitted testimony. The court listed ten factors to consider when assessing such testimony:

1. The level of training in the clinical uses and forensic applications of hypnosis by the person performing the hypnosis;

2. The hypnotist's independence from law enforcement investigators, prosecution, and defense;
3. The existence of a record of any information given or known by the hypnotist concerning the case prior to the hypnosis session;
4. The existence of a written or recorded account of the facts as the hypnosis subject remembers them prior to undergoing hypnosis;
5. The creation of recordings of all contacts between the hypnotist and the subject;
6. The presence of persons other than the hypnotist and the subject during any phase of the hypnosis session, as well as the location of the session;
7. The appropriateness of the induction and memory retrieval techniques used;
8. The appropriateness of using hypnosis on the kind of memory loss involved;
9. The existence of any evidence to corroborate the hypnotically enhanced testimony; and
10. The presence or absence of overt or subtle cuing or suggestion of answers during the hypnotic session.

g. *Psychological Profiling*

Williams v. State, 895 S.W.2d 363, 366 (Tex. Crim. App. 1994) (expert testimony that defendant's tests indicated he did not fit profile of type of person who would commit offense properly excluded).

Coleman v. State, 440 S.W.3d 218, 226 (Tex. App.—Houston [14th Dist.] 2013, no pet.) (defendant did not satisfy his burden of showing by clear and convincing evidence during the gatekeeping hearing the reliability of his expert's methodology for determining whether defendant fit the profile of someone who would be susceptible to giving a false confession).

h. *Accident Reconstruction Evidence*

Rhomer v. State, 522 S.W.3d 13 (Tex. App.—San Antonio 2017), *aff'd*, 569 S.W.3d 664 (Tex. Crim. App. 2019) ("Generally, police officers are not qualified to render expert opinions regarding accidents based on their position as police officers alone.").

Lopez-Juarez v. Kelly, 348 S.W.3d 10, 20 (Tex. App.—Texarkana 2011, pet. denied) (whether a police officer is qualified to testify as an expert on accident reconstruction depends on the facts of each case).

Pilgrim's Pride Corp. v. Smoak, 134 S.W.3d 880, 890 (Tex. App.—Texarkana 2004, pet. denied) (officer not qualified to give expert opinion on reconstruction of accident).

i. *Biomechanic Evidence*

Gainsco County Mut. Ins. Co. v. Martinez, 27 S.W.3d 97, 104 (Tex. App.—San Antonio 2000, pet. dism'd by agr.) (harmless error to allow officer to testify about vehicle speed and force of impact where officer was not sufficiently qualified).

Smelser v. Norfolk S. Ry., Co., 105 F.3d 299 (6th Cir.), *cert. denied*, 522 U.S. 817 (1997) (court erred in allowing biomechanic expert to offer opinion regarding medical causation of injury).

J.B. Hunt Transp., Inc. v. Gen. Motors Corp., 243 F.3d 441 (8th Cir. 2001) (accident reconstruction expert whose opinion was based upon examining photographs of vehicles was properly excluded as unreliable and speculative under *Daubert*; in addition, evidence of another passenger's "minor injuries" properly excluded as irrelevant).

Clark v. Takata Corp., 192 F.3d 750 (7th Cir. 1999) (opinion of expert in biomechanics properly excluded where rested on unproven assumptions and not supported by reliable methodology).

Finchum v. Ford Motor Co., 57 F.3d 526 (7th Cir. 1995) (although accident reconstruction and biomechanics expert was permitted to testify at length, his videotaped experiment evidence depicting crash test dummy was properly excluded where conditions of experiment were not sufficiently similar to those of actual incident). *See also People v. Dellinger*, 163 Cal. App. 3d 284 (1984) (*Kelly* test not met regarding biomechanic testing of anthropomorphic dummy and "finite element analysis" to determine force involved in victim's head injury); but cf. *People v. Roehler*, 167 Cal. App. 3d 353 (1985) (use of test evidence on dummy allowed, not to show cause of injury, but to corroborate conclusions of medical witnesses); *Clemente v. Blumenberg*, 705 N.Y.S.2d 792 (1999) (studies relied upon by biomechanic expert regarding claimed noninjuries in low-speed accident held unreliable); *Smelser v. Norfolk S. Ry., Co.*, 105 F.3d 299 (6th Cir.), *cert. denied*, 522 U.S. 817 (1997) (court erred in allowing biomechanic expert to offer opinion regarding medical causation of injury).

j. Statistical Evidence—Exclusion of Confusing Evidence

Texas Rule of Evidence 403 states:

> Although relevant, evidence may be excluded if its probative value is substantially outweighed by the danger of unfair prejudice, *confusion of the issues*, or *misleading the jury*, or by considerations of undue delay, or needless presentation of cumulative evidence. (Emphasis added.)

Luensmann v. Zimmer-Zampese & Assocs., Inc., 103 S.W.3d 594, 597 (Tex. App.—San Antonio 2003, no pet.) (trial court did not abuse its discretion by excluding evidence regarding a statutory presumption, as misleading to the jury).

Reeves v. State, 969 S.W.2d 471, 490 (Tex. App.—Waco 1998, pet. ref'd), *cert. denied*, 526 U.S. 1068 (1999) (exclusion of testimony on crucial point where inherent tendency to confuse issues).

i. Disapproved Statistical Evidence

Taylor v. Tex. Dep't of Protective & Regulatory Servs., 160 S.W.3d 641, 651 (Tex. App.—Austin 2005, pet. denied) ("[W]ith regard to evaluating matters within the psychological or sociological sciences [in parental termination cases,] ... a social study does not lend itself to evaluation by the *Robinson* factors because it is an inherently subjective endeavor and is not susceptible to scientific replication or statistical or rate of error analysis").

Matthews v. State, 960 S.W.2d 750, 756 (Tex. App.—Tyler 1997, no pet.) (seat belt fatality statistics inadmissible as irrelevant).

McDonald v. Webb, 510 S.W.2d 670, 674 (Tex. Civ. App.—Corpus Christi 1974, no writ) (exclusion of testimony of cotton market where based on statistics).

McBeth v. Tex. & Pac. Ry. Co., 414 S.W.2d 45, 53 (Tex. Civ. App.—Fort Worth 1967), *cert. denied*, 390 U.S. 987 (1968) (exclusion of manual showing statistics on stopping distances under various conditions).

ii. Statistical Significance Requirements

Merrell Dow Pharm., Inc. v. Havner, 953 S.W.2d 706, 716 (Tex. 1997), *cert. denied*, 523 U.S. 1119 (1998) (setting out statistical-significance requirements for determining reliability and admissibility of causation evidence).

In re Allied Chem. Corp., 227 S.W.3d 652, 656 (Tex. 2007) (orig. proceeding) (claimants in a mass toxic tort action must have an expert who can answer "why [an epidemiological] study is reliable, and how the plaintiffs' exposure is similar to that of the study's subjects. An expert must also exclude other causes with reasonable certainty.").

City of Austin v. Chandler, 428 S.W.3d 398, 410 (Tex. App.—Austin 2014, no pet.) ("[I]n disparate-impact cases, after identifying a specific employment practice, causation must be proved; that is, the plaintiff must offer statistical evidence of a kind and degree sufficient to show that the practice in question has caused the complained of disparity ... the statistical disparities must be sufficiently substantial that they raise such an inference of causation.").

Austin v. Kerr-McGee Ref. Corp., 25 S.W.3d 280, 287 (Tex. App.—Texarkana 2000, no writ) (exclusion of statistical evidence that did not meet statistical-significance requirements).

iii. Statistics in Products Liability and Negligence Cases

Gen. Elec. Co. v. Joiner, 522 U.S. 136 (1997) (no error excluding evidence of study related to exposure to carcinogens where study did not demonstrate statistically significant link between exposure to carcinogen and increase in cancer).

Merck & Co. v. Garza, 347 S.W.3d 256, 263 (Tex. 2011) ("[W]hile the controlled, experimental, and prospective nature of clinical trials undoubtedly make them more reliable than retroactive, observational studies, both must show a statistically significant doubling of the risk in order to be some evidence that a drug more likely than not caused a particular injury.").

Merck & Co. v. Garza, 347 S.W.3d 256, 263 (Tex. 2011) (clinical trials and epidemiological studies must show a statistically significant doubling of the risk in order to be some evidence that a drug more likely than not caused a particular injury).

Washington v. Armstrong World Indus., Inc., 839 F.2d 1121 (5th Cir. 1988) (opinion speculative and inadmissible where based upon statistical possibility that could not be ruled out, but in contrast to results of tests performed on specific plaintiff by other experts).

iv. Statistics in Employment Discrimination Cases

City of Austin v. Chandler, 428 S.W.3d 398, 410 (Tex. App.—Austin 2014, no pet.) ("[I]n disparate-impact cases, after identifying a specific employment practice, causation must be proved; that is, the plaintiff must offer statistical evidence of a kind and degree sufficient to show that the practice in question has caused the complained of disparity ... the statistical disparities must be sufficiently substantial that they raise such an inference of causation.").

Armstrong v. Norris Cylinder Co., 922 S.W.2d 210, 212 (Tex. App.—Texarkana 1996, writ dism'd w.o.j.) (statistics by themselves insufficient to establish discrimination).

4. *Opposing Authorities—Approved Tests*

- DNA Typing. [*Kelly v. State*, 824 S.W.2d 568, 569 (Tex. Crim. App. 1992)]
- Footprint Identification [*Hurrelbrink v. State*, 46 S.W.3d 350, 353 (Tex. App.—Amarillo 2001, pet. ref'd)]
- Bite-Mark Identification [*Spence v. State*, 795 S.W.2d 743, 750 (Tex. Crim. App. 1990), *cert. denied*, 499 U.S. 932 (1991)]
- Fingerprint Testing [*Todd v. State*, 342 S.W.2d 575, 577 (Tex. Crim. App. 1961) (expert qualified to testify as expert)]
- HGN Sobriety Tests [*Quinney v. State*, 99 S.W.3d 853, 857 (Tex. App.—Houston [14th Dist.] 2003, no pet.); but see *State v. Rudd*, 255 S.W.3d 293, 301 (Tex. App.—Waco 2008, pet. ref'd) (to be reliable, evidence regarding horizontal gaze nystagmus (HGN) must satisfy three criteria: (1) underlying scientific theory must be valid; (2) technique applying theory must be valid; and (3) technique must have been applied properly on occasion in question)]
- Battered Spouse Syndrome [*Scugoza v. State*, 949 S.W.2d 360, 363 (Tex. App.—San Antonio 1997, no pet.)]
- Abused Child Characteristics [*Hitt v. State*, 53 S.W.3d 697, 707 (Tex. App.—Austin 2001, pet. ref'd)]
- Munchausen Syndrome by Proxy [*Reid v. State*, 964 S.W.2d 723, 730 (Tex. App.—Amarillo 1998, pet ref'd)]
- Handwriting Analysis [*Bratt v. State*, 41 S.W. 622, 622 (Tex. Crim. App. 1897) (expert qualified)

a. *Hedonic Damages*

Golden Eagle Archery, Inc. v. Jackson, 116 S.W.3d 757, 764 (Tex. 2003) ("We are persuaded that in the proper case, when the evidence supports such a submission, loss of enjoyment of life fits best among the factors a fact-finder may consider in assessing damages for physical impairment. Indeed, if other elements such as pain, suffering, mental anguish, and disfigurement are submitted, there is little left for which to compensate under the category of physical impairment other than loss of enjoyment of life.").

Primoris Energy Services Corp. v. Myers, 569 S.W.3d 745 (Tex. App.—Houston [1st Dist.] 2018, no pet.) ("[T]he commonly-understood meaning of 'physical' is 'of or relating to the body'.... And 'impair' is commonly understood to mean 'to diminish in quantity, value, excellence, or strength'.... More generally, Texas courts have recognized that physical impairment damages can compensate for physical injuries that affect the plaintiff's activities or lead to loss of enjoyment of life.").

PNS Stores, Inc. v. Munguia, 484 S.W.3d 503, 514 (Tex. App.—Houston [14th Dist.] 2016, no pet.) ("Physical impairment, sometimes called loss of enjoyment of life, encompasses the loss of the injured party's former lifestyle.... To receive physical impairment damages, the plaintiff must prove that (1) he incurred injuries that are distinct from, or extend beyond, injuries compensable through other damage elements, and (2) these distinct injuries have had a substantial effect.").

Huston v. United Parcel Service, Inc., 434 S.W.3d 630, 640 (Tex. App.—Houston [1st Dist.] 2014, pet. denied) ("[I]ssues such as physical impairment are necessarily speculative, and it is particularly within the jury's province to resolve these matters and determine the amounts attributable thereto.").

Enright v. Goodman Distribution, Inc., 330 S.W.3d 392, 402 (Tex. App.—Houston [14th Dist.] 2010, no pet.) (physical impairment damages "can encompass both economic and noneconomic losses, and can include hedonic damages, or loss of enjoyment of life").

Rentech Steel, L.L.C. v. Teel, 299 S.W.3d 155, 166 (Tex. App.—Eastland 2009, pet. dism'd) ("[D]amages for physical impairment encompass the loss of enjoyment of life, the effect of which must be substantial and extend beyond any pain, suffering, mental anguish, lost wages, or diminished earning capacity.").

Gen. Motors Corp. v. Burry, 203 S.W.3d 514, 554 (Tex. App.—Fort Worth 2006, pet. denied) ("[L]oss of enjoyment of life encompasses the loss of the injured party's former lifestyle, for purposes of awarding damages for future physical impairment.").

Patlyek v. Brittain, 149 S.W.3d 781, 785 (Tex. App.—Austin 2004, pet. denied) (damages for physical impairment can include hedonic damages).

b. Polygraph Evidence

Harty v. State, 229 S.W.3d 849, 851 (Tex. App.—Texarkana 2007, pet. ref'd) (party's admission made during the course of a polygraph examination is generally admissible).

i. Stipulation of Parties

Wright v. State, 154 S.W.3d 235, 239 (Tex. App.—Texarkana 2005, pet. ref'd) ("[S]tatements made during a polygraph pretest interview, during the polygraph examination itself, or during an interview after the examination, may be admissible evidence, but the proper procedure for introducing such evidence before the jury is to redact from such evidence all references to the polygraph examination.").

c. Battered Spouse Syndrome

Fielder v. State, 756 S.W.2d 309, 321 (Tex. Crim. App. 1988) (trial court should have allowed psychologist to testify why woman would endure abusive situation).

Salinas v. State, 426 S.W.3d 318, 327 (Tex. App.—Houston [14th Dist.] 2014), rev'd on other grounds, 464 S.W.3d 363 (Tex. 2015) (expert testimony that it is common for domestic abuse victims to recant or minimize allegations of abuse was relevant to understanding why the complainant may have changed his account of the incident that led to the defendant's prosecution).

Dixon v. State, 244 S.W.3d 472 (Tex. App.—Houston [14th Dist.] 2007, pet. ref'd) (testimony pertaining to the behavior of abuse victims as an appropriate subject for expert testimony).

Dixon v. State, 244 S.W.3d 472, 479 (Tex. App.—Houston [14th Dist.] 2007, pet. ref'd) (police officer's testimony regarding the behavior of victims of family violence was appropriate for expert testimony in aggravated assault trial, where officer's field of expertise was legitimate, and officer's testimony was within the scope of his expertise and properly relied on observations made during his experience with victims of family violence).

d. Abused Child Characteristics

Morris v. State, 361 S.W.3d 649, 669 (Tex. Crim. App. 2011) (grooming of children for sexual molestation is a legitimate subject of expert testimony).

Chavez v. State, 324 S.W.3d 785, 789 (Tex. App.—Eastland 2010, no pet.) ("[E]xpert testimony that a child exhibits behavioral characteristics that have been empirically shown to be common among children who been sexually abused is relevant and admissible.... Such testimony is not objectionable on the ground that it bolsters the credibility of the child complainant.").

DeLeon v. State, 322 S.W.3d 375, 382 (Tex. App.—Houston [14th Dist.] 2010, pet. ref'd) (expert testimony that identifies certain physical or behavioral manifestations of sexual abuse and relates those characteristics to the complainant is admissible even if the complainant has not been impeached).

Reyes v. State, 274 S.W.3d 724, 730 (Tex. App.—San Antonio 2008, pet. ref'd) (in a criminal case involving a child victim, a court may admit expert testimony that a child exhibits behavioral characteristics that have been empirically shown to be common among children who have been abused).

Isenhower v. State, 261 S.W.3d 168, 179 (Tex. App.—Houston [14th Dist.] 2008, no pet.) ("[E]vidence of an extraneous offense is admissible to explain why a victim of sexual assault did not make a prompt outcry.").

Reynolds v. State, 227 S.W.3d 355, 365 n.11 (Tex. App.—Texarkana 2007, no pet.) ("[E]xpert's testimony that a child witness did not exhibit the traits of manipulation is not a direct comment on the truth of the child's allegations and thus is admissible.").

Reynolds v. State, 227 S.W.3d 355, 365 (Tex. App.—Texarkana 2007, no pet.) (it is not error for a social worker to opine that a child was not fantasizing when the child related allegations of sexual abuse during a forensic interview).

Fox v. State, 175 S.W.3d 475, 482 (Tex. App.—Texarkana 2005, pet. ref'd) (an expert witness may not testify that a witness is truthful, but an expert may testify that a child exhibits symptoms consistent with sexual abuse).

e. *Hypnosis Evidence*

Texas Occupations Code Section 1701.403 states:

Investigative Hypnosis

(a) The commission may establish minimum requirements for the training, testing, and certification of peace officers who use investigative hypnosis.

(b) A peace officer may not use a hypnotic interview technique unless the officer:
  (1) completes a training course approved by the commission; and
  (2) passes an examination administered by the commission that is designed to test the officer's knowledge of investigative hypnosis.

(c) The commission may issue a professional achievement or proficiency certificate to an officer who meets the requirements of Subsection (b).

Spence v. State, 795 S.W.2d 743, 750 (Tex. Crim. App. 1990), *cert. denied*, 499 U.S. 932 (1991) (trial court did not err admitting hypnotically enhanced testimony of witness).

f. *Accident Reconstruction and Biomechanics*

Rhomer v. State, 522 S.W.3d 13, (Tex. App.—San Antonio 2017), *aff'd*, 569 S.W.3d 664 (Tex. Crim. App. 2019) ("[P]olice officers are qualified to testify regarding accident reconstruction if they are trained in the science about which they will testify and possess the high degree of knowledge sufficient to qualify as an expert.").

Nabors Well Services, Ltd v. Romero, 508 S.W.3d 512, 531 (Tex. App.—El Paso 2016, pet. denied) ("Biomechanical experts are commonly designated when a plaintiff or defendant wish to prove that a particular kind of injury might or might not result from an auto collision at a particular speed.... Biomechanical experts also appear in cases when a driver is attempting to prove that the malfunction of seat belt enhanced their injury from an accident.... And ... biomechanical experts are used when the defendant attempts to demonstrate a plaintiff's injury was caused by the failure to use a seat-belt.").

Nabors Well Services, Ltd v. Romero, 508 S.W.3d 512, 531 (Tex. App.—El Paso 2016, pet. denied) ("Texas law does not per se disqualify a properly qualified biomechanical expert, who otherwise meets the requirements of Rule 702, from expressing opinions that will assist the jury in deciding injury causation questions.").

Nabors Well Services, Ltd v. Romero, 508 S.W.3d 512, 531 (Tex. App.—El Paso 2016, pet. denied) ("A properly qualified biomechanical engineer, with the proper foundation and analysis, may explain why and to what degree certain injuries are more likely experienced in rollover accidents when a person fails to use a seat belt.").

Lopez-Juarez v. Kelly, 348 S.W.3d 10, 20 (Tex. App.—Texarkana 2011, pet. denied) ("[M]athematical modeling [by expert witness] is not required in all accident reconstructions.... In simple automobile accidents, the accident reconstruction can be conducted without mathematical modeling.").

City of Paris v. McDowell, 79 S.W.3d 601, 606 (Tex. App.—Texarkana 2002, pet. ref'd) (testimony by expert in biomechanics permitted).

Chavers v. State, 991 S.W.2d 457, 461 (Tex. App.—Houston [1st Dist.] 1999, pet. ref'd) (expert testimony reconstructing accident, including speed of vehicles, allowed).

Trailways, Inc. v. Clark, 794 S.W.2d 479, 482 (Tex. App.—Corpus Christi 1990, writ denied) (expert permitted to testify about accident reconstruction and vehicle speed).

g. *Statistics Evidence*

Hinojosa v. State, 4 S.W.3d 240, 250 (Tex. Crim. App. 1999, no pet.) (statistical evaluation of DNA evidence not excludable as incomplete).

Griffith v. State, 976 S.W.2d 241, 247 (Tex. App.—Amarillo 1998, pet. ref'd) (State not required to call mathematical expert as condition for admission of statistical evidence).

Owens-Corning Fiberglas Corp. v. Malone, 916 S.W.2d 551, 563 (Tex. App.—Houston [1st Dist.] 1996), *aff'd*, 972 S.W.2d 35 (Tex. 1998) (admission of hearsay in form of statistics not reversible error).

i. Where Relevant

Lewis v. Southmore Sav. Ass'n, 480 S.W.2d 180, 186 (Tex. 1972) (publications of statistical compilations admissible if proper predicate shown).

Baker Hughes Oilfield Operations, Inc. v. Williams, 360 S.W.3d 15, 30 (Tex. App.—Houston [1st Dist.] 2011, pet. denied) (statistical evidence may be relevant in evaluating claims of racial discrimination in some cases brought under the Texas Commission on Human Rights Act).

h. *Evidence That Is Not "Novel"*

Harris v. Belue, 974 S.W.2d 386, 392 (Tex. App.—Tyler 1998, pet. denied) (expert's conclusion that gynecologist performing laparoscopic-assisted vaginal hysterectomy fired errant staple that caused obstruction in patient's small bowel was a straightforward medical deduction based upon physical facts, which did not have to satisfy standard for admission of novel scientific evidence).

II. Sample Motions

A. Motion to Exclude Evidence of Statistical Analysis

NO. _____

	§	
_____	§	IN THE DISTRICT COURT
	§	
v.	§	_____ JUDICIAL COURT
	§	
_____	§	_____ COUNTY, TEXAS

Motion to Exclude Statistical Evidence

Comes now _____, Plaintiff in this cause, and files this, his Motion to Exclude Statistical Evidence, and in support thereof, Plaintiff would show the Court the following:

1.
FACTUAL BACKGROUND

This is a products liability action arising from a failed "seatback" on the Plaintiff's 2012 Ranchster automobile. The underlying accident occurred on February 2, 2019, when Plaintiff's vehicle, which was stopped at a red light, was rear-ended by a mid-sized sedan at a speed of approximately 35 miles per hour. As a result of the accident, the Plaintiff's driver-side seatback failed and threw the Plaintiff head-first into the rear seat, breaking the Plaintiff's C-2 vertebrae.

The issue raised by this motion relates to an internal report prepared by the Defendant automobile manufacturer entitled "Low-Speed Seatback Failure: A Statistical Report" ("Report"). This Report is a compilation of repair records for the 2013 and 2014 model years of the Ranchster vehicle, analyzing seatback failure in rear-end accidents at speeds from 1 to 15 miles per hour. Not surprisingly, this self-serving document, prepared in anticipation of this litigation, shows no seatback failure at such low speeds.

By this motion, the Plaintiff seeks to exclude this Report as irrelevant, confusing, and prejudicial.

2.
THIS COURT MAY EXCLUDE IRRELEVANT EVIDENCE

Texas Rule of Evidence 402 states that "evidence which is not relevant is inadmissible." Relevant evidence is defined by Texas Rule of Evidence 401 as "having any tendency to make the existence of any fact that is of consequence to the determination of the action more probable or less probable than it would be without the evidence." *See Torrington v. Stutzman*, 46 S.W.3d 829, 845 (Tex. 2000). Irrelevant evidence is not admissible. *Morale v. State*, 557 S.W.3d 569, 573 (Tex. 2018); *Diamond Offshore Services Ltd. v. Williams*, 542 S.W.3d 539, 549 (Tex. 2018).

Evidence may be properly excluded where not relevant to matters at issue. *See Morale v. State,* 557 S.W.3d 569, 573 (Tex. 2018). Plaintiff's immigration or residence status is not relevant to the issues in the case. *See TXI Transp. Co. v. Hughes,* 306 S.W.3d 230, 234 (Tex. 2010); *Zamarron v. Adame,* 864 S.W.2d 173, 175 (Tex. App.—El Paso 1993, reh'g overruled, writ denied) (plaintiff's immigration status irrelevant).

In the present case, Defendant's Report is clearly irrelevant and should be excluded. The Report is a compilation of repair records relating to seatback failure for the 2013 and 2014 model years of the Ranchster vehicle. The Plaintiff's vehicle is a 2012 model—manufactured prior to the adoption of a more rigid seatback design which was added beginning with the 2013 models. Furthermore, the Report focuses on seatback failure in accidents of 1 to 15 miles per hour. The Plaintiff's accident occurred at rate of 35 miles per hour, a much greater rate of speed.

Because the Report has no rational bearing on the facts of this case, it is clearly irrelevant and should be excluded. Further, as is discussed below, because of this clear lack of relevance, there is a great danger that the jurors will be confused, to the detriment of the Plaintiff.

3.
THIS COURT MAY EXCLUDE CONFUSING OR PREJUDICIAL STATISTICAL EVIDENCE

Texas Rule of Evidence 403 states: "[a]lthough relevant, evidence may be excluded if its probative value is substantially outweighed by the danger of unfair prejudice, confusion of the issues, or misleading the jury, or by considerations of undue delay, or needless presentation of cumulative evidence." *Brookshire Bros., Ltd. v. Aldridge,* 438 S.W.3d 9, 26 (Tex. 2014) (evidence that raises a risk of prejudice and confusion of the jury should be excluded); *Farmers Texas County Mutual Insurance Co. v. Pagan,* 453 S.W.3d 454, (Tex. App.—Houston [14th Dist.] 2014, no pet.) (evidence should have been excluded where its probative value was outweighed by danger of confusion of issues and misleading jury).

The Court may exclude irrelevant, unreliable or potentially confusing statistical evidence. *Gen. Elec. Co. v. Joiner,* 522 U.S. 136 (1997) (no error excluding evidence of study related to exposure to carcinogens where study did not demonstrate statistically significant link between exposure to carcinogen and increase in cancer); *Merrell Dow Pharm., Inc. v. Havner,* 953 S.W.2d 706, 716 (Tex. 1997), *cert. denied,* 523 U.S. 1119 (1998) (setting out statistical-significance requirements for determining the reliability and admissibility of causation evidence); *Austin v. Kerr-McGee Ref. Corp.,* 25 S.W.3d 280, 287 (Tex. App.—Texarkana 2000, no writ) (exclusion of statistical evidence that did not meet statistical-significance requirements).

In the present case, the Defendant's Report contains the type of misleading and confusing "pseudoscientific speculations" that should be excluded.

The Report contains an internal analysis of seatback failure at rates of speed significantly lower than the speed of the subject accident. In addition, the Report analyzes accidents with newer Ranchster models, manufactured after important safety features were added to prevent exactly the type of failure that occurred in this case. Because of key differences between the analyzed data and the facts of this case, there is a very real danger that the jurors will be confused by the Report's findings, which shows no seatback failure in newer Ranchster vehicles.

The Report, which was prepared in anticipation of this litigation, <u>excludes key data</u> regarding the rate of speed and the model year involved in the subject accident. To allow this evidence would create undue prejudice to the plaintiff based upon the danger of jury confusion, while adding absolutely nothing of material value for the jury's consideration.

As such, it is respectfully requested that the Court exclude the Report and any mention of the findings contained therein.

Dated: _____*(Date)*_____

By: _____

_____*(Name of Counsel)*_____

Attorneys for Plaintiff,

_____*(Name of Plaintiff)*_____

B. Motion to Exclude Evidence of Hypnosis

NO. _____

	§	
_____	§	IN THE DISTRICT COURT
	§	
v.	§	_____ JUDICIAL COURT
	§	
_____	§	_____ COUNTY, TEXAS

Motion to Exclude Evidence of Hypnosis Results or Testing

Comes now _____, Plaintiff in this cause, and files this, his Motion to Exclude Evidence of Hypnosis Results or Testing, and in support thereof, Plaintiff would show the Court the following:

1.
FACTUAL BACKGROUND

This is a wrongful death action for damages arising from the untimely death of Plaintiff, an eighteen-year-old college student, who suffered a severe asthma attack and died from asphyxiation when Defendant, Plaintiff's roommate, denied Plaintiff his prescribed inhaler treatment during a hazing ritual during rush week at State College. The incident occurred on the night of August 23, 2019, when the Plaintiff suffered severe inflammation of the throat, a collapsed lung, a bleeding esophagus, loss of oxygen to the brain, and a cornea rupture to the right eye due to the strain on Plaintiff's body prior to death. Plaintiff's family seeks recovery of medical expenses, recovery for future lost earnings, pain, and suffering. This Motion seeks to preclude the defendant from attempting to present irrelevant, prejudicial, and junk science evidence relating to the defendant's hypnotic interview at the time of trial. Defendant's hypnotic interview includes two separate denials by defendant of any knowledge that Plaintiff used prescription drugs for asthma and a separate statement made by defendant indicating Defendant's participation in the hazing ritual was "minimal." Defendant admits to being present when Plaintiff's death occurred but claims no knowledge of the whereabouts of Plaintiff's medicine. No ambulance was called until after Plaintiff passed out and stopped breathing.

2.
DEFENDANT'S HYPNOTIC INTERVIEW IS NOT RELEVANT TO ANY MATERIAL ISSUE IN THIS CASE

Texas Rule of Evidence 402 states that "evidence which is not relevant is inadmissible." Relevant evidence is defined by Texas Rule of Evidence 401 as "having any tendency to make the existence of any fact that is of consequence to the determination of the action more probable or less probable than it would be without the evidence." *See Torrington v. Stutzman*, 46 S.W.3d 829, 845 (Tex. 2000). Irrelevant evidence is not admissible. *Morale v. State*, 557 S.W.3d 569, 573 (Tex. 2018); *Diamond Offshore Services Ltd. v. Williams*, 542 S.W.3d 539, 549 (Tex. 2018).

Evidence may be properly excluded where not relevant to matters at issue. *See Morale v. State,* 557 S.W.3d 569, 573 (Tex. 2018). Plaintiff's immigration or residence status is not relevant to the issues in the case. *See TXI Transp. Co. v. Hughes*, 306 S.W.3d 230, 234 (Tex. 2010); *Zamarron v. Adame*, 864 S.W.2d 173, 175 (Tex. App.—El Paso 1993, reh'g overruled, writ denied) (plaintiff's immigration status irrelevant).

Evidence of defendant's hypnotic interview is irrelevant as to any issue in this case. Hypnotic interviews are rarely relevant and may only be admitted under a clear and convincing standard of evidence with the burden on the defendant to show cause. *Zani v. State*, 758 S.W.2d 233, 744 (Tex. Crim. App. 1988). The admission of hypnotically enhanced testimony is only allowed if, after consideration of the totality of the circumstances, the trial court should find by clear and convincing evidence that hypnosis neither rendered the witness's post-hypnotic memory untrustworthy nor substantially impaired the ability of the opponent fairly to test the witness's recall by cross-examination.

Several factors are used to determine whether the hypnotic recall is trustworthy. These factors are:

(1) The level of training in clinical uses and forensic applications of hypnosis by the person performing the hypnosis;
(2) The hypnotist's independence from investigators, prosecution, and defense;
(3) The existence of record of any information given or known by hypnotist concerning case prior to the hypnosis session;
(4) The existence of a written or recorded account of the facts as the subject remembers them prior to undergoing hypnosis;
(5) The creation of recordings of all contacts between the hypnotist and the subject;

(6) The presence of persons other than the hypnotist and the subject during any phase of the session, as well as the location of session;
(7) The appropriateness of the induction and memory retrieval techniques used;
(8) The appropriateness of using hypnosis for kind of memory loss involved; and
(9) The existence of any evidence to corroborate hypnotically enhanced testimony.

Zani v. State, 758 S.W.2d 233, 744 (Tex. Crim. App. 1988). *See also State v. Medrano*, 127 S.W.3d 781, 786 (Tex. Crim. App. 2004).

In the present case, defendant has failed to carry the burden of proof because none of the factors in *Zani v. State*, 758 S.W.2d 233, 744 (Tex. Crim. App. 1988), were satisfied prior to defendant's attempt to introduce the hypnotic interview in question. Because the defendant has not offered any proof in order to satisfy the court that the procedural safeguards were met in relation to defendant's own interview, the burden was left unsatisfied and defendant's hypnotic interview should therefore be rendered inadmissible as irrelevant. Defendant has also made no showing as to the purpose or relevance of defendant's hypnotic interview in this case. As such, admission of the interview would not be helpful to a jury and should be excluded.

3.
ADMISSION OF HYPNOTIC INTERVIEW WOULD CREATE UNDUE PREJUDICE TO PLAINTIFF

Texas Rule of Evidence 403 states: "[a]lthough relevant, evidence may be excluded if its probative value is substantially outweighed by the danger of unfair prejudice, confusion of the issues, or misleading the jury, or by considerations of undue delay, or needless presentation of cumulative evidence." *Brookshire Bros., Ltd. v. Aldridge*, 438 S.W.3d 9, 26 (Tex. 2014) (evidence that raises a risk of prejudice and confusion of the jury should be excluded); *Farmers Texas County Mutual Insurance Co. v. Pagan*, 453 S.W.3d 454, (Tex. App.—Houston [14th Dist.] 2014, no pet.) (evidence should have been excluded where its probative value was outweighed by danger of confusion of issues and misleading jury).

Texas Rule of Evidence 403 justifies the preclusion of the hypnotic evidence in this case. In the present case, Plaintiff's concern is that upon allowing the admission of defendant's hypnotic interview, reasonable jury members would become misled by evidence that holds no probative value. As a result, prejudice against Plaintiff is inevitable especially if irrelevant hypnotic evidence put forth by the defendant is paraded in front of the jury.

4.
DEFENDANT'S HYPNOTIC INTERVIEW SHOULD BE EXCLUDED AS JUNK SCIENCE NOT SATISFYING *DAUBERT*

Texas has adopted the *Daubert* test to determine the admissibility of expert testimony based on novel scientific evidence. See *E.I. du Pont de Nemours and Co. v. Robinson*, 923 S.W.2d 549, 557 (Tex. 1995); *Daubert v. Merrell Dow Pharmaceuticals, Inc.*, 509 U.S. 579, 113 S. Ct. 2786 (1993). Under the test, the proponent of novel scientific evidence must establish the proper foundation of admissibility including: (1) the extent to which the theory has been or can be tested; (2) the extent to which the technique relies upon the subjective interpretation of the expert; (3) whether the theory has been subjected to peer review and/or publication; (4) the technique's potential rate of error; (5) whether the underlying theory or technique has been generally accepted as valid by the relevant scientific community; and (6) the nonjudicial uses that have been made of the theory or technique.

The misuse of scientific evidence in a courtroom is a serious problem. Although hypnosis has known therapeutic value, it is not known as a method of producing accurate recollection of past events, as defendant would attempt to show in court. It is for this reason that Texas courts have adopted the list of procedural safeguards previously discussed. Principally, the court in *Zani v. State*, 758 S.W.2d 233, 744 (Tex. Crim. App. 1988), held that a party attempting to introduce hypnotic testimony has the burden of establishing admissibility by clear and convincing evidence. Defendant failed to address the threshold safeguards 1-4 and by simply applying the same concerns the court in *Zani* shared to the facts in this case, the *Daubert* standard is not met by defendant.

5.
CONCLUSION

Based upon all of the above, the highly prejudicial nature of defendant's hypnotic interview, and failure of the defendant to satisfy the burden of proof in this case, exclusion of reference to the defendant's hypnotic interview is proper in this case as well as any testimony defendant's hypnotist seeks to offer at trial.

Dated: _____*(Date of Motion)*_____

By: _____

_____*(Name of Counsel)*_____

Attorneys for Plaintiff,

_____*(Name of Plaintiff)*_____

C. Motion to Exclude Expert Testimony

NO. _____

	§	IN THE DISTRICT COURT
	§	
v.	§	_____ JUDICIAL COURT
	§	
	§	_____ COUNTY, TEXAS

Motion to Exclude Expert Testimony

Comes now _____, Plaintiff in this cause, and file this, his Motion to Exclude Expert Testimony, and in support thereof, Plaintiff would show the Court the following:

1.
FACTUAL BACKGROUND

This is a tort case arising out of an incident that occurred when Plaintiff's child was injured on a school playground. Plaintiff brought this suit against the school and the manufacturers of the playground equipment and seeks damages for injuries the child suffered. On September 6, 2018, Plaintiff's child climbed between the safety railings on the highest part of the playground and fell, injuring herself. Plaintiff seeks to introduce evidence, in the form of expert testimony, that the playground design was not safe for children. Plaintiff's expert witness is not an engineer, but rather a building contractor who also sells playground equipment.

By this motion, Defendant seeks an order precluding the introduction of any evidence, references to evidence, testimony, or argument relating to Plaintiff's expert witness. This motion is based upon the grounds that Plaintiff's expert witness is unqualified and therefore his testimony is inadmissible pursuant to Texas Rule of Evidence 702, the testimony is based on speculation, and that the evidence is unduly prejudicial

2.
THIS COURT MAY EXCLUDE EVIDENCE IN ADVANCE OF TRIAL BY WAY OF AN IN LIMINE MOTION

The Court has the inherent power to grant a motion in limine to exclude evidence which could be objected to at trial, either as irrelevant or subject to exclusion as unduly prejudicial. *Vela v. Wagner & Brown, Ltd.*, 203 S.W.3d 37, 54 (Tex. App.—San Antonio 2006, no pet.); *Greenberg Traurig of New York, P.C. v. Moody*, 161 S.W.3d 56, 91 (Tex. App.—Houston [14th Dist.] 2004); *Weidner v. Sanchez*, 14 S.W.3d 353, 363 (Tex. App.—Houston [14th Dist.] 2000, no pet.).

Moreover, the court may hear and determine the question of the admissibility of evidence outside the presence or hearing of the jury. *See Weidner v. Sanchez*, 14 S.W.3d 353, 363 (Tex. App.—Houston [14th Dist.] 2000, no pet.); *Kendrix v. S. Pac. Transp. Co.*, 907 S.W.2d 111, 113 (Tex. App.—Beaumont 1995, writ denied); Texas Rule of Civil Procedure 166; and Texas Rules of Evidence 103 and 104.

3.
WITNESS IS NOT QUALIFIED AS AN EXPERT PURSUANT TO RULE 702

Texas Rule of Evidence Rule 702 sets out the basic requirements for expert qualification, as follows:

> If scientific, technical, or other specialized knowledge will assist the trier of fact to understand the evidence or to determine a fact in issue, a witness qualified as an expert by knowledge, skill, experience, training, or education, may testify thereto in the form of an opinion or otherwise.

The fact that a witness has knowledge, skill, expertise, or training does not necessarily mean that the witness can assist the trier of fact. *In re Commitment of Bohannan,* 388 S.W.3d 296, 304 (Tex. 2012), *cert. denied,* 133 S. Ct. 2747 (May 28, 2013). Credentials alone do not qualify an expert to testify. *In re Commitment of Bohannan,* 388 S.W.3d 296, 304 (Tex. 2012), *cert. denied,* 133 S. Ct. 2747 (May 28, 2013). Trial courts are required to ensure that those who purport to be experts truly have expertise regarding the actual subject upon which they are offering an opinion. *In re Commitment of Bohannan,* 388 S.W.3d 296, 304 (Tex. 2012), *cert. denied,* 133 S. Ct. 2747 (May 28, 2013). The test for determining whether an expert is qualified is whether the offering party has established that the expert has knowledge, skill, experience, training, or education regarding the specific issue before the court, which would qualify the expert to give an opinion on that particular subject. *In re Commitment of Bohannan,* 388 S.W.3d 296, 304 (Tex. 2012), *cert. denied,* 133 S. Ct. 2747 (May 28, 2013).

In *Schronk v. Laerdal Med. Corp.,* 440 S.W.3d 250, 257 (Tex. App.—Waco 2013, pet. denied), the court held that a proferred expert witness was not qualified to testify. The case was against the manufacturer of an automatic external defibrillator (AED) after emergency medical technicians were unable to resuscitate a decedent with the device. The expert was offered as an expert in the field of medical devices and was expected to testify to alleged marketing or design defects in the manufacturer's automatic external defibrillator (AED) or its battery. The witness had Bachelor's and Master's degrees in management and a "unique" Doctorate in the field of medical-technology studies from "Union Graduate School and University," and his doctorate focused on the relationship between the medical industry and Food and Drug Administration regulation. He worked as Director of Technical Services for a company called Medtronic, Inc. for nine years, and independently studied for and passed an exam to become a member of the Society of Manufacturing Engineers. However, he was not an engineer, not a registered professional engineer, not licensed by a Board of Engineers, nor an expert in various engineering areas. The expert admitted that he was not a medical doctor, was not certified in emergency medicine, was not an expert in cardiopulmonary resuscitation or defibrillation, has never been employed by a firm that manufactures AEDs or batteries, has never designed or developed an AED or battery, has never formulated warnings applicable to the operation of an AED, has never published any articles on the design or use of AEDs, has never received training or actually used an AED, and had neither examined nor tested the AED or battery used in the case.

In this case, Plaintiff's expert witness will try to establish that because the witness has construction experience and is familiar with different models of playground equipment, he is qualified to testify to the safety of the playground equipment's design. While Plaintiff's witness may have familiarity with different types of playground equipment, he is not an engineer and has no experience with the safety and design of such equipment. As in *Schronk,* a witness's experience in a particular field does not make that witness an expert in all areas of that field. The witness's lack of "knowledge, skill, experience, training or education" in the safety and design of playground equipment makes his testimony as an expert witness inadmissible under Texas Rule of Evidence 702.

4.
PLAINTIFF'S EXPERT TESTIMONY IS BASED ON SPECULATION

Texas case law establishes that conclusory and speculative expert testimony is irrelevant and insufficient to support a verdict. *Coastal Transp. Co., Inc. v. Crown Cent. Petroleum Corp.,* 136 S.W.3d 227, 232 (Tex. 2004). Opinion testimony that is conclusory or speculative is not relevant evidence, because it does not tend to make the existence of a material fact more probable or less probable. *Coastal Transp. Co., Inc. v. Crown Cent. Petroleum Corp.*, 136 S.W.3d 227, 232 (Tex. 2004); *Russell Equestrian Ctr., Inc. v. Miller,* 406 S.W.3d 243, 247 (Tex. App.—San Antonio 2013, no pet.).

In the present matter, Plaintiff's expert witness's opinion that the playground equipment is not safe is based solely on his own opinions and not any scientific data or analysis. Expert opinion based on speculation rather than reasoned analysis is of no assistance to the jury. Further, a trial court is not required to admit evidence connected to existing data only by the expert's ipse dixit. *Cooper Tire & Rubber Co. v. Mendez,* 204 S.W.3d 797, 805 (Tex. 2006); *Taber v. Roush,* 316 S.W.3d 139, 148 (Tex. App.—Houston [14th Dist.] 2010, no pet.). The testimony of Plaintiff's expert witness does not meet the standards for admission of expert testimony and is inadmissible.

5.
THIS COURT MAY EXCLUDE PREJUDICIAL EVIDENCE PURSUANT TO RULE 403

Texas Rule of Evidence 403 states: "[a]lthough relevant, evidence may be excluded if its probative value is substantially outweighed by the danger of unfair prejudice, confusion of the issues, or misleading the jury, or by considerations of undue delay, or needless presentation of cumulative evidence." *Brookshire Bros., Ltd. v. Aldridge,* 438 S.W.3d 9, 26 (Tex. 2014) (evidence that raises a risk of prejudice and confusion of the jury should be excluded); *Farmers Texas County Mutual Insurance Company v. Pagan,* 453 S.W.3d 454, (Tex. App.—Houston [14th Dist.] 2014, no pet.) (evidence should have been excluded where its probative value was outweighed by danger of confusion of issues and misleading jury).

Texas Rule of Evidence 403 justifies the preclusion of the requested evidence in this case. The fact that Plaintiff's witness will testify as an "expert" that the playground equipment was unsafe would mislead the jury as to fault and the amount of damages, if any. The evidence relating to Plaintiff's expert witness should be excluded.

6.
CONCLUSION

Based on the foregoing, Defendant respectfully requests that this Court enter an order excluding any and all evidence, references to evidence, testimony, or argument relating to Plaintiff's expert witness in this matter.

Dated: _____ *(Date of Motion)* _____

By: _____

_____ *(Name of Counsel)* _____

Attorneys for Defendant,

_____ *(Name of Defendant)* _____

CHAPTER 6

Discovery Motions

I. Motion Authorities
   A. Motion for Evidentiary Sanctions
      1. Suggested Motion Text
      2. Motion Summary
      3. Supporting Authorities
         a. Misuse of Discovery Process
            i. Evidence Sanctions
            ii. Issue Sanctions
            iii. "Death Penalty" Sanctions (Terminating Sanctions)
         b. When Prior Order Is Unnecessary
         c. Monetary Sanctions
         d. Depositions
            i. Evidentiary Sanctions
            ii. Monetary Sanctions
            iv. "Death Penalty" Sanctions
         e. Interrogatories
            i. Evidentiary Sanctions
            ii. Monetary Sanctions
            iii. "Death Penalty" Sanctions
         f. Production Requests
            i. Evidentiary Sanctions
            ii. Monetary Sanctions
            iii. "Death Penalty" Sanctions
         g. Mental and Physical Examinations
            i. "Death Penalty" Cases
         h. Requests for Admission
            i. Deeming Matters Admitted for Lack of Response
            ii. "Death Penalty" Sanctions
         i. Other Grounds
      4. Opposing Authorities
         a. "Death Penalty" Sanctions
         b. Interrogatories
         c. Matters Deemed Admitted
         d. Depositions
         e. Production Requests
   B. Motion to Conclusively Establish Matters
      1. Suggested Motion Text
      2. Motion Summary

3. Supporting Authorities
      a. Purpose of Discovery
   4. Opposing Authorities
  C. Motion to Exclude Evidence of Claims Denied in Discovery
   1. Suggested Motion Text
   2. Motion Summary
   3. Supporting Authorities
      a. Prejudicial Evidence—No Need to Show Unfair Surprise
         i. Unfair Surprise
      b. Where Privilege Raised in Discovery
      c. Matters Not in Dispute
      d. Other Grounds
   4. Opposing Authorities
  D. Motion Regarding Expert Declarations and Expert Depositions
   1. Suggested Motion Text
   2. Motion Summary
   3. Supporting Authorities
      a. Time for Disclosure of Expert Information
      b. Evidentiary Sanctions
      c. Deficient Declaration
      d. Undisclosed Witness
      e. Opinions Not Referenced in Discovery
   4. Opposing Authorities
      a. Continuance to Depose Expert
      b. No Unfair Surprise
      c. Minor Change in Testimony
      d. Opportunity to Redepose Experts
II. Sample Motions
  A. Motion to Exclude Evidence of Claim Denied During Discovery
  B. Opposition to Defendant's Motion to Limit Plaintiff's Expert's Opinions
  C. Motion to Exclude Evidence of Medical Bills for Services Obtained After [Date]

I. Motion Authorities

A. Motion for Evidentiary Sanctions

1. Suggested Motion Text

Alternative One (Sanction Precluding Evidence):

> (*Name of Moving Party*) hereby moves this Court for an order precluding (*Name of Party*) from introducing or mentioning evidence relating to (*Describe Evidence to Be Excluded*). The motion is based upon the grounds that [name of party] misused the discovery process by (*Describe Discovery Abuse, e.g., Failing to Appear for a Deposition*) and therefore an evidence sanction, pursuant to Texas Rule of Civil Procedure 215.2(b)(4), is an appropriate remedy.

Alternative Two (Issue Sanction Establishing Facts):

>(*Name of Moving Party*) hereby moves this Court for an order that (*Describe Facts to Be Established*) shall be taken as established at the time of trial in this matter. The motion is based upon the grounds that (*Name of Party*) misused the discovery process by (*Describe Discovery Abuse, e.g., Failing to Comply With Proper Discovery Requests or Orders*) and therefore may be sanctioned by way of an issue sanction, pursuant to Texas Rule of Civil Procedure 215.2(b)(3).

Alternative Three (Issue Sanction Prohibiting Party From Supporting or Opposing Claim or Defense):

>(*Name of Moving Party*) hereby moves this Court for an order prohibiting (*Name of Party*) from supporting or opposing the following (*Claims or Defenses*): (*List Claims or Defenses Forming Basis of Requested Sanction, Relating to Offending Party's Discovery Abuse*). The motion is based upon the grounds that (*Name of Party*) misused the discovery process by (*Describe Discovery Abuse, e.g., Violating Two Court Orders to Appear for Deposition and Negligently Destroying Key Evidence*) and therefore may be sanctioned by way of an issue sanction, pursuant to Texas Rule of Civil Procedure 215.2(b)(4).

Alternative Four (Terminating Sanction):

>(*Name of Moving Party*) hereby moves this Court for an order (*Describe Desired Terminating Sanction, e.g., Striking the Pleadings, Staying Further Proceedings, Dismissing the Action, Rendering Default Judgment, etc.*). The motion is based upon the grounds that (*Name of Party*) misused the discovery process in an egregious fashion by (*Describe Discovery Abuse, e.g., Violating Two Court Orders to Appear for Deposition and Intentionally Destroying Key Evidence*) and therefore may be sanctioned by way of a terminating sanction, pursuant to Texas Rule of Civil Procedure 215.2(b)(5).

2. Motion Summary

This motion is based upon Texas Rule of Civil Procedure 215, which provides the authority for evidence, issue, and terminating, or "death penalty" sanctions against parties who have misused the discovery process. See Tex. R. Civ. P. 215.1 to 215.5; *Cire v. Cummings*, 134 S.W.3d 835, 839 (Tex. 2003) (terminating sanction); *Rundle v. Comm'n for Lawyer Discipline*, 1 S.W.3d 209, 215 (Tex. App.—Amarillo 1999, no pet.) (evidence sanction); *Swain v. Sw. Bell Yellow Pages, Inc.*, 998 S.W.2d 731, 733 (Tex. App.—Fort Worth 1999, no pet.) (issue sanction); *Pena v. Williams*, 547 S.W.2d 671, 673 (Tex. Civ. App.—San Antonio 1977, no writ.) (terminating sanction).

>*Note: This chapter provides general authorities for obtaining discovery sanctions [6:3] as well as authorities for abuses arising from the following specific discovery types:*

- *Depositions;*
- *Interrogatories;*
- *Production Requests;*
- *Mental and Physical Examinations;*
- *Requests for Admission.*

3. Supporting Authorities

Texas Rule of Civil Procedure 215.2 states:

> If a party or an officer, director, or managing agent of a party or a person designated under Rules 199.2(b)(1) or 200.1(b) to testify on behalf of a party fails to comply with proper discovery requests or to obey an order to provide or permit discovery, including an order made under Rules 204 or 215.1, the court in which the action is pending may, after notice and hearing, make such orders in regard to the failure as are just, and among others the following:
>
> (1) an order disallowing any further discovery of any kind or of a particular kind by the disobedient party;
>
> (2) an order charging all or any portion of the expenses of discovery or taxable court costs or both against the disobedient party or the attorney advising him;
>
> (3) an order that the matters regarding which the order was made or any other designated facts shall be taken to be established for the purposes of the action in accordance with the claim of the party obtaining the order;
>
> (4) an order refusing to allow the disobedient party to support or oppose designated claims or defenses, or prohibiting him from introducing designated matters in evidence;
>
> (5) an order striking out pleadings or parts thereof, or staying further proceedings until the order is obeyed, or dismissing with or without prejudice the action or proceedings or any part thereof, or rendering a judgment by default against the disobedient party;
>
> (6) in lieu of any of the foregoing orders or in addition thereto, an order treating as a contempt of court the failure to obey any orders except an order to submit to a physical or mental examination;
>
> (7) when a party has failed to comply with an order under Rule 204 requiring him to appear or produce another for examination, such orders as are listed in paragraphs (1), (2), (3), (4), or (5) of this subdivision, unless the person failing to comply shows that he is unable to appear or to produce such person for examination.
>
> In lieu of any of the foregoing orders or in addition thereto, the court shall require the party failing to obey the order or the attorney advising him, or both, to pay, at such time as ordered by the court,

the reasonable expenses, including attorney fees, caused by the failure, unless the court finds that the failure was substantially justified or that other circumstances make an award of expenses unjust. Such an order shall be subject to review on appeal from the final judgment.

Misuses of the discovery process, as provided by Texas Rule of Civil Procedure 215.1(b), include:

- failing to appear before an officer who is to take the deposition [215.1(b)(2)(A)];
- failing to answer a question propounded or submitted upon oral examination or written questions [215.1(b)(2)(B)];
- failing to serve answers or objections to interrogatories, requests for inspection, or other permitted discovery [215.2(b)(3)];
- giving an evasive or incomplete answer to discovery [215.1(c)].

a. Misuse of Discovery Process

Altesse Healthcare Solutions, Inc. v. Wilson, 540 S.W.3d 570, 572 (Tex. 2018) ("Trial courts have broad authority to impose appropriate sanctions on recalcitrant litigants ... That authority is not, however, without limits ... a direct relationship must exist between the offensive conduct and the sanction imposed.").

Altesse Healthcare Solutions, Inc. v. Wilson, 540 S.W.3d 570, 572 (Tex. 2018) ("[A] court imposing sanctions must seek to ensure that the punishment fits the crime.").

Horizon Health Corp. v. Acadia Healthcare Co., Inc., 520 S.W.3d 848, (Tex. 2017) ("Sanctions may be imposed, after notice and a hearing, on parties who refuse to respond, or who give inadequate responses, to valid discovery requests or orders.... For purposes of these provisions, evasive or incomplete answers are treated as a failure to answer.").

Horizon Health Corp. v. Acadia Healthcare Co., 520 S.W.3d 848, (Tex. 2017) ("[S]anctions may be appropriate even when a party eventually complies with a discovery request.").

Horizon Health Corp. v. Acadia Healthcare Co., 520 S.W.3d 848, (Tex. 2017) (discovery sanctions "must further one of the recognized purposes of discovery sanctions ... and must be 'just,' no more severe than required to further their legitimate purposes, and specifically related to the harm done by the condemned conduct").

Petroleum Solutions, Inc. v. Head, 454 S.W.3d 482, 489 (Tex. 2014); *Brookshire Bros. v. Aldridge,* 438 S.W.3d 9, 21 (Tex. 2014) (in issuing sanctions for discovery abuse, two elements should be considered: first, a direct relationship must exist between the offensive conduct, the offender, and the sanction imposed, which means that the sanction must be directed against the wrongful conduct and toward remedying the prejudice suffered by the innocent party; second, a sanction must not be excessive, which means it should be no more severe than necessary to satisfy its legitimate purpose, and requires the trial court to consider the availability of lesser sanctions and, in all but the most exceptional cases, actually test the lesser sanctions).

Brookshire Bros. v. Aldridge, 438 S.W.3d 9, 21 (Tex. 2014) (the remedial purpose supporting the imposition of a spoliation remedy is to restore the parties to a rough approximation of their positions if all evidence were available).

Paradigm Oil, Inc. v. Retamco Operating, Inc., 372 S.W.3d 177, 184 (Tex. 2012) ("[T]wo factors mark the bounds of a 'just' sanction. First, a direct relationship between the offensive conduct and the sanction imposed must exist... Second, the sanction imposed must not be excessive.").

PR Invs. & Specialty Retailers, Inc. v. State, 251 S.W.3d 472, 481 (Tex. 2008) (discovery sanction should be no more severe than necessary to satisfy its legitimate purposes, and courts must consider the availability of less stringent sanctions and whether such lesser sanctions would fully promote compliance).

Shops at Legacy (Inland) L.P. v. Fine Autographs & Memorabilia Retail Stores, Inc., 418 S.W.3d 229, 232 (Tex. App.—Dallas 2013, no pet.) (if a trial court finds a party is abusing the discovery process in seeking, making, or resisting discovery, then the trial court may, after notice and hearing, impose any appropriate sanction authorized by Rule 215.2(b)(1)-(5) and (8)).

Shops at Legacy (Inland) L.P. v. Fine Autographs & Memorabilia Retail Stores, Inc., 418 S.W.3d 229, 232 (Tex. App.—Dallas 2013, no pet.) ("[W]hen determining whether a trial court's imposition of sanctions was just, an appellate court considers the following two standards: (1) whether there is a 'direct relationship' between the abusive conduct and the sanction imposed; and (2) whether the sanction is excessive.").

In re M.J.M., 406 S.W.3d 292, 296 (Tex. App.—San Antonio 2013, no pet.) (sanctions for discovery abuse serve three legitimate purposes: (1) to secure compliance with the discovery rules; (2) to deter other litigants from similar misconduct; and (3) to punish violators).

In re M.J.M., 406 S.W.3d 292, 296 (Tex. App.—San Antonio 2013, no pet.) (whether discovery sanctions are just depends on two factors; first, a direct relationship must exist between the offensive conduct and the sanction imposed; and second, the sanction imposed must not be excessive).

PopCap Games, Inc. v. MumboJumbo, LLC, 350 S.W.3d 699, 718 (Tex. App.—Dallas 2011, pet. denied) (good-cause exception allows a trial judge to excuse a party's failure to comply with discovery obligations in difficult or impossible circumstances; however, inadvertence of counsel, lack of surprise, or uniqueness of the excluded evidence do not constitute good cause).

In re Kings Ridge Homeowners Ass'n, Inc., 303 S.W.3d 773, 783 (Tex. App.—Fort Worth 2009, orig. proceeding) ("[P]urposes of [Rule 193.6] are to promote responsible assessment of settlement and prevent trial by ambush.").

Buck v. Estate of Buck, 291 S.W.3d 46, 55 (Tex. App.—Corpus Christi 2009, no pet.) ("[T]o determine whether discovery sanctions are just, the court applies a two-prong test.... The first prong requires that a direct relationship exists between the offensive conduct and the sanction imposed.... The sanction must be directed against the abuse and toward remedying the prejudice caused an innocent party.... Under this prong, the trial court should attempt to determine if the offensive conduct is attributable to the attorney, the party, or both.... The second prong requires that the sanctions 'fit the crime'; in other words, they should not be excessive.... Sanctions which are so severe that they preclude presentation on the merits should not be assessed absent a party's bad faith or counsel's flagrant disregard for the responsibilities of discovery under the rules.").

Scott Bader, Inc. v. Sandstone Prods., Inc., 248 S.W.3d 802, 812 (Tex. App.—Houston [1st Dist.] 2008, no pet.) ("Rule of Civil Procedure 215.2 allows a trial court to enter 'just' sanctions for a party's failure to comply with a discovery order or request.").

Scott Bader, Inc. v. Sandstone Prods., Inc., 248 S.W.3d 802, 812 (Tex. App.—Houston [1st Dist.] 2008, no pet.) (for a discovery sanction to be "just," there must be a direct nexus among the offensive conduct, the offender, and the sanction imposed, the sanction must be directed against the abuse and toward remedying the prejudice caused to the innocent party, and the sanction should be visited upon the offender).

Scott Bader, Inc. v. Sandstone Prods., Inc., 248 S.W.3d 802, 812 (Tex. App.—Houston [1st Dist.] 2008, no pet.) (sanction imposed for discovery abuse should be no more severe than necessary to satisfy its legitimate purposes, which include securing compliance with discovery rules, deterring other litigants from similar misconduct, and punishing violators).

Scott Bader, Inc. v. Sandstone Prods., Inc., 248 S.W.3d 802, 812 (Tex. App.—Houston [1st Dist.] 2008, no pet.) (trial courts must consider less stringent discovery sanctions and whether such lesser sanctions would fully promote compliance with discovery rules).

Tidrow v. Roth, 189 S.W.3d 408, 412 (Tex. App.—Dallas 2006, no pet.) (choice of discovery sanctions is left to the sound discretion of the trial judge, but the sanction imposed must be just).

Cass v. Stephens, 156 S.W.3d 38, 78 (Tex. App.—El Paso 2004, pet. denied), *cert. denied*, 552 U.S. 819 (2007) (trial court did not abuse discretion by imposing $978,492.00 for discovery sanctions against party who failed to comply with discovery).

i. Evidence Sanctions

Paradigm Oil, Inc. v. Retamco Operating, Inc., 372 S.W.3d 177, 184 (Tex. 2012) (sanctions that preclude the admission of evidence intrude upon the fact-finding process of a trial just as much as a default judgment on liability).

Paradigm Oil, Inc. v. Retamco Operating, Inc., 372 S.W.3d 177, 184 (Tex. 2012) (destruction of evidence that directly and significantly impairs a party's ability to prove damages might reasonably justify a sanction preventing a party from presenting evidence in the damages portion of a trial).

Arshad v. American Express Bank, FSB, 580 S.W.3d 798, 807 (Tex. App.—Houston [14th Dist.] 2019, no pet.) ("A party who fails to make, amend, or supplement a discovery response in a timely manner may not offer the testimony of a witness, other than a party, who was not timely identified, unless the court finds that there was good cause for the failure or the failure will not unfairly surprise or unfairly prejudice another party.").

Arshad v. American Express Bank, FSB, 580 S.W.3d 798, 807 (Tex. App.—Houston [14th Dist.] 2019, no pet.) ("The burden of establishing good cause or lack of unfair surprise or unfair prejudice rests on the party seeking to call the witness, and the record must support such findings.").

In Interest of D.W.G.K., 558 S.W.3d 671, 680 (Tex. App.—Texarkana 2018, pet. denied) ("[T]he purposes of Rule 193.6 [excluding evidence that is not properly disclose] are threefold: (1) to promote responsible assessment of settlement, (2) to prevent trial by ambush, and (3) to give the other party the opportunity to prepare rebuttal to expert testimony.").

In Interest of D.W.G.K., 558 S.W.3d 671, 680 (Tex. App.—Texarkana 2018, pet. denied) ("[I]n order to establish the absence of unfair prejudice, the party seeking to call an untimely disclosed witness or introduce untimely disclosed evidence must establish that, notwithstanding the late disclosure, the other party had enough evidence to reasonably assess settlement, to avoid trial by ambush, and to prepare rebuttal to expert testimony.").

In re M.J.M., 406 S.W.3d 292, 296 (Tex. App.—San Antonio 2013, no pet.) (depending on the circumstances, an order excluding essential evidence may constitute a death penalty sanction).

Duff v. Spearman, 322 S.W.3d 869, 877 (Tex. App.—Beaumont 2010, pet. denied) ("[T]rial court, in remedying discovery abuse, has the right to determine in the first instance whether to deem facts as being established in determining an appropriate sanction for discovery misconduct.").

In re Kings Ridge Homeowners Ass'n, Inc., 303 S.W.3d 773, 783 (Tex. App.—Fort Worth 2009, orig. proceeding) ("[P]urposes of [Rule 193.6] are to promote responsible assessment of settlement and prevent trial by ambush.").

Duerr v. Brown, 262 S.W.3d 63, 76 (Tex. App.—Houston [14th Dist.] 2008, no pet.) (failure to provide expert information as required by the rules is sanctionable by exclusion of that expert's report).

In re Commitment of Marks, 230 S.W.3d 241, 245 (Tex. App.—Beaumont 2007, no pet.) (offender did not "request a finding of good cause or a finding of no unfair surprise or prejudice to the State prior to the time he rested, nor made an offer of proof to show surprise" for failure to disclose substance of expert testimony).

Chau v. Riddle, 212 S.W.3d 699, 704 (Tex. App.—Houston [1st Dist.] 2006), *rev'd on other grounds*, 254 S.W.3d 453 (Tex. 2008) (exclusion of re-designated expert anesthesiologist was appropriate sanction for failure by parents of newborn infant to de-designate previously named expert, in order to comply with docket control order that indicated only one expert per specialty).

Aguilar v. Morales, 162 S.W.3d 825, 832 (Tex. App.—El Paso 2005, pet. denied) (trial court properly struck expert witness for discovery abuse).

Swain v. Sw. Bell Yellow Pages, Inc., 998 S.W.2d 731, 733 (Tex. App.—Fort Worth 1999, no pet.) (customer was precluded from introducing evidence of damages at trial where he failed to respond to discovery requests on the issue of damages).

Rundle v. Comm'n for Lawyer Discipline, 1 S.W.3d 209, 215 (Tex. App.—Amarillo 1999, no pet.) (exclusion of witness' testimony for failure to comply with discovery).

ii. Issue Sanctions

Paradigm Oil, Inc. v. Retamco Operating, Inc., 372 S.W.3d 177, 184 (Tex. 2012) (trial court should have discretion to bar a defendant's participation, such as at the damages hearing, if such a sanction is necessary to remedy discovery abuse, but even so, such an extreme sanction must be carefully tailored to comport with the requirements of TransAmerican and due process).

Shops at Legacy (Inland) L.P. v. Fine Autographs & Memorabilia Retail Stores, Inc., 418 S.W.3d 229, 232 (Tex. App.—Dallas 2013, no pet.) (among discovery sanctions available under Rule 215.2 are orders "striking out pleadings or parts thereof," "dismissing with or without prejudice the actions or proceedings or any part thereof," and "rendering a judgment by default against the disobedient party").

Duff v. Spearman, 322 S.W.3d 869, 877 (Tex. App.—Beaumont 2010, pet. denied) ("[T]rial court, in remedying discovery abuse, has the right to determine in the first instance whether to deem facts as being established in determining an appropriate sanction for discovery misconduct.").

Swain v. Sw. Bell Yellow Pages, Inc., 998 S.W.2d 731, 733 (Tex. App.—Fort Worth 1999, no pet.) (a customer was precluded from introducing evidence of damages at trial where he failed to respond to discovery requests on issue of damages).

iii. "Death Penalty" Sanctions (Terminating Sanctions)

An order dismissing the action or striking a party's pleadings for failure to comply with discovery is referred to as a "death penalty" sanction. "Death penalty" sanctions prevent the presentation of the merits of a party's case by striking pleadings, dismissing an action, or entering a default judgment. See Tex. R. Civ. P. 215.2(b)(5); *TransAmerican Natural Gas v. Powell*, 811 S.W.2d 913, 917 (Tex. 1991).

Altesse Healthcare Solutions, Inc. v. Wilson, 540 S.W.3d 570, 572 (Tex. 2018) ("[S]o-called death-penalty sanctions, under which the offending party essentially loses the case because of the sanction, are generally reserved for the most egregious cases in which the offending party's conduct justifies a presumption that its claims lack merit.").

Cire v. Cummings, 134 S.W.3d 835, 839 (Tex. 2004) (refusal to comply with discovery and destruction of evidence warranted death penalty sanction).

Braden v. Downey, 811 S.W.2d 922, 929 (Tex. 1991) (discovery rules authorize orders establishing facts, prohibiting claims or defenses, or otherwise terminating presentation on merits).

Hogg v. Lynch, Chappell & Alsup, P.C., 553 S.W.3d 55, 70 (Tex. App.—El Paso 2018, no pet.) ("Death penalty sanctions implicate due process concerns and may be imposed as an initial sanction only in exceptional cases in which lesser sanctions would not promote compliance.").

Hogg v. Lynch, Chappell & Alsup, P.C., 553 S.W.3d 55, 70 (Tex. App.—El Paso 2018, no pet.) ("Ascertaining whether an order is an outcome determinative sanction requires evidence to be presented concerning whether the case could be proven under the terms of the order; the sanctioned party's allegations alone are not enough to meet this requirement.").

Shops at Legacy (Inland) L.P. v. Fine Autographs & Memorabilia Retail Stores, Inc., 418 S.W.3d 229, 232 (Tex. App.—Dallas 2013, no pet.) (among discovery sanctions available under Rule 215.2 are orders "striking out pleadings or parts thereof," "dismissing with or without prejudice the actions or proceedings or any part thereof," and "rendering a judgment by default against the disobedient party").

Shops at Legacy (Inland) L.P. v. Fine Autographs & Memorabilia Retail Stores, Inc., 418 S.W.3d 229, 232 (Tex. App.—Dallas 2013, no pet.) (discovery sanctions that adjudicate a claim and preclude presentation of the merits of the case are often referred to as "death penalty" sanctions).

In re M.J.M., 406 S.W.3d 292, 296 (Tex. App.—San Antonio 2013, no pet.) (death penalty sanction" is any sanction that adjudicates a claim and precludes the presentation of the merits of the case).

In re M.J.M., 406 S.W.3d 292, 296 (Tex. App.—San Antonio 2013, no pet.) (Rule 215.2(b)(5) of the Texas Rules of Civil Procedure expressly authorizes "death penalty" sanctions, including "an order striking out pleadings," an order "dismissing with or without prejudice the action or proceedings," or an order "rendering judgment by default against the disobedient party").

In re M.J.M., 406 S.W.3d 292, 296 (Tex. App.—San Antonio 2013, no pet.) (depending on the circumstances, an order excluding essential evidence may constitute a death penalty sanction).

In re Le, 335 S.W.3d 808, 813 (Tex. App.—Houston [14th Dist.] 2011, orig. proceeding) ("[I]n imposing 'death penalty' discovery sanctions, the trial court may properly consider everything that has occurred during the history of the litigation and is not limited to considering only the last violation of the discovery rules.").

Davenport v. Scheble, 201 S.W.3d 188, 195 (Tex. App.—Dallas 2006, review denied) (death penalty sanctions were appropriate for knowing concealment of material information).

HRN, Inc. v. Shell Oil Co., 102 S.W.3d 205, 218 (Tex. App.—Houston [14th Dist.] 2003), *rev'd on other grounds*, 144 S.W.3d 429 (Tex. 2004) (terminating sanction appropriate for repeated failure to comply with discovery).

Magnuson v. Mullen, 65 S.W.3d 815, 823 (Tex. App.—Fort Worth 2002, pet. denied) (dismissal of plaintiff's lawsuit, with prejudice was warranted as a sanction for failure to comply with discovery).

In re Dynamic Health, Inc., 32 S.W.3d 876, 881(Tex. App.—Texarkana 2000, orig. proceeding) (trial court properly imposed death penalty sanction as a result of a party's repeated failure to comply with discovery, after lesser sanctions proved ineffective).

b. When Prior Order Is Unnecessary

Texas Rule of Civil Procedure 215.1(b) states:

> (b) *Motion*
> (1) If a party or other deponent which is a corporation or other entity fails to make a designation under Rules 199.2(b)(1) or 200.1(b); or
> (2) If a party, or other deponent, or a person designated to testify on behalf of a party or other deponent fails:
> (A) to appear before the officer who is to take his deposition, after being served with a proper notice; or
> (B) to answer a question propounded or submitted upon oral examination or upon written questions; or
> (3) if a party fails:
> (A) to serve answers or objections to interrogatories submitted under Rule 197, after proper service of the interrogatories; or
> (B) to answer an interrogatory submitted under Rule 197; or
> (C) to serve a written response to a request for inspection submitted under Rule 196 after proper service of the request; or
> (D) to respond that discovery will be permitted as requested or fails to permit discovery as requested in response to a request for inspection submitted under Rule 196;
>
> the discovering party may move for an order compelling a designation, an appearance, an answer or answers, or inspection or production in accordance with the request, or apply to the court in which the action is pending for the imposition of any sanction authorized by Rule 215.2(b) *without the necessity of first having obtained a court order compelling such discovery.* (Emphasis added.)

In re First Transit Inc., 499 S.W.3d 584 (Tex. App.—Houston [14th Dist.] 2016, orig. proceeding [mand. denied) ("Death penalty sanctions may be imposed in the first instance only when they are clearly justified and it is fully apparent that no lesser sanctions would promote compliance with the rules.").

Shops at Legacy (Inland) L.P. v. Fine Autographs & Memorabilia Retail Stores, Inc., 418 S.W.3d 229, 232 (Tex. App.—Dallas 2013, no pet.) (the trial court need not test the effectiveness of each available lesser sanction by actually imposing the lesser sanction on the party before issuing the death penalty; instead the trial court must analyze the available sanctions and offer a reasoned explanation as to the appropriateness of the sanction imposed).

In re Estate of Preston, 346 S.W.3d 137, 157 (Tex. App.—Fort Worth 2011, no pet.) ("[I]n cases of exceptional misconduct, the trial court is not required to test lesser sanctions before striking pleadings ... so long as the record reflects that the trial court considered lesser sanctions before striking pleadings and the party's conduct justifies the presumption that its claims lack merit.... This means that a trial court must analyze the available sanctions and offer a reasoned explanation as to the appropriateness of the sanction imposed.").

Teate v. CBL/Parkdale Mall, LP, 262 S.W.3d 486, 492 (Tex. App.—Beaumont 2008, no pet.) ("[T]rial court need not test the effectiveness of each available lesser sanction by actually imposing the lesser sanction on the party before issuing the death penalty; rather, the trial court must analyze the available sanctions and offer a reasoned explanation as to the appropriateness of the sanction imposed.").

c. *Monetary Sanctions*

Clark v. Clark, 546 S.W.3d 268, 273 (Tex. App.—El Paso 2017, no pet.) ("[A]n award under Rule 215.1(d) is not a penalty.... Rather, the rule functions to reimburse the movant for the expenses incurred in advancing the motion.").

Prize Energy Res., L.P. v. Cliff Hoskins, Inc., 345 S.W.3d 537, 575 (Tex. App.—San Antonio 2011, no pet.) ("[Defendants] were not required to specifically plead for monetary damages [for discovery abuse] because courts possess inherent powers to discipline attorney behavior through the imposition of sanctions sua sponte in appropriate cases.").

d. *Depositions*

Texas Rule of Civil Procedure 215.1 governs a party's failure to appear at a deposition and states in pertinent part:

> A party, upon reasonable notice to other parties and all other persons affected thereby, may apply for sanctions or an order compelling discovery as follows:
>
> ...
>
> (b)(2) If a party, or other deponent, or a person designated to testify on behalf of a party or other deponent fails:
>
> (A) to appear before the officer who is to take his deposition, after being served with a proper notice;
>
> ...
>
> the discovering party may move for an order compelling a designation, an appearance, an answer or answers, or inspection or production in accordance with the request, or apply to the court in which the action is pending for the imposition of any sanction authorized by Rule 215.2(b) without the necessity of first having obtained a court order compelling such discovery.
>
> When taking a deposition on oral examination, the proponent of the question may complete or adjourn the examination before he applies for an order.
>
> If the court denies the motion in whole or in part, it may make such protective order as it would have been empowered to make on a motion pursuant to Rule 192.6.

(b) *Evasive or Incomplete Answer.* For purposes of this subdivision an evasive or incomplete answer is to be treated as a failure to answer.

(c) *Disposition of Motion to Compel: Award of Expenses.* If the motion is granted, the court shall, after opportunity for hearing, require a party or deponent whose conduct necessitated the motion or the party or attorney advising such conduct or both of them to pay, at such time as ordered by the court, the moving party the reasonable expenses incurred in obtaining the order, including attorney fees, unless the court finds that the opposition to the motion was substantially justified or that other circumstances make an award of expenses unjust. Such an order shall be subject to review on appeal from the final judgment.

If the motion is denied, the court may, after opportunity for hearing, require the moving party or attorney advising such motion to pay to the party or deponent who opposed the motion the reasonable expenses incurred in opposing the motion, including attorney fees, unless the court finds that the making of the motion was substantially justified or that other circumstances make an award of expenses unjust.

If the motion is granted in part and denied in part, the court may apportion the reasonable expenses incurred in relation to the motion among the parties and persons in a just manner.

In determining the amount of reasonable expenses, including attorney fees, to be awarded in connection with a motion, the trial court shall award expenses which are reasonable in relation to the amount of work reasonably expended in obtaining an order compelling compliance or in opposing a motion which is denied.

i. Evidentiary Sanctions

Smith v. Southwest Feed Yards, 835 S.W.2d 89, 90 (Tex. 1992) (court may exclude testimony for failure to comply with discovery unless good cause is shown).

Mid Continent Lift & Equipment, LLC v. J. McNeill Pilot Car Service, 537 S.W.3d 660, 670 (Tex. App.—Austin 2017, no pet.) ("[T]he concepts of 'surprise' and 'prejudice' that the district court was charged with applying, or more precisely the concepts of 'unfair surprise' and 'unfair prejudice' to which Rule 193.6 actually refers, contemplate not merely factual inquiry but also a degree of judgment or weighing that is informed by the underlying purposes of Rule 193.6's automatic exclusion and the Texas discovery rules as a whole. These purposes include ensuring that parties receive notice of the witnesses and evidence their opponents intend to present at trial, thereby promoting realistic assessment of settlement prospects and preventing 'trial by ambush.' A related underlying policy, emphasized in the current (1999) version of the Texas discovery rules, is that these disclosures should generally be completed within fixed and clear deadlines that precede, but operate independently of, any trial date.").

Good v. Baker, 339 S.W.3d 260, 281 (Tex. App.—Texarkana 2011, pet. denied) (rule requiring that witnesses be disclosed in response to a discovery request "is mandatory, and the penalty of exclusion of evidence is automatic, absent a showing of (1) good cause, (2) lack of unfair surprise, or (3) unfair prejudice").

Adams v. Allstate County Mut. Ins. Co., 199 S.W.3d 509, 513 (Tex. App.—Houston [1st Dist.] 2006, pet. denied) (striking affidavit of chiropractor's assistant on reasonableness of medical services was a just discovery sanction for eluding automobile insurer's attempts to depose assistant).

ii. Monetary Sanctions

Canine, Inc. v. Golla, 380 S.W.3d 189, 196 (Tex. App.—Dallas 2012, pet. denied) (awarding attorney's fees for a party's attendance at a deposition had a direct nexus to the conduct involved, which was the other party's changed deposition testimony and her incomplete answers given therein).

Blake v. Dorado, 211 S.W.3d 429, 432 (Tex. App.—El Paso 2006, no pet.) (defendants were entitled to an order requiring plaintiffs to pay expenses incurred in obtaining an order to compel discovery).

Lopez v. La Madeline of Tex., Inc., 200 S.W.3d 854, 865 (Tex. App.—Dallas 2006, no pet.) ("[B]oth sanction [of discovery expenses and court costs and sanction of charging party with reasonable expenses, including attorney's fees] are designed to remedy the abuse by compensating the aggrieved party for expenses incurred in the litigation.").

Braden v. S. Main Bank, 837 S.W.2d 733, 740 (Tex. App.—Houston [14th Dist.] 1992, writ denied) (Rule 215.3 authorizes monetary fines as sanctions for failing to comply with discovery).

iii. "Death Penalty" Sanctions

TransAmerican Natural Gas v. Powell, 811 S.W.2d 913, 917 (Tex. 1991) (death penalty sanctions authorized for various discovery abuses).

Braden v. Downey, 811 S.W.2d 922, 929 (Tex. 1991) (terminating sanctions are authorized by discovery rules).

Magnuson v. Mullen, 65 S.W.3d 815, 823 (Tex. App.—Fort Worth 2002, pet. denied) (trial court did not abuse its discretion in dismissing defamation suit as a discovery sanction, where the plaintiff persistently refused to provide disclosures, to answer requests for discovery, and to appear for his deposition).

Sharpe v. Kilcoyne, 962 S.W.2d 697, 7012 (Tex. App.—Fort Worth 1998, no writ) (striking a defendant's pleadings and entering a default judgment was proper where the defendant twice failed to appear for deposition and left the country).

e. *Interrogatories*

Texas Rule of Civil Procedure 215.1 governs the failure to serve timely responses to interrogatories and states in pertinent part:

> A party, upon reasonable notice to other parties and all other persons affected thereby, may apply for sanctions or an order compelling discovery as follows:
>
> ...
>
> (b)(3) if a party fails:
>   (A) to serve answers or objections to interrogatories submitted under Rule 197; or
>   (B) to answer an interrogatory submitted under Rule 197;
> ...
>
> the discovering party may move for an order compelling a designation, an appearance, an answer or answers, or inspection or production in accordance with the request, or apply to the court in which the action is pending for the imposition of any sanction authorized by Rule 215.2(b) without the necessity of first having obtained a court order compelling such discovery.

Pjetrovic v. Home Depot, 411 S.W.3d 639, 700 (Tex. App.—Texarkana 2013, no pet.) (a party is entitled to prepare for trial assured that a witness will not be called because opposing counsel has not identified him or her in response to a proper interrogatory).

In re Barnes, 956 S.W.2d 746, 748 (Tex. App.—Corpus Christi 1997, orig. proceeding) (court may impose sanctions for party's failure to answer interrogatories).

i. Evidentiary Sanctions

Rogers v. Stell, 835 S.W.2d 100, 101 (Tex. 1992) (exclusion of testimony by defendant who did not disclose she would be testifying at trial in response to interrogatory where no good cause shown).

Burnett Ranches, Ltd v. Cano Petroleum, 289 S.W.3d 862, 871 (Tex. App.—Amarillo 2009, pet. denied) (trial court did not abuse its discretion in refusing to allow late designation of expert witnesses, absent evidence that the witnesses considered themselves as experts in that area).

Duerr v. Brown, 262 S.W.3d 63, 76 (Tex. App.—Houston [14th Dist.] 2008, no pet.) (failure to provide expert information as required by the rules is sanctionable by exclusion of that expert's report).

Phan v. Addison Spectrum, L.P., 244 S.W.3d 892, 899 (Tex. App.—Dallas 2008, no pet.) (trial court did not abuse its discretion in precluding plaintiff's expert testimony on attorney's fees incurred, where "plaintiff never responded to propounded discovery requests that she would be offering expert testimony on any issue ... [and], when asked by the trial court why she never supplemented her discovery responses, plaintiff gave no reason and made no showing that her failure to disclose any experts would not unfairly surprise or prejudice defendants").

Nealy v. Southlawn Palms Apartments, 196 S.W.3d 386, 394 (Tex. App.—Houston [1st Dist.] 2006, no pet.) (evidence should have been excluded at trial for lack of sufficient answer to interrogatory).

ii. Monetary Sanctions

Wal-Mart Stores, Inc. v. Lynch, 981 S.W.2d 353, 355 (Tex. App.—Texarkana 1998, pet. denied) (trial court did not abuse discretion imposing $5,000 discovery sanction for failing to verify supplemental answers to interrogatories).

Braden v. S. Main Bank, 837 S.W.2d 733, 740 (Tex. App.—Houston [14th Dist.] 1992, writ denied) (monetary fines are authorized as sanctions under Tex. R. Civ. P. 215.3).

iii. "Death Penalty" Sanctions

Andras v. Mem'l Hosp. Sys., 888 S.W.2d 567, 572 (Tex. App.—Houston [1st Dist] 1994, writ denied) (discovery sanctions of striking pleadings and dismissing case not too severe).

Altus Communications, Inc. v. Meltzer & Martin, Inc., 829 S.W.2d 878, 884 (Tex. App.—Dallas 1992, no writ) ("[M]ultiple discovery violations may be factor in authorizing sanctions such as striking pleadings or entry of default judgment.").

Pena v. Williams, 547 S.W.2d 671, 673 (Tex. Civ. App.—San Antonio 1977, no writ) (orders striking pleadings are just when a party refuses to answer questions propounded in an interrogatory after being directed to do so by the court).

f. Production Requests

Texas Rule of Civil Procedure 215.1(b)(2)(B) governs the failure to timely respond to request for productions and states in pertinent part:

> A party, upon reasonable notice to other parties and all other persons affected thereby, may apply for sanctions or an order compelling discovery as follows:
>
> > (b)(2) If a party, or other deponent, or a person designated to testify on behalf of a party or other deponent fails:
> > (A) to answer a question propounded or submitted upon oral examination or upon written questions.

Brookshire Bros. v. Aldridge, 438 S.W.3d 9, 21 (Tex. 2014) (a spoliation analysis involves a two-step judicial process: (1) the trial court must determine, as a question of law, whether a party spoliated evidence; and (2) if spoliation occurred, the court must assess an appropriate remedy).

Petroleum Solutions, Inc. v. Head, 454 S.W.3d 482, 489 (Tex. 2014); *Brookshire Bros. v. Aldridge*, 438 S.W.3d 9, 21 (Tex. 2014) (to conclude that a party spoliated evidence, the court must find that (1) the spoliating party had a duty to reasonably preserve evidence, and (2) the party intentionally or negligently breached that duty by failing to do so).

Petroleum Solutions, Inc. v. Head, 454 S.W.3d 482, 489 (Tex. 2014); *Brookshire Bros. v. Aldridge*, 438 S.W.3d 9, 21 (Tex. 2014) (upon a finding of spoliation, the trial court has broad discretion to impose a remedy that, as with any discovery sanction, must be proportionate; that is, it must relate directly to the conduct giving rise to the sanction and may not be excessive; key considerations in imposing a remedy are the level of culpability of the spoliating party and the degree of prejudice, if any, suffered by the nonspoliating party).

Petroleum Solutions, Inc. v. Head, 454 S.W.3d 482, 489 (Tex. 2014); *Brookshire Bros. v. Aldridge,* 438 S.W.3d 9 (Tex. 2014) (in considering the prejudice suffered as a result of spoliation, the court is to consider the relevance of the spoliated evidence to key issues in the case, the harmful effect of the evidence on the spoliating party's case (or, conversely, whether the evidence would have been helpful to the nonspoliating party's case), and whether the spoliated evidence was cumulative of other competent evidence that may be used instead of the spoliated evidence).

Brookshire Bros. v. Aldridge, 438 S.W.3d 9, 21 (Tex. 2014) (spectrum of remedies that may be imposed for spoliation range from an award of attorney's fees to the dismissal of the lawsuit).

Brookshire Bros. v. Aldridge, 438 S.W.3d 9, 21 (Tex. 2014) (courts have broad discretion to utilize a variety of remedies to address spoliation, including the spoliation instruction).

Brookshire Bros. v. Aldridge, 438 S.W.3d 9, 21 (Tex. 2014) (when evidence is lost, altered, or destroyed, trial courts have the discretion to impose an appropriate remedy so that the parties are restored to a rough approximation of what their positions would have been were the evidence available).

Brookshire Bros. v. Aldridge, 438 S.W.3d 9, 21 (Tex. 2014) (spoliation is essentially a particularized form of discovery abuse, in that it ultimately results in the failure to produce discoverable evidence, and discovery matters are also within the sole province of the trial court).

Brookshire Bros. v. Aldridge, 438 S.W.3d 9, 21 (Tex. 2014) (sanctions enumerated under Rule 215.2 are available for spoliation of evidence, as well as other remedies such as the spoliation instruction).

Brookshire Bros. v. Aldridge, 438 S.W.3d 9, 21 (Tex. 2014) (a party's intentional destruction of evidence may, absent evidence to the contrary, be sufficient by itself to support a finding that the spoliated evidence is both relevant and harmful to the spoliating party).

Miner Dederick Constr., LLP v. Gulf Chemical & Metallurgical Corp., 403 S.W.3d 451, 465 (Tex. App.—Houston [1st Dist.] 2013), pet. denied per curiam, 455 S.W.3d 164 (Tex. 2015) ("[A] party knows or reasonably should know that there is a substantial chance a claim will be filed if a reasonable person would conclude from the severity of the incident, and other circumstances surrounding it, that there was a substantial chance for litigation at the time of the alleged spoliation.").

Miner Dederick Constr., LLP v. Gulf Chemical & Metallurgical Corp., 403 S.W.3d 451, 465 (Tex. App.—Houston [1st Dist.] 2013), pet. denied per curiam, 455 S.W.3d 164 (Tex. 2015) ("[A] party should not be able to subvert the discovery process and the fair administration of justice simply by destroying evidence before a claim is actually filed.").

Miner Dederick Constr., LLP v. Gulf Chemical & Metallurgical Corp, 403 S.W.3d 451, 465 (Tex. App.—Houston [1st Dist.] 2013), pet. denied per curiam, 455 S.W.3d 164

(Tex. 2015) (although it need not take extraordinary measures to preserve evidence, a party has a duty to exercise reasonable care in preserving potentially relevant evidence).

Miner Dederick Constr., LLP v. Gulf Chemical & Metallurgical Corp., 403 S.W.3d 451, 465 (Tex. App.—Houston [1st Dist.] 2013), pet. denied per curiam, 455 S.W.3d 164 (Tex. 2015) ("[C]laim that the evidence was destroyed in the ordinary course of business will not excuse the obligation to preserve when a party's duty to preserve evidence arises before the destruction.").

Miner Dederick Constr., LLP v. Gulf Chemical & Metallurgical Corp., 403 S.W.3d 451, 465 (Tex. App.—Houston [1st Dist.] 2013), pet. denied per curiam, 455 S.W.3d 164 (Tex. 2015) ("[I]mplicit in the duty to exercise reasonable care in preserving evidence is the duty to refrain from altering or changing the evidence's condition or integrity.").

Duff v. Spearman, 322 S.W.3d 869, 877 (Tex. App.—Beaumont 2010, pet. denied) ("[I]f a trial court determines that a party has failed to preserve documents that it is on notice to preserve, the trial court may take affirmative measures to correct the effects of the spoliation... The affirmative measures can range from a jury instruction on the spoliation presumption to, in the most egregious case, death penalty sanctions.").

Duff v. Spearman, 322 S.W.3d 869, 877 (Tex. App.—Beaumont 2010, pet. denied) (there is no one remedy that is appropriate for every incidence of spoliation; the trial court must respond appropriately based upon the particular facts of each individual case).

Clark v. Randalls Food, 317 S.W.3d 351, 356 (Tex. App.—Houston [1st Dist.] 2010, pet. denied) ("[I]nquiry as to whether a spoliation sanction or presumption is justified requires a court to consider (1) whether there was a duty to preserve evidence, (2) whether the alleged spoliator breached that duty, and (3) whether the spoliation prejudiced the nonspoliator's ability to present its case or defense.").

> Note: Discovery sanctions for failing to comply with a request for production are covered generally under the rule for written or oral questions. See generally Texas Rules of Civil Procedure 196, et seq., for specific requirements regarding requests for production. Note also that a prior order may not be required before moving for sanctions for discovery violations.

i. Evidentiary Sanctions

Vela v. Wagner & Brown, Ltd., 203 S.W.3d 37, 58 (Tex. App.—San Antonio 2006, no pet.) ("[E]xpert is required to preserve his work product and the party who retained the expert may be sanctioned if the expert destroys his work product.").

City of Fort Worth v. Gay, 977 S.W.2d 814, 817 (Tex. App.—Fort Worth 1998, no pet.) (when a witness or expert is not properly designated, party cannot offer that testimony).

Grossnickle v. Grossnickle, 935 S.W.2d 830, 840 (Tex. App.—Texarkana 1996, writ denied) ("[W]hen a party fails to identify evidence timely in response to a discovery request, the trial court must exclude all evidence not properly identified in discovery.").

ii. Monetary Sanctions

Chevron Phillips Chem. Co. LP v. Kingwood Crossroads, L.P., 346 S.W.3d 37, 68 (Tex. App.—Houston [14th Dist.] 2011, pet. denied) (trial court did not abuse its discretion by imposing monetary discovery sanction of attorney's fees, where some evidence indicated that the party failed to produce all requested emails on a subject, an order was rendered to aid in the discovery of the emails, and the party made known at the outset of the electronic search that it did not intend to fully comply with the order).

Trahan v. Lone Star Title Co. of El Paso, Inc., 247 S.W.3d 269, 278 (Tex. App.—El Paso 2007, pet. denied) (monetary penalty, as a discovery sanction, was not too severe for legitimate purposes of punishment and deterrence).

iii. "Death Penalty" Sanctions

Brookshire Bros. v. Aldridge, 438 S.W.3d 9, 21 (Tex. 2014) (courts have broad discretion to utilize a variety of remedies to address spoliation, including the spoliation instruction).

Brookshire Bros. v. Aldridge, 438 S.W.3d 9, 21 (Tex. 2014) (because the spoliation instruction itself is given to compensate for the absence of evidence that a party had a duty to preserve, its very purpose is to nudge or tilt the jury toward a finding adverse to the alleged spoliator).

Brookshire Bros., Ltd. v. Aldridge, 438 S.W.3d 9, 21 (Tex. 2014) (spoliation instruction often ends litigation because it is too difficult a hurdle for the spoliator to overcome).

Brookshire Bros. v. Aldridge, 438 S.W.3d 9, 21 (Tex. 2014) (spoliation instruction is among the harshest sanctions a trial court may utilize to remedy an act of spoliation and can be tantamount to a death penalty sanction).

Brookshire Bros. v. Aldridge, 438 S.W.3d 9, 21 (Tex. 2014) (a party must intentionally spoliate evidence in order for a spoliation instruction to constitute an appropriate remedy).

Brookshire Bros. v. Aldridge, 438 S.W.3d 9, 21 (Tex. 2014) ("intentional" spoliation, often referenced as "bad faith" or "willful" spoliation, means that the party acted with the subjective purpose of concealing or destroying discoverable evidence, and includes the concept of "willful blindness," which encompasses the scenario in which a party does not directly destroy evidence known to be relevant and discoverable, but nonetheless allows for its destruction).

Brookshire Bros. v. Aldridge, 438 S.W.3d 9, 21 (Tex. 2014) (spoliation instruction may be proper if the act of spoliation, although merely negligent, so prejudices the nonspoliating party that it is irreparably deprived of having any meaningful ability to present a claim or defense).

g. *Mental and Physical Examinations*

Texas Rule of Civil Procedure 215.2 governs the failure to serve timely responses to demands for examinations or requests for medical records and the failure to submit to an examination and states in pertinent part:

> (b) If a party or an officer, director, or managing agent of a party or a person designated under Rules 199.2(b)(1) or 200.1(b) to testify on behalf of a party fails to comply with proper discovery requests or to obey an order to provide or permit discovery, including an order made under Rules 204 or 215.1, the court in which the action is pending may, after notice and hearing, make such order in regard to the failure as a just, and among others the following:
>
> ...
>
> (7) when a party has failed to comply with an order under Rule 204 requiring him to appear or produce for examination, such orders as are listed in paragraphs (1), (2), (3), (4) or (5) of this subdivision, unless the person failing to comply shows that he is unable to appear or to produce such person for examination.

i. "Death Penalty" Cases

Allied Resources v. Mo-Vac Serv. Co., 871 S.W.2d 773, 775 (Tex. App.—Corpus Christi 1994, writ denied) (death penalty sanctions are just when entire discovery process marked by delay, avoidance, and obstruction).

Luxenberg v. Marshall, 835 S.W.2d 136, 141 (Tex. App.—Dallas 1992, orig. proceeding) (death penalty sanctions proper when record demonstrates bad faith in litigation process as a whole, as well as prior imposition of lesser sanctions).

h. *Requests for Admission*

Texas Rule of Civil Procedure 215.4 states in pertinent part:

> (a) A party who has requested an admission under Rule 198 may move to determine the sufficiency of the answer or objection. For purposes of this subdivision an evasive or incomplete answer may be treated as a failure to answer. Unless the court determines that an objection is justified, it shall order that an answer be served. If the court determines that an answer does not comply with the requirements of Rule 198, it may order either that the matter is admitted or than an amended answer be served. The provisions of Rule 215.1(d) apply to the award of expenses incurred in relation to the motion.
>
> (b) If a party fails to admit the genuineness of any document or the truth of any matter as requested under Rule 198 and if the party requesting the admissions thereafter proves the genuineness of the document or the truth of the matter, he may apply to the court for an order requiring the other party to pay him the reasonable expenses incurred in making that proof, including reasonable attorney fees. The court shall make the order unless it find that
>
>   (1) the request was held objectionable pursuant to Rule 193, or
>
>   (2) the admission sought was of no substantial importance, or
>
>   (3) the party failing to admit had a reasonable ground to believe

that he might prevail on the matter, or (4) there was other good reason for the failure to admit.

i. Deeming Matters Admitted for Lack of Response

In Interest of N.L.W., 534 S.W.3d 102, 111 (Tex. App.—Texarkana 2017, no pet.) ("[I]n the event a party does not serve responses to requests for admissions within thirty days, the matters in the requests are deemed admitted against that party.... Any matter admitted is conclusively established unless the trial court, on motion of the party, permits the withdrawal or amendment of the admission.").

In Interest of N.L.W., 534 S.W.3d 102, 111 (Tex. App.—Texarkana 2017, no pet.) ("[A]n admitted fact constitutes a judicial admission, and the answering party may not then introduce evidence to controvert it.").

In Interest of N.L.W., 534 S.W.3d 102, 111 (Tex. App.—Texarkana 2017, no pet.) ("[J]udicial admission is an assertion of fact that acts as a formal waiver of proof... Thus, a judicial admission is conclusive upon the party making it, and it relieves the opposing party's burden of proving the admitted fact, and bars the admitting party from disputing it.").

In Interest of N.L.W., 534 S.W.3d 102, 111 (Tex. App.—Texarkana 2017, no pet.) ("When a judicial admission regarding the ultimate issue occurs, it removes the ultimate issue from further consideration. In that instance, the judicial admission negates the existence of a material fact regarding the ultimate issue so completely that it conclusively establishes the movant's right to judgment as a matter of law.").

Time Warner, Inc. v. Gonzalez, 441 S.W.3d 661, 665 (Tex. App.—San Antonio 2014, pet. denied) (ordinarily, the burden of showing good cause and no undue prejudice lies with the party seeking withdrawal of deemed admissions).

Time Warner, Inc. v. Gonzalez, 441 S.W.3d 661, 665 (Tex. App.—San Antonio 2014, pet. denied) (undue prejudice as a result of the proposed withdrawal of admissions depends on whether withdrawing an admission or filing a late response will delay trial or significantly hamper the opposing party's ability to prepare for it).

Lucas v. Clark, 347 S.W.3d 800, 803 (Tex. App.—Austin 2011, pet. denied) ("[G]enerally, when a party fails to respond to a request for admission, either by timely answer, written objection, or motion to file late answers, the facts contained in the request are deemed admitted.").

Oliphant Financial, LLC v. Galaviz, 299 S.W.3d 829, 838 (Tex. App.—Dallas 2009, no pet.) (plaintiff may serve a request for admissions as part of its petition, and when the defendant fails to file an answer or other response, those requests are deemed admitted).

Oliphant Financial, LLC v. Galaviz, 299 S.W.3d 829, 838 (Tex. App.—Dallas 2009, no pet.) (facts that have been deemed admitted may not be contradicted by evidence at the trial).

Morgan v. Timmers Chevrolet, Inc., 1 S.W.3d 803, 805 (Tex. App.—Houston [1st Dist.] 1999, pet. denied) (requests for admission deemed admitted where defendant did not respond to them).

State v. Carillo, 885 S.W.2d 212, 216 (Tex. App.—San Antonio 1994, no writ) (party may not refuse to answer request for admission on basis of insufficient evidence where there is in fact sufficient evidence to admit or deny).

ii. "Death Penalty" Sanctions

Ramirez v. Otis Elevator Co., 837 S.W.2d 405, 409 (Tex. App.—Dallas 1992, writ denied) (finding no abuse of discretion in trial court's order striking pleadings for failing to comply with discovery).

i. Other Grounds

Other possible grounds for excluding evidence arising from discovery abuses include:

- Prejudicial;
- Confusing or misleading;
- Cumulative;
- Lost or destroyed evidence.

4. Opposing Authorities

Brookshire Bros. v. Aldridge, 438 S.W.3d 9, 21 (Tex. 2014) (the remedy crafted by the trial court for spoliation must be proportionate when weighing the culpability of the spoliating party and the prejudice to the nonspoliating party).

Paradigm Oil, Inc. v. Retamco Operating, Inc., 372 S.W.3d 177, 184 (Tex. 2012) (sanctions for discovery abuse should not be dispensed as arbitrary monetary penalties unrelated to any harm).

Arshad v. American Express Bank, FSB, 580 S.W.3d 798, 808 (Tex. App.—Houston [14th Dist.] 2019, no pet.) (the rule excluding a witness who has not been disclosed does not apply to a corporate party witness).

Shops at Legacy (Inland) L.P. v. Fine Autographs & Memorabilia Retail Stores, Inc., 418 S.W.3d 229, 232 (Tex. App.—Dallas 2013, no pet.) (a sanction imposed for discovery abuse should be no more severe than necessary to satisfy its legitimate purposes; it follows that a court must consider the availability of less stringent sanctions and whether such lesser sanctions would fully promote compliance).

In re M.J.M., 406 S.W.3d 292, 296 (Tex. App.—San Antonio 2013, no pet.) (discovery sanctions must be "just").

PopCap Games, Inc. v. MumboJumbo, LLC, 350 S.W.3d 699, 718 (Tex. App.—Dallas 2011, pet. denied) (good-cause exception allows a trial judge to excuse a party's failure to comply with discovery obligations in difficult or impossible circumstances; however, the inadvertence of counsel, lack of surprise, or the uniqueness of the excluded evidence do not constitute good cause).

Union Carbide Corp. v. Martin, 349 S.W.3d 137, 145 (Tex. App.—Dallas 2011, no pet.) ("[L]esser sanctions must first be tested to determine whether they are adequate to secure compliance with discovery rules, deterrence of future discovery abuse, and punishment of the offender.").

Hernandez v. Sovereign Cherokee Nation Tejas, 343 S.W.3d 162, 171 (Tex. App.—Dallas 2011, pet. denied) (discovery sanction is excessive if lesser sanctions would have served the purposes of compliance, deterrence, and punishment).

Duerr v. Brown, 262 S.W.3d 63, 76 (Tex. App.—Houston [14th Dist.] 2008, no pet.) ("[T]o avoid the sanction [of the exclusion of an expert report for failure to provide expert information, a party] has to demonstrate that failure to make such disclosures would not unfairly surprise or prejudice the other party, or that failure to make such disclosures is for good cause.").

In re Commitment of Marks, 230 S.W.3d 241, 245 (Tex. App.—Beaumont 2007, no pet.) (trial court has discretion to determine whether a party calling a witness has met its discovery burden of showing good cause for failing to disclose general substance of opinion testimony).

Hooper v. Chittaluru, 222 S.W.3d 103, 110 (Tex. App.—Houston [14th Dist.] 2006, pet. denied) (exclusion of evidence for failure to timely disclose is not appropriate if there is no surprise to the opposing parties).

In re Commitment of Larkin, 127 S.W.3d 930, 932 (Tex. App.—Beaumont 2004, no pet.) (trial court abused discretion striking party's pleading before attempting to impose lesser sanctions).

Finlay v. Olive, 77 S.W.3d 520, 525 (Tex. App.—Houston [1st Dist.] 2002, no pet.) (trial court abused discretion imposing discovery sanctions without providing notice and hearing to offending party).

Straitway Transp., Inc. v. Mundorf, 6 S.W.3d 734, 740 (Tex. App.—Corpus Christi 1999, pet. denied) (trial court properly determined a party had good cause for not supplementing interrogatory responses with witness's address where the party made a showing on the record that he did not know address at issue and could not have determined it with reasonable diligence).

Roberts v. Golden Crest Waters, Inc., 1 S.W.3d 291, 293 (Tex. App.—Corpus Christi 1999, no pet.) (exclusion of plaintiff's witnesses for failure to comply with pretrial discovery was abuse of discretion).

AIU Ins. Co. v. Mehaffy, 942 S.W.2d 796, 802 (Tex. App.—Beaumont 1997, no writ) (court erred making unauthorized sanction).

Ramirez v. Otis Elevator Co., 837 S.W.2d 405, 410 (Tex. App.—Dallas 1992, writ denied) (trial court abuses discretion if sanctions imposed do not further purpose of securing purpose of discovery rules, deterring discovery violations, and punishing those who violated discovery rules).

a. "Death Penalty" Sanctions

Brookshire Bros. v. Aldridge, 438 S.W.3d 9, 21 (Tex. 2014) (when a party is inherently prevented from having the merits of its case adjudicated, constitutional due process is implicated).

Brookshire Bros. v. Aldridge, 438 S.W.3d 9, 21 (Tex. 2014) (spoliation instruction is among the harshest sanctions a trial court may utilize to remedy an act of spoliation and can be tantamount to a death penalty sanction).

PR Invs. & Specialty Retailers, Inc. v. State, 251 S.W.3d 472, 481 (Tex. 2008) (discovery sanction should be no more severe than necessary to satisfy its legitimate purposes, and courts must consider the availability of less stringent sanctions and whether such lesser sanctions would fully promote compliance).

TransAmerican Natural Gas v. Powell, 811 S.W.2d 913, 917 (Tex. 1991) (severe sanctions may not be imposed where lesser sanction would satisfy purpose for which sanction is being imposed).

Shops at Legacy (Inland) L.P. v. Fine Autographs & Memorabilia Retail Stores, Inc., 418 S.W.3d 229, 232 (Tex. App.—Dallas 2013, no pet.) ("death penalty" sanctions are harsh and may be imposed as an initial sanction only in the most egregious and exceptional cases when they are clearly justified, and it is fully apparent that no lesser sanctions would promote compliance with the rules).

Shops at Legacy (Inland) L.P. v. Fine Autographs & Memorabilia Retail Stores, Inc., 418 S.W.3d 229, 232 (Tex. App.—Dallas 2013, no pet.) (the trial court record must include some explanation to justify the granting of "death penalty" sanctions).

In re M.J.M., 406 S.W.3d 292, 296 (Tex. App.—San Antonio 2013, no pet.) ("death penalty" sanctions are limited by constitutional due process).

In re M.J.M., 406 S.W.3d 292, 296 (Tex. App.—San Antonio 2013, no pet.) ("death penalty" sanction cannot be used to adjudicate the merits of claims or defenses unless the offending party's conduct during discovery justifies a presumption that its claims or defenses lack merit).

In re M.J.M., 406 S.W.3d 292, 296 (Tex. App.—San Antonio 2013, no pet.) (before assessing death penalty sanctions, trial courts must first consider the availability of less stringent sanctions and whether such lesser sanctions would be adequate to promote compliance, deterrence, and punishment of the offender; the record in such a case must show that the trial court considered the availability of less stringent sanctions, and in all but the most exceptional cases, that the trial court tested a less stringent sanction before striking a party's pleadings).

In re M.J.M., 406 S.W.3d 292, 296 (Tex. App.—San Antonio 2013, no pet.) (to show that the trial court has considered less stringent sanctions, "the record should contain some explanation of the appropriateness of the sanctions imposed").

Gunn v. Fuqua, 397 S.W.3d 358, 366 (Tex. App.—Dallas 2013, pet. denied) ("[D]eath penalty sanctions are harsh and may be imposed as an initial sanction only in the most egregious and exceptional cases when they are clearly justified and it is fully apparent that no lesser sanctions would promote compliance with the rules.").

Gunn v. Fuqua, 397 S.W.3d 358, 366 (Tex. App.—Dallas 2013, pet. denied) (for "death penalty" sanctions to be just, the trial court "must determine that 'a party's hindrance of the discovery process justifies a presumption that its claims or defenses lack merit'").

Gunn v. Fuqua, 397 S.W.3d 358, 366 (Tex. App.—Dallas 2013, pet. denied) ("[S]anctions which terminate or inhibit the presentation of the merits of a party's claim must be reserved for circumstances in which a party has so abused the rules of procedure, despite imposition of lesser sanctions, that the party's position can be presumed to lack merit and it would be unjust to permit the party to present the substance of that position before the court.").

Min Rong Zheng v. Bridgestone Firestone N. Am. Tire, L.L.C., 284 S.W.3d 890, 893 (Tex. App.—Eastland 2009, no pet.) ("[D]eath penalty sanctions should not be used to deny a trial on the merits unless the guilty party's conduct is so bad that it justifies a presumption that its claims or defenses lack merit.").

In re Commitment of Larkin, 127 S.W.3d 930, 932 (Tex. App.—Beaumont 2004, no pet.) (trial court abused discretion striking party's pleading before attempting to impose lesser sanctions).

Roberts v. Golden Crest Waters, Inc., 1 S.W.3d 291, 293 (Tex. App.—Corpus Christi 1999, no pet.) (death penalty sanctions not proper for failure to file pretrial statement).

b. Interrogatories

Rogers v. Stell, 835 S.W.2d 100, 101 (Tex. 1992) (testimony allowed of undisclosed witness where party did not respond to interrogatory but properly identified herself as person with knowledge of relevant facts).

Straitway Transp., Inc. v. Mundorf, 6 S.W.3d 734, 740 (Tex. App.—Corpus Christi 1999, pet. denied) (trial court properly determined a party had good cause for not supplementing interrogatory responses with witness's address where the party made a showing on the record that he did not know address at issue and could not have determined it with reasonable diligence).

In Interest of C.S., 977 S.W.2d 729, 732 (Tex. App.—Fort Worth 1998, pet. denied) (failure to update interrogatory answers did not require sanction of exclusion of witness' testimony where the witness could be easily located).

In re Barnes, 956 S.W.2d 746, 748 (Tex. App.—Corpus Christi 1997, orig. proceeding) (severe sanctions for failing to timely answer interrogatories was inappropriate in the absence of bad faith or counsel's callous disregard of discovery rules).

c. Matters Deemed Admitted

Marino v. King, 355 S.W.3d 629, 634 (Tex. 2011) ("[C]onstitutional imperatives favor the determination of cases on their merits rather than on harmless procedural defaults. Using deemed admissions as the basis for summary judgment does not avoid the due-process requirement of flagrant bad faith or callous disregard, which is the showing necessary to support a merits-preclusive sanction; it merely incorporates the requirement as an element of the movant's summary-judgment burden.").

Wheeler v. Green, 157 S.W.3d 439, 443 (Tex. 2005) ("[T]rial courts have broad discretion to permit or deny withdrawal of deemed admissions, but they cannot do so arbitrarily, unreasonably, or without reference to guiding rules or principles").

Time Warner, Inc. v. Gonzalez, 441 S.W.3d 661, 665 (Tex. App.—San Antonio 2014, pet. denied) (a trial court has discretion to permit a party to withdraw an admission if: (a) the party shows good cause for the withdrawal; (b) the court finds that the other party will not be unduly prejudiced; and (c) presentation of the lawsuit's merits is served by the withdrawal).

Time Warner, Inc. v. Gonzalez, 441 S.W.3d 661, 665 (Tex. App.—San Antonio 2014, pet. denied) ("good cause" for withdrawing admissions can be shown when a party's failure to answer was accidental or the result of a mistake, rather than intentional or the result of conscious indifference; even a slight excuse will suffice, especially when delay or prejudice to the opposing party will not result).

Time Warner, Inc. v. Gonzalez, 441 S.W.3d 661, 665 (Tex. App.—San Antonio 2014, pet. denied) ("good cause" for withdrawing admissions exists when due process concerns are implicated by deemed admissions that act as a merits-preclusive discovery sanction, absent bad faith or callous disregard on the part of the party requesting withdrawal).

Time Warner, Inc. v. Gonzalez, 441 S.W.3d 661, 665 (Tex. App.—San Antonio 2014, pet. denied) (when due process concerns are involved in deeming admissions, the burden of showing bad faith is on the party opposing withdrawal of the admissions).

Time Warner, Inc. v. Gonzalez, 441 S.W.3d 661, 665 (Tex. App.—San Antonio 2014, pet. denied) (when the party requesting merits-based admissions knew or should have known that the admissions were improper in this regard, that party cannot be said to have relied on the admissions in deciding not to otherwise develop evidence; while that party may be prejudiced by the withdrawal of the admissions during the trial, that prejudice is not "undue").

Tommy Gio, Inc. v. Dunlop, 348 S.W.3d 503, 508 (Tex. App.—Dallas 2011, pet. denied) ("good cause" for withdrawal or amendment of a deemed admission is established by showing the failure involved was an accident or mistake, not intentional or the result of conscious indifference).

Lucas v. Clark, 347 S.W.3d 800, 803 (Tex. App.—Austin 2011, pet. denied) (overly broad, merits-preclusive requests for admissions are improper and may not result in deemed admissions).

d. Depositions

Serv. Corp. Int'l v. Aragon, 268 S.W.3d 112, 123 (Tex. App.—Eastland 2008, pet. denied) (trial court did not abuse its discretion by not excluding expert psychologist's trial testimony on ground that he had not supplemented his deposition testimony before trial, since psychologist was not retained expert).

Fethkenher v. Kroger Co., 139 S.W.3d 24, 35 (Tex. App.—Fort Worth 2004, no pet.) (discovery sanctions were excessive for alleged failure to produce a party for deposition).

e. Production Requests

Brookshire Bros. v. Aldridge, 438 S.W.3d 9, 21 (Tex. 2014) (upon a finding of spoliation, the trial court has broad discretion to impose a remedy that, as with any discovery sanction, must be proportionate; that is, it must relate directly to the conduct giving rise to the sanction and may not be excessive).

Brookshire Bros. v. Aldridge, 438 S.W.3d 9, 21 (Tex. 2014) (harsh remedy of a spoliation instruction is warranted only when the trial court finds that the spoliating party acted with the specific intent of concealing discoverable evidence, and that a less severe remedy would be insufficient to reduce the prejudice caused by the spoliation).

Brookshire Bros. v. Aldridge, 438 S.W.3d 9, 21 (Tex. 2014) (a failure to preserve evidence with a negligent mental state may only underlie a spoliation instruction in the rare situation in which a nonspoliating party has been irreparably deprived of any meaningful ability to present a claim or defense).

Brookshire Bros. v. Aldridge, 438 S.W.3d 9, 21 (Tex. 2014) (spoliation instruction is an important remedy, but its use can affect the fundamental fairness of the trial in ways as troubling as the spoliating conduct itself).

Brookshire Bros. v. Aldridge, 438 S.W.3d 9, 21 (Tex. 2014) (a party alleging spoliation bears the burden of establishing that the nonproducing party had a duty to preserve the evidence; the standard governing the duty to preserve resolves two related inquiries: when the duty is triggered and the scope of that duty).

Petroleum Solutions, Inc. v. Head, 454 S.W.3d 482, 489 (Tex. 2014); *Brookshire Bros. v. Aldridge,* 438 S.W.3d 9, 21 (Tex. 2014) (a duty to preserve evidence arises only when a party knows or reasonably should know that there is a substantial chance that a claim will be filed and that evidence in its possession or control will be material and relevant to that claim; a "substantial chance of litigation" arises when litigation is more than merely an abstract possibility or unwarranted fear).

Brookshire Bros. v. Aldridge, 438 S.W.3d 9, 21 (Tex. 2014) (the party seeking a remedy for spoliation must demonstrate that the other party breached its duty to preserve material and relevant evidence).

Brookshire Bros. v. Aldridge, 438 S.W.3d 9, 21 (Tex. 2014) (negligent spoliation is not enough to support a finding that the spoliated evidence was relevant and harmful to the spoliating party without some proof about what the destroyed evidence would show).

Brookshire Bros. v. Aldridge, 438 S.W.3d 9, 21 (Tex. 2014) (spoliation instruction is among the harshest sanctions a trial court may utilize to remedy an act of spoliation and can be tantamount to a death penalty sanction).

Brookshire Bros. v. Aldridge, 438 S.W.3d 9, 21 (Tex. 2014) (evidence considered by the trial court in making spoliation findings usually has no bearing on the facts that are of consequence to the determination of the action from the jury's perspective, and thus should not be admitted into evidence before the jury).

In re Methodist Primary Care Group, 553 S.W.3d 709, 721 (Tex. App.—Houston [14th Dist.] 2018, orig. proceeding) ("[A] party cannot be compelled to produce (or sanctioned for failing to produce) that which it has not been requested to produce").

Sanders Oil & Gas, Ltd. v. Big Lake Kay Construction, Inc., 554 S.W.3d 79, 97 (Tex. App.—El Paso 2018, no pet.) ("An opposing party must demonstrate that the non-producing party had a duty to preserve the evidence in question before any failure to produce evidence may be viewed as a discovery abuse.").

Sanders Oil & Gas, Ltd. v. Big Lake Kay Construction, Inc., 554 S.W.3d 79, 97 (Tex. App.—El Paso 2018, no pet.) ("[D]uty [to preserve evidence] is not so encompassing as to require a litigant to keep or retain every document in its possession, however, a party should not be able to subvert the discovery process and the fair administration of justice simply by destroying evidence before a claim is actually filed.").

Miner Dederick Constr., LLP v. Gulf Chemical & Metallurgical Corp., 403 S.W.3d 451, 465 (Tex. App.—Houston [1st Dist.] 2013), pet. denied per curiam, 455 S.W.3d 164 (Tex. 2015) ("[I]nquiry regarding whether a spoliation sanction or presumption is justified requires a court to consider (1) whether there was a duty to preserve evidence, (2) whether the alleged spoliator breached that duty; and (3) whether the spoliation prejudiced the non-spoliator's ability to present its case or defense.").

Miner Dederick Constr., LLP v. Gulf Chemical & Metallurgical Corp., 403 S.W.3d 451, 465 (Tex. App.—Houston [1st Dist.] 2013), pet. denied per curiam, 455 S.W.3d 164 (Tex. 2015) ("[D]uty to preserve evidence is not raised unless (1) a party knows or reasonably should know that there is a substantial chance a claim will be filed, and (2) evidence is relevant and material.").

Miner Dederick Constr., LLP v. Gulf Chemical & Metallurgical Corp., 403 S.W.3d 451, 465 (Tex. App.—Houston [1st Dist.] 2013), pet. denied per curiam, 455 S.W.3d 164 (Tex. 2015) ("[S]poliator can defend against an assertion of negligent or intentional destruction by providing explanations to justify its failure to preserve evidence.").

Matlock Place Apartments, L.P. v. Druce, 369 S.W.3d 355, 380 (Tex. App.—Fort Worth 2012, pet. denied) ("[B]efore any failure to produce material evidence may be viewed as discovery abuse, the opposing party must establish that the nonproducing party had a duty to preserve the evidence in question.... There must be a sufficient foundational showing that the party who destroyed the evidence had notice both of the potential claim and of the evidence's potential relevance thereto.").

In re Estate of Preston, 346 S.W.3d 137, 157 (Tex. App.—Fort Worth 2011, no pet.) (when a motion for sanctions asserts that a respondent to a discovery request has failed to produce a document within its possession, custody, or control, the movant has the burden to prove the assertion).

Gilmore v. SCI Tex. Funeral Svcs., Inc., 234 S.W.3d 251, 263 n.12 (Tex. App.—Waco 2007, pet. denied) ("[I]f a particular item has been lost or destroyed before a request for production is served, it is no longer in the party's possession and its nonproduction necessarily cannot constitute a discovery violation.").

Roberts v. Whitfill, 191 S.W.3d 348, 361 (Tex. App.—Waco 2006, no pet.) ("[B]efore any failure to produce material evidence may be viewed as discovery abuse, the opposing party must establish that the nonproducing party had a duty to preserve the evidence in question, and such a duty arises only when a party knows or reasonably should know that there is a substantial chance that a claim will be filed and that evidence in its possession or control will be material and relevant to that claim.").

B. Motion to Exclude Conclusively Established Matters

1. Suggested Motion Text

(*Name of Moving Party*) hereby moves this Court for an order that all matters admitted by (*Name of Party*) in response to (*Name of Moving Party*)'s requests for admissions (*or List Each Admission by Set and Number*) be conclusively established at trial. The motion is based upon the ground that each admission is deemed established pursuant to Texas Rule of Civil Procedure 198.3.

2. Motion Summary

This motion is based upon the express authority of Texas Rule of Civil Procedure 198.3, which provides that any matter admitted in response to a request for admission is "conclusively established against the party making the admission."

Note that this motion is unnecessary if the admitting party acknowledges the admitted matters as undisputed at the commencement of trial. Consider other strategic reasons for not bringing the motion, such as saving the admission to impeach the credibility of a party who might contradict prior admissions while testifying.

3. Supporting Authorities

Texas Rule of Civil Procedure 198.3 states in pertinent part:

> Any admission made by a party under this rule may be used solely in the pending action and not in any other proceeding. A matter admitted under this rule is conclusively established as the party making the admission unless the court permits the party to withdraw or amend the admission. The court may permit the party to withdraw or amend the admission if:
>
> (a) the party shows good cause for the withdrawal or amendment; and
> (b) the court finds that the parties relying upon the responses and deemed admissions will not be unduly prejudiced and that the presentation of the merits of the action will be subserved by permitting the party to amend or withdraw the admission.

a. Purpose of Discovery

Jampole v. Touchy, 673 S.W.2d 569, 573 (Tex. 1984, orig. proceeding), *disapproved of on other grounds by Walker v. Packer*, 827 S.W.2d 833 (Tex. 1992) (purpose of discovery is to "seek the truth, so that disputes may be decided by what the facts reveal, not by what facts are concealed. For this reason, discovery is not limited to information that will be admissible at trial."). (Citations omitted.)

In Interest of N.L.W., 534 S.W.3d 102, 111 (Tex. App.—Texarkana 2017, no pet.) ("[I]n the event a party does not serve responses to requests for admissions within thirty days, the matters in the requests are deemed admitted against that party.... Any matter admitted is conclusively established unless the trial court, on motion of the party, permits the withdrawal or amendment of the admission.").

In Interest of N.L.W., 534 S.W.3d 102, 111 (Tex. App.—Texarkana 2017, no pet.) ("[A]n admitted fact constitutes a judicial admission, and the answering party may not then introduce evidence to controvert it.").

In Interest of N.L.W., 534 S.W.3d 102, 111 (Tex. App.—Texarkana 2017, no pet.) ("[J]udicial admission is an assertion of fact that acts as a formal waiver of proof... Thus, a judicial admission is conclusive upon the party making it, and it relieves the opposing party's burden of proving the admitted fact, and bars the admitting party from disputing it.").

In Interest of N.L.W., 534 S.W.3d 102, 111 (Tex. App.—Texarkana 2017, no pet.) ("When a judicial admission regarding the ultimate issue occurs, it removes the ultimate issue from further consideration. In that instance, the judicial admission negates the existence of a material fact regarding the ultimate issue so completely that it conclusively establishes the movant's right to judgment as a matter of law.").

Duff v. Spearman, 322 S.W.3d 869, 877 (Tex. App.—Beaumont 2010, pet. denied) ("[W]hen requests for admissions are used as intended—addressing uncontroverted matters or evidentiary ones like the authenticity or admissibility of documents—deeming admissions by default is unlikely to compromise presentation of the merits. Nevertheless, due process concerns arise when a party uses deemed admissions to preclude presentation of the merits of a case.").

DeSoto Wildwood Dev., Inc. v. City of Lewisville, 184 S.W.3d 814, 822 (Tex. App.—Fort Worth 2006, no pet.) ("[A] matter clearly admitted in a request for admissions is conclusively established and cannot be controverted.").

Miller v. Kennedy & Minshew, Prof'l Corp., 142 S.W.3d 325, 348 (Tex. App.—Fort Worth 2003, pet. denied) (purpose of discovery of experts is to give opposing party sufficient information to allow cross-examination of expert and to prepare rebuttal).

In re Dynamic Health, Inc., 32 S.W.3d 876, 881 (Tex. App.—Texarkana 2000, orig. proceeding) (purpose of discovery is to ensure each party has full knowledge of facts and issues prior to trial).

4. Opposing Authorities

Time Warner, Inc. v. Gonzalez, 441 S.W.3d 661, 665 (Tex. App.—San Antonio 2014, pet. denied) (a trial court has discretion to permit a party to withdraw an admission if: (a) the party shows good cause for the withdrawal, (b) the court finds that the other party will not be unduly prejudiced, and (c) presentation of the lawsuit's merits is served by the withdrawal).

Time Warner, Inc. v. Gonzalez, 441 S.W.3d 661, 665 (Tex. App.—San Antonio 2014, pet. denied) ("good cause" for withdrawing admissions can be shown when a party's failure to answer was accidental or the result of a mistake, rather than intentional or the result of conscious indifference; even a slight excuse will suffice, especially when delay or prejudice to the opposing party will not result).

Time Warner, Inc. v. Gonzalez, 441 S.W.3d 661, 665 (Tex. App.—San Antonio 2014, pet. denied) ("good cause" for withdrawing admissions exists when due process concerns are implicated by deemed admissions that act as a merits-preclusive discovery sanction, absent bad faith or callous disregard on the part of the party requesting withdrawal).

Time Warner, Inc. v. Gonzalez, 441 S.W.3d 661, 665 (Tex. App.—San Antonio 2014, pet. denied) (when due process concerns are involved in deeming admissions, the burden of showing bad faith is on the party opposing withdrawal of the admissions).

Time Warner, Inc. v. Gonzalez, 441 S.W.3d 661, 665 (Tex. App.—San Antonio 2014, pet. denied) (when the party requesting merits-based admissions knew or should have known that the admissions were improper in this regard, that party cannot be said to have relied on the admissions in deciding not to otherwise develop evidence; while that party may be prejudiced by the withdrawal of the admissions during the trial, that prejudice is not "undue").

Duff v. Spearman, 322 S.W.3d 869, 877 (Tex. App.—Beaumont 2010, pet. denied) (trial court's discretion in deeming a request for admissions to have been admitted is limited by due process).

Petree v. Southern Farm Bureau Cas. Ins. Co., 315 S.W.3d 254, 259 (Tex. App.—Corpus Christi 2010, no pet.) (absent flagrant bad faith or callous disregard for discovery rules, due process bars merits-preclusive sanctions).

Scott Bader, Inc. v. Sandstone Prods., Inc., 248 S.W.3d 802, 812 (Tex. App.—Houston [1st Dist.] 2008, no pet.) (trial court should have considered lesser discovery sanctions on defendant, before ordering that jury would be instructed that defendant's product did not meet specifications and that product specifications provided by defendant to plaintiff had been modified).

Methodist Hosp. of Dallas v. Mid-Century Ins. Co. of Tex., 195 S.W.3d 844, 846 (Tex. App.—Dallas 2006, no pet.) ("[D]iscovery admissions constitute competent summary judgment evidence only if they are referred to or incorporated in the summary judgment motion and they are used against the party who filed them.").

Neal v. Wisc. Hard Chrome, Inc., 173 S.W.3d 891, 894 (Tex. App.—Texarkana 2005, no pet.) (answers to requests for admissions merely constituting admissions of law are not binding on the court).

C. Motion to Exclude Evidence of Claims Denied in Discovery

1. Suggested Motion Text

(*Name of Moving Party*) hereby moves this Court for an order prohibiting (*Name of Party*) from introducing or mentioning any evidence relating to (*Describe Claim or Claims Denied During Discovery*). The motion is based upon the ground that (*Name of Party*) denied that a claim would be pursued on this matter in response to (_Describe Discovery Propounded by Moving Party_) and therefore (_Name of Moving Party_) assumed the matter would not be litigated. Any introduction of evidence on this issue will create unfair surprise and a substantial danger of undue prejudice to (_Name of Moving Party_).

2. Motion Summary

This motion seeks to prevent unfair surprise at trial caused by the introduction of evidence on claims denied during discovery. Such surprise can be prejudicial, justifying evidence preclusion. *See Magnuson v. Mullen*, 65 S.W.3d 815, 823 (Tex. App.—Fort Worth 2002, pet. denied) (plaintiff frustrated defendant's attempt to define litigation through discovery process and therefore, dismissal of plaintiff's lawsuit, with prejudice, was warranted as sanction for failure to comply with discovery).

3. Supporting Authorities

Texas Rule of Evidence 403 states that relevant evidence "may be excluded if its probative value is substantially outweighed by the danger of unfair prejudice, confusion of the issues, or misleading the jury, or by considerations of undue delay, or needless presentation of cumulative evidence." *See Diamond Offshore Services Ltd. v. Williams*, 542 S.W.3d 539, 549 (Tex. 2018); *Brookshire Bros. v. Aldridge*, 438 S.W.3d 9, 34 (Tex. 2014); *Hernandez v. State*, 390 S.W.3d 310, 323 (Tex. Crim. App. 2012).

a. Prejudicial Evidence—No Need to Show Unfair Surprise

Sharp v. Broadway Nat'l Bank, 784 S.W.2d 669, 671 (Tex. 1990) (lack of unfair surprise is not sufficient to demonstrate good cause for late disclosure of experts, and without a showing of good cause for the late disclosure, the experts should have been excluded).

i. Unfair Surprise

Texas Rule of Civil Procedure 193.6 governs the failure to timely respond and its effect on trial and states in pertinent part:

> (a) *Exclusion of Evidence and Exceptions.* A party who fails to make, amend, or supplement a discovery response in a timely manner may not introduce in evidence the material or information that was not timely disclosed, or offer the testimony of a witness (other than a named party) who was not timely identified, unless the court finds that:
> (1) there was good cause for the failure to timely make, amend, or supplement the discovery response; or
> (2) the failure to timely make, amend, or supplement the discovery response will not unfairly surprise or unfairly prejudice the other parties.

(b) *Burden of Establishing Exception.* The burden of establishing good cause or the lack of unfair surprise or unfair prejudice is on the party seeking to introduce the evidence or call the witness....

PopCap Games, Inc. v. MumboJumbo, LLC, 350 S.W.3d 699, 718 (Tex. App.—Dallas 2011, pet. denied) (fact that a party needs an expert to establish its cause of action does not establish that other parties will not be unfairly surprised by the late designation of an expert).

PopCap Games, Inc. v. MumboJumbo, LLC, 350 S.W.3d 699, 718 (Tex. App.—Dallas 2011, pet. denied) (offering other parties an opportunity to depose a late—designated expert does not ensure the absence of unfair surprise or prejudice).

Concept Gen. Contracting, Inc. v. Asbestos Maint. Servs., Inc., 346 S.W.3d 172, 180 n.2 (Tex. App.—Amarillo 2011, pet. denied) ("withholding of evidence that is necessary to respond to a discovery request results in the exclusion of that evidence").

Good v. Baker, 339 S.W.3d 260, 271 (Tex. App.—Texarkana 2011, pet. denied) (rule requiring that witnesses be disclosed in response to a discovery request "is mandatory, and the penalty of exclusion of evidence is automatic, absent a showing of (1) good cause, (2) lack of unfair surprise, or (3) unfair prejudice").

Good v. Baker, 339 S.W.3d 260, 271 (Tex. App.—Texarkana 2011, pet. denied) (burden of establishing good cause or lack of unfair surprise for the failure to disclose a witness pursuant to a discovery request is on the party seeking to introduce the witness's testimony).

Dyer v. Cotton, 333 S.W.3d 703, 717 (Tex. App.—Houston [1st Dist.] 2010, no pet.) ("[The] purpose of Rule 193.6 is to require complete responses to discovery so as to promote responsible assessment of settlement and prevent trial by ambush.").

Capital Metro. Transp. Auth./Cent. of Tenn. Ry. & Navigation Co. v. Cent. of Tenn. Ry. & Navigation Co., 114 S.W.3d 573, 583 (Tex. App.—Austin 2003, pet. denied) (evidence of damages for failure to disclose information until shortly before trial properly excluded where court implicitly found unfair surprise from late disclosure).

Ersek v. Davis & Davis, P.C., 69 S.W.3d 268, 272 (Tex. App.—Austin 2002, pet. denied) (expert not properly disclosed was properly excluded where testimony would have unfairly surprised opposing party).

Magnuson v. Mullen, 65 S.W.3d 815, 823 (Tex. App.—Fort Worth 2002, pet. denied) (plaintiff frustrated defendant's attempt to define litigation through discovery process and dismissal of plaintiff's lawsuit, with prejudice, was warranted as sanction for failure to comply with discovery).

Matagorda County Hosp. Dist. v. Burwell, 94 S.W.3d 75, 82 (Tex. App.—Corpus Christi 2002), *rev'd on other grounds,* 189 S.W.3d 738 (Tex. 2006) (witness testimony not disclosed in timely manner properly excluded based upon unfair surprise to opposing party).

F & H Invs. Inc. v. State, 55 S.W.3d 663, 671 (Tex. App.—Waco 2001, no pet.) (trial court abused discretion not excluding undisclosed evidence and witnesses that represented unfair surprise to opposing party).

b. Where Privilege Raised in Discovery

West v. Solito, 563 S.W.2d 240, 246 (Tex. 1978) (trial court could not order discovery without first determining whether attorney-client privilege applied).

In re Lavernia Nursing Facility, Inc., 12 S.W.3d 566, 570 (Tex. App.—San Antonio 1999, orig. proceeding) (trial court had authority to order privileged material be disclosed as sanction for discovery abuse).

In re Monsanto Co., 998 S.W.2d 917, 925 (Tex. App.—Waco 1999, orig. proceeding) (attorney-client and work product privileges did not apply to protect documents from discovery; mere listing of a privilege does not prove privilege).

In re Anderson, 973 S.W.2d 410, 411 (Tex. App.—Eastland 1998, orig. proceeding) (generally privileged matters are undiscoverable).

c. Matters Not in Dispute

Exxon Pipeline Co. v. Zwahr, 88 S.W.3d 623, 629 (Tex. 2002) (evidence that has no relationship to any issue in the case is not admissible as it is irrelevant).

Brown v. State, 757 S.W.2d 739, 741 (Tex. Crim. App. 1988) (evidence of victim's emotional trauma following rape irrelevant where only disputed issue was identity of rapist, not fact of rape).

Palomo v. State, 925 S.W.2d 329, 337 (Tex. App.—Corpus Christi 1996, no pet.) (evidence defendant had tattoo suggesting gang membership irrelevant and should not have been admitted where defendant did not contest issue of gang membership).

d. Other Grounds

Other possible grounds for excluding matters denied during discovery include:

- Time-wasting;
- Confusing or misleading;
- Irrelevant;
- Collateral to issues in case

4. Opposing Authorities

Sharp v. Broadway Nat'l Bank, 784 S.W.2d 669, 671 (Tex. 1990) (absence of surprise alone does not satisfy good cause exception to sanction of automatic exclusion).

Dyer v. Cotton, 333 S.W.3d 703, 717 (Tex. App.—Houston [1st Dist.] 2010, no pet.) ("[A]lthough exclusion of testimony is a harsh consequence for failure to timely disclose or supplement, the good cause exception allows the trial court to excuse the failure to comply in difficult or impossible circumstances.").

Brunelle v. TXVT Ltd. P'ship, 198 S.W.3d 476, 477 (Tex. App.—Dallas 2006, no pet.) (trial court must not exclude testimony of nondisclosed witness if offeror shows good cause or lack of unfair surprise or prejudice).

In re CFWC Religious Ministries, Inc., 143 S.W.3d 891, 893 (Tex. App.—Beaumont 2004, orig. proceeding) (privileged documents should not have been compelled to be disclosed where other means of cross-examining opposing party's expert).

Miller v. Kennedy & Minshew, Prof'l Corp., 142 S.W.3d 325, 348 (Tex. App.—Fort Worth 2003, pet. denied) (expert testimony from two witnesses not properly disclosed was proper where substance of testimony did not cause opposing party unfair surprise).

Bellino v. Comm'n for Lawyer Discipline, 124 S.W.3d 380, 384 (Tex. App.—Dallas 2003, reh'g overruled, pet. stricken) (witness not disclosed in timely fashion properly permitted to testify where opposing party not unfairly surprised).

Henson v. Citizens Bank of Irving, 549 S.W.2d 446, 448 (Tex. Civ. App.—Eastland 1977, no writ) (trial court erred dismissing suit before directing plaintiff to answer questions where plaintiff claimed privilege against self-incrimination).

D. Motion Regarding Expert Declarations and Expert Depositions

1. Suggested Motion Text

Alternative One [Limiting of Testimony]

> (*Name of Moving Party*) hereby moves this Court for an order excluding any and all evidence, references to evidence, testimony or argument relating to the testimony of (*Name of Witness*) with respect to (*Describe Testimony and Evidence to Be Excluded*). The motion is based upon the ground that (*Describe Grounds, e.g., the Testimony Related to Matters Not Disclosed in the Opposition's Expert Designations*) and therefore allowing such testimony would create unfair surprise and prejudice to the moving party.

Alternative Two [Undisclosed Witness]

> (*Name of Moving Party*) hereby moves this Court for an order precluding (*Name of Witness*) from testifying at the trial of this matter based upon the fact that (*Opposing Party*) failed to properly designate said witness pursuant to Texas Rule of Civil Procedure 194.2(f). This Court has the clear authority to preclude the testimony of said witness to prevent unfair surprise and prejudice to the moving party.

2. Motion Summary

This motion seeks to exclude expert witness testimony based upon a deficiency in the required expert witness declarations. See Texas Rule of Civil Procedure 194.2(f). These challenges typically arise where there has been a nondisclosure of experts, improper description of expected testimony, or the expert fails to provide complete opinions at the time of his or her deposition.

3. *Supporting Authorities*

Texas Rule of Civil Procedure 194.2 states in pertinent part:

> A party may request disclosure of any or all of the following:
>
> ...
>
> (f) for any testifying expert:
> (1) the expert's name, address, and telephone number;
> (2) the subject matter on which the expert will testify;
> (3) the general substance of the expert's mental impressions and opinions and a brief summary of the basis for them, or if the expert is not retained by, employed by, or otherwise subject to the control of the responding party, documents reflecting such information;
> (4) if the expert is retained by, employed by, or otherwise subject to the control of the responding party:
> (g) all documents, tangible things, reports, models, or data compilations that have been provided to, reviewed by, or prepared by or for the expert in anticipation of the expert's testimony; and
> (h) the expert's current resume and bibliography.

Reid Road Mun. Util. Dist. No. 2 v. Speedy Stop Food Stores, Ltd., 337 S.W.3d 846, 851(Tex. 2011) (witness who will be giving opinion evidence about a property's fair market value must be disclosed and designated as an expert pursuant to discovery and other applicable rules).

Beinar v. Deegan, 432 S.W.3d 398, 404 (Tex. App.—Dallas 2014, no pet.) (the duty to supplement or amend an expert's opinions arises when a party learns that its previous responses to written discovery were incomplete or inaccurate when made or are no longer complete or correct).

Beinar v. Deegan, 432 S.W.3d 398, 404 (Tex. App.—Dallas 2014, no pet.) (a party must amend or supplement any written report of an expert that is retained, employed, or controlled).

Bexar County Appraisal Dist. v. Abdo, 399 S.W.3d 248, 256 (Tex. App.—San Antonio 2012, no pet.) (purpose of Rule 194.2(f)'s expert disclosure requirements is to give the opposing party sufficient information about the expert's opinions to prepare to cross-examine the expert and to prepare expert rebuttal evidence).

PopCap Games, Inc. v. MumboJumbo, LLC, 350 S.W.3d 699, 718 (Tex. App.—Dallas 2011, pet. denied) (fact that a party needs an expert to establish its cause of action does not establish that other parties will not be unfairly surprised by the late designation of an expert).

PopCap Games, Inc. v. MumboJumbo, LLC, 350 S.W.3d 699, 718 (Tex. App.—Dallas 2011, pet. denied) (offering other parties an opportunity to depose a late-designated expert does not ensure the absence of unfair surprise or prejudice).

In re M.H., 319 S.W.3d 137, 146 (Tex. App.—Waco 2010, no pet.) (trial court has discretion to determine whether party satisfies its burden to establish lack of unfair surprise or unfair prejudice in attempting to admit expert testimony without adequate pretrial disclosure of mental impressions and opinions, but the court's finding must be supported by the record).

Burnett Ranches, Ltd v. Cano Petroleum, 289 S.W.3d 862, 871 (Tex. App.—Amarillo 2009, pet. denied) (trial court did not abuse its discretion in refusing to allow late designation of expert witnesses, absent evidence that the witnesses considered themselves as experts in that area).

Duerr v. Brown, 262 S.W.3d 63, 76 (Tex. App.—Houston [14th Dist.] 2008, no pet.) (failure to provide expert information as required by the rules is sanctionable by exclusion of that expert's report).

Satterwhite v. Safeco Land Title of Tarrant, 853 S.W.2d 202, 205 (Tex. App.—Fort Worth 1993, writ denied) ("[The] usual sanction for failure to supplement expert witness information is exclusion of testimony.").

> *Note that sanctions for failure to comply with discovery requests for expert information are covered in the general rule imposing sanctions for failure to comply with oral or written deposition questions under Tex. R. Civ. P. 215.1(b)(2)(B), or interrogatories under Tex. R. Civ. P. 215.1(b)(3).*

a. Time for Disclosure of Expert Information

Texas Rule of Civil Procedure 195.2 states:

> Unless otherwise ordered by the court, a party must designate experts—that is, furnish information requested under Rule 194.2(f)—by the later of the following two dates: 30 days after the request is served, or—
>
> (a) with regard to all experts testifying for a party seeking affirmative relief, 90 days before the end of the discovery period;
> (b) with regard to all other experts, 60 days before the end of the discovery period.

In re First Transit Inc., 499 S.W.3d 584, (Tex. App.—Houston [14th Dist.] 2016, orig. proceeding [mand. denied]) ("A failure to disclose the expert's opinions and to provide a brief summary of the basis of the opinions triggers the automatic exclusion sanctions of Rule 193.6, absent a showing of good cause for such failure or lack of surprise or prejudice.")

Burnett Ranches, Ltd v. Cano Petroleum, 289 S.W.3d 862, 871 (Tex. App.—Amarillo 2009, pet. denied) (trial court did not abuse its discretion in refusing to allow late designation of expert witnesses as experts, absent evidence that witnesses considered themselves as experts in that area).

Cunningham v. Columbia/St. David's Healthcare Sys., L.P., 185 S.W.3d 7, 14 (Tex. App.—Austin 2005, no pet.) (even if a party knows the substance of an expert witness's opinions, the nondesignated expert should not be permitted to testify because the party is not on notice that the witness will be called and, thus, cannot adequately prepare).

Ersek v. Davis & Davis, P.C., 69 S.W.3d 268, 272 (Tex. App.—Austin 2002, pet. denied) (expert not properly disclosed was properly excluded where testimony would have unfairly surprised opposing party).

Snider v. Stanley, 44 S.W.3d 713, 715 (Tex. App.—Beaumont 2001, pet. denied) (testimony of expert not disclosed in timely fashion properly excluded).

b. Evidentiary Sanctions

Duerr v. Brown, 262 S.W.3d 63, 76 (Tex. App.—Houston [14th Dist.] 2008, no pet.) (failure to provide expert information as required by the rules is sanctionable by exclusion of that expert's report).

Cunningham v. Columbia/St. David's Healthcare Sys., L.P., 185 S.W.3d 7, 14 (Tex. App.—Austin 2005, no pet.) (nondesignated expert's affidavit cannot be considered as summary judgment evidence absent a showing of good cause or a lack of unfair surprise or prejudice).

Snider v. Stanley, 44 S.W.3d 713, 715 (Tex. App.—Beaumont 2001, pet. denied) (testimony of expert not disclosed in timely fashion properly excluded).

Satterwhite v. Safeco Land Title of Tarrant, 853 S.W.2d 202, 205 (Tex. App.—Fort Worth 1993, writ denied) (usual sanction for failure to supplement expert witness information is exclusion of testimony).

Brook v. Brook, 865 S.W.2d 166, 170 (Tex. App.—Corpus Christi 1993), *aff'd*, 881 S.W.2d 297 (1994) (failure to disclose the subject of an expert's testimony will result in sanctions).

c. Deficient Declaration

Moore v. Mem'l Hermann Hosp. Sys., Inc., 140 S.W.3d 870, 874 (Tex. App.—Houston [14th Dist.] 2004, no pet.) (substance of treating physician's proposed rebuttal testimony not properly disclosed and therefore, properly excluded).

Ersek v. Davis & Davis, P.C., 69 S.W.3d 268, 272 (Tex. App.—Austin 2002, pet. denied) (expert not properly disclosed was properly excluded where testimony would have unfairly surprised opposing party).

Satterwhite v. Safeco Land Title of Tarrant, 853 S.W.2d 202, 205 (Tex. App.—Fort Worth 1993, writ denied) (usual sanction for failure to supplement expert witness information is exclusion of testimony).

d. Undisclosed Witness

Reid Road Mun. Util. Dist. No. 2 v. Speedy Stop Food Stores, Ltd., 337 S.W.3d 846, 851 (Tex. 2011) (witness who will be giving opinion evidence about a property's fair market value must be disclosed and designated as an expert pursuant to discovery and other applicable rules).

Ersek v. Davis & Davis, P.C., 69 S.W.3d 268, 272 (Tex. App.—Austin 2002, pet. denied) (expert not properly disclosed was properly excluded where testimony would have unfairly surprised opposing party).

e. Opinions Not Referenced in Discovery

The following citations may support a motion to exclude portions of expert testimony relating to opinions not disclosed during discovery. The motion is usually made when it is anticipated that the expert will testify to new opinions formed after the discovery, even after responding in the negative to questions such as: "Do you have any other opinions not yet expressed?"

Kingsley Properties, LP v. San Jacinto Title Services of Corpus Christi, LLC, 501 S.W.3d 344, 353 (Tex. App.—Corpus Christi 2016, no pet.) ("When an expert changes his opinion about a material issue after being deposed, the party must supplement discovery.").

Beinar v. Deegan, 432 S.W.3d 398, 404 (Tex. App.—Dallas 2014, no pet.) (a party must not be allowed to present a material alteration of an expert's opinion that would constitute a surprise attack).

Pilgrim's Pride Corp. v. Smoak, 134 S.W.3d 880, 902 (Tex. App.—Texarkana 2004, pet. denied) (offering party must timely disclose material change in an expert's opinion is to give the other party an opportunity to prepare a rebuttal).

Moore v. Mem'l Hermann Hosp. Sys., Inc., 140 S.W.3d 870, 874 (Tex. App.—Houston [14th Dist.] 2004, no pet.) (substance of treating physician's proposed rebuttal testimony not properly disclosed and therefore, properly excluded).

Brook v. Brook, 865 S.W.2d 166, 170 (Tex. App.—Corpus Christi 1993), *aff'd*, 881 S.W.2d 297 (1994) (failure to disclose subject of expert's testimony will result in sanctions).

4. Opposing Authorities

Miller v. Kennedy & Minshew, Prof'l Corp., 142 S.W.3d 325, 348 (Tex. App.—Fort Worth 2003, pet. denied) (expert testimony from two witnesses not properly disclosed allowed where substance of testimony did not cause opposing party unfair surprise).

Beard Family P'ship v. Commercial Indem. Ins. Co., 116 S.W.3d 839, 850 (Tex. App.—Austin 2003, no pet.) (trial court did not abuse discretion allowing expert witness not timely disclosed to testify where failure to disclose inadvertent and opposing party not unfairly surprised).

Gutierrez v. Gutierrez, 86 S.W.3d 729, 736 (Tex. App.—El Paso 2002, no pet.) (witness properly allowed to testify as expert, even though only disclosed as a fact witness, where opposing party not unfairly surprised).

Vaughn v. Ford Motor Co., 91 S.W.3d 387, 392 (Tex. App.—Eastland 2002, pet. denied) (exclusion of expert witnesses for failure to disclose substance of opinions excessive).

a. Continuance to Depose Expert

Texas Rule of Civil Procedure 193.6 states in pertinent part:

> (a) *Continuance.* Even if the party seeking to introduce the evidence or call the witness fails to carry the burden [of showing an exception to the rule that evidence is barred if not timely disclosed] under paragraph (b) [of Rule 193.6)], the court may grant a continuance or temporarily postpone the trial to allow a response to be made, amended, or supplemented, and to allow opposing parties to conduct discovery regarding any new information presented by that response.

b. No Unfair Surprise

Miller v. Kennedy & Minshew, Prof'l Corp., 142 S.W.3d 325, 348 (Tex. App.—Fort Worth 2003, pet. denied) (expert testimony from two witnesses not properly disclosed was proper where substance of testimony did not cause opposing party unfair surprise).

Beard Family P'ship v. Commercial Indem. Ins. Co., 116 S.W.3d 839, 850 (Tex. App.—Austin 2003, no pet.) (trial court did not abuse discretion allowing expert witness not timely disclosed to testify where failure to disclose inadvertent and opposing party not unfairly surprised).

Bellino v. Comm'n for Lawyer Discipline, 124 S.W.3d 380, 384 (Tex. App.—Dallas 2003, reh'g overruled, pet. stricken) (witness not disclosed in timely fashion properly permitted to testify where opposing party not unfairly surprised).

Gutierrez v. Gutierrez, 86 S.W.3d 729, 736 (Tex. App.—El Paso 2002, no pet.) (witness properly allowed to testify as expert, even though only disclosed as fact witness, where opposing party not unfairly surprised).

c. Minor Change in Testimony

Southwestern Energy Production Co. v. Berry-Helfand, 491 S.W.3d 699, 718 (Tex. 2016) ("Subject to timely disclosure and supplementation requirements under our rules of civil procedure, experts can continue to refine calculations and perfect expert reports.").

Kingsley Properties, LP v. San Jacinto Title Services of Corpus Christi, LLC, 501 S.W.3d 344, 353 (Tex. App.—Corpus Christi 2016, no pet.) ("[T]he discovery rules do not prevent experts from refining calculations and perfecting reports through the time of trial.").

Beinar v. Deegan, 432 S.W.3d 398, 404 (Tex. App.—Dallas 2014, no pet.) (the rule requiring supplementation does not prevent an expert from refining calculations and perfecting a report through the time of trial).

Vela v. Wagner & Brown, Ltd., 203 S.W.3d 37, 58 (Tex. App.—San Antonio 2006, no pet.) (testimony of an expert should not be barred as a violation of discovery rules because a change in some minor detail of the person's work was not disclosed before trial).

d. *Opportunity to Redepose Experts*

Note: Allowing an additional deposition of the subject expert may be a satisfactory remedy to cure any potential prejudice. In opposing the other party's motion for sanctions for failing to disclose the substance of the expert's opinions, counsel should offer to make his or her experts available for additional depositions, as necessary.

II. Sample Motions
A. Motion to Exclude Evidence of Claim Denied During Discovery

NO. _____

	§	
_____	§	IN THE DISTRICT COURT
	§	
v.	§	_____ JUDICIAL COURT
	§	
_____	§	_____ COUNTY, TEXAS

Motion to Exclude Evidence of Claim Denied During Discovery

Come now _____, Plaintiff in this cause, and file this, her Motion to Exclude Evidence of Claims Denied During discovery, and in support would show the Court the following:

I.
FACTUAL BACKGROUND

This action arises from a rear-end automobile accident between Plaintiff and Defendant that occurred on September 18, 2016. As a result of the accident, Plaintiff claims to have sustained neck and back injuries and lost wages.

On June 12, 2017, Defendant noticed Plaintiff's deposition. The notice, in part, requested that Plaintiff produce documents pertaining to his wage loss claim. A copy of the deposition notice is attached hereto as exhibit "A." When asked at the deposition whether he had any documents to support the claim, Plaintiff responded "None." When asked whether he was seeking reimbursement for lost wages, the Plaintiff responded, "I'm not sure, no." Relevant portions of Plaintiff's deposition transcripts are attached hereto as Exhibit "B." See Exhibit "B" at Lines 10-15.

On August 21, 2017, Defendant served First Demand for Inspection of Documents ("Inspection Demand"), asking, at Request No. 2, for "Any and all documents pertaining to your claim for lost wages or lost earning capacity." A copy of Defendant's Inspection Demand is attached hereto as exhibit "C." In Plaintiff's response to Request No. 2 of the Inspection Demand, Plaintiff responded "None." A copy of Plaintiff's response to Defendant's Inspection Demand is attached hereto as exhibit "D."

Up until the date of the pretrial conference in this matter—just ten (10) days before trial on January 10, 2019—Plaintiff had provided no documents to support a claim for loss of earnings or earning capacity. At the pretrial conference, Plaintiff's counsel indicated that Plaintiff would be offering several payroll documents at trial relating to Plaintiff's earnings history.

By this motion, Defendant seeks an order excluding any and all evidence pertaining to Plaintiff's wage loss claim.

2.
THIS COURT MAY EXCLUDE PREJUDICIAL EVIDENCE IN ADVANCE OF TRIAL BY WAY OF AN IN LIMINE MOTION

The Court has the inherent power to grant a motion in limine to exclude evidence which could be objected to at trial, either as irrelevant or subject to exclusion as unduly prejudicial. *Wackenhut Corp. v. Gutierrez*, 453 S.W.3d 917, 920 n.3 (Tex. 2016); *In re BCH Development, LLC*, 525 S.W.3d 920, 925 (Tex. App.—Dallas 2017, orig. proceeding). Texas Rule of Evidence 403 allows the court to exclude evidence where there is a substantial danger that the probative value will be outweighed by the danger of undue prejudice. *See Diamond Offshore Services Ltd. v. Williams*, 542 S.W.3d 539, 549 (Tex. 2018); *Brookshire Bros. v. Aldridge*, 438 S.W.3d 9, 34 (Tex. 2014).

Moreover, the court may hear and determine the question of the admissibility of evidence outside the presence or hearing of the jury. *See Weidner v. Sanchez*, 14 S.W.3d 353, 363 (Tex. App.—Houston [14th Dist.] 2000, no pet.); *Kendrix v. S. Pac. Transp. Co.*, 907 S.W.2d 111, 113 (Tex. App.—Beaumont 1995, writ denied); Texas Rule of Civil Procedure 166; and Texas Rules of Evidence 103 and 104.

3.
EVIDENCE OF PLAINTIFF'S LOST WAGE CLAIM SHOULD BE EXCLUDED TO PREVENT UNFAIR SURPRISE TO DEFENDANT

To avoid unfair surprise, the Court may exclude evidence on issues where discovery responses and actions of counsel led opposing counsel to believe those issues would not be litigated. *Capital Metro. Transp. Auth./Cent. of Tenn. Ry. & Navigation Co. v. Cent. of Tenn. Ry. & Navigation Co.* 114 S.W.3d 573, 583 (Tex. App.—Austin 2003, pet. denied) (evidence of damages for failure to disclose information until shortly before trial properly excluded where court implicitly found unfair surprise from late disclosure); *Magnuson v. Mullen*, 65 S.W.3d 815, 823 (Tex. App.—Fort Worth 2002, pet. denied) (plaintiff frustrated defendant's attempt to define litigation through discovery process and therefore, dismissal of plaintiff's lawsuit, with prejudice, warranted as sanction for failure to comply with discovery); *Matagorda County Hosp. Dist. v. Burwell*, 94 S.W.3d 75, 82 (Tex. App.—Corpus Christi 2002), *rev'd on other grounds*, 189 S.W.3d 738 (Tex. 2006) (witness testimony not disclosed in timely manner properly excluded where unfair surprise to opposing party).

The court is within its power to preclude a party from introducing documents not discovered by the opposing party, where relevant evidence is not disclosed during discovery. *See*

F & H Invs. Inc. v. State, 55 S.W.3d 663, 671 (Tex. App.—Waco 2001, no pet.) (trial court abused discretion not excluding undisclosed evidence and witnesses where unfair surprise to opposing party).

In the present case, Plaintiff's statements and actions led Defendant to reasonably believe that Plaintiff would not be pursuing the wage loss claim. Plaintiff responded at his deposition that he would not be seeking reimbursement for his lost wages claim. See Exhibit "B" at Lines 10-15. Plaintiff produced no documentation that would support the claim, despite several formal discovery requests by Defendant. See Exhibits "A," "C," and "D."

The first indication that Plaintiff would be offering any evidence on the lost wages claim was at the Issue Conference—just days before the commencement of trial and after the discovery cut-off date. Clearly, Plaintiff knew or should have known that these documents existed when asked at deposition or through other discovery requests. Failure to produce the documents suggests strongly that they were suppressed by the Plaintiff.

The Defendant will suffer undue prejudice if Plaintiff is permitted to testify or introduce any documentation at trial to support his claim for lost wages. As such, this court should exclude any and all evidence, including any mention of evidence, relating to Plaintiff's lost wage claim.

4.
PLAINTIFF'S LOST WAGE EVIDENCE WAS NOT DISPUTED THROUGHOUT DISCOVERY

Texas Rule of Evidence 402 states that "evidence which is not relevant is inadmissible." Relevant evidence is defined by Texas Rule of Evidence 401 as "having any tendency to make the existence of any fact that is of consequence to the determination of the action more probable or less probable than it would be without the evidence." *See Torrington v. Stutzman*, 46 S.W.3d 829, 845 n.13 (Tex. 2000). Irrelevant evidence is not admissible. *Morale v. State*, 557 S.W.3d 569, 573 (Tex. 2018); *Diamond Offshore Services Ltd. v. Williams*, 542 S.W.3d 539, 549 (Tex. 2018).

The Court may exclude evidence on matters that are not in dispute. *Palomo v. State*, 925 S.W.2d 329, 337 (Tex. App.—Corpus Christi 1996, no pet.) (evidence defendant had tattoo suggesting gang membership irrelevant and should not have been admitted where defendant did not contest issue of gang membership); *Brown v. State*, 757 S.W.2d 739 (Tex. Crim. App. 1988) (evidence of victim's emotional trauma following rape irrelevant where only disputed issue was identity of rapist, not fact of rape).

In the present case, the Plaintiff testified under oath at his deposition that he was not seeking reimbursement for lost wages. See Exhibit "B" at Lines 10-15. The Plaintiff's failure to provide supporting documentation, despite several proper discovery requests by Defendant, further supports this fact. See Exhibits "A," "C," and "D."

Plaintiff's clear indication throughout the discovery process, and up until just ten (10) days before trial, was that he was not seeking reimbursement for lost wages. It would be unfair and prejudicial to allow Plaintiff, at this late date, to present evidence on an issue which, until days before the start of trial, was not in dispute.

The Court should therefore exclude any and all evidence, including any mention of evidence, relating to Plaintiff's wage loss claim.

5.
Conclusion

Based on the foregoing, Defendant respectfully requests that this Court exclude any testimony or documentary evidence, or mention of any evidence, regarding Plaintiff's claim for wage loss.

Dated: _____ *(Date)* _____

By: _____

_____ *(Name of Counsel)* _____

Attorneys for Defendant,

_____ *(Name of Defendant)* _____

B. Opposition to Defendant's Motion to Limit Plaintiff's Expert's Opinions

NO. _____

	§	IN THE DISTRICT COURT
_____	§	
	§	_____ JUDICIAL COURT
v.	§	
_____	§	_____ COUNTY, TEXAS

Opposition to Defendant's Motion to Limit Plaintiff's Expert's Opinions

Comes now _____, Plaintiff in this cause, and file this, her Opposition to Defendant's Motion to Limit Plaintiff's Expert's Opinions, and in support would show the Court the following:

1.
FACTUAL BACKGROUND

This case is a medical malpractice and wrongful death action whereby it is alleged that Defendants negligently misdiagnosed and treated the decedent, allowing decedent to become gravely ill and die from complications from pneumonia.

Expert depositions were conducted for all three of Plaintiff's designated medical experts approximately two months ago. Each deposition in this serious medical malpractice case took approximately two hours. This motion concerns Defendants' attempts to exclude key testimony from Plaintiff's expert witnesses. Plaintiff submits that Defendants never conducted any meaningful inquiry relating to the disputed testimony when the depositions were taken. Near the conclusion of each of Plaintiff's expert depositions, Defendants' counsel asked the following general question: "Do you have any other opinions not yet expressed?"

Defendants' motion in limine seeks to limit Plaintiff's expert testimony to those opinions and conclusions testified to at their depositions, and secondly, to exclude testimony based upon material available but not provided to or reviewed by them prior to their depositions.

For the reasons and authorities cited below, Plaintiff respectfully urges this Court to reject the Defendants' overbroad motions. In the alternative, Plaintiff requests a brief continuance to allow Defendants to re-depose Plaintiff's experts to obtain the information they claim was withheld from them at the time of the original depositions.

2.
THE DEFENSE INTERPRETATION OF THE LAW WOULD REWARD DEFENDANTS FOR TAKING INSUFFICIENTLY THOROUGH DEPOSITIONS

Defendants are asking the Court to preclude an expert from saying anything that he has not already said in his deposition. This is clearly contrary to the law and would create a possible loophole in the expert discovery statute. A defendant would simply have to ask very few questions and thereby block the expert from testifying about anything other than what he was asked. Surely the Defendants cannot possibly be asking the Court to make such a ruling.

This is particularly true in instances, such as here, where Defendants insisted on asking overbroad, catch-all questions such as "do you have any other opinions not yet expressed," rather than asking questions about the specific areas about which an expert could reasonably have an opinion in this case. Indeed, in numerous instances in this case, the defense did so over Plaintiff's objection and despite Plaintiff's statement that they were welcome to inquire into remaining areas. They should not expect to use that catch-all question in a way to rule out other opinions the expert might present at trial.

Even more importantly, this motion is universally propounded by defendants in medical malpractice actions in order to gain an unfair litigation advantage. Unlike most other litigation, in medical malpractice actions, the defendants have virtually all the facts regarding the incident in question in their possession or control while plaintiffs have none. Through discovery, plaintiffs seek to elicit as much of this information as possible, and the defendants typically vigorously resist such discovery. Then, almost without exception, at the time of the deposition of plaintiffs' expert witnesses, there will be some information that plaintiffs have not managed to uncover, and that defendants are withholding and plan to make part of their trial strategy. Knowing that they plan to introduce such information, they nonetheless intentionally fail to ask plaintiffs' experts questions based on this withheld information. Alternatively, the defendants insist on priority in taking depositions and then introduce, for the first time at the subsequent deposition of defendants' experts, theories that plaintiffs could not have reasonably foreseen and for which plaintiffs' experts could not have formulated an opinion. Defendants next propound the standard motion and seek to use it as an offensive weapon, preventing plaintiffs' experts from responding to new facts which are brought out by defendants in their defense claims for the first time at trial or at subsequent depositions.

In the present case, Defendants' experts concocted totally outlandish theories with absolutely no medical basis, which Plaintiff's experts would not have dreamed they should address. These defense opinions, such as the notion that decedent suffered from an encephalitis (inflammation of the brain) and myocarditis (inflammation of the heart muscle) and that these conditions, rather than the pneumonia Plaintiffs' experts found as actual treating physicians, caused decedent's death, were not offered until after the depositions of Plaintiff's experts were taken.

To the extent no questions were asked on subjects that Plaintiff's witnesses could not reasonably be expected to predict, Defendants should not be rewarded for taking an insufficiently thorough deposition. Accordingly, at the very least, the ruling on the motion should be deferred until the time a specific question is asked and the Court can determine whether such information was material to the particular expert's deposition in this case.

3.
THE DEFENDANTS SHOULD NOT BE SURPRISED BY THE TESTIMONY OF THE PLAINTIFF'S EXPERT AND THUS, THE TESTIMONY SHOULD BE ADMISSIBLE

Texas law authorizes the Plaintiff's expert to testify in the instant matter, despite the fact that the exact nature of the opinion was not expressed at the Plaintiff's expert's deposition, when the opposing party should not be surprised by the testimony. For example, in *Beard Family P'ship v. Commercial Indem. Ins. Co.*, 116 S.W.3d 839, 850 (Tex. App.—Austin 2003, no pet.), the court held that the trial court did not abuse its discretion by allowing an expert witness who was not timely disclosed to testify because the failure was inadvertent and the opposing party was not unfairly surprised.

Similarly, in *Miller v. Kennedy & Minshew, Prof'l Corp.*, 142 S.W.3d 325, 348 (Tex. App.—Fort Worth 2003, pet. denied), expert testimony from two witnesses who were not properly disclosed was held to be proper where the substance of their testimony did not cause the opposing party unfair surprise. *See also State v. Target Corp.*, 194 S.W.3d 46 (Tex. App.—Waco 2006, no pet.) (even if party's supplementation of discovery thirty-one days before trial to include additional witnesses and expert information were untimely, exclusion of expert testimony that related to supplemented discovery was unwarranted because opposition would not have been unfairly surprised or prejudiced); *Bellino v. Comm'n for Lawyer Discipline*, 124 S.W.3d 380, 384 (Tex. App.—Dallas 2003, reh'g overruled, pet. stricken) (witness not disclosed in timely fashion was properly permitted to testify where opposing party was not unfairly surprised); *Llanes v. Davila*, 133 S.W.3d 635 (Tex. App.—Corpus Christi 2003, pet. denied) (trial court did not abuse its discretion allowing expert testimony despite incomplete disclosure of substance of testimony where opposing party was not unfairly surprised by testimony); *Gutierrez v. Gutierrez*, 86 S.W.3d 729, 736 (Tex. App.—El Paso 2002, no pet.) (witness properly allowed to testify as expert, even though witness was only disclosed as fact witness, where opposing party was not unfairly surprised).

In the instant matter, Plaintiff or his experts have not engaged in any abuse of discovery or any activity that could be construed as waiver or warrant estoppel. The Defendants' motion is clearly a shotgun attempt at excluding relevant expert testimony based upon an overbroad reading of existing law. To allow the exclusion of Plaintiff's expert's testimony would only serve to harm the Plaintiff and reward the Defendants for an incomplete deposition.

4.
ALTERNATIVELY, THIS COURT SHOULD ALLOW DEFENDANTS TO RE-DEPOSE PLAINTIFF'S EXPERTS

If this Court feels that Defendants have met their burden in bringing this motion, Plaintiff respectfully requests that a brief continuance be allowed so that Defendants may re-depose Plaintiff's medical experts for the limited purpose of allowing Defendants to obtain the alleged missing information they failed to discover in the first deposition.

Texas law supports Plaintiff's request for a continuance. See Texas Rule of Civil Procedure 193.6; *Mauzey v. Sutliff*, 125 S.W.3d 71 (Tex. App.—Austin 2003, pet. denied) (no error in allowing expert to testify, despite inadequate disclosure of substance of testimony, where opposing party failed to take deposition of expert and failed to make motion to compel or for continuance).

In this case, good cause exists to allow the requested continuance. Plaintiff has not engaged in any improper behavior and has, in fact, been totally forthright in all discovery. A clear reading of the disputed expert deposition transcripts shows that Plaintiff's experts were similarly forthright in their responses to all of Defendants' questions. Plaintiff should not be penalized because Defendants failed to take a thorough deposition the first time around.

Plaintiff does not believe that additional depositions are even necessary. However, in the spirit of cooperation, Plaintiff will allow the depositions to be retaken, only for the limited purpose of allowing Defendants to do follow-up inquiry only on those issues addressed in their moving papers. Any additional matter would clearly a last-minute "fishing expedition" and should be restricted.

5.
CONCLUSION

For the foregoing reasons, the Court should deny Defendants' motion as overbroad. To the extent that the Court is inclined to grant Defendants' Motion, it should not extend to opinions that Plaintiff's experts did not give because they were not asked or because they did not have that information available to them at the time of the taking of their deposition. In the alternative, the Court should order that limited new depositions be scheduled for Plaintiff's medical experts.

Dated: _____ *(Date)* _____

By: _____

_____ *(Name of Counsel)* _____

Attorneys for Plaintiff,

_____ *(Name of Plaintiff)* _____

C. Motion to Exclude Evidence of Medical Bills for Services Obtained After [Date]

NO. _____

	§	IN THE DISTRICT COURT
_____	§	
	§	
v.	§	_____ JUDICIAL COURT
	§	
_____	§	_____ COUNTY, TEXAS

Motion to Exclude Evidence of Medical Bills for Services Obtained After [Date]

Comes now _____, Defendant in this cause, and file this, his Motion to Exclude Evidence of Medical Bills for Services Obtained After ___ [date], and in support would show the Court the following:

1.
FACTUAL BACKGROUND

This action arises from an incident on May 10, 2017, when the Plaintiff allegedly slipped and fell in the Defendant's supermarket. As a result of the incident, Plaintiff claims to have sustained neck and back injuries and lost wages.

On February 2018, Defendant served upon Plaintiff certain requests to admit facts. Said requests to admit included a request to admit the fact that there were no medical bills for services obtained after October 15, 2017, that resulted from the incident at issue in this case. A copy of the Requests to Admit and the Proof of Service of them is attached hereto as Exhibit A. Plaintiff failed to timely respond to the requests to admit that were served upon him. The Plaintiff's failure to respond to the requests to admit have resulted in deemed admissions of them and therefore, any evidence related to medical bills for services that were obtained after October 15, 2007, is prejudicial, irrelevant, and inadmissible.

This case is now set for trial on _____, 2019. Up until the date of the final pretrial on ___, 2019, just one week before the scheduled trial, Plaintiff had provided no evidence of medical bills for services that were obtained after October 15, 2017. At the pretrial conference, Plaintiff's counsel indicated that Plaintiff would be offering evidence related to medical bills for services that were obtained after October 15, 2017.

By this motion, Defendant seeks an order excluding any and all evidence pertaining to Plaintiff's claim related to medical bills for services that were obtained after October 15, 2017.

2.
PLAINTIFF'S FAILURE TO RESPOND TO DEFENDANT'S REQUESTS
TO ADMIT RESULTED IN DEEMED ADMISSIONS OF THOSE FACTS

Pursuant to Texas Rule of Civil Procedure 198.1, Defendant was authorized to serve the requests to admit upon Plaintiff. Specifically, Rule 198.1 provides:

"A party may serve on another party—no later than 30 days before the end of the discovery period—written requests that the other party admit the truth of any matter within the scope of discovery, including statements of opinion or of fact or of the application of law to fact, or the genuineness of any documents served with the request or otherwise made available for inspection and copying. Each matter for which an admission is requested must be stated separately. Once the admissions were served upon plaintiff, he was required by law to respond to them within 30 days after service of the request."

Tex. R. Civ. P. 198.2. In fact, Rule 198.2 provides that unless the responding party states an objection or asserts a privilege, the responding party must specifically admit or deny the request or explain in detail the reasons that the responding party cannot admit or deny the request. A response must fairly meet the substance of the request. The responding party may qualify an answer, or deny a request in part, only when good faith requires. Lack of information or knowledge is not a proper response unless the responding party states that a reasonable inquiry was made but that the information known or easily obtainable is insufficient to enable the responding party to admit or deny. An assertion that the request presents an issue for trial is not a proper response. If a response is not timely served, the request is considered admitted without the necessity of a court order.

In this case, Plaintiff did not respond to the requests to admit in a timely fashion. Furthermore, he has never provided a good faith basis for an extension of time to answer the requests to admit. As a result, the Plaintiff must be deemed to have admitted the facts as contained in Exhibit A. *See Cont'l Carbon Co. v. Sea-Land Serv., Inc.*, 27 S.W.3d 184, 189 (Tex. App.—Dallas 2000, pet. denied) (deemed admissions, resulting from a party's failure to answer a request for admissions, are judicial admissions and may not be controverted with testimony); *Morgan v. Timmers Chevrolet, Inc.*, 1 S.W.3d 803, 805 (Tex. App.—Houston [1st Dist.] 1999, pet. denied) (requests for admission deemed admitted where defendant did not respond to them).

For the foregoing reasons, this Court should determine that Plaintiff has admitted that there are no medical bills for services that were obtained after October 15, 2007, as a result of the incident that is at issue in this case. As such, any evidence related to such medical bills should be excluded from the trial in this case.

3.
PLAINTIFF'S MEDICAL BILLS FOR SERVICES OBTAINED AFTER THE REQUESTED DATE ARE IRRELEVANT TO THIS ACTION

Due to the fact that Plaintiff has admitted that there are no medical bills for services obtained after October 15, 2017, that resulted from the incident at issue in this case, any such evidence should be excluded as irrelevant to this cause of action. Texas Rule of Evidence 401 defines relevancy as evidence having any tendency to make the existence of any fact that is of consequence to the determination of the action more probable or less probable than it would be without the evidence.

Evidence may be properly excluded where it is not relevant to matters at issue. *Exxon Pipeline Co. v. Zwahr*, 88 S.W.3d 623, 629 (Tex. 2002) (evidence that has no relationship to any issue in the case is not admissible as it is irrelevant).

In the present case, as was discussed above, the Plaintiff has admitted, through deemed admissions, that there are no medical bills for services obtained after October 15, 2017, that resulted from the incident at issue in this case. It would be unfair and prejudicial to allow Plaintiff, at this late date, to present evidence on an issue that, until days before the start of trial, was not in dispute. Thus, the Court should therefore exclude any and all evidence, including any mention of evidence, relating to medical bills for services that were obtained after October 15, 2017, as irrelevant to the issues in this case.

4.
THIS COURT MAY EXCLUDE PREJUDICIAL EVIDENCE IN ADVANCE OF TRIAL BY WAY OF AN IN LIMINE MOTION

Evidence should be excluded when the prejudicial impact of the evidence outweighs the probative value of it. Texas Rule of Evidence 403 states: "Although relevant, evidence may be excluded if its probative value is substantially outweighed by the danger of unfair prejudice, confusion of the issues, or misleading the jury, or by considerations of undue delay, waste of time, or needless presentation of cumulative evidence."

In fact, Texas cases have excluded evidence when the prejudicial impact of the evidence outweighed the probative value of it. *See e.g. Strauss v. Cont'l Airlines, Inc.*, 67 S.W.3d 428, 448(Tex. App.—Houston [14th Dist.] 2002, no pet.) (not abuse of trial court's discretion to exclude psychiatric records as irrelevant and unduly prejudicial). Moreover, the Court should determine whether to exclude this evidence outside of the presence of the jury in order to prevent the jury from hearing about inadmissible material. Specifically, Texas Rule of Evidence 103(c) provides: "Hearing of Jury.—In jury cases, proceedings shall be conducted, to the extent practicable, so as to prevent inadmissible evidence from being suggested to the jury by any means, such as making statements or offers of proof or asking questions in the hearing of the jury."

Furthermore, as was discussed above, Plaintiff has admitted, through deemed admissions, that there are no medical bills for services that were obtained after October 15, 2017, as a result of the incident that is at issue in this case. It would be unfair and prejudicial to allow Plaintiff, at this late date, to present evidence on an issue that, until days before the start of trial, was not in dispute. Thus, the Court should therefore exclude any and all evidence, including any mention of evidence, relating to medical bills for services that were obtained after October 15, 2017, as unfairly prejudicial to Defendant.

5.
EVIDENCE OF PLAINTIFF'S MEDICAL BILLS FOR SERVICES OBTAINED AFTER THE REQUESTED DATE SHOULD BE EXCLUDED TO PREVENT UNFAIR SURPRISE TO DEFENDANT

To avoid unfair surprise, the Court may exclude evidence on issues where discovery responses and actions of counsel led opposing counsel to believe those issues would not be litigated. Texas Rule of Civil Procedure 193.6 governs the failure to timely respond and its effect on trial and states in pertinent part:

(a) Exclusion of Evidence and Exceptions. A party who fails to make, amend, or supplement a discovery response in a timely manner may not introduce in evidence the material or information that was not timely disclosed, or offer the testimony of a witness (other than a named party) who was not timely identified, unless the court finds that:
 (1) there was good cause for the failure to timely make, amend, or supplement the discovery response; or
 (2) the failure to timely make, amend, or supplement the discovery response will not unfairly surprise or unfairly prejudice the other parties.
(b) Burden of Establishing Exception. The burden of establishing good cause or the lack of unfair surprise or unfair prejudice is on the party seeking to introduce the evidence or call the witness.

See Capital Metro. Transp. Auth./Cent. of Tenn. Ry. & Navigation Co. v. Cent. of Tenn. Ry. & Navigation Co., 114 S.W.3d 573, 583 (Tex. App.—Austin 2003, pet. denied) (evidence of damages for failure to disclose information until shortly before trial properly excluded where court implicitly found unfair surprise from late disclosure); *Matagorda County Hosp. Dist. v. Burwell*, 94 S.W.3d 75, 82 (Tex. App.—Corpus Christi 2002), *rev'd on other grounds*, 189 S.W.3d 738 (Tex. 2006) (witness testimony not disclosed in timely manner properly excluded based upon unfair surprise to opposing party).

Furthermore, the Court is within its power to preclude a party from introducing documents not discovered by the opposing party, where the relevant evidence is not disclosed during discovery. *See Avila v. State*, 252 S.W.3d 632 (Tex. App.—Tyler 2008, no pet.) (exclusion of immigration document that was signed by respondents' client showing that respondents provided immigration services as requested was an appropriate sanction for respondents' failure to produce the document during discovery).

In the present case, Plaintiff's statements and actions led defense counsel to reasonably believe that Plaintiff would not be pursuing a claim for medical bills for services obtained after October 15, 2017. The first indication that Plaintiff would be offering any evidence on this issue was at the final pretrial conference, just days before the commencement of trial and after the discovery cut-off date. Moreover, as was discussed above, Plaintiff has admitted, through deemed admissions, that there are no medical bills for services obtained after October 15, 2017, that resulted from the incident at issue in this case. It would be unfair and prejudicial to allow Plaintiff, at this late date, to present evidence on an issue that, until days before the start of trial, was not in dispute. Thus, the Court should therefore exclude any and all evidence, including any mention of evidence, relating to medical bills for services that were obtained after October 15, 2017, to prevent unfair surprise to Defendant.

6.
CONCLUSION

Based on the foregoing, Defendant respectfully requests that this Court exclude any testimony or documentary evidence, or mention of any evidence, regarding Plaintiff's claim for medical bills for services that were obtained after October 15, 2017.

Dated: _____ *(Date)* _____

By: _____

_____ *(Name of Counsel)* _____

Attorneys for Defendant,

_____ *(Name of Defendant)* _____

CHAPTER 7

Character Evidence

I. Motion Authorities
   A. Overview of Character Evidence
      1. Admissible Character Evidence
      2. Character Evidence Subject to Exclusion
      3. Evidence Rule Limitations in Criminal Cases
   B. Motion to Exclude Character Evidence Used for Impeachment
      1. Suggested Motion Text
      2. Motion Summary
      3. Supporting Authorities
         a. Exclusion of Improper Impeachment Evidence
            i. Alcohol Consumption
            ii. Arrests or Misdemeanor Convictions
            iii. Drug Use
            iv. Felony Convictions
            v. Fraudulent Acts
            vii. Good Character of Witness
            viii. Religious Belief
            ix. Sexual Preference or Behavior
         b. Other Grounds
      4. Opposing Authorities
         a. Witness Perceptions
         b. Impeachment
            i. Balancing Test
            ii. Identity
            iii. Rebuttal
            iv. Witness Veracity/Moral Turpitude
            v. Context Evidence
            vi. Clarify False Impression
   C. Motion to Exclude Character Evidence Used to Prove Conduct
      1. Suggested Motion Text
      2. Motion Summary
      3. Supporting Authorities
         a. Care or Skill in Negligence Cases
         b. Crimes Evidence
         d. Other Grounds
      4. Opposing Authorities
         a. Relevant to Material Issue
         b. Witness Impeachment

            c. Trait at Issue
            d. Permitted by Statute
      D. Motion to Exclude Evidence of Prior Felony Conviction
         1. Suggested Motion Text
         2. Motion Summary
         3. Supporting Authorities
            a. Balancing Prejudicial Effect of Felony Evidence
            b. Disposition to Commit Crime
            c. Must Reflect on Credibility
            d. Exclusion of Improper Character Evidence
            e. Other Grounds
         4. Opposing Authorities
            a. Texas Code of Criminal Procedure Art. 38.37
            b. Moral Turpitude
II. Sample Motions
   A. Motion to Exclude Evidence of Alcohol Use of Witness
   B. Opposition to Motion to Exclude Inflammatory Evidence

I. Motion Authorities

A. Overview of Character Evidence

Before making a motion to exclude character evidence, users should familiarize themselves with the rules of admissibility of such evidence, which can be confusing. For helpful commentary, see Texas Rules of Evidence, Rules 404 to 406, 412, and 609 to 610.

The following sections provide a brief overview of the statutory basis for admitting or excluding character evidence.

1. Admissible Character Evidence

Generally, character evidence is admissible if relevant and not specifically restricted by statute. Texas Rule of Evidence 608(a) states:

> The credibility of a witness may be attacked or supported by evidence in the form of opinion or reputation, but subject to these limitations: (1) the evidence may refer only to character for truthfulness or untruthfulness; and (2) evidence of truthful character is admissible only after the character of the witness for truthfulness has been attacked by opinion or reputation evidence or otherwise.

Texas Rule of Evidence 405 further states:

> (a) Reputation or Opinion. In all cases in which evidence of a person's character or character trait is admissible, proof may be made by testimony as to reputation or by testimony in the form of an opinion. In a criminal case, to be qualified to testify at the guilt stage of trial concerning the character or character trait

of an accused, a witness must have been familiar with the reputation, or with the underlying facts or information upon which the opinion is based, prior to the day of the offense. In all cases where testimony is admitted under this rule, on cross-examination inquiry is allowable into relevant specific instances of conduct.

(b) Specific Instances of Conduct. In cases in which a person's character or character trait is an essential element of a charge, claim or defense, proof may also be made of specific instances of that person's conduct.

Note: Evidence of custom or habit is admissible pursuant to Texas Rule of Evidence 406, even where a person's character is inadmissible.

If the case involves a sexual offense, the reader should also be aware that Texas Rule of Evidence 412 applies to limit the admissibility of certain evidence regarding the victim's prior sexual conduct.

2. Character Evidence Subject to Exclusion

Texas Rule of Evidence 608 restricts certain character evidence when used to attack or support witness credibility. Texas Rule of Evidence 404 restricts the extent to which character evidence may be used as circumstantial evidence to prove conduct. Note that Texas Rule of Evidence 609(a) expressly allows evidence of prior felony convictions involving moral turpitude for impeachment purposes, subject to the time limit contained in Rule 609(b), although this evidence may be excluded when found to be prejudicial.

3. Evidence Rule Limitations in Criminal Cases

Texas Rule of Evidence 405(a) states in pertinent part:

> In a criminal case, to be qualified to testify at the guilt stage of trial concerning the character or character trait of an accused, a witness must have been familiar with the reputation, or with the underlying facts or information upon which the opinion is based, prior to the day of the offense.

B. Motion to Exclude Character Evidence Used for Impeachment

1. Suggested Motion Text

(*Name of Moving Party*) hereby moves this Court for an order excluding any and all evidence, references to evidence, testimony or argument relating to the character or trait of (*Name of Witness*) for (*Describe the Character or Trait Evidence at Issue, e.g., the Witness's Habits Regarding Consumption of Alcohol*) where such evidence will be used for impeachment purposes. The motion is based upon the grounds that the evidence is irrelevant to the issues in this case, is expressly prohibited for impeachment purposes by Texas Rule of Evidence 608 and will create a substantial danger of undue prejudice to (*Name of Moving Party*).

2. Motion Summary

This motion is used to exclude character evidence of specific instances of a person's conduct, where used for impeachment purposes. The motion is based upon the express authority of Texas Rules of Evidence 608, 402, and 403, and cases such as *Lagrone v. State*, 942 S.W.2d 602, 613 (Tex. Crim. App. 1997), *cert. denied*, 522 U.S. 917 (1997). This chapter includes citations for the exclusion of character evidence in commonly disputed areas, such as alcohol and drug use, arrests and misdemeanors, felony convictions, sexual behavior, religious belief, etc.

3. Supporting Authorities

Texas Rule of Evidence 403 states that relevant evidence "may be excluded if its probative value is substantially outweighed by the danger of unfair prejudice, confusion of the issues, or misleading the jury, or by considerations of undue delay, or needless presentation of cumulative evidence." *See Diamond Offshore Services Ltd. v. Williams*, 542 S.W.3d 539, 549 (Tex. 2018); *Brookshire Bros. v. Aldridge*, 438 S.W.3d 9, 34 (Tex. 2014); *Hernandez v. State*, 390 S.W.3d 310, 323 (Tex. Crim. App. 2012).

a. Exclusion of Improper Impeachment Evidence

Texas Rule of Evidence 608(a) states:

> The credibility of a witness may be attacked or supported by evidence in the form of opinion or reputation, but subject to these limitations: (1) the evidence may refer only to character for truthfulness or untruthfulness; and (2) evidence of truthful character is admissible only after the character of the witness for truthfulness has been attacked by opinion or reputation evidence or otherwise.

Texas Rule of Evidence 608(b) states:

> Specific instances of the conduct of a witness, for the purpose of attacking or supporting the witness' credibility, other than conviction of crime as provided in Rule 609, may not be inquired into on cross-examination of the witness nor proved by extrinsic evidence.

Texas Rule of Evidence 404(b) states:

> Evidence of other crimes, wrongs or acts is not admissible to prove the character of a person in order to show action in conformity therewith. It may, however, be admissible for other purposes, such as proof of motive, opportunity, intent, preparation, plan, knowledge,

identity, or absence of mistake or accident, provided that upon timely request by the accused in a criminal case, reasonable notice is given in advance of trial of intent to introduce in the State's case-in-chief such evidence other than that arising in the same transaction.

Pierson v. State, 426 S.W.3d 763, 772 (Tex. Crim. App. 2014), *cert. denied,* 574 U.S. 885 (2014) (the general rule is that impeachment on a collateral matter is impermissible).

Pierson v. State, 426 S.W.3d 763, 772 (Tex. Crim. App. 2014), *cert. denied,* 574 U.S. 885 (2014) (the proponent of evidence has the burden to show that the question is anything more than a prelude to impeachment on a collateral matter and an impermissible attempt to attack the complaining witness's general credibility with evidence of specific instances of conduct).

Ex parte Martinez, 330 S.W.3d 891, 902 (Tex. Crim. App. 2011) (gang-related evidence tends to be irrelevant and prejudicial if not accompanied by testimony that puts the evidence into context).

TXI Transp. Co. v. Hughes, 306 S.W.3d 230, 241 (Tex. 2010) (statements concerning a party's immigration status were inadmissible because it was a collateral matter and thus not relevant to proving a material issue in the case).

TXI Transp. Co. v. Hughes, 306 S.W.3d 230, 241 (Tex. 2010) (specific instances of conduct may not be used for purposes of impeachment).

Hammer v. State, 296 S.W.3d 555, 563 (Tex. Crim. App. 2009) (witness's general character for truthfulness or credibility may not be attacked by cross examining the witness, or offering extrinsic evidence, concerning specific prior instances of untruthfulness).

Michael v. State, 235 S.W.3d 723, 726 (Tex. Crim. App. 2007) (if an inconsistent statement is not used to show that a witness is of dishonest character, then testimony explaining that witness's character for truthfulness should not be allowed).

Martinez v. State, 17 S.W.3d 677, 688 (Tex. Crim. App. 2000) (trial court properly excluded evidence of offenses not resulting in convictions where evidence offered to impeach witness).

Reighley v. State, 585 S.W.3d 98, 105 (Tex. App.—Amarillo 2019, pet. ref'd) ("Because a defendant should be tried only for the crime he is charged with committing and not for having criminal propensities, extraneous offense evidence is generally inadmissible.").

Reighley v. State, 585 S.W.3d 98, 105 (Tex. App.—Amarillo 2019, pet. ref'd) ("Rule 404(b) prohibits the use of evidence of a crime, wrong, or other act to prove a person's bad character and that, on a particular occasion, the person acted in accordance with that character.").

Lumsden v. State, 564 S.W.3d 858 (Tex. App.—Fort Worth 2018, pet. ref'd), cert. denied, 139 S.Ct. 2018 (2019) ("Generally, prior offenses are inadmissible for impeachment purposes unless the offense resulted in a final conviction for either a felony or a crime involving moral turpitude and the conviction is not too remote in time.").

Canada v. State, 547 S.W.3d 4, 21 (Tex. App.—Austin 2017, no pet.) ("Although Rule 608 allows for 'a witness's credibility' to 'be attacked or supported by testimony about the witness's reputation for having a character for truthfulness or untruthfulness, or by testimony in the form of an opinion about that character,' 'a party may not inquire into or offer extrinsic evidence to prove specific instances of the witness's conduct in order to attack or support the witness's character for truthfulness.'").

Alford v. State, 495 S.W.3d 63, 68 (Tex. App.—Houston [14th Dist.] 2016, pet. ref'd) ("Rule 608(b) provides that a witness's credibility may not be attacked with specific instances of past conduct, with exceptions not at issue here.... This means that a cross-examiner may not elicit testimony that a witness has lied in the past for the sole purpose of showing that the witness is generally dishonest and should not be believed in the current case.").

Smith v. State, 436 S.W.3d 353, 375 (Tex. App.—Houston [14th Dist.] 2014, pet. ref'd) (trial court may limit the extent of cross-examination for the purpose of challenging credibility).

Andrews v. State, 429 S.W.3d 849, 855 (Tex. App.—Texarkana 2014, pet. ref'd) ("[A] trial court may properly limit the scope of cross-examination to prevent harassment, prejudice, confusion of the issues, harm to the witness, and repetitive or marginally relevant interrogation.").

Smith v. State, 420 S.W.3d 207, 219 (Tex. App.—Houston [1st Dist.] 2013, pet. ref'd) (evidence of extraneous offenses is not admissible to prove the character of a person in order to show that he acted in conformity therewith).

Freeman v. State, 413 S.W.3d 198, 206 (Tex. App.—Houston [14th Dist.] 2013, pet. ref'd) ("[A] witness's character for truthfulness may not be attacked by offering extrinsic evidence concerning specific prior instances of untruthfulness.").

Sandoval v. State, 409 S.W.3d 259, 292 (Tex. App.—Austin 2013, no pet.) ("[I]f a witness's general character for truthfulness has been attacked, Rule of Evidence 608(a) allows, for purposes of rehabilitation, the presentation of opinion or reputation evidence of that witness's good character for truthfulness.... However, a lay witness may not, under Rule 608, testify to the complainant's truthfulness in the particular allegations.").

Sandoval v. State, 409 S.W.3d 259, 292 (Tex. App.—Austin 2013, no pet.) ("[T]estimony of the truthfulness of a witness's testimony or the truthfulness of allegations is inadmissible because it does more than assist the trier of fact to understand the evidence or to determine a fact in issue; it decides an issue for the jury.").

Clay v. State, 390 S.W.3d 1, 13 (Tex. App.—Texarkana 2012, pet. ref'd) (Rules of Evidence limit evidence of specific instances of conduct of a witness for the purpose of attacking the witness's credibility other than by proof of conviction of a crime).

Huerta v. State, 359 S.W.3d 887, 894 (Tex. App.—Houston [14th Dist.] 2012, no pet.) (details of a prior conviction are generally inadmissible for impeachment purposes).

In re O.O.A., 358 S.W.3d 352, 357 (Tex. App.—Houston [14th Dist.] 2011, no pet.) ("[P]erson's sexual orientation, standing alone, has no bearing on his or her propensity for truthfulness.").

Smith v. State, 352 S.W.3d 55, 64 (Tex. App.—Fort Worth 2011, no pet.) (right to confront witnesses "does not mean that a defendant can explore every possible line of inquiry.... Rather, the Confrontation Clause guarantees an opportunity for effective cross-examination, not cross-examination that is effective in whatever way, and to whatever extent, the defense might wish.").

Smith v. State, 352 S.W.3d 55, 64 (Tex. App.—Fort Worth 2011, no pet.) ("[C]ourts have the discretion to limit cross-examination as inappropriate for a number of reasons, including the prevention of harassment, prejudice, confusion of the issues, and marginally relevant interrogation.").

Smith v. State, 352 S.W.3d 55, 64 (Tex. App.—Fort Worth 2011, no pet.) ("[P]roponent of evidence to show bias must show that the evidence is relevant; the proponent does this by demonstrating that a nexus, or logical connection, exists between the witness's testimony and the witness's potential motive to testify in favor of the other party.").

McMillon v. State, 294 S.W.3d 198, 203 (Tex. App.—Texarkana 2009, no pet.) (witness's general character for truthfulness may be shown only through reputation or opinion testimony).

McMillon v. State, 294 S.W.3d 198, 203 (Tex. App.—Texarkana 2009, no pet.) (witness's general character for truthfulness or credibility may not be attacked either by cross-examining him or by offering extrinsic evidence concerning specific prior instances of untruthfulness).

Toliver v. State, 279 S.W.3d 391, 395 n.3 (Tex. App.—Texarkana 2009, pet. ref'd) (extraneous-offense evidence may not be considered by the jury unless there is sufficient evidence to support a finding the defendant committed the extraneous offense beyond a reasonable doubt).

Stafford v. State, 248 S.W.3d 400, 411 (Tex. App.—Beaumont 2008, pet. ref'd) ("[I]ssue regarding the general credibility of a witness or the accused is not a material issue in the sense that it will justify the admission of inherently prejudicial evidence of details of an extraneous offense committed by the witness or the accused.").

Tapps v. State, 257 S.W.3d 438, 466 (Tex. App.—Austin 2008), *aff'd*, 294 S.W.3d 175 (Tex. Crim. App. 2009) (evidence that does not have relevance apart from character conformity is inadmissible).

Pollard v. State, 255 S.W.3d 184, 189 (Tex. App.—San Antonio 2008), *aff'd*, 277 S.W.3d 25 (Tex. Crim. App. 2009) ("[C]haracter evidence offered simply because it is background evidence offered to help the jury understand the offense, but which otherwise conflicts with the proscription of Rule 404(b) [other crimes], is not admissible.... This is because when extraneous offenses are introduced as background evidence, there is a real danger that they will be viewed by the jury as impermissible character evidence.").

Stafford v. State, 248 S.W.3d 400, 411 (Tex. App.—Beaumont 2008, pet. ref'd) ("[I]ssue regarding the general credibility of a witness or the accused is not a material issue in the sense that it will justify the admission of inherently prejudicial evidence of details of an extraneous offense committed by the witness or the accused.").

i. Alcohol Consumption

Gibbs v. State, 385 S.W.2d 258, 259 (Tex. Crim. App. 1965) (impeachment evidence that witness was terminated from employment for driving while intoxicated properly excluded where no evidence that witness had been convicted for intoxicated driving and did not represent crime of moral turpitude).

Holland v. State, 60 Tex.Crim. 117, 119, 131 S.W. 563 (Tex. Crim. App. 1910) (trial court improperly allowed impeachment of witness by evidence that someone had previously brought alcohol to her house and she drank it).

Bituminous Cas. Corp. v. Martin, 478 S.W.2d 206, 209 (Tex. Civ. App.—El Paso 1972, writ ref'd n.r.e.) (evidence of drinking habit properly excluded as impeachment evidence where no showing that drinking related to incidents in question).

ii. Arrests or Misdemeanor Convictions

Meadows v. State, 455 S.W.3d 166, 170 (Tex. Crim. App. 2015) ("Evidence of a prior conviction is inadmissible if more than ten years has elapsed since the later of the date of conviction or release of the witness from the confinement imposed for that conviction 'unless the court determines, in the interests of justice, that the probative value of the conviction supported by specific facts and circumstances substantially outweighs its prejudicial effect.'... In deciding whether, in the interests of justice, the probative value of a remote conviction substantially outweighs its prejudicial effect, a court may consider all relevant specific facts and circumstances, including whether intervening convictions dilute the prejudice of that remote conviction.").

Martinez v. State, 17 S.W.3d 677, 688 (Tex. Crim. App. 2000) (trial court properly excluded evidence of offenses not resulting in convictions where evidence offered to impeach witness).

Beltran v. State, 517 S.W.3d 243, 252 (Tex. App.—San Antonio 2017, no pet.) ("[T]he fact that a witness is facing a pending charge or a change in probation status is not relevant for showing bias or motive to testify absent some 'causal connection' or 'logical relationship'.... The evidence must show a causal connection between the elicited testimony and the existence of a plea agreement, or testimony showing the witness believes a deal exists in the pending matter. In the context of cross-examination of a witness with pending charges, for the evidence to be admissible, the proponent must establish some causal connection or logical relationship between the pending charges and the witness's 'vulnerable relationship' or potential bias or prejudice for the State, or testimony at trial."

Smith v. State, 436 S.W.3d 353, 375 (Tex. App.—Houston [14th Dist.] 2014, pet. ref'd) (the fact of a prior conviction is generally admissible to impeach a witness, but details of the conviction are generally inadmissible for purposes of impeachment).

Urtado v. State, 333 S.W.3d 418, 429 (Tex. App.—Austin 2011, pet. ref'd) ("[A] misdemeanor conviction for interference with an emergency call [does not] represent a crime of moral turpitude.").

Jabari v. State, 273 S.W.3d 745, 753 (Tex. App.—Houston [1st Dist.] 2008, no pet.) ("[The] fact of a prior conviction is generally admissible to impeach a witness if that crime was a felony or involved moral turpitude.... However, the details of the conviction are generally inadmissible for the purpose of impeachment.").

Arnold v. State, 36 S.W.3d 542, 547 (Tex. App.—Tyler 2000, pet. ref'd) ("[C]riminally negligent homicide is not a crime of moral turpitude.").

Hilliard v. State, 881 S.W.2d 917, 921 (Tex. App.—Fort Worth 1994, no pet.) (trial court properly prevented defendant from cross examining witness about conviction for driving while intoxicated and alleged prior bad acts not resulting in conviction).

Lape v. State, 893 S.W.2d 949, 955 (Tex. App.—Houston [14th Dist.] 1994, pet. ref'd) (a misdemeanor conviction for lying to an officer by making a false police report was a crime of moral turpitude and properly allowed as impeachment evidence).

Hutson v. State, 843 S.W.2d 106, 107 (Tex. App.—Texarkana 1992, no pet.) (criminal trespass not crime of moral turpitude).

Patterson v. State, 783 S.W.2d 268, 272 (Tex. App.—Houston [14th Dist.] 1989, pet. ref'd) (reckless conduct conviction not admissible as impeachment where not a felony and did not involve moral turpitude)

iii. Drug Use

Gonzalez v. State, 544 S.W.3d 363, 371 (Tex. Crim. App. 2018) ("[E]vidence of drug use is not relevant if it does not apply to a 'fact of consequence.'").

Gonzalez v. State, 544 S.W.3d 363, 371 (Tex. Crim. App. 2018) ("[A]ny relevance of ... evidence [of drug use] necessarily depends upon the ability to infer intoxicating effects from the fact of consumption of the controlled substance.... The strength of that inference will naturally depend upon such factors as when the drug was taken, how much of it was taken, how long the effects of the particular drug last, and whether intoxication with a particular drug is such a common occurrence that its recognition requires no expertise.").

Lagrone v. State, 942 S.W.2d 602, 613 (Tex. Crim. App. 1997), *cert. denied*, 522 U.S. 917 (1997) (trial court properly excluded evidence of witness's drug use where offered as impeachment evidence and no showing that person was impaired at time of events in question).

Ramirez v. State, 802 S.W.2d 674, 676 (Tex. Crim. App. 1990) (trial court erred allowing impeachment of a witness by evidence of prior heroin use).

Goodnight v. State, 820 S.W.2d 254, 259 (Tex. App.—Beaumont 1991, no pet.) (trial court did not abuse discretion excluding evidence that witnesses were convicted of delivering controlled substances to the same officer and informant involved in the case where extrinsic evidence regarding specific instances of conduct may not be used to impeach credibility).

iv. Felony Convictions

Texas Rule of Evidence 609 provides the general rule that evidence of felony convictions may be used to attack witness credibility. However, felony conviction evidence should be excluded where the probative value is outweighed by the danger of undue prejudice. See Texas Rule of Evidence 609(a); *Enriquez v. State*, 56 S.W.3d 596, 601 (Tex. App.—Corpus Christi 2001, pet. ref'd). Such evidence may also be excluded where used to show a disposition to commit a similar crime or where the sole purpose is to show bad moral character. *Theus v. State*, 845 S.W.2d 874, 877 (Tex. Crim. App. 1992).

Texas Rule of Evidence 609 excludes felony convictions under certain listed circumstances:

> Time Limit. Evidence of a conviction under this rule is not admissible if a period of more than ten years has elapsed since the date of the conviction or of the release of the witness from the confinement imposed for that conviction, whichever is the later date, unless the court determines, in the interests of justice, that the probative value of the conviction supported by specific facts and circumstances substantially outweighs its prejudicial effect.
>
> (b) Effect of Pardon, Annulment, or Certificate of Rehabilitation. Evidence of a conviction is not admissible under this rule if:
>   (1) based on the finding of the rehabilitation of the person convicted, the conviction has been the subject of a pardon, annulment, certificate of rehabilitation, or other equivalent procedure, and that person has not been convicted of a subsequent crime which was classified as a felony or involved moral turpitude, regardless of punishment;
>   (2) probation has been satisfactorily completed for the crime for which the person was convicted, and that person has not been convicted of a subsequent crime which was classified as a felony or involved moral turpitude, regardless of punishment; or
>   (3) based on a finding of innocence, the conviction has been the subject of a pardon, annulment, or other equivalent procedure.
> (c) Juvenile Adjudications. Evidence of juvenile adjudications is not admissible, except for proceedings conducted pursuant to Title III, Family Code, in which the witness is a party, under this rule unless required to be admitted by the Constitution of the United States or Texas.
> (d) Pendency of Appeal. Pendency of an appeal renders evidence of a conviction inadmissible.
> (e) Notice. Evidence of a conviction is not admissible if after timely written request by the adverse party specifying the witness or witnesses, the proponent fails to give to the adverse party sufficient advance written notice of intent to use such evidence to provide the adverse party with a fair opportunity to contest the use of such evidence.

v. Fraudulent Acts

TXI Transp. Co. v. Hughes, 306 S.W.3d 230, 241 (Tex. 2010) (specific instances of conduct may not be used for purposes of impeachment).

Eris v. Phares, 39 S.W.3d 708, 717 (Tex. App.—Houston [1st Dist.] 2001, pet. denied) (trial court erred admitting evidence party had been fired from job where accused of stealing).

Lape v. State, 893 S.W.2d 949, 955 (Tex. App.—Houston [14th Dist.] 1994, pet. ref'd) (specific instances of witness lying in the past are not admissible to impeach a witness).

vi. Good Character of Witness

Texas Rule of Evidence 608(a) states:

> The credibility of a witness may be attacked or supported by evidence in the form of opinion or reputation, but subject to these limitations:
>
> (1) *the evidence may refer only to character for truthfulness or untruthfulness*; and
> (2) *evidence of truthful character is admissible only after the character of the witness for truthfulness has been attacked by opinion or reputation evidence or otherwise.* (Emphasis added.)

Nassouri v. State, 503 S.W.3d 416, 419 (Tex. App.—San Antonio 2016, no pet.) ("Bolstering occurs when one item of evidence is improperly used by a party to add credence or weight to some earlier unimpeached piece of evidence offered by the same party.").

Mack v. State, 928 S.W.2d 219, 225 (Tex. App.—Austin 1996, pet. ref'd) ("[E]vidence of the victim's peaceful character may only be offered in rebuttal to defense evidence that the victim was the first aggressor.").

Garcia v. State, 819 S.W.2d 667, 668 (Tex. App.—Corpus Christi 1991, no pet.) (defendant properly prohibited from offering specific factual instances to support claim of good character).

But note that an accused may be permitted to offer reputation evidence of his or her good character related to a trait in issue for the purpose of suggesting that he or she would not have been likely to commit the crime at issue. See, e.g., Wade v. State, *803 S.W.2d 806, 807 (Tex. App.—Fort Worth 1991, no pet.);* Carnley v. United States, *274 F.2d 68, 69 (5th Cir. 1960).*

vii. Religious Belief

Texas Rule of Evidence 610 states:

> Evidence of the beliefs or opinions of a witness on matters of religion is not admissible for the purpose of showing that by reason of their nature the witness' credibility is impaired or enhanced.

Ramirez v. State, 264 S.W.2d 99, 412 (Tex. Crim. App. 1953) (witness should not have been allowed to be impeached by evidence suggesting lack of religious belief).

Nassouri v. State, 503 S.W.3d 416, 419 (Tex. App.—San Antonio 2016, no pet.) ("Evidence of a witness's religious beliefs or opinions is not admissible to attack or support the witness's credibility.").

See also Tex. Const. art. 1, § 5 which states, in relevant part, "[n]o person shall be disqualified to give evidence in any of the Courts of this State on account of his religious opinions, or for the want of any religious belief...." Tex. Code Crim. Proc. art. 1.17 further states, in relevant part, "[n]o person shall be disqualified to give evidence in any court of this State on account of his religious opinions, or for the want of any religious belief...."

    viii. Sexual Preference or Behavior

Waffle House, Inc. v. Williams, 313 S.W.3d 796, 812 n.77 (Tex. 2010) (evidence of sexual behavior outside of what society deems acceptable is inherently inflammatory).

Waffle House, Inc. v. Williams, 313 S.W.3d 796, 812 (Tex. 2010) (in determining whether sexually provocative speech is admissible, the court should carefully weigh the applicable considerations).

In re O.O.A., 358 S.W.3d 352, 357 (Tex. App.—Houston [14th Dist.] 2011, no pet.) ("[A] person's sexual orientation, standing alone, has no bearing on his or her propensity for truthfulness.").

Tinlin v. State, 983 S.W.2d 65, 69 (Tex. App.—Fort Worth 1998, pet. ref'd) (in sexual assault case, defendant properly prevented from questioning victim about prior accusation of sexual abuse made by her against another individual that did not result in a prosecution).

Norrid v. State, 925 S.W.2d 342, 347 (Tex. App.—Fort Worth 1996, no pet.) (no error in restricting defendant's cross examination of victim regarding extra-marital affair). *See also Casterline v. State*, 736 S.W.2d 207, 212 (Tex. App.—Corpus Christi 1987, pet. ref'd) (defendant properly prevented from cross examining witness regarding extra-marital affair).

Ramos v. State, 819 S.W.2d 939, 942 (Tex. App.—Corpus Christi 1991, pet. ref'd) (trial court properly prevented defendant from impeaching witnesses with evidence of prior sexual misconduct).

    b. Other Grounds

Other possible grounds for excluding improper character evidence include:

- Collateral to issues in case;
- Confusing or misleading;
- Solely intended to create an emotional bias;
- Inadmissible hearsay.

4. Opposing Authorities

Texas Rule of Evidence 404(a) expressly allows for the introduction of character trait evidence:

> (a) **Character Evidence Generally**. Evidence of a person's character or character trait is not admissible for the purpose of proving action in conformity therewith on a particular occasion, except:

(1) *Character of accused*. Evidence of a pertinent character trait offered:
    (A) by an accused in a criminal case, or by the prosecution to rebut the same, or
    (B) by a party accused in a civil case of conduct involving moral turpitude, or by the accusing party to rebut the same;
(2) *Character of victim*. In a criminal case and subject to Rule 412, evidence of a pertinent character trait of the victim of the crime offered by an accused, or by the prosecution to rebut the same, or evidence of peaceable character of the victim offered by the prosecution in a homicide case to rebut evidence that the victim was the first aggressor; or in a civil case, evidence of character for violence of the alleged victim of assaultive conduct offered on the issue of self-defense by a party accused of the assaultive conduct, or evidence of peaceable character to rebut the same.
....

Jones v. State, 571 S.W.3d 764 (Tex. Crim. App. 2019) ("The failure to affirmatively establish the fact sought does not prevent the cross-examination from having probative value in regard to the witness' credibility. An unbelievable denial of the existence of a fact can be even more probative as to lack of credibility than an affirmative admission of the fact.").

Jones v. State, 571 S.W.3d 764 (Tex. Crim. App. 2019) ("[A] defendant need not secure an admission of bias to justify broaching the subject in cross-examination.").

Jones v. State, 571 S.W.3d 764 (Tex. Crim. App. 2019) ("[A] biased witness may well deny that the circumstances gave him a motive to testify falsely.... But the witness may nevertheless be questioned about the potential for bias so engendered.").

Jones v. State, 571 S.W.3d 764 (Tex. Crim. App. 2019) ("The Texas Rules of Evidence permit the defendant to cross-examine a witness for his purported bias, interest, and motive without undue limitation or arbitrary prohibition.").

Gonzalez v. State, 544 S.W.3d 363, 371 (Tex. Crim. App. 2018) ("[E]vidence of intoxication at the time of a murder can be relevant in a given case ... evidence of extraneous offenses can be admissible to show the context and circumstances in which the criminal act occurred.").

Reighley v. State, 585 S.W.3d 98, 105 (Tex. App.—Amarillo 2019, pet. ref'd) ("Rule 404(b) "allows evidence of other crimes, wrongs, or acts if the evidence has relevance apart from character conformity.... Some examples of relevance apart from character conformity include intent, absence of mistake, or lack of accident.... Uses such as mistake and accident are admissible in rebuttal of a defensive theory").

Jones v. State, 540 S.W.3d 16, 25 (Tex. App.—Houston [1st Dist.] 2017), rev'd on other grounds, 571 S.W.3d 764 (Tex. Crim. App. 2019) ("Cross-examination serves three general purposes: to identify the witness with the community so that independent testimony regarding the witness's reputation for veracity may be sought, to allow the jury to assess the credibility of the witness, and to allow facts to be brought out tending to discredit the witness by showing that his testimony was untrue or biased.").

Jones v. State, 540 S.W.3d 16, 25 (Tex. App.—Houston [1st Dist.] 2017), rev'd on other grounds, 571 S.W.3d 764 (Tex. Crim. App. 2019) ("Cross-examination is, by its nature, exploratory, and there is no general requirement that the defendant indicate the purpose of his inquiry.... Rather, the defendant should be granted a wide latitude even though he is unable to state what facts he expects to prove through his cross-examination.").

Jones v. State, 540 S.W.3d 16, 25 (Tex. App.—Houston [1st Dist.] 2017), rev'd on other grounds, 571 S.W.3d 764 (Tex. Crim. App. 2019) ("The main and essential purpose of confrontation is to secure for the opponent the opportunity of cross-examination, as this is the principal means by which the believability of a witness and the truth of his testimony are tested... The defendant is not only permitted to delve into the witness's story to test his perceptions and memory but is traditionally allowed to impeach or discredit the witness.").

Jones v. State, 540 S.W.3d 16, 25 (Tex. App.—Houston [1st Dist.] 2017), rev'd on other grounds, 571 S.W.3d 764 (Tex. Crim. App. 2019) ("The scope of appropriate cross-examination is necessarily broad.... It encompasses all facts and circumstances that, tested by human experience, tend to show that the witness may shade his testimony for the purpose of establishing one side of the cause only.... Accordingly, a defendant is entitled to pursue all avenues of cross-examination reasonably calculated to expose a motive, bias, or interest for the witness's testimony.").

Beltran v. State, 517 S.W.3d 243, 252 (Tex. App.—San Antonio 2017, no pet.) ("[T]he introduction of a prior crime is admissible to attack the witness's credibility or possible bias.").

Linney v. State, 401 S.W.3d 764, 772 (Tex. App.—Houston [14th Dist.], pet. ref'd) (scope of cross-examination in Texas is broad and extends to facts that may affect the witness's credibility).

Cunningham v. Hughes & Luce, L.L.P., 312 S.W.3d 62, 72 (Tex. App.—El Paso 2010, no pet.) (evidence concerning client's criminal past, in client's legal malpractice suit, was relevant to issues in case).

Dudzik v. State, 276 S.W.3d 554, 560 (Tex. App.—Waco 2008, pet. ref'd) ("[E]vidence of the victim's violent character is relevant to support a claim that the victim was the first aggressor, even if the defendant was unaware of the victim's violent character.... However, for this theory to apply, the defendant must first offer evidence of an actual act of aggression by the victim at the time of the offense.").

Stafford v. State, 248 S.W.3d 400, 411 (Tex. App.—Beaumont 2008, pet. ref'd) (extraneous misconduct evidence is not inadmissible if the evidence is relevant to a fact of consequence apart from its tendency to show conduct in conformity with character).

Lape v. State, 893 S.W.2d 949, 955 (Tex. App.—Houston [14th Dist.] 1994, pet. ref'd) (evidence that a witness had made false reports of sexual abuse in the past regarding the same alleged victim should have been admissible, even though the conviction for a false report was a misdemeanor).

a. *Witness Perceptions*

Lagrone v. State, 942 S.W.2d 602, 613 (Tex. Crim. App. 1997), *cert. denied*, 522 U.S. 917 (1997) ("We have held that a witness' credibility is only subject to attack on cross-examination when their perceptual capacity is physically impaired by the intoxicating effects of alcohol or drugs during their observation of pertinent events." (Citations omitted.)).

Russell v. State, 84 Tex.Crim. 245, 250, 209 S.W. 671 (Tex. Crim. App. 1919) (impeachment evidence that defendant was intoxicated at time of events was proper).

Goodwin v. State, 91 S.W.3d 912, 917 (Tex. App.—Fort Worth 2002, no pet.) (evidence victim had been in mental hospital inadmissible where no showing that reasons for hospitalization affected her ability to recall or testify).

Bituminous Cas. Corp. v. Martin, 478 S.W.2d 206, 209 (Tex. Civ. App.—El Paso 1972, writ ref'd n.r.e.) (witness may be impeached by evidence that witness was drunk at time of events in question).

Russell v. State, 84 Tex.Crim. 245, 250, 209 S.W. 671 (Tex. Crim. App. 1919) (impeachment evidence that defendant was intoxicated at time of events was proper).

b. Impeachment

Jones v. State, 571 S.W.3d 764 (Tex. Crim. App. 2019) ("The failure to affirmatively establish the fact sought does not prevent the cross-examination from having probative value in regard to the witness' credibility. An unbelievable denial of the existence of a fact can be even more probative as to lack of credibility than an affirmative admission of the fact.").

Jones v. State, 571 S.W.3d 764 (Tex. Crim. App. 2019) ("[A] defendant need not secure an admission of bias to justify broaching the subject in cross-examination.").

Jones v. State, 571 S.W.3d 764 (Tex. Crim. App. 2019) ("[A] biased witness may well deny that the circumstances gave him a motive to testify falsely.... But the witness may nevertheless be questioned about the potential for bias so engendered").

Jones v. State, 571 S.W.3d 764 (Tex. Crim. App. 2019) ("The Texas Rules of Evidence permit the defendant to cross-examine a witness for his purported bias, interest, and motive without undue limitation or arbitrary prohibition.").

Jones v. State, 571 S.W.3d 764 (Tex. Crim. App. 2019) (While "a showing by the proponent of the cross-examination that the circumstances he wishes to call to the witness's attention in fact give rise to an inference of undue influence or bias—even if the witness denies any actual shading of his testimony" is required, "such a principle cannot be applied too rigorously, since, generally speaking, the Texas Rules of Evidence permit the defendant to cross-examine a witness for his purported bias, interest, and motive without undue limitation or arbitrary prohibition.... Too strict an adherence to this 'logical relationship'/'causal connection' principle would undermine Alford's constitutional mandate—and Rule 613(b)'s implicit assumption—that a defendant be permitted to explore any plausible basis for witness bias, whether or not the witness is willing to admit to it.").

Pierson v. State, 426 S.W.3d 763, 772 (Tex. Crim. App. 2014), *cert. denied*, 574 U.S. 885 (2014) (while the general rule is that impeachment on a collateral matter is impermissible, sometimes the rules of evidence must give way to a defendant's Sixth Amendment right to confront his or her accuser).

Johnson v. State, 433 S.W.3d 546, 552 (Tex. Crim. App. 2014) ("[T]o be considered 'relevant,' the proffered evidence need not definitively prove the bias alleged—it need only 'make the existence' of bias more probable or less probable than it would be without the evidence.").

Bowley v. State, 310 S.W.3d 431, 434 (Tex. Crim. App. 2010) (by choosing to testify, a defendant puts his or her character for veracity, (as opposed to moral character) in issue).

Billodeau v. State, 277 S.W.3d 34, 40 (Tex. Crim. App. 2009) ("[R]elevant facts that occurred before a witness testifies at trial are admissible for impeachment purposes if permitted by the Rules of Evidence or the Confrontation Clause.").

Billodeau v. State, 277 S.W.3d 34, 40 (Tex. Crim. App. 2009) ("[W]itness's credibility does not escape scrutiny at a criminal trial because the witness can be shown to have displayed unprincipled qualities of his or her character only after the date of the charged offense.").

Billodeau v. State, 277 S.W.3d 34, 42 (Tex. Crim. App. 2009) ("[P]ossible animus, motive, or ill will of a prosecution witness who testifies against a defendant is never a collateral or irrelevant inquiry, and the defendant is entitled, subject to reasonable restrictions, to show any relevant fact that might tend to establish ill feeling, bias, motive, interest, or animus on the part of any witness testifying against him.").

Reighley v. State, 585 S.W.3d 98, 105 (Tex. App.—Amarillo 2019, pet. ref'd) ("Rule 404(b) "allows evidence of other crimes, wrongs, or acts if the evidence has relevance apart from character conformity.... Some examples of relevance apart from character conformity include intent, absence of mistake, or lack of accident.... Uses such as mistake and accident are admissible in rebuttal of a defensive theory.").

Richard Nugent and CAO, Inc. v. Estate of Ellickson, 543 S.W.3d 243, 261 (Tex. App.—Houston [14th Dist.] 2018, no pet.) ("The impeachment value of crimes involving deception is greater than that for crimes involving violence.").

Richard Nugent and CAO, Inc. v. Estate of Ellickson, 543 S.W.3d 243, 261 (Tex. App.—Houston [14th Dist.] 2018, no pet.) ("If the past crime and the conduct at issue in the civil case are similar, the third factor militates against admission").

Jones v. State, 540 S.W.3d 16, 25 (Tex. App.—Houston [1st Dist.] 2017), rev'd on other grounds, 571 S.W.3d 764 (Tex. Crim. App. 2019) ("[E]xposure of a witness' motivation in testifying is a proper and important function of the constitutionally protected right of cross-examination.").

Jones v. State, 540 S.W.3d 16, 25 (Tex. App.—Houston [1st Dist.] 2017), rev'd on other grounds, 571 S.W.3d 764 (Tex. Crim. App. 2019) ("The possible animus, motive, or ill will of a prosecution witness who testified against the defendant is never a collateral or irrelevant inquiry, and the defendant is entitled, subject to reasonable restrictions, to show any relevant fact that might tend to establish ill feeling, bias, motive, interest, or animus on the part of any witness testifying against him.").

Beltran v. State, 517 S.W.3d 243, 252 (Tex. App.—San Antonio 2017, no pet.) ("[T]he introduction of a prior crime is admissible to attack the witness's credibility or possible bias.").

Andrews v. State, 429 S.W.3d 849, 855 (Tex. App.—Texarkana 2014, pet. ref'd) (whether a witness brought a civil suit against a defendant arising from the same incident for which the defendant is on trial is generally admissible as tending to show interest and bias on the part of the witness).

Andrews v. State, 429 S.W.3d 849, 855 (Tex. App.—Texarkana 2014, pet. ref'd) ("[U]nder certain circumstances, evidence of the complainant's civil suit against a third party may also be relevant to show bias.... Relevance of such evidence is derived from its impeachment value to show motive to give false testimony based on a witness's desire to recover damages or other relief.").

Linney v. State, 401 S.W.3d 764, 772 (Tex. App.—Houston [14th Dist.], pet. ref'd) (a defendant is entitled to pursue all avenues of cross-examination reasonably calculated to expose a motive, bias, or interest for the witness to testify).

Pierson v. State, 398 S.W.3d 406, 415 (Tex. App.—Texarkana 2013), *aff'd*, 426 S.W.3d 763 (Tex. Crim. App. 2014), *cert. denied*, 574 U.S. 885 (2014) (Rule 613, which permits the use of "extrinsic evidence to show bias or interest," is an exception to Rule 608).

Gomez v. State, 380 S.W.3d 830, 835 n.8 (Tex. App.—Houston [14th Dist] 2012, pet. ref'd) (evidence of other crimes or misconduct may be admissible as proof of motive, opportunity, intent, preparation, plan, knowledge, identity, or absence of mistake or accident).

Huerta v. State, 359 S.W.3d 887, 894 (Tex. App.—Houston [14th Dist.] 2012, no pet.) (temporal proximity of prior offense and current offense will favor admission of prior crime evidence for impeachment purposes if the past crime is recent and if the witness has demonstrated a propensity for running afoul of the law).

Huerta v. State, 359 S.W.3d 887, 894 (Tex. App.—Houston [14th Dist.] 2012, no pet.) (crimes involving deception have a higher impeachment value than crimes of violence).

Salinas v. State, 368 S.W.3d 550, 557 (Tex. App.—Houston [14th Dist.] 2011), *aff'd*, 369 S.W.3d 176 (Tex. Crim. App. 2012), *aff'd*, 570 U.S. 178 (2013) ("[I]f a defendant testifies, his pre-arrest silence can be used to impeach him ... [without violating] his Fifth Amendment privilege against self-incrimination.").

Smith v. State, 352 S.W.3d 55, 64 (Tex. App.—Fort Worth 2011, no pet.) ("[T]he Sixth Amendment right to confront witnesses includes the right to cross-examine them to attack their general credibility or to show their possible bias, self-interest, or motives in testifying.").

Smith v. State, 352 S.W.3d 55, 64 (Tex. App.—Fort Worth 2011, no pet.) ("[P]ossible animus, motive, or ill will of a prosecution witness who testifies against the defendant is never a collateral or irrelevant inquiry, and the defendant is entitled, subject to reasonable restrictions, to show any relevant fact that might tend to establish ill feeling, bias, motive, interest, or animus on the part of any witness testifying against the defendant.").

Smith v. State, 352 S.W.3d 55, 64 (Tex. App.—Fort Worth 2011, no pet.) ("[A] defendant is entitled to pursue all avenues of cross-examination reasonably calculated to expose a motive, bias, or interest for the witness to testify, and therefore, the scope of appropriate cross-examination is necessarily broad.").

Smith v. State, 355 S.W.3d 138, 154 (Tex. App.—Houston [1st Dist.] 2011, pet. ref'd) ("[G]ang membership is admissible to show bias, motive, or intent, or to refute a defensive theory.").

Thomas v. State, 312 S.W.3d 732, 739 (Tex. App.—Houston [1st Dist.] 2009, pet. ref'd) (impeachment value of crimes that involve deception or moral turpitude is greater than for offenses that involve violence).

Hennessey v. State, 268 S.W.3d 153, 159 (Tex. App.—Waco 2008, pet. ref'd) (if a defendant testifies, her pre-arrest silence can be used to impeach her).

Dickson v. State, 246 S.W.3d 733, 742 (Tex. App.—Houston [14th Dist.] 2007, pet. ref'd) ("To be admissible to show identity [in a criminal prosecution], an extraneous offense must be so similar to the offense-at-issue that the offenses are marked as the accused's handiwork.... Sufficient similarity may be shown by proximity in time and place or by a common mode of committing the offenses.").

Dickson v. State, 246 S.W.3d 733, 742 (Tex. App.—Houston [14th Dist.] 2007, pet. ref'd) ("[E]xtraneous offenses may be sufficiently similar to prove identity when there is either proximity in time and place or a common mode of committing the offense.").

Dickson v. State, 246 S.W.3d 733, 742 (Tex. App.—Houston [14th Dist.] 2007, pet. ref'd) ("[A]lthough evidence that an accused has pattern of committing offenses could implicate the prohibition on using extraneous offenses to prove conformity with bad character, where identity is an issue in a criminal prosecution, evidentiary rules make exception for the introduction of extraneous offenses bearing same *modus operandi.*").

Dickson v. State, 246 S.W.3d 733, 742 (Tex. App.—Houston [14th Dist.] 2007, pet. ref'd) ("[I]mpeachment of a witness's identification testimony raises the issue of identity for which extraneous offense evidence is admissible.").

Perry v. State, 236 S.W.3d 859, 865 (Tex. App.—Texarkana 2007, no pet.) (Rule 608(b) "precludes attacks on a witness's credibility by way of specific instances of conduct, except for certain criminal convictions.... However, a jury is entitled to hear evidence as to the mental status of the witness and the extent of his or her mental impairment.").

Perry v. State, 236 S.W.3d 859, 865 (Tex. App.—Texarkana 2007, no pet.) ("[M]ental capacity of a witness is the proper subject of consideration and impeachment as bearing upon the witness's credibility.... Therefore, the right of cross examination includes the right to impeach the witness with evidence that might go to any impairment or disability affecting the witness's credibility.").

Perry v. State, 236 S.W.3d 859, 865 (Tex. App.—Texarkana 2007, no pet.) ("[C]ross-examination of a testifying state's witness to show that the witness has suffered a recent mental illness or disturbance is proper, provided that such mental illness or disturbance is such that it might tend to reflect on the witness's credibility.").

Perry v. State, 236 S.W.3d 859, 865 (Tex. App.—Texarkana 2007, no pet.) ("[A]vailable, relevant adverse evidence that might affect a co-defendant's credibility should be admitted so that the jury might use it in making the determination of how much weight it should give the co-defendant's testimony.").

Miller v. State, 196 S.W.3d 256, 268 (Tex. App.—Fort Worth 2006, pet. ref'd) ("[C]rimes that involve deception have a higher impeachment value than crimes involving violence, the latter having a higher potential for prejudice.").

Fox v. State, 115 S.W.3d 550, 568 (Tex. App.—Houston [14th Dist.] 2002, pet. ref'd) (evidence that witness had extra-marital affair proper to demonstrate witness's bias).

Hilliard v. State, 881 S.W.2d 917, 921 (Tex. App.—Fort Worth 1994, no pet.) (defendant should have been permitted to impeach witness with evidence of prior bad act by her son where incident relevant to suggest bias by witness).

Bituminous Cas. Corp. v. Martin, 478 S.W.2d 206, 209 (Tex. Civ. App.—El Paso 1972, writ ref'd n.r.e.) (witness may be impeached by evidence that witness was drunk at time of events in question).

Russell v. State, 84 Tex.Crim. 245, 250, 209 S.W. 671 (Tex. Crim. App. 1919) (impeachment evidence that defendant was intoxicated at time of events was proper).

i. Balancing Test

Reighley v. State, 585 S.W.3d 98, 105 (Tex. App.—Amarillo 2019, pet. ref'd); *Green v. State*, 589 S.W.3d 250, 259 (Tex. App.—Houston [14th Dist.] Aug. 6, 2019, no pet. h.) (Under Rule 403, the trial court is to consider several relevant factors, including: "1. how compellingly evidence of the extraneous offense serves to make a fact of consequence more or less probable; 2. the extraneous offense's potential to impress the jury in some irrational but indelible way; 3. the trial time that the proponent will require to develop evidence of the extraneous misconduct; and 4. the proponent's need for the extraneous transaction evidence.").

Bryant v. State, 534 S.W.3d 471, 473 (Tex. App.—Corpus Christi 2017, pet. ref'd) ("In weighing the probative value of a conviction against its prejudicial effect, we consider the following nonexclusive list of factors: (1) the impeachment value of the prior crime; (2) the temporal proximity of the past crime relative to the charged offense and the witness's subsequent history; (3) the similarity between the past crime and the offense being prosecuted; (4) the importance of the defendant's testimony; and (5) the importance of the credibility issue.").

Toliver v. State, 279 S.W.3d 391, 395 (Tex. App.—Texarkana 2009, pet. ref'd) ("[R]elevant criteria in determining whether prejudice of an extraneous offense substantially outweighs its probative value include: (1) how compellingly the extraneous offense evidence serves to make a fact of consequence more or less probable; (2) the potential the other offense evidence has to impress the jury in some irrational, but nevertheless, indelible way; (3) the time the proponent will need to develop the evidence; and (4) the force of the proponent's need for the evidence to prove a fact of consequence.").

Toliver v. State, 279 S.W.3d 391, 395 (Tex. App.—Texarkana 2009, pet. ref'd) (determination on probative value versus prejudicial effect is reversed rarely and only after a clear abuse of discretion because the trial court is in a superior position to gauge the impact of the relevant evidence).

Stafford v. State, 248 S.W.3d 400, 411 (Tex. App.—Beaumont 2008, pet. ref'd) ("[T]he term 'probative value' refers to the inherent probative force of an item of evidence, i.e., how strongly it serves to make more or less probable the existence of a fact of consequence to the litigation, coupled with the proponent's need for that item of evidence.").

Grant v. State, 247 S.W.3d 360, 366 (Tex. App.—Austin 2008, pet. ref'd) ("[The] trial court has a wide measure of discretion in deciding whether to admit into evidence a previous conviction to impeach testimony, and such a ruling is reviewed for an abuse of discretion.").

Isenhower v. State, 261 S.W.3d 168, 177 (Tex. App.—Houston [14th Dist.] 2008, no pet.) ("[F]actors to be considered [in balancing probative value of evidence of extraneous acts against the unfair prejudice of admission] include: (1) how compellingly the extraneous offense evidence serves to make a fact of consequence more or less probable; (2) the potential the other offense evidence has to impress the jury in some irrational but nevertheless indelible way; (3) the time the proponent will need to develop the evidence, during which the jury will be distracted from consideration of the indicted offense; and (4) the force of the proponent's need for this evidence to prove a fact of consequence, i.e., whether the proponent has other probative evidence available to him to help establish this fact, and whether the fact related to an issue in dispute.").

ii. Identity

Segundo v. State, 270 S.W.3d 79, 86 (Tex. Crim. App. 2008), *cert. denied*, 558 U.S. 828 (2009) ("trial judge has considerable latitude in determining that identity is disputed", for the purpose of determining whether evidence of uncharged misconduct is admissible to prove identity).

Segundo v. State, 270 S.W.3d 79, 86 (Tex. Crim. App. 2008), *cert. denied*, 558 U.S. 828 (2009) (identity "may be placed in dispute by a defendant's opening statement or cross-examination as well as by affirmative evidence offered by the defense").

Segundo v. State, 270 S.W.3d 79, 86 (Tex. Crim. App. 2008), *cert. denied*, 558 U.S. 828 (2009) ("[T]he impeachment was particularly damaging or effective in light of all of the evidence presented is not the question.... The question is whether the impeachment raised the issue of identity, and if it did, extraneous offenses that are relevant to the issue of identity.").

Segundo v. State, 270 S.W.3d 79, 86 (Tex. Crim. App. 2008), *cert. denied*, 558 U.S. 828 (2009) ("[E]vidence of extraneous acts of misconduct may be admissible if (1) the uncharged act is relevant to a material issue in the case and (2) the probative value of that evidence is not significantly outweighed by its prejudicial effect.").

Casey v. State, 215 S.W.3d 870, 881 (Tex. Crim. App. 2007) ("[I]n the context of extraneous offenses, "*modus operandi*" refers to a defendant's distinctive and idiosyncratic manner of committing criminal acts.").

Casey v. State, 215 S.W.3d 870, 881 (Tex. Crim. App. 2007) ("Although the *modus operandi* theory of admissibility under Rule 404(b) usually refers to evidence offered to prove the identity of a specific person, its use is not so limited in the law.... M*odus operandi* may also encompass the 'doctrine of chances theory to show lack of consent, motive, and the manner of committing an offense").

Distefano v. State, 532 S.W.3d 25, 31 (Tex. App.—Houston [14th Dist.] 2016, pet. ref'd) ("A claim that an extraneous offense is relevant to show a signature crime is often a shorthand way of saying it is relevant to show the identity of the perpetrator of the charged offense, his modus operandi, or the absence of a mistake or accident.").

Distefano v. State, 532 S.W.3d 25, 31 (Tex. App.—Houston [14th Dist.] 2016, pet. ref'd) ("When an extraneous offense is offered as emblematic of a signature crime, the common characteristics or the device used in each offense must be so unusual and distinctive to be like a 'signature.'... No rigid rules dictate what constitute sufficient similarities; rather, the common characteristics may be proximity in time and place, mode of commission of the crimes, the person's dress, or any other elements that mark both crimes as having been committed by the same person ..., If the similarities are generic, i.e., typical to this type of crime, they will not constitute a signature crime.... Sometimes, however, the signature can be one unique characteristic.").

McGregor v. State, 394 S.W.3d 90, 118 (Tex. App.—Houston [1st Dist.] 2012, pet. ref'd) ("[W]hen the extraneous offense is introduced to prove identity by comparing common characteristics, it must be so similar to the charged offense that the offenses illustrate the defendant's distinctive and idiosyncratic manner of committing criminal acts.").

McGregor v. State, 394 S.W.3d 90, 118 (Tex. App.—Houston [1st Dist.] 2012, pet. ref'd) ("[E]xtraneous offense evidence is admissible to prove identity when the common characteristics of each offense are so unusual as to act as the defendant's signature.... The signature must be apparent from a comparison of the circumstances in both cases.").

Isenhower v. State, 261 S.W.3d 168, 177 (Tex. App.—Houston [14th Dist.] 2008, no pet.) ("[O]therwise inadmissible extraneous evidence may be admissible for other purposes including proving motive, opportunity, intent, preparation, plan, knowledge, identity, absence of mistake, or accident.").

iii. Rebuttal

Richardson v. State, 328 S.W.3d 61, 71 (Tex. App.—Fort Worth 2010, pet. ref'd) ("[B]y raising a defensive theory, the defendant 'opens the door' for the State to offer rebuttal testimony regarding an extraneous offense if the extraneous offense has common characteristics with the offense for which the defendant was on trial.").

Espinosa v. State, 328 S.W.3d 32, 42 (Tex. App.—Corpus Christi 2010, pet. ref'd) ("[E]xtraneous-offense evidence may be admissible when a defendant raises an affirmative defense or a defensive issue that negates one of the elements of the crime.").

Alberts v. State, 302 S.W.3d 495, 507 (Tex. App.—Texarkana 2009, no pet.) ("[G]eneral evidence supporting truthful character may be liberally employed to respond to attacks on truthful character: there need only be a loose fit between the rebuttal evidence and the predicate attacks on character, [and in this context,] the use of questions designed to call a witness's character for truthfulness into doubt can be considered a predicate attack.").

Alberts v. State, 302 S.W.3d 495, 507 (Tex. App.—Texarkana 2009, no pet.) ("[T]est for determining whether a witness's credibility was attacked is whether a reasonable juror would believe that a witness's character for truthfulness has been attacked by evidence from other witnesses, or statements of counsel, e.g., during voir dire or opening statements.").

Isenhower v. State, 261 S.W.3d 168, 177 (Tex. App.—Houston [14th Dist.] 2008, no pet.) (rebuttal of a defensive theory is one of the permissible purposes for which relevant evidence of an extraneous offense may be admitted).

Isenhower v. State, 261 S.W.3d 168, 177 (Tex. App.—Houston [14th Dist.] 2008, no pet.) (trial court does not abuse its discretion in admitting extraneous offense evidence to rebut a defensive theory of "frame-up" or retaliation).

Johnson v. State, 263 S.W.3d 405, 426 (Tex. App.—Beaumont 2008, pet. ref'd) ("[C]riminal acts that are designed to reduce the likelihood of prosecution, conviction, or incarceration for the offense on trial are admissible under rule governing other crimes evidence, as showing consciousness of guilt.").

iv. Witness Veracity/Moral Turpitude

The use of character evidence to impeach a witness's honesty or veracity, or their opposites, has been statutorily approved by Texas Rule of Evidence 608(a):

> The credibility of a witness may be attacked or supported by evidence in the form of opinion or reputation, but subject to these limitations: (1) *the evidence may refer only to character for truthfulness or untruthfulness*; and (2) *evidence of truthful character is admissible only after the character of the witness for truthfulness has been attacked by opinion or reputation evidence or otherwise.* (Emphasis added.)

Hammer v. State, 296 S.W.3d 555, 563 (Tex. Crim. App. 2009) (witness's general character for truthfulness or credibility may not be attacked by cross-examining him, or offering extrinsic evidence, concerning specific prior instances of untruthfulness).

Michael v. State, 235 S.W.3d 723, 726 (Tex. Crim. App. 2007) (when a witness's credibility has been attacked by any one of the five forms of impeachment, the sponsoring party may rehabilitate the witness only in direct response to the attack).

Michael v. State, 235 S.W.3d 723, 726 (Tex. Crim. App. 2007) (witness's character for truthfulness may be rehabilitated with "good character" witnesses only when the witness's general character for truthfulness has been attacked).

Michael v. State, 235 S.W.3d 723, 726 (Tex. Crim. App. 2007) ("[I]f an inconsistent statement is used to show that a witness is of dishonest character, then it follows that the opposing party should be allowed to rehabilitate this witness through testimony explaining that witness's character for truthfulness.").

Sandoval v. State, 409 S.W.3d 259, 292 (Tex. App.—Austin 2013, no pet.) ("[I]f a witness's general character for truthfulness has been attacked, Rule of Evidence 608(a) allows, for purposes of rehabilitation, the presentation of opinion or reputation evidence of that witness's good character for truthfulness.").

Lester v. State, 366 S.W.3d 214, 214 (Tex. App.—Waco 2011, pet. ref'd) ("[O]ffenses involving dishonesty or false statement are crimes involving 'moral turpitude,' which may be used to impeach a witness.").

Ludwig v. State, 969 S.W.2d 22, 28 (Tex. App.—Fort Worth 1998, pet. ref'd) (evidence of defendant's prior misdemeanor convictions for violating order of protection properly used to impeach him where offenses involved moral turpitude).

Lape v. State, 893 S.W.2d 949, 955 (Tex. App.—Houston [14th Dist.] 1994, pet. ref'd) (evidence that a witness had made false reports of sexual abuse in the past regarding the same alleged victim should have been admissible, even though the conviction for false report was a misdemeanor).

Polk v. State, 865 S.W.2d 627, 630 (Tex. App.—Fort Worth 1993, pet. ref'd) (trial court did not abuse discretion allowing defendant to be impeached by evidence of conviction for misdemeanor indecent exposure where offense involved moral turpitude).

v. Context Evidence

Pollard v. State, 255 S.W.3d 184, 189 (Tex. App.—San Antonio 2008), *aff'd*, 277 S.W.3d 25 (Tex. Crim. App. 2009) ("[T]o determine whether contextual evidence is admissible, the [Court] first determines whether the evidence is directed at a consequential fact, thus making the evidence relevant.... If the evidence in question is relevant, the Court of Appeals next determines whether the evidence is admissible as an exception or 'other purpose' under Rule 404(b).").

Smith v. State, 316 S.W.3d 688, 698 (Tex. App.—Fort Worth 2010, pet. ref'd) ("same transaction contextual evidence" is evidence reflecting the context in which a criminal act occurred).

Smith v. State, 316 S.W.3d 688, 698 (Tex. App.—Fort Worth 2010, pet. ref'd) (use of same transaction contextual evidence "is a recognition that events do not occur in a vacuum, and a jury has a right to hear what occurred immediately before and after the offense in order to realistically evaluate the evidence").

Smith v. State, 316 S.W.3d 688, 698 (Tex. App.—Fort Worth 2010, pet. ref'd); *Pollard v. State*, 255 S.W.3d 184, 189 (Tex. App.—San Antonio 2008), *aff'd*, 277 S.W.3d 25 (Tex. Crim. App. 2009) (when several crimes are intermixed or connected and testimony regarding one crime cannot be given without showing the other crimes, or it would be impracticable to do so, the evidence may be deemed admissible as "same transaction contextual evidence").

Dickson v. State, 246 S.W.3d 733, 742 (Tex. App.—Houston [14th Dist.] 2007, pet. ref'd) ("[C]ontextual evidence is admissible when several offenses are so intermixed or connected as to form a single, indivisible criminal transaction, such that in narrating the one, it is impracticable to avoid describing the other.").

Dickson v. State, 246 S.W.3d 733, 742 (Tex. App.—Houston [14th Dist.] 2007, pet. ref'd) ("contextual evidence is admissible in a criminal prosecution only when an offense would make little or no sense without extraneous offense evidence").

Swarb v. State, 125 S.W.3d 672, 682 (Tex. App.—Houston [1st Dist.] 2003, pet. dism'd) (evidence of an arrest warrant for an extraneous offense was admissible as context evidence).

vi. Clarify False Impression

Lumsden v. State, 564 S.W.3d 858 (Tex. App.—Fort Worth 2018, pet. ref'd), cert. denied, 139 S.Ct. 2018 (2019) ("[A]n exception [to the preclusion of prior offense evidence] arises when a defendant testifies and leaves a false impression as to the extent of his prior arrests, convictions, charges against him, or 'trouble' with the police generally.... In such a case, the defendant is deemed to have 'opened the door' to an inquiry into the veracity of his testimony, and evidence of the defendant's prior criminal record is admissible to correct the false impression.").

Lumsden v. State, 564 S.W.3d 858 (Tex. App.—Fort Worth 2018, pet. ref'd), cert. denied, 139 S.Ct. 2018 (2019) ("[T]he false impression the State seeks to rebut [via prior offense evidence] must be created by the defendant through direct examination.... However, when a defendant voluntarily testifies on cross-examination concerning his prior criminal record, without any prompting or maneuvering on the part of the State, and in so doing leaves a false impression with the jury, the State is allowed to correct that false impression by introducing evidence of the defendant's prior criminal record.").

Lumsden v. State, 564 S.W.3d 858 (Tex. App.—Fort Worth 2018, pet. ref'd), cert. denied, 139 S.Ct. 2018, 204 L.Ed.2d 224 (2019) ("[I]f the 'opening door' testimony is volunteered by the defendant on cross-examination, it must be volunteered without any prompting or maneuvering by the State.").

Caldwell v. State, 356 S.W.3d 42, 50 (Tex. App.—Texarkana 2011, no pet.) ("[The] exception to the prohibition against impeachment through a prior conviction arises when the testimony of a witness during direct examination 'opens the door' or leaves a false impression with the jury as to the extent of the witness's prior arrests, convictions, charges, or trouble with the police.").

Caldwell v. State, 356 S.W.3d 42, 50 (Tex. App.—Texarkana 2011, no pet.) ("[I]n determining whether a false impression was created, [the court] must examine the testimony in context, rather than in a vacuum.").

Hernandez v. State, 351 S.W.3d 156, 160 (Tex. App.—Texarkana 2011, pet. ref'd) ("[A]s a general rule, specific acts of misconduct may not be introduced to impeach a party or a witness.... However, when a party produces evidence tending to create a false impression of his or her law-abiding behavior, he opens the door on his otherwise irrelevant past criminal history, and opposing counsel may introduce evidence tending to rebut the false impression.").

Grant v. State, 247 S.W.3d 360, 366 (Tex. App.—Austin 2008, pet. ref'd) (defendant "may open the door to an otherwise irrelevant criminal history when he creates a false impression of law-abiding behavior, allowing the State to expose the falsehood").

Grant v. State, 247 S.W.3d 360, 366 (Tex. App.—Austin 2008, pet. ref'd) ("[T]o open the door to the use of prior crimes for the purposes of impeachment, a witness must do more than just imply that he abides by the law, and must in some way convey the impression that he has never committed a crime.").

Grant v. State, 247 S.W.3d 360, 366 (Tex. App.—Austin 2008, pet. ref'd) ("[F]alse-impression exception [to the prohibition of the use of criminal convictions more than ten years old to impeach a witness] is a narrow one, and any statements that are alleged to have left a false impression must be viewed in context.").

Grant v. State, 247 S.W.3d 360, 366 (Tex. App.—Austin 2008, pet. ref'd) ("[I]n analyzing the applicability of the false-impression exception [to the prohibition of the use of criminal convictions more than ten years old to impeach a witness], reviewing courts consider the defendant's statement in relation to the question asked, examine how broadly the question asked could be interpreted, and analyze the relationship between the question asked and the major substantive issues in the trial.").

C. Motion to Exclude Character Evidence Used to Prove Conduct

1. Suggested Motion Text

(*Name of Moving Party*) hereby moves this Court for an order excluding any and all evidence, references to evidence, testimony, or argument relating to the character or trait of (*Name of Witness*) for (*Describe the Character or Trait Evidence at Issue, e.g., the Prior Arrest of Defendant for Possession of Marijuana*).

The motion is based upon the grounds that the character evidence is irrelevant to the issues in this case, is prohibited by Texas Rule of Evidence 404 to prove conduct and will create a substantial danger of undue prejudice to (*Name of Moving Party*).

2. Motion Summary

This motion is based on the express authority of Texas Rule of Evidence 404, which makes evidence of person's character or trait inadmissible when offered to prove his or her conduct on a specific occasion. *See In re L.R.*, 84 S.W.3d 701, 706 (Tex. App.—Houston [1st Dist.] 2002, no pet.).

3. Supporting Authorities

Gonzalez v. State, 544 S.W.3d 363, 371 (Tex. Crim. App. 2018) ("If evidence of prior bad acts is not relevant apart from supporting an inference of character conformity, it is absolutely inadmissible.")

Ex parte Martinez, 330 S.W.3d 891, 902 (Tex. Crim. App. 2011) (gang-related evidence tends to be irrelevant and prejudicial if not accompanied by testimony that puts the evidence into context).

Worthy v. State, 312 S.W.3d 34, 41 (Tex. Crim. App. 2010) (pretrial notice of same-transaction contextual evidence is not required under Article 37.07, § 3(g)).

Page v. State, 213 S.W.3d 332, 336 (Tex. Crim. App. 2006) (evidence of extraneous offense showed pattern of distinctive conduct).

Reighley v. State, 585 S.W.3d 98, 103 (Tex. App.—Amarillo 2019, pet. ref'd) ("[S]pecific instances of conduct may not be admitted to establish an inference that the accused did or did not commit the charged offense.").

Reighley v. State, 585 S.W.3d 98, 103-04 (Tex. App.—Amarillo 2019, pet. ref'd) ("[T]he status of being a murderer or a pedophile is not a 'character trait.'").

Griffis v. State, 441 S.W.3d 599, 609 (Tex. App.—San Antonio 2014, pet. ref'd), cert. denied, 136 S.Ct. 58 (2015) ("[C]ontextual evidence, or same-transaction evidence, is admissible only when the offense would make little or no sense without also bringing in that evidence, and it is admissible only to the extent that it is necessary to the jury's understanding of the offense.").

Smith v. State, 420 S.W.3d 207, 219 (Tex. App.—Houston [1st Dist.] 2013, pet. ref'd) (evidence of extraneous offenses is not admissible to prove the character of a person in order to show that he acted in conformity therewith).

Mason v. State, 416 S.W.3d 720, 740 (Tex. App.—Houston [14th Dist.] 2013, pet. ref'd) ("[E]xtraneous offense evidence is admissible under both Rules 404(b) and 403 if that evidence satisfies a two-prong test: whether the evidence is relevant to a fact of consequence in the case apart from its tendency to prove conduct in conformity with character and whether the probative value of the evidence is substantially outweighed by unfair prejudice.").

Newland v. State, 363 S.W.3d 205 (Tex. App.—Waco 2011, pet. ref'd) ("bolstering" is the introduction of evidence that the witness is believable without that evidence being relevant to the proceeding; thus, bolstering is generally prohibited).

Hernandez v. State, 351 S.W.3d 156, 160 (Tex. App.—Texarkana 2011, pet. ref'd) (a general rule is that specific acts of misconduct may not be introduced to impeach a party or a witness).

Haagensen v. State, 346 S.W.3d 758 (Tex. App.—Texarkana 2011, no pet.) (accused must be tried only for the offense charged; the accused may not be tried for a collateral crime or for being a criminal generally).

Barnett v. State, 344 S.W.3d 6 (Tex. App.—Texarkana 2011, pet. ref'd) (improper "bolstering" occurs when one item of evidence is improperly used by a party to add credence or weight to some earlier unimpeached piece of evidence offered by the same party).

Jackson v. State, 320 S.W.3d 873 (Tex. App.—Texarkana 2010, pet. ref'd) (accused must be tried only for the offense with which he or she is charged and may not be tried for a collateral crime or for being a criminal generally).

Jackson v. State, 320 S.W.3d 873 (Tex. App.—Texarkana 2010, pet. ref'd) (extraneous offense evidence is inherently prejudicial, tends to confuse the issues, and forces the accused to defend himself against charges not part of the present case against him).

Stafford v. State, 248 S.W.3d 400, 411 (Tex. App.—Beaumont 2008, pet. ref'd) (generally, evidence that does not have relevance apart from character conformity is inadmissible).

Biagas v. State, 177 S.W.3d 161 (Tex. App.—Houston [1st Dist.] 2005, pet. ref'd) (trial court did not err excluding evidence of defendant's reputation for truthfulness and honesty where proffered testimony included evidence of specific instances of conduct by defendant; character trait is not considered element of felony theft).

In re L.R., 84 S.W.3d 701, 706 (Tex. App.—Houston [1st Dist.] 2002, no pet.) (harmless error where evidence of a school record was improperly admitted suggesting a person acted in conformity with prior behaviors on the day of the charged incident).

Peters v. State, 93 S.W.3d 347 (Tex. App.—Houston [14th Dist.] 2002, pet. denied) (where only issue was consent to search in case involving possession of cocaine, trial court should not have admitted evidence of shotgun and marijuana found in room where evidence represented improper character evidence).

Tamez v. State, 48 S.W.3d 295 (Tex. App.—San Antonio 2001, no pet.) (in case involving driving while intoxicated, evidence that defendant had been convicted for same offense on six other occasions was improper and prejudicial where only two of convictions were necessary to raise offense to felony status and defendant had offered to stipulate to two prior convictions).

Lam v. State, 25 S.W.3d 233 (Tex. App.—San Antonio 2000, no pet.) (evidence of young girl's underwear and bra and pornographic videotape found in defendant's room represented impermissible character evidence and should not have been admitted in trial for murder and aggravated assault with a deadly weapon).

Coleman v. State, 935 S.W.2d 467 (Tex. App.—Tyler 1996, writ ref'd) (testimony of specific instances of provocative behavior by victim properly excluded by trial court where prosecution had not raised issue of victim's character and defendant's self-defense theory did not need proof of victim's character as essential element of theory).

Mack v. State, 928 S.W.2d 219, 225 (Tex. App.—Austin 1996, pet. ref'd) ("[E]vidence of the victim's peaceful character may only be offered in rebuttal to defense evidence that the victim was the first aggressor.").

Hilliard v. State, 881 S.W.2d 917, 921(Tex. App.—Fort Worth 1994, no pet.) (trial court erred admitting pictures of a victim's injuries from an assault when the defendant was charged with retaliation but not for the actual assault where the evidence was irrelevant and could allow the jury to convict based on conduct other than the charged conduct).

Serv. Lloyds Ins. Co. v. Martin, 855 S.W.2d 816 (Tex. App.—Dallas 1993, no writ) (trial court did not abuse discretion excluding evidence that party had lied on employment application where evidence was improper impeachment on a collateral issue and represented improper attempt to suggest party had bad character and was likely to have acted in conformity with that bad character in incident in question).

Rogers v. State, 853 S.W.2d 29 (Tex. Crim. App. 1993, writ dism'd) (evidence of defendant's use, possession, or sale of marijuana in case involving burglary and possession of methamphetamine improper character evidence and should not have been admitted).

Wiggins v. State, 778 S.W.2d 877, 885 (Tex. App.—Dallas 1989, writ ref'd) (harmless error to admit evidence of defendant's reputation for honesty where not relevant to charge of aggravated sexual assault).

Spector v. State, 746 S.W.2d 946 (Tex. App.—Austin 1988, writ ref'd) (evidence of defendant's character for truthfulness and honesty properly excluded in case involving possession of marijuana where traits not relevant to offense and prosecution had not impeached defendant with respect to those traits).

a. Care or Skill in Negligence Cases

Felix v. Gonzalez, 87 S.W.3d 574 (Tex. App.—San Antonio 2002, pet. denied) (trial court should not have admitted evidence of prior accident to suggest driver was negligent during incident in question).

Waldon v. City of Longview, 855 S.W.2d 875 (Tex. App.—Tyler 1993, no writ) (evidence of past accidents or negligence properly excluded where offered to suggest conduct in conformity with past acts during events in question).

Lovelace v. Sabine Consol., Inc., 733 S.W.2d 648 (Tex. App.—Houston [14th Dist.] 1987, writ denied) (evidence of past negligence not admissible to suggest negligence in incidents at issue).

b. Crimes Evidence

Lopez v. State, 253 S.W.3d 680 (Tex. Crim. App. 2008) (two extraneous drug offenses to which defendant had admitted guilt in a prior prosecution, and which, in the prior prosecution, had been taken into account when sentencing defendant for the primary offense and then had been dismissed, did not constitute prior "convictions," for purposes of impeachment of defendant in a subsequent prosecution).

Smith v. State, 420 S.W.3d 207, 219 (Tex. App.—Houston [1st Dist.] 2013, pet. ref'd) (to raise a defensive theory sufficient to open the door to the introduction of extraneous-offense evidence, cross-examination responses must undermine the State's testimony and effectively place in controversy a fact that testimony was offered to prove).

Mason v. State, 416 S.W.3d 720, 740 (Tex. App.—Houston [14th Dist.] 2013, pet. ref'd) ("[W]hen extraneous offense is introduced to prove identity by comparing common characteristics, it must be so similar to the charged offense that the offenses illustrate the defendant's distinctive and idiosyncratic manner of committing criminal acts.").

Jackson v. State, 320 S.W.3d 873 (Tex. App.—Texarkana 2010, pet. ref'd) (accused must be tried only for the offense with which he or she is charged and may not be tried for a collateral crime or for being a criminal generally).

Jackson v. State, 320 S.W.3d 873 (Tex. App.—Texarkana 2010, pet. ref'd) (extraneous offense evidence is inherently prejudicial, tends to confuse the issues, and forces the accused to defend himself against charges not part of the present case against him).

Dickson v. State, 246 S.W.3d 733, 742 (Tex. App.—Houston [14th Dist.] 2007, pet. ref'd) (raising the issue of identity in a criminal prosecution does not automatically render extraneous offenses admissible).

Booker v. State, 103 S.W.3d 521 (Tex. App.—Fort Worth 2003, pet. ref'd) (trial court did not abuse discretion determining other offenses sufficiently similar to demonstrate identity).

Hilliard v. State, 881 S.W.2d 917, 921 (Tex. App.—Fort Worth 1994, no pet.) (the trial court erred admitting pictures of a victim's injuries from an assault when the defendant was charged with retaliation but not for actual assault where the evidence was irrelevant and could allow the jury to convict based on conduct other than the charged conduct).

c. *Other grounds*
- Collateral to issues in case;
- Confusing or misleading;
- Solely intended to create an emotional bias;
- Improper impeachment evidence;
- Improper felony conviction;
- Inadmissible hearsay.

4. Opposing Authorities

Booker v. State, 103 S.W.3d 521, 530 (Tex. App.—Fort Worth 2003, pet. ref'd) (trial court's decision whether other crimes sufficiently similar to prove identity entitled to deference and should be upheld if "within the zone of reasonable disagreement"). *See also Murray v. State*, 840 S.W.2d 675, 678 (Tex. App.—Tyler 1992, no writ) (trial court's decision to admit or exclude evidence of other offenses should be upheld as long as within "zone of reasonable disagreement").

Daggett v. State, 103 S.W.3d 444, 447 (Tex. App.—San Antonio 2002) *vacated on other grounds*, 187 S.W.3d 444 (Tex. Crim. App. 2005) (appellate court review of trial court's decision to admit evidence of other crimes or wrongs reviewed for abuse of discretion).

a. *Relevant to Material Issue*

Texas Rule of Evidence 404 states:

> (a) **Character Evidence.**
> (1) *Prohibited Uses.* **Evidence** of a person's character or character trait is not admissible to prove that on a particular occasion the person acted in accordance with the character or trait.
> (2) *Exceptions for an Accused.*
> (A) In a criminal case, a defendant may offer **evidence** of the defendant's pertinent trait, and if the **evidence** is admitted, the prosecutor may offer **evidence** to rebut it.
> (B) In a civil case, a party accused of conduct involving moral turpitude may offer **evidence** of the party's pertinent trait, and if the **evidence** is admitted, the accusing party may offer evidence to rebut it.
> (3) *Exceptions for a Victim.*
> (A) In a criminal case, subject to the limitations in **Rule** 412, a defendant may offer **evidence** of a victim's pertinent trait, and if the **evidence** is admitted, the prosecutor may offer **evidence** to rebut it.
> (B) In a homicide case, the prosecutor may offer **evidence** of the victim's trait of peacefulness to rebut **evidence** that the victim was the first aggressor.
> (C) In a civil case, a party accused of assaultive conduct may offer **evidence** of the victim›s trait of violence to prove

self-defense, and if the **evidence** is admitted, the accusing party may offer **evidence** of the victim›s trait of peacefulness.

(4) *Exceptions for a Witness.* **Evidence** of a witness's character may be admitted under **Rules** 607, 608, and 609.

(5) *Definition of "Victim."* In this **rule**, "victim" includes an alleged victim.

(b) **Crimes, Wrongs, or Other Acts**.

(1) *Prohibited Uses.* **Evidence** of a crime, wrong, or other act is not admissible to prove a person's character in order to show that on a particular occasion the person acted in accordance with the character.

(2) *Permitted Uses; Notice in Criminal Case.* This **evidence** may be admissible for another purpose, such as proving motive, opportunity, intent, preparation, plan, knowledge, identity, absence of mistake, or lack of accident. On timely request by a defendant in a criminal case, the prosecutor must provide reasonable notice before trial that the prosecution intends to introduce such **evidence**—other than that arising in the same transaction—in its case-in-chief.

Dabney v. State, 492 S.W.3d 309, 317 (Tex. Crim. App. 2016) ("Rule 404(b) is a rule of inclusion rather than exclusion—it excludes only evidence that is offered solely for proving bad character and conduct in conformity with that bad character.").

Billodeau v. State, 277 S.W.3d 34, 42 (Tex. Crim. App. 2009) ("[P]ossible animus, motive, or ill will of a prosecution witness who testifies against a defendant is never a collateral or irrelevant inquiry, and the defendant is entitled, subject to reasonable restrictions, to show any relevant fact that might tend to establish ill feeling, bias, motive, interest, or animus on the part of any witness testifying against him.").

Page v. State, 213 S.W.3d 332, 336 (Tex. Crim. App. 2006) ("[E]xtraneous offense evidence is admissible to prove identity when the common characteristics of each offense are so unusual as to act as the defendant's 'signature' ... the 'signature' must be apparent from a comparison of the circumstances in both cases.").

Page v. State, 213 S.W.3d 332, 336 (Tex. Crim. App. 2006) ("[F]acts of extraneous offenses showed a pattern of conduct sufficiently distinctive to constitute a 'signature,' a distinctive and idiosyncratic manner of committing criminal acts, and thereby qualif[ied] as an exception to the general rule precluding the admission of extraneous-offense evidence.").

Reighley v. State, 585 S.W.3d 98, 105 (Tex. App.—Amarillo 2019, pet. ref'd) ("[Rule 404(b)] allows evidence of other crimes, wrongs, or acts if the evidence has relevance apart from character conformity.... Some examples of relevance apart from character conformity include intent, absence of mistake, or lack of accident.... Uses such as mistake and accident are admissible in rebuttal of a defensive theory.").

Green v. State, 589 S.W.3d 250, 258 (Tex. App.—Houston [14th Dist.] 2019, pet. ref'd) ("[I]n a case ... in which the defendant adduces evidence of self-defense, the defendant may offer evidence of the victim's reputation, opinion testimony, and evidence of specific prior acts of violence by the victim to show the reasonableness of the defendant's claim of apprehension of danger from the victim.... This is called 'communicated character' because the defendant is aware of the victim's violent tendencies and perceives a danger posed by the victim, regardless of whether the danger is real or not.").

Green v. State, 589 S.W.3d 250, 258 (Tex. App.—Houston [14th Dist.] 2019, pet. ref'd) ("communicated character evidence in the form of the victim's specific acts of violence is admissible under Rule 404 to show the defendant's state of mind").

Griffis v. State, 441 S.W.3d 599, 609 (Tex. App.—San Antonio 2014, pet. ref'd), cert. denied, 136 S.Ct. 58 (2015) (because the jury is entitled to hear relevant surrounding facts and the circumstances of the charged offense, some extraneous misconduct evidence is admissible).

Smith v. State, 420 S.W.3d 207, 219 (Tex. App.—Houston [1st Dist.] 2013, pet. ref'd) (evidence of extraneous offenses may be admissible for purposes of establishing proof of motive, opportunity, intent, preparation, plan, knowledge, identity, or absence of mistake or accident).

Smith v. State, 420 S.W.3d 207, 219 (Tex. App.—Houston [1st Dist.] 2013, pet. ref'd); Mason v. State, 416 S.W.3d 720, 740 (Tex. App.—Houston [14th Dist.] 2013, pet. ref'd) (extraneous-offense evidence is admissible to rebut a defensive theory as when raised in an opening statement or through the cross-examination of the State's witnesses).

Smith v. State, 420 S.W.3d 207, 219 (Tex. App.—Houston [1st Dist.] 2013, pet. ref'd) ("[I]ntent can be characterized as a contested issue for purposes of justifying the admission of extraneous offense evidence if the required intent for the primary offense cannot be inferred from the act itself or if the defendant presents evidence to rebut the inference that the required intent existed.").

Smith v. State, 420 S.W.3d 207, 219 (Tex. App.—Houston [1st Dist.] 2013, pet. ref'd) ("[I]ntent is most clearly in issue when the defendant argues that the charged offense was unintentional or the result of an accident.").

Smith v. State, 420 S.W.3d 207, 221 (Tex. App.—Houston [1st Dist.] 2013, pet. ref'd) ("[W]hen extraneous evidence is offered on the issue of intent ... there is less need to show significant similarity between the facts of the other incidents and those of the case being tried.... The degree of similarity simply need not be as great if offered to prove the issue of intent.").

Mason v. State, 416 S.W.3d 720, 740 (Tex. App.—Houston [14th Dist.] 2013, pet. ref'd) (extraneous-offense evidence may be admissible when a defendant raises a defensive issue that negates one of the elements of the offense).

Mason v. State, 416 S.W.3d 720, 740 (Tex. App.—Houston [14th Dist.] 2013, pet. ref'd) ("[A] party may introduce evidence of other crimes, wrongs, or acts if such evidence logically serves to make more or less probable an elemental fact, an evidentiary fact that inferentially leads to an elemental fact, or defensive evidence that undermines an elemental fact.").

Mason v. State, 416 S.W.3d 720, 740 (Tex. App.—Houston [14th Dist.] 2013, pet. ref'd) ("[C]ross examination places identity at issue if it implies the witness's identification of the defendant is not trustworthy.").

Mason v. State, 416 S.W.3d 720, 740 (Tex. App.—Houston [14th Dist.] 2013, pet. ref'd) ("[W]hen extraneous offense is introduced to prove identity by comparing common characteristics, it must be so similar to the charged offense that the offenses illustrate the defendant's distinctive and idiosyncratic manner of committing criminal acts.... Such extraneous offense evidence is admissible to prove identity when the common characteristics of each offense are so unusual as to act as the defendant's 'signature.'").

Agbogwe v. State, 414 S.W.3d 820, 836 (Tex. App.—Houston [1st Dist.] 2013, no pet.) ("[A]bsent a request for notice [of intent to introduce evidence of other bad acts] under Rule 404(b), the State is not required to give such notice.").

Agbogwe v. State, 414 S.W.3d 820, 836 (Tex. App.—Houston [1st Dist.] 2013, no pet.) ("Rule 404(b) does not expressly require the State to provide written notice of its intent to introduce evidence of extraneous misconduct.").

McGregor v. State, 394 S.W.3d 90, 118 (Tex. App.—Houston [1st Dist.] 2012, pet. ref'd) ("[W]hen the extraneous offense is introduced to prove identity by comparing common characteristics, it must be so similar to the charged offense that the offenses illustrate the defendant's distinctive and idiosyncratic manner of committing criminal acts.").

McGregor v. State, 394 S.W.3d 90, 118 (Tex. App.—Houston [1st Dist.] 2012, pet. ref'd) ("[E]xtraneous offense evidence is admissible to prove identity when the common characteristics of each offense are so unusual as to act as the defendant's signature.... The signature must be apparent from a comparison of the circumstances in both cases.").

Gomez v. State, 380 S.W.3d 830, 835 n.8 (Tex. App.—Houston [14th Dist] 2012, pet. ref'd) (evidence of other crimes or misconduct may be admissible as proof of motive, opportunity, intent, preparation, plan, knowledge, identity, or absence of mistake or accident).

Desormeaux v. State, 362 S.W.3d 233, 238 (Tex. App.—Beaumont 2012, no pet.) ("'[S]ame transaction contextual evidence' is evidence that imparts to the trier of fact information essential to understanding the context and circumstances of events which, although legally separate offenses, are blended or interwoven.").

Hidrogo v. State, 352 S.W.3d 27, 31 (Tex. App.—Eastland 2011, pet. ref'd) ("[W]hen identity is an issue ... extraneous offense evidence may be admitted to prove identity if the extraneous offense is so similar to the offense at issue that the offenses are marked as the accused's handiwork.").

Hidrogo v. State, 352 S.W.3d 27, 31 (Tex. App.—Eastland 2011, pet. ref'd) ("[S]ufficient similarity of an extraneous offense to a charged offense may be shown by proximity in time and place or by a common mode of committing the offenses.").

Smith v. State, 337 S.W.3d 354, 360 (Tex. App.—Eastland 2011), *aff'd sub nom. Watson v. State,* 369 S.W.3d 865 (Tex. Crim. App. 2012) ("[A] dog's prior bad acts were admissible to show that the dog's attack in this case was unprovoked and also, to the extent that appellant knew of the dog's prior bad acts, to show that appellant acted with criminal negligence in failing to secure the dog.").

Stine v. State, 300 S.W.3d 52, 59 (Tex. App.—Texarkana 2009, pet. dism'd) (to be admissible as extraneous-offense evidence, "the statement must have reflected a crime or bad act to which [the defendant] was connected").

Thomas v. State, 226 S.W.3d 697, 702 (Tex. App.—Corpus Christi 2007, pet. dism'd) (evidence of a party's other crimes, wrongs, or acts is admissible to show a plan or scheme).

Booker v. State, 103 S.W.3d 521, 530 (Tex. App.—Fort Worth 2003, pet. ref'd) (trial court did not abuse discretion determining that other offenses sufficiently similar to demonstrate identity; note that appellate court held one of prior offenses should have been excluded under Rule 403 balancing test).

Brown v. State, 96 S.W.3d 508, 511 (Tex. App.—Austin 2002, no pet.) (evidence of other sexual assaults properly admitted to demonstrate intent and lack of consent).

Daggett v. State, 103 S.W.3d 444, 448 (Tex. App.—San Antonio 2002), *vacated*, 187 S.W.3d 444 (Tex. Crim. App. 2005) (evidence of prior acts of sexual abuse admissible to demonstrate common scheme or plan).

Ludwig v. State, 969 S.W.2d 22, 28 (Tex. App.—Fort Worth 1998, pet. ref'd) (evidence of defendant's prior misdemeanor convictions for violating order of protection properly used to prove intent).

Murray v. State, 840 S.W.2d 675, 678 (Tex. App.—Tyler 1992, no writ) (evidence of drug paraphernalia relevant to rebut defendant's claim of intoxication by accidentally inhaling gas fumes at time of offense).

Vasquez v. State, 814 S.W.2d 773, 776 (Tex. App.—Houston [14th Dist.] 1991, writ ref'd) (evidence of unrelated thefts and robberies admissible to demonstrate identity and plan).

Wiggins v. State, 778 S.W.2d 877, 885 (Tex. App.—Dallas 1989, writ ref'd) (evidence of defendant's prior sexual assault relevant to demonstrate intent and lack of consent).

> *Note: Rule 404 is limited by a trial court's discretion to exclude probative but prejudicial evidence under Texas Rule of Evidence 403.* See Booker v. State, *103 S.W.3d 521, 530 (Tex. App.—Fort Worth 2003, pet. ref'd).*

b. *Witness Impeachment*

Williamson v. State, 356 S.W.3d 1, 22 (Tex. App.—Houston [1st Dist.] 2010, pet. ref'd) ("Rule 404(b) is a rule of inclusion rather than exclusion. The rule excludes only that evidence that is offered or will be used solely for the purpose of proving bad character and hence conduct in conformity with that bad character.").

Fox v. State, 115 S.W.3d 550, 568 (Tex. App.—Houston [14th Dist.] 2002, pet. ref'd) (evidence that witness had extra-marital affair proper to demonstrate witness's bias).

Hilliard v. State, 881 S.W.2d 917, 921 (Tex. App.—Fort Worth 1994, no pet.) (defendant should have been permitted to impeach witness with evidence of prior bad act by her son where the incident was relevant to suggest witness bias).

Bituminous Cas. Corp. v. Martin, 478 S.W.2d 206, 209 (Tex. Civ. App.—El Paso 1972, writ ref'd n.r.e.) (witness may be impeached by evidence that witness was drunk at time of events in question).

Russell v. State, 84 Tex.Crim. 245, 250, 209 S.W. 671 (Tex. Crim. App. 1919) (impeachment evidence that defendant intoxicated at time of events proper).

c. Trait at Issue

Texas Rule of Evidence 404(a) expressly allows for the introduction of character trait evidence and provides in pertinent part:

> (1) *Character of accused.* Evidence of a pertinent character trait offered:
>   (A) by an accused in a criminal case, or by the prosecution to rebut the same, or
>   (B) by a party accused in a civil case of conduct involving moral turpitude, or by the accusing party to rebut the same.
> (2) *Character of victim.* In a criminal case and subject to Rule 412, evidence of a pertinent character trait of the victim of the crime offered by an accused or by the prosecution to rebut the same, or evidence of peaceable character of the victim offered by the prosecution in a homicide case to rebut evidence that the victim was the first aggressor; or in a civil case, evidence of character for violence of the alleged victim of assaultive conduct offered on the issue of self-defense by a party accused of the assaultive conduct, or evidence of peaceable character to rebut the same....

Texas Rule of Evidence 405 states:

> (a) **Reputation or Opinion**. In all cases in which evidence of a person's character or character trait is admissible, proof may be made by testimony as to reputation or by testimony in the form of an opinion. In a criminal case, to be qualified to testify at the guilt stage of trial concerning the character or character trait of an accused, a witness must have been familiar with the reputation, or with the underlying facts or information upon which the opinion is based, prior to the day of the offense. In all cases where testimony is admitted under this rule, on cross-examination inquiry is allowable into relevant specific instances of conduct.
> (b) **Specific Instances of Conduct**. In cases in which a person's character or character trait is an essential element of a charge, claim or defense, proof may also be made of specific instances of that person's conduct.

Reighley v. State, 585 S.W.3d 98, 103 (Tex. App.—Amarillo 2019, pet. ref'd) ("If evidence of a person's character or character trait is admissible, proof may be made through reputation or opinion testimony.").

Reighley v. State, 585 S.W.3d 98, 103 (Tex. App.—Amarillo 2019, pet. ref'd) ("[I]n a prosecution for a crime of violence, the defendant's character for peacefulness is relevant because evidence establishing that a defendant possesses a peaceful character makes it less likely that he committed the crime charged.").

Reighley v. State, 585 S.W.3d 98, 103 (Tex. App.—Amarillo 2019, pet. ref'd) ("A defendant's reputation for peacefulness or non-aggressive behavior is an appropriate inquiry in a murder prosecution.").

Reighley v. State, 585 S.W.3d 98, 103 (Tex. App.—Amarillo 2019, pet. ref'd) ("[A] defendant charged with sexual assault of a child is entitled to offer evidence of his good character for moral and safe relations with small children or young girls.").

Burke v. State, 371 S.W.3d 252, 261 (Tex. App.—Houston [1st Dist.] 2011, pet. ref'd, untimely filed) ("The right of a party to cross-examine a character witness on specific instances of conduct is subject to certain limitations.... First, the incidents inquired about must be relevant to the character traits at issue.... Second, the alleged bad act must have a basis in fact.").

Burke v. State, 371 S.W.3d 252, 261 (Tex. App.—Houston [1st Dist.] 2011, pet. ref'd, untimely filed) ("[T]he foundation for inquiring into the specific instances of conduct should be laid outside the jury's presence so that the judge will have an opportunity to rule on the propriety of asking them.... Specific instances should not, however, be proven before the jury.").

Smith v. State, 337 S.W.3d 354, 360 (Tex. App.—Eastland 2011), *aff'd sub nom. Watson v. State,* 369 S.W.3d 865 (Tex. Crim. App. 2012) ("[The] dog's prior bad acts were admissible to show that the dog's attack in this case was unprovoked and also, to the extent that appellant knew of the dog's prior bad acts, to show that appellant acted with criminal negligence in failing to secure the dog.").

Stafford v. State, 248 S.W.3d 400, 411 (Tex. App.—Beaumont 2008, pet. ref'd) (witness's testimony describing defendant as impatient, anxious, angry, aggravated, and controlling toward his wife, murder victim, was within purview of rule on admissibility of evidence of other crimes, wrongs, or acts).

Wade v. State, 803 S.W.2d 806, 807 (Tex. App.—Fort Worth 1991, no pet.) (harmless error not allowing defendant to introduce witness testimony that he had never seen defendant possess drugs where testimony represented evidence of pertinent trait for charged offense).

d. *Permitted by Statute*

Article 38.37 of the Texas Code of Criminal Procedure states:

> Sec. 1. This article applies to a proceeding in the prosecution of a defendant for an offense under the following provisions of the Penal Code, if committed against a child under 17 years of age:
>
> (1) Chapter 21 (Sexual Offenses);
> (2) Chapter 22 (Assaultive Offenses);
> (3) Section 25.02 (Prohibited Sexual Conduct);
> (4) Section 43.25 (Sexual Performance by a Child) or

(5) an attempt or conspiracy to commit an offense listed in this section.

Sec. 2. *Notwithstanding Rules 404 and 405, Texas Rules of Criminal Evidence, evidence of other crimes, wrongs, or acts committed by the defendant against the child who is the victim of the alleged offense shall be admitted for its bearing on relevant matters, including:*

(1) *the state of mind of the defendant and the child; and*
(2) *the previous and subsequent relationship between the defendant and the child.*

Sec. 3. On timely request by the defendant, the state shall give the defendant notice of the state's intent to introduce in the case in chief evidence described by Section 2 in the same manner as the state is required to give notice under Rule 404(b), Texas Rules of Criminal Evidence.

Sec. 4. This article does not limit the admissibility of evidence of extraneous crimes, wrongs, or acts under any other applicable law. (Emphasis added.)

Gutierrez v. State, 585 S.W.3d 599, 612 (Tex. App.—Houston [14th Dist.] 2019, no pet.) ("Section 2 of [article 38.37] makes admissible evidence that the defendant has committed a separate offense listed in the statute against any person for any bearing the evidence has on relevant matters, including the character of the defendant and acts performed in conformity with the character of the defendant.... A defendant's possession of child pornography is one of the listed offenses that may be admissible under Section 2.... The list of offenses does not include public lewdness or any other offense that might include the possession of bestiality pornography involving adults.").

Gutierrez v. State, 585 S.W.3d 599, 612 (Tex. App.—Houston [14th Dist.] 2019, no pet.) ("Before evidence of an offense listed in [article 38.37] Section 2 may be introduced, the trial court must conduct a hearing outside the presence of the jury to determine whether the evidence likely to be admitted at trial will be adequate to support a finding by the jury that the defendant committed the separate offense beyond a reasonable doubt.... Furthermore, the State must give the defendant notice of the State's intent to introduce evidence under Article 38.37 before trial.").

Distefano v. State, 532 S.W.3d 25, 31 (Tex. App.—Houston [14th Dist.] 2016, pet. ref'd) ("When evidence of a defendant's extraneous acts is relevant under article 38.37, the trial court still is required to conduct a Rule 403 balancing test upon proper objection or request.").

Lara v. State, 513 S.W.3d 135, 141 (Tex. App.—Houston [14th Dist.] 2016, no pet.) (article 38.37 "supersedes application of Rule 404(b), making admissible extraneous offense evidence that Rule 404(b) does not").

Lara v. State, 513 S.W.3d 135, 141 (Tex. App.—Houston [14th Dist.] 2016, no pet.) ("[A]rticle 38.37 allows the jury to consider that evidence's bearing on 'relevant matters,' including the state of mind of the defendant and the child, the previous and subsequent relationship between the defendant and the child, and the character of the defendant and acts performed in conformity with the character of the defendant.").

Alvarez v. State, 491 S.W.3d 362, 367 (Tex. App.—Houston [1st Dist.] 2016, pet. ref'd) ("In the context of sexual assault of a child … the special circumstances surrounding the sexual assault of a child victim outweigh normal concerns associated with evidence of extraneous acts.").

Alvarez v. State, 491 S.W.3d 362, 367 (Tex. App.—Houston [1st Dist.] 2016, pet. ref'd) ("Under Article 38.37, the State is allowed to provide evidence of other children who the defendant has sexually assaulted for any bearing the evidence has on relevant matters, including the character of the defendant and acts performed in conformity with the character of the defendant.").

Alvarez v. State, 491 S.W.3d 362, 367 (Tex. App.—Houston [1st Dist.] 2016, pet. ref'd) ("Before [article 38.37] evidence is admitted … the defendant is protected by "numerous procedural safeguards.… First, the State must give the defendant 30 days' notice of its intent to introduce the evidence.… Second, the trial court must conduct a hearing out of the jury's presence to determine that the evidence likely to be admitted will support a jury finding that the defendant committed the separate offense beyond a reasonable doubt.").

D. Motion to Exclude Evidence of Prior Felony Conviction

1. Suggested Motion Text

(*Name of Moving Party*) hereby moves this Court for an order excluding any and all evidence, references to evidence, testimony, or argument relating to a prior felony conviction by (*Name of Witness*) for (*Describe Nature of Conviction*) that occurred on or about (*Date of Conviction*). The motion is based upon the grounds that the probative value of the evidence is substantially outweighed by the risk of undue prejudice to (*Name of Moving Party*) and therefore should be excluded.

2. Motion Summary

This motion is used to exclude inadmissible evidence of felony convictions. While Texas Rule of Evidence 609(a) expressly allows the use of felony convictions to impeach the credibility of a witness, this section also provides that the evidence can be admitted only if "the court determines that the probative value of admitting this evidence outweighs its prejudicial effect to a party." *Garcia v. State*, 150 S.W.3d 598, 616 (Tex. App.—San Antonio 2004), *rev'd on other grounds*, 201 S.W.3d 695 (Tex. Crim. App. 2006), *cert. denied*, 549 U.S. 1224 (2007); *Booker v. State*, 103 S.W.3d 521, 530 (Tex. App.—Fort Worth 2003, pet. ref'd).

3. Supporting Authorities

Evidence of other crimes may also be excluded under Texas Rule of Evidence 404(b), which states:

(b) **Other Crimes, Wrongs or Acts.** *Evidence of other crimes, wrongs or acts is not admissible to prove the character of a person* *in order to show action in conformity therewith.* It may, however, be admissible for other purposes, such as proof of motive, opportunity, intent, preparation, plan, knowledge, identity, or absence of mistake or accident, provided that upon timely request by the accused in a criminal case, reasonable notice is given in advance of trial of intent to introduce in the State's case-in-chief such evidence other than that arising in the same transaction. (Emphasis added.)

Evidence of crimes may be excluded where used for purposes other than to impeach the witness, such as to prove one's disposition to commit a similar crime or to show "bad moral character." *See Garcia v. State*, 150 S.W.3d 598, 616 (Tex. App.—San Antonio 2004), *rev'd on other grounds*, 201 S.W.3d 695 (Tex. Crim. App. 2006), *cert. denied*, 549 U.S. 1224 (2007) (evidence of prior "car dumping" incident between defendant and his wife, with defendant stopping the car, pushing wife out of the car, and driving away, was admissible as prior bad act evidence, in prosecution of defendant for murdering wife, for purpose of illustrating the nature and circumstances of their relationship immediately before the murder, i.e., that they had separated, had attempted to reconcile, and had sought marriage counseling, but instead were in the process of divorcing).

In addition, other crime evidence may be excluded under subdivisions (b) through (f) of Texas Rule of Evidence 609, which state:

> (b) **Time Limit.** Evidence of a conviction under this rule is not admissible if a period of more than ten years has elapsed since the date of the conviction or of the release of the witness from the confinement imposed for that conviction, whichever is the later date, unless the court determines, in the interests of justice, that the probative value of the conviction supported by specific facts and circumstances substantially outweighs its prejudicial effect.
>
> (c) **Effect of Pardon, Annulment, or Certificate of Rehabilitation.** Evidence of a conviction is not admissible under this rule if:
>   (1) based on the finding of the rehabilitation of the person convicted, the conviction has been the subject of a pardon, annulment, certificate of rehabilitation, or other equivalent procedure, and that person has not been convicted of a subsequent crime which was classified as a felony or involved moral turpitude, regardless of punishment;
>   (2) probation has been satisfactorily completed for the crime for which the person was convicted, and that person has not been convicted of a subsequent crime which was classified as a felony or involved moral turpitude, regardless of punishment; or
>   (3) based on a finding of innocence, the conviction has been the subject of a pardon, annulment, or other equivalent procedure.
>
> (d) **Juvenile Adjudications.** Evidence of juvenile adjudications is not admissible, except for proceedings conducted pursuant to Title III, Family Code, in which the witness is a party, under this

rule unless required to be admitted by the Constitution of the United States or Texas.

(e) **Pendency of Appeal**. Pendency of an appeal renders evidence of a conviction inadmissible.

(f) **Notice**. Evidence of a conviction is not admissible if after timely written request by the adverse party specifying the witness or witnesses, the proponent fails to give to the adverse party sufficient advance written notice of intent to use such evidence to provide the adverse party with a fair opportunity to contest the use of such evidence.

a. Balancing Prejudicial Effect of Felony Evidence

McGregor v. State, 394 S.W.3d 90, 118 (Tex. App.—Houston [1st Dist.] 2012, pet. ref'd) ("[W]ithout a high degree of similarity, the probative value of the extraneous offense evidence is outweighed by its prejudicial effect.... Sufficient similarity may be shown by proximity in time and place or by a common mode of committing the offenses.").

Huerta v. State, 359 S.W.3d 887, 894 (Tex. App.—Houston [14th Dist.] 2012, no pet.) (when weighing the probative value of a conviction against its prejudicial effect, a court "considers the following set of nonexclusive factors: (1) the impeachment value of the prior crime, (2) the proximity of the past crime relative to the charged offense and the witness's subsequent history, (3) the similarity between the past crime and the offense being prosecuted, (4) the importance of the defendant's testimony, and (5) the importance of the credibility issue").

Perry v. State, 236 S.W.3d 859, 865 (Tex. App.—Texarkana 2007, no pet.) ("unfair prejudice," as used in the rule providing that evidence may be excluded if its probative value is substantially outweighed by the danger of unfair prejudice, refers to a tendency to suggest a decision on an improper basis, commonly, though not necessarily, an emotional one).

Hankins v. State, 180 S.W.3d 177 (Tex. App.—Austin 2005, pet. ref'd) (probative value of evidence of defendant's prior felony conviction for manufacture and distribution of cannabis did not substantially outweigh its prejudicial effect, as required for evidence to be admissible for impeachment purposes in assault trial).

Garcia v. State, 150 S.W.3d 598, 616 (Tex. App.—San Antonio 2004), *rev'd on other grounds,* 201 S.W.3d 695 (Tex. Crim. App. 2006), *cert. denied,* 549 U.S. 1224 (2007) (evidence of prior "car dumping" incident between defendant and his wife, with defendant stopping the car, pushing wife out of the car, and driving away, was admissible as prior bad act evidence, in prosecution of defendant for murdering wife, for purpose of illustrating the nature and circumstances of their relationship immediately before the murder, i.e., that they had separated, had attempted to reconcile, and had sought marriage counseling, but instead were in the process of divorcing).

Booker v. State, 103 S.W.3d 521, 530 (Tex. App.—Fort Worth 2003, pet. ref'd) (trial court did not abuse discretion determining other offenses were sufficiently similar to demonstrate identity; note that appellate court held one of prior offenses should have been excluded under Rule 403 balancing test as unduly prejudicial, confusing, and time-consuming).

b. Disposition to Commit Crime

Garcia v. State, 150 S.W.3d 598, 616 (Tex. App.—San Antonio 2004), *rev'd on other grounds*, 201 S.W.3d 695 (Tex. Crim. App. 2006), *cert. denied*, 549 U.S. 1224 (2007) (trial court erred allowing evidence regarding defendant's prior offense where prior offense not sufficiently similar to charged offense and evidence could lead jury to convict defendant based on belief he was bad person).

Enriquez v. State, 56 S.W.3d 596, 601 (Tex. App.—Corpus Christi 2001, pet. ref'd) (trial court erred admitting three prior drug-related convictions where evidence could allow jury to convict defendant based upon propensity to commit offense).

c. Must Reflect on Credibility

Theus v. State, 845 S.W.2d 874, 877 (Tex. Crim. App. 1992, writ denied) (defendant's prior arson conviction did not have bearing on the issue of credibility in case involving possession and delivery of a controlled substance and was more prejudicial than probative and thus, should have been excluded when offered as impeachment).

d. Exclusion of Improper Character Evidence

Texas Rule of Evidence 608(a) states:

> The credibility of a witness may be attacked or supported by evidence in the form of opinion or reputation, but subject to these limitations: (1) the evidence may refer only to character for truthfulness or untruthfulness; and (2) evidence of truthful character is admissible only after the character of the witness for truthfulness has been attacked by opinion or reputation evidence or otherwise.

Texas Rule of Evidence 608(b) states:

> Specific instances of the conduct of a witness, for the purpose of attacking or supporting the witness' credibility, other than conviction of crime as provided in Rule 609, may not be inquired into on cross-examination of the witness nor proved by extrinsic evidence.

Smith v. State, 436 S.W.3d 353, 375 (Tex. App.—Houston [14th Dist.] 2014, pet. ref'd) (fact of prior conviction is generally admissible to impeach a witness, but details of conviction are generally inadmissible for purposes of impeachment).

Garcia v. State, 150 S.W.3d 598, 616 (Tex. App.—San Antonio 2004), *rev'd on other grounds*, 201 S.W.3d 695 (Tex. Crim. App. 2006), *cert. denied*, 549 U.S. 1224 (2007) (trial court erred allowing evidence regarding defendant's prior offense where prior offense not sufficiently similar to charged offense and evidence could lead jury to convict defendant based on belief he was bad person).

Enriquez v. State, 56 S.W.3d 596, 601 (Tex. App.—Corpus Christi 2001, pet. ref'd) (trial court erred admitting three prior drug-related convictions where evidence could allow jury to convict defendant based upon propensity to commit offense).

e. Other Grounds

See the following sections for other possible grounds to support a motion to exclude crimes evidence:

- Collateral to issues in case;
- Confusing or misleading;
- Solely intended to create an emotional bias;
- Irrelevant;
- Inadmissible character evidence used to impeach witness;
- Inadmissible character evidence used to prove conduct;
- Inadmissible hearsay;
- Statute violation;
- Prior D.W.I.

4. *Opposing Authorities*

Texas Rule of Evidence 609 (a) states:

> (a) **General Rule**. For the purpose of attacking the credibility of a witness, evidence that the witness has been convicted of a crime shall be admitted if elicited from the witness or established by public record but only if the crime was a felony or involved moral turpitude, regardless of punishment, and the court determines that the probative value of admitting this evidence outweighs its prejudicial effect to a party.

Murray v. Tex. Dep't of Family & Protect. Servs., 294 S.W.3d 360, 370 (Tex. App.—Austin 2009, no pet.) (evidence of use of illegal drugs and of prior convictions properly allowed as evidence regarding the best interests of a child).

Polk v. State, 865 S.W.2d 627, 630 (Tex. App.—Fort Worth 1993, pet. ref'd) (trial court did not abuse discretion allowing evidence of old murder conviction to impeach defendant, over defendant's objection that remote in time).

But see Texas Rule of Evidence 609(b) through (f) for exceptions to Rule 609(a)'s general rule.

a. *Texas Code of Criminal Procedure Art. 38.37*

Article 38.37 of the Texas Code of Criminal Procedure states:

> Sec. 1. This article applies to a proceeding in the prosecution of a defendant for an offense under the following provisions of the Penal Code, if committed against a child under 17 years of age:
>
> (1) Chapter 21 (Sexual Offenses);
> (2) Chapter 22 (Assaultive Offenses);
> (3) Section 25.02 (Prohibited Sexual Conduct);
> (4) Section 43.25 (Sexual Performance by a Child); or

(5) an attempt or conspiracy to commit an offense listed in this section.

Sec. 2. *Notwithstanding Rules 404 and 405, Texas Rules of Criminal Evidence, evidence of other crimes, wrongs, or acts committed by the defendant against the child who is the victim of the alleged offense shall be admitted for its bearing on relevant matters, including*:

(1) the state of mind of the defendant and the child; and
(2) *the previous and subsequent relationship between the defendant and the child.*

Sec. 3. On timely request by the defendant, the state shall give the defendant notice of the state's intent to introduce in the case in chief evidence described by Section 2 in the same manner as the state is required to give notice under Rule 404(b), Texas Rules of Criminal Evidence.

Sec. 4. This article does not limit the admissibility of evidence of extraneous crimes, wrongs, or acts under any other applicable law. (Emphasis added.)

b. *Moral Turpitude*

Crimes of "moral turpitude" are properly used for impeachment. See generally Texas Rule of Evidence 609; *Polk v. State*, 865 S.W.2d 627, 630 (Tex. App.—Fort Worth 1993, pet. ref'd) (trial court did not abuse discretion allowing defendant to be impeached by evidence of conviction for misdemeanor indecent exposure where offense involved moral turpitude).

II. Sample Motions

A. Motion to Exclude Evidence of Alcohol Use of Witness

NO. _____

_____	§	IN THE DISTRICT COURT
	§	
v.	§	_____ JUDICIAL COURT
	§	
_____	§	_____ COUNTY, TEXAS

Motion to Exclude Evidence of Alcohol Use of Witness

Comes now _____, Plaintiff in this cause, and file this, her Motion to Exclude Evidence of Alcohol Use of Witness, and in support would show the Court the following:

I.
FACTUAL BACKGROUND

This case involves a civil action for damages arising from the alleged wrongful imprisonment of the Plaintiff, who was detained for three hours in Defendant's department store after witnesses observed him shoplifting.

A key issue in this case relates to the credibility of one of the percipient witnesses, Percy Appient, an undercover security guard employed by the Defendant. The Defendant anticipates that the Plaintiff will seek to admit evidence relating to this witness's prior treatment for alcoholism. According to the testimony of this witness, he has been "clean and sober" for three years, and it is undisputed that he was not drinking at the time he observed the Plaintiff's actions.

By this motion, the Defendant seeks to exclude any alcohol evidence regarding this witness.

2.
THE COURT MAY EXCLUDE PREJUDICIAL EVIDENCE

Evidence should be excluded when the prejudicial impact of the evidence outweighs the probative value of it. Texas Rule of Evidence 403 states: "Although relevant, evidence may be excluded if its probative value is substantially outweighed by the danger of unfair prejudice, confusion of the issues, or misleading the jury, or by considerations of undue delay, waste of time, or needless presentation of cumulative evidence."

3.
THE COURT MAY EXCLUDE IRRELEVANT EVIDENCE

Texas Rule of Evidence 402 states that "evidence which is not relevant is inadmissible." Relevant evidence is defined by Texas Rule of Evidence 401 as "having any tendency to make the existence of any fact that is of consequence to the determination of the action more probable or less probable than it would be without the evidence." *See Torrington v. Stutzman,* 46 S.W.3d 829, 845 (Tex. 2000). Irrelevant evidence is not admissible. *Morale v. State,* 557 S.W.3d 569, 573 (Tex. 2018); *Diamond Offshore Services Ltd. v. Williams,* 542 S.W.3d 539, 549 (Tex. 2018).

Evidence may be properly excluded where not relevant to matters at issue. *See Morale v. State,* 557 S.W.3d 569, 573 (Tex. 2018). Plaintiff's immigration or residence status is not relevant to the issues in the case. *See TXI Transp. Co. v. Hughes,* 306 S.W.3d 230, 234 (Tex. 2010); *Zamarron v. Adame,* 864 S.W.2d 173, 175 (Tex. App.—El Paso 1993, reh'g overruled, writ denied) (plaintiff's immigration status irrelevant). In the present case, evidence of the witness's prior alcoholism is irrelevant to the issues in the case and should be excluded.

4.
THIS COURT MAY EXCLUDE IMPROPER CHARACTER EVIDENCE

Texas Rule of Evidence 608(b) states: "[s]pecific instances of the conduct of a witness, for the purpose of attacking or supporting the witness' credibility, other than conviction of crime as provided in Rule 609, may not be inquired into on cross-examination of the witness nor proved by extrinsic evidence."

Evidence of the drinking habits of a witness is inadmissible absent a showing that the witness had been drinking prior to or contemporaneous to the event in question. *Gibbs v. State*, 385 S.W.2d 258, 259 (Tex. Crim. App. 1965) (impeachment evidence that witness terminated from employment for driving while intoxicated properly excluded where no evidence witness had been convicted for intoxicated driving and did not represent crime of moral turpitude); *Holland v. State*, 60 Tex.Crim. 117, 119, 131 S.W. 563 (Tex. Crim. App. 1910) (trial court improperly allowed impeachment of witness by evidence that someone had previously brought alcohol to her house, and she drank it).

In the present case, any evidence of Mr. Appient's prior treatment for alcoholism is clearly irrelevant and inadmissible. There is absolutely no evidence that he had consumed any alcohol prior to observing the Plaintiff's actions, and certainly his past conduct has no bearing on the issues in this action. To allow such evidence would raise a red herring regarding the witness's ability to accurately perceive the subject events and his credibility.

To avoid undue prejudice to the Defendant, it is respectfully requested that this motion be granted and that any reference to Mr. Appient's prior drinking habits be excluded.

Dated: _____ *(Date)* _____

By: _____

_____ *(Name of Counsel)* _____

Attorneys for Defendant,

_____ *(Name of Defendant)* _____

CHARACTER EVIDENCE   319

B. Opposition to Motion to Exclude Inflammatory Evidence

NO. _____

	§	IN THE DISTRICT COURT
_____	§	
v.	§	_____ JUDICIAL COURT
	§	
_____	§	_____ COUNTY, TEXAS

Opposition to Motion to Exclude Inflammatory Evidence

Comes now _____, Plaintiff in this cause, and file this, her Motion to Exclude Inflammatory Evidence, and in support would show the Court the following:

1.
FACTUAL BACKGROUND

This is a breach of contract case between Plaintiff and Defendant, a dog breeder. Defendant represented himself as a top dog breeder specializing in raising champion show breeds as well as "designer" and hypoallergenic breeds. In 2018, the five Plaintiffs entered into contracts with Defendant to purchase puppies. After experiencing health problems with their dogs, Plaintiffs conducted genetic testing. The results demonstrated that none of the dogs possessed champion breeding, nor were they hypoallergenic.

Thereafter, Plaintiffs instituted this action against Defendant for breach of contract. Plaintiffs intend to introduce evidence of Defendant's dishonesty through the testimony of Defendant's former employees. Defendant has filed a motion to exclude this evidence as inflammatory. This opposition is based upon the grounds that the testimony is admissible opinion and reputation evidence of Defendant's character pursuant to Texas Rule of Evidence 608.

2.
OPINION AND REPUTATION EVIDENCE IS ADMISSIBLE PURSUANT
TO RULE 608

The use of character evidence to impeach a witness's honesty or veracity, or their opposites, has been statutorily approved by Texas Rule of Evidence 608, which states in relevant part as follows:

> The credibility of a witness may be attacked or supported by evidence in the form of opinion or reputation, but subject to these limitations: (1) the evidence may refer only to character for truthfulness or untruthfulness, and (2) evidence of truthful character is admissible only after the character of the witness for truthfulness has been attacked by opinion or reputation evidence or otherwise.

In the case of *Cunningham v. Hughes & Luce, L.L.P.*, 312 S.W.3d 62, 72 (Tex. App.—El Paso 2010, no pet.), evidence concerning a client's criminal past was admissible in the client's legal malpractice suit because it was relevant to the issues in the case.

In the present matter, Plaintiffs' witnesses, who are former employees of Defendant, will testify that Defendant has a reputation for dishonesty in the community. The witnesses satisfy the requirements of Rule 608. The fact that Defendant's reputation for dishonesty in the community does not support his case, and will not endear him to the jury, does not mean that the testimony is inadmissible. Accordingly, this court should deny Defendant's motion to exclude the testimony of the former employees.

3.
EVIDENCE IS NOT UNDULY PREJUDICIAL PURSUANT TO RULE 403

Texas Rule of Evidence 403 states that the court may only exclude relevant evidence "if its probative value is substantially outweighed by the danger of undue prejudice, confusion of the issues, or misleading the jury, or by considerations of undue delay, or needless presentation of cumulative evidence."

As noted by the Texas Supreme Court, "testimony is not inadmissible on the sole ground that it is 'prejudicial' because in our adversarial system, much of a proponent's evidence is legitimately intended to wound the opponent." *Bay Area Healthcare Group, Ltd. v. McShane*, 239 S.W.3d 231, 234 (Tex. 2007). The party moving for exclusion of "prejudicial" evidence must show that the evidence is unduly prejudicial. *Id.*

In the present case, Rule 403 does not justify the exclusion of the testimony of Defendant's former employees. While testimony of Defendant's reputation for dishonesty is prejudicial, it is not unduly prejudicial: the probative value of this testimony is not substantially outweighed by the danger of undue prejudice. Consequently, the evidence is not inadmissible, and Defendant's motion should be denied.

4.
EVIDENCE IS RELEVANT PURSUANT TO RULES 401 AND 402

Texas Rule of Evidence 402 states that "evidence which is not relevant is inadmissible." Relevant evidence is defined by Texas Rule of Evidence 401 as "having any tendency to make the existence of any fact that is of consequence to the determination of the action more probable or less probable than it would be without the evidence." *See Torrington v. Stutzman*, 46 S.W.3d 829, 845 (Tex. 2000). Irrelevant evidence is not admissible. *Morale v. State*, 557 S.W.3d 569, 573 (Tex. 2018); *Diamond Offshore Services Ltd. v. Williams*, 542 S.W.3d 539, 549 (Tex. 2018).

Evidence may be properly excluded where not relevant to matters at issue. *See Morale v. State,* 557 S.W.3d 569, 573 (Tex. 2018). Plaintiff's immigration or residence status is not relevant to the issues in the case. *See TXI Transp. Co. v. Hughes*, 306 S.W.3d 230, 234 (Tex. 2010); *Zamarron v. Adame*, 864 S.W.2d 173, 175 (Tex. App.—El Paso 1993, reh'g overruled, writ denied) (plaintiff's immigration status irrelevant). In this case, Defendant's reputation in the community for dishonesty is relevant to Defendant's misrepresentation of his dogs to Plaintiffs. In other words, the testimony of Defendant's former employees makes a fact of consequence to the determination of the action more probable than it would be without the evidence. The former employees' testimony is admissible pursuant to Texas Rule of Evidence 401.

5.
CONCLUSION

Based on the foregoing, Plaintiffs respectfully request that this Court enter an order denying Defendant's motion to exclude inflammatory evidence.

Dated: _____ *(Date of Motion)* _____

By: _____

_____ *(Name of Counsel)* _____

Attorneys for Plaintiff,

_____ *(Name of Plaintiff)* _____

CHAPTER 8

Witness Evidence

I. Motion Authorities
   A. Motion to Exclude Improper Expert Opinion
      1. Suggested Motion Text
      2. Motion Summary
      3. Supporting Authorities
         a. Not Reliable
         b. Hypothetical Questions
         c. Inadmissible Hearsay
            i. Opinions of Others
            ii. Statements of Others
            iii. Treatises, Documents, and Texts
         d. Legal Questions
            i. Compare: Ultimate Issues
         e. Matters of Common Experience
         f. Not Reasonably Relied on by Experts
         g. Not Perceived or Personally Known
         h. Speculation or Conjecture
         i. Usurping Jury Function
         j. Irrelevant Matters
         k. Conclusory Testimony
         l. Burden of Proof
         m. Other Grounds
      4. Opposing Authorities
         a. Hearsay
            i. Statements of Others
            ii. Treatises, Documents, and Texts
         b. Hypothetical Questions
         c. Legal Questions vs. Ultimate Issues
   B. Motion to Exclude Testimony of Nonqualified Expert
      1. Suggested Motion Text
      2. Motion Summary
      3. Supporting Authorities
         a. Examples
         b. Qualification of Experts in Health Care Liability Cases
            i. Examples
         c. Other Grounds
      4. Opposing Authorities
         a. Health Care Liability Cases

C. Motion to Exclude Opinion of Nonexpert
   1. Supporting Motion Text
   2. Motion Summary
   3. Supporting Authorities
      a. Lack of Personal Knowledge
      b. Legal Opinions
      c. Not Based on Perceptions of Witness
      d. Not Helpful to Jury
      e. Speculative or Conjectural
      f. Other Grounds
   4. Opposing Authorities
      a. Sanity/Mental Condition or Capacity
      b. Health
      c. Age, Size, Quality
      d. Damages
      e. Personal Knowledge
      f. Causation
      g. Hearsay
D. Motion to Exclude Testimony of Incompetent Witness
   1. Suggested Motion Text
   2. Motion Summary
   3. Supporting Authorities
      a. Inability to Express or Tell Truth
         i. Children
      b. Lack of Mental Competence/Insanity
      c. Lack of Personal Knowledge of Subject Matter
      d. Other Grounds
   4. Opposing Authorities
      a. Children
      b. Mental Competence/Insanity
      c. Dead Man's Rule
E. Motion to Exclude Testimony of Judge, Arbitrator, Mediator, or Juror
   1. Suggested Motion Text
   2. Motion Summary
   3. Supporting Authorities—Judges
      a. Arbitrators
      b. Jurors
   4. Opposing Authorities—Judges
      a. Arbitrators
      b. Jurors
F. Motion to Exclude Witness From Courtroom Prior to Testifying
   1. Suggested Motion Text
   2. Motion Summary
   3. Supporting Authorities
   4. Opposing Authorities
      a. Cannot Exclude a Party
      b. Exclusion of Testimony Is Improper
      c. Welfare of a Child

G. Motion to Exclude Comment on Exercise of Privilege Not to Testify
   1. Suggested Motion Text
   2. Motion Summary
   3. Supporting Authorities
   4. Opposing Authorities
      a. Civil Consequences of Silence
      b. Harmless Error
H. Motion to Exclude Evidence of Failure to Call Witness
   1. Suggested Motion Text
   2. Motion Summary
   3. Supporting Authorities
      a. Where Witness Was Equally Available to Both Parties
      b. Where Comments Would Invite Speculation
      c. Where Witness Was Not Available
      d. Other Grounds
   4. Opposing Authorities
      a. Failure to Call Material Witness
I. Motion to Exclude Hearsay Evidence
   1. Suggested Motion Text
   2. Motion Summary
   3. Supporting Authorities
      a. Purpose of Rule
      b. Written Hearsay
   4. Opposing Authorities
      a. Purpose of Exceptions to the Hearsay Rule
      b. Nonhearsay Evidence
      c. Nonassertive Conduct
      d. Multiple Hearsay
      e. Hearsay to Impeach Credibility or Rehabilitate Witness

II. Sample Motions
   A. Motion to Exclude Speculative Expert Opinion
   B. Motion to Exclude Reference to Failure to Call Witness
   C. Motion to Exclude Testimony and Opinions of Medical Doctor

I. Motion Authorities

A. Motion to Exclude Improper Expert Opinion

1. Suggested Motion Text

(*Name of Moving Party*) hereby moves this Court for an order excluding any and all testimony, references to testimony, or argument based upon the testimony of (*Name of Witness*) relating to (*Describe Improper Opinion Sought to Be Excluded, e.g., the Witness's Opinion of the Legal Interpretation of the Jury Instructions in This Case*). The motion is based upon the ground that the subject matter of the witness's opinion testimony is improper and is therefore inadmissible.

2. Motion Summary

This motion is used to exclude the opinion of an expert witness that is based upon improper matter. Texas Rule of Evidence 702 limits an expert opinion to those subjects that "will assist the trier of fact to understand the evidence or to determine a fact in issue. *See GTE Sw. v. Bruce*, 998 S.W.2d 605, 620 (Tex. 1999). Under Texas Rule of Evidence 702, the witness must be qualified as an expert based upon "knowledge, skill, experience, training or education," in order to provide expert opinions. See generally, Texas Rule of Evidence 702 and cases cited below.

3. Supporting Authorities

Texas Rule of Evidence 702 states:

> If scientific, technical, or other specialized knowledge will assist the trier of fact to understand the evidence or to determine a fact in issue, a witness qualified as an expert by knowledge, skill, experience, training, or education may testify thereto in the form of an opinion or otherwise.

Dallas Morning News, Inc. v. Hall, 579 S.W.3d 370, 379 (Tex. 2019) ("Testimony by an expert witness is admissible only if the expert's scientific, technical, or other specialized knowledge will help the trier of fact to understand the evidence or to determine a fact in issue.").

Morale v. State, 557 S.W.3d 569, 575 (Tex. 2018) ("[E]xpert testimony in condemnation cases is inadmissible if it relates to remote, speculative, and conjectural uses of the property that are not reflected in the present market value of the property.").

Gunn v. McCoy, 554 S.W.3d 645, 666 (Tex. 2018) ("To testify as an expert, a witness must be qualified, and the proposed testimony must be relevant to the issues in the case and based upon a reliable foundation.").

Gunn v. McCoy, 554 S.W.3d 645, 666 (Tex. 2018) ("Expert testimony may also be unreliable if there is simply too great an analytical gap between the data relied upon and the opinion proffered.... [Courts] are not required to ignore fatal gaps in an expert's analysis or assertions that are simply incorrect, and such a flaw in an expert's reasoning renders the scientific testimony unreliable and, legally, no evidence.").

Rogers v. Zanetti, 518 S.W.3d 394, 405 (Tex. 2017) ("An expert's familiarity with the facts is not alone a satisfactory basis for his or her opinion.").

Wolfe v. State, 509 S.W.3d 325, 335 (Tex. Crim. App. 2017) ("For expert testimony to be admissible ... the proponent of the expert scientific evidence must demonstrate by clear and convincing evidence that the testimony is sufficiently reliable and relevant to help the jury in reaching accurate results.... In other words, the proponent must prove two prongs: (1) the testimony is based on a reliable scientific foundation, and (2) it is relevant to the issues in the case.").

Wolfe v. State, 509 S.W.3d 325, 335 (Tex. Crim. App. 2017) ("[There are] three criteria for reliability that the proponent of scientific evidence must prove [are]: (1) the underlying scientific theory must be valid; (2) the technique applying the theory must be valid; and (3) the technique must have been properly applied on the occasion in question.").

Wolfe v. State, 509 S.W.3d 325, 335 (Tex. Crim. App. 2017) ("Unreliable scientific evidence is inadmissible because it simply will not assist the jury to understand the evidence or accurately determine a fact in issue; such evidence obfuscates rather than leads to an intelligent evaluation of the facts.").

Southwestern Energy Production Company v. Berry-Helfand, 491 S.W.3d 699, 717 (Tex. 2016) ("[A]n expert must connect the data relied on and his or her opinion and show how that data is valid support for the opinion reached ... If there is too great an analytical gap between the data relied on and the expert's opinion, the expert's testimony is unreliable.").

Enbridge Pipelines (East Texas) L.P. v. Avinger Timber, LLC, 386 S.W.3d 256, 261 (Tex. 2012) (an expert's testimony must be relevant to the issues and based upon a reliable foundation).

In re Commitment of Bohannan, 388 S.W.3d 296, 304 (Tex. 2012) (an expert must be qualified by knowledge, skill, experience, training, or education to assist the trier of fact to understand the evidence or to determine a fact in issue).

In re Commitment of Bohannan, 388 S.W.3d 296, 304 (Tex. 2012) (that a witness has knowledge, skill, expertise, or training does not necessarily mean that the witness can assist the trier of fact).

In re Commitment of Bohannan, 388 S.W.3d 296, 304 (Tex. 2012) (credentials alone do not qualify an expert to testify).

In re Commitment of Bohannan, 388 S.W.3d 296, 304 (Tex. 2012) (the test is whether the offering party has established that the expert has knowledge, skill, experience, training, or education regarding the specific issue before the court, which would qualify the expert to give an opinion on that particular subject).

Merck & Co. v. Garza, 347 S.W.3d 256, 262 (Tex. 2011) (if the foundational data underlying expert opinion testimony are unreliable, an expert will not be permitted to base an opinion on that data because any opinion drawn from that data is likewise unreliable).

Barshaw v. State, 342 S.W.3d 91, 93 (Tex. Crim. App. 2011) (expert testimony that a particular class of persons to which the victim belongs is truthful is not expert testimony of the kind that will assist the jury, as is required by Texas Rule of Evidence 702, and is thus inadmissible).

Reid Road Mun. Util. Dist. No. 2 v. Speedy Stop Food Stores, Ltd., 337 S.W.3d 846, 854 (Tex. 2011) (witness is testifying as an expert witness when the witness's testimony, in substance, is based on special knowledge, skill, experience, training, or education in a particular subject).

Reid Road Mun. Util. Dist. No. 2 v. Speedy Stop Food Stores, Ltd., 337 S.W.3d 846, 854 (Tex. 2011) (when the main substance of the witness's testimony is based on application of the witness's specialized knowledge, skill, experience, training, or education to the witness's familiarity with the property, then the testimony will generally be expert testimony within the scope of Rule 702, and a witness giving such testimony must be properly disclosed and designated as an expert and the witness's testimony is subject to scrutiny under rules regarding experts and expert opinion).

Reid Road Mun. Util. Dist. No. 2 v. Speedy Stop Food Stores, Ltd., 337 S.W.3d 846, 854 (Tex. 2011) (subject to the provisions of Rule 701, a witness who will be giving opinion evidence about a property's fair market value must be disclosed and designated as an expert pursuant to discovery and other applicable rules).

Reid Road Mun. Util. Dist. No. 2 v. Speedy Stop Food Stores, Ltd., 337 S.W.3d 846, 854 (Tex. 2011) (testimony that was based on the witness's expertise—"knowledge, background, education and experience"—not the witness's personal familiarity with the property, was properly excluded because the witness was not timely disclosed as an expert).

Dynegy Midstream Servs. Ltd. P'ship v. Apache Corp., 294 S.W.3d 164, 170 (Tex. 2009) (experts have a proper, if confined, role in litigation, but it is not to supply parol evidence to vary or contradict the terms of unambiguous contracts).

Cooper Tire & Rubber Co. v. Mendez, 204 S.W.3d 797, 800 (Tex. 2006) (expert testimony is admissible if the expert is qualified, and the testimony is relevant and based on a reliable foundation).

Exxon Pipeline Co. v. Zwahr, 88 S.W.3d 623, 628 (Tex. 2002) (reliability requirement of Rule of Evidence governing the admission of expert testimony focuses on the principles, research, and methodology underlying an expert's conclusions, and under this requirement, expert testimony is unreliable if it is not grounded in the methods and procedures of science and is no more than subjective belief or unsupported speculation).

Exxon Pipeline Co. v. Zwahr, 88 S.W.3d 623, 628 (Tex. 2002) (expert testimony is unreliable if there is too great an analytical gap between the data the expert relies upon and the opinion offered, and in applying this reliability standard the trial court does not decide whether the expert's conclusions are correct, but rather, the trial court determines whether the analysis used to reach those conclusions is reliable).

Gammill v. Jack Williams Chevrolet, Inc., 972 S.W.2d 713, 727 (Tex. 1998) (too great of analytical gap between expert's theories and conclusions and therefore not reliable).

E.I. du Pont de Nemours & Co. v. Robinson, 923 S.W.2d 549, 557 (Tex. 1995) (scientific evidence not grounded "in the methods and procedures of science" is no more than "subjective belief or unsupported speculation").

Jordan v. State, 928 S.W.2d 550, 554 (Tex. Crim. App. 1996) (under Texas law, scientific evidence must be relevant and reliable to be admissible, and Texas standard for reliability adopted in *Kelly* case is similar to *Daubert* standard adopted under federal law; held that trial court should have admitted expert evidence regarding reliability of eyewitness identification). *See Daubert v. Merrell Dow Pharm., Inc.*, 509 U.S. 579 (1993).

Kelly v. State, 824 S.W.2d 568, 572 (Tex. Crim. App. 1992) (evidence must be relevant and reliable to be admissible; note: held that DNA evidence should have been admitted).

Brown v. State, 580 S.W.3d 755, 765 (Tex. App.—Houston [14th Dist.] 2019, pet. ref'd) ("[A]n expert is not permitted to give a direct opinion on the truthfulness of a witness.... This type of testimony is inadmissible because it does more than 'assist the trier of fact to understand the evidence or to determine a fact in issue;' it decides an issue for the jury.").

Brown v. State, 580 S.W.3d 755, 765 (Tex. App.—Houston [14th Dist.] 2019, pet. ref'd) ("[A] witness's expert opinion on the truthfulness of a criminal defendant during an investigation is ... inadmissible.... This rule equally applies to expert and lay witness testimony.").

Equistar Chemicals, LP v. ClydeUnion DB, Ltd., 579 S.W.3d 505, 511 (Tex. App.—Houston [14th Dist.] 2019, pet. denied) ("To be admissible, an expert's opinion testimony must have a reliable foundation.").

Equistar Chemicals, LP v. ClydeUnion DB, Ltd., 579 S.W.3d 505, 511 (Tex. App.—Houston [14th Dist.] 2019, pet. denied) ("Expert testimony is not reliable if there is too great an analytical gap between the data on which the expert relies and the opinion offered.... Whether an analytical gap exists is largely determined by comparing the facts the expert relied on, the facts in the record, and the expert's ultimate opinion.... An analytical gap exists if the expert's opinion is based on assumed facts that vary materially from the facts in the record.").

R&M Mixed Beverage Consultants, Inc. v. Safe Harbor Benefits, Inc., 578 S.W.3d 218 (Tex. App.—El Paso 2019) (expert testimony not admissible because it would not have helped the trier of fact to understand the evidence or to determine a fact in issue).

Burke v. State, 371 S.W.3d 252, 258 (Tex. App.—Houston [1st Dist.] 2011, pet. ref'd, untimely filed) (expert testimony does not assist the jury if it constitutes a direct opinion on the truthfulness of a child complainant's allegations).

Taber v. Roush, 316 S.W.3d 139, 147 (Tex. App.—Houston [14th Dist.] 2010, no pet.) (if expert's scientific evidence is not reliable, it is not evidence).

Von Hohn v. Von Hohn, 260 S.W.3d 631, 636 (Tex. App.—Tyler 2008, no pet.) (if the trial court determines that the proffered expert testimony is relevant and reliable, it must then determine whether to exclude the evidence because its probative value is outweighed by the danger of unfair prejudice, confusion of the issues, or misleading the jury, or by considerations of undue delay, or needless presentation of cumulative evidence).

Green v. State, 55 S.W.3d 633, 637 (Tex. App.—Tyler 2001, pet. ref'd), *cert. denied*, 535 U.S. 958 (2002), *aff'd*, 116 S.W.3d 26 (Tex. 2003) (defendant failed to show proposed expert was reliable where expert failed to show what authorities in field were relied upon for opinions).

> *Note: Texas no longer follows the Frye "general acceptance" test.* See Frye v. United States, *293 F. 1013 (D.C. Cir. 1923). Instead, whether an underlying technique or theory has been generally accepted is just one factor to consider in determining the admissibility of scientific evidence.* See E.I. du Pont de Nemours & Co. v. Robinson, *923 S.W.2d*

549, 557 (Tex. 1995) (listing seven factors to consider in determining admissibility of expert testimony); Sears, Roebuck & Co. v. Kunze, 996 S.W.2d 416, 424 (Tex. App.—Beaumont 1999, writ denied) (applying seven factors to test evidence).

a. Not Reliable

Kumho Tire Co. v. Carmichael, 526 U.S. 137, 147 (1999) (*Daubert* standard for determining reliability of testimony stating scientific conclusions may apply to both scientists and nonscientists).

Morale v. State, 557 S.W.3d 569, 575 (Tex. 2018) ("[E]xpert testimony in condemnation cases is inadmissible if it relates to remote, speculative, and conjectural uses of the property that are not reflected in the present market value of the property.").

Gunn v. McCoy, 554 S.W.3d 645, 666 (Tex. 2018) ("An expert's opinion may be considered unreliable if it is based on assumed facts that vary materially from the actual facts, or if it is based on tests or data that do not support the conclusions reached.... In either instance, the opinion is not probative evidence.").

Gunn v. McCoy, 554 S.W.3d 645, 666 (Tex. 2018) ("[I]f the record contains no evidence supporting an expert's material factual assumptions, or if such assumptions are contrary to conclusively proven facts, opinion testimony founded on those assumptions is not competent evidence.").

Gunn v. McCoy, 554 S.W.3d 645, 666 (Tex. 2018) ("Expert testimony may also be unreliable if there is simply too great an analytical gap between the data relied upon and the opinion proffered.... [Courts] are not required to ignore fatal gaps in an expert's analysis or assertions that are simply incorrect, and such a flaw in an expert's reasoning renders the scientific testimony unreliable and, legally, no evidence.").

Rogers v. Zanetti, 518 S.W.3d 394, 405 (Tex. 2017) ("When an expert's opinion is based on assumed facts that vary materially from the actual, undisputed facts, the opinion is without probative value and cannot support a verdict or judgment.").

Wolfe v. State, 509 S.W.3d 325, 335 (Tex. Crim. App. 2017) ("([There are] three criteria for reliability that the proponent of scientific evidence must prove: (1) the underlying scientific theory must be valid; (2) the technique applying the theory must be valid; and (3) the technique must have been properly applied on the occasion in question.").

Wolfe v. State, 509 S.W.3d 325, 335 (Tex. Crim. App. 2017) ("[A] nonexclusive list of factors [to consider in making] a finding of reliability: (1) the extent to which the underlying scientific theory and technique are accepted as valid by the relevant scientific community, if such a community can be ascertained; (2) the qualifications of the testifying experts; (3) the existence of literature supporting or rejecting the underlying scientific theory and technique; (4) the potential rate of error of the technique; (5) the availability of other experts to test and evaluate the technique; (6) the clarity with which the underlying scientific theory and technique can be explained to the court; and (7) the experience and skill of the person who applied the technique on the occasion in question.... In weighing these factors as a means of assessing reliability, the focus is to determine whether the evidence has its basis in sound scientific methodology such that testimony about 'junk science' is weeded out.").

Wolfe v. State, 509 S.W.3d 325, 335 (Tex. Crim. App. 2017) ("Unreliable scientific evidence is inadmissible because it simply will not assist the jury to understand the evidence or accurately determine a fact in issue; such evidence obfuscates rather than leads to an intelligent evaluation of the facts.").

Wolfe v. State, 509 S.W.3d 325, 335 (Tex. Crim. App. 2017) ("In sorting untested or invalid theories from those that are grounded in 'good' science, trial judges are called upon to serve as gatekeepers ... The trial court's essential gatekeeping role is to ensure that evidence that is unreliable because it lacks a basis in sound scientific methodology is not admitted.").

Southwestern Energy Production Company v. Berry-Helfand, 491 S.W.3d 699, 717 (Tex. 2016) ("Courts must rigorously examine the validity of the facts and assumptions on which [expert] testimony is based.").

Southwestern Energy Production Company v. Berry-Helfand, 491 S.W.3d 699, 717 (Tex. 2016) ("[A]n expert must connect the data relied on and his or her opinion and show how that data is valid support for the opinion reached ... If there is too great an analytical gap between the data relied on and the expert's opinion, the expert's testimony is unreliable.").

Hous. Unlimited, Inc. Metal Processing v. Mel Acres Ranch, 443 S.W.3d 820, 832–33 (Tex. 2014) ("[I]f an expert's opinion is unreliable because it is based on assumed facts that vary from the actual facts, the opinion is not probative evidence. This does not mean that an expert's factual assumptions must be uncontested or established as a matter of law. If the evidence conflicts, it is the province of the jury to determine which evidence to credit. Nor does it mean that parties must prove up every inconsequential assumption on which their expert relies.").

Bostic v. Georgia-Pacific Corp., 439 S.W.3d 332, 340 (Tex. 2013) (an expert's opinion must be based on sufficient facts and data).

Bostic v. Georgia-Pacific Corp., 439 S.W.3d 332, 340 (Tex. 2013) (if the expert's scientific testimony is not reliable, it is not evidence; also, the underlying scientific technique or principle relied upon by an expert must be reliable).

Bostic v. Georgia-Pacific Corp., 439 S.W.3d 332, 340 (Tex. 2013) (in a product liability case, proof that a defendant's product more than doubled the plaintiff's risk of injury must be shown through reliable expert testimony that is based on epidemiological studies or similarly reliable scientific testimony).

Enbridge Pipelines (East Texas) L.P. v. Avinger Timber, LLC, 386 S.W.3d 256, 261 (Tex. 2012) (expert testimony is unreliable if there is too great an analytical gap between the data the expert relies upon and the opinion offered).

In re Commitment of Bohannan, 388 S.W.3d 296, 304 (Tex. 2012) (determining whether an expert's theory or technique is reliable requires consideration of all pertinent factors, including: (1) the extent to which the theory has been or can be tested, (2) the extent to which the technique relies upon the subjective interpretation of the expert, (3) whether the theory has been subjected to peer review and/or publication, (4) the technique's potential rate of error, (5) whether the underlying theory or technique has been generally accepted as valid by the relevant scientific community, and (6) the non-judicial uses that have been made of the theory or technique).

Merck & Co. v. Garza, 347 S.W.3d 256, 262 (Tex. 2011) (if the foundational data underlying expert opinion testimony are unreliable, an expert will not be permitted to base an opinion on that data because any opinion drawn from that data is likewise unreliable).

Merck & Co. v. Garza, 347 S.W.3d 256, 262 (Tex. 2011) (expert's testimony is unreliable even when the underlying data are sound if the expert draws conclusions from that data based on flawed methodology).

Merck & Co. v. Garza, 347 S.W.3d 256, 262 (Tex. 2011) (flaw in an expert's reasoning from the data may render reliance on a study unreasonable and render the inferences drawn therefrom dubious; under that circumstance, the expert's scientific testimony is unreliable and, legally, no evidence).

Whirlpool Corp. v. Camacho, 298 S.W.3d 631, 641 (Tex. 2009) (testing is not always required to support an expert's opinion, but lack of relevant testing to the extent it was possible, either by the expert or others, is one factor that points toward a determination that an expert opinion is unreliable and inadmissible).

State v. Cent. Expressway Sign Assocs., 302 S.W.3d 866, 870 (Tex. 2009) (to be relevant, the expert's opinion must be based on the facts; to be reliable, the expert's opinion must be based on sound reasoning and methodology).

Ford Motor Co. v. Ledesma, 242 S.W.3d 32, 39 (Tex. 2007) (expert testimony is unreliable, and therefore inadmissible, if it is based on unreliable data, or if the expert draws conclusions from underlying data based on flawed methodology).

Ford Motor Co. v. Ledesma, 242 S.W.3d 32, 39 (Tex. 2007) (expert testimony is unreliable, and therefore inadmissible, if there is simply too great an analytical gap between the data and the opinion proffered).

Ford Motor Co. v. Ledesma, 242 S.W.3d 32, 39 (Tex. 2007) (expert's opinion is unreliable, and therefore inadmissible, if based solely upon his subjective interpretation of the facts).

Cooper Tire & Rubber Co. v. Mendez, 204 S.W.3d 797, 800 (Tex. 2006) (testimony on theory that wax contamination caused tire failure was legally insufficient to establish manufacturing defect in product liability action because the theory was unreliable).

Mack Trucks, Inc. v. Tamez, 206 S.W.3d 572, 578 (Tex. 2006) (in determining the reliability of an expert's testimony, the trial court should undertake a rigorous examination of the facts on which the expert relies, the method by which the expert draws an opinion from those facts, and how the expert applies the facts and methods to the case at hand).

Jordan v. State, 928 S.W.2d 550, 554 (Tex. Crim. App. 1996) (under Texas law, scientific evidence must be relevant and reliable to be admissible; Texas standard for reliability adopted in *Kelly* case similar to *Daubert* standard adopted under federal law; note: held that trial court should have admitted expert evidence regarding reliability of eyewitness identification). *See Daubert v. Merrell Dow Pharm., Inc.*, 509 U.S. 579 (1993).

Equistar Chemicals, LP v. ClydeUnion DB, Ltd., 579 S.W.3d 505, 511 (Tex. App.—Houston [14th Dist.] 2019, pet. denied) ("To be admissible, an expert's opinion testimony must have a reliable foundation.").

Equistar Chemicals, LP v. ClydeUnion DB, Ltd., 579 S.W.3d 505, 511 (Tex. App.—Houston [14th Dist.] 2019, pet. denied) ("Expert testimony is not reliable if there is too great an analytical gap between the data on which the expert relies and the opinion offered.... Whether an analytical gap exists is largely determined by comparing the facts the expert relied on, the facts in the record, and the expert's ultimate opinion.... An analytical gap exists if the expert's opinion is based on assumed facts that vary materially from the facts in the record.").

Equistar Chemicals, LP v. ClydeUnion DB, Ltd., 579 S.W.3d 505, 511 (Tex. App.—Houston [14th Dist.] 2019, pet. denied) ("Expert testimony is not reliable if there is too great an analytical gap between the data on which the expert relies and the opinion offered.... Whether an analytical gap exists is largely determined by comparing the facts the expert relied on, the facts in the record, and the expert's ultimate opinion ... An analytical gap exists if the expert's opinion is based on assumed facts that vary materially from the facts in the record.").

Key Energy Servs., LLC v. Shelby Cnty. Appraisal Dist., 428 S.W.3d 133, 142 (Tex. App.—Tyler 2014, pet. denied) (expert testimony is unreliable if it is based on unreliable data, or if the expert draws conclusions from his underlying data based on flawed methodology).

Schronk v. Laerdal Med. Corp., 440 S.W.3d 250, 258 (Tex. App.—Waco 12, 2013, pet. denied) (to constitute evidence of causation, an expert opinion must rest in reasonable medical probability, which is determined by the substance and context of the opinion, and does not turn on semantics or on the use of a particular term or phrase; "reasonable medical probability" or "reasonable probability" means that it is more likely than not that the ultimate harm or condition resulted from the negligence of one or more defendants).

City of Alton v. Sharyland Water Supply Corp., 402 S.W.3d 867, 876 (Tex. App.—Corpus Christi 2013, pet. denied) (expert testimony lacking a proper foundation is incompetent, and its admission is an abuse of discretion).

Bekendam v. State, 398 S.W.3d 358, 362 (Tex. App.—Fort Worth 2013, no pet.) (to be considered reliable, evidence derived from a scientific theory must satisfy three criteria: (a) the underlying scientific theory must be valid, (b) the technique applying the theory must be valid, and (c) the technique must have been properly applied on the occasion in question).

U.S. Renal Care, Inc. v. Jaafar, 345 S.W.3d 600, 607 (Tex. App.—San Antonio 2011, pet. denied) (expert testimony is unreliable if it is based on unreliable data, if the expert draws conclusions from underlying data based on flawed methodology, or if the testimony lacks proper foundation).

U.S. Renal Care, Inc. v. Jaafar, 345 S.W.3d 600, 607 n.7 (Tex. App.—San Antonio 2011, pet. denied) ("[U]nder the analytical gap approach for determining the reliability of expert witness testimony, the focus is on the experience of the expert and an examination of whether there is too great an analytical gap between the data and the opinion proffered.").

U.S. Renal Care, Inc. v. Jaafar, 345 S.W.3d 600, 607 n.8 (Tex. App.—San Antonio 2011, pet. denied) (each material part of an expert's theory must be reliable).

U.S. Renal Care, Inc. v. Jaafar, 345 S.W.3d 600, 608 (Tex. App.—San Antonio 2011, pet. denied) ("[I]n its gate-keeping function, courts are to rigorously examine the validity of facts and assumptions on which the testimony is based, as well as the principles, research, and methodology underlying the expert's conclusions and the manner in which the principles and methodologies are applied by the expert to reach the conclusions.").

State v. Dominguez, 425 S.W.3d 411, 423 (Tex. App.—Houston [1st Dist.] 2011, pet. ref'd) (when addressing fields that are based upon experience or training as opposed to scientific methods, the appropriate questions for assessing reliability are (1) whether the field of expertise is a legitimate one, (2) whether the subject matter of the expert's testimony is within the scope of the field, and (3) whether the expert's testimony properly relies upon or utilizes the principles involved in the field).

Taber v. Roush, 316 S.W.3d 139, 147 (Tex. App.—Houston [14th Dist.] 2010, no pet.) (when an expert's underlying scientific technique or principle is unreliable, the expert's opinion is no more than subjective belief or unsupported speculation and is inadmissible).

Lincoln v. Clark Freight Lines, Inc., 285 S.W.3d 79, 83 (Tex. App.—Houston [1st Dist.] 2009, no pet.) (expert testimony must be shown to be reliable before it is admitted).

Lincoln v. Clark Freight Lines, Inc., 285 S.W.3d 79, 83 (Tex. App.—Houston [1st Dist.] 2009, no pet.) (unreliable scientific or technical evidence is of no assistance to the jury and is therefore inadmissible).

Lincoln v. Clark Freight Lines, Inc., 285 S.W.3d 79, 83 (Tex. App.—Houston [1st Dist.] 2009, no pet.) (if an expert relies on unreliable foundational data, any opinion drawn from that data is likewise unreliable, and therefore inadmissible).

Collini v. Pustejovsky, 280 S.W.3d 456, 465 (Tex. App.—Fort Worth 2009, no pet.) (to justify the submission of expert opinion testimony under the rules of evidence, the proponent of the opinion must show that the opinion is reliable).

Exxon Mobil Corp. v. Altimore, Prod. Liab. Rep., 256 S.W.3d 415, 424 (Tex. App.—Houston [14th Dist.] 2008, no pet.) (whenever scientific evidence is required to establish any element of a cause of action, that evidence must be scientifically reliable).

Hernandez v. State, 127 S.W.3d 206, 218 (Tex. App.—Houston [1st Dist.] 2003, pet. ref'd) (trial court did not abuse discretion excluding proposed expert testimony where defendant failed to demonstrate testimony sufficiently reliable).

Green v. State, 55 S.W.3d 633, 637 (Tex. App.—Tyler 2001, pet. ref'd), *cert. denied*, 535 U.S. 958 (2002), *aff'd*, 116 S.W.3d 26 (Tex. 2003) (defendant failed to show proposed expert on false confessions reliable where expert failed to show what authorities in field were relied upon for opinions).

Green v. State, 55 S.W.3d 633, 637 (Tex. App.—Tyler 2001, pet. ref'd), *cert. denied*, 535 U.S. 958 (2002), *aff'd*, 116 S.W.3d 26 (Tex. 2003) (trial court improperly relied upon unreliable expert evidence where insufficient showing that underlying methodology supporting evidence accepted as valid in scientific field).

Franco v. State, 25 S.W.3d 26, 29 (Tex. App.—El Paso 2000, pet. ref'd) (scientific testimony must be reliable and outside general knowledge of lay persons).

Purina Mills, Inc. v. Odell, 948 S.W.2d 927, 933 (Tex. App.—Texarkana 1997, pet. denied) (the party offering expert testimony must show that the testimony is relevant and based on reliable foundation).

b. Hypothetical Questions

Clark Equip. Co. v. Pitner, 923 S.W.2d 117, 123 (Tex. App.—Houston [14th Dist.] 1996, writ denied) (trial court did not abuse discretion excluding expert's hypothetical testimony where insufficient evidence to support hypothetical).

Crawford v. Deets, 828 S.W.2d 795, 799 (Tex. App.—Fort Worth 1992, writ denied) (trial court properly excluded hypothetical questions not supported by evidence).

Sabelli v. Sec. Ins. Co. of New Haven, 372 S.W.2d 348, 351 (Tex. Civ. App. 1963, writ ref'd n.r.e.) (trial court properly excluded hypothetical question based upon facts not in evidence) *See also Gulf Oil Corp. v. Walker*, 288 S.W.2d 173, 186 (Tex. Civ. App. 1956, no writ) (trial court did not err excluding hypothetical testimony based upon facts not supported by evidence).

c. Inadmissible Hearsay

Dallas Morning News, Inc. v. Hall, 579 S.W.3d 370, 379 (Tex. 2019) ("[H]earsay—an out-of-court statement offered to prove the truth of the matter asserted—is inadmissible.").

Hooper v. Torres, 790 S.W.2d 757, 761 (Tex. App.—El Paso 1990, writ denied) (portion of medical report representing summaries of findings by other physicians inadmissible).

Cornelison v. Aggregate Haulers, Inc., 777 S.W.2d 542, 545 (Tex. App.—Fort Worth 1989, writ denied) (trial court committed harmless error admitting statement from medical records regarding cause of incident where record did not establish who made statement at issue and whether individual had personal knowledge of events).

i. Opinions of Others

Hooper v. Torres, 790 S.W.2d 757, 761 (Tex. App.—El Paso 1990, writ denied) (portion of medical report representing summaries of findings by other physicians inadmissible).

ii. Statements of Others

Cornelison v. Aggregate Haulers, Inc., 777 S.W.2d 542, 545 (Tex. App.—Fort Worth 1989, writ denied) (trial court committed harmless error admitting statement from medical records regarding cause of incident where record did not establish who made statement at issue and whether individual had personal knowledge of events).

But see Texas Rule of Evidence 703, which states:

> The facts or data in the particular case upon which an expert bases an opinion or inference may be those perceived by, reviewed by, or made known to the expert at or before the hearing. If of a type

reasonably relied upon by experts in the particular field in forming opinions or inferences upon the subject, the facts or data need not be admissible in evidence.

iii. Treatises, Documents, and Texts

Deramus v. Thornton, 160 Tex. 494, 505, 333 S.W.2d 824 (Tex. 1960) (orig. proceeding) (copies of newspaper articles hearsay and could not be considered in mandamus proceeding).

Elder v. State, 614 S.W.2d 136, 137 (Tex. Crim. App. 1981) (newspaper article found at appellant's house inadmissible hearsay).

Duncan v. State, 140 Tex.Crim. 606, 609, 146 S.W.2d 749 (Tex. Crim. App. 1940) (newspaper report on murder victim inadmissible hearsay).

Simms v. Sw. Tex. Methodist Hosp., 535 S.W.2d 192, 198 (Tex. Civ. App.—San Antonio 1976, writ ref'd n.r.e.) (statements contained in treatises, books, etc. inadmissible hearsay; exclusion of excerpts from writings as hearsay).

Atchison, Topeka & Santa Fe Ry. Co. v. Ham, 454 S.W.2d 451, 461(Tex. Civ. App.—Austin 1970, writ ref'd n.r.e.) (newspaper article properly excluded as hearsay).

Houston Packing Co. v. Griffith, 164 S.W. 431, 434 (Tex. Civ. App.—San Antonio 1914, no writ) (newspaper market quotes offered as evidence of market value should have been rejected as hearsay).

Poling v. San Antonio & A.P. Ry. Co., 32 Tex. Civ. App. 487, 490 75 S.W. 69 (Tex. Civ. App.—San Antonio 1903, writ ref'd) (newspaper account of proceedings of Board of Medical Examiners inadmissible hearsay).

d. Legal Questions

Gonzalez v. VATR Constr. LLC, 418 S.W.3d 777, 786 (Tex. App.—Dallas 2013, no pet.) (an expert witness may not testify to his opinion on a pure question of law).

Williams v. State, 417 S.W.3d 162, 182 (Tex. App.—Houston [1st Dist.] 2013, pet. ref'd) (no witness is competent to voice an opinion as to guilt or innocence of a criminal defendant).

Great W. Drilling, Ltd. v. Alexander, 305 S.W.3d 688, 696 (Tex. App.—Eastland 2009, no pet.) (no witness is authorized to offer an opinion on a pure question of law).

Schronk v. City of Burleson, 387 S.W.3d 692, 705 (Tex. App.—Waco 2009, pet. denied) (lay witness may not give legal conclusions or interpret the law to the jury).

Methodist Hosp. v. Zurich American Ins. Co., 329 S.W.3d 510, 524 n.15 (Tex. App.—Houston [14th Dist.] 2009, pet. denied) (in breach of contract action against workers' compensation insurer for its alleged breach of duty to defend, insurer's obligations under the policy were matter of contract interpretation and a question of law for the court—not subject to a witness's opinion).

Welder v. Welder, 794 S.W.2d 420, 532 (Tex. App.—San Antonio 1996, no pet.) (trial court properly excluded accountant's opinion on legal question of law).

Taylor v. State, 774 S.W.2d 31, 34 (Tex. App.—Houston [14th Dist.] 1989, writ ref'd) (harmless error to allow police officer's testimony on defendant's mental state where improper opinion on issue for jury to determine).

Dieter v. Baker Serv. Tools, a Div. of Baker Int'l, Inc., 776 S.W.2d 781, 784 (Tex. App.—Corpus Christi 1989, writ denied) (expert's affidavit filed in opposition to summary judgment motion irrelevant, not necessary to assist jury, and represented improper legal conclusion).

i. Compare: Ultimate Issues

Texas Rule of Evidence 704 states that "[t]estimony in the form of an opinion or inference otherwise admissible is not objectionable because it embraces an ultimate issue to be decided by the trier of fact." However, even under this statutory authority, the trial court maintains the discretion to exclude testimony as not helpful to the jury, speculative, irrelevant, or as improper under other principles of evidentiary law. The following cases provide examples of such "ultimate issue" testimony held to be inappropriate.

Burke v. State, 371 S.W.3d 252, 258 (Tex. App.—Houston [1st Dist.] 2011, pet. ref'd, untimely filed) (expert testimony does not assist the jury if it constitutes a direct opinion on the truthfulness of a child complainant's allegations).

Burke v. State, 371 S.W.3d 252, 258 (Tex. App.—Houston [1st Dist.] 2011, pet. ref'd, untimely filed) (expert's bare opinion that she believes, or believed, a child complainant's testimony to be true is excludable).

Paradigm Oil, Inc. v. Retamco Operating, Inc., 242 S.W.3d 67, 74 (Tex. App.—San Antonio 2007, pet. denied) (for an expert's opinion testimony on an ultimate issue to be competent, it must not be speculative or conclusory).

Holden v. Weidenfeller, 929 S.W.2d 124, 134 (Tex. App.—San Antonio 1996, writ denied) ("For a mixed question of law and fact to be admissible, it must meet the requirements applicable to expert testimony in general, and, in particular, it must be helpful to the trier of fact.").

e. *Matters of Common Experience*

Texas Rule of Evidence 702 provides:

> If scientific, technical, or other specialized knowledge *will assist the trier of fact to understand the evidence or to determine a fact in issue*, a witness qualified as an expert by knowledge, skill, experience, training, or education may testify thereto in the form of an opinion or otherwise. (Emphasis added.)

GTE Sw. v. Bruce, 998 S.W.2d 605, 620 (Tex. 1999) (expert testimony may be excluded on issue where jury is equally competent to form opinion, or specialized or technical knowledge not necessary).

Great W. Drilling, Ltd. v. Alexander, 305 S.W.3d 688, 696 (Tex. App.—Eastland 2009, no pet.) (in instances in which the jury is equally competent to form an opinion about the ultimate fact issues or the expert's testimony is within the common knowledge of the jury, the trial court should exclude the expert's testimony).

Burns v. Baylor Health Sys., 125 S.W.3d 589, 594 (Tex. App.—El Paso 2003, no pet.) (when a jury is equally competent to form an opinion about the ultimate fact issues or the expert's testimony is within the common knowledge of the jury, the trial court should exclude the expert's testimony).

f. Not Reasonably Relied on by Experts

Texas Rule of Evidence 703 provides:

> The facts or data in the particular case upon which an expert bases an opinion or inference may be those perceived by, reviewed by, or made known to the expert at or before the hearing. *If of a type reasonably relied upon by experts in the particular field in forming opinions or inferences upon the subject, the facts or data need not be admissible in evidence.* (Emphasis added.)

Bostic v. Georgia-Pacific Corp., 439 S.W.3d 332, 340 (Tex. 2013) (in addition to being relevant, the underlying scientific technique or principle relied on by the expert must be reliable).

Leonard v. State, 385 S.W.3d 570, 582 (Tex. Crim. App. 2012) (expert's opinion was improper because it was based solely on unreliable polygraph results).

Duncan-Hubert v. Mitchell, 310 S.W.3d 92, 102 (Tex. App.—Dallas 2010, pet. denied) (scientific evidence that is not grounded in methods and procedures of science is no more than subjective belief or unsupported speculation and is unreliable, and thus is inadmissible under the rule governing the admission of expert testimony).

Lincoln v. Clark Freight Lines, Inc., 285 S.W.3d 79, 83 (Tex. App.—Houston [1st Dist.] 2009, no pet.) (scientific evidence that is not grounded in the methods and procedures of science is no more than subjective belief or unsupported speculation and is therefore inadmissible).

g. Not Perceived or Personally Known

Texas Rule of Evidence 602 states:

> A witness may not testify to a matter *unless evidence is introduced sufficient to support a finding that the witness has personal knowledge of the matter.* Evidence to prove personal knowledge may, but need not, consist of the testimony of the witness. *This rule is subject to the provision of Rule 703, relating to opinion testimony by expert witnesses.* (Emphasis added.)

Dallas Morning News, Inc. v. Hall, 579 S.W.3d 370, 379 (Tex. 2019) ("A witness may testify to a matter only if the evidence supports a finding that the witness has personal knowledge of the matter.").

Amberson v. State, 552 S.W.3d 321, 329 (Tex. App.—Corpus Christi 2018, pet. ref'd) ("[H]elpful testimony by a witness who does not possess personal knowledge of the events about which he or she is testifying is expert testimony" not lay testimony.).

Hooper v. Torres, 790 S.W.2d 757, 761 (Tex. App.—El Paso 1990, writ denied) (portion of medical report representing summaries of findings by other physicians inadmissible).

Cornelison v. Aggregate Haulers, Inc., 777 S.W.2d 542, 545 (Tex. App.—Fort Worth 1989, writ denied) (trial court committed harmless error admitting statement from medical records regarding cause of incident where record did not establish who made statement at issue and whether individual had personal knowledge of events; "Statements contained in a medical record as to how an accident happened or where it happened, age, medical history, etc. are not admissible as a business-record exception to the hearsay rule, because the party making the entry in the record does not have personal knowledge as to these matters, and the statements do not become trustworthy just because it is hospital routine to record them." (Citations omitted.)).

h. *Speculation or Conjecture*

Morale v. State, 557 S.W.3d 569, 575 (Tex. 2018) ("[E]xpert testimony in condemnation cases is inadmissible if it relates to remote, speculative, and conjectural uses of the property that are not reflected in the present market value of the property.").

Gunn v. McCoy, 554 S.W.3d 645, 666 (Tex. 2018) ("[I]f no basis for the opinion is offered, or the basis offered provides no support, the opinion is merely a conclusory statement and cannot be considered probative evidence, regardless of whether there is no objection.").

Rogers v. Zanetti, 518 S.W.3d 394, 405 (Tex. 2017) ("When an expert's opinion is based on assumed facts that vary materially from the actual, undisputed facts, the opinion is without probative value and cannot support a verdict or judgment.").

Bustamante v. Ponte, 529 S.W.3d 447, 462 (Tex. 2016) ("An expert's testimony is conclusory if the witness simply states a conclusion without an explanation or factual substantiation.... If no basis for the opinion is offered, or the basis offered provides no support, the opinion is merely a conclusory statement and cannot be considered probative evidence, regardless of whether there is no objection.").

Bustamante v. Ponte, 529 S.W.3d 447, 462 (Tex. 2016) ("[A]n expert's testimony is conclusory if the expert merely gives an unexplained conclusion or asks the jury to 'take my word for it' because of his or her status as an expert.").

Bostic v. Georgia-Pacific Corp., 439 S.W.3d 332, 340 (Tex. 2013) (scientific evidence that is not grounded in the methods and procedures of science is no more than subjective belief or unsupported speculation).

Natural Gas Pipeline Co. of America v. Justiss, 397 S.W.3d 150, 156 (Tex. 2012) (testimony is speculative if it is based on guesswork or conjecture).

Natural Gas Pipeline Co. of America v. Justiss, 397 S.W.3d 150, 156 (Tex. 2012) (opinion testimony that is conclusory or speculative is not relevant evidence, because it does not tend to make the existence of a material fact more probable or less probable).

Natural Gas Pipeline Co. of America v. Justiss, 397 S.W.3d 150, 156 (Tex. 2012) (if a property owner's estimate is speculative, "the owner's testimony may be of such minimal probative force to warrant a judge's refusal even to submit the issue to the jury").

Wal-Mart Stores, Inc. v. Merrell, 313 S.W.3d 837, 840 (Tex. 2010) (expert's failure to explain or adequately disprove alternative theories of causation makes his or her own theory speculative and conclusory).

Cooper Tire & Rubber Co. v. Mendez, 204 S.W.3d 797, 800 (Tex. 2006) (scientific testimony is unreliable if it is not grounded in the methods and procedures of science and amounts to no more than a subjective belief or unsupported speculation).

Coastal Transp. Co. v. Crown Cent. Petroleum Corp., 136 S.W.3d 227, 232 (Tex. 2004) (conclusory and speculative expert testimony irrelevant and insufficient to overcome directed verdict motion by opposing party).

Gammill v. Jack Williams Chevrolet, Inc., 972 S.W.2d 713, 727 (Tex. 1998) (expert's opinions speculative and unreliable).

Tuttle v. Builes, 572 S.W.3d 344 (Tex. App.—Eastland 2019) (a property "owner's valuation testimony must be relevant ... [and] an owner's valuation testimony is not relevant if it is conclusory or speculative").

Tuttle v. Builes, 572 S.W.3d 344 (Tex. App.—Eastland 2019) (property valuations may not be based solely on a property owner's ipse dixit").

Tuttle v. Builes, 572 S.W.3d 344 (Tex. App.—Eastland 2019) ("[A] property owner may not simply echo the phrase 'market value' and state a number to substantiate his valuation.... His subjective opinion, by itself, will not provide relevant evidence of value.... Instead, to be relevant, the witness must provide the factual basis on which his opinion rests.... Evidence of price paid, nearby sales, tax valuations, appraisals, online resources, and any other relevant factors may be offered to support the valuation.").

Integrated of Amarillo, Inc. v. Kirkland, 424 S.W.3d 131, 135 (Tex. App.—Amarillo 2014, no pet.); *Schronk v. Laerdal Med. Corp.*, 440 S.W.3d 250, 258 (Tex. App.—Waco 2013, pet. denied) (opinion testimony that is conclusory or speculative is not relevant evidence because it does not tend to make the existence of a material fact more probable or less probable).

Russell Equestrian Ctr., Inc. v. Miller, 406 S.W.3d 243, 247 (Tex. App.—San Antonio 2013, no pet.) (opinion testimony that is conclusory or speculative is not relevant evidence, because it does not tend to make the existence of a material fact more probable or less probable).

Russell Equestrian Ctr., Inc. v. Miller, 406 S.W.3d 243, 247 (Tex. App.—San Antonio 2013, no pet.) (conclusory or speculative testimony is incompetent and cannot support a judgment).

Russell Equestrian Ctr., Inc. v. Miller, 406 S.W.3d 243, 247 (Tex. App.—San Antonio 2013, no pet.) (when the testimony is challenged as conclusory or speculative and therefore non-probative on its face, there is no need to go beyond the face of the record to test its reliability).

THI of Tex. at Lubbock I, LLC v. Perea, 329 S.W.3d 548, 563 n.25 (Tex. App.—Amarillo 2010, pet. denied) ("perhaps" and "possibly" in a medical expert's testimony indicate conjecture, speculation, or mere possibility, rather than qualified opinions based on reasonable medical probability).

DMC Valley Ranch, L.L.C. v. HPSC, Inc., 315 S.W.3d 898, 905 (Tex. App.—Dallas 2010, no pet.) (expert testimony is considered conclusory or speculative when it has no factual substantiation in the record).

Duncan-Hubert v. Mitchell, 310 S.W.3d 92, 102 (Tex. App.—Dallas 2010, pet. denied) (scientific evidence that is not grounded in methods and procedures of science is no more than subjective belief or unsupported speculation and is unreliable, and thus is inadmissible under the rule governing the admission of expert testimony).

Plunkett v. Conn. Gen. Life Ins. Co., 285 S.W.3d 106, 118 (Tex. App.—Dallas 2009, pet. denied) ("[C]ompetent expert medical causation evidence, whether expressed in testimony or in medical records, must be grounded in reasonable medical probability, not speculation or conjecture.").

State Off. of Risk Mgmt. v. Larkins, 258 S.W.3d 686, 692 (Tex. App.—Waco 2008, no pet.) ("[I]n the medical context, expert testimony that is not based on reasonable medical probability, but relies instead on possibility, speculation, or surmise, does not assist the jury and cannot support a judgment.").

Paradigm Oil, Inc. v. Retamco Operating, Inc., 242 S.W.3d 67, 74 (Tex. App.—San Antonio 2007, pet. denied) (expert opinion that has no factual substantiation in the record is speculative or conclusory).

Paradigm Oil, Inc. v. Retamco Operating, Inc., 242 S.W.3d 67, 74 (Tex. App.—San Antonio 2007, pet. denied) (for an expert's opinion testimony on an ultimate issue to be competent, it must not be speculative or conclusory).

Paradigm Oil, Inc. v. Retamco Operating, Inc., 242 S.W.3d 67, 74 (Tex. App.—San Antonio 2007, pet. denied) (expert opinion testimony on damages must be supported by objective facts, figures or data from which the amount may be ascertained with reasonable certainty; if it is not, it is speculative and conclusory and will not support a judgment).

LMC Complete Auto., Inc. v. Burke, 258 S.W.3d 686, 692 (Tex. App.—Houston [1st Dist.] 2007, pet. denied) ("In the medical context, expert testimony that is not based on reasonable medical probability, but relies instead on possibility, speculation, or surmise, does not assist the jury and cannot support a judgment.").

Quiroz ex rel. Quiroz v. Covenant Health Sys., 234 S.W.3d 74, 87 (Tex. App.—El Paso 2007, pet. denied) (opinion based on unreliable scientific data is inadmissible as it is nothing more than the expert's subjective belief or speculation).

Walker v. Thomasson Lumber Co., 203 S.W.3d 470, 475 (Tex. App.—Houston [14th Dist.] 2006, no pet.) ("[T]o be reliable, an expert's testimony must be grounded in scientific method and procedure such that it amounts to more than subjective belief or unsupported speculation.").

Naegeli Transp. v. Gulf Electroquip, Inc., 853 S.W.2d 737, 741 (Tex. App.—Houston [14th Dist.] 1993, writ denied) ("[E]xpert testimony cannot be based on mere guess or speculation, but must have a proper factual basis.").

i. Usurping Jury Function

Sandoval v. State, 409 S.W.3d 259, 281 (Tex. App.—Austin 2013, no pet.) ("the State may not elicit expert testimony that a particular child is telling the truth, or that child complainants as a class are worthy of belief.... Nor may an expert offer an opinion on the truthfulness of a child complainant's allegations," because such testimony "crosses the line" between evidence that will genuinely assist the jury and that which usurps the jury's function to judge the credibility of witnesses).

Holden v. Weidenfeller, 929 S.W.2d 124, 134 (Tex. App.—San Antonio 1996, writ denied) ("For a mixed question of law and fact to be admissible, it must meet the requirements applicable to expert testimony in general, and, in particular, it must be helpful to the trier of fact.").

Taylor v. State, 774 S.W.2d 31, 34 (Tex. App.—Houston [14th Dist.] 1989, writ ref'd) ("[A] witness may not give an opinion as to [a party's mental state] or the truth or falsity of other testimony.").

j. Irrelevant Matters

Gunn v. McCoy, 554 S.W.3d 645, 666 (Tex. 2018) ("[I]f no basis for the opinion is offered, or the basis offered provides no support, the opinion is merely a conclusory statement and cannot be considered probative evidence, regardless of whether there is no objection.").

Rogers v. Zanetti, 518 S.W.3d 394, 405 (Tex. 2017) ("When an expert's opinion is based on assumed facts that vary materially from the actual, undisputed facts, the opinion is without probative value and cannot support a verdict or judgment.").

Bustamante v. Ponte, 529 S.W.3d 447, 462 (Tex. 2016) ("An expert's testimony is conclusory if the witness simply states a conclusion without an explanation or factual substantiation.... If no basis for the opinion is offered, or the basis offered provides no support, the opinion is merely a conclusory statement and cannot be considered probative evidence, regardless of whether there is no objection.").

Exxon Pipeline Co. v. Zwahr, 88 S.W.3d 623, 628 (Tex. 2002) (relevance requirement for expert testimony, which incorporates traditional relevancy analysis under the Rules of Evidence, is met if the expert testimony is sufficiently tied to the facts of the case that it will aid the jury in resolving a factual dispute).

Exxon Pipeline Co. v. Zwahr, 88 S.W.3d 623, 628 (Tex. 2002) (evidence that has no relationship to any issue in the case does not satisfy the Rule of Evidence governing the admission of expert testimony, and thus inadmissible under the Rules of Evidence requiring that evidence be relevant, as well).

Enbridge Pipelines (East Texas) L.P. v. Avinger Timber, LLC, 386 S.W.3d 256, 261 (Tex. 2012) (a trial court must act as an evidentiary gatekeeper to exclude irrelevant and unreliable expert evidence).

Fleming v. Kinney ex rel. Shelton, 395 S.W.3d 917, 928 (Tex. App.—Houston [14th Dist.] 2013, pet. denied) (an expert may state an opinion on a mixed question of law and fact if the opinion is limited to the relevant issues and is based on proper legal concepts).

Integrated of Amarillo, Inc. v. Kirkland, 424 S.W.3d 131, 135 (Tex. App.—Amarillo 2014, no pet.); *Schronk v. Laerdal Med. Corp.*, 440 S.W.3d 250, 258 (Tex. App.—Waco 2013, pet. denied) (opinion testimony that is conclusory or speculative is not relevant evidence because it does not tend to make the existence of a material fact more probable or less probable).

Schronk v. Laerdal Med. Corp., 440 S.W.3d 250, 258 (Tex. App.—Waco 2013, pet. denied) (to be relevant, the expert's opinion must be based on the facts).

Goss v. Kellogg Brown & Root, Inc., 232 S.W.3d 816, 819 (Tex. App.—Houston [14th Dist.] 2007, pet. denied) (to be relevant, expert testimony must be so sufficiently tied to the facts of the case that it will aid the jury in resolving a factual dispute).

Kelly v. State, 824 S.W.2d 568, 572 (Tex. Crim. App. 1992) (proponent of novel scientific evidence must show evidence is relevant).

Nguyen v. State, 21 S.W.3d 609, 612 (Tex. App.—Houston [1st Dist.] 2000, pet. ref'd) (insufficient factual foundation existed to make an expert's testimony relevant).

Associated Carriages, Inc. v. Int'l Bank of Commerce, 37 S.W.3d 69, 74 (Tex. App.—San Antonio 2000, pet. denied) (proposed deposition testimony of expert regarding corporate law properly excluded as irrelevant).

Purina Mills, Inc. v. Odell, 948 S.W.2d 927, 933 (Tex. App.—Texarkana 1997, pet. denied) (the party offering expert testimony must show that the testimony is relevant and based on a reliable foundation).

Dieter v. Baker Serv. Tools, a Div. of Baker Int'l, Inc., 776 S.W.2d 781, 784 (Tex. App.—Corpus Christi 1989, writ denied) (expert's affidavit filed in opposition to summary judgment motion irrelevant, not necessary to assist jury, and represented improper legal conclusion).

k. *Conclusory Testimony*

Gunn v. McCoy, 554 S.W.3d 645, 666 (Tex. 2018) ("[I]f no basis for the opinion is offered, or the basis offered provides no support, the opinion is merely a conclusory statement and cannot be considered probative evidence, regardless of whether there is no objection.").

Rogers v. Zanetti, 518 S.W.3d 394, 405 (Tex. 2017) ("[E]ven when some basis is offered for an opinion, if that basis does not, on its face, support the opinion, the opinion is still conclusory.").

Bustamante v. Ponte, 529 S.W.3d 447, 462 (Tex. 2016) ("An expert's testimony is conclusory if the witness simply states a conclusion without an explanation or factual substantiation.... If no basis for the opinion is offered, or the basis offered provides no support, the opinion is merely a conclusory statement and cannot be considered probative evidence, regardless of whether there is no objection.").

Bustamante v. Ponte, 529 S.W.3d 447, 462 (Tex. 2016) ("[A]n expert's testimony is conclusory if the expert merely gives an unexplained conclusion or asks the jury to 'take my word for it' because of his or her status as an expert.").

Wal-Mart Stores, Inc. v. Merrell, 313 S.W.3d 837, 840 (Tex. 2010) (expert's failure to explain or adequately disprove alternative theories of causation makes his or her own theory speculative and conclusory).

Cooper Tire & Rubber Co. v. Mendez, 204 S.W.3d 797, 800 (Tex. 2006) (engineer's testimony was legally insufficient to establish existence of manufacturing defect that caused tire failure where it was conclusory, subjective, and unsupported by testing or studies).

Coastal Transp. Co., v. Crown Cent. Petroleum Corp., 136 S.W.3d 227, 232 (Tex. 2004) (conclusory and speculative expert testimony irrelevant and insufficient to overcome directed verdict motion by opposing party).

Subsea 7 Port Isabel, LLC v. Port Isabel Logistical Offshore Terminal, Inc., 593 S.W.3d 859, 874 (Tex. App.—Corpus Christi 2019, pet. filed) ("[I]n order for a property owner to qualify as a witness to the damages to his property, his testimony must show that it refers to market, rather than intrinsic or some other value of the property.... When the evidence does not indicate the factual basis behind the owner's valuation, the testimony is conclusory and will be legally insufficient to sustain a judgment.").

Tuttle v. Builes, 572 S.W.3d 344 (Tex. App.—Eastland 2019) (a property "owner's valuation testimony must be relevant ... [and] an owner's valuation testimony is not relevant if it is conclusory or speculative").

Tuttle v. Builes, 572 S.W.3d 344 (Tex. App.—Eastland 2019) ("[P]roperty valuations may not be based solely on a property owner's ipse dixit.").

Tuttle v. Builes, 572 S.W.3d 344 (Tex. App.—Eastland 2019) ("[A] property owner may not simply echo the phrase 'market value' and state a number to substantiate his valuation.... His subjective opinion, by itself, will not provide relevant evidence of value.... Instead, to be relevant, the witness must provide the factual basis on which his opinion rests.... Evidence of price paid, nearby sales, tax valuations, appraisals, online resources, and any other relevant factors may be offered to support the valuation.").

Integrated of Amarillo, Inc. v. Kirkland, 424 S.W.3d 131, 135 (Tex. App.—Amarillo 2014, no pet.) (opinion testimony that is conclusory or speculative is objectionable and inadmissible as lacking relevance because it does not tend to make the existence of a material fact more probable or less probable).

iLight Techs. Inc. v. Clutch City Sports & Entertainment, L.P., 414 S.W.3d 842, 847 (Tex. App.—Houston [1st Dist.] 2013, pet. denied) (expert opinions must be supported by facts in evidence, not conjecture).

Russell Equestrian Ctr., Inc. v. Miller, 406 S.W.3d 243, 247 (Tex. App.—San Antonio 2013, no pet.) (opinion testimony that is conclusory or speculative is not relevant evidence, because it does not tend to make the existence of a material fact more probable or less probable).

Russell Equestrian Ctr., Inc. v. Miller, 406 S.W.3d 243, 247 (Tex. App.—San Antonio 2013, no pet.) (conclusory or speculative testimony is incompetent and cannot support a judgment).

Russell Equestrian Ctr., Inc. v. Miller, 406 S.W.3d 243, 247 (Tex. App.—San Antonio 2013, no pet.) (when the testimony is challenged as conclusory or speculative and therefore non-probative on its face, there is no need to go beyond the face of the record to test its reliability).

Russell Equestrian Ctr., Inc. v. Miller, 406 S.W.3d 243, 247 (Tex. App.—San Antonio 2013, no pet.) (even when some basis is offered for an opinion, if that basis does not, on its face, support the opinion, the opinion is still conclusory).

Qui Phuoc Ho v. MacArthur Ranch, LLC, 395 S.W.3d 325, 333 (Tex. App.—Dallas 2013, no pet) (expert's testimony is conclusory as a matter of law if the witness simply states a conclusion without an explanation or factual substantiation).

Custom Transit, L.P. v. Flatrolled Steel, Inc., 375 S.W.3d 337, 356 (Tex. App.—Houston [14th Dist.] 2012, no pet.) ("[I]f testing of critical aspects of an expert's testimony has not taken place either by the expert or others in the relevant scientific or expert community, then an explanation of why it has not is an important consideration in evaluating the expert opinions and determining whether they are substantially more than merely the expert's conclusory, subjective opinion.").

Houston Cab Co. v. Fields, 249 S.W.3d 741, 749 (Tex. App.—Beaumont 2008, no pet.) ("[W]hen it is apparent that the expert testimony is conclusory, it is deemed non-probative.").

Houston Cab Co. v. Fields, 249 S.W.3d 741, 749 (Tex. App.—Beaumont 2008, no pet.) (expert testimony taxicab driver was not a safe driver was too conclusory to be given probative value).

U.S. Fire Ins. Co. v. Scottsdale Ins. Co., 264 S.W.3d 160, 172 (Tex. App.—Dallas 2008, no pet.) (expert opinion is conclusory when it offers an opinion with no factual substantiation, as an expert must explain how he or she reached the conclusion).

Paradigm Oil, Inc. v. Retamco Operating, Inc., 242 S.W.3d 67, 74 (Tex. App.—San Antonio 2007, pet. denied) (expert opinion that has no factual substantiation in the record is speculative or conclusory).

Kettle v. Baylor Med. Ctr. at Garland, 232 S.W.3d 832, 844 (Tex. App.—Dallas 2007, pet. denied) ("[C]onclusory opinion testimony is not evidence.").

United Svcs. Auto. Ass'n v. Croft, 175 S.W.3d 457, 463 (Tex. App.—Dallas 2005, no pet.) (an expert opinion is conclusory when it offers an opinion with no factual substantiation).

l. Burden of Proof

Wolfe v. State, 509 S.W.3d 325, 335 (Tex. Crim. App. 2017) ("[There are] three criteria for reliability that the proponent of scientific evidence must prove: (1) the underlying scientific theory must be valid; (2) the technique applying the theory must be valid; and (3) the technique must have been properly applied on the occasion in question.").

Mack Trucks, Inc. v. Tamez, 206 S.W.3d 572, 578 (Tex. 2006) (because the party sponsoring the expert bears the burden of showing that the expert's testimony is admissible, the burden of presenting understandable evidence that will persuade the trial court to admit the expert's testimony is on the presenting party).

Gammill v. Jack Williams Chevrolet, Inc., 972 S.W.2d 713, 727 (Tex. 1998); *Menafee v. Ohman*, 323 S.W.3d 509, 514 (Tex. App.—Fort Worth 2010, no pet.) (party offering the expert's testimony bears the burden to prove that the witness is qualified and must demonstrate that the witness possesses special knowledge as to the very matter on which he or she proposes to give an opinion).

Russell Equestrian Ctr., Inc. v. Miller, 406 S.W.3d 243, 247 (Tex. App.—San Antonio 2013, no pet.) (proponent of expert testimony bears the burden of showing the testimony is admissible).

Foster v. Richardson, 303 S.W.3d 833, 844 (Tex. App.—Fort Worth 2009, no pet.) ("[T]here is no validity, if there ever was, to the notion that every licensed medical doctor should be automatically qualified to testify as an expert on every medical question. The proponent of the testimony has the burden to show that the expert possesses special knowledge as to the very matter on which he or she proposes to give an opinion.").

Rogers v. Alexander, 244 S.W.3d 370, 383 (Tex. App.—Dallas 2007, no pet.) ("[O]ffering party must establish that an expert has knowledge, skill, experience, or education regarding the specific issue before the court which would qualify the expert to give an opinion on that particular subject.").

Baylor Univ. Med. Ctr. v. Biggs, 237 S.W.3d 909, 915 (Tex. App.—Dallas 2007, pet. denied) ("[T]o comply with section 74.401's requirements, the proponent of the expert's testimony has the burden to show that the expert has knowledge, skill, experience, training, or education regarding the specific issue before the court which would qualify the expert to give an opinion on that particular subject.").

Mem'l Hermann Healthcare Sys. v. Burrell, 230 S.W.3d 755, 757 (Tex. App.—Houston [14th Dist.] 2007, no pet.) (proponent of expert has burden to show that the expert is qualified).

Chester v. El-Ashram, 228 S.W.3d 909, 912 (Tex. App.—Dallas 2007, no pet.) (proponent of the expert's testimony has the burden to show that the expert possesses special knowledge as to the very matter on which he or she proposes to give an opinion; what is required is that the offering party establish that the expert has knowledge, skill, experience, training, or education regarding the specific issue before the court that would qualify the expert to give an opinion on that particular subject).

m. *Other Grounds*

Other possible grounds for excluding expert testimony include:

- Prejudicial;
- Time-wasting;
- Confusing or misleading;
- Cumulative;
- Irrelevant;
- Collateral to issues in case;
- Improper foundation;
- Improper test evidence;

- Improper expert qualifications;
- Inadmissible hearsay.

4. Opposing Authorities

Texas Rule of Evidence 703 states:

> The facts or data in the particular case upon which an expert bases an opinion or inference may be those perceived by, reviewed by, or made known to the expert at or before the hearing. If of a type reasonably relied upon by experts in the particular field in forming opinions or inferences upon the subject, the facts or data need not be admissible in evidence.

Morale v. State, 557 S.W.3d 569, 575 (Tex. 2018) ("[A]n expert's opinion may assume facts established by legally sufficient evidence.").

Gunn v. McCoy, 554 S.W.3d 645, 666 (Tex. 2018) ("Litigants in Texas are afforded a broad right to make strategic decisions when introducing evidence at trial, and they are entitled to present experts in a manner of their choosing, so long as it is consistent with the Texas Rules of Civil Procedure and the Texas Rules of Evidence.").

Gunn v. McCoy, 554 S.W.3d 645, 666 (Tex. 2018) ("An expert's factual assumptions must [not] be uncontested or established as a matter of law—if the evidence conflicts, it is normally the province of the jury to determine which evidence to credit.").

In re National Lloyds Insurance Company, 532 S.W.3d 794, 815 (Tex. 2017) (orig. proceeding) ("[W]hen a witness is properly disclosed and designated as an expert and the main substance of the witness's testimony is based on specialized knowledge, skill, experience, training, and education, the testimony will generally be expert testimony within the scope of Rule 702.").

Wolfe v. State, 509 S.W.3d 325, 335 (Tex. Crim. App. 2017) ("The trial court's gatekeeping function under Rule 702 does not supplant cross-examination as the traditional and appropriate means of attacking shaky but admissible evidence.").

Garcia v. Gomez, 319 S.W.3d 638, 642 (Tex. 2010) ("An attorney's testimony about the reasonableness of his or her own fees is not like other expert witness testimony. Although rooted in the attorney's experience and expertise, it also consists of the attorney's personal knowledge about the underlying work and its particular value to the client. The testimony is similar to that of a property owner whose personal knowledge qualifies him to give an opinion about his own property's value.... The attorney's testimony is not objectionable as merely conclusory because the opposing party, or that party's attorney, likewise has some knowledge of the time and effort involved and if the matter is truly in dispute, may effectively question the attorney regarding the reasonableness of his fee.").

Templeton v. Dreiss, 961 S.W.2d 645, 672 (Tex. App.—San Antonio 1998, pet. denied) (trial court did not err admitting lawyer's expert opinion regarding technical meaning of certain words in document).

Lyondell Petrochemical Co. v. Fluor Daniel, Inc., 888 S.W.2d 547, 555 (Tex. App.—Houston [1st Dist.] 1994, writ denied) (trial court should have allowed testimony that contractor violated OSHA).

a. Hearsay

Texas Rule of Evidence 703 states:

> The facts or data in the particular case upon which an expert bases an opinion or inference may be those perceived by, reviewed by, or made known to the expert at or before the hearing. If of a type reasonably relied upon by experts in the particular field in forming opinions or inferences upon the subject, the facts or data need not be admissible in evidence.

Burroughs Wellcome Co. v. Crye, 907 S.W.2d 497, 499 (Tex. 1995) (diagnosis contained in medical records admissible as business record; note that the records were insufficient to prove reasonably probable causation where the context of the records that the suggested notations were merely recitations of statements and the opinions of others).

In re Marriage of Bivins, 393 S.W.3d 893, 901 (Tex. App.—Waco 2012, pet. denied) (experts are permitted to use evidence that may otherwise be hearsay in rendering their opinions).

Reyes v. State, 48 S.W.3d 917, 922 (Tex. App.—Fort Worth 2001, no pet.) (hearsay statements in medical records made for purposes of seeking treatment properly admitted).

Castaneda v. State, 28 S.W.3d 685, 693 (Tex. App.—Corpus Christi 2000, pet. ref'd) (medical records of victim, including victim's description of incident, admissible as business records).

Glenn v. C & G Elec., Inc., 977 S.W.2d 686, 689 (Tex. App.—Fort Worth 1998, pet. denied) (medical records containing opinions and diagnoses made by physicians properly admitted into evidence as business records).

Moyer v. State, 948 S.W.2d 525, 528 (Tex. App.—Fort Worth 1997, pet. ref'd) (subjective statements of patient to paramedic admissible as statements made for purposes of diagnosis).

Welder v. Welder, 794 S.W.2d 420, 532 (Tex. App.—Corpus Christi 1990, no pet.) (accountant could testify to nature of certain assets even if records relied upon to form opinion were not admissible into evidence).

i. Statements of Others

Castaneda v. State, 28 S.W.3d 685, 693 (Tex. App.—Corpus Christi 2000, pet. ref'd) (medical records of victim, including victim's description of incident, admissible as business records).

Moyer v. State, 948 S.W.2d 525, 528 (Tex. App.—Fort Worth 1997, pet. ref'd) (subjective statements of patient to paramedic admissible as statements made for purposes of diagnosis).

Hooper v. Torres, 790 S.W.2d 757, 761 (Tex. App.—El Paso 1990, writ denied) (portion of medical report representing summaries of findings by other physicians inadmissible).

ii. Treatises, Documents, and Texts

McMillen Feed, Inc. v. Harlow, 405 S.W.2d 123, 136 (Tex. Civ. App.—Austin 1966, writ ref'd n.r.e.) (charts contained in magazine admissible as exceptions to hearsay rule).

Gilmore v. State, 666 S.W.2d 136, 149 (Tex. App.—Amarillo 1983, writ ref'd) (admission of newspaper articles did not violate hearsay rule).

b. Hypothetical Questions

Eldred v. State, 431 S.W.3d 177, 186 (Tex. App.—Texarkana 2014, no pet.) (hypothetical questions are relevant when the facts of the hypothetical match the facts of the case being tried).

Celotex Corp. v. Tate, 797 S.W.2d 197, 203 (Tex. App.—Corpus Christi 1990, writ dism'd by agr.) (expert testimony based upon hypothetical information admissible to assist the jury in its calculation of damages).

Soriano v. Medina, 648 S.W.2d 426, 429 (Tex. App.—San Antonio 1983, no writ) (testimony based upon hypothetical question proper when hypothetical supported by sufficient facts in evidence).

Roth v. Law, 579 S.W.2d 949, 954 (Tex. Civ. App.—Corpus Christi 1979, writ ref'd n.r.e.) (hypothetical questions asked of experts proper where supported by evidence).

Weingarten, Inc. v. Tripplett, 530 S.W.2d 653, 656 (Tex. Civ. App.—Beaumont 1975, writ ref'd n.r.e.) (hypothetical question properly restricted to facts in evidence, inferences from evidence, and facts that later came into evidence).

Burns v. Bridge Eng'g Corp., 465 S.W.2d 427, 431 (Tex. Civ. App.—Houston [14th Dist.] 1971, writ ref'd n.r.e.) (hypothetical fairly based upon one party's theory of evidence is proper).

Tex. Emp. Ins. Ass'n v. Steadman, 415 S.W.2d 211, 215 (Tex. Civ. App.—Amarillo 1967, writ ref'd n.r.e.) (hypothetical question asked of expert proper where supported by evidence).

c. Legal Questions vs. Ultimate Issues

Texas Rule of Evidence 704 states:

> Testimony in the form of an opinion or inference otherwise admissible is not objectionable because it embraces an ultimate issue to be decided by the trier of fact.

Ex parte Nailor, 149 S.W.3d 125, 134 (Tex. Crim. App. 2004) (police officer could provide testimony that embraced ultimate issue).

Merrill v. Sprint Waste Services LP, 527 S.W.3d 663, 670 (Tex. App.—Houston [14th Dist.] 2017, no pet.) ("Rule of Evidence 704 ... abolished the common law rule that a witness cannot invade the province of the jury by offering an opinion on liability.").

Williams v. State, 417 S.W.3d 162, 182 (Tex. App.—Houston [1st Dist.] 2013, pet. ref'd) ("[O]pinion testimony that is otherwise admissible is not objectionable solely because it embraces an ultimate issue to be decided by the trier of fact.").

Burke v. State, 371 S.W.3d 252, 258 (Tex. App.—Houston [1st Dist.] 2011, pet. ref'd, untimely filed) (testimony by an expert witness that provides useful background information to aid the jury in evaluating the testimony of another witness is admissible).

Burke v. State, 371 S.W.3d 252, 258 (Tex. App.—Houston [1st Dist.] 2011, pet. ref'd, untimely filed) (opinion testimony that is otherwise admissible is not objectionable solely because it embraces an ultimate opinion to be decided by the trier of fact).

Great W. Drilling, Ltd. v. Alexander, 305 S.W.3d 688, 696 (Tex. App.—Eastland 2009, no pet.) (expert witness may offer an opinion on a mixed question of law and fact when a standard or measure is fixed by law and the question is whether the person or conduct measures up to that standard).

Taylor v. Tex. Dep't of Protective & Regulatory Servs., 160 S.W.3d 641, 650 (Tex. App.—Austin 2005, pet. denied) (social worker qualified to testify as to ultimate issue).

B. Motion to Exclude Testimony of Nonqualified Expert

1. Suggested Motion Text

(*Name of Moving Party*) hereby moves this Court for an order excluding any and all testimony, references to testimony, or argument relating to the testimony of (*Name of Witness*) that (*Describe Improper Testimony, e.g., the Decedent Died as a Result of Drowning*). The motion is based upon the ground that the witness lacks the requisite knowledge, skill, experience, training, or education to properly testify on this subject and therefore the testimony is inadmissible).

2. Motion Summary

This motion is used to exclude expert testimony of a witness lacking the necessary background qualifications to testify on the stated areas of expertise. The motion is based upon the express authority of Texas Rule of Evidence 702 which requires that the witness be "qualified as an expert by knowledge, skill, experience, training, or education."

This motion is typically presented at what is referred to as a *Robinson* hearing, named after the leading case of *E.I. du Pont de Nemours & Co. v. Robinson*, 923 S.W.2d 549, 557 (Tex. 1995).

3. Supporting Authorities

Texas Rule of Evidence 702 states:

> If scientific, technical, or other specialized knowledge will assist the trier of fact to understand the evidence or to determine a fact in issue, *a witness qualified as an expert by knowledge, skill, experience, training, or education* may testify thereto in the form of an opinion or otherwise. (Emphasis added.)

Gunn v. McCoy, 554 S.W.3d 645, 666 (Tex. 2018) ("To testify as an expert, a witness must be qualified, and the proposed testimony must be relevant to the issues in the case and based upon a reliable foundation.").

Rogers v. Zanetti, 518 S.W.3d 394, 405 (Tex. 2017) ("[T]he assurance of familiarity and credibility is not a 'demonstrable and reasoned basis' upon which to evaluate [an expert's] opinion.... An ipse dixit is still an ipse dixit even if offered by the most trustworthy of sources.").

Rogers v. Zanetti, 518 S.W.3d 394, 405 (Tex. 2017) ("An expert's familiarity with the facts is not alone a satisfactory basis for his or her opinion.").

Bustamante v. Ponte, 529 S.W.3d 447, 462 (Tex. 2016) ("[A]n expert's simple ipse dixit is insufficient to establish a matter; rather, the expert must explain the basis of the statements to link the conclusions to the facts.").

Bustamante v. Ponte, 529 S.W.3d 447, 462 (Tex. 2016) ("[A]n expert's testimony is conclusory if the expert merely gives an unexplained conclusion or asks the jury to 'take my word for it' because of his or her status as an expert.").

Wolfe v. State, 509 S.W.3d 325, 335 (Tex. Crim. App. 2017) ("Unreliable scientific evidence is inadmissible because it simply will not assist the jury to understand the evidence or accurately determine a fact in issue; such evidence obfuscates rather than leads to an intelligent evaluation of the facts.").

In re Commitment of Bohannan, 388 S.W.3d 296, 304 (Tex. 2012) (an expert must be qualified by knowledge, skill, experience, training, or education to assist the trier of fact to understand the evidence or to determine a fact in issue).

In re Commitment of Bohannan, 388 S.W.3d 296, 304 (Tex. 2012) (that a witness has knowledge, skill, expertise, or training does not necessarily mean that the witness can assist the trier of fact).

In re Commitment of Bohannan, 388 S.W.3d 296, 304 (Tex. 2012) (credentials alone do not qualify an expert to testify).

In re Commitment of Bohannan, 388 S.W.3d 296, 304 (Tex. 2012) (the test is whether the offering party has established that the expert has knowledge, skill, experience, training, or education regarding the specific issue before the court, which would qualify the expert to give an opinion on that particular subject).

Reid Road Mun. Util. Dist. No. 2 v. Speedy Stop Food Stores, Ltd., 337 S.W.3d 846, 854 (Tex. 2011) (to the provisions of Rule 701, a witness who will be giving opinion evidence about a property's fair market value must be disclosed and designated as an expert pursuant to discovery and other applicable rules).

In re McAllen Med. Ctr., 275 S.W.3d 458, 463 (Tex. 2008, orig. proceeding) (there is no validity to the notion that every licensed medical doctor should be automatically qualified to testify as an expert on every medical question).

Gen. Motors Corp. v. Iracheta, 161 S.W.3d 462, 470 (Tex. 2006) (expert testimony inadmissible as expert not qualified).

Gammill v. Jack Williams Chevrolet, Inc., 972 S.W.2d 713, 727 (Tex. 1998) (no error in determining one of mechanical engineers unqualified to testify as expert on subject matter at issue).

Equistar Chemicals, LP v. ClydeUnion DB, Ltd., 79 S.W.3d 505, 511 (Tex. App.—Houston [14th Dist.] 2019, pet. denied) ("To be competent evidence, an expert's opinion must have a demonstrable and reasoned basis on which to evaluate the opinion.... When an expert's opinion is based on assumed facts that vary materially from the actual, undisputed facts, the opinion is without probative value and cannot support a verdict or judgment.").

Carter v. State, 575 S.W.3d 892 (Tex. App.—Amarillo 2019, pet. granted) ("[Q]ualifying a witness as an expert normally implicates a two-step procedure.... First, it must be shown that the witness has a sufficient background in a particular field, which background encompasses the matter on which the witness is to give an opinion.... The second step gauges the relationship between the subject matter at issue and the expert's familiarity with it; that is, it must be shown that the expert's background is tailored to the specific area of expertise in which the expert desires to testify.").

Grismore v. Texas Spine & Joint Hospital, Ltd., PAC, 578 S.W.3d 684 (Tex. App.—Tyler 2019, no pet.) ("Not every licensed medical doctor is automatically qualified to testify as an expert on every medical question, and the proponent of that testimony must show that the expert possesses special knowledge regarding the matter on which he proposes to give an opinion.").

Schronk v. Laerdal Med. Corp., 440 S.W.3d 250, 258 (Tex. App.—Waco 2013, pet. denied) (whether a witness is qualified as an expert is a preliminary question for the trial court to determine).

Menafee v. Ohman, 323 S.W.3d 509, 514 (Tex. App.—Fort Worth 2010, no pet.) (offering party must demonstrate that the expert "has knowledge, skill, experience, training, or education regarding the specific issue before the court which would qualify the expert to give an opinion on that particular subject").

Great W. Drilling, Ltd. v. Alexander, 305 S.W.3d 688, 696 (Tex. App.—Eastland 2009, no pet.) (expert opinion testimony is admissible if that testimony will assist the trier-of-fact to determine a fact in issue, provided the expert is qualified as an expert by knowledge, skill, experience, training, or education; the expert's testimony must also be relevant to the issues in the case and must be based upon a reliable foundation).

Foster v. Richardson, 303 S.W.3d 833, 844 (Tex. App.—Fort Worth 2009, no pet.) ("[T]here is no validity, if there ever was, to the notion that every licensed medical doctor should be automatically qualified to testify as an expert on every medical question. The proponent of the testimony has the burden to show that the expert possesses special knowledge as to the very matter on which he or she proposes to give an opinion.").

Champion v. Great Dane Ltd. P'ship, 286 S.W.3d 533, 544 (Tex. App.—Houston [14th Dist.] 2009, no pet.) ("if the expert is not qualified to offer a particular opinion in a particular case, then the expert's testimony is not admissible because it does not rise above mere speculation, and, accordingly, does not offer genuine assistance to the jury").

Champion v. Great Dane Ltd. P'ship, 286 S.W.3d 533, 544 (Tex. App.—Houston [14th Dist.] 2009, no pet.) ("[W]hether an expert is qualified under Rule 702 is a preliminary matter to be determined by the trial court ... [which] must ensure that those who purport to be experts truly have expertise concerning the actual subject matter about which they are offering an opinion.... General experience in a specialized field is insufficient to qualify a witness as an expert.").

Spin Doctor Golf, Inc. v. Paymentech, L.P., 296 S.W.3d 354, 359 (Tex. App.—Dallas 2009, pet. denied) ("[I]n deciding if expert is qualified, trial courts must ensure that those who purport to be experts truly have expertise concerning the actual subject about which they are offering an opinion.").

Spin Doctor Golf, Inc. v. Paymentech, L.P., 296 S.W.3d 354, 359 (Tex. App.—Dallas 2009, pet. denied) (general experience in a specialized field does not qualify a witness as an expert).

Collini v. Pustejovsky, 280 S.W.3d 456, 465 (Tex. App.—Fort Worth 2009, no pet.) (in health care liability cases, "to be qualified, an expert must have knowledge, skill, experience, training, or education regarding the specific issue before the court that would qualify the expert to give an opinion on that particular subject").

Collini v. Pustejovsky, 280 S.W.3d 456, 465 (Tex. App.—Fort Worth 2009, no pet.) ("[The] party offering the witness as an expert on causation must establish that the witness is qualified to testify under Rule 702.").

MCI Sales and Serv., Inc. v. Hinton, 272 S.W.3d 17, 30 (Tex. App.—Waco 2008), *aff'd*, 329 S.W.3d 475 (Tex. 2010), *cert. denied*, 131 S. Ct. 2903 (2011) ("[T]o establish a witness's expert qualifications, the party calling the witness must show that the expert has knowledge, skill, experience, training, or education regarding the specific issue before the court which would qualify the expert to give an opinion on that particular subject.").

Castillo v. August, 248 S.W.3d 874, 881 (Tex. App.—El Paso 2008, no pet.) (not every licensed medical doctor is automatically qualified to testify as an expert on every medical question; the issue is the expert's familiarity with the specific subject matter in question).

Castillo v. August, 248 S.W.3d 874, 881 (Tex. App.—El Paso 2008, no pet.) (fact that an expert is not a specialist in the particular area at issue does not necessarily disqualify him or her from providing an expert opinion on a medical question).

Farishta v. Tenet Healthsystem Hospitals Dallas, Inc., 224 S.W.3d 448, 455 (Tex. App.—Fort Worth 2007, no pet.) ("[N]onphysician may not opine on medical causation matters.").

Palafox v. Silvey, 247 S.W.3d 310, 316 (Tex. App.—El Paso 2007, no pet.) (in deciding whether an expert is qualified, the trial court must ensure those who purport to be experts truly have expertise concerning the actual subject about which they are offering an opinion; trial court is not required to admit opinion evidence which is connected to the existing data by the *ipse dixit* of the expert).

Praytor v. Ford Motor Co., 97 S.W.3d 237, 245 (Tex. App.—Houston [14th Dist.] 2002, no pet.) (trial court properly determined insufficient foundation to qualify certain witnesses as expert witnesses).

a. Examples

Gammill v. Jack Williams Chevrolet, Inc., 972 S.W.2d 713, 727 (Tex. 1998) (no error determining one of mechanical engineers not qualified to testify as expert on subject matter at issue).

Broders v. Heise, 924 S.W.2d 148, 152 (Tex. 1996) (trial court did not abuse discretion determining witness lacked qualifications to provide expert opinion on causation).

Bailey v. Amaya Clinic, Inc., 402 S.W.3d 355, 365 (Tex. App.—Houston [14th Dist.] 2013, no pet.) ("[A] board-certified dermatologist, although generally qualified to opine as to the standard of care for dermatologists, was not qualified to opine as to the standard of care for weight-loss health care providers.").

Praytor v. Ford Motor Co., 97 S.W.3d 237, 245 (Tex. App.—Houston [14th Dist.] 2002, no pet.) (trial court properly determined insufficient foundation to qualify certain witnesses as expert witnesses).

Franco v. State, 25 S.W.3d 26, 29 (Tex. App.—El Paso 2000, pet. ref'd) (harmless error where trial court improperly allowed confusing, misleading, and prejudicial blood spatter evidence by unqualified expert).

Nixon v. State, 937 S.W.2d 610, 612 (Tex. App.—Houston [1st Dist.] 1996, no writ) (harmless error for court to admit opinion of witness who lived near property and invested in other property where not qualified to provide expert opinion on cost of repairing damaged property).

Celotex Corp. v. Tate, 797 S.W.2d 197, 203 (Tex. App.—Corpus Christi 1990, writ dism'd by agr.) (harmless error allowing opinion of expert where expert did not possess any special knowledge to allow him to provide value of damages for loss of "guidance and counsel").

Handel v. Long Trusts, 757 S.W.2d 848, 851 (Tex. App.—Texarkana 1988, no writ) (insufficient foundation provided to establish witness was qualified as expert).

b. Qualification of Experts in Health Care Liability Cases

Tex. Civ. Prac. & Rem. Code §§ 74.001 et seq. govern health care liability cases. A "health care liability claim" is a "cause of action against a health care provider or physician for treatment, lack of treatment, or other claimed departure from accepted standards of medical care, or health care, or safety or professional or administrative services directly related to health care, which proximately results in injury to or death of a claimant, whether the claimant's claim or cause of action sounds in tort or contract." Tex. Civ. Prac. & Rem. Code § 74.001(a)(13). "Health care provider" means "any person, partnership, professional association, corporation, facility, or institution duly licensed, certified, registered, or chartered by the State of Texas to provide health care, including a registered nurse, a dentist, a podiatrist, a pharmacist, a chiropractor, an optometrist, or a health care institution," and the phrase also includes "an officer, director, shareholder, member, partner, manager, owner, or affiliate of a health care provider or physician and an employee, independent contractor, or agent of a health care provider or physician acting in the course and scope of the employment or contractual relationship." Tex. Civ. Prac. & Rem. Code § 74.001(a)(12).

Claims Against Physicians

In a suit involving a health care liability claim against a physician:

> a person may qualify as an expert witness on the issue of whether the physician departed from accepted standards of medical care only if the proposed expert is a physician who:
>
> (1) is practicing medicine at the time such testimony is given or was practicing medicine at the time the claim arose;
> (2) has knowledge of accepted standards of medical care for the diagnosis, care, or treatment of the illness, injury, or condition involved in the claim; and
> (3) is qualified on the basis of training or experience to offer an expert opinion regarding those accepted standards of medical care.

Tex. Civ. Prac. & Rem. Code §§ 74.401(a).

"Practicing medicine" or "medical practice" includes training residents or students at an accredited school of medicine or osteopathy or serving as a consulting physician to other physicians who provide direct patient care, upon the request of such other physicians. Tex. Civ. Prac. & Rem. Code § 74.401(b). In determining whether a witness is qualified on the basis of training or experience, the court shall consider whether, at the time the claim arose or at the time the testimony is given, the witness is board certified or has other substantial training or experience in an area of medical practice relevant to the claim and is actively practicing medicine in rendering medical care services relevant to the claim. Tex. Civ. Prac. & Rem. Code § 74.401(c).

The court may depart from those criteria if, under the circumstances, the court determines that there is a good reason to admit the expert's testimony. In such circumstances, the court must state on the record the reason for admitting the testimony if the court departs from the criteria. Tex. Civ. Prac. & Rem. Code § 74.401(d).

Claims Against Health Care Providers

Tex. Civ. Prac. & Rem. Code § 74.402(b) provides that, "in a suit involving a health care liability claim against a health care provider, a person may qualify as an expert witness on the issue of whether the health care provider departed from accepted standards of care only if the person:

> (1) is practicing health care in a field of practice that involves the same type of care or treatment as that delivered by the defendant health care provider, if the defendant health care provider is an individual, at the time the testimony is given or was practicing that type of health care at the time the claim arose;
> (2) has knowledge of accepted standards of care for health care providers for the diagnosis, care, or treatment of the illness, injury, or condition involved in the claim; and
> (3) is qualified on the basis of training or experience to offer an expert opinion regarding those accepted standards of health care."

In such cases, "practicing health care" includes training health care providers in the same field as the defendant health care provider at an accredited educational institution or serving as a consulting health care provider and being licensed, certified, or registered in the same field as the defendant health care provider." Tex. Civ. Prac. & Rem. Code § 74.402(a). In determining whether a witness is qualified on the basis of training or experience, the court will consider whether, at the time the claim arose or at the time the testimony is given, the witness "(1) is certified by a licensing agency of one or more states of the United States or a national professional certifying agency, or has other substantial training or experience, in the area of health care relevant to the claim; and (2) is actively practicing health care in rendering health care services relevant to the claim." Tex. Civ. Prac. & Rem. Code § 74.402(c).

The court may depart from these criteria if, under the circumstances, the court determines that there is good reason to admit the expert's testimony. The court shall state on the record the reason for admitting the testimony if the court departs from the criteria. Tex. Civ. Prac. & Rem. Code § 74.402(d). These provisions do not prevent a health care provider who is a defendant, or an employee of the defendant health care provider, from qualifying as an expert. Tex. Civ. Prac. & Rem. Code § 74.402(e).

Experts on Causation in Health Care Liability Claims

Tex. Civ. Prac. & Rem. Code § 74.403(a) sets out specific qualifications for experts who propose to testify as to causation in health care liability claims.

> [A] person may qualify as an expert witness on the issue of the causal relationship between the alleged departure from accepted standards of care and the injury, harm, or damages claimed only if the person is a physician and is otherwise qualified to render opinions on that causal relationship under the Texas Rules of Evidence.

Further:

> in a suit involving a health care liability claim against a dentist, a person may qualify as an expert witness on the issue of the causal relationship between the alleged departure from accepted standards of care and the injury, harm, or damages claimed if the person is a

dentist or physician and is otherwise qualified to render opinions on that causal relationship under the Texas Rules of Evidence.

Tex. Civ. Prac. & Rem. Code § 74.403(b).
Similarly:

> in a suit involving a health care liability claim against a podiatrist, a person may qualify as an expert witness on the issue of the causal relationship between the alleged departure from accepted standards of care and the injury, harm, or damages claimed if the person is a podiatrist or physician and is otherwise qualified to render opinions on that causal relationship under the Texas Rules of Evidence.

Tex. Civ. Prac. & Rem. Code § 74.403(c).

Gunn v. McCoy, 554 S.W.3d 645, 666 (Tex. 2018) (in a medical negligence case, "to avoid being conclusory, an expert must, to a reasonable degree of medical probability, explain how and why the negligence caused the injury").

Gunn v. McCoy, 554 S.W.3d 645, 666 (Tex. 2018) ("[W]hen the evidence demonstrates that there are other plausible causes of the injury or condition that could be negated, the plaintiff must offer evidence excluding those causes with reasonable certainty.").

Gunn v. McCoy, 554 S.W.3d 645, 666 (Tex. 2018) ("]W]hen the facts support several possible conclusions, only some of which establish that the defendant's negligence caused the plaintiff's injury, the expert must explain to the fact finder why those conclusions are superior based on verifiable medical evidence, not simply the expert's opinion.").

Bustamante v. Ponte, 529 S.W.3d 447, 462 (Tex. 2016) ("[W]hen equally likely causes for an injury are present, an expert must explain why one cause and not the other was the proximate cause of the injury.").

Grismore v. Texas Spine & Joint Hospital, Ltd., PAC, 578 S.W.3d 684 (Tex. App.—Tyler 2019, no pet.) ("Not every licensed medical doctor is automatically qualified to testify as an expert on every medical question, and the proponent of that testimony must show that the expert possesses special knowledge regarding the matter on which he proposes to give an opinion.").

Martinez-Partido v. Methodist Speciality & Transplant Hosp., 327 S.W.3d 274, 278 (Tex. App.—San Antonio 2010, no pet.) (plaintiff offering expert medical testimony in a medical malpractice action must establish that the expert has expertise regarding the specific issue before the court which would qualify the expert to give an opinion on that particular subject).

Hayes v. Carroll, 314 S.W.3d 494, 504 (Tex. App.—Austin 2010, no pet.) ("[W]hether a physician qualifies as an expert is determined by comparing the area in which the witness has such knowledge, skill, experience, or training with the subject matter of the proposed testimony. The focus is on the 'fit' between the subject matter at issue and the expert's familiarity of the subject matter, and not on a comparison of the expert's specialty or experience with that of the defendant.").

Dingler v. Tucker, 301 S.W.3d 761 (Tex. App.—Fort Worth 2009, pet. denied), abrogated on other grounds by *Zanchi v Lane*, 408 S.W.3d 373 (Tex. 2013) ("[I]n delineating the statutory qualifications for a chapter 74 expert, the statute does not focus on the defendant physician's area of expertise but on the condition involved in the claim.... That is, the applicable standard of care and an expert's ability to opine on it is dictated by the medical condition involved in the claim and by the expert's familiarity and experience with that condition.").

House v. Jones, 275 S.W.3d 926, 929 (Tex. App.—Dallas 2009, pet. denied) ("[E]very licensed doctor does not qualify automatically to testify as an expert on every medical question.... On the other hand, the expert need not be a specialist in the particular branch of the profession for which the testimony is offered.").

Chester v. El-Ashram, 228 S.W.3d 909, 912 (Tex. App.—Dallas 2007, no pet.) (only a physician who satisfies specific requirements may qualify as an expert witness on the issue of whether another physician departed from accepted standards of medical care in a health care liability claim against that physician for injury to a patient).

Chester v. El-Ashram, 228 S.W.3d 909, 912 (Tex. App.—Dallas 2007, no pet.) (proponent of the expert's testimony has the burden to show that the expert possesses special knowledge as to the very matter on which the expert proposes to give an opinion; what is required is that the offering party establish that the expert has knowledge, skill, experience, training, or education regarding the specific issue before the court which would qualify the expert to give an opinion on that particular subject).

Chester v. El-Ashram, 228 S.W.3d 909, 912 (Tex. App.—Dallas 2007, no pet.) (trial court does not abuse its discretion by excluding the testimony of an expert physician when that physician has not been shown to be qualified to treat an injury like the one at issue in medical malpractice action).

Chester v. El-Ashram, 228 S.W.3d 909, 912 (Tex. App.—Dallas 2007, no pet.) (when the evidence shows the expert physician has not performed the procedure at issue in many years and has not taught the procedure, the trial court does not abuse its discretion by excluding the expert's testimony in medical malpractice action).

i. Examples

Bailey v. Amaya Clinic, Inc., 402 S.W.3d 355, 365 (Tex. App.—Houston [14th Dist.] 2013, no pet.) ("[A] board-certified dermatologist, although generally qualified to opine as to the standard of care for dermatologists, was not qualified to opine as to the standard of care for weight-loss health care providers.").

Kelly v. Rendon, 255 S.W.3d 665, 675 (Tex. App.—Houston [14th Dist.] 2008, no pet.) ("the reports [of two nurses], standing alone, [could] not meet the statutory expert report requirement on medical causation" because the nurses were not qualified to give an opinion on medical causation).

c. Other Grounds

Other possible grounds for excluding expert testimony include:

- Prejudicial;
- Time-wasting;

- Confusing or misleading;
- Cumulative;
- Irrelevant;
- Collateral to issues in case;
- Improper foundation;
- Improper test evidence;
- Improper expert qualifications;
- Inadmissible hearsay.

4. Opposing Authorities

Ex parte Owens, 515 S.W.3d 891, 898 (Tex. Crim. App. 2017) (police "officers need not have been experts in identifying marihuana to testify that the substance found was marihuana").

Crosstex North Texas Pipeline, L.P. v. Gardiner, 505 S.W.3d 580, 611 (Tex. 2016) ("Expert testimony may aid the factfinder, but a landowner is also competent to testify to the value of his property if he is familiar with its fair market value.").

Reid Road Mun. Util. Dist. No. 2 v. Speedy Stop Food Stores, Ltd., 337 S.W.3d 846, 854 (Tex. 2011) (under the Property Owner Rule, a property owner is qualified to testify to the value of her property even if she is not an expert and would not be qualified to testify to the value of other property; this is based on the presumption that a property owner is familiar with her property and its value).

State v. Cent. Expressway Sign Assocs., 302 S.W.3d 866, 870 (Tex. 2009) (trial court abuses its discretion in excluding expert testimony if the testimony is relevant to the issues in the case and is based on a reliable foundation).

Subsea 7 Port Isabel, LLC v. Port Isabel Logistical Offshore Terminal, Inc., 593 S.W.3d 859, 874 (Tex. App.—Corpus Christi 2019, pet. filed) ("A property owner may testify to the value of his property, even if the owner could not qualify to testify about the value of like property belonging to someone else.... But in order for a property owner to qualify as a witness to the damages to his property, his testimony must show that it refers to market, rather than intrinsic or some other value of the property.").

Tuttle v. Builes, 572 S.W.3d 344 (Tex. App.—Eastland 2019) ("Under [the property owner] rule, a property owner may testify about the value of his property.... The rule creates a rebuttable presumption that a landowner is personally familiar with his property and knows its fair rental value and, thus, is qualified to express an opinion about that value.... As such, the property owner is permitted an exception to the general rule that a witness must first establish his qualifications to opine on land values before he may testify.").

Schronk v. Laerdal Med. Corp., 440 S.W.3d 250, 258 (Tex. App.—Waco 2013, pet. denied) (the approach to assessing reliability must be flexible depending on the nature of the evidence).

Pjetrovic v. Home Depot, 411 S.W.3d 639, 648 (Tex. App.—Texarkana 2013, no pet.) ("[U]nder what is known as the 'property owner's rule,' a property owner can testify to the market value of his own property.").

Tenet Hospitals Ltd. v. Barnes, 329 S.W.3d 537, 546 (Tex. App.—El Paso 2010, no pet.) ("[I]f a physician states he is familiar with the standard of care and responsibilities and requirements for physician's assistants, and he has worked with, interacted with, and supervised physician's assistants, the physician is qualified on the issue of whether the health care provider departed from the accepted standards of care for health care providers.... A physician is not required to state he or she is familiar with the core standards for nurse practitioners or physician's assistants.").

Newman v. Graham, 316 S.W.3d 197, 201 (Tex. App.—Dallas 2010, no pet.) ("[W]hen the offering party shows a subject is substantially developed in more than one field, testimony can come from a qualified medical expert in any of those fields").

Kettle v. Baylor Med. Ctr. at Garland, 232 S.W.3d 832, 844 (Tex. App.—Dallas 2007, pet. denied) ("when a subject is substantially developed in more than one medical field, testimony can come from a qualified expert in any of those fields, provided the offering party can establish expertise regarding the specific issue before the court.").

Gen. Motors Corp. v. Burry, 203 S.W.3d 514, 526 (Tex. App.—Fort Worth 2006, pet. denied) (witness with the appropriate knowledge, skill, experience, training, or education is qualified to testify as an expert).

Burns v. Baylor Health Sys., 125 S.W.3d 589, 594 (Tex. App.—El Paso 2003, no pet.) (trial court abused discretion striking evidence of expert's opinion where party's expert qualified as expert).

State v. Northborough Ctr., Inc., 987 S.W.2d 187, 193 (Tex. App.—Houston [14th Dist.] 1999, pet. ref'd) (witness did not need to be licensed professional to give expert opinion).

Waldie v. State, 923 S.W.2d 152, 157 (Tex. App.—Beaumont 1996, no writ) (witness qualified as expert based upon work experience).

Butler v. State, 892 S.W.2d 138, 140 (Tex. App.—Texarkana 1994, pet. denied) (trial court abused discretion excluding expert testimony on sole basis witness was not licensed in State).

Glasscock v. Income Prop. Svcs., Inc., 888 S.W.2d 176, 180 (Tex. App.—Houston [1st Dist.] 1994, writ dism'd by agr.) (witness not required to have college degree in order to qualify as expert).

Petrolia Ins. Co. v. Everett, 719 S.W.2d 639, 641 (Tex. App.—El Paso 1986, no writ) (witness qualified as expert by experience even though witness had limited education).

a. Health Care Liability Cases

Benge v. Williams, 548 S.W.3d 466, 471 (Tex. 2018) ("[W]hile there is no validity, if there ever was, to the notion that every licensed medical doctor should be automatically qualified to testify as an expert on every medical question, the TMLA's test for expert qualifications should not be too narrowly drawn. Indeed, the test cannot be rigidly applied because it is expressly nonexclusive.").

Benge v. Williams, 548 S.W.3d 466, 471 (Tex. 2018) ("The TMLA requires that an expert testifying on whether a physician departed from accepted standards of medical care must have been 'practicing medicine' either when the claim arose or when the testimony was given. Under the Act, practicing medicine includes, but is not limited to, training residents or students at an accredited school of medicine or osteopathy or serving as a consulting physician to other physicians who provide direct patient care, upon the request of such other physicians. 'Physician' in this context and for our purposes means a person licensed to practice medicine in the United States.").

Bustamante v. Ponte, 529 S.W.3d 447, 462 (Tex. 2016) ("[W]hen the only evidence of a vital fact is circumstantial, the expert cannot merely draw possible inferences from the evidence and state that 'in medical probability' the injury was caused by the defendant's negligence.").

Bioderm Skin Care, LLC v. Sok, 426 S.W.3d 753, 762 (Tex. 2014) ("[E]xpert testimony does not necessarily have to be proffered by a licensed physician to constitute expert health care testimony in a health care liability case.").

Grismore v. Texas Spine & Joint Hospital, Ltd., PAC, 578 S.W.3d 684 (Tex. App.—Tyler 2019, no pet.) ("[T]here are certain standards of medical care that apply to multiple schools of practice and any medical doctor.... If the subject matter is common to and equally recognized in all areas of practice, no specialized knowledge is required and any physician familiar with the standard may testify as to the standard of care.").

Grismore v. Texas Spine & Joint Hospital, Ltd., PAC, 578 S.W.3d 684 (Tex. App.—Tyler 2019, no pet.) ("It is axiomatic that a hospital should remove recalled medical devices from its inventory and not allow the surgical implantation of a recalled medical device in patients at its facility; thus, it is reasonable to conclude that this concept is both common to all fields of practice and within the common sense of a layperson.").

Harvey v. Kindred Healthcare Operating, Inc., 578 S.W.3d 638 (Tex. App.—Houston [14th Dist.] 2019, no pet.) ("A physician is qualified to testify as an expert regarding whether a nonphysician healthcare provider departed from the accepted standards of care when the physician states she is familiar with the standard of care (1) for both nurses and physicians and (2) for the prevention and treatment of the illness, injury, or condition involved in the claim.").

Harvey v. Kindred Healthcare Operating, Inc., 578 S.W.3d 638 (Tex. App.—Houston [14th Dist.] 2019, no pet.) ("[W]hen a physician states that she is familiar with the standard of care and requirements for nonphysician healthcare providers and that she has worked with, interacted with, and supervised such healthcare providers, she is qualified to opine regarding whether the healthcare provider departed from the accepted standards of care.").

TTHR, L.P. v. Coffman, 338 S.W.3d 103, 112 (Tex. App.—Fort Worth 2011, no pet.) (the first requirement of section 74.402, requiring that the expert must be practicing health care in a field of practice that involves the same type of care or treatment as that delivered by the defendant health care provider, applies only when the defendant is an individual and does not apply when the defendant is a hospital).

TTHR, L.P. v. Coffman, 338 S.W.3d 103, 112 (Tex. App.—Fort Worth 2011, no pet.) (qualified expert in medical liability case regarding improper release of a laboratory report would be an individual who has knowledge of the accepted standards of care for providers regarding the confidentiality of medical records and the necessary training or experience to offer an expert opinion).

Newman v. Graham, 316 S.W.3d 197, 201 (Tex. App.—Dallas 2010, no pet.) ("[A] medical expert with a different specialty than the defendant physician may testify so long as the subject of inquiry is common to and equally recognized and developed in both fields.").

Menafee v. Ohman, 323 S.W.3d 509, 514 (Tex. App.—Fort Worth 2010, no pet.) (physician who is not of the same school of medicine as the defendant in a health care liability action is competent to testify as an expert to the standard of care if physician has practical knowledge of what is usually and customarily done by a practitioner under circumstances similar to those confronting the defendant).

House v. Jones, 275 S.W.3d 926, 929 (Tex. App.—Dallas 2009, pet. denied) ("if ... a subject of inquiry is substantially developed in more than one field, a qualified expert in any of those fields may testify.... If an area is common to and equally recognized and developed in all fields of practice, any physician familiar with the subject may testify as to the standard of care.").

Chester v. El-Ashram, 228 S.W.3d 909, 912 (Tex. App.—Dallas 2007, no pet.) ("[A]n expert from a different field from the defendant physician may testify in medical malpractice action so long as the subject of inquiry is common to and equally recognized and developed in both fields ... when the offering party shows a subject is substantially developed in more than one field, testimony can come from a qualified expert in any of those fields.").

Simonson v. Keppard, 225 S.W.3d 868, 875 (Tex. App.—Dallas 2007, no pet.) (surgeon's "expert report established that he [had] experience in both his own field of neurosurgery and [a defendant doctors'] field of emergency medicine" and as such, expert was "qualified to opine on the standard of care for [defendant doctors]").

C. Motion to Exclude Opinion of Nonexpert

1. Suggested Motion Text

(*Name of Moving Party*) hereby moves this Court for an order excluding any and all testimony, reference to testimony, or argument relating to the testimony of (*Name of Witness*) that (*Describe Opinion Testimony to Be Excluded, e.g., Defendant Suffers From Alzheimer's Disease*). The motion is based upon the ground that a nonexpert may not testify on such matters, pursuant to Texas Rule of Evidence 701, and therefore this testimony is inadmissible.

2. Motion Summary

This motion is used to exclude improper opinion testimony of a lay witness. The motion is based upon the statutory authority and case law interpretations of Texas Rule of Evidence 701. *See Colls v. Price's Creameries*, 244 S.W.2d 900, 909 (Tex. Civ. App.—El Paso 1951, writ ref'd n.r.e.). Rule 701 has slightly broadened the lay opinion testimony procedure. *Austin v. State*, 794 S.W.2d 408, 410 (Tex. App.—Austin 1990, writ ref'd). Examples of inadmissible lay opinion evidence include testimony on legal conclusions [*Lum v. State*, 903 S.W.2d 365, 369 (Tex. App.—Texarkana 1995, writ ref'd)], and matters beyond common knowledge [*Hernandez v. Tex. Employers Ins. Ass'n*, 783 S.W.2d 250, 252 (Tex. App.—Corpus Christi 1989, no writ)].

3. Supporting Authorities

Texas Rule of Evidence 701 states:

> If the witness is not testifying as an expert, the witness' testimony in the form of opinions or inferences is limited to those opinions or inferences which are
>
> (a) rationally based on the perception of the witness and
> (b) helpful to a clear understanding of the witness' testimony or the determination of a fact in issue.

Note: An objection to lay opinion testimony may be based on the standard set in Rule 701, e.g., not based on personal knowledge or not helpful. This type of objection will be stronger if it is supported with an explanation of why the lay opinion is not rational or not helpful.

a. Lack of Personal Knowledge

Texas Rule of Evidence 602 states:

> A witness may not testify to a matter *unless evidence is introduced sufficient to support a finding that the witness has personal knowledge of the matter*. Evidence to prove personal knowledge may, but need not, consist of the testimony of the witness. This rule is subject to the provision of Rule 703, relating to opinion testimony by expert witnesses. (Emphasis added.)

Texas Rule of Evidence 701 states:

> If the witness is not testifying as an expert, the witness' testimony in the form of opinions or inferences is limited to those opinions or inferences which are
>
> (a) *rationally based on the perception of the witness* and
> (b) helpful to a clear understanding of the witness' testimony or the determination of a fact in issue. (Emphasis added.)

Dallas Morning News, Inc. v. Hall, 579 S.W.3d 370, 379 (Tex. 2019) ("A witness may testify to a matter only if the evidence supports a finding that the witness has personal knowledge of the matter.").

Reid Road Mun. Util. Dist. No. 2 v. Speedy Stop Food Stores, Ltd., 337 S.W.3d 846, 854 (Tex. 2011) (an officer of a corporate general partner who had general knowledge of Speedy Stop's property did not fall into the category of entity representatives to whom the Property Owner Rule applies, and did not qualify to testify to the value of Property under the Property Owner Rule).

Subsea 7 Port Isabel, LLC v. Port Isabel Logistical Offshore Terminal, Inc., 593 S.W.3d 859, 874 (Tex. App.—Corpus Christi 2019, pet. filed) ("[F]or a property owner to qualify as a witness to the damages to his property, his testimony must show that it refers to market, rather than intrinsic or some other value of the property.... When the evidence does not indicate the factual basis behind the owner's valuation, the testimony is conclusory and will be legally insufficient to sustain a judgment.").

Tuttle v. Builes, 572 S.W.3d 344 (Tex. App.—Eastland 2019) ("[A] property owner may not simply echo the phrase 'market value' and state a number to substantiate his valuation.... His subjective opinion, by itself, will not provide relevant evidence of value.... Instead, to be relevant, the witness must provide the factual basis on which his opinion rests.... Evidence of price paid, nearby sales, tax valuations, appraisals, online resources, and any other relevant factors may be offered to support the valuation.").

Merrill v. Sprint Waste Services LP, 527 S.W.3d 663, 670 (Tex. App.—Houston [14th Dist.] 2017, no pet.) ("An opinion will satisfy the personal knowledge requirement if it is an interpretation of the witness's objective perception of event.").

Merrill v. Sprint Waste Services LP, 527 S.W.3d 663, 670 (Tex. App.—Houston [14th Dist.] 2017, no pet.) ("An opinion is rationally based on perception if a reasonable person could draw that opinion under the circumstances.").

Hurst v. State, 406 S.W.3d 617, 622 (Tex. App.—Eastland 2013, no pet.) ("[F]or lay opinion testimony to be admissible, the opinion must be (1) rationally based on the perception of the witness and (2) helpful to better understand the witness's testimony or to determine a fact issue.").

Hurst v. State, 406 S.W.3d 617, 622 (Tex. App.—Eastland 2013, no pet.) ("[L]ay opinion witness must have personal knowledge of the events that inform the opinion, and second, the opinion must be rationally based on that knowledge.").

Anthony Equip. Corp. v. Irwin Steel Erectors, Inc., 115 S.W.3d 191, 206 (Tex. App.—Dallas 2003, pet. dism'd) (witness lacked requisite personal knowledge to provide opinion as lay witness regarding cost of equipment repair).

Cornelison v. Aggregate Haulers, Inc., 777 S.W.2d 542, 545 (Tex. App.—Fort Worth 1989, writ denied) ("Statements contained in a medical record as to how an accident happened or where it happened, age, medical history, etc. are not admissible as a business-record exception to the hearsay rule, because the party making the entry in the record does not have personal knowledge as to these matters, and the statements do not become trustworthy just because it is hospital routine to record them." (Citations omitted.)).

Dieter v. Baker Serv. Tools, a Div. of Baker Int'l, Inc., 776 S.W.2d 781, 784 (Tex. App.—Corpus Christi 1989, writ denied) (affidavits filed by lay witnesses in opposition to summary judgment motion were speculative and conclusory and failed to assert any facts that were the basis of the witnesses' opinions).

Handel v. Long Trusts, 757 S.W.2d 848, 851 (Tex. App.—Texarkana 1988, no writ) (witness to provide an opinion as lay witness where lacked personal knowledge).

b. Legal Opinions

Leitch v. Hornsby, 935 S.W.2d 114, 119 (Tex. 1996) (lay opinion testimony not admissible where witness seeks to offer opinion on subject that calls for expertise).

Carr v. Radkey, 393 S.W.2d 806, 810 (Tex. 1965) (lay opinion testimony not admissible where witness seeks to testify on mixed question of law and fact and does not understand underlying legal standard).

Schronk v. City of Burleson, 387 S.W.3d 692, 705 (Tex. App.—Waco 2009, pet. denied) (lay witness may not give legal conclusions or interpret the law to the jury).

Rogers v. Crossroads Nursing Serv., Inc., 13 S.W.3d 417, 419 (Tex. App.—Corpus Christi 1999, no pet.) (lay witness cannot testify on standard of care for physician).

Lum v. State, 903 S.W.2d 365, 369 (Tex. App.—Texarkana 1995, writ ref'd) (lay opinions expressed in terms of legal definitions and conclusions or testimony amounting to little more than choosing sides on case's outcome not admissible).

Mowbray v. State, 788 S.W.2d 658 (Tex. App.—Corpus Christi 1990, writ ref'd), *cert. denied*, 521 U.S. 1120 (1997) (lay testimony on legal conclusions not admissible).

Dieter v. Baker Serv. Tools, a Div. of Baker Int'l, Inc., 776 S.W.2d 781, 784 (Tex. App.—Corpus Christi 1989, writ denied) (affidavits filed by lay witnesses in opposition to summary judgment motion regarding foreseeability speculative and conclusory and failed to assert any facts that were basis of witnesses' opinions).

Montoya v. Am. Employers' Ins. Co., 426 S.W.2d 661, 663 (Tex. Civ. App.—El Paso 1968, writ ref'd n.r.e.) (lay testimony that injuries suffered were permanent was not admissible).

Lee v. Lee, 413 S.W.2d 931, 938 (Tex. Civ. App.—Fort Worth 1967), *judgment aff'd in part, rev'd in part on other grounds*, 424 S.W.2d 609 (Tex. 1968) (lay witness cannot testify on sanity or insanity unless he accompanies his opinion with a recital of the facts upon which it is based").

c. Not Based on Perceptions of Witness

Texas Rule of Evidence 701(a) provides that a nonexpert may give opinion testimony that is "rationally based on the perception of the witness."

Fairow v. State, 943 S.W.2d 895, 899 (Tex. Crim. App. 1997) (opinions not capable of being formed from events underlying opinion must be excluded).

Bigby v. State, 892 S.W.2d 864, 889 (Tex. Crim. App. 1994), *cert. denied*, 515 U.S. 1162 (1995) (requirement that testimony be based on "perception of the witness" presumes underlying facts were observed or experienced by witness).

Merrill v. Sprint Waste Services LP, 527 S.W.3d 663, 670 (Tex. App.—Houston [14th Dist.] 2017, no pet.) ("the requirement that an opinion be rationally based on the perceptions of the witness is composed of two parts: (1) the witness must establish personal knowledge of the events from which her opinion is drawn; and (2) the opinion drawn must be rationally based on that knowledge").

Merrill v. Sprint Waste Services LP, 527 S.W.3d 663, 670 (Tex. App.—Houston [14th Dist.] 2017, no pet.) ("An opinion is rationally based on perception if a reasonable person could draw that opinion under the circumstances.").

Clark v. State, 305 S.W.3d 351, 357 (Tex. App.—Houston [14th Dist.] 2010), *aff'd,* 365 S.W.3d 333 (Tex. Crim. App. 2012) ("[F]or lay testimony to be based on a witness's perception, the witness must have personally experienced or observed the event; the witness may also make reasonable inferences based on his perceptions.").

Lum v. State, 903 S.W.2d 365, 369 (Tex. App.—Texarkana 1995, writ ref'd) (lay opinion not admissible in criminal case unless rationally based on perception of witness).

Bigby v. State, 892 S.W.2d 864, 889 (Tex. Crim. App. 1994), *cert. denied,* 515 U.S. 1162 (1995) ("[B]y requiring the testimony to be based on the 'perception of the witness', the rule presumes the underlying facts were observed or experienced by witness.").

d. *Not Helpful to Jury*

Steve v. State, 614 S.W.2d 137, 139 (Tex. Crim. App. 1981) (lay opinion testimony not admissible where jury is equally well-positioned to draw inferences from underlying data).

Merrill v. Sprint Waste Services LP, 527 S.W.3d 663, 670 (Tex. App.—Houston [14th Dist.] 2017, no pet.) ("Courts balance general evidentiary considerations of relevance and consider the complexity of the information from which the opinion was drawn to determine the helpfulness of the lay opinion.... If the opinion is a shorthand rendition of the facts, then the opinion is likely to be helpful because it distills what otherwise might be difficult for the witness to describe in detail.".

e. *Speculative or Conjectural*

Bd. of Trs. of Fire & Police Retiree Health Fund v. Towers, Perrin, Forster & Crosby, Inc., 191 S.W.3d 185, 193 (Tex. App.—San Antonio 2005, pet. denied) ("[A] speculative opinion, such as an opinion on what someone else was thinking at a specific time, does not help the jury either to understand the witness's testimony better, or decide the question of the other person's intent. Mere conjecture does not assist the jury.").

Pooler v. Klobassa, 413 S.W.2d 768, 770 (Tex. Civ. App.—San Antonio 1967) (lay witness cannot testify to purely speculative or conjectural opinions).

Subsea 7 Port Isabel, LLC v. Port Isabel Logistical Offshore Terminal, Inc., 593 S.W.3d 859, 874 (Tex. App.—Corpus Christi 2019, pet. filed) ("[F]or a property owner to qualify as a witness to the damages to his property, his testimony must show that it refers to market, rather than intrinsic or some other value of the property.... When the evidence does not indicate the factual basis behind the owner's valuation, the testimony is conclusory and will be legally insufficient to sustain a judgment.").

Tuttle v. Builes, 572 S.W.3d 344 (Tex. App.—Eastland 2019) ("[Property] owner's valuation testimony must be relevant ... [and] an owner's valuation testimony is not relevant if it is conclusory or speculative").

Tuttle v. Builes, 572 S.W.3d 344 (Tex. App.—Eastland 2019) ("property valuations may not be based solely on a property owner's ipse dixit").

Tuttle v. Builes, 572 S.W.3d 344 (Tex. App.—Eastland 2019) ("[A] property owner may not simply echo the phrase 'market value' and state a number to substantiate his valuation.... His subjective opinion, by itself, will not provide relevant evidence of value ... Instead, to be relevant, the witness must provide the factual basis on which his opinion rests ... Evidence of price paid, nearby sales, tax valuations, appraisals, online resources, and any other relevant factors may be offered to support the valuation.").

f. Other Grounds

Other possible grounds for excluding lay witness testimony include:

- Prejudicial;
- Time-wasting;
- Confusing or misleading;
- Cumulative;
- Irrelevant;
- Collateral to issues in case;
- Improper foundation;
- Improper test evidence;
- Improper expert qualifications;
- Inadmissible hearsay.

4. Opposing Authorities

Texas Rule of Evidence 701 states:

> If the witness is not testifying as an expert, the witness' testimony in the form of opinions or inferences is limited to those opinions or inferences which are
>
> (a) *rationally based on the perception of the witness* and
> (b) helpful to a clear understanding of the witness' testimony or the determination of a fact in issue. (Emphasis added.)

Reid Road Mun. Util. Dist. No. 2 v. Speedy Stop Food Stores, Ltd., 337 S.W.3d 846, 854 (Tex. 2011) (not all witnesses who are experts necessarily testify as experts; a witness may have special knowledge, skill, experience, training, or education in a particular subject, but testify only to matters based on personal perception and opinions).

Reid Road Mun. Util. Dist. No. 2 v. Speedy Stop Food Stores, Ltd., 337 S.W.3d 846, 854 (Tex. 2011) (if a witness is testifying to matters based on personal perception and opinion, witness's testimony is not expert testimony for purposes of Rule 702, and the witness need not be designated or identified as an expert).

Osborn v. State, 92 S.W.3d 531, 538 (Tex. Crim. App. 2002) ("[I]f the witness perceived events and formed an opinion that a reasonable person could draw from the facts then the first part of the rule [relating to lay opinion testimony] is met. If the opinion is also helpful to the trier-of-fact to understand the witness's testimony or aids in the determination of a fact in issue, then the opinion is admissible under Rule 701.").

Fairow v. State, 943 S.W.2d 895, 899 (Tex. Crim. App. 1997) (opinions rationally based on perception are ones that a reasonable person could draw under the circumstances).

Subsea 7 Port Isabel, LLC v. Port Isabel Logistical Offshore Terminal, Inc., 593 S.W.3d 859, 874 (Tex. App.—Corpus Christi 2019, pet. filed) ("[T]he Property Owner Rule falls under Texas Rule of Evidence 701, which allows a lay witness to provide opinion testimony if it is (a) rationally based on the witness's perception and (b) helpful to a clear understanding of the witness's testimony or the determination of a fact in issue.").

Subsea 7 Port Isabel, LLC v. Port Isabel Logistical Offshore Terminal, Inc., 593 S.W.3d 859, 874 (Tex. App.—Corpus Christi 2019, pet. filed) ("Under the Property Owner Rule, an owner's valuation testimony fulfills the same role that expert testimony does; however, that testimony is based on personal knowledge rather than merely on expertise.").

Tuttle v. Builes, 572 S.W.3d 344 (Tex. App.—Eastland 2019) ("Under [the property owner] rule, a property owner may testify about the value of his property.... The rule creates a rebuttable presumption that a landowner is personally familiar with his property and knows its fair rental value and, thus, is qualified to express an opinion about that value.... As such, the property owner is permitted an exception to the general rule that a witness must first establish his qualifications to opine on land values before he may testify.").

Merrill v. Sprint Waste Services LP, 527 S.W.3d 663, 670 (Tex. App.—Houston [14th Dist.] 2017, no pet.) ("Lay witness opinion testimony is admissible as long as it is rationally based on the witness's perception and helpful to understanding clearly the witness's testimony or determining a fact in issue.").

Merrill v. Sprint Waste Services LP, 527 S.W.3d 663, 670 (Tex. App.—Houston [14th Dist.] 2017, no pet.) ("[T]he requirement that an opinion be rationally based on the perceptions of the witness is composed of two parts: (1) the witness must establish personal knowledge of the events from which her opinion is drawn; and (2) the opinion drawn must be rationally based on that knowledge.").

City of San Antonio Bd. of Adjustment v. Reilly, 429 S.W.3d 707, 715 (Tex. App.—San Antonio 2014, no pet.) ("[A] non-expert witness may offer opinion testimony when it is rationally based on his perception and helpful to a clear understanding of his testimony or the determination of a fact issue.").

Melendez v. Houston Indep. School Dist., 418 S.W.3d 701, 707 n.1 (Tex. App.—Houston [14th Dist.] 2013, no pet.) ("lay witnesses may testify about subjects rationally within their own perception").

Siller v. LPP Mortg., Ltd., 264 S.W.3d 324, 328 (Tex. App.—San Antonio 2008, no pet.) ("[A] jury confronted with conflicting evidence may choose to believe one witness and disbelieve others, it may resolve inconsistencies in the testimony of any witness, or it may accept lay testimony over that of experts.").

Fairow v. State, 943 S.W.2d 895, 899 (Tex. Crim. App. 1997) (opinions rationally based on perception are ones that a reasonable person could draw under the circumstances).

a. Sanity/Mental Condition or Capacity

Texas courts have permitted lay witnesses to offer their opinions regarding the defendant's ability to distinguish between right and wrong, the sanity of a person, and culpable mental states.

Fairow v. State, 943 S.W.2d 895, 899 (Tex. Crim. App. 1997) (lay witness may give opinion as to third party's culpable mental state).

Bigby v. State, 892 S.W.2d 864, 889 (Tex. Crim. App. 1994), *cert. denied*, 515 U.S. 1162 (1995) (lay witness may testify to opinion that individual is legally insane).

Jackson v. State, 822 S.W.2d 18, 30 (Tex. Crim. App. 1990), *cert. denied*, 509 U.S. 921 (1993) (lay opinion as to mental attitude or emotional state was admissible).

Fuller v. State, 423 S.W.2d 924, 929 (Tex. Crim. App. 1968) ("[It was] error to exclude opinion of a nonexpert witness as to the sanity of the defendant, where such witness has first stated the facts on which his opinion is based, and it appears that his opinion will be justified by his opportunities for observing the conduct of the defendant.").

In re Cervantes, 300 S.W.3d 865, 876 (Tex. App.—Waco 2009, orig. proceeding) ("[L]ay testimony is admissible on the issue of a person's capacity to sign a legal document.").

b. Health

Rivera v. White, 234 S.W.3d 802, 806 n.2 (Tex. App.—Texarkana 2007, no pet.) (in establishing damages, a lay person is competent to testify about his or her own pain and suffering).

Dickson v. Minnesota Mut. Life Ins. Co., 562 S.W.2d 925, 929 (Tex. Civ. App.—Tyler 1978, no writ) (lay opinion testimony permitted on "good health" in cases involving insurance provisions requiring "good health").

Emerson v. State, 880 S.W.2d 759, 763 (Tex. Crim. App. 1994), *cert. denied*, 513 U.S. 931 (1994) (lay opinion testimony by police office generally admissible to prove whether defendant was intoxicated).

McCown v. State, 192 S.W.3d 158, 163 (Tex. App.—Fort Worth 2006, pet. ref'd) ("[A] witness does not have to be an expert to testify that a person he or she observes is intoxicated by alcohol; therefore, lay opinion testimony by a police officer that a person is intoxicated is probative evidence that a person was 'drunk.'").

Tex. Dep't of Pub. Safety v. Struve, 79 S.W.3d 796, 803 (Tex. App.—Corpus Christi 2002, pet. denied) (police officer's lay opinion that person was intoxicated proper where based upon officer's observations, rather than from experience and training).

c. Age, Size, Quality

McMillan v. State, 754 S.W.2d 422, 425 (Tex. App.—Eastland 1988, writ ref'd) ("[O]pinions of lay witnesses, when competent, are admissible concerning estimates of age, size, quality, time, and estimates of distance and speed.").

d. Damages

Crosstex North Texas Pipeline, L.P. v. Gardiner, 505 S.W.3d 580, 611 (Tex. 2016) ("Expert testimony may aid the factfinder, but a landowner is also competent to testify to the value of his property if he is familiar with its fair market value.").

Subsea 7 Port Isabel, LLC v. Port Isabel Logistical Offshore Terminal, Inc., 593 S.W.3d 859, 874 (Tex. App.—Corpus Christi 2019, pet. filed) ("A property owner may testify to the value of his property, even if the owner could not qualify to testify about the value of like property belonging to someone else.... But in order for a property owner to qualify as a witness to the damages to his property, his testimony must show that it refers to market, rather than intrinsic or some other value of the property.").

Tuttle v. Builes, 572 S.W.3d 344 (Tex. App.—Eastland 2019) ("[A] property owner may not simply echo the phrase 'market value' and state a number to substantiate his valuation.... His subjective opinion, by itself, will not provide relevant evidence of value.... Instead, to be relevant, the witness must provide the factual basis on which his opinion rests.... Evidence of price paid, nearby sales, tax valuations, appraisals, online resources, and any other relevant factors may be offered to support the valuation.").

Motor Car Classics, LLC v. Abbott, 316 S.W.3d 223 (Tex. App.—Texarkana 2010, no pet.) (property owner can testify as to the market value of his or her property even though owner cannot qualify to testify about the value of like property belonging to someone else).

Red Sea Gaming, Inc. v. Block Invs. (Nevada) Co., 338 S.W.3d 562 (Tex. App.—El Paso 2010, pet. denied) (property owner is qualified to testify to the market value of his or her property, and the testimony must indicate that the owner's assessment is based on the market and not on the intrinsic value of the property to owner).

Penner Cattle, Inc. v. Cox, 287 S.W.3d 370 (Tex. App.—Eastland 2009, pet. denied) (opinions or estimates of lost profits in a breach of contract action may be competent evidence if that opinion or estimate is based on objective facts, figures, or data from which the amount of lost profits may be ascertained).

Am. Heritage, Inc. v. Nevada Gold & Casino, Inc., 259 S.W.3d 816 (Tex. App.—Houston [1st Dist.] 2008, no pet.) (Executive of company facilitating casino financing services could testify regarding damages sustained when company and developer entered into contract under which company was to use its best efforts to procure financing in return for half of profits of casino, and developer repudiated contract before facilitator could perform, when basis for testimony was profit information released by developer after casino began operations, despite claim that executive lacked sufficient information regarding casino's operations; contract repudiation barred executive from obtaining more detailed information).

Royce Homes, L.P. v. Humphreys, 244 S.W.3d 570 (Tex. App.—Beaumont 2008, pet. denied) (when the owner is familiar with his or her property's value, the owner of the property can testify to its market value, even if owner could not qualify to testify about the value of like property belonging to someone else).

Rivera v. White, 234 S.W.3d 802, 806 n.2 (Tex. App.—Texarkana 2007, no pet.) (in establishing damages, a lay person is competent to testify about his or her own pain and suffering).

Akin, Gump, Strauss, Hauer & Feld, L.L.P. v. Nat'l Dev. & Research Corp., 232 S.W.3d 883 (Tex. App.—Dallas 2007), *rev'd on other grounds*, 299 S.W.3d 106 (Tex. 2009) (property owner may testify about the market value of his or her property if testimony shows owner is familiar with the market value and owner's opinion is based on that market value).

Sierad v. Barnett, 164 S.W.3d 471 (Tex. App.—Dallas 2005, no pet.) (lay witness could testify as to value of property).

Barraza v. Koliba, 933 S.W.2d 164 (Tex. App.—San Antonio 1996, writ denied) (lay opinion testimony on value of real property admissible).

Coker v. Burghardt, 833 S.W.2d 306, 310 (Tex. App.—Dallas 1992, writ denied) (lay witness may give opinion on amount of damages provided he testifies about matters within knowledge).

McMillan v. State, 754 S.W.2d 422, 425 (Tex. App.—Eastland 1988, writ ref'd) (lay opinion testimony admissible on estimates of value).

e. Personal Knowledge

Crosstex North Texas Pipeline, L.P. v. Gardiner, 505 S.W.3d 580, 611 (Tex. 2016) ("Expert testimony may aid the factfinder, but a landowner is also competent to testify to the value of his property if he is familiar with its fair market value.").

Reid Road Mun. Util. Dist. No. 2 v. Speedy Stop Food Stores, Ltd., 337 S.W.3d 846, 854 (Tex. 2011) (not all witnesses who are experts necessarily testify as experts; a witness may have special knowledge, skill, experience, training, or education in a particular subject, but testify only to matters based on personal perception and opinions).

Reid Road Mun. Util. Dist. No. 2 v. Speedy Stop Food Stores, Ltd., 337 S.W.3d 846, 854 (Tex. 2011) (if a witness is testifying to matters based on personal perception and opinion, witness's testimony is not expert testimony for purposes of Rule 702, and the witness need not be designated or identified as an expert).

Reid Road Mun. Util. Dist. No. 2 v. Speedy Stop Food Stores, Ltd., 337 S.W.3d 846, 854 (Tex. 2011) (under the Property Owner Rule, a property owner is qualified to testify to the value of her property even if she is not an expert and would not be qualified to testify to the value of other property; this is based on the presumption that a property owner is familiar with her property and its value).

Reid Road Mun. Util. Dist. No. 2 v. Speedy Stop Food Stores, Ltd., 337 S.W.3d 846, 854 (Tex. 2011) (with regard to property owned by an entity, the Property Owner Rule allows officer in a management position with duties that at least in some part relate to the property at issue, or an employee of the entity in a substantially equivalent position, to testify as to value of the property).

Smith v. State, 683 S.W.2d 393, 404 (Tex. Crim. App. 1984) ("[W]itness may give opinion regarding matters within his or her common knowledge.").

Subsea 7 Port Isabel, LLC v. Port Isabel Logistical Offshore Terminal, Inc., 593 S.W.3d 859, 874 (Tex. App.—Corpus Christi 2019, pet. filed) ("Based on the presumption that an owner is familiar with his property and its value, the Property Owner Rule is an exception to the requirement that a witness must otherwise establish his qualifications to express an opinion on land values.").

Subsea 7 Port Isabel, LLC v. Port Isabel Logistical Offshore Terminal, Inc., 593 S.W.3d 859, 874 (Tex. App.—Corpus Christi 2019, pet. filed) ("Under the Property Owner Rule, an owner's valuation testimony fulfills the same role that expert testimony does; however, that testimony is based on personal knowledge rather than merely on expertise.").

Subsea 7 Port Isabel, LLC v. Port Isabel Logistical Offshore Terminal, Inc., 593 S.W.3d 859, 874 (Tex. App.—Corpus Christi 2019, pet. filed) ("[W]hile valuation testimony may not be based solely on a property owner's ipse dixit, the Property Owner Rule establishes that an owner is automatically qualified to provide such testimony.").

Merrill v. Sprint Waste Services LP, 527 S.W.3d 663, 670 (Tex. App.—Houston [14th Dist.] 2017, no pet.) ("Courts balance general evidentiary considerations of relevance and consider the complexity of the information from which the opinion was drawn to determine the helpfulness of the lay opinion.... If the opinion is a shorthand rendition of the facts, then the opinion is likely to be helpful because it distills what otherwise might be difficult for the witness to describe in detail.").

Merrill v. Sprint Waste Services LP, 527 S.W.3d 663, 670 (Tex. App.—Houston [14th Dist.] 2017, no pet.) ("Eyewitness opinion testimony can be helpful if it assists the jury in making a factual determination regarding something the eyewitness saw.").

Twin City Fire Ins. Co. v. Vega-Garcia, 223 S.W.3d 762, 772 (Tex. App.—Dallas 2007, pet. denied) (attorney could testify as to time estimates based on notes and past experience in performing similar work).

Anderson v. Mkt. St. Dev., Ltd., 944 S.W.2d 776, 779 (Tex. App.—Eastland 1997, writ denied) ("[The] risk of injury from a protruding screw next to a moving conveyor belt was within common knowledge of laypersons.").

Jones v. State, 843 S.W.2d 92, 99 (Tex. App.—Dallas 1992, writ ref'd) (testimony that knife is deadly weapon capable of causing injury within common knowledge of lay witness).

f. Causation

Merrill v. Sprint Waste Services LP, 527 S.W.3d 663, 670 (Tex. App.—Houston [14th Dist.] 2017, no pet.) ("[A] lay opinion can establish causation when general experience and common sense will enable a layperson to determine, with reasonable probability, the causal relationship between the event and condition.").

Minn. Min. & Mfg. Co. v. Atterbury, 978 S.W.2d 183, 190 (Tex. App.—Texarkana 1998, pet. denied) ("[A] lay opinion is adequate to prove causation where general experience and common sense enables a layman to determine with reasonable probability the causal relationship between the event and the condition.").

Purina Mills, Inc. v. Odell, 948 S.W.2d 927, 933 (Tex. App.—Texarkana 1997, pet. denied) (lay opinion is adequate to prove causation where general experience and common sense enables layperson to determine causal relationship between event and condition with reasonable probability).

g. Hearsay

Coker v. Burghardt, 833 S.W.2d 306, 310 (Tex. App.—Dallas 1992, writ denied) (lay witness opinion may be based on hearsay provided witness has personal knowledge of facts forming opinion; lay witness allowed to give opinion on costs where familiarized himself with repair costs by going to various car repair shops).

D. Motion to Exclude Testimony of Incompetent Witness

1. Suggested Motion Text

(*Name of Moving Party*) hereby moves this Court for an order excluding any and all testimony, reference to testimony, or argument relating to the testimony of (*Name of Witness*). The motion is based upon the grounds that (*Describe Facts Supporting Claim That Witness is Incompetent to Testify, e.g., the Witness is Only Five Years Old and is Incapable of Relating the Incident*) and therefore, the witness is incompetent to testify.

2. Motion Summary

This motion is used to exclude the testimony of any witness who is incompetent under the law. The motion is based upon Texas Rules of Evidence 601 and 602 and supporting case law. Rule 601 disqualifies persons who are "insane" at the time of their testimony or at the time of the incident and children who do not appear to possess sufficient intellect to relate the facts of the incident. Rule 602 requires that people testify from personal knowledge, subject to Rule 703 (expert witnesses).

3. Supporting Authorities

Texas Rule of Evidence 601 governs the competency and incompetency of witnesses and states:

(a) **General Rule**. Every person is competent to be a witness except as otherwise provided in these rules. The following witnesses shall be incompetent to testify in any proceeding subject to these rules:
  (1) *Insane persons*. Insane persons who, in the opinion of the court, are in an insane condition of mind at the time when they are offered as a witness, or who, in the opinion of the court, were in that condition when the events happened of which they are called to testify.
  (2) *Children*. Children or other persons who, after being examined by the court, appear not to possess sufficient intellect to relate transactions with respect to which they are interrogated.
(b) "Dead Man's Rule" in Civil Actions. In civil actions by or against executors, administrators, or guardians, in which judgment may be rendered for or against them as such, neither party shall be allowed to testify against the others as to any oral statement by the testator, intestate or ward, unless that testimony to the oral statement is corroborated or unless the witness is called at the trial to testify thereto by the opposite party; and, the provisions of this article shall extend to and include all actions by or against the heirs or legal representatives of a decedent based in whole or in part on such oral statement. Except for the foregoing, a

witness is not precluded from giving evidence of or concerning any transaction with, any conversations with, any admissions of, or statement by, a deceased or insane party or person merely because the witness is a party to the action or a person interested in the event thereof. The trial court shall, in a proper case, where this rule prohibits an interested party or witness from testifying, instruct the jury that such person is not permitted by the law to give evidence relating to any oral statement by the deceased or ward unless the oral statement is corroborated or unless the party or witness is called at the trial by the opposite party.

Gilley v. State, 418 S.W.3d 114, 121 (Tex. Crim. App. 2014), *cert. denied*, 574 U.S. 830 (2014) ("[T]he competency of a child-witness is a preliminary question for the trial court to determine under Rule 104(a) of the Texas Rules of Evidence, and the trial court is not bound by the Rules of Evidence in making that determination.").

a. *Inability to Express or Tell Truth*

In re R.M.T., 352 S.W.3d 12, 21 (Tex. App.—Texarkana 2011, no pet.) ("[T]o demonstrate witness incompetency under Rule 601, it must be shown that the witness lacked the ability to perceive the relevant events, recall and narrate those events at the time of trial, or that the witness lacked the capacity to understand the obligation of the oath.").

Kokes v. College, 148 S.W.3d 384, 389 (Tex. App.—Beaumont 2004, no pet.) ("The issue of competency under Rule 601 is whether a witness has the ability to perceive the relevant events, recollect the events, and narrate adequately that recollection[;]" note: party who had been found incapacitated in probate proceeding remained competent to give deposition).

i. Children

Texas Rule of Evidence 601 states in relevant part:

Competency and Incompetency of Witnesses

(a) **General Rule**. Every person is competent to be a witness except as otherwise provided in these rules. The following witnesses shall be incompetent to testify in any proceeding subject to these rules:

...

(2) *Children. Children or other persons who, after being examined by the court, appear not to possess sufficient intellect to relate transactions with respect to which they are interrogated.* (Emphasis added.)

Gilley v. State, 418 S.W.3d 114, 121 (Tex. Crim. App. 2014), *cert. denied*, 574 U.S. 830 (2014) (children are incompetent to testify if, after being examined by the court, they appear not to possess sufficient intellect to relate transactions with respect to which they are interrogated).

Gilley v. State, 418 S.W.3d 114, 121 (Tex. Crim. App. 2014), *cert. denied*, 574 U.S. 830 (2014) (besides gauging the sufficiency of the child-witness's cognitive ability to relate relevant facts, as specifically contemplated by Rule 601(a)(2), a trial court may also inquire whether a child-witness possesses the capacity to appreciate the obligations of the oath—or can at least distinguish the truth from a lie).

Gilley v. State, 418 S.W.3d 114, 121 (Tex. Crim. App. 2014), *cert. denied*, 574 U.S. 830 (2014) (trial court has discretion to permit the parties to participate in the Rule 601(a)(2) examination, and may even allow the parties themselves to propound the questions, so long as the trial court itself makes an independent ruling on competency based on that questioning).

Baldit v. State, 522 S.W.3d 753, 761 (Tex. App.—Houston [1st Dist.] 2017, no pet.) ("[A] person, such as a child, is not competent to testify if, upon examination by the trial court, the court finds that the person lacks sufficient intellect to testify concerning the matters in issue.").

Baldit v. State, 522 S.W.3d 753, 761 (Tex. App.—Houston [1st Dist.] 2017, no pet.) ("When a party challenges the competency of a child witness, the trial court must consider whether the child witness possesses (1) the ability to intelligently observe the events in question at the time of the occurrence, (2) the capacity to recollect the events, and (3) the capacity to narrate the events.... The third element involves the ability to understand the moral responsibility to tell the truth, to understand the questions posed, and to frame intelligent answers.").

b. *Lack of Mental Competence/Insanity*

Texas Rule of Evidence 601 states in relevant part:

Competency and Incompetency of Witnesses

(a) **General Rule.** Every person is competent to be a witness except as otherwise provided in these rules. The following witnesses shall be incompetent to testify in any proceeding subject to these rules:

(1) *Insane persons. Insane persons who, in the opinion of the court, are in an insane condition of mind at the time when they are offered as a witness, or who, in the opinion of the court, were in that condition when the events happened of which they are called to testify.* (Emphasis added.)

Hogan v. State, 440 S.W.3d 211, 213 (Tex. App.—Houston [14th Dist.] 2013, pet. ref'd) (in determining whether a witness has sufficient intellect to relate transactions with respect to which he is being interrogated, the court will consider whether the witness possesses (1) the ability to intelligently observe the events in question at the time of the occurrence, (2) the capacity to recollect the events, and (3) the capacity to narrate the events).

In re R.M.T., 352 S.W.3d 12, 21 (Tex. App.—Texarkana 2011, no pet.) (adjudication of insanity of a witness creates a rebuttable presumption of insanity).

Hunter v. NCNB Tex. Nat'l Bank, 857 S.W.2d 722, 727 (Tex. App.—Houston [14th Dist.] 1993, reh'g denied) (trial court did not err excluding evidence from witness who had previously been adjudicated incompetent where party offering evidence failed to rebut presumption arising from prior adjudication of witness's incompetence).

Mobil Oil Corp. v. Floyd, 810 S.W.2d 321, 324 (Tex. App.—Beaumont 1991, orig. proceeding) (presumption arises from previous finding of incompetency but may be rebutted; testimony of neurologist sufficient to rebut presumption that person previously found incompetent was incompetent for purposes of giving deposition where testimony proved that witness "is capable of understanding the oath, and can recall and narrate events. This being so it results in [the party] being able to examine him under oath for discovery purposes *although such testimony may or may not be admissible at trial.*" (Emphasis added.)).

c. *Lack of Personal Knowledge of Subject Matter*

Texas Rule of Evidence 602 states:

> A witness may not testify to a matter *unless evidence is introduced sufficient to support a finding that the witness has personal knowledge of the matter.* Evidence to prove personal knowledge may, but need not, consist of the testimony of the witness. This rule is subject to the provision of Rule 703, relating to opinion testimony by expert witnesses. (Emphasis added.)

Texas Rule of Evidence 701 states:

> If the witness is not testifying as an expert, the witness' testimony in the form of opinions or inferences is limited to those opinions or inferences which are
>
> (a) *rationally based on the perception of the witness* and
> (b) helpful to a clear understanding of the witness' testimony or the determination of a fact in issue. (Emphasis added.)

Dallas Morning News, Inc. v. Hall, 579 S.W.3d 370, 379 (Tex. 2019) ("A witness may testify to a matter only if the evidence supports a finding that the witness has personal knowledge of the matter").

Bigby v. State, 892 S.W.2d 864, 889 (Tex. Crim. App. 1994), *cert. denied*, 515 U.S. 1162 (1995) (requirement that testimony be based on "perception of the witness" presumes underlying facts were observed or experienced by witness).

Merrill v. Sprint Waste Services LP, 527 S.W.3d 663, 670 (Tex. App.—Houston [14th Dist.] 2017, no pet.) ("An opinion will satisfy the personal knowledge requirement if it is an interpretation of the witness's objective perception of event.").

Myre v. Meletio, 307 S.W.3d 839, 845 (Tex. App.—Dallas 2010, pet. denied) ("[T]estimony based solely on conjecture and speculation is incompetent.").

Anthony Equip. Corp. v. Irwin Steel Erectors, Inc., 115 S.W.3d 191, 206 (Tex. App.—Dallas 2003, pet. dism'd) (witness lacked requisite personal knowledge to provide opinion as lay witness regarding cost of equipment repair).

Lum v. State, 903 S.W.2d 365, 369 (Tex. App.—Texarkana 1995, writ ref'd) (lay opinion not admissible in criminal case unless rationally based on witness's perception).

Cornelison v. Aggregate Haulers, Inc., 777 S.W.2d 542, 545 (Tex. App.—Fort Worth 1989, writ denied) ("Statements contained in a medical record as to how an accident happened or where it happened, age, medical history, etc. are not admissible as a business-record exception to the hearsay rule, because the party making the entry in the record does not have personal knowledge as to these matters, and the statements do not become trustworthy just because it is hospital routine to record them." (Citations omitted.)).

McMillan v. State, 754 S.W.2d 422, 425 (Tex. App.—Eastland 1988, pet. ref'd) (lay opinion based on hearsay not admissible where witness lacks personal knowledge of underlying facts).

Handel v. Long Trusts, 757 S.W.2d 848, 851 (Tex. App.—Texarkana 1988, no writ) (witness lacked personal knowledge and therefore unable to provide opinion as lay witness).

Dieter v. Baker Serv. Tools, a Div. of Baker Int'l, Inc., 776 S.W.2d 781, 784 (Tex. App.—Corpus Christi 1989, writ denied) (affidavits filed by lay witnesses in opposition to summary judgment motion speculative and conclusory and failed to assert any facts that were basis of witnesses' opinions).

d. Other Grounds

Other possible grounds for excluding lay witness testimony include:

- Prejudicial;
- Time-wasting;
- Confusing or misleading;
- Irrelevant;
- Collateral to issues in case;
- Improper foundation;
- Improper test evidence;
- Improper expert qualifications;
- Inadmissible hearsay.

4. Opposing Authorities

Gilley v. State, 418 S.W.3d 114, 121 (Tex. Crim. App. 2014), *cert. denied*, 574 U.S. 830 (2014) (the party seeking to exclude the witness from testifying must raise the issue of his competency and shoulders the burden of establishing incompetency).

Baldit v. State, 522 S.W.3d 753, 761 (Tex. App.—Houston [1st Dist.] 2017, no pet.) ("Generally, every person is presumed competent to testify.").

Hogan v. State, 440 S.W.3d 211, 213 (Tex. App.—Houston [14th Dist.] 2013, pet. ref'd) (every person is presumed competent to testify).

In re R.M.T., 352 S.W.3d 12, 21 (Tex. App.—Texarkana 2011, no pet.) (burden of proof rests on the party who claims a witness is incompetent due to insanity to show the existence of insanity by a preponderance of the evidence).

Mobil Oil Corp. v. Floyd, 810 S.W.2d 321, 324 (Tex. App.—Beaumont 1991, orig. proceeding) (presumption arising from previous finding of incompetency can be rebutted).

a. Children

Pipkin v. Kroger Texas, L.P., 383 S.W.3d 655, 668 (Tex. App.—Houston [14th Dist.] 2012, pet. denied) ("[T]here is no age below which a child is automatically deemed incompetent to testify.").

Pipkin v. Kroger Texas, L.P., 383 S.W.3d 655, 668 (Tex. App.—Houston [14th Dist.] 2012, pet. denied) (when a trial court determines whether a child is competent to testify at trial, it considers (1) the competence of the child to observe intelligently the events in question at the time of the occurrence, (2) the child's capacity to recollect the events, and (3) the child's capacity to narrate the facts).

Davis v. State, 268 S.W.3d 683, 699 (Tex. App.—Fort Worth 2008, pet. ref'd) (once the competency of a child witness is challenged, a trial court must assure itself that the child has (1) the ability to intelligently observe the events in question at the time of the occurrence, (2) the capacity to recollect the events, and (3) the capacity to narrate the events; the third element requires that the witness is able to understand the questions asked, frame intelligent answers to those questions, and understand the moral responsibility to tell the truth).

De Los Santos v. State, 219 S.W.3d 71, 80 (Tex. App.—San Antonio 2006, no pet.) (considerations in determining a child witness's capacity to narrate involve both an ability to understand the questions asked and to frame intelligent answers and a moral responsibility to tell the truth).

De Los Santos v. State, 219 S.W.3d 71, 80 (Tex. App.—San Antonio 2006, no pet.) (there is no certain age below which a child is automatically deemed incompetent to testify).

De Los Santos v. State, 219 S.W.3d 71, 80 (Tex. App.—San Antonio 2006, no pet.) (in evaluating a child witness's competency, the court examines the child's responses to qualification questions as well as the child's entire testimony).

Woods v. State, 14 S.W.3d 445, 451 (Tex. App.—Fort Worth 2000, no pet.) (child who was eight years old at the time of the events was competent to testify and any discrepancies or confusion in the testimony affected the weight of the testimony and not the admissibility of it).

Upton v. State, 894 S.W.2d 426, 429 (Tex. App.—Amarillo 1995, pet. ref'd) (child witness was competent to testify, despite being unable to define the word, "lie" because she stated that a person who lies would go to jail).

Hollinger v. State, 911 S.W.2d 35, 38 (Tex. App.—Tyler 1995, pet. ref'd) (trial court did not abuse its discretion by finding that a four-year-old victim was competent to testify).

Rodriguez v. State, 772 S.W.2d 167, 171 (Tex. App.—Houston [14th Dist.] 1989, pet. ref'd) (no error where witness competency hearing held in front of jury, and defendant did not object to procedure at trial).

State ex rel. Holmes v. Lanford, 764 S.W.2d 593, 594 (Tex. App.—Houston [14th Dist.] 1989, orig. proceeding), *motion to file mandamus denied* (trial court did not have authority to order psychological examination of four-year-old victim in criminal case to determine competency as witness; "no in-depth psychological probing is necessary" to determine if child has intellect to relate events).

Dufrene v. State, 853 S.W.2d 86, 88 (Tex. App.—Houston [14th Dist.] 1993, pet. ref'd) ("A child is considered competent to testify unless it appears to the Court that she does not possess sufficient intellect to relate the transaction about which she will testify ... The child no longer needs to understand the 'obligation of the oath.'... The Court must simply impress on her mind the duty of being 'truthful.'").

Macias v. State, 776 S.W.2d 255, 256 (Tex. App.—San Antonio 1989, pet. ref'd) (five-and-a-half-year-old competent to testify about events even though she had trouble placing events into time frame; note: prior requirement that child understand meaning of oath to be competent to testify repealed in 1986).

> *Note that a party waives any objection to competency by failing to raise the issue at trial or to ask for a competency hearing.* See McGinn v. State, *961 S.W.2d 161, 166 (Tex. Crim. App. 1998)*, cert. denied, *525 U.S. 967 (1998);* Hill v. State, *3 S.W.3d 249, 253 (Tex. App.—Waco 1999, pet. ref'd);* Grayson v. State, *786 S.W.2d 504, 505 (Tex. App.—Dallas 1990, no pet.).*

b. *Mental Competence/Insanity*

Moody v. State, 543 S.W.3d 309, 314 (Tex. App.—Eastland 2017, pet. ref'd) ("There is nothing in the law that automatically disqualifies an autistic witness, nor do inconsistencies automatically lower evidence below the required standard.").

Hogan v. State, 440 S.W.3d 211, 213 (Tex. App.—Houston [14th Dist.] 2013, pet. ref'd) (if an intellectually disabled person possesses sufficient intelligence to receive correct impressions of events she sees, retains clear recollection of them, and is able to communicate them through some means, then there is no reason for rejecting her testimony).

Hogan v. State, 440 S.W.3d 211, 213 (Tex. App.—Houston [14th Dist.] 2013, pet. ref'd) (a witness is not rendered incompetent merely because there are inconsistencies in her testimony).

Kokes v. College, 148 S.W.3d 384, 389 (Tex. App.—Beaumont 2004, no pet.) (party been found incapacitated in probate proceeding remained competent to give deposition).

Mobil Oil Corp. v. Floyd, 810 S.W.2d 321, 324 (Tex. App.—Beaumont 1991, orig. proceeding) (neurologist's testimony sufficient to rebut presumption that person previously found incompetent was incompetent for purposes of giving deposition; testimony proved that witness "is capable of understanding the oath, and can recall and narrate events. This being so it results in [the party] being able to examine him under oath for discovery purposes although such testimony may or may not be admissible at trial.").

Rodriguez v. State, 772 S.W.2d 167, 171 (Tex. App.—Houston [14th Dist.] 1989, pet. ref'd) (witness who previously suffered nervous breakdown and had Alzheimer's disease competent to testify where witness could relate facts of incident, despite some confusion and inconsistency in testimony).

c. Dead Man's Rule

Fraga v. Drake, 276 S.W.3d 55, 61 (Tex. App.—El Paso 2008, no pet.) (Dead Man's Rule does not prohibit testimony concerning statements by the deceased that are properly corroborated).

Fraga v. Drake, 276 S.W.3d 55, 61 (Tex. App.—El Paso 2008, no pet.) ("The [Dead Man's] rule does not prohibit testimony concerning statements by the deceased that are properly corroborated.... Corroborating evidence must tend to support some of the material allegations or issues that are raised by the pleadings and testified to by the witness whose evidence is sought to be corroborated.... It may come from any other competent witness or other legal source, including documentary evidence.... Corroborating evidence need not be sufficient standing alone, but must tend to confirm and strengthen the testimony of the witness and show the probability of its truth.").

Fraga v. Drake, 276 S.W.3d 55, 61 (Tex. App.—El Paso 2008, no pet.) (under the Dead Man's Rule, "it is sufficient if the corroborating evidence shows conduct by the deceased that is generally consistent with the testimony concerning the deceased's statements").

Coleman v. Coleman, 170 S.W.3d 231, 238 (Tex. App.—Dallas 2005, pet. denied) (Dead Man's Rule "does not prohibit testimony concerning statements by the deceased that are properly corroborated.... Corroborating evidence must tend to support some of the material allegations or issues that are raised by the pleadings and testified to by the witness whose evidence is sought to be corroborated").

E. Motion to Exclude Testimony of Judge, Arbitrator, Mediator, or Juror

1. Suggested Motion Text

(*Name of Moving Party*) hereby moves this Court for an order excluding any and all testimony, reference to testimony, or argument relating to the testimony of (*Name of Witness*). The motion is based upon the ground that the witness has served as (*a/an*) (*Judge/Arbitrator/Mediator/Juror*) in a related proceeding (*or Describe Date and Nature of Proceeding*) and therefore the witness is incompetent to testify.

2. Motion Summary

This motion is used to exclude the testimony of a judge, arbitrator, mediator, or juror.

3. Supporting Authorities—Judges

Texas Rule of Evidence 605 states:

Competency of Judge as a Witness

The judge presiding at the trial may not testify in that trial as a witness. No objection need be made in order to preserve the point.

Canon 2 of the Texas Code of Judicial Conduct states in relevant part:

Avoiding Impropriety and the Appearance of Impropriety in All of the Judge's Activities

A. A judge shall comply with the law and *should act at all times in a manner that promotes public confidence in the integrity and impartiality of the judiciary.*
B. A judge shall not allow any relationship to influence judicial conduct or judgment. A judge shall not lend the prestige of judicial office to advance the private interests of the judge or others; nor shall a judge convey or permit others to convey the impression that they are in a special position to influence the judge. *A judge shall not testify voluntarily as a character witness.* (Emphasis added.)

Texas Code of Criminal Procedure, article 38.05, states:

In ruling upon the admissibility of evidence, the judge shall not discuss or comment upon the weight of the same or its bearing in the case, but shall simply decide whether or not it is admissible; *nor shall he, at any stage of the proceeding previous to the return of the verdict, make any remark calculated to convey to the jury his opinion of the case.* (Emphasis added.)

Joachim v. Chambers, 815 S.W.2d 234, 237 (Tex. 1991) (orig. proceeding) (trial court abused discretion allowing judge to testify as expert witness where testimony was prohibited by Canon 2 of the Texas Code of Judicial Conduct).

In re Daugherty, 558 S.W.3d 272, 278 (Tex. App.—Dallas 2018, orig. proceeding) ("The presiding judge may not testify as a witness at the trial. A party need not object to a presiding judge testifying to preserve the issue.").

Orion Enters., Inc. v. Pope, 927 S.W.2d 654, 660 (Tex. App.—San Antonio 1996, orig. proceeding) (first judge's affidavit submitted to second judge regarding reasons behind ruling improper where testimony could still be considered improper based upon Canon 2 of the Texas Code of Judicial Conduct, even though first judge may not have been incompetent as witness under Texas Rule of Evidence 605).

a. Arbitrators

Tex. Civ. Prac. & Rem. Code Section 154.073 states:

(a) Except as provided by Subsections (c), (d), (e), and (f), *a communication relating to the subject matter of any civil or criminal dispute made by a participant in an alternative dispute resolution procedure, whether before or after the institution of formal judicial proceedings, is confidential, is not subject to disclosure, and may not be used as evidence against the participant in any judicial or administrative proceeding.*

(b) Any record made at an alternative dispute resolution procedure is confidential, and *the participants or the third party facilitating the procedure may not be required to testify in any proceedings relating to or arising out of the matter in dispute or be subject to process requiring disclosure of confidential information or data relating to or arising out of the matter in dispute.*

(c) An oral communication or written material used in or made a part of an alternative dispute resolution procedure is admissible or discoverable if it is admissible or discoverable independent of the procedure.

(d) A final written agreement to which a governmental body, as defined by Section 552.003, Government Code, is a signatory that is reached as a result of a dispute resolution procedure conducted under this chapter is subject to or excepted from required disclosure in accordance with Chapter 552, Government Code.

(e) If this section conflicts with other legal requirements for disclosure of communications, records, or materials, the issue of confidentiality may be presented to the court having jurisdiction of the proceedings to determine, in camera, whether the facts, circumstances, and context of the communications or materials sought to be disclosed warrant a protective order of the court or whether the communications or materials are subject to disclosure.

(f) This section does not affect the duty to report abuse or neglect under Subchapter B, Chapter 261, Family Code, and abuse, exploitation, or neglect under Subchapter C, Chapter 48, Human Resources Code.

(g) This section applies to a victim-offender mediation by the Texas Department of Criminal Justice as described in Article 56.13, Code of Criminal Procedure. (Emphasis added.)

b. Jurors

Texas Rule of Evidence 606 states:

Competency of Juror as a Witness

(a) **At the Trial**. *A member of the jury may not testify as a witness before that jury in the trial of the case in which the juror is sitting* *as a juror.* If the juror is called so to testify, the opposing party shall be afforded an opportunity to object out of the presence of the jury.

(b) **Inquiry Into Validity of Verdict or Indictment.** Upon an inquiry into the validity of a verdict or indictment, *a juror may not testify as to any matter or statement occurring during the jury's deliberations, or to the effect of anything on any juror's mind or emotions or mental processes, as influencing any juror's assent to or dissent from the verdict or indictment. Nor may a juror's affidavit or any statement by a juror concerning any matter about which the juror would be precluded from testifying be admitted in evidence for any of these purposes.* However, a juror may testify: (1) whether any outside influence was improperly brought to bear upon any juror; or (2) to rebut a claim that the juror was not qualified to serve. (Emphasis added.)

Colyer v. State, 428 S.W.3d 117, 125 (Tex. Crim. App. 2014) (except for (1) an "outside influence" that is (2) improperly brought to bear upon a juror, Rule 606(b) continues to prohibit juror testimony to impeach a verdict).

Colyer v. State, 428 S.W.3d 117, 125 (Tex. Crim. App. 2014) ("Rule 606(b) inquiry is limited to that which occurs both outside of the jury room and outside of the jurors' personal knowledge and experience. External events or information, unrelated to the trial, which happen to cause jurors to feel personal pressure to hasten (or end) deliberations are not 'outside influences' because those pressures are caused by a juror's personal and emotional reaction to information that is irrelevant to the trial issues.").

Ford Motor Co. v. Castillo, 279 S.W.3d 656, 666 (Tex. 2009) ("[R]easons for rules prohibiting unfettered probing into jury deliberations include: (1) keeping jury deliberations private to encourage candid discussion of a case; (2) protecting jurors from post-trial harassment or tampering; (3) preventing a disgruntled juror whose view did not prevail from overturning the verdict; and (4) protecting the need for finality.").

Lewis v. State, 911 S.W.2d 1, 11 (Tex. Crim. App. 1995) (trial court did not err excluding evidence of one juror's perception of what another juror (foreman) said, where actual juror allegedly improperly influenced by what foreman said testified about effect of statements on her).

Lincicome v. State, 3 S.W.3d 644, 647 (Tex. App.—Amarillo 1999, no pet.) (newspaper article quoting juror on jurors' thought processes during portions of deliberations insufficient to undermine verdict where article did not show that information from outside had improperly influenced verdict).

Speer v. State, 890 S.W.2d 87, 89 (Tex. App.—Houston [1st Dist.] 1994, pet. ref'd) (in considering sufficiency of evidence relating to jury instructions, appellate court would not consider jurors' affidavits about thought processes).

Brown v. State, 804 S.W.2d 566, 569 (Tex. App.—Houston [14th Dist.] 1991, pet. ref'd) ("[J]urors are incompetent to impeach their verdict by affidavit or testimony about their mental processes during deliberations but may testify as to any matter that is relevant to the validity of the verdict or indictment.... A matter is relevant to the validity of the verdict or indictment if it concerns an overt act which constitutes jury misconduct under Tex. R. App. P. 30(b) and its predecessor Tex. C. Crim. P. Ann. art. 40.03.").

Baldonado v. State, 745 S.W.2d 491, 493 (Tex. App.—Corpus Christi 1988, pet. ref'd) (juror affidavit of juror's own thought process insufficient to justify new trial where no actual misconduct shown by it).

4. Opposing Authorities—Judges

a. Arbitrators

Tex. Civ. Prac. & Rem. Code Section 154.073 governs alternative dispute resolutions and states in relevant part:

> ...
> Any record made at an alternative dispute resolution procedure is confidential, and the participants or the third party facilitating the procedure *may not be required to testify* in any proceedings relating to or arising out of the matter in dispute or be subject to process requiring disclosure of confidential information or data relating to or arising out of the matter in dispute.
>
> (b) *An oral communication or written material used in or made a part of an alternative dispute resolution procedure is admissible or discoverable if it is admissible or discoverable independent of the procedure.*
>
> ...
>
> (e) *If this section conflicts with other legal requirements for disclosure of communications, records, or materials, the issue of confidentiality may be presented to the court having jurisdiction of the proceedings to determine, in camera, whether the facts, circumstances, and context of the communications or materials sought to be disclosed warrant a protective order of the court or whether the communications or materials are subject to disclosure.* (Emphasis added.)

> Note that based upon section (b), above, it would appear that an argument could be made that if the parties agree, the testimony should be allowed. Also, based upon section (e) above, there are situations where the trial court can order the communications or materials to be disclosed.

Knapp v. Wilson N. Jones Mem'l Hosp., 281 S.W.3d 163, 172 (Tex. App.—Dallas 2009, no pet.) ("[S]ection 154.073 does not create a blanket of confidentiality nor is it so broad as to bar all evidence regarding everything that occurs at arbitration from being presented in the trial court.").

Knapp v. Wilson N. Jones Mem'l Hosp., 281 S.W.3d 163, 172 (Tex. App.—Dallas 2009, no pet.) ("[I]f the communication or written material does not relate to the subject matter of the dispute, or does not relate to or arise out of the matter in dispute, it may not be confidential, under section 154.073(a) and (b) of the Texas Civil Practice and Remedies Code.").

Knapp v. Wilson N. Jones Mem'l Hosp., 281 S.W.3d 163, 172 (Tex. App.—Dallas 2009, no pet.) ("[D]isclosure regarding arbitration proceedings may be warranted when a party does not seek discovery of arbitration evidence to obtain additional funds from another party to the arbitration or to establish any liability of the other party after the dispute has been peaceably resolved, but proposes to offer the arbitration evidence in a separate case against a separate party to prove a claim that is factually and legally unrelated to the arbitration claims.").

Knapp v. Wilson N. Jones Mem'l Hosp., 281 S.W.3d 163, 172 (Tex. App.—Dallas 2009, no pet.) ("[D]isclosure [regarding arbitration proceedings] may be warranted in a case alleging a new and independent cause of action, if disclosure of the confidential communications or written materials will not disturb the settlement in the underlying arbitration.").

b. *Jurors*

Texas Rule of Evidence 606(b) states in relevant part:

> **Inquiry Into Validity of Verdict or Indictment.** Upon an inquiry into the validity of a verdict or indictment, ... a juror may testify: (1) whether any outside influence was improperly brought to bear upon any juror; or (2) to rebut a claim that the juror was not qualified to serve.

Colyer v. State, 428 S.W.3d 117, 125 (Tex. Crim. App. 2014) ("'[O]utside influence' on which juror may testify includes factual or legal information conveyed to the jurors by a bailiff or some other unauthorized person who intends to affect the deliberations.").

McQuarrie v. State, 380 S.W.3d 145, 150 (Tex. Crim. App. 2012) (under Rule of Evidence 606(b), "a juror may testify about whether any outside influence was improperly brought to bear upon any juror or to rebut a claim that the juror was not qualified to serve").

McQuarrie v. State, 380 S.W.3d 145, 150 (Tex. Crim. App. 2012) ("[A]n 'outside influence' is something outside of both the jury room and the juror.").

McQuarrie v. State, 380 S.W.3d 145, 150 (Tex. Crim. App. 2012) ("[T]he conduct of the jurors may be of such a character as not only to defeat the rights of litigants but it may directly affect the administration of public justice.").

McQuarrie v. State, 380 S.W.3d 145, 150 (Tex. Crim. App. 2012) ("internet research [conducted by juror] constituted an 'outside influence'" about which juror testimony was allowed).

Ford Motor Co. v. Castillo, 279 S.W.3d 656, 666 (Tex. 2009) (discovery involving jurors should ordinarily be limited to facts and evidence relevant to (1) whether any outside influence was improperly brought to bear upon any juror, and (2) rebuttal of a claim that a juror was not qualified to serve).

Golden Eagle Archery, Inc. v. Jackson, 24 S.W.3d 362, 370 (Tex. 2003) (juror may testify about "improper contacts with individuals outside the jury," or "matters or statements not occurring during the course of the jury's deliberations").

Editorial Caballero, S.A. de C.V. v. Playboy Enters., Inc., 359 S.W.3d 318, 324 (Tex. App.—Corpus Christi 2012, pet. denied) (juror may testify about improper contacts with individuals outside the jury or matters or statements not occurring during the course of the jury's deliberations).

Brandt v. Surbur, 194 S.W.3d 108, 134 (Tex. App.—Corpus Christi 2006, pet. denied) (upon claim of juror misconduct, a juror may testify about improper contacts with individuals outside the jury, or matters or statements not occurring during the course of the jury's deliberations; however, a juror may not testify as to any matter or statement occurring during the course of the jury's deliberations or to the effect of anything upon his or any other juror's mind or emotions).

Hampton v. State, 838 S.W.2d 337, 339 (Tex. App.—Houston [1st Dist.] 1992, no pet.) (affidavit from attorney citing juror as source of alleged juror misconduct proper support for defendant's new trial motion).

Martin v. State, 823 S.W.2d 726, 729 (Tex. App.—Waco 1992, pet. ref'd) (affidavit from juror regarding information another juror shared with other jurors during deliberations was considered with respect to whether juror had committed overt act of misconduct).

Baldonado v. State, 745 S.W.2d 491, 493 (Tex. App.—Corpus Christi 1988, pet. ref'd) (juror testimony regarding alleged misconduct considered when deciding whether to grant defendant's request for new trial).

F. Motion to Exclude Witness From Courtroom Prior to Testifying

1. Suggested Motion Text

(<u>*Name of Moving Party*</u>) hereby moves this Court for an order restricting (<u>*Name of Witness(es)*</u>) from entering the courtroom until called to testify. The motion is based upon the ground that (<u>State Basis for Exclusion of Witness, e.g., the Witnesses Will Be Testifying on Similar Matters and Allowing One to Hear the Questions and Answers of Another Will Undermine the Moving Party's Cross-examination</u>) and therefore this court should exclude the named witness[es] pursuant to Texas Rule of Evidence 614.

2. Motion Summary

This motion is used to exclude a witness from the courtroom while another witness is testifying. The principal basis for making the motion is to avoid the risk that the witness will be unfairly educated on the forthcoming interrogation. The motion is based upon the authority of Texas Rule of Evidence 614.

3. Supporting Authorities

Texas Rule of Evidence 614 states:

At the request of a party the court shall order witnesses excluded so that they cannot hear the testimony of other witnesses, and it may make the order of its own *motion*. This rule does not authorize exclusion of:

(1) a party who is a natural person or in civil cases the spouse of such natural person;
(2) an officer or employee of a party in a civil case or a defendant in a criminal case that is not a natural person designated as its representative by its attorney;
(3) a person whose presence is shown by a party to be essential to the presentation of the party's cause; or
(4) the victim in a criminal case, unless the victim is to testify and the court determines that the victim's testimony would be materially affected if the victim hears other testimony at the trial." (Emphasis added).

Russell v. State, 155 S.W.3d 176, 180 (Tex. Crim. App. 2005) ("State's designating a witness as a "case agent" does not make the witness one whom a trial court may not exclude from the courtroom under Rule 614.").

Drilex Sys., Inc. v. Flores, 1 S.W.3d 112, 117 (Tex. 1999) ("The burden rests with the party seeking to exempt an expert witness from the Rule's exclusion requirement to establish that the witness's presence is essential.").

Garcia v. State, 553 S.W.3d 645, 646 (Tex. App.—Texarkana 2018, pet. ref'd) ("At a party's request, the court must order witnesses excluded so that they cannot hear other witnesses' testimony.").

Parks v. State, 463 S.W.3d 166, 174 (Tex. App.—Houston [14th Dist.] 2015, no pet.) ("The purpose of the [witness sequestration] rule is to prevent the testimony of one witness from influencing the testimony of another.").

Parks v. State, 463 S.W.3d 166, 174 (Tex. App.—Houston [14th Dist.] 2015, no pet.) ("The party seeking to exempt a witness [from the exercise of the Rule] has the burden of showing that the claimed exception applies.").

Allen v. State, 436 S.W.3d 815, 822 (Tex. App.—Texarkana 2014, pet. ref'd) ("Rule 614 of the Texas Rules of Evidence, the witness sequestration rule, prevents witnesses from tailoring their testimony to fit that of other witnesses and enhances the jury's ability to detect falsehood by exposing inconsistencies in testimony.").

Allen v. State, 436 S.W.3d 815, 822 (Tex. App.—Texarkana 2014, pet. ref'd) ("Rule 614 requires a trial court to exclude testifying witnesses from the courtroom unless the witness is (1) a party or the spouse of a party in a civil case, (2) an officer or employee of a legal entity named in the lawsuit who has been designated as the entity's representative for purposes of the trial, (3) a person whose presence is shown by a party to be essential to the presentation of the party's cause, or (4) the victim in a criminal case, unless the victim is to testify and the court determines that the victim's testimony would be materially affected by hearing other trial testimony.").

Allen v. State, 436 S.W.3d 815, 822 (Tex. App.—Texarkana 2014, pet. ref'd) ("[A] party claiming an exemption under the witness sequestration rule bears the burden of showing that the exemption applies.").

Allen v. State, 436 S.W.3d 815, 822 (Tex. App.—Texarkana 2014, pet. ref'd) ("[A] conclusory statement that the witness's presence is "essential and necessary" does not meet the burden to show that an exception under Rule 614 applies.").

Willet v. Cole, 249 S.W.3d 585, 590 (Tex. App.—Waco 2008, no pet.) ("[The] purpose of the rule is to prevent witnesses from colluding about their testimony and to prevent witnesses from tailoring their answers in response to that of other witnesses.").

Emenhiser v. State, 196 S.W.3d 915, 923 (Tex. App.—Fort Worth 2006, pet. ref'd) ("[I]n determining whether to disqualify a witness who has violated the Rule, the trial court must balance the interests of the State and the accused, consider alternative sanctions, and consider the benefit and detriment arising from a disqualification in light of the nature and weight of the testimony to be offered.").

Minor v. State, 91 S.W.3d 824, 829 (Tex. App.—Fort Worth 2002, pet. ref'd) (trial court has discretion excluding witness's testimony who violated exclusionary order during guilt/innocence phase).

Longoria v. State, 148 S.W.3d 657, 660 (Tex. App.—Houston [14th Dist.] 2004, pet. ref'd) ("[O]ne of the purposes of the rule is to prevent witness from modifying testimony based upon testimony of other witnesses.").

Phillips v. State, 64 S.W.3d 458, 460 (Tex. App.—Houston [1st Dist.] 2001, no pet.) (trial court had discretion to exclude defendant's investigator's testimony after he violated exclusion order, even though defendant claimed that excluded testimony was crucial to his case).

In re K.M.B., 91 S.W.3d 18, 28 (Tex. App.—Fort Worth 2002, no pet.) (trial court had discretion to exclude testimony of witness who violated exclusion order where excluded testimony was not crucial to defense).

Jasso v. State, 699 S.W.2d 658, 661 (Tex. App.—San Antonio 1985, pet. ref'd) (trial court had discretion to allow testimony of witness been in courtroom during trial).

Pena v. State, 662 S.W.2d 430, 434 (Tex. App.—Corpus Christi 1983, no pet.) (trial court did not abuse discretion allowing individual present in courtroom during trial).

Tell v. State, 908 S.W.2d 535, 542 (Tex. App.—Waco 1997) (trial court erred allowing witness to testify after being present during trial where prosecutor's conclusory statement that witness's presence was essential was insufficient to prove his presence was in fact essential).

4. Opposing Authorities

Drilex Sys., Inc. v. Flores, 1 S.W.3d 112, 117 (Tex. 1999) ("The burden rests with the party seeking to exempt an expert witness from the Rule's exclusion requirement to establish that the witness's presence is essential.").

Garcia v. State, 553 S.W.3d 645, 646 (Tex. App.—Texarkana 2018, pet. ref'd) ("A trial court is without authority to exclude a qualifying witness unless the court determines her testimony would be materially affected if she heard the other testimony at trial.... In the absence of such a showing, a trial court does not err in allowing the witness to remain in the courtroom.").

Lopez v. State, 960 S.W.2d 948, 953 (Tex. App.—Houston [1st Dist.] 1998, pet. ref'd) (trial court did not abuse discretion excluding testimony of two defense witnesses for violation of exclusion order).

Holloman v. State, 942 S.W.2d 773, 774 (Tex. App.—Beaumont 1997, no pet.) (trial court had discretion to allow testimony of witness who violated exclusion rule where nature of witness's actual testimony at trial had not been anticipated prior to trial).

Tell v. State, 908 S.W.2d 535, 542 (Tex. App.—Fort Worth 1995) (harmless error where defendant's investigator should have been exempted from the exclusion order).

White v. State, 867 S.W.2d 921, 927 (Tex. App.—Houston [1st Dist.] 1993, no pet.) (no per se rule that trial court must exclude testimony of witness for violating exclusion order).

Beasley v. State, 810 S.W.2d 838, 842 (Tex. App.—Fort Worth 1991, pet. ref'd) (trial court did not abuse discretion allowing witnesses to testify despite violation of sequestration order where no showing that testimony was affected by violation and defendant was not prejudiced).

Kelley v. State, 817 S.W.2d 168, 171 (Tex. App.—Austin 1991, pet. ref'd) (trial court had discretion to exempt lead investigator from exclusion order after prosecutor demonstrated witness's presence in courtroom was essential).

Sallings v. State, 789 S.W.2d 408, 416 (Tex. App.—Dallas 1990, pet. ref'd) (trial court had discretion to allow testimony of witness in courtroom during trial where testimony was not anticipated at time of exclusion order).

Floyd v. State, 662 S.W.2d 683, 684 (Tex. App.—Eastland 1983, no pet.) (trial court had discretion to allow witness to testify after talking to another witness outside of courtroom where no showing that discussion had influenced witness's testimony in any way).

Pena v. State, 662 S.W.2d 430, 434 (Tex. App.—Corpus Christi 1983, no pet.) (trial court did not abuse discretion allowing individual present in courtroom during trial to testify in rebuttal).

a. Cannot Exclude a Party

Texas Rule of Evidence 614 states:

> At the request of a party the court shall order witnesses excluded so that they cannot hear the testimony of other witnesses, and it may make the order of its own motion. *This rule does not authorize exclusion of:*
>
> (1) *a party who is a natural person or in civil cases the spouse of such* natural *person*;
> (2) an officer or employee of a party in a civil case or a defendant in a criminal case that is not a natural person designated as its representative by its attorney;
> (3) a person whose presence is shown by a party to be essential to the presentation of the party's cause; or

> (4) the victim in a criminal case, unless the victim is to testify and the court determines that the victim's testimony would be materially affected if the victim hears other testimony at the trial. (Emphasis added.)

Similarly, Tex. R. Civ. P. 267(b) states:

> This rule does not authorize exclusion of (1) a party who is a natural person or the spouse of such natural person, or (2) an officer or employee of a party that is not a natural person and who is designated as its representative by its attorney, or (3) a person whose presence is shown by a party to be essential to the presentation of the cause.

b. *Exclusion of Testimony Is Improper*

Webb v. State, 766 S.W.2d 236, 244 (Tex. Crim. App. 1989) (trial court abused discretion excluding testimony of witness who violated exclusion order where witness's testimony was crucial to defense; there was no evidence that defense was aware of violation at time occurred, and defense did not know of relevance of witness's testimony at time of violation).

Allen v. State, 436 S.W.3d 815, 823 (Tex. App.—Texarkana 2014, pet. ref'd) (expert witnesses expected to testify in an expert capacity only, and not to the facts of the case, should typically be exempt so that they can form opinions based on more accurate factual assumptions).

c. *Welfare of a Child*

Texas Code of Criminal Procedure article 38.074, § 3 provides that, in cases involving the testimony of a child in any hearing or proceeding in the prosecution of any offense, other than the testimony of a child in a hearing or proceeding in a criminal case in which that child is the defendant

> (b) On the motion of any party ... the court shall allow ... a support person to be present in close proximity to the child during the child's testimony if the court finds by a preponderance of the evidence that:
> (1) the child cannot reliably testify without the possession of the item or presence of the support person, as applicable; and
> (2) granting the motion is not likely to prejudice the trier of fact in evaluating the child's testimony.
> (c) A support person who is present during a child's testimony may not:
> (1) obscure the child from the view of the defendant or the trier of fact;
> (2) provide the child with an answer to any question asked of the child; or
> (3) assist or influence the testimony of the child.

Garcia v. State, 553 S.W.3d 645, 646 (Tex. App.—Texarkana 2018, pet. ref'd) ("Article 36.03 was enacted as a part of 2001 legislation strengthening the ability of crime victims and particular witnesses to participate in certain criminal justice proceedings.").

Garcia v. State, 553 S.W.3d 645, 646 (Tex. App.—Texarkana 2018, pet. ref'd) ("Article 36.03 places the burden on the party seeking exclusion of a witness to make an offer of proof to justify the exclusion. Thus, legal guardians of crime victims should generally be permitted to stay in the courtroom.").

G. Motion to Exclude Comment on Exercise of Privilege Not to Testify

1. Suggested Motion Text

(*Name of Moving Party*) hereby moves this Court for an order excluding any and all evidence, references to evidence, testimony, or argument relating to the fact that (*Name of Party*) exercised a right not to testify. The motion is based upon the ground that the witness has a Constitutional right not to testify and commenting on that fact is restricted by Texas Code of Criminal Procedure, Article 38.08.

2. Motion Summary

This motion is used to exclude any comment or evidence regarding the exercise of a witness' constitutional right not to testify. The motion is based upon the express authority of Texas Code of Criminal Procedure, Article 38.08, and related case authority. *Trevino v. State*, 979 S.W.2d 78 (Tex. App.—Austin 1998, pet. ref'd).

3. Supporting Authorities

Texas Code of Criminal Procedure, Article 38.08, states:

Defendant may testify

Any defendant in a criminal action shall be permitted to testify in his own behalf therein, *but the failure of any defendant to so testify shall not be taken as a circumstance against him, nor shall the same be alluded to or commented on by counsel in the cause.* (Emphasis added.)

Randolph v. State, 353 S.W.3d 887, 891 (Tex. Crim. App. 2011) ("[C]omment on defendant's failure to testify violates both the state and federal constitutions as well as state statutory law.").

Randolph v. State, 353 S.W.3d 887, 892 (Tex. Crim. App. 2011) ("State could not argue, at either the guilt or punishment stage of trial, that the defendant denied responsibility for the crime simply because he pled not guilty; that would be an impermissible comment on the failure to testify.").

Randolph v. State, 353 S.W.3d 887, 892 (Tex. Crim. App. 2011) ("[C]omment on the defendant's failure to show remorse is generally not proper if the defendant testifies at the guilt stage and presents some defense, but does not testify at the punishment phase.").

Whitehead v. State, 437 S.W.3d 547, 551 (Tex. App.—Texarkana 2014, pet. ref'd) (to violate the right against self-incrimination, the offending language must be viewed from the jury's standpoint, and the implication that the comment referred to the defendant's failure to testify must be clear; the test is whether the language used was manifestly intended or was of such a character that the jury would necessarily and naturally take it as a comment on the defendant's failure to testify).

Gately v. State, 321 S.W.3d 72, 79 (Tex. App.—Eastland 2010, no pet.) (comment on a defendant's failure to testify offends the Texas and United States Constitutions, as well as Texas statutory law).

Lopez v. State, 314 S.W.3d 54, 62 (Tex. App.—San Antonio 2010), *pet. stricken,* No. PD-0332-10, 2010 WL 3431129 (Tex. Crim. App. 2010) ("[P]rosecutorial argument is considered a comment on a defendant's failure to testify when the language used was manifestly intended or was of such a character that the jury would necessarily and naturally take it as a comment on the defendant's failure to testify.... It is not sufficient that the language used might impliedly or indirectly be so construed.").

Andrade v. State, 246 S.W.3d 217, 230 (Tex. App.—Houston [14th Dist.] 2007, pet. ref'd) ("[C]omment by the prosecutor on a defendant's failure to show remorse can sometimes be a comment on his or her failure to testify.").

Campbell v. State, 900 S.W.2d 763, 766 (Tex. App.—Waco 1995, no pet.) (failure to object to comment on defendant's failure to testify does not waive error for review; prosecutor's comment that defendant "hadn't explained" why he was in possession of certain evidence was improper comment on defendant's failure to testify and constituted harmless error).

4. Opposing Authorities

Randolph v. State, 353 S.W.3d 887, 891 (Tex. Crim. App. 2011) ("[I]n assessing whether the defendant's Fifth Amendment right has been violated, courts must view the State's argument from the jury's standpoint and resolve any ambiguities in the language in favor of it being a permissible argument; the implication that the State referred to the defendant's failure to testify must be a clear and necessary one.").

Randolph v. State, 353 S.W.3d 887, 891 (Tex. Crim. App. 2011) ("[T]he test [for whether there has been an impermissible comment on the failure to testify] is whether the language used was manifestly intended or was of such a character that the jury would necessarily and naturally take it as a comment on the defendant's failure to testify.... In applying this standard, the context in which the comment was made must be analyzed to determine whether the language used was of such character.").

Randolph v. State, 353 S.W.3d 887, 892 (Tex. Crim. App. 2011) (comments about the defendant's failure to testify are permissible if they constitute a fair response to the defendant's claims or assertions).

Randolph v. State, 353 S.W.3d 887, 895 (Tex. Crim. App. 2011) (prosecutor may comment on any testimony given by the defendant in the guilt stage, and, if the defendant expressly or impliedly denies criminal responsibility during that testimony, the prosecutor may comment on that denial).

Busby v. State, 253 S.W.3d 661, 666 (Tex. Crim. App. 2008), *cert. denied*, 129 S. Ct. 625 (2008) ("[The] test for determining whether prosecutorial argument is a comment on a defendant's failure to testify is whether the language used was manifestly intended or was of such a character that the jury would necessarily and naturally take it as a comment on the defendant's failure to testify.... It is not sufficient that the language used might impliedly or indirectly be so construed.").

Beal v. State, 520 S.W.2d 907, 912 (Tex. Crim. App. 1975) (comment that defendant had no witnesses to testify about alibi was not improper comment on defendant's failure to testify where evidence could have been offered through other witnesses).

Turner v. State, 504 S.W.2d 843, 845 (Tex. Crim. App. 1974) (based upon context of comment, prosecutor's comment during punishment phase that defendant did not wince or move when verdict was read and did not assert that he was not guilty, was not improper comment on defendant's failure to testify)

Nowlin v. State, 507 S.W.2d 534, 536 (Tex. Crim. App. 1974) (a prosecutor's comment that the only witnesses were those presented by the State was not an improper comment on the defendant's failure to testify).

Whitehead v. State, 437 S.W.3d 547, 551 (Tex. App.—Texarkana 2014, pet. ref'd) (a comment that is an implied or indirect allusion to the defendant's failure to testify is not a violation of the right against self-incrimination).

Whitehead v. State, 437 S.W.3d 547, 551 (Tex. App.—Texarkana 2014, pet. ref'd) (calling attention to the absence of evidence that only the defendant could produce will result in reversal only if the remark can be construed to refer to appellant's failure to testify and not to the defense's failure to produce evidence).

Hennessey v. State, 268 S.W.3d 153, 159 (Tex. App.—Waco 2008, pet. ref'd) (if a defendant testifies, pre-arrest silence can be used to impeach him or her).

Crocker v. State, 248 S.W.3d 299, 304 (Tex. App.—Houston [1st Dist.] 2007, pet. ref'd) (prosecutor's comment amounts to an impermissible comment on a defendant's failure to testify only if, when viewed from the jury's standpoint, the comment is manifestly intended to be, or is of such character that a typical jury would naturally and necessarily take it to be, a comment on the defendant's failure to testify).

Crocker v. State, 248 S.W.3d 299, 304 (Tex. App.—Houston [1st Dist.] 2007, pet. ref'd) ("[I]t is not sufficient that the comment might be construed as an implied or indirect allusion to a defendant's failure to testify.... Where the remark calls the jury's attention to the absence of evidence that only a defendant's testimony could supply, however, the conviction is subject to reversal.").

Weyandt v. State, 35 S.W.3d 144, 157 (Tex. App.—Houston [14th Dist.] 2000, no pet.) (prosecutor's "inadvertent transposition of the defendant's name for that of a witness being called to testify does not rise to the level of being a comment on appellant's failure to testify").

a. Civil Consequences of Silence

Texas Rule of Evidence 513 states:

> Comment Upon or Inference From Claim of Privilege; Instruction
>
> (a) Comment or Inference Not Permitted. Except as permitted in Rule 504(b)(2), the claim of a privilege, whether in the present proceeding or upon a prior occasion, is not a proper subject of comment by judge or counsel, and no inference may be drawn therefrom.
>
> (b) Claiming Privilege Without Knowledge of Jury. In jury cases, proceedings shall be conducted, to the extent practicable, so as to facilitate the making of claims of privilege without the knowledge of the jury.
>
> (c) *Claim of Privilege Against Self-Incrimination in Civil Cases. Paragraphs (a) and (b) shall not apply with respect to a party's claim, in the present civil proceeding, of the privilege against self-incrimination.*
>
> (d) Jury Instruction. Except as provided in Rule 504(b)(2) and in paragraph (c) of this Rule, upon request any party against whom the jury might draw an adverse inference from a claim of privilege is entitled to an instruction that no inference may be drawn therefrom. (Emphasis added.)

Flournoy v. Wilz, 228 S.W.3d 674, 677 (Tex. 2007) (jury may draw adverse inferences against parties who refuse to testify in response to probative evidence offered against them as the Fifth Amendment does not preclude the inference where the privilege against self-incrimination is claimed by a party to a civil cause).

Craycroft v. Crawford, 285 S.W. 275, 282 (Tex. 1926) (silence can be taken as admission where person would have spoken in response to another party's statements if statements were untrue).

P.C. as next friend of C.C. v. E.C., 594 S.W.3d 459, 462 (Tex. App.—Fort Worth 2019, no pet.) ("[I]n a civil case, a factfinder may draw negative inferences from a party's invocation of the Fifth Amendment privilege against self-incrimination.").

P.C. as next friend of C.C. v. E.C., 594 S.W.3d 459, 462 (Tex. App.—Fort Worth 2019, no pet.) ("[A] party in a civil case who uses the privilege to protect relevant information, instead of to avoid subjecting himself to criminal responsibility, converts the Fifth Amendment privilege from shield to sword against the other party who needs that information.").

P.C. as next friend of C.C. v. E.C., 594 S.W.3d 459, 462 (Tex. App.—Fort Worth 2019, no pet.) ("[T]he adverse inference goes into effect when a party in a civil action refuses to testify in response to probative evidence offered against him.").

In re Commitment of Gipson, 580 S.W.3d 476, 487 No. 03-18-00332-CV, 2019 WL 3367549 (Tex. App.—Austin 2019, no pet.) ("[A]lthough the jury [in a civil case] is free to draw a negative inference [from invoking the Fifth Amendment privilege], a claim of privilege is not a substitute for relevant evidence.").

Brauss v. Triple M Holding GmbH, 411 S.W.3d 614, 623 (Tex. App.—Dallas 2013, pet. denied) ("[I]n a civil case, a fact finder may draw negative inferences from a party's assertion of the privilege against self-incrimination.").

Brauss v. Triple M Holding GmbH, 411 S.W.3d 614, 623 (Tex. App.—Dallas 2013, pet. denied) ("[T]he Fifth Amendment does not forbid adverse inferences against parties to civil actions when they refuse to testify in response to probative evidence offered against them.").

Webb v. Maldonado, 331 S.W.3d 879, 883 (Tex. App.—Dallas 2011, pet. denied) ("[I]n a civil case, a fact finder may draw negative inferences from a party's assertion of the privilege against self-incrimination.").

Murray v. Tex. Dep't of Family & Protect. Servs., 294 S.W.3d 360, 367 (Tex. App.—Austin 2009, no pet.) ("[I]n a civil case, the fact finder may draw reasonable inferences from a party's assertion of the privilege against self-incrimination.... That does not change merely because there are pending criminal charges arising out of the same conduct.").

Blake v. Dorado, 211 S.W.3d 429, 433 (Tex. App.—El Paso 2006, no pet.) ("[A] claim of privilege [against self-incrimination] is not a substitute for relevant evidence.").

Wenk v. City Nat'l Bank, 613 S.W.2d 345, 349 (Tex. Civ. App.—Tyler 1981, no writ) (that defendant did not say anything to bank about inaccuracy of statements sent monthly could be admitted to demonstrate admission of accuracy of statements).

b. Harmless Error

Shears v. State, 895 S.W.2d 456, 463 (Tex. App.—Tyler 1995, no pet.) (prosecutor's comment on defendant's failure to testify harmless error).

Ellis v. State, 877 S.W.2d 380, 385 (Tex. App.—Houston [14th Dist.] 1992, pet. ref'd) (prosecutor may comment on defendant's failure to call material witness and argue inference that witness would be adverse to defendant's position).

H. Motion to Exclude Evidence of Failure to Call Witness

1. Suggested Motion Text

(*Name of Moving Party*) hereby moves this Court for an order excluding any and all evidence, references to evidence, testimony, or argument relating to (*Name of Moving Party*)'s decision not to call certain witnesses to testify at trial. The motion is based upon the grounds that the evidence is speculative, irrelevant and the probative value is substantially outweighed by the risk of undue prejudice to (*Name of Moving Party*).

2. Motion Summary

This motion is used to exclude evidence or inferences relating to a party's failure to call a witness. Where a party chooses not to call a certain witness, this fact generally may not be commented upon by the opposition if the witness was not available to testify [*McKee v. State*, 116 Tex.Crim. 232, 235, 34 S.W.2d 592 (Tex. Crim. App. 1930)], or where it would invite juror speculation [*McKenzie v. State*, 617 S.W.2d 211, 221 (Tex. Crim. App. 1981)].

3. Supporting Authorities

Texas Rule of Evidence 403 states that the court may only exclude relevant evidence "if its probative value is substantially outweighed by the danger of undue prejudice, confusion of the issues, or misleading the jury, or by considerations of undue delay, or needless presentation of cumulative evidence."

a. Where Witness Was Equally Available to Both Parties

Askew v. State, 59 Tex.Crim. 152, 153, 127 S.W. 1037 (Tex. Crim. App. 1910) (trial court erred allowing prosecutor to cross-examine defendant about absent eyewitnesses where no showing defendant was responsible for keeping witnesses away from trial).

b. Where Comment Would Invite Speculation

Mosley v. State, 686 S.W.2d 180, 183 (Tex. Crim. App. 1985) (prosecutor may comment on witnesses the defendant failed to call but may not speculate about what they would say; comments held to be proper).

McKenzie v. State, 617 S.W.2d 211, 221 (Tex. Crim. App. 1981) (prosecutor may comment on uncalled witnesses but may not speculate regarding what witnesses would say if called).

Askew v. State, 59 Tex.Crim. 152, 153, 127 S.W. 1037 (Tex. Crim. App. 1910) (trial court erred allowing prosecutor to cross-examine defendant about absent eyewitnesses where no showing defendant was responsible for keeping witnesses away from trial).

Johnson v. State, 649 S.W.2d 111, 117 (Tex. App.—San Antonio 1983), *aff'd*, 662 S.W.2d 368 (Tex. Crim. App. 1984) ("[P]rosecutor may not imply that an absent witness was afraid to testify due to the defendant.").

c. Where Witness Was Not Available

Texas Rule of Evidence 513 states:

> Comment Upon or Inference From Claim of Privilege; Instruction
>
> (a) **Comment or Inference Not Permitted.** *Except as permitted in Rule 504(b)(2), the claim of a privilege, whether in the present proceeding or upon a prior occasion, is not a proper subject of comment by judge or counsel, and no inference may be drawn therefrom.*
> (b) **Claiming Privilege Without Knowledge of Jury.** In jury cases, proceedings shall be conducted, to the extent practicable, so as to facilitate the making of claims of privilege without the knowledge of the jury.

(c) **Claim of Privilege Against Self-Incrimination in Civil Cases**. Paragraphs (a) and (b) shall not apply with respect to a party's claim, in the present civil proceeding, of the privilege against self-incrimination.

(d) **Jury Instruction**. Except as provided in Rule 504(b)(2) and in paragraph (c) of this Rule, upon request any party against whom the jury might draw an adverse inference from a claim of privilege is entitled to an instruction that no inference may be drawn therefrom. (Emphasis added.)

Hendricks v. State, 640 S.W.2d 932, 937 (Tex. Crim. App. 1982) ("[W]hile the prosecution may normally comment on the failure of the defendant to call a witness, it may not do so where the witness is unavailable through no fault of the defendant.").

McKee v. State, 116 Tex.Crim. 232, 235, 34 S.W.2d 592 (Tex. Crim. App. 1930) (comment on defendant's failure to call wife as witness was improper where defendant's wife was recovering from miscarriage and trial judge denied defendant's request for continuance).

Ramirez v. State, 112 Tex.Crim. 332, 333, 16 S.W.2d 814 (Tex. Crim. App. 1929) (improper to allow prosecutor to comment on defendant's failure to call wife to testify where wife was also codefendant).

McQueen v. State, 984 S.W.2d 712, 717 (Tex. App.—Texarkana 1998, no pet.) (prosecutor may not comment on defendant's failure to call witness if witness unavailable to defendant;). *See also Reese v. State*, 905 S.W.2d 631 (Tex. App.—Texarkana 1995, pet. ref'd).

But see Texas Rule of Evidence 504(b), which states that "[f]ailure by an accused to call the accused's spouse as a witness, where other evidence indicates that the spouse could testify to relevant matters, is a proper subject of comment by counsel."

d. Other Grounds

Other possible grounds for excluding comment on uncalled witnesses include:

- Confusing or misleading;
- Solely intended to create an emotional bias;
- Irrelevant;
- Collateral to issues in case;
- Inadmissible hearsay.

4. Opposing Authorities

Jackson v. State, 17 S.W.3d 664, 675 (Tex. Crim. App. 2000) (prosecutor's comment that defendant's failure to produce expert held proper where comment does not refer to defendant's failure to testify).

Albiar v. State, 739 S.W.2d 360, 363 (Tex. Crim. App. 1987) (where defendant fails to produce available evidence, proper to presume evidence would be unfavorable to defendant).

Baines v. State, 401 S.W.3d 104, 107 (Tex. App.—Houston [14th Dist.] 2011, no pet.) ("prosecutor may properly comment on a defendant's failure to produce evidence, as long as the remarks do not fault the defendant for failing to testify").

Corpus v. State, 30 S.W.3d 35, 41 (Tex. App.—Houston [14th Dist.] 2000, pet. ref'd) (prosecutor may properly comment on defendant's failure to call material witness and argue that jury may infer witness was not called because testimony would be unfavorable to defendant).

Shears v. State, 895 S.W.2d 456, 464 (Tex. App.—Tyler 1995, no pet.) (prosecutor could refer to defendant's failure to produce witnesses and could suggest that absent witnesses would be adverse to defendant).

Ellis v. State, 877 S.W.2d 380, 385 (Tex. App.—Houston [1st Dist.] 1994, pet. ref'd) (prosecutor may comment on defendant's failure to call material witness and argue inference that witness would be adverse to defendant's position).

McDuffie v. State, 854 S.W.2d 195, 217 (Tex. App.—Beaumont 1993, pet. ref'd) (prosecutor could comment on defendant's failure to produce his wife as witness, even though she could invoke spousal privilege); see also Texas Rule of Evidence 504(b) ("Failure by an accused to call the accused's spouse as a witness, where other evidence indicates that the spouse could testify to relevant matters, is a proper subject of comment by counsel.").

Albiar v. State, 739 S.W.2d 360, 363 (Tex. Crim. App. 1987) (where defendant fails to produce available evidence, proper to presume evidence would be unfavorable to defendant).

a. Failure to Call Material Witness

Albiar v. State, 739 S.W.2d 360, 363 (Tex. Crim. App. 1987) (prosecutor could comment on defendant's failure to call available and material witness to support alibi defense).

Caron v. State, 162 S.W.3d 614, 617 (Tex. App.—Houston [14th Dist.] 2005, no pet.) (during jury argument, State may comment on appellant's failure to present evidence in appellant's favor).

Corpus v. State, 30 S.W.3d 35, 42 (Tex. App.—Houston [14th Dist.] 2000, pet. ref'd) (prosecutor may properly comment on defendant's failure to call material witness and argue that jury may infer that witness was not called because testimony would be unfavorable to defendant).

McQueen v. State, 984 S.W.2d 712, 717 (Tex. App.—Texarkana 1998, no pet.) (prosecutor can comment on defendant's failure to call witness, even if State also subpoenaed witness).

I. Motion to Exclude Hearsay Evidence

1. *Suggested Motion Text*

(<u>Name of Moving Party</u>) hereby moves this Court for an order excluding any and all evidence, references to evidence, testimony, or argument relating to (<u>Describe Hearsay Evidence to Be Excluded</u>).

The motion is based upon the grounds that the evidence is hearsay not within any recognized exception and is therefore inadmissible.

2. Motion Summary

This motion is used to exclude hearsay evidence that does not fall within one of the recognized hearsay exceptions. The motion is based upon the express authority of Texas Rule of Evidence 802 (the "hearsay rule") and related statutory and case authority. *Clark v. State*, 947 S.W.2d 650 (Tex. App.—Fort Worth 1997, pet. ref'd).

3. Supporting Authorities

Texas Rule of Evidence 802 states:

> Hearsay is not admissible except as provided by statute or these rules or by other rules prescribed pursuant to statutory authority. Inadmissible hearsay admitted without objection shall not be denied probative value merely because it is hearsay.

Texas Rule of Evidence 801(a) defines a "statement" as:

> A "statement" is (1) an oral or written verbal expression or (2) non-verbal conduct of a person, if it is intended by the person as a substitute for verbal expression.

Texas Rule of Evidence 801(d) defines "hearsay" as:

> A statement, other than one made by the declarant while testifying at the trial or hearing, offered in evidence to prove the truth of the matter asserted.

Dallas Morning News, Inc. v. Hall, 579 S.W.3d 370, 379 (Tex. 2019) ("[H]earsay—an out-of-court statement offered to prove the truth of the matter asserted—is inadmissible.").

Sanchez v. State, 354 S.W.3d 476, 484 (Tex. Crim. App. 2011) (hearsay is inadmissible unless it falls into one of the exceptions in the rules of evidence, or it is allowed by other rules prescribed pursuant to statutory authority, including the provision of code of civil procedure permitting testimony of outcry witness).

Fischer v. State, 252 S.W.3d 375, 381 (Tex. Crim. App. 2008) ("[I]f the declarant has had time to reflect upon the event and the conditions he observed, this lack of contemporaneity diminishes the reliability of the statements regarding the event and renders them inadmissible under the [present sense impression exception to the hearsay] rule.").

Fischer v. State, 252 S.W.3d 375, 381 (Tex. Crim. App. 2008) ("[O]nce reflective narratives, calculated statements, deliberate opinions, conclusions, or conscious 'thinking-it-through' statements enter the picture, the present sense impression exception to the hearsay rule no longer allows their admission.").

Fischer v. State, 252 S.W.3d 375, 381 (Tex. Crim. App. 2008) ("'[T]hinking about it' destroys the unreflective nature required of a present sense impression.").

Fischer v. State, 252 S.W.3d 375, 382 (Tex. Crim. App. 2008) ("[F]actual observations, narrations, opinions, and conclusions made by a citizen or bystander that might be intended by the declarant to be made with an eye toward future litigation or evidentiary use are inadmissible under the [present sense impression exception to the] rule.").

Wheatfall v. State, 882 S.W.2d 829, 836 (Tex. Crim. App. 1994) (prosecutor's testimony about uninvestigated claim that another individual looked like sketch identified as representing defendant properly excluded as hearsay).

Allen v. State, 436 S.W.3d 815, 823 (Tex. App.—Texarkana 2014, pet. ref'd) (hearsay is not admissible at trial except as provided by statute or by the Texas Rules of Evidence).

Zhu v. Lam, 426 S.W.3d 333, 342 (Tex. App.—Houston [14th Dist.] 2014, no pet.) ("[P]roponent of hearsay evidence has the burden of showing that the testimony fits within an exception to the general rule prohibiting the admission of hearsay evidence.").

Certain Underwriters at Lloyd's, London v. Chicago Bridge & Iron Co., 406 S.W.3d 326, 340 (Tex. App.—Beaumont 2013, pet. denied) ("[A] statement constitutes hearsay when it is made out of court and is offered into evidence to prove the truth of the matter asserted.").

Farlow v. Harris Methodist Fort Worth Hosp., 284 S.W.3d 903, 910 (Tex. App.—Fort Worth 2009, pet. denied) (for a hearsay statement made by an agent or servant to be admissible as admission by a party-opponent, the proponent of its admission must show that the statement was made by an employee or agent acting within the scope of authority).

Clark v. State, 282 S.W.3d 924, 929 (Tex. App.—Beaumont 2009, no pet.) ("[F]or hearsay to be admissible, the statement must fit into an exception provided by a statute or the Rules of Evidence.").

Bryant v. State, 282 S.W.3d 156, 163 (Tex. App.—Texarkana 2009, pet. ref'd) ("[P]roponent of hearsay testimony has the burden of laying the proper predicate and establishing its admissibility.... The trial court must then determine the applicability of the proffered justification for the admission of hearsay testimony and, if additionally requested, perform the requisite relevancy balancing test by comparing the probative value of the hearsay testimony against its danger for unfair prejudice.").

Dietz v. State, 123 S.W.3d 528, 532 (Tex. App.—San Antonio 2003, pet. ref'd) (proposed testimony from defendant's mother and friend was inadmissible as hearsay where the testimony based upon the defendant's out of court statements to witnesses).

Clark v. State, 947 S.W.2d 650, 654 (Tex. App.—Fort Worth 1997, pet. ref'd) (testimony that did not satisfy hearsay exception for statements against interest properly excluded where the statement was not against a codefendant's interest).

Peden v. State, 917 S.W.2d 941, 947 (Tex. App.—Fort Worth 1996, pet. ref'd) (testimony of witnesses that victim told them he and defendant were dealing drugs improper hearsay).

Callahan v. State, 937 S.W.2d 553, 559 (Tex. App.—Texarkana 1996, no pet.) (defendant's doctor's written summary of findings was hearsay).

For an expanded discussion, see Comments, Texas Rule of Evidence Annotated 802; see also 2A Goode, Wellborn and Sharlot, Texas Practice: Courtroom Handbook on Texas Evidence 448 (2000 ed.), Rules 802, et seq.

a. Purpose of Rule

Fischer v. State, 207 S.W.3d 846, 852 (Tex. App.—Houston [14th Dist.] 2006), *aff'd,* 252 S.W.3d 375 (Tex. Crim. App. 2008) (general rule against the admission of hearsay statements is based on their inherent unreliability).

Utsey v. State, 921 S.W.2d 451, 456 (Tex. App.—Texarkana 1996, pet. ref'd) ("Hearsay evidence is inadmissible under the confrontation clause of the Sixth Amendment unless the evidence either falls within a firmly rooted hearsay exception or is supported by a particular guarantee of trustworthiness.").

Green v. State, 876 S.W.2d 226, 228 (Tex. App.—Beaumont 1994, no pet.) ("The basic reason for excluding hearsay is its inherent unreliability[;]" evidence was proper under an exception to the hearsay rule).

b. Written Hearsay

Texas Rule of Evidence 802 states:

> Hearsay is not admissible except as provided by statute or these rules or by other rules prescribed pursuant to statutory authority. Inadmissible hearsay admitted without objection shall not be denied probative value merely because it is hearsay.

Texas Rule of Evidence 801(a) defines a "statement" as:

> A "statement" is (1) an oral *or written* verbal expression or (2) nonverbal conduct of a person, if it is intended by the person as a substitute for verbal expression. (Emphasis added.)

Kratz v. Exxon Corp., 890 S.W.2d 899, 905 (Tex. App.—El Paso 1994, no writ) (statements not within the public records exception to the hearsay rule were properly excluded).

Tex. Dep't of Pub. Safety v. Nesmith, 559 S.W.2d 443, 447 (Tex. Civ. App.—Corpus Christi 1977, no writ) (to be admissible, writing must fall within some exception to hearsay rule even if authentic).

Simms v. Sw. Tex. Methodist Hosp., 535 S.W.2d 192, 198 (Tex. Civ. App.—San Antonio 1976, writ ref'd n.r.e.) (statements contained in treatises, books, etc., inadmissible hearsay; excerpts from writings excluded as hearsay).

> *See also Texas Rule of Evidence 803(8)(B), which specifically excludes matters observed by police officers and other law enforcement personnel in criminal cases from the public records exception to the hearsay rule.*

4. Opposing Authorities

Note: The hearsay rule and the rule's many statutory exceptions are an expansive area of evidence law that cannot be briefly encapsulated in this text. The citations below provide only general support for an opposition to a motion to exclude hearsay evidence. For complete citations, see Texas Rules of Evidence 801, et. seq. For a detailed discussion of the hearsay rule and hearsay exceptions, see Texas Rules of Evidence Annotated 801 and 802; see also Texas Rules of Evidence Handbook, 30 Houston L. Rev. 954 (1993); 2A Goode, Wellborn and Sharlot, Texas Practice: Courtroom Handbook on Texas Evidence *452 (2000 Edition).*

Texas Rule of Evidence 803 states:

Hearsay Exceptions: Availability of Declarant Immaterial

The following are not excluded by the hearsay rule, even though the declarant is available as a witness:

(1) **Present Sense Impression**. A statement describing or explaining an event or condition made while the declarant was perceiving the event or condition, or immediately thereafter.

(2) **Excited Utterance**. A statement relating to a startling event or condition made while the declarant was under the stress of excitement caused by the event or condition.

(3) **Then Existing Mental, Emotional, or Physical Condition**. A statement of the declarant's then existing state of mind, emotion, sensation, or physical condition (such as intent, plan, motive, design, mental feeling, pain, or bodily health), but not including a statement of memory or belief to prove the fact remembered or believed unless it relates to the execution, revocation, identification, or terms of declarant's will.

(4) **Statements for Purposes of Medical Diagnosis or Treatment**. Statements made for purposes of medical diagnosis or treatment and describing medical history, or past or present symptoms, pain, or sensations, or the inception or general character of the cause or external source thereof insofar as reasonably pertinent to diagnosis or treatment.

(5) **Recorded Recollection**. A memorandum or record concerning a matter about which a witness once had personal knowledge but now has insufficient recollection to enable the witness to testify fully and accurately, shown to have been made or adopted by the witness when the matter was fresh in the witness' memory and to reflect that knowledge correctly, unless the circumstances of preparation cast doubt on the document's trustworthiness. If admitted, the memorandum or record may be read into evidence but may not itself be received as an exhibit unless offered by an adverse party

(6) **Records of Regularly Conducted Activity.** A memorandum, report, record, or data compilation, in any form, of acts, events, conditions, opinions, or diagnoses, made at or near the time by, or from information transmitted by, a person with knowledge, if kept in the course of a regularly conducted business activity, and if it was the regular practice of that business activity to make the memorandum, report, record, or data compilation, all as shown by the testimony of the custodian or other qualified witness, or by affidavit that complies with Rule 902(10), unless the source of information or the method or circumstances of preparation indicate lack of trustworthiness. "Business" as used in this paragraph includes any and every kind of regular organized activity whether conducted for profit or not.

(7) **Absence of Entry in Records Kept in Accordance With the Provisions of Paragraph (6)**. Evidence that a matter is not included in the memoranda, reports, records, or data compilations, in any form, kept in accordance with the provisions of paragraph (6), to prove the nonoccurrence or nonexistence of the matter, if the matter was of a kind of which a memorandum, report, record, or data compilation was regularly made and preserved, unless the sources of information or other circumstances indicate lack of trustworthiness.

(8) **Public Records and Reports.** Records, reports, statements, or data compilations, in any form, of public offices or agencies setting forth:
(A) the activities of the office or agency;
(B) matters observed pursuant to duty imposed by law as to which matters there was a duty to report, excluding in criminal cases matters observed by police officers and other law enforcement personnel; or
(C) in civil cases as to any party and in criminal cases as against the state, factual findings resulting from an investigation made pursuant to authority granted by law; unless the sources of information or other circumstances indicate lack of trustworthiness.

(9) **Records of Vital Statistics.** Records or data compilations, in any form, of births, fetal deaths, deaths, or marriages, if the report thereof was made to a public office pursuant to requirements of law.

(10) **Absence of Public Record or Entry**. To prove the absence of a record, report, statement, or data compilation, in any form, or the nonoccurrence or nonexistence of a matter of which a record, report, statement, or data compilation, in any form, was regularly made and preserved by a public office or agency, evidence in the form of a certification in accordance with Rule 902, or testimony, that diligent search failed to disclose the record, report statement, or data compilation, or entry.

(11) **Records of Religious Organizations.** Statements of births, marriages, divorces, deaths, legitimacy, ancestry, relationship

by blood or marriage, or other similar facts of personal or family history, contained in a regularly kept record of a religious organization.

(12) **Marriage, Baptismal, and Similar Certificates**. Statements of fact contained in a certificate that the maker performed a marriage or other ceremony or administered a sacrament, made by a member of the clergy, public official, or other person authorized by the rules or practices of a religious organization or by law to perform the act certified, and purporting to have been issued at the time of the act or within a reasonable time thereafter.

(13) **Family Records**. Statements of fact concerning personal or family history contained in family Bibles, genealogies, charts, engravings on rings, inscriptions on family portraits, engravings on urns, crypts, or tombstones, or the like.

(14) **Records of Documents Affecting an Interest in Property**. The record of a document purporting to establish or affect an interest in property, as proof of the content of the original recorded document and its execution and delivery by each person by whom it purports to have been executed, if the record is a record of a public office and an applicable statute authorizes the recording of documents of that kind in that office.

(15) **Statements in Documents Affecting an Interest in Property**. A statement contained in a document purporting to establish or affect an interest in property if the matter stated was relevant to the purpose of the document, unless dealings with the property since the document was made have been inconsistent with the truth of the statement or the purport of the document.

(16) **Statements in Ancient Documents**. Statements in a document in existence twenty years or more the authenticity of which is established.

(17) **Market Reports, Commercial Publications**. Market quotations, tabulations, lists, directories, or other published compilations, generally used and relied upon by the public or by persons in particular occupations.

(18) **Learned Treatises**. To the extent called to the attention of an expert witness upon cross-examination or relied upon by the expert in direct examination, statements contained in published treatises, periodicals, or pamphlets on a subject of history, medicine, or other science or art established as a reliable authority by the testimony or admission of the witness or by other expert testimony or by judicial notice. If admitted, the statements may be read into evidence but may not be received as exhibits.

(19) **Reputation Concerning Personal or Family History**. Reputation among members of a person's family by blood, adoption, or marriage, or among a person's associates, or in the community, concerning a person's birth, adoption, marriage, divorce, death, legitimacy, relationship by blood, adoption, or marriage, ancestry, or other similar fact of personal or family history.

(20) **Reputation Concerning Boundaries or General History.** Reputation in a community, arising before the controversy, as to boundaries of or customs affecting lands in the community, and reputation as to events of general history important to the community or state or nation in which located.
(21) **Reputation as to Character.** Reputation of a person's character among associates or in the community.
(22) **Judgment of Previous Conviction.** In civil cases, evidence of a judgment, entered after a trial or upon a plea of guilty (but not upon a plea of nolo contendere), judging a person guilty of a felony, to prove any fact essential to sustain the judgment of conviction. In criminal cases, evidence of a judgment, entered after a trial or upon a plea of guilty or nolo contendere, adjudging a person guilty of a criminal offense, to prove any fact essential to sustain the judgment of conviction, but not including, when offered by the state for purposes other than impeachment, judgments against persons other than the accused. In all cases, the pendency of an appeal renders such evidence inadmissible.
(23) **Judgment as to Personal, Family, or General History, or Boundaries.** Judgments as proof of matters of personal, family or general history, or boundaries, essential to the judgment, if the same would be provable by evidence of reputation.
(24) **Statement Against Interest.** A statement which was at the time of its making so far contrary to the declarant's pecuniary or proprietary interest, or so far tended to subject the declarant to civil or criminal liability, or to render invalid a claim by the declarant against another, or to make the declarant an object of hatred, ridicule, or disgrace, that a reasonable person in declarant's position would not have made the statement unless believing it to be true. In criminal cases, a statement tending to expose the declarant to criminal liability is not admissible unless corroborating circumstances clearly indicate the trustworthiness of the statement.

Texas Rule of Evidence 804 states:

Hearsay Exceptions; Declarant Unavailable

(a) **Definition of Unavailability.** "Unavailability as a witness" includes situations in which the declarant:
  (1) is exempted by ruling of the court on the ground of privilege from testifying concerning the subject matter of the declarant's statement;
  (2) persists in refusing to testify concerning the subject matter of the declarant's statement despite an order of the court to do so;
  (3) testifies to a lack of memory of the subject matter of the declarant's statement;

(4) is unable to be present or to testify at the hearing because of death or then existing physical or mental illness or infirmity; or

(5) is absent from the hearing and the proponent of the declarant's statement has been unable to procure the declarant's attendance or testimony by process or other reasonable means.

A declarant is not unavailable as a witness if the declarant's exemption, refusal, claim of lack of memory, inability, or absence is due to the procurement or wrong-doing of the proponent of the declarant's statement for the purpose of preventing the witness from attending or testifying.

(b) **Hearsay Exceptions**. The following are not excluded if the declarant is unavailable as a witness:

Former testimony. In civil cases, testimony given as a witness at another hearing of the same or a different proceeding, or in a deposition taken in the course of another proceeding, if the party against whom the testimony is now offered, or a person with a similar interest, had an opportunity and similar motive to develop the testimony by direct, cross, or redirect examination. In criminal cases, testimony given as a witness at another hearing of the same or a different proceeding, if the party against whom the testimony is now offered had an opportunity and similar motive to develop the testimony by direct, cross, or redirect examination. In criminal cases the use of depositions is controlled by Chapter 39 of the Code of Criminal Procedure.

(1) Dying declarations. A statement made by a declarant while believing that the declarant's death was imminent, concerning the cause or circumstances of what the declarant believed to be impending death.

(2) Statement of personal or family history.
   (A) A statement concerning the declarant's own birth, adoption, marriage, divorce, legitimacy, relationship by blood, adoption, or marriage, ancestry, or other similar fact of personal or family history even though declarant had no means of acquiring personal knowledge of the matter stated; or
   (B) A statement concerning the foregoing matters, and death also, of another person, if the declarant was related to the other by blood, adoption, or marriage or was so intimately associated with the other's family as to be likely to have accurate information concerning the matter declared.

Fischer v. State, 252 S.W.3d 375, 381 (Tex. Crim. App. 2008) (present sense impression exception to the hearsay rule is based upon the premise that the contemporaneity of the event and the declaration ensures reliability of the statement).

Walter v. State, 267 S.W.3d 883, 891 (Tex. Crim. App. 2008) (rule governing the hearsay exception for statements against penal interest sets out a two-step foundation requirement for admissibility. First, the trial court must determine whether the statement, considering all the circumstances, subjects the declarant to criminal liability and whether the declarant realized this when making that statement. Second, the court must determine whether there are sufficient corroborating circumstances that clearly indicate the trustworthiness of the statement).

Walter v. State, 267 S.W.3d 883, 891 (Tex. Crim. App. 2008) ("if the declarant does not recognize the disserving nature of the statement when it is made, the statement indicates ignorance, not trustworthiness; such statements are not admissible" under the statement against penal interest exception).

Walter v. State, 267 S.W.3d 883, 891 (Tex. Crim. App. 2008) ("[S]statements against penal interest fall into three general categories: Some inculpate only the declarant ... others inculpate equally both the declarant and a third party, such as a co-defendant ... still others inculpate both the declarant and third party, but also shift blame by minimizing the speaker's culpability.... A confession, conversation, or narrative, even a short one, might mix together all three types of statements.").

Walter v. State, 267 S.W.3d 883, 891 (Tex. Crim. App. 2008) ("[A]n admission against a co-defendant declarant's interest can be admissible against the defendant so long as it is also sufficiently against the declarant's interest to be reliable.").

Walter v. State, 267 S.W.3d 883, 891 (Tex. Crim. App. 2008) ("[B]oth statements that are directly against the declarant's interest and collateral 'blame-sharing' statements may be admissible [under the statements against penal interest exception], if corroborating circumstances clearly indicate their trustworthiness. "Blame-shifting" statements that minimize the speaker's culpability are not, absent extraordinary circumstances, admissible under the rule.").

Simien v. Unifund CCR Partners, 321 S.W.3d 235, 240 (Tex. App.—Houston [1st Dist.] 2010, no pet.) (pursuant to hearsay exception for business records, "a document authored or created by a third party may be admissible as business records of a different business if: (1) the document is incorporated and kept in the course of the testifying witness's business; (2) that business typically relies upon the accuracy of the contents of the document; and (3) the circumstances otherwise indicate the trustworthiness of the document").

Simien v. Unifund CCR Partners, 321 S.W.3d 235, 240 (Tex. App.—Houston [1st Dist.] 2010, no pet.) ("[A]lthough a second business's confirmation of the accuracy of first business's records is one way to support admissibility under hearsay rule, another way is to show that the second business reasonably relied on the accuracy of the first business's records.").

Riddle v. Unifund CCR Partners, 298 S.W.3d 780, 783 (Tex. App.—El Paso 2009, no pet.) ("[B]usiness records that have been created by one entity, but which have become another entity's primary record of the underlying transaction may be admissible pursuant to [the business records exception to the hearsay rule].").

Clark v. State, 282 S.W.3d 924, 930 (Tex. App.—Beaumont 2009, no pet.) ("'excited utterance' exception to the rule excluding hearsay is a statement relating to a startling event or condition made while the declarant was under the stress of excitement caused by the event or condition.").

Clark v. State, 282 S.W.3d 924, 930 (Tex. App.—Beaumont 2009, no pet.) ("[I]n determining whether a hearsay statement is admissible as an excited utterance, the court may consider the length of time between the occurrence and the statement, the declarant's demeanor, whether the statement is made in response to a question, and whether the statement is self-serving.... The critical determination is whether the declarant was still dominated by the emotions, excitement, fear, or pain of the event or condition at the time of the statement.").

Martinez v. Midland Credit Mgmt., Inc., 250 S.W.3d 481, 484 (Tex. App.—El Paso 2008, no pet.) ("Business records that have been created by one entity, but which have become another entity's primary record of the underlying transaction may be admissible pursuant to [the business records exception to the hearsay rule].... [A] document can comprise the records of another business if the second business determines the accuracy of the information generated by the first business.").

Avila v. State, 252 S.W.3d 632, 636 (Tex. App.—Tyler 2008, no pet.) (records that would otherwise be hearsay are admissible under business records exception if the following four requirements are met: 1) the records were kept in the course of a regularly conducted business activity; 2) it was the regular practice of that business activity to make the records; 3) the records were made at or near the time of the event being recorded; and 4) the person making the records or submitting the information had personal knowledge of the events being recorded).

TXI Transp. Co. v. Hughes, 224 S.W.3d 870, 889 (Tex. App.—Fort Worth 2007), *rev'd on other grounds*, 306 S.W.3d 230 (Tex. 2010) ("Generally, accident reports prepared by investigating officers—possessing sufficient training in accident reconstruction—are admissible under Rule 803(8) as an exception to the hearsay rule.").

Menefree v. State, 211 S.W.3d 893, 905 (Tex. App.—Texarkana 2006, pet. ref'd) ("it is not permissible to admit hearsay evidence regarding facts that reveal why the declarant was afraid" under state of mind hearsay exception).

Corrales v. Dep't of Family & Protective Servs., 155 S.W.3d 478, 485 (Tex. App.—El Paso 2004, no writ) (police reports containing statements of witnesses not present and available for cross examination admissible in termination of parental rights case).

Reyes v. State, 48 S.W.3d 917, 922 (Tex. App.—Fort Worth 2001, no pet.) (medical records properly admitted as business records).

Castaneda v. State, 28 S.W.3d 685, 693 (Tex. App.—Corpus Christi 2000, pet. ref'd) (medical records of victim, including victim's description of incident, admissible as business records).

Glenn v. C & G Elec., Inc., 977 S.W.2d 686, 689 (Tex. App.—Fort Worth 1998, pet. denied) (medical records properly admitted as business records).

Bee v. State, 974 S.W.2d 184, 188 (Tex. App.—San Antonio 1998, no pet.) (witness's testimony at prior trial admissible under former testimony exception to hearsay rule).

Moyer v. State, 948 S.W.2d 525, 528 (Tex. App.—Fort Worth 1997, pet. ref'd) (subjective statements of patient to paramedic admissible as statements made for purposes of diagnosis).

Gilmore v. State, 666 S.W.2d 136, 149 (Tex. App.—Amarillo 1983, writ ref'd) (admission of newspaper articles did not violate hearsay rule).

McMillen Feed, Inc. v. Harlow, 405 S.W.2d 123, 136 (Tex. Civ. App.—Austin 1966, writ ref'd n.r.e.) (charts contained in magazine admissible as exceptions to hearsay rule).

a. Purpose of Exceptions to the Hearsay Rule

Fischer v. State, 252 S.W.3d 375, 381 (Tex. Crim. App. 2008) ("[T]he rationale for the [present sense impression] exception is that the contemporaneity of the statement with the event that it describes eliminates all danger of faulty memory and virtually all danger of insincerity.").

Fischer v. State, 252 S.W.3d 375, 381 (Tex. Crim. App. 2008) (present sense impression exception "is predicated on the notion that the utterance is a reflex product of immediate sensual impressions, unaided by retrospective mental processes. It is instinctive, rather than deliberate").

Walter v. State, 267 S.W.3d 883, 891 (Tex. Crim. App. 2008) (exceptions to the hearsay rule "stem from the notion that the four hearsay dangers of faulty perception, faulty memory, miscommunication, and insincerity are either absent or minimal in certain situations").

Walter v. State, 267 S.W.3d 883, 891 (Tex. Crim. App. 2008) ("[S]tatements made in [the situations or under the specified circumstances under exceptions to the hearsay rule] carry such sufficient, independent, circumstantial guarantees of trustworthiness that the rule deems cross-examination unnecessary.").

Walter v. State, 267 S.W.3d 883, 891 (Tex. Crim. App. 2008) (exception to the hearsay rule for statements against pecuniary, penal, or social interest "stems from the commonsense notion that people ordinarily do not say things that are damaging to themselves unless they believe they are true").

Muttoni v. State, 25 S.W.3d 300, 305 (Tex. App.—Austin 2000, no pet.) ("The common factor among these firmly rooted hearsay exceptions is recognition of their proven trustworthiness over a substantial period of time.... When a hearsay statement does not fall into a firmly rooted exception, evidence that it bears other 'particularized guarantees of trustworthiness' may make it sufficiently reliable to satisfy the Confrontation Clause[;]" appellate court held trial judge erred by finding statement at issue to be admissible).

b. Nonhearsay Evidence

Texas Rule of Evidence 801(e) states:

> **Statements Which Are Not Hearsay.** A statement is not hearsay if:
>
> (1) *Prior statement by witness*. The declarant testifies at the trial or hearing and is subject to cross-examination concerning the statement, and the statement is:
>   (A) inconsistent with the declarant's testimony, and was given under oath subject to the penalty of perjury at a trial,

hearing, or other proceeding except a grand jury proceeding in a criminal case, or in a deposition;
(B) consistent with the declarant's testimony and is offered to rebut an express or implied charge against the declarant of recent fabrication or improper influence or motive;
(C) one of identification of a person made after perceiving the person; or
(D) taken and offered in a criminal case in accordance with Code of Criminal Procedure article 38.071.
(2) *Admission by party-opponent.* The statement is offered against a party and is:
(A) the party's own statement in either an individual or representative capacity;
(B) a statement of which the party has manifested an adoption or belief in its truth;
(C) a statement by a person authorized by the party to make a statement concerning the subject;
(C) a statement by the party's agent or servant concerning a matter within the scope of the agency or employment, made during the existence of the relationship; or
(E) a statement by a co-conspirator of a party during the course and in furtherance of the conspiracy.
(3) *Depositions.* In a civil case, it is a deposition taken in the same proceeding, as same proceeding is defined in Rule of Civil Procedure 203.6(b). Unavailability of deponent is not a requirement for admissibility.

Texas Rule of Evidence 801(d) states:

Hearsay. "Hearsay" is a statement, other than one made by the declarant while testifying at the trial or hearing, *offered in evidence to prove the truth of the matter asserted.* (Emphasis added.)

Reid Road Mun. Util. Dist. No. 2 v. Speedy Stop Food Stores, Ltd., 337 S.W.3d 846, 854 (Tex. 2011) (where a party has used a document made by a third party in such a way as amounts to an approval of its contents, such statement may be received against him as an admission by adoption and is nonhearsay).

Reid Road Mun. Util. Dist. No. 2 v. Speedy Stop Food Stores, Ltd., 337 S.W.3d 846, 854 (Tex. 2011) (because a utility manifested its belief in and approval of an appraiser's opinion as to a party's damages, by calling him as a witness to testify to the special commissioners regarding that opinion and proffering his written appraisal to them in support of his testimony, the appraisal was admissible against the district as a nonhearsay admission by adoption).

Langham v. State, 305 S.W.3d 568, 580 (Tex. Crim. App. 2010) (typically, hearsay offered as "background evidence is admissible, not because it has particularly compelling probative value with respect to the elements of the alleged offense, but simply because it provides the jury with perspective, so that the jury is equipped to evaluate, in proper context, other evidence that more directly relates to elemental facts. But, it is not necessary to go into elaborate detail in setting the evidentiary scene, and there is an inherent danger in doing so.").

PNP Petroleum I, LP v. Taylor, 438 S.W.3d 723, 735 (Tex. App.—San Antonio 2014, pet. denied) (deletions and revisions in lease drafts were offered to show what was said, not for the truth of what was said, and thus was not hearsay).

Lyle v. State, 418 S.W.3d 901, 903 (Tex. App.—Houston [14th Dist.] 2013, no pet.) (an extrajudicial statement or writing that is offered for the purpose of showing what was said rather than for the truth of the matter stated therein does not constitute hearsay).

Lyle v. State, 418 S.W.3d 901, 903 (Tex. App.—Houston [14th Dist.] 2013, no pet.) (although a police officer's testimony may be inadmissible due to hearsay, an officer may describe statements made by others for the purpose of showing why the defendant became a suspect and to explain the events and circumstances leading to the defendant's arrest).

Certain Underwriters at Lloyd's, London v. Chicago Bridge & Iron Co., 406 S.W.3d 326, 340 (Tex. App.—Beaumont 2013, pet. denied) (evidence offered to show that a party had notice is not inadmissible hearsay).

Lozano v. State, 359 S.W.3d 790, 820 (Tex. App.—Fort Worth 2012, pet. ref'd) (statements offered for the purpose of showing what was said, and not for the truth of the matter asserted, do not constitute hearsay).

Black v. State, 358 S.W.3d 823, 831 (Tex. App.—Fort Worth 2012, pet. ref'd) ("[S]creensaver picture of what appeared to be methamphetamine was not a statement; it was therefore not hearsay.").

Johnson v. State, 425 S.W.3d 344, 346 (Tex. App.—Houston [1st Dist.] 2011, pet. ref'd) ("[S]tatement is not hearsay if its relevancy does not hinge on its truthfulness.").

Limited Logistics Servs., Inc. v. Villegas, 268 S.W.3d 141, 146 (Tex. App.—Corpus Christi 2008, no pet.) ("[A] signed instrument, such as a contract, that creates legal rights is not hearsay because it has legal effect independent of the truth of any statement contained in it.").

Stafford v. State, 248 S.W.3d 400, 407 (Tex. App.—Beaumont 2008, pet. ref'd) ("[O]ut-of-court statement which is not offered to prove the truth of the matter asserted therein, but is offered for some other reason, is not hearsay.").

c. Nonassertive Conduct

Texas Rule of Evidence 801(a) states:

> **Statement.** A "statement" is (1) an oral or written verbal expression or (2) *nonverbal conduct of a person, if it is intended by the person as a substitute for verbal expression.* (Emphasis added.)

Mega Child Care, Inc. v. Tex. Dep't of Protective & Regulatory Servs., 29 S.W.3d 303, 311 (Tex. App.—Houston [14th Dist.] 2000, no pet.) (pointing gestures admissible, where not offered for truth of what was asserted by gestures).

Johnson v. State, 987 S.W.2d 79, 90 (Tex. App.—Houston [14th Dist.] 1998, pet. ref'd) (act of seeking medical assistance admissible as nonverbal conduct).

d. Multiple Hearsay

Texas Rule of Evidence 805 states:

> Hearsay included within hearsay is not excluded under the hearsay rule if each part of the combined statements conforms with an exception to the hearsay rule provided in these rules.

Green v. State, 839 S.W.2d 935, 942 (Tex. App.—Waco 1992, pet. ref'd) (hearsay within hearsay admissible where both portions of hearsay fell within exception to hearsay rule).

e. Hearsay to Impeach Credibility or Rehabilitate Witness

Texas Rule of Evidence 801(e) states in relevant part:

> **Statements Which Are Not Hearsay.** A statement is not hearsay if:
>
> (1) Prior statement by witness. The declarant testifies at the trial or hearing and is subject to cross-examination concerning the statement, and the statement is:
>   (A) inconsistent with the declarant's testimony, and was given under oath subject to the penalty of perjury at a trial, hearing, or other proceeding except a grand jury proceeding in a criminal case, or in a deposition;
>   (B) consistent with the declarant's testimony and is offered to rebut an express or implied charge against the declarant of recent fabrication or improper influence or motive;
>   (C) one of identification of a person made after perceiving the person; or
>   (D) taken and offered in a criminal case in accordance with Code of Criminal Procedure article 38.071.

Wisdom v. State, 143 S.W.3d 276, 281 (Tex. App.—Waco 2004, no pet.) (prior statement by witness admissible as prior consistent statement).

Bolden v. State, 967 S.W.2d 895, 898 (Tex. App.—Fort Worth 1998, pet. ref'd) (prior consistent statement admissible to rehabilitate impeached witness).

Turro v. State, 950 S.W.2d 390, 404 (Tex. App.—Fort Worth 1997, pet. ref'd) ("[A]dmission of a prior consistent statement [is proper] to rebut allegations of improper influence or motive.").

II. Sample Motions
A. Motion to Exclude Speculative Expert Opinion

NO. _____

	§	IN THE DISTRICT COURT
_____	§	
v.	§	_____ JUDICIAL COURT
	§	
_____	§	_____ COUNTY, TEXAS

Motion to Exclude Speculative Expert Opinion

Comes now _____, Plaintiff in this cause, and file this, her Motion to Exclude Speculative Expert Opinion, and in support thereof, Plaintiff would show the Court the following:

1.
FACTUAL BACKGROUND

This matter arises from a serious accident that occurred in the Defendant's garage on or about December 24, 2018.

The accident occurred when the Plaintiff slipped and fell in a puddle of oil on the concrete floor of the Defendant's garage, striking the back of her head on the ground as she fell. As a result of the accident, the Plaintiff has incurred serious head injuries, with long-term memory loss and other neurological deficiencies. She has no recollection of how the fall occurred. There were no witnesses to the accident or the Plaintiff's actions immediately prior to the accident.

A major issue in this case is whether the Plaintiff was running or walking when the incident occurred. The Plaintiff anticipates that Defendant's expert witness, a mechanical engineer, will attempt to testify how the fall occurred, based solely upon grease stains on the Plaintiff's shoes and clothing.

By this motion, the Plaintiff seeks to exclude any testimony as to how the fall occurred, since any such testimony would be too speculative to be reliable.

2.
THIS COURT MAY PRECLUDE EVIDENCE WHERE THE PROBATIVE VALUE
IS SUBSTANTIALLY OUTWEIGHED BY THE DANGER OF UNDUE PREJUDICE

Texas Rule of Evidence 403 states: "[a]lthough relevant, evidence may be excluded if its probative value is substantially outweighed by the danger of unfair prejudice, confusion of the issues, or misleading the jury, or by considerations of undue delay, or needless presentation of cumulative evidence." *Brookshire Bros. v. Aldridge*, 438 S.W.3d 9, 26 (Tex. 2014) (evidence that raises a risk of prejudice and confusion of the jury should be excluded); *Farmers Texas County Mutual Insurance Co. v. Pagan*, 453 S.W.3d 454, (Tex. App.—Houston [14th Dist.]

2014, no pet.) (evidence should have been excluded where its probative value was outweighed by danger of confusion of issues and misleading jury).

In the present case, any testimony relating to how the fall occurred would be purely speculative, as is discussed in more detail below. Allowing such evidence would create unfair and significant prejudice to the Plaintiff, and therefore should be excluded.

3.
THIS COURT MAY EXCLUDE AN EXPERT'S OPINION WHERE BASED UPON SPECULATION OR CONJECTURE

Texas Rule of Evidence 703 states in relevant part, "[t]he facts or data in the particular case upon which an expert bases an opinion or inference <u>may be those perceived by, reviewed by, or made known to the expert at or before the hearing</u>." (Emphasis added.)

An expert may not base his or her opinion on speculation or conjecture. *Cooper Tire & Rubber Co. v. Mendez*, 204 S.W.3d 797, 800 (Tex. 2006) (scientific testimony is unreliable if it is not grounded in the methods and procedures of science, and amounts to no more than a subjective belief or unsupported speculation); *Gammill v. Jack Williams Chevrolet, Inc.*, 972 S.W.2d 713, 727 (Tex. 1998) (expert's opinions speculative and unreliable); *Naegeli Transp. v. Gulf Electroquip, Inc.*, 853 S.W.2d 737, 741 (Tex. App.—Houston [14th Dist.] 1993, writ denied) (expert testimony cannot be based on mere guess or speculations); *Cent. Mut. Ins. Co. v. D.&B., Inc.*, 340 S.W.2d 525 (Tex. Civ. App.—Waco 1960, writ ref'd n.r.e.) (evidence speculative and not proper subject of expert opinion testimony); *Harris v. State*, 137 S.W. 373 (Tex. Crim. App. 1911, no pet.) (testimony on experiments not admissible where based on speculative hypothetical theories).

An expert's opinion may also be excluded if it is not shown to be reliable. *Cooper Tire & Rubber Co. v. Mendez*, 204 S.W.3d 797, 800 (Tex. 2006) (testimony on theory that wax contamination caused tire failure was legally insufficient to establish manufacturing defect in product liability action because the theory was unreliable); *Mack Trucks, Inc. v. Tamez*, 206 S.W.3d 572, 578 (Tex. 2006) (in determining the reliability of an expert's testimony, the trial court should undertake a rigorous examination of the facts on which the expert relies, the method by which the expert draws an opinion from those facts, and how the expert applies the facts and methods to the case at hand).

In the present case, the Defendant's expert is hindered by the same type of problems that rendered the testimony in the above-referenced cases inadmissible. The defense expert will attempt to determine how the fall occurred, and specifically, whether the Plaintiff was running or walking at the time based <u>solely</u> upon the oil marks on the Plaintiff's clothing and shoes.

Too much critical evidence is missing to allow this expert to render a reliable opinion, in that:

1. There were no witnesses to the accident or the events leading up to the accident. Due to the severity of the Plaintiff's injuries, she has no recollection of how the incident occurred.

2. Immediately after the accident, the Defendant cleaned up the oil spill, eliminating the best possible evidence for analysis: the location, direction, and length of the slide marks. The Defendant has testified that he has no recollection, one way or another, of any slide marks.
3. The expert's tests and analysis on the Plaintiff's clothing occurred more than twelve (12) months after the accident date. Prior to conducting the testing, the articles of clothing were stored in a large plastic trash bag in the Plaintiff's closet. Since the oil almost certainly transferred to new areas of the clothing while stored in the bag, any tests attempting to reconstruct the incident based upon the location of the stains would be totally speculative.

Based upon the foregoing, it is unclear how the defense expert can render an opinion on this crucial evidence based upon anything other than conjecture, speculation, and simple guesswork. As such, it is again requested that the Court exclude any testimony of Defendant's expert relating to how the incident occurred.

Dated: _____ *(Date)* _____

                         Respectfully submitted,

                         By: _____

                              (Name of Counsel)

                         Attorneys for Plaintiff,

                              (Name of Plaintiff)

B. Motion to Exclude Reference to Failure to Call Witness

NO. _____

_____	§	IN THE DISTRICT COURT
	§	
v.	§	_____ JUDICIAL COURT
	§	
_____	§	_____ COUNTY, TEXAS

Motion to Exclude Reference to Failure to Call Witness

Comes now _____, Plaintiff in this cause, and file this, his Motion to Exclude Reference to a Failure to Call Witness, and in support thereof, Plaintiff would show the Court the following:

1.
FACTUAL BACKGROUND

This action involves a dog bite incident whereby the Plaintiff was injured and permanently disfigured as a result of an attack by the Defendant's German Shepherd. Following this incident, the Plaintiff sought treatment by five physicians, including the attending emergency room physician (Dr. Carter), Plaintiff's primary care doctor (Dr. Kaiser), a plastic surgeon (Dr. Nippentuck), and two orthopedic surgeons (Dr. Bones and Dr. Fixit).

The Plaintiff has chosen to call Dr. Carter, Dr. Fixit, and Dr. Nippentuck to testify at trial. To avoid needless duplication of evidence, the Plaintiff has chosen not to call the remaining witnesses.

This motion seeks to preclude the Defendant from making reference to the fact that the other two treating physicians will not be called to testify in this matter, or to speculate as to what the witnesses who was not called might have said on the stand.

2.
EVIDENCE MAY BE EXCLUDED

Texas Rule of Evidence 403 states: "[a]lthough relevant, evidence may be excluded if its probative value is substantially outweighed by the danger of unfair prejudice, confusion of the issues, or misleading the jury, or by considerations of undue delay, or needless presentation of cumulative evidence." *Brookshire Bros. v. Aldridge*, 438 S.W.3d 9, 26 (Tex. 2014) (evidence that raises a risk of prejudice and confusion of the jury should be excluded); *Farmers Texas County Mutual Insurance Co. v. Pagan*, 453 S.W.3d 454, (Tex. App.—Houston [14th Dist.] 2014, no pet.) (evidence should have been excluded where its probative value was outweighed by danger of confusion of issues and misleading jury).

3.
ANY REFERENCE TO THE TESTIMONY OF UNCALLED WITNESSES WOULD BE PURE SPECULATION

The Court may exclude evidence that is wholly speculative. *See McKenzie v. State*, 617 S.W.2d 211, 221 (Tex. Crim. App. 1981) (prosecutor may comment on uncalled witnesses but may not speculate regarding what witnesses would say if called); *Garza v. State*, 18 S.W.3d 813 (Tex. App.—Fort Worth 2000, pet. ref'd); *In the Matter of V.M.D.*, 974 S.W.2d 332 (Tex. App.—San Antonio 1998, no writ). A party may not speculate as to what a witness who was not called might say. *Johnson v. State*, 649 S.W.2d 111, 116 (Tex. App.—San Antonio 1983), aff'd, 662 S.W.2d 368 (Tex. Crim. App. 1984) (prosecutor's argument implying certain witnesses weren't called that would have been adverse to defendant improper where asked jury to speculate about allegedly missing witnesses); *McKenzie v. State*, 617 S.W.2d 211, 221 (Tex. Crim. App. 1981) (prosecutor may comment on uncalled witnesses but may not speculate regarding what witnesses would say if called).

In the present case, any comments regarding the Plaintiff's failure to call a treating physician would invite exactly the type of speculation forbidden by the above-mentioned cases. As such, the evidence should be excluded.

4. CALLING THE OTHER TREATING PHYSICIANS WOULD CREATE NEEDLESS DUPLICATION OF EVIDENCE

Texas Rule of evidence 403 states: "[a]lthough relevant, evidence may be excluded if its probative value is substantially outweighed by the danger of unfair prejudice, confusion of the issues, or misleading the jury, <u>or by considerations of undue delay, or needless presentation of cumulative evidence</u>." (Emphasis added.) See generally *Gigliobianco v. State*, 210 S.W.3d 637, 640 (Tex. Crim. App. 2006); *Nissan Motor Co. v. Armstrong*, 145 S.W.3d 131, 138 (Tex. 2004).

In the present case, the witnesses who will testify will provide ample proof of all of the Plaintiff's claims in this case. To call the additional witnesses would only unnecessarily delay the proceedings and add needless expense to all parties involved. As such, there is no need to call those witnesses and the Plaintiff should not be penalized for exercising such judicial economy.

5. CONCLUSION

Based on the foregoing, it is respectfully requested that the Court issue the accompanying In Limine Order as prayed.

Dated: _____ *(Date)* _____

By: _____

_____ *(Name of Counsel)* _____

Attorneys for Plaintiff,

_____ *(Name of Plaintiff)* _____

C. Motion to Exclude Testimony and Opinions of Medical Doctor

NO. _____

	§	IN THE DISTRICT COURT
_____	§	
	§	
v.	§	_____ JUDICIAL COURT
	§	
_____	§	_____ COUNTY, TEXAS

Motion to Exclude Testimony and Opinions of Medical Doctor

Comes now _____, Plaintiff in this cause, and file this, her Motion to Exclude Testimony and Opinions of Medical Doctor, and in support thereof, Plaintiff would show the Court the following:

1.
FACTUAL BACKGROUND

This action is a medical malpractice claim wherein Plaintiff alleges that she was permanently disabled as a result of surgery that was allegedly improperly performed by defendant on Plaintiff's back, on August 13, 2018.

During the discovery of this matter, Plaintiff disclosed Dr. Benjamin Smith as an expert witness who would provide an opinion regarding her current physical condition. However, during his deposition, in September of 2019, Dr. Benjamin Smith specifically testified, "I have no knowledge [with regard to her [the Plaintiff's] current condition]." In addition, he stated that his opinion with respect to the Plaintiff's long-term prognosis "would be speculative." A copy of the relevant portions of the deposition of Dr. Benjamin Smith is attached hereto, as Exhibit A.

By this motion, Plaintiff seeks an order excluding evidence of opinions, testimony, or argument relating to Dr. Benjamin Smith.

2.
THIS COURT MAY EXCLUDE PREJUDICIAL AND MISLEADING EVIDENCE IN ADVANCE OF TRIAL BY WAY OF AN IN LIMINE MOTION

The Court has the inherent power to grant a motion in limine to exclude evidence which could be objected to at trial, either as irrelevant or subject to exclusion as unduly prejudicial. *Wackenhut Corp. v. Gutierrez*, 453 S.W.3d 917, 920 n.3 (Tex. 2016); *In re BCH Development, LLC*, 525 S.W.3d 920, 925 (Tex. App.—Dallas 2017, orig. proceeding). Texas Rule of Evidence 403 allows the court to exclude evidence where there is a substantial danger that the probative value will be outweighed by the danger of undue prejudice. *See Diamond Offshore Services Ltd. v. Williams*, 542 S.W.3d 539, 549 (Tex. 2018); *Brookshire Bros. v. Aldridge*, 438 S.W.3d 9, 34 (Tex. 2014).

Texas Rule of Evidence 403 states: "[a]lthough relevant, evidence may be excluded if its probative value is substantially outweighed by the danger of unfair prejudice, confusion of the issues, or misleading the jury, or by considerations of undue delay, or needless presentation of cumulative evidence." *Brookshire Bros. v. Aldridge*, 438 S.W.3d 9, 26 (Tex. 2014) (evidence that raises a risk of prejudice and confusion of the jury should be excluded); *Farmers Texas County Mutual Insurance Co. v. Pagan*, 453 S.W.3d 454, (Tex. App.—Houston [14th Dist.] 2014, no pet.) (evidence should have been excluded where its probative value was outweighed by danger of confusion of issues and misleading jury).

Moreover, the court may hear and determine the question of the admissibility of evidence outside the presence or hearing of the jury. *See Weidner v. Sanchez*, 14 S.W.3d 353, 363 (Tex. App.—Houston [14th Dist.] 2000, no pet.); *Kendrix v. S. Pac. Transp. Co.*, 907 S.W.2d 111, 113 (Tex. App.—Beaumont 1995, writ denied); Texas Rule of Civil Procedure 166; and Texas Rules of Evidence 103 and 104.

In the instant matter, it is clear that any testimony or opinions of Dr. Benjamin Smith as they relate to the Plaintiff's current condition would be prejudicial and misleading to the jury, because he testified, "I have no knowledge [with regard to her [the Plaintiff's] current condition]. Thus, this Court should enter an order excluding any and all evidence, references to evidence, opinions, testimony, or argument relating to Dr. Benjamin Smith in the trial for this matter.

3.
THIS COURT MAY EXCLUDE THE TESTIMONY AND OPINIONS OF DR. BENJAMIN SMITH AS REPRESENTING IMPROPER SPECULATION

It is improper to provide an opinion to the jury that is based upon speculation or conjecture. *See Cooper Tire & Rubber Co. v. Mendez*, 204 S.W.3d 797, 800 (Tex. 2006); *Coastal Transp. Co. v. Crown Cent. Petroleum Corp.*, 136 S.W.3d 227, 232 (Tex. 2004) (conclusory and speculative expert testimony irrelevant and insufficient to overcome directed verdict motion by opposing party).

The deposition testimony of Dr. Benjamin Smith, as described above, shows that his opinions are improperly speculative and based upon unproven assumptions and thus, his opinions and testimony should be excluded from the evidence at this trial.

4.
EVIDENCE OF THE TESTIMONY AND OPINIONS OF DR. BENJAMIN SMITH SHOULD BE EXCLUDED TO PREVENT UNFAIR SURPRISE TO DEFENDANT

To avoid unfair surprise, the Court may exclude evidence on issues where discovery responses and actions of counsel led opposing counsel to believe those issues would not be litigated. *See Capital Metro. Transp. Auth./Cent. of Tenn. Ry. & Navigation Co. v. Cent. of Tenn. Ry. & Navigation Co.*, 114 S.W.3d 573, 583 (Tex. App.—Austin 2003, pet. denied) (evidence of damages for failure to disclose information until shortly before trial properly excluded where court implicitly found unfair surprise from late disclosure).

In the present case, Plaintiff's statements and actions led defense counsel to reasonably believe that Dr. Benjamin Smith had no knowledge regarding Plaintiff's condition. It would be unfair and prejudicial to allow Plaintiff, at this late date, to present evidence from Dr. Benjamin Smith on that issue. Thus, the Court should therefore exclude any and all evidence, including any mention of evidence, relating to Dr. Benjamin Smith, to prevent unfair surprise to Defendant.

5.
CONCLUSION

Based on the foregoing, Defendant respectfully requests that this Court exclude any testimony or documentary evidence, or mention of any evidence, or argument relating to Dr. Benjamin Smith.

Dated: _____ *(Date)* _____

By: _____

_____ *(Name of Counsel)* _____

Attorneys for Defendant,

_____ *(Name of Defendant)* _____

CHAPTER 9

Trial Presentation

I. Motion Authorities
   A. Motion to Prevent Improper Voir Dire
      1. Suggested Motion Text
      2. Motion Summary
      3. Supporting Authorities
         a. Preconditioning
            i. Preconditioning on Issue of Amount of Damages
         b. Educating Jury on the Law
         c. Insurance References
         d. Improper Commitment to a Position
         e. References to "Lawsuit Crisis"
         f. Other Statutory Limitations on Voir Dire
      4. Opposing Authorities
         a. Constitutional Considerations
         b. Court's Discretion
         c. References to Insurance
   B. Motion to Exclude Improper Argument in Opening Statement
      1. Suggested Motion Text
      2. Motion Summary
      3. Supporting Authorities
         a. Other Grounds
      4. Opposing Authorities
   C. Motion to Exclude Premature Rebuttal of Affirmative Defenses
      1. Suggested Motion Text
      2. Motion Summary
      3. Supporting Authorities
      4. Opposing Authorities
   D. Motion to Exclude Reference to Lost or Destroyed Evidence
      1. Suggested Motion Text
      2. Motion Summary
      3. Supporting Authorities
         a. Accidental Destruction of Evidence
         b. Intentional Destruction or Suppression of Evidence
         c. Negative Presumption
         d. Other Grounds

4. Opposing Authorities
E. Motion to Exclude Arbitration Evidence and Findings
  1. Suggested Motion Text
  2. Motion Summary
  3. Supporting Authorities
     a. Other Grounds
  4. Opposing Authorities
F. Motion to Exclude Evidence of Damages in Bifurcated Trial
  1. Suggested Motion Text
  2. Motion Summary
  3. Supporting Authorities
     a. Other Grounds
  4. Opposing Authorities
G. Motion to Preclude "Golden Rule" Argument
  1. Suggested Motion Text
  2. Motion Summary
  3. Supporting Authorities
     a. Other Grounds
  4. Opposing Authorities
H. Motion to Exclude Improper Terminology
  1. Suggested Motion Text
  2. Motion Summary
  3. Supporting Authorities
     a. Exclusion of Ultimate Issue Evidence
        i. General Admissibility of Ultimate Issue Opinions
     b. Usurping Jury Function
  4. Opposing Authorities
II. Sample Motions
A. Motion to Exclude Reference to Lost or Destroyed Evidence

I. Motion Authorities

A. Motion to Exclude Improper Voir Dire

1. Suggested Motion Text

(*Name of Moving Party*) hereby moves this Court for an order prohibiting counsel for (*Name Party*) from conducting any voir dire that relates to (*Describe Anticipated Improper Voir Dire Questions, e.g., Educating the Jury on the State of the Governing Law in This Case*). The motion is based upon the ground that (*State Basis for Belief That Improper Voir Dire Will Occur, e.g., Opposing Counsel's Proposed Voir Dire Questions Listed Inappropriate Matters, Including a Description of the Pleadings and Statements of Law*) and if allowed, would unfairly precondition the jury in this case.

2. Motion Summary

This motion is used to restrict counsel from asking improper questions during voir dire. The motion is based upon leading cases in this area. *See Babcock v. Nw. Mem'l Hosp.*, 767 S.W.2d 705, 707 (Tex. 1989); *Tacon Mech. Contractors, Inc. v. Grant Sheet Metal, Inc.*, 889 S.W.2d 666, 675 (Tex. App.—Houston [14th Dist.] 1994, writ denied); *Gulf States Utils. Co. v. Reed*, 659 S.W.2d 849, 856 (Tex. App.—Houston [14th Dist.] 1983, writ ref'd n.r.e.).

> *Note: Facts that might warrant a motion on this issue include past attorney misconduct, information on proposed voir dire questionnaires, comments of counsel, etc. Be prepared to back up your motion with a detailed declaration or consider making the motion orally at a sidebar during voir dire, if necessary.*

3. Supporting Authorities

Texas Rule of Civil Procedure 230, states:

> In examining a juror, he shall not be asked a question the answer to which may show that he has been convicted of an offense which disqualifies him, or that he stands charged by some legal accusation with theft or any felony.

Jacobs v. State, 560 S.W.3d 205, 210 (Tex. Crim. App. 2018) ("[A] trial judge has broad discretion in the manner it chooses to conduct voir dire, both as to the topics that will be addressed, and the form and substance of the questions that will be employed to address them.").

Jacobs v. State, 560 S.W.3d 205, 210 (Tex. Crim. App. 2018) ("[T]he Constitution does not always entitle a defendant to have questions posed during voir dire specifically directed to matters that conceivably might prejudice him... Instead, the State's obligation to impanel an impartial jury generally can be satisfied by less than an inquiry into the specific prejudice feared by the defendant.").

Jacobs v. State, 560 S.W.3d 205, 210 (Tex. Crim. App. 2018) ("[N]either the Texas constitutional guarantee of 'trial by an impartial jury' nor the Texas constitutional guarantee 'of being heard' by counsel grants a more expansive right to pose specific questions in jury selection than what is already guaranteed by the federal Constitution.").

Palacio v. State, 580 S.W.3d 447, 450 (Tex. App.—Houston [14th Dist.] 2019, pet. ref'd) ("The trial court has broad discretion over the jury-selection process.").

Evans v. State, 440 S.W.3d 107, 114 (Tex. App.—Waco 2013, pet. ref'd) (a trial court retains discretion to restrict voir dire questions that are confusing, misleading, vague and broad, or are improper commitment questions).

Contreras v. State, 440 S.W.3d 85, 88 (Tex. App.—Waco 2012, pet. dism'd, untimely filed) ("[T]rial judge may prohibit as improper a voir dire question that is so vague or broad in nature as to constitute a global fishing expedition.").

K.J. v. USA Water Polo, Inc., 383 S.W.3d 593, 601 (Tex. App.—Houston [14th Dist.] 2012, pet. denied) (primary purpose of voir dire is to inquire about specific views that would prevent or substantially impair jurors from performing their duty in accordance with their instructions and oath).

McBride v. State, 359 S.W.3d 683, 689 (Tex. App.—Houston [14th Dist.] 2011, pet. ref'd) ("question [to the venire members during jury selection] is 'improper if it: (1) attempts to commit the juror to a particular verdict based on particular facts' (a commitment question), or (2) 'is so vague or broad in nature as to constitute a global fishing expedition.'").

Zavala v. State, 401 S.W.3d 171, 175 (Tex. App.—Houston [14th Dist.] 2011, pet. ref'd) ("[S]cope of permissible voir dire examination is necessarily broad to enable litigants to discover bias or prejudice so that they may make challenges for cause or peremptory challenges.... But questions that are not intended to discover bias or prejudice and instead seek only to determine how jurors would respond to the anticipated evidence and commit them to a specific verdict on that evidence are not proper.").

Dewalt v. State, 307 S.W.3d 437, 457 (Tex. App.—Austin 2010, pet. ref'd) ("[P]roper [voir dire] question is one which seeks to discover a venire members' views on an issue applicable to the case.").

Thompson v. State, 267 S.W.3d 514, 517 (Tex. App.—Austin 2008, pet. ref'd) ("[T]rial court may impose reasonable restrictions on the exercise of voir dire examination.").

Gulf States Utils. Co. v. Reed, 659 S.W.2d 849, 856 (Tex. App.—Houston [14th Dist.] 1983, writ ref'd n.r.e.) (improper during voir dire for attorney to comment on personal lives of families of parties or parties' attorneys).

Brown v. Poff, 387 S.W.2d 101, 104 (Tex. Civ. App.—El Paso 1965, writ ref'd n.r.e.) (attorney may not attempt to commit prospective juror to particular verdict amount).

Green v. Ligon, 190 S.W.2d 742, 746 (Tex. Civ. App.—Fort Worth 1945, writ ref'd n.r.e.) (trial judge may exercise sound discretion to impose reasonable limitations on scope of attorney's voir dire examination to prevent questioning on matters with only remote or tenuous connection to potentially relevant attitudes or biases or unduly time-consuming in light of potential for exposing significant prejudice).

Tex. & New Orleans R.R. Co. v. Lide, 117 S.W.2d 479, 480 (Tex. Civ. App.—Waco 1938, no writ) (improper during voir dire for attorney to attempt to foster sympathy for or prejudice against a party by appealing to prospective jurors to decide case on basis of comparative wealth of parties).

Campbell v. Campbell, 215 S.W. 134, 137 (Tex. Civ. App.—Dallas 1919, writ ref'd.) (attorney may not ask questions of prospective juror that would require juror to disclose personal views on particular issues and committing juror to certain views or conclusions; in will contest, improper for attorney to ask jurors if they would be influenced by testator's disinheriting certain family members).

> *Note: Counsel should also be sure to check the local rules for the jurisdiction in which the trial is heard, which may place additional restrictions on voir dire. For example, Rule 3.26 of the Harrison County Rules of*

Practice states that *"all counsel with cases to be tried will be expected to take notice of the preceding voir dire examinations. Repetition of previous voir dire questions will not be permitted."*

See also Rule 403 of the Texas Rules of Evidence, which states:

> *Although relevant, evidence may be excluded if its probative value is substantially outweighed by the danger of unfair prejudice, confusion of the issues, or misleading the jury, or by considerations of undue delay, or needless presentation of cumulative evidence.*

a. Preconditioning

Davis v. State, 349 S.W.3d 517, 518 (Tex. Crim. App. 2011) ("[A] commitment question is a question that commits a prospective juror to resolve or to refrain from resolving an issue a certain way after learning of a particular fact.").

Mims v. State, 434 S.W.3d 265, 271 (Tex. App.—Houston [1st Dist.] 2014, no pet.) ("[Q]uestions attempting to commit venire members to give mitigating or aggravating effect to particular facts are improper.").

Hawkins v. State, 278 S.W.3d 396, 401 (Tex. App.—Eastland 2008, no pet.) ("[I]t is impermissible to attempt to bind or to commit a prospective juror to a verdict based upon a hypothetical set of facts.").

In re Travelers Lloyds of Tex. Ins. Co., 273 S.W.3d 368, 374 (Tex. App.—San Antonio 2008, orig. proceeding) ("[V]oir dire inquiries may address bias or prejudice, but may not be used to address how specific evidence such as settlement offer evidence may affect a verdict.").

Tex. Employers Ins. Ass'n. v. Loesch, 538 S.W.2d 435, 442 (Tex. Civ. App.—Waco 1976, writ ref'd n.r.e.) (improper during voir dire for attorney to advise jurors of effect of answers on judgment).

Brown v. Poff, 387 S.W.2d 101, 104 (Tex. Civ. App.—El Paso 1965, writ ref'd n.r.e.) (attorney may not attempt to commit prospective juror to particular verdict amount).

Lassiter v. Bouche, 41 S.W.2d 88, 90 (Tex. Civ. App.—Dallas 1931, writ ref'd) (attorney may not attempt to commit prospective juror to amount of weight to give to particular piece of evidence).

i. Preconditioning on Issue of Amount of Damages

Brown v. Poff, 387 S.W.2d 101, 104 (Tex. Civ. App.—El Paso 1965, writ ref'd n.r.e.) (attorney may not attempt to commit prospective juror to particular verdict amount).

Tex. & New Orleans R.R. Co. v. Lide, 117 S.W.2d 479, 480 (Tex. Civ. App.—Waco 1938, no writ) (improper during voir dire for attorney to attempt to foster sympathy for or prejudice against party by appealing to prospective jurors to decide case on basis of comparative wealth of parties).

b. Educating Jury on the Law

Tex. Employers Ins. Ass'n. v. Loesch, 538 S.W.2d 435, 442 (Tex. Civ. App.—Waco 1976, writ ref'd n.r.e.) (improper during voir dire for attorney to advise jurors of effect of answers on judgment).

Robinson v. Lovell, 238 S.W.2d 294, 298 (Tex. Civ. App.—Galveston, 1951, writ ref'd n.r.e.) (trial court abuses discretion permitting counsel to advise jury of legal consequences of any of its findings).

Lassiter v. Bouche, 41 S.W.2d 88, 90 (Tex. Civ. App.—Dallas 1931, writ ref'd) (attorney may not attempt to commit prospective juror to amount of weight to give to particular piece of evidence).

c. Insurance References

A.J. Miller Trucking Co. v. Wood, 474 S.W.2d 763, 766 (Tex. Civ. App.—Tyler 1971, writ ref'd n.r.e.) (improper for attorney to inject subject of insurance into voir dire examination and reversible error per se).

d. Improper Commitment to a Position

Davis v. State, 313 S.W.3d 317, 346 (Tex. Crim. App. 2010) ("[C]ommitment question during voir dire is one that commits a prospective juror to resolve, or refrain from resolving, an issue a certain way after learning a particular fact. Often, a commitment question requires a 'yes' or 'no' answer, and one or both possible answers commits a juror to resolve an issue in a particular way.").

Sanchez v. State, 165 S.W.3d 707, 712 (Tex. Crim. App. 2005) ("[I]mproper commitment question attempts to create a bias or prejudice in the venireperson before he or she has heard the evidence, whereas a proper voir dire question attempts to discover a venireperson's preexisting bias or prejudice.").

Sandoval v. State, 571 S.W.3d 392 (Tex. App.—Houston [1st Dist.] 2019, no pet.) ("Improper commitment questions are prohibited to ensure that the jury will listen to the evidence with an open mind—a mind that is impartial and without bias or prejudice—and render a verdict based upon that evidence.").

Sandoval v. State, 571 S.W.3d 392 (Tex. App.—Houston [1st Dist.] 2019, no pet.) ("Commitment questions require a venireman to promise that he will base his verdict or course of action on some specific set of facts before he has heard any evidence, much less all of the evidence in its proper context.").

Sandoval v. State, 571 S.W.3d 392 (Tex. App.—Houston [1st Dist.] 2019, no pet.) ("Commitment questions are those that commit a prospective juror to resolve, or to refrain from resolving, an issue a certain way after learning a particular fact.").

Sandoval v. State, 571 S.W.3d 392 (Tex. App.—Houston [1st Dist.] 2019, no pet.) ("[F]or determining whether a voir dire question is an improper commitment question ... [f]irst, the trial court must determine whether a particular question is in fact a commitment question.... Second, if it is a commitment question, then the court must decide whether it is nevertheless a proper commitment question.... To determine whether the question is a proper commitment question, the court first inquires whether one of the possible answers to the question gives rise to a valid challenge for cause.... If it does not, then the question is not proper and should be disallowed by the trial court.... Third, if the commitment question gives rise to a valid challenge for cause, then the court must determine whether the question contains only those facts necessary to test whether a prospective juror is challengeable for cause.").

Evans v. State, 440 S.W.3d 107, 114 (Tex. App.—Waco 2013, pet. ref'd) (a trial court retains discretion to restrict voir dire questions that are confusing, misleading, vague, and broad, or are improper commitment questions).

Evans v. State, 440 S.W.3d 107, 114 (Tex. App.—Waco 2013, pet. ref'd) (a commitment question is one that commits a prospective juror to resolve, or refrain from resolving, an issue a certain way after learning a particular fact).

Evans v. State, 440 S.W.3d 107, 114 (Tex. App.—Waco 2013, pet. ref'd) (a commitment question often requires a "yes" or "no" answer and the answer commits a juror to resolve an issue in a particular way).

Contreras v. State, 2440 S.W.3d 85, 88 (Tex. App.—Waco 2012, pet. dism'd, untimely filed) (an otherwise proper question is impermissible if the question attempts to commit the juror to a particular verdict based on particular facts).

Hailey v. State, 413 S.W.3d 457, 492 (Tex. App.—Fort Worth 2012, pet. ref'd) (commitment questions "commit a prospective juror to resolve, or to refrain from resolving, an issue a certain way after learning a particular fact").

Hailey v. State, 413 S.W.3d 457, 492 (Tex. App.—Fort Worth 2012, pet. ref'd) ("[A]lthough commitment questions are generally phrased to elicit a 'yes' or 'no' answer, an open-ended question can be a commitment question if the question asks the prospective juror to set the hypothetical parameters for his decision-making.").

K.J. v. USA Water Polo, Inc., 383 S.W.3d 593, 601 (Tex. App.—Houston [14th Dist.] 2012, pet. denied) ("commitment question" has been defined as "one that commits a prospective juror to resolve, or refrain from resolving, an issue a certain way after learning a particular fact").

K.J. v. USA Water Polo, Inc., 383 S.W.3d 593, 601 (Tex. App.—Houston [14th Dist.] 2012, pet. denied) (questions that are not intended to discover bias against the law or prejudice for or against the defendant, but rather seek only to determine how jurors would respond to the anticipated evidence and commit them to a specific verdict based on that evidence are not proper).

K.J. v. USA Water Polo, Inc., 383 S.W.3d 593, 601 (Tex. App.—Houston [14th Dist.] 2012, pet. denied) (it is improper to ask jurors what their verdict would be if certain facts were proved).

Rodriguez-Flores v. State, 351 S.W.3d 612, 622 (Tex. App.—Austin 2011, pet. ref'd) (court determines whether a question propounded to venire panelists is a proper commitment question using a three-part inquiry: (1) "the court must decide whether the propounded question is a commitment question—that is, whether it asks a prospective juror to resolve or to refrain from resolving an issue a certain way after learning a particular fact"; (2) the court must decide "whether the question includes facts that lead to a valid challenge for cause"; and (3) the court must "determine whether a potentially proper question includes only those facts that lead to a valid challenge for cause").

Kennedy v. State, 255 S.W.3d 684, 688 (Tex. App.—Eastland 2008, no pet.) ("[C]ommitment questions are those that commit a prospective juror to resolve, or to refrain from resolving, an issue a certain way after learning a particular fact.").

Duffey v. State, 249 S.W.3d 507, 512 (Tex. App.—Waco 2007, pet. ref'd) ("[C]ommitment question is proper if one of the possible answers to that question gives rise to a valid challenge for cause.").

Duffey v. State, 249 S.W.3d 507, 512 (Tex. App.—Waco 2007, pet. ref'd) ("[F]or a commitment question to be proper, one of the possible answers to the question must give rise to a valid challenge for cause.").

In re Commitment of Barbee, 192 S.W.3d 835, 846 (Tex. App.—Beaumont 2006, no pet.) ("[W]hen trial court determines that proffered question's substance is confusing, or seeks to elicit pre-commitment from jury, counsel should propose different question or specific area of inquiry to preserve error on desired line of inquiry; absent such effort, trial court is not required to formulate question.").

Lassiter v. Bouche, 41 S.W.2d 88, 90 (Tex. Civ. App.—Dallas 1931, writ ref'd) (trial court properly sustained objections to voir dire questions designed to commit jurors to weight they would give to certain evidence).

Campbell v. Campbell, 215 S.W. 134, 137 (Tex. Civ. App.—Dallas 1919, writ ref'd) (voir dire question that elicits juror's views on certain facts, thereby committing juror to certain views or conclusions, is improper).

e. References to "Lawsuit Crisis"

Babcock v. Nw. Mem'l Hosp., 767 S.W.2d 705, 707 (Tex. 1989) (trial court committed reversible error refusing to allow voir dire questions concerning alleged "liability insurance crisis" and "lawsuit crisis").

f. Other Statutory Limitations on Voir Dire

Tex. Civ. Prac. & Rem. Code § 33.013(d) (jury not to be made aware through voir dire or any other means that certain conduct enumerated in statute governing contribution among codefendants is defined in Texas Penal Code).

Tex. Civ. Prac. & Rem. Code § 41.008(e) (provisions of statute limiting recovery of exemplary damages may not be made known to jury by any means, including voir dire).

4. Opposing Authorities

Jacobs v. State, 560 S.W.3d 205, 210 (Tex. Crim. App. 2018) ("[i]n capital-punishment cases, the Constitution requires more than 'general fairness and follow the law questions' for the purpose of exposing those in the venire who automatically would vote for the death penalty.").

Hyundai Motor Co. v. Vasquez, 189 S.W.3d 743, 756 (Tex. 2006) ("[J]urors should not base their verdicts on matters that are irrelevant, inadmissible, or unfairly prejudicial, and counsel is entitled to frame voir dire inquiries that ensure that the seated jury will not do so.").

Babcock v. Nw. Mem'l Hosp., 767 S.W.2d 705, 707 (Tex. 1989) (although voir dire is "largely within the sound discretion of the trial judge," trial court "abuses discretion when denial of right to ask proper question prevents determination of whether grounds exist to challenge for cause or denies intelligent use of peremptory challenges").

Martin v. State, 200 S.W.3d 635, 640 (Tex. Crim. App. 2006) ("Both the State and the defense may voir dire the jury concerning the range of punishment for both a felony and misdemeanor DWI.").

Collier v. State, 959 S.W.2d 621, 623 (Tex. Crim. App. 1997) ("[A] question is proper if seeks to discover a venireperson's views on an issue applicable to the case.").

Linnell v. State, 935 S.W.2d 426, 428 (Tex. Crim. App. 1996) ("[T]he permissible areas of questioning the venire in order to exercise peremptory challenges are broad and cannot be unnecessarily limited.").

Palacio v. State, 580 S.W.3d 447, 450 (Tex. App.—Houston [14th Dist.] 2019, pet. ref'd) ("The trial court abuses its discretion when it permits an improper [voir dire] question to be asked.").

Hill v. State, 426 S.W.3d 868, 875 (Tex. App.—Eastland 2014, no pet.) ("[A] juror must be able to consider the full range of punishment for an offense, and a defendant's voir dire question about a juror's ability to do so is generally proper.").

Barnett v. State, 420 S.W.3d 188, 191 (Tex. App.—Amarillo 2013, no pet.) ("[T]he voir dire process is designed to ensure, as much as possible, that an intelligent, alert, disinterested, impartial, and truthful jury will perform the duty assigned to it.").

Evans v. State, 440 S.W.3d 107, 114 (Tex. App.—Waco 2013, pet. ref'd) (not all commitment questions are improper; where the law requires a certain type of commitment from jurors, such as considering the full range of punishment, an attorney may ask prospective jurors to commit to following the law in that regard; also, for a commitment question to be proper, one of the possible answers to that question must give rise to a valid challenge for cause).

Santiesteban-Pileta v. State, 421 S.W.3d 9, 16 (Tex. App.—Waco 2013, pet. ref'd) (voir dire question "is proper if it seeks to discover a juror's views on an issue applicable to the case").

Hailey v. State, 413 S.W.3d 457, 492 (Tex. App.—Fort Worth 2012, pet. ref'd) ("It is permissible to use fact-specific hypotheticals to explain the application of the law.").

Thompson v. State, 267 S.W.3d 514, 517 (Tex. App.—Austin 2008, pet. ref'd) ("[I]n order to allow counsel to effectively assist the defendant and to help ensure an impartial jury by intelligently exercising challenges to the jury panelists, the permissible areas of questioning the venire in order to exercise peremptory challenges are broad and cannot be unnecessarily limited.").

Urista v. Bed, Bath & Beyond, Inc., 245 S.W.3d 591, 596 (Tex. App.—Houston [1st Dist.] 2007, no pet.) ("[V]oir dire examination allows parties to expose possible improper juror biases that form the basis for disqualification and enables parties to intelligently exercise their peremptory strikes.").

Braxton v. State, 226 S.W.3d 602, 603 (Tex. App.—Houston [1st Dist.] 2007, pet. dism'd) ("[T]o determine whether a voir dire question is a proper commitment question, the trial court first inquires whether one of the possible answers to the question gives rise to a valid challenge for cause.... If does not, then the question is not proper and should be disallowed by the trial court.... If the commitment question gives rise to a valid challenge for cause, then the trial court must determine whether the question contains only those facts necessary to test whether a prospective juror is challengeable for cause.").

Abbott v. State, 196 S.W.3d 334, 341 (Tex. App.—Waco 2006, pet. ref'd) ("[P]art of the constitutional guarantee to the right to an impartial jury includes adequate voir dire to identify unqualified jurors.").

Sw. Elec. Power. Co. v. Martin, 844 S.W.2d 229, 237 (Tex. App.—Texarkana 1992, writ denied) ("Texas courts permit a broad range of inquiries on voir dire.").

Campbell v. Campbell, 215 S.W. 134, 137 (Tex. Civ. App.—Dallas 1919, writ ref'd.) (though trial court is subject to certain limitations, general rule is "utmost freedom on examination on voir dire should be permitted in order to discover any interest, bias, opinion, or other fact tending to disqualify or affect the impartiality of prospective jurors towards or concerning the controversy which they are to determine or the parties thereto, both for the purpose of challenging the juror for cause, and as an aid to the intelligent exercise of the right of peremptory challenge").

> *See also Section 74.053 of the Texas Civil Practice and Remedies Code, which states as follows:*
>
> > Pleadings in a suit based on a health care liability claim shall not specify an amount of money claimed as damages. The defendant may file a special exception to the pleadings on the ground the suit is not within the court's jurisdiction, in which event the plaintiff shall inform the court and defendant in writing of the total dollar amount claimed. *This section does not prevent a party from mentioning the total dollar amount claimed in examining prospective jurors on voir dire or in argument to the court or jury.* (Emphasis added.)

a. Constitutional Considerations

Jacobs v. State, 560 S.W.3d 205, 210 (Tex. Crim. App. 2018) (for voir dire questions to be constitutionally compelled, "it is not enough that such questions might be helpful. Rather, the trial court's failure to ask these questions must render the defendant's trial fundamentally unfair").

Jacobs v. State, 560 S.W.3d 205, 210 (Tex. Crim. App. 2018) ("[T]here may be instances when a judge's limitation on voir dire is so substantial as to warrant labeling the error as constitutional in dimension.").

Babcock v. Nw. Mem'l Hosp., 767 S.W.2d 705, 707 (Tex. 1989) (trial court's refusal to allow questions directed at exposing bias or prejudice during voir dire violates constitutional right to fair and impartial jury).

Hill v. State, 426 S.W.3d 868, 875 (Tex. App.—Eastland 2014, no pet.) ("[T]he 'right to counsel' under the Texas constitution includes the right to pose proper questions during voir dire examination.").

Hill v. State, 426 S.W.3d 868, 875 (Tex. App.—Eastland 2014, no pet.) ("[T]he right to be heard at voir dire is a right to participate in the proceedings in a certain way. The denial of that participation is the constitutional violation, even if it is later determined that the defense was not compromised by that denial.").

Scott v. State, 419 S.W.3d 698, 701 (Tex. App.—Texarkana 2013, no pet.) ("[T]he constitutional guarantee of the right to an impartial jury includes adequate voir dire to identify unqualified jurors.").

b. Court's Discretion

Murff v. Pass, 249 S.W.3d 407, 411 (Tex. 2008) ("because trial judges are present in the courtroom and are in the best position to evaluate the sincerity and attitude of individual panel members, they are given wide latitude in both conducting voir dire proceedings ... and in determining whether a panel member is impermissibly partial"; therefore, an appellate court must consider the entire examination in reviewing whether a trial court abused its discretion in deciding that a juror was or was not disqualified).

Hyundai Motor Co. v. Vasquez, 189 S.W.3d 743, 747 (Tex. 2006) (it is proper for a trial court to exclude a voir dire question that previews relevant evidence and inquires of prospective jurors whether such evidence is outcome determinative).

Cortez v. HCCI-San Antonio, Inc., 159 S.W.3d 87, 92 (Tex. 2005) (voir dire examination is largely within the sound discretion of the trial judge).

Collier v. State, 959 S.W.2d 621, 623 (Tex. Crim. App. 1997) (trial judge has wide discretion in controlling voir dire examination).

In re Commitment of Smith, 422 S.W.3d 802, 807 (Tex. App.—Beaumont 2014, pet. denied) ("[A] court abuses its discretion when its denial of the right to ask a proper question prevents determination of whether grounds exist to challenge for cause or denies intelligent use of peremptory challenges.").

Santiesteban-Pileta v. State, 421 S.W.3d 9, 16 (Tex. App.—Waco 2013, pet. ref'd) ("[A] trial court abuses its discretion when it prohibits a proper question about a proper area of inquiry.").

Smith v. Dean, 232 S.W.3d 181, 189 (Tex. App.—Fort Worth 2007, pet. denied) ("[V]oir dire examination is largely within the sound discretion of the trial court, and broad latitude is allowed for examination.").

Vann v. State, 216 S.W.3d 881, 884 (Tex. App.—Fort Worth 2007, no pet.) ("[T]rial court abuses its discretion during voir dire when it prohibits a proper question on a proper area of inquiry.").

c. References to Insurance

Brentwood Fin. Corp. v. Lamprecht, 736 S.W.2d 836, 841 (Tex. App.—San Antonio 1987, writ ref'd n.r.e.) (mention of insurance during voir dire does not require reversal "unless the error is reasonably calculated to cause and probably did cause the rendition of an improper judgment").

Meyers v. Searcy, 488 S.W.2d 509, 515 (Tex. Civ. App.—San Antonio 1972, no writ) ("[I]njection of insurance into a case is not ground for reversal unless, from a review of the entire record, the appellate court is convinced that the injection of insurance probably caused the rendition of an improper judgment.").

B. Motion to Exclude Improper Argument in Opening Statement

1. Suggested Motion Text

(*Name of Moving Party*) hereby moves this Court for an order prohibiting counsel for (*Name Party*) from mentioning (*Describe Anticipated Improper Matter*) during opening statement. The motion is based upon the ground that (*State Basis for Belief That Improper Comments Will Be Made, e.g., Opposing Counsel Made Several Inappropriate Comments in the Preliminary Statement of His Trial Brief*), which, if allowed at trial, would create a substantial danger of undue prejudice to (*Name of Moving Party*).

2. Motion Summary

This motion is used to prevent counsel from mentioning improper matter in opening statement that would tend to unduly prejudice the moving party. The motion is based upon Texas Rule of Civil Procedure 265, the court's discretionary authority to exclude prejudicial evidence under Texas Rule of Evidence 403, and leading cases. *See Guerrero v. Smith*, 864 S.W.2d 797, 799 (Tex. App.—Houston [14th Dist.] 1993).

> *Note: Facts that might warrant a motion on this issue include past attorney misconduct, comments made by opposing counsel at arbitration, inappropriate material found in a trial brief, etc.*

3. Supporting Authorities

Texas Rule of Civil Procedure 265 states in pertinent part:

> The trial of cases before a jury shall proceed in the following order unless the court should, for good cause stated in the record, otherwise direct:
> The party upon whom rests the burden of proof on the whole case *shall state to the jury briefly the nature of his claim or defense and what said party expects to prove and the relief sought.* Immediately thereafter, *the adverse party may make a similar statement, and intervenors and other parties will be accorded similar rights* in the order determined by the court. (Emphasis added.)

Guillory v. State, 397 S.W.3d 864, 868 (Tex. App.—Houston [14th Dist.] 2013, no pet.) ("[T]he purpose of an opening statement is to allow defense counsel to tell the jury the nature of the defenses relied upon and the facts expected to be proved in their support.").

Guillory v. State, 397 S.W.3d 864, 868 (Tex. App.—Houston [14th Dist.] 2013, no pet.) (opening statement is "used to communicate to the jury the party's theory of the case in order to aid the jury to evaluate and understand the evidence as it is being presented").

Guillory v. State, 397 S.W.3d 864, 868 (Tex. App.—Houston [14th Dist.] 2013, no pet.) ("[The] character and extent of [opening] statement are subject to the control of the trial court.").

Smith v. State, 114 S.W.3d 66, 71 (Tex. App.—Eastland 2003, pet. ref'd) (a prosecutor's comment during opening statement describing the effect of an offense on victims was improper; but the error was cured by the trial judge's instructions to disregard comments).

Hullaby v. State, 911 S.W.2d 921, 927 (Tex. App.—Fort Worth 1995, writ ref'd) (prosecutor's reference to gang evidence improper but was cured by evidence supporting comment eventually introduced and it did not deny defendant a fair trial).

Ruiz v. State, 891 S.W.2d 302, 305 (Tex. App.—San Antonio 1995, pet. ref'd) (a prosecutor's opening statement that a child victim was there to tell the truth was not so prejudicial that defendant denied fair trial; defendant objected to remark, and trial judge told jury that opening statements are not evidence).

Guerrero v. Smith, 864 S.W.2d 797, 799 (Tex. App.—Houston [14th Dist.] 1993) (Rule 265 "does not afford counsel the right to detail to the jury the evidence which he intends to offer, nor to read or display the documents and photographs he proposes to offer. Where counsel is allowed to detail expectations in the opening statement, he places matters before the jury without the determination of their admissibility. This practice misleads and confuses the jurors as between counsel's mere expectations and evidence that is actually admitted.").

a. Other Grounds

Other possible grounds for excluding improper matter in opening statement include:

- Prejudicial;
- Time-wasting;
- Confusing or misleading;
- Solely intended to create an emotional bias;
- Irrelevant.

4. Opposing Authorities

Guillory v. State, 397 S.W.3d 864, 868 (Tex. App.—Houston [14th Dist.] 2013, no pet.) (a criminal defendant has a statutory right to make an opening statement after the State's opening statement).

Lillard v. State, 994 S.W.2d 747, 751 (Tex. App.—Eastland 1999, pet. ref'd) ("To constitute reversible error, the prosecutor's comment in his opening statement has to be so egregious that its prejudicial effect cannot be cured by an instruction to disregard.").

Norton v. State, 930 S.W.2d 101, 103 (Tex. App.—Amarillo 1996, writ ref'd) ("Statements made by counsel generally will not constitute reversible error unless, in light of the record as a whole, the statements are extreme or manifestly improper, violative of a mandatory statute, or inject new facts harmful to the accused into the proceedings.").

Ruiz v. State, 891 S.W.2d 302, 305 (Tex. App.—San Antonio 1995, pet. ref'd) (a prosecutor's opening statement that a child victim was there to tell the truth was not so prejudicial that defendant denied fair trial; defendant objected to remark, and trial judge told jury that opening statements are not evidence).

C. Motion to Exclude Premature Rebuttal of Affirmative Defenses

1. *Suggested Motion Text*

Defendant hereby moves this Court for an order prohibiting plaintiff from presenting any and all evidence, references to evidence or testimony rebutting defendant's affirmative defenses during plaintiff's case-in-chief. The motion is based upon the ground that the moving party is informed and believes that opposing counsel will improperly present evidence out of order based upon [state facts to support claim regarding improper order of evidence, e.g., opposing counsel's similar conduct at arbitration or in prior trials], which would unfairly and prejudicially undermine defendant's case-in-chief.

2. *Motion Summary*

This motion is used to prevent the plaintiff from undermining defendant's evidence by offering rebuttal evidence prior to defendant's case-in-chief. The motion is based upon the statutory provision governing the order of proof at trial [Texas Rule of Civil Procedure 265] and to prevent prejudice and jury confusion [Texas Rule of Evidence 403].

> *Note: Where facts, such as past attorney misconduct, suggest that the motion is warranted, be prepared to include a detailed, fact-based declaration.*

3. *Supporting Authorities*

Texas Rule of Civil Procedure 265 governs the order of proceedings on trial by jury and states in pertinent part:

> The trial of cases before a jury shall proceed in the following order unless the court should, for good cause stated in the record, otherwise direct:

...
(b) The party upon whom rests the burden of proof on the whole case shall then introduce his evidence.
(c) The adverse party shall briefly state the nature of his claim or defense and what said party expects to prove and the relief sought unless he has already done so.
(d) *He shall then introduce his evidence.*
...
(f) The parties shall then be confined to rebutting testimony on each side. (Emphasis added.)

Russell v. State, 904 S.W.2d 191, 194 (Tex. App.—Amarillo 1995, writ ref'd) ("[T]he defense of entrapment is not available to a defendant who denies that he committed the offense charged.... The defense is not available in such instances because entrapment necessarily assumes the act charged was committed".).

Hemsell v. Summers, 153 S.W.2d 305, .309 (Tex. Civ. App.—Amarillo 1941, no writ) ("It is well established in this and most other jurisdictions in this country that the proper order in which evidence should be introduced is for the plaintiff, movant or relator first to introduce all of the evidence which he expects to adduce in support of the allegations of his petition or motion. This should be done before the defendant or respondent begins the introduction of his testimony. After the defendant, or respondent, has offered such testimony as he desires to offer in support of his defense, the plaintiff or moving party is permitted to introduce evidence of a rebutting nature only.").

Other possible grounds supporting this motion include:

- Time-wasting (Sections 2:7 to 2:10);
- Confusing or misleading (Sections 2:11 to 2:14);
- Solely intended to create an emotional bias (Sections 2:15 to 2:21);
- Cumulative (Sections 2:22 to 2:46);
- Improper impeachment evidence (Sections 7:1 to 7:3).

4. Opposing Authorities

Dabney v. State, 492 S.W.3d 309, 317 (Tex. Crim. App. 2016) ("Because Appellant presented his defensive theory in opening statements, the State could use extraneous-offense evidence to rebut this theory in its case-in-chief rather than waiting until the defense rested.").

Baker v. Sturgeon, 361 S.W.2d 610, 614 (Tex. Civ. App.—Texarkana 1962, no writ) (trial court has discretion to control order of trial and did not abuse discretion allowing plaintiff to present evidence in rebuttal that could have been presented in case-in-chief).

Travelers Ins. Co. v. Hurst, 358 S.W.2d 883, 886 (Tex. Civ. App.—Texarkana 1962, writ ref'd n.r.e.) (trial court had discretion to allow party to present rebuttal testimony out of order).

Hemsell v. Summers, 153 S.W.2d 305, 309 (Tex. Civ. App.—Amarillo 1941, no writ) (due to circumstances of case, trial judge had discretion to vary rules regarding order of presentation).

Plunkett v. Simmons, 63 S.W.2d 313, 315 (Tex. Civ. App.—Waco 1933, writ dism'd) (trial court had discretion to require interveners to present evidence before defendants).

Cameron Compress Co. v. Jacobs, 10 S.W.2d 1040, 1042 (Tex. Civ. App.—Austin 1928, writ refused) (trial court had discretion to allow plaintiff to prove defendant's negligence during rebuttal).

D. Motion to Exclude Reference to Lost or Destroyed Evidence

1. Suggested Motion Text

(*Name of Moving Party*) hereby moves this Court for an order excluding any and all evidence, references to evidence, testimony, or argument relating to (*Describe Lost or Destroyed Evidence*). The motion is based upon the ground that (*State Basis for Belief That Evidence Was Lost or Destroyed*), and therefore, if allowed to be introduced, (*Name of Moving Party*) will be unfairly prejudiced and surprised at trial.

2. Motion Summary

This motion is used to restrict a party from unfairly utilizing or referring to evidence that was willfully or negligently lost, destroyed, or tampered with. The motion is based upon the authority of Texas Rule of Civil Procedure 215.2, Texas Rule of Evidence 403, and leading cases supporting exclusion and/or a presumption that the evidence would be unfavorable to the nonproducing party. *See Tex. Elec. Co-op. v. Dillard*, 171 S.W.3d 201, 209 (Tex. App.—Tyler 2005, no pet.); *Grossnickle v. Grossnickle*, 935 S.W.2d 830, 840 (Tex. App.—Texarkana 1996, writ denied).

3. Supporting Authorities

Texas Rule of Civil Procedure 215.2 states in pertinent part:

> If a party or an officer, director, or managing agent of a party or a person designated under Rules 199.2(b)(1) or 200.1(b) to testify on behalf of a party fails to comply with proper discovery requests or to obey an order to provide or permit discovery, including an order made under Rules 204 or 215.1, the court in which the action is pending may, after notice and hearing, make such orders in regard to the failure as are just, and among others the following:
>
> . . .
>
> (3) an order that the matters regarding which the order was made or any other designated facts shall be taken to be established for the purposes of the action in accordance with the claim of the party obtaining the order;
>
> (4) an order refusing to allow the disobedient party to support or oppose designated claims or defenses, or prohibiting him from introducing designated matters in evidence;

(5) an order striking out pleadings or parts thereof, or staying further proceedings until the order is obeyed, or dismissing with or without prejudice the action or proceedings or any part thereof, or rendering a judgment by default against the disobedient party.

Texas Rule of Evidence 1004 states in pertinent part:

The original is not required, and other evidence of the contents of a writing, recording, or photograph is admissible if:

(a) **Originals Lost or Destroyed**. All originals are lost or have been destroyed, *unless the proponent lost or destroyed them in bad faith*;

(b) **Original Not Obtainable**. No original can be obtained by any available judicial process or procedure;

(c) **Original Outside the State**. No original is located in Texas;

(d) **Original in Possession of Opponent**. At a time when an original was under the control of the party against whom offered, that party was put on notice, by the pleadings or otherwise, that the content would be a subject of proof at the hearing, and that party does not produce the original at the hearing; or

(e) **Collateral Matters**. The writing, recording or photograph is not closely related to a controlling issue. (Emphasis added.)

Grossnickle v. Grossnickle, 935 S.W.2d 830, 840 (Tex. App.—Texarkana 1996, writ denied) (trial court must exclude evidence where party fails to identify evidence in response to discovery request).

a. Accidental Destruction of Evidence

Petroleum Solutions, Inc. v. Head, 454 S.W.3d 482, 488 (Tex. 2014); *Brookshire Bros. v. Aldridge,* 438 S.W.3d 9, 22 (Tex. 2014) (to conclude that a party spoliated evidence, the court must find that (1) the spoliating party had a duty to reasonably preserve evidence, and (2) the party intentionally or negligently breached that duty by failing to do so).

Petroleum Solutions, Inc. v. Head, 454 S.W.3d 482, 488 (Tex. 2014); *Brookshire Bros. v. Aldridge,* 438 S.W.3d 9, 22 (Tex. 2014) (upon a finding of spoliation, the trial court has broad discretion to impose a remedy that, as with any discovery sanction, must be proportionate; that is, it must relate directly to the conduct giving rise to the sanction and may not be excessive; key considerations in imposing a remedy are the level of culpability of the spoliating party and the degree of prejudice, if any, suffered by the nonspoliating party).

Petroleum Solutions, Inc. v. Head, 454 S.W.3d 482, 488 (Tex. 2014); *Brookshire Bros. v. Aldridge*, 438 S.W.3d 9, 22 (Tex. 2014) (in considering the prejudice suffered as a result of spoliation, the court is to consider the relevance of the spoliated evidence to key issues in the case, the harmful effect of the evidence on the spoliating party's case (or, conversely, whether the evidence would have been helpful to the nonspoliating party's case), and whether the spoliated evidence was cumulative of other competent evidence that may be used instead of the spoliated evidence).

Brookshire Bros. v. Aldridge, 438 S.W.3d 9, 22 (Tex. 2014) ("[T]he remedial purpose undergirding the imposition of a spoliation remedy under Texas law is to restore the parties to a rough approximation of their positions if all evidence were available.").

Brookshire Bros. v. Aldridge, 438 S.W.3d 9, 22 (Tex. 2014) ("[A] spoliation analysis involves a two-step judicial process: (1) the trial court must determine, as a question of law, whether a party spoliated evidence, and (2) if spoliation occurred, the court must assess an appropriate remedy.").

Brookshire Bros. v. Aldridge, 438 S.W.3d 9, 22 (Tex. 2014) ("[S]pectrum of remedies that may be imposed for spoliation range from an award of attorney's fees to the dismissal of the lawsuit.").

Brookshire Bros. v. Aldridge, 438 S.W.3d 9, 22 (Tex. 2014) ("[C]ourts have broad discretion to utilize a variety of remedies to address spoliation, including the spoliation instruction.").

Brookshire Bros. v. Aldridge, 438 S.W.3d 9, 22 (Tex. 2014) ("[W]hen evidence is lost, altered, or destroyed, trial courts have the discretion to impose an appropriate remedy so that the parties are restored to a rough approximation of what their positions would have been were the evidence available.").

Brookshire Bros. v. Aldridge, 438 S.W.3d 9, 22 (Tex. 2014) (sanctions enumerated under Rule 215.2 are available for spoliation of evidence, as well as other remedies such as the spoliation instruction).

Brookshire Bros. v. Aldridge, 438 S.W.3d 9, 22 (Tex. 2014) ("[A] party's intentional destruction of evidence may, absent evidence to the contrary, be sufficient by itself to support a finding that the spoliated evidence is both relevant and harmful to the spoliating party.").

Brookshire Bros. v. Aldridge, 438 S.W.3d 9, 25 (Tex. 2014) ("[S]poliation instruction may be proper if the act of spoliation, although merely negligent, so prejudices the nonspoliating party that it is irreparably deprived of having any meaningful ability to present a claim or defense.").

Tony Gullo Motors I, L.P. v. Chapa, 212 S.W.3d 299, 306 (Tex. 2006) ("[S]poliation of evidence normally supports an inference only that the evidence was unfavorable, not that it was created *ab initio* with fraudulent intent.").

In re Xterra Construction, LLC, 582 S.W.3d 652, 662 (Tex. App.—Waco 2019, orig. proceeding [mand. dism'd]) ("[T]o find that spoliation occurred, the trial court must make affirmative determinations as to two elements. First, the party who failed to produce evidence must have had a duty to preserve the evidence.... Such a duty arises only when a party knows or reasonably should know that there is a substantial chance that a claim will be filed and that evidence in its possession or control will be material and relevant to that claim.... Second, the nonproducing party must have breached its duty to reasonably preserve material and relevant evidence.... A party cannot breach its duty to preserve without at least acting negligently.").

Knoderer v. State Farm Lloyds, 515 S.W.3d 21, 40 (Tex. App.—Texarkana 2017, pet. denied) ("One of the principle [sic] reasons spoliation evidence should be not be admitted is 'the tendency of such evidence to skew the focus of the trial from the merits to the conduct of the spoliating party thereby raising a significant risk of both prejudice and confusion of the issues.'").

Miner Dederick Constr., LLP v. Gulf Chemical & Metallurgical Corp., 403 S.W.3d 451, 465 (Tex. App.—Houston [1st Dist.] 2013), pet. denied per curiam, 455 S.W.3d 164 (Tex. 2015) ("[The] inquiry regarding whether a spoliation sanction or presumption is justified requires a court to consider (1) whether there was a duty to preserve evidence, (2) whether the alleged spoliator breached that duty, and (3) whether the spoliation prejudiced the non-spoliator's ability to present its case or defense.").

Miner Dederick Constr., LLP v. Gulf Chemical & Metallurgical Corp., 403 S.W.3d 451, 465 (Tex. App.—Houston [1st Dist.] 2013), pet. denied per curiam, 455 S.W.3d 164 (Tex. 2015) ("[A] party knows or reasonably should know that there is a substantial chance a claim will be filed if a reasonable person would conclude from the severity of the incident, and other circumstances surrounding it, that there was a substantial chance for litigation at the time of the alleged spoliation.").

Miner Dederick Constr., LLP v. Gulf Chemical & Metallurgical Corp., 403 S.W.3d 451, 465 (Tex. App.—Houston [1st Dist.] 2013), pet. denied per curiam, 455 S.W.3d 164 (Tex. 2015) ("[A] party should not be able to subvert the discovery process and the fair administration of justice simply by destroying evidence before a claim is actually filed.").

Miner Dederick Constr., LLP v. Gulf Chemical & Metallurgical Corp., 403 S.W.3d 451, 465 (Tex. App.—Houston [1st Dist.] 2013), pet. denied per curiam, 455 S.W.3d 164 (Tex. 2015) ("[T]o show that the evidence is relevant and material, a party must demonstrate that the alleged spoliator knew or should have reasonably known that the evidence would be relevant to the action.").

Miner Dederick Constr., LLP v. Gulf Chemical & Metallurgical Corp., 403 S.W.3d 451, 465 (Tex. App.—Houston [1st Dist.] 2013), pet. denied per curiam, 455 S.W.3d 164 (Tex. 2015) ("[A]lthough it need not take extraordinary measures to preserve evidence, a party has a duty to exercise reasonable care in preserving potentially relevant evidence.").

Miner Dederick Constr., LLP v. Gulf Chemical & Metallurgical Corp., 403 S.W.3d 451, 465 (Tex. App.—Houston [1st Dist.] 2013), pet. denied per curiam, 455 S.W.3d 164 (Tex. 2015) ("[A] claim that the evidence was destroyed in the ordinary course of business will not excuse the obligation to preserve when a party's duty to preserve evidence arises before the destruction.").

Miner Dederick Constr., LLP v. Gulf Chemical & Metallurgical Corp., 403 S.W.3d 451, 465 (Tex. App.—Houston [1st Dist.] 2013), pet. denied per curiam, 455 S.W.3d 164 (Tex. 2015) ("[I]mplicit in the duty to exercise reasonable care in preserving evidence is the duty to refrain from altering or changing the evidence's condition or integrity.").

Miner Dederick Constr., LLP v. Gulf Chemical & Metallurgical Corp., 403 S.W.3d 451, 465 (Tex. App.—Houston [1st Dist.] 2013), pet. denied per curiam, 455 S.W.3d 164 (Tex. 2015) (in determining whether spoliation of evidence affected a party's ability to present his claim or defense, the court "look[s] to a variety of circumstances such as (1) the relevancy of the missing evidence and (2) the availability of other evidence to take the place of the missing information").

Tex. Elec. Co-op. v. Dillard, 171 S.W.3d 201, 208 (Tex. App.—Tyler 2005, no pet.) ("A spoliation instruction is an instruction given to the jury outlining permissible inferences they may make against a party who has lost, altered, or destroyed evidence.").

Fuller v. Preston State Bank, 667 S.W.2d 214, 220 (Tex. App.—Dallas 1983, writ ref'd n.r.e.) ("A party is entitled to show that the opposing party has destroyed documents that would bear on a crucial issue in the case, since the destruction of relevant evidence raises a presumption that the evidence would have been unfavorable to the spoliator.").

b. *Intentional Destruction or Suppression of Evidence*

Texas Rule of Evidence 1004 states in pertinent part:

> The original is not required, and other evidence of the contents of a writing, recording, or photograph is admissible if:
>
> (a) **Originals Lost or Destroyed**. All originals are lost or have been destroyed, *unless the proponent lost or destroyed them in bad faith*[.] (Emphasis added.)

Petroleum Solutions, Inc. v. Head, 454 S.W.3d 482, 488 (Tex. 2014); *Brookshire Bros. v. Aldridge,* 438 S.W.3d 9, 22 (Tex. 2014) (to conclude that a party spoliated evidence, the court must find that (1) the spoliating party had a duty to reasonably preserve evidence, and (2) the party intentionally or negligently breached that duty by failing to do so).

Brookshire Bros. v. Aldridge, 438 S.W.3d 9, 22 (Tex. 2014) (generally, a party must intentionally spoliate evidence in order for a spoliation instruction to constitute an appropriate remedy).

Brookshire Bros. v. Aldridge, 438 S.W.3d 9, 22 (Tex. 2014) ("[I]ntentional spoliation, often referenced as 'bad faith' or 'willful' spoliation, means that the party acted with the subjective purpose of concealing or destroying discoverable evidence. This includes the concept of 'willful blindness,' which encompasses the scenario in which a party does not directly destroy evidence known to be relevant and discoverable, but nonetheless allows for its destruction.").

Brookshire Bros. v. Aldridge, 438 S.W.3d 9, 22 (Tex. 2014) (when evidence is lost, altered, or destroyed, trial courts have the "discretion to impose an appropriate remedy so that the parties are restored to a rough approximation of what their positions would have been were the evidence available").

Brookshire Bros. v. Aldridge, 438 S.W.3d 9, 22 (Tex. 2014) (sanctions enumerated under Rule 215.2 are available for spoliation of evidence, as well as other remedies such as the spoliation instruction).

Wal-Mart Stores, Inc. v. Johnson, 106 S.W.3d 718, 722 (Tex. 2003) (spoliation of evidence "presumption arises when the party controlling the missing evidence cannot explain its failure to produce it").

Matlock Place Apartments, L.P. v. Druce, 369 S.W.3d 355, 380 (Tex. App.—Fort Worth 2012, pet. denied) ("[A] trial court may be guided by the following three factors in determining whether a spoliation presumption is justified: (1) whether there was a duty to preserve evidence, (2) whether the alleged spoliator either negligently or intentionally spoliated evidence, and (3) whether the spoliation prejudiced the nonspoliator's ability to present its case or defense.").

Ham v. Equity Residential Prop. Mgmt. Servs. Corp., 315 S.W.3d 627, 631 (Tex. App.—Dallas 2010, pet. denied) ("[S]poliation is the deliberate destruction of, failure to produce, or failure to explain the nonproduction of relevant evidence, which, if proved, may give rise to a presumption that the missing evidence would be unfavorable to the spoliator.").

Ham v. Equity Residential Prop. Mgmt. Servs. Corp., 315 S.W.3d 627, 631 (Tex. App.—Dallas 2010, pet. denied); *Clark v. Randalls Foods, Inc.*, 317 S.W.3d 351, 356 (Tex. App.—Houston [1st Dist.] 2010, pet. denied) (in analyzing denial of a spoliation presumption motion, appellate court considers: (1) whether there was a duty to preserve evidence; (2) whether the alleged spoliator breached that duty; and whether the spoliation prejudiced the non-spoliator's ability to present its case).

Buckeye Retirement Co., LLC, Ltd. v. Bank of Am., N.A., 239 S.W.3d 394, 401 (Tex. App.—Dallas 2007, no pet.) ("[I]ntentional destruction or spoliation of evidence relevant to a case may, in the trial court's discretion, give rise to a presumption that the destroyed evidence would not have been favorable to its destroyer.... The presumption may be rebutted by a showing that the evidence in question was not destroyed with a fraudulent purpose or intent.").

Tex. Elec. Co-op v. Dillard, 171 S.W.3d 201, 208 (Tex. App.—Tyler 2005, no pet.) ("[P]arty who has deliberately destroyed evidence is presumed to have done so because evidence was unfavorable to its case.").

Fuller v. Preston State Bank, 667 S.W.2d 214, 220 (Tex. App.—Dallas 1983, writ ref'd n.r.e.) ("A party is entitled to show that the opposing party has destroyed documents that would bear on a crucial issue in the case, since the destruction of relevant evidence raises a presumption that the evidence would have been unfavorable to the spoliator.").

c. Negative Presumption

Ham v. Equity Residential Prop. Mgmt. Servs. Corp., 315 S.W.3d 627, 631 (Tex. App.—Dallas 2010, pet. denied) (spoliation "may give rise to a presumption that the missing evidence would be unfavorable to the spoliator").

Tex. Elec. Co-op. v. Dillard, 171 S.W.3d 201, 208 (Tex. App.—Tyler 2005, no pet.) (trial court did not abuse discretion instructing jury it could presume destroyed evidence would be unfavorable to party who destroyed it).

Fuller v. Preston State Bank, 667 S.W.2d 214, 220 (Tex. App.—Dallas 1983, writ ref'd n.r.e.) ("A party is entitled to show that the opposing party has destroyed documents that would bear on a crucial issue in the case, since the destruction of relevant evidence raises a presumption that the evidence would have been unfavorable to the spoliator.").

H.E. Butt Grocery Co. v. Bruner, 530 S.W.2d 340, 344 (Tex. Civ. App. 1975, writ dism'd by agr.) (intentional destruction of evidence leads to presumption destroyed evidence would have been unfavorable to party who destroyed it).

d. Other Grounds

Other possible grounds for excluding references to lost or destroyed evidence may include:

- Time-wasting;
- Confusing or misleading;
- Solely intended to create an emotional bias;
- Cumulative;
- Irrelevant;
- Improper foundation;
- Discovery sanctions.

4. Opposing Authorities

Texas Rule of Evidence 1004 states in pertinent part:

> The original is not required, and other evidence of the contents of a writing, recording, or photograph is admissible if:
>
> (a) **Originals Lost or Destroyed**. All originals are lost or have been destroyed, unless the proponent lost or destroyed them in bad faith;
>
> (b) **Original Not Obtainable**. No original can be obtained by any available judicial process or procedure;
>
> (c) **Original Outside the State**. No original is located in Texas;
>
> (d) **Original in Possession of Opponent**. At a time when an original was under the control of the party against whom offered, that party was put on notice, by the pleadings or otherwise, that the content would be a subject of proof at the hearing, and that party does not produce the original at the hearing; or
>
> (e) **Collateral Matters**. The writing, recording or photograph is not closely related to a controlling issue.

Petroleum Solutions, Inc. v. Head, 454 S.W.3d 482, 488 (Tex. 2014); *Brookshire Bros. v. Aldridge*, 438 S.W.3d 9, 20 (Tex. 2014) (a duty to preserve evidence arises only when a party knows or reasonably should know that there is a substantial chance that a claim will be filed and that evidence in its possession or control will be material and relevant to that claim; a "substantial chance of litigation" arises when litigation is more than merely an abstract possibility or unwarranted fear).

Brookshire Bros. v. Aldridge, 438 S.W.3d 9, 22 (Tex. 2014) ("[H]arsh remedy of a spoliation instruction is warranted only when the trial court finds that the spoliating party acted with the specific intent of concealing discoverable evidence, and that a less severe remedy would be insufficient to reduce the prejudice caused by the spoliation.").

Brookshire Bros. v. Aldridge, 438 S.W.3d 9, 14 (Tex. 2014) ("[A] failure to preserve evidence with a negligent mental state may only underlie a spoliation instruction in the rare situation in which a nonspoliating party has been irreparably deprived of any meaningful ability to present a claim or defense.").

Brookshire Bros. v. Aldridge, 438 S.W.3d 9, 17 (Tex. 2014) (spoliation instruction "is an important remedy, but its use can affect the fundamental fairness of the trial in ways as troubling as the spoliating conduct itself").

Brookshire Bros. v. Aldridge, 438 S.W.3d 9, 20 (Tex. 2014) ("[A] party alleging spoliation bears the burden of establishing that the nonproducing party had a duty to preserve the evidence.... The standard governing the duty to preserve resolves two related inquiries: when the duty is triggered and the scope of that duty.").

Brookshire Bros. v. Aldridge, 438 S.W.3d 9, 22 (Tex. 2014) ("negligent spoliation could not enough to support a finding [that the spoliated evidence was relevant and harmful to the spoliating party] without some proof about what the destroyed evidence would show").

Brookshire Bros. v. Aldridge, 438 S.W.3d 9, 22 (Tex. 2014) (spoliation instruction is among the "harshest sanctions a trial court may utilize to remedy an act of spoliation" and can be "tantamount to a death penalty sanction").

Brookshire Bros. v. Aldridge, 438 S.W.3d 9, 22 (Tex. 2014) ("evidence considered by the trial court in making [spoliation] findings often has no bearing on the facts that are of consequence to the determination of the action from the jury's perspective" and thus should not be admitted into evidence before the jury).

Wal-Mart Stores, Inc. v. Johnson, 106 S.W.3d 718, 722 (Tex. 2003) (trial court abused discretion giving spoliation instruction where party did not know or have reason to know evidence would be relevant and no negative presumption arose from party destroying it).

Miner Dederick Constr., LLP v. Gulf Chemical & Metallurgical Corp., 403 S.W.3d 451, 465 (Tex. App.—Houston [1st Dist.] 2013), pet. denied per curiam, 455 S.W.3d 164 (Tex. 2015) ("[The] duty to preserve evidence is not raised unless: (1) a party knows or reasonably should know that there is a substantial chance a claim will be filed, and (2) evidence is relevant and material.").

Miner Dederick Constr., LLP v. Gulf Chemical & Metallurgical Corp., 403 S.W.3d 451, 465 (Tex. App.—Houston [1st Dist.] 2013), pet. denied per curiam, 455 S.W.3d 164 (Tex. 2015) ("[A] spoliator can defend against an assertion of negligent or intentional destruction by providing explanations to justify its failure to preserve evidence.").

Walker v. Thomasson Lumber Co., 203 S.W.3d 470, 477 (Tex. App.—Houston [14th Dist.] 2006, no pet.) ("[T]o raise the spoliation issue, the party seeking the presumption that the missing evidence would be unfavorable to the spoliator bears the burden of establishing that the alleged spoliator had a duty to preserve the evidence in question.").

Martinez v. Abbott Labs. & Abbott Labs., Inc., 146 S.W.3d 260, 270 (Tex. App.—Fort Worth 2004, pet. denied) (party did not know or have reason to know evidence would be relevant and no negative presumption arose from party destroying it).

Lively v. Blackwell, 51 S.W.3d 637, 643 (Tex. App.—Tyler 2001, pet. denied) (where no evidence that a party had either intentionally or negligently destroyed evidence, the other party was not entitled to a presumption that the evidence at issue would have been unfavorable to the party who had had control over it).

Doe v. Mobile Video Tapes, Inc., 43 S.W.3d 40, 56 (Tex. App.—Corpus Christi 2001, no pet.) (evidence destroyed in the regular course of business, rather than in an intentional or negligent fashion, did not give rise to the presumption that the evidence would have been unfavorable to party who destroyed it and did not mandate its exclusion).

Brewer v. Dowling, 862 S.W.2d 156, 159 (Tex. App.—Fort Worth 1993, writ denied) (failure to produce evidence lost rather than intentionally or accidentally destroyed did not give rise to presumption evidence would have been unfavorable to party who did not produce it).

E. Motion to Exclude Arbitration Evidence and Findings

1. Suggested Motion Text

(*Name of Moving Party*) hereby moves this Court for an order excluding any and all evidence, references to evidence, testimony, or argument relating to the findings, award, evidence or any other matter arising from a prior arbitration in this matter (*or Describe Specific Arbitration and Date*). The motion is based upon the grounds that any such evidence is explicitly barred by Texas Statutes Annotated, Title 7, Section 154.073.

2. Motion Summary

This motion is used to exclude any evidence, findings or awards arising from a prior arbitration in the subject case. The motion is based upon the express authority of Texas Statutes Annotated, Title 7, Section 154.073.

3. Supporting Authorities

Tex. Civ. Prac. & Rem. Code Section 154.073, states:

> (a) Except as provided by Subsections (c), (d), (e), and (f), *a communication relating to the subject matter of any civil or criminal dispute made by a participant in an alternative dispute resolution procedure, whether before or after the institution of formal judicial proceedings, is confidential, is not subject to disclosure, and may not be used as evidence against the participant in any judicial or administrative proceeding.*

(b) *Any record made at an alternative dispute resolution procedure is confidential, and the participants or the third party facilitating the procedure may not be required to testify in any proceedings relating to or arising out of the matter in dispute or be subject to process requiring disclosure of confidential information or data relating to or arising out of the matter in dispute.*

(c) An oral communication or written material used in or made a part of an alternative dispute resolution procedure is admissible or discoverable if it is admissible or discoverable independent of the procedure.

(d) A final written agreement to which a governmental body, as defined by Section 552.003, Government Code, is a signatory that is reached as a result of a dispute resolution procedure conducted under this chapter is subject to or excepted from required disclosure in accordance with Chapter 552, Government Code.

(e) If this section conflicts with other legal requirements for disclosure of communications, records, or materials, the issue of confidentiality may be presented to the court having jurisdiction of the proceedings to determine, in camera, whether the facts, circumstances, and context of the communications or materials sought to be disclosed warrant a protective order of the court or whether the communications or materials are subject to disclosure.

(f) This section does not affect the duty to report abuse or neglect under Subchapter B, Chapter 261, Family Code, and abuse, exploitation, or neglect under Subchapter C, Chapter 48, Human Resources Code.

(g) This section applies to a victim-offender mediation by the Texas Department of Criminal Justice as described in Article 56.13, Code of Criminal Procedure. (Emphasis added.)

a. *Other Grounds*

Other possible grounds for excluding arbitration evidence include:

- Prejudicial;
- Time-wasting;
- Confusing or misleading;
- Cumulative;
- Irrelevant;
- Improper foundation;
- Inadmissible hearsay.

4. *Opposing Authorities*

Tex. Civ. Prac. & Rem. Code Section 154.073, regarding alternative dispute resolutions, states in relevant part, as follows:

(b) Any record made at an alternative dispute resolution procedure is confidential, and the participants or the third party facilitating the procedure *may not be required to testify* in any proceedings relating to or arising out of the matter in dispute or be subject to process requiring disclosure of confidential information or data relating to or arising out of the matter in dispute.

(c) *An oral communication or written material used in or made a part of an alternative dispute resolution procedure is admissible or discoverable if it is admissible or discoverable independent of the procedure.*

...

(e) *If this section conflicts with other legal requirements for disclosure of communications, records, or materials, the issue of confidentiality may be presented to the court having jurisdiction of the proceedings to determine, in camera, whether the facts, circumstances, and context of the communications or materials sought to be disclosed warrant a protective order of the court or whether the communications or materials are subject to disclosure.* (Emphasis added.)

Note: Based upon section (b), above, it would appear that an argument could be made that if the parties agree, the testimony should be allowed. Also, based upon section (e) above, the trial court can order the communications or materials to be disclosed in certain situations.

Knapp v. Wilson N. Jones Mem'l Hosp., 281 S.W.3d 163, 173 (Tex. App.—Dallas 2009, no pet.) ("[S]ection 154.073 does not create a blanket of confidentiality, nor is it so broad as to bar all evidence regarding everything that occurs at arbitration from being presented in the trial court.").

Knapp v. Wilson N. Jones Mem'l Hosp., 281 S.W.3d 163, 173 (Tex. App.—Dallas 2009, no pet.) ("[I]f the communication or written material does not relate to the subject matter of the dispute, or does not relate to or arise out of the matter in dispute, it may not be confidential, under section 154.073.").

Knapp v. Wilson N. Jones Mem'l Hosp., 281 S.W.3d 163, 173 (Tex. App.—Dallas 2009, no pet.) ("Disclosure [regarding arbitration proceedings] may be warranted when a party does not seek discovery of arbitration evidence to obtain additional funds from another party to the arbitration or to establish any liability of the other party after the dispute has been peaceably resolved, but proposes to offer the arbitration evidence in a separate case against a separate party to prove a claim that is factually and legally unrelated to the arbitration claims").

Knapp v. Wilson N. Jones Mem'l Hosp., 281 S.W.3d 163, 173 (Tex. App.—Dallas 2009, no pet.) ("[D]isclosure [regarding arbitration proceedings] may be warranted in a case alleging a new and independent cause of action, if disclosure of the confidential communications or written materials will not disturb the settlement in the underlying arbitration.").

F. Motion to Exclude Evidence of Damages in Bifurcated Trial

1. Suggested Motion Text

(*Name of Moving Party*) hereby moves this Court for an order excluding any and all evidence, references to evidence, testimony, or argument relating to plaintiff's damages during the liability phase of this trial. The motion is based upon the ground that this case has been bifurcated so that liability and damages will be tried separately, and thus any evidence on damages presented during the liability phase is irrelevant and immaterial to the liability issues.

2. Motion Summary

This motion is used to prevent the potential prejudice that may occur where a plaintiff's damages are referenced in the liability phase of a bifurcated trial. The motion is based upon the authority of Texas Rule of Civil Procedure 174 and supporting case law.

Note: This motion presupposes that damages and liability have been bifurcated by prior order. If no bifurcation motion has been made, see Texas Rule of Civil Procedure 174 and Texas Civil Practice and Remedies Code, Section 41.009.

3. Supporting Authorities

Texas Rule of Civil Procedure 174 states in pertinent part:

> (b) Separate Trials. The court in furtherance of convenience or to avoid prejudice may order a separate trial of any claim, cross-claim, counterclaim, or third-party claim, or of any separate issue or of any number of claims, cross-claims, counterclaims, third-party claims, or issues.

Section 41.009 of the Texas Civil Practice and Remedies Code governs bifurcated trials and states:

> (a) On motion by a defendant, the court shall provide for a bifurcated trial under this section. A motion under this subsection shall be made prior to voir dire examination of the jury or at a time specified by a pretrial court order issued under Rule 166, Texas Rules of Civil Procedure.
> (b) In an action with more than one defendant, the court shall provide for a bifurcated trial on motion of any defendant.
> (c) In the first phase of a bifurcated trial, the trier of fact shall determine:
> (1) liability for compensatory and exemplary damages; and
> (2) the amount of compensatory damages.

> (d) If liability for exemplary damages is established during the first phase of a bifurcated trial, the trier of fact shall, in the second phase of the trial, determine the amount of exemplary damages to be awarded, if any.

But see Iley v. Hughes, 158 Tex. 362, 363, 311 S.W.2d 648 (Tex. 1958) (Rule 174(b) does not authorize trial court to bifurcate issues of liability and damages in personal injury cases).

Sw. Ref. Co. v. Bernal, 22 S.W.3d 425, 442 (Tex. 2000) (punitive damages should not be decided until after liability and actual damages are resolved).

Transp. Ins. Co. v. Moriel, 879 S.W.2d 10, 30 (Tex. 1994) (issue of amount of punitive damages must be bifurcated from issues of liability for actual damages and punitive damages).

State v. Wood Oil Distrib., Inc., 751 S.W.2d 863, 865 (Tex. 1988, reh'g denied) ("The question of whether there has been a material and substantial impairment of access or whether there exists merely the issue of circuity of travel is a question of law, not of fact. *It is incumbent upon the trial court to make this determination prior to trial and to control the admission of evidence accordingly.* Thus, the introduction of evidence on damages due to inconvenience suffered by a property owner as a result of circuity of travel is improper as a matter of law since it is a non-compensable matter." (Emphasis added.)).

In re K.M.T., 415 S.W.3d 573, 576 (Tex. App.—Texarkana 2013, no pet.) (Rule 174(b) permits a trial court to order separate trials for any claim or issue in furtherance of convenience or to avoid prejudice).

In re K.M.T., 415 S.W.3d 573, 576 (Tex. App.—Texarkana 2013, no pet.) (an order for a separate trial (bifurcation) leaves the lawsuit intact but enables the court to hear and determine one or more issues without trying all controverted issues at the same hearing).

Beverly Enters. of Tex., Inc. v. Leath, 829 S.W.2d 382, 387 (Tex. App.—Waco 1992, writ withdrawn) (decision whether separate trial on issue of punitive damages within trial court's discretion; trial court did not abuse discretion denying request to order separate trial for issue).

Simpson v. Phillips Pipe Line Co., 603 S.W.2d 307, 312 (Tex. Civ. App.—Beaumont 1980, writ ref'd n.r.e.) (trial judge's order for separate trial on issue of damages proper and served purposes of judicial convenience and avoidance of prejudice).

a. Other Grounds

Other possible grounds for excluding damages evidence in the liability phase of trial include:

- Prejudicial;
- Time-wasting;
- Confusing or misleading;

- Solely intended to create an emotional bias;
- Cumulative;
- Irrelevant.

4. Opposing Authorities

Iley v. Hughes, 158 Tex. 362, 363, 311 S.W.2d 648 (Tex. 1958) (Rule 174(b) does not authorize trial court to bifurcate issues of liability and damages in personal injury cases).

Pacesetter Corp. v. Barrickman, 885 S.W.2d 256, 262 (Tex. App.—Tyler 1994, no writ) (trial court did not abuse its discretion by refusing to conduct separate trials regarding liability and punitive damages, even though this decision allowed for admission of evidence that one party had a high net worth).

Mo. Pac. R.R. Co. v. Lemon, 861 S.W.2d 501, 528 (Tex. App.—Houston [14th Dist.] 1993, writ dism'd by agr.) (trial court did not abuse discretion denying request to bifurcate trial on issue of punitive damages where refusal to bifurcate did not prejudice party requesting bifurcation).

Beverly Enters. of Tex., Inc. v. Leath, 829 S.W.2d 382, 387 (Tex. App.—Waco 1992, writ withdrawn) (decision whether separate trial on issue of punitive damages within trial court's discretion; trial court did not abuse discretion denying request to order separate trial for issue).

G. Motion to Preclude "Golden Rule" Argument

1. Suggested Motion Text

(*Name of Moving Party*) hereby moves this Court for an order restricting plaintiff's counsel from making any inquiry, comment, or argument before the jury that suggests that jurors should base plaintiff's damages on an amount that the jurors would charge to endure similar injuries. The motion is based upon the ground that (*Describe Basis for Belief That Counsel Will Engage in Such Conduct, e.g., Counsel Made This Same Argument at a Prior Arbitration*) and that any such argument is prohibited by law and will create a substantial danger of undue prejudice to (*Name of Moving Party*).

2. Motion Summary

This motion is used to prevent unfair prejudice to the defendant in personal injury actions, where plaintiff's counsel asks the jury to calculate pain and suffering damages based upon what the jurors would "charge" to endure a similar injury. This practice, known as the "golden rule argument," has been rejected by Texas courts and is clearly prejudicial under a Texas Rule of Evidence 403 balancing. *See World Tire Co. v. Brown*, 644 S.W.2d 144, 146 (Tex. App.—Houston [14th Dist.] 1982, writ ref'd n.r.e.).

3. Supporting Authorities

World Tire Co. v. Brown, 644 S.W.2d 144, 146 (Tex. App.—Houston [14th Dist.] 1982, writ ref'd n.r.e.) (while merely arguing "golden rule" in closing arguments is not improper as it cuts both ways, "the argument here went beyond that and amounted to a direct appeal to the jury to consider the case from an improper viewpoint, because its effect was to ask the members of the jury to put themselves into the plaintiff's shoes and to give the plaintiff what *they* would *want* if they were injured, rather than what the evidence showed *plaintiff* was *entitled* to receive as compensation").

City of Houston v. Jean, 517 S.W.2d 596, 600 (Tex. Civ. App.—Houston [1st Dist.] 1974, writ ref'd n.r.e.) (trial court sustained opposing party's objection to golden rule argument, curing error).

a. Other Grounds

Other possible grounds for excluding the golden rule argument include:

- Confusing or misleading;
- Solely intended to create an emotional bias;
- Irrelevant.

4. Opposing Authorities

Linder v. State, 828 S.W.2d 290, 303 (Tex. App.—Houston [1st Dist.] 1992, pet. ref'd, reh'g on pet. denied) (prosecutor's argument was proper summation of evidence and not improper golden rule argument, even though referred to jurors in second person and asked if they could imagine situation from victim's perspective).

City of Houston v. Jean, 517 S.W.2d 596, 600 (Tex. Civ. App.—Houston [1st Dist.] 1974, writ ref'd n.r.e.) (error caused by a golden rule argument, is generally cured by proper instructions).

Ravel v. Couravallos, 245 S.W.2d 731, 734 (Tex. Civ. App.—Austin 1952, no writ) (argument of "I don't know how rich you are, but I have a grandbaby, and I would appreciate the fact that I could buy a diaper for a few cents less than somebody can go down to Buttreys and probably buy a sateen finished diaper. I want my diapers for my baby as cheap as I can get them, and I know your jurors want the same thing," was not improper golden rule argument where price of diapers was not actual issue in case).

H. Motion to Exclude Improper Terminology

1. Suggested Motion Text

(*Name of Moving Party*) hereby moves this Court for an order excluding the mention in the presence of the jury, by counsel, witnesses, or any other person in the courtroom, of the following word [or phrase] or words with related meaning or effect: (*Describe Terms to Be Excluded, e.g., "Independent Medical Examiner"*).

The motion is based upon the grounds that (*Describe Grounds, e.g., the Words are Confusing and Meaningless and Create the Improper*

Impression That the Witness Being Referenced is Truly "Independent" When in Fact He is a Paid Expert Hired by the Defense), and therefore any mention of this terminology will unfairly prejudice the moving party.

2. Motion Summary

This motion is used to exclude evidence of improper, irrelevant, confusing, or conclusory terms by witnesses, counsel, or any other person in the presence of the jury. The motion is based upon a combination of authorities found throughout this text, including prejudice [Sections 2:1 to 2:6], juror confusion [Sections 2:11 to 2:14], limitations on juror preconditioning [Section 9:4], restrictions against witness testimony on legal issues [Sections 8:6, 8:103(c)(1)(ii)], and avoidance of usurping of the jury function [Section 8:18].

Certain "loaded" words may also be subject to exclusion, based upon their potential to confuse or create prejudicial inferences. For example, it may be inappropriate for the defense to use the terms "frivolous lawsuit" in describing plaintiff's case to a jury during voir dire or at any time during the presentation of evidence or argument. Or, it may be improper for plaintiff's counsel to use the terms "litigation doctor" to describe a defense medical expert. Similarly, counsel's use of the word "tap" to describe a low-impact automobile accident might be construed as misleading since the forces and sounds involved in even a very small accident are inconsistent with the commonly understood meaning of the word "tap." One might argue that the sickening sound of two cars colliding in even a very small accident has no relationship to the gentle sound of a pencil tapping a table, and thus any usage of this term during trial simply has too much potential to mislead.

In seeking to limit certain terms of art by qualified experts, the moving party should clarify that the motion is not an attempt to prohibit the expert from testifying on facts or opinions that properly touch on ultimate issues, but rather, the motion seeks to prevent an expert from prejudicially using loaded terminology designed to precondition or confuse the jurors or words that might improperly or prematurely suggest that certain jury questions have already been decided.

3. Supporting Authorities

Carr v. Radkey, 393 S.W.2d 806, 813 (Tex. 1965) (lay opinion testimony not admissible where witness seeks to testify on mixed question of law and fact and does not understand underlying legal standard).

Fleming v. Kinney ex rel. Shelton, 395 S.W.3d 917, 928 (Tex. App.—Houston [14th Dist.] 2013, pet. denied) ("[An] expert ... may not testify on pure questions of law.").

Fleming v. Kinney ex rel. Shelton, 395 S.W.3d 917, 928 (Tex. App.—Houston [14th Dist.] 2013, pet. denied) ("[An] expert is not allowed to testify directly to his understanding of the law, but may only apply legal terms to his understanding of the factual matters in issue.").

Fleming v. Kinney ex rel. Shelton, 395 S.W.3d 917, 928 (Tex. App.—Houston [14th Dist.] 2013, pet. denied) ("[I]t is not the role of the expert witness to define the particular legal principles applicable to a case; that is the role of the trial court.").

Great W. Drilling, Ltd. v. Alexander, 305 S.W.3d 688, 696 (Tex. App.—Eastland 2009, no pet.) ("[N]o witness is authorized to offer an opinion on a pure question of law.").

Schronk v. City of Burleson, 387 S.W.3d 692, 705 (Tex. App.—Waco 2009, pet. denied) ("[L]ay witness may not give legal conclusions or interpret the law to the jury.").

Luensmann v. Zimmer-Zampese & Assocs., Inc., 103 S.W.3d 594, 597 (Tex. App.—San Antonio 2003, no pet.) (trial court did not abuse discretion excluding evidence on statutory presumption as misleading to jury).

Dickerson v. DeBarbieris, 964 S.W.2d 680, 690 (Tex. App.—Houston [14th Dist.] 1998, no pet) (trial court properly excluded expert testimony on legal effect of document where opinion would represent opinion on legal question).

Holden v. Weidenfeller, 929 S.W.2d 124, 134 (Tex. App.—San Antonio 1996, writ denied) (trial court did not abuse discretion excluding attorney's expert opinion involving mixed question of law and fact and bearing on ultimate issue where no proof that expert was more qualified to assess issue than trial judge).

Lum v. State, 903 S.W.2d 365, 370 (Tex. App.—Texarkana 1995, writ ref'd) (lay opinions expressed in terms of legal definitions and conclusions or testimony amounting to little more than choosing sides on outcome of case not admissible).

United Gas Pipe Line Co. v. Mueller Eng'g Corp., 809 S.W.2d 597, 602 (Tex. App.—Corpus Christi 1991, writ denied) (expert's opinion regarding meaning of contract improper where it represented opinion on a legal question).

Mowbray v. State, 788 S.W.2d 658, 668 (Tex. App.—Corpus Christi 1990), *cert. denied*, 498 U.S. 1101 (1991) (lay testimony on legal conclusions not admissible).

Welder v. Welder, 794 S.W.2d 420, 433 (Tex. App.—Corpus Christi 1990, no pet.) (trial court properly excluded opinion of accountant on legal question about his interpretation of case law).

Dieter v. Baker Serv. Tools, a Div. of Baker Int'l, Inc., 776 S.W.2d 781, 783 (Tex. App.—Corpus Christi 1989, writ denied) (affidavit filed by expert in opposition to summary judgment motion irrelevant, not necessary to assist jury, and represented improper legal conclusion).

Montoya v. Am. Employers' Ins. Co., 426 S.W.2d 661, 663 (Tex. Civ. App.—El Paso 1968, writ ref'd n.r.e.) (lay testimony that injuries permanent not admissible).

a. Exclusion of Ultimate Issue Evidence

Texas Rule of Evidence 704 states: "[t]estimony in the form of an opinion or inference otherwise admissible is not objectionable because it embraces an ultimate issue to be decided by the trier of fact." Even under this statutory authority, however, the trial court maintains the discretion to exclude testimony as not helpful to the jury, speculative, irrelevant, or as improper under other principles of evidentiary law. The following cases provide examples of such "ultimate issue" testimony that was held to be inappropriate.

Carr v. Radkey, 393 S.W.2d 806, 813 (Tex. 1965) (lay opinion testimony not admissible where witness seeks to testify on mixed question of law and fact and does not understand underlying legal standard).

Burke v. State, 371 S.W.3d 252, 258 (Tex. App.—Houston [1st Dist.] 2011, pet. ref'd, untimely filed) ("[E]xpert testimony does not assist the jury if it constitutes a direct opinion on the truthfulness of a child complainant's allegations.").

Burke v. State, 371 S.W.3d 252, 258 (Tex. App.—Houston [1st Dist.] 2011, pet. ref'd, untimely filed) ("[E]xpert's bare opinion that she believes, or believed, a child complainant's testimony to be true is excludable.").

Holden v. Weidenfeller, 929 S.W.2d 124, 134 (Tex. App.—San Antonio 1996, writ denied) (trial court did not abuse discretion excluding attorney's expert opinion involving mixed question of law and fact and bearing on ultimate issue where no proof that expert was more qualified to assess issue than trial judge).

Montoya v. Am. Employers' Ins. Co., 426 S.W.2d 661, 663 (Tex. Civ. App.—El Paso 1968, writ ref'd n.r.e.) (lay testimony that injuries are permanent not admissible).

i. General Admissibility of Ultimate Issue Opinions

Texas Rule of Evidence 704 states that "[t]estimony in the form of an opinion or inference otherwise admissible is not objectionable because it embraces an ultimate issue to be decided by the trier of fact."

b. *Usurping Jury Function*

Holden v. Weidenfeller, 929 S.W.2d 124, 134 (Tex. App.—San Antonio 1996, writ denied) (trial court did not abuse discretion excluding attorney's expert opinion involving mixed question of law and fact and bearing on ultimate issue where no proof expert more qualified to assess issue than trial judge).

4. *Opposing Authorities*

Texas Rule of Evidence 704 states:

> Testimony in the form of an opinion or inference otherwise admissible is not objectionable because it embraces an ultimate issue to be decided by the trier-of-fact.

Texas Rule of Evidence 703 states:

> The facts or data in the particular case upon which an expert bases an opinion or inference may be those perceived by, reviewed by, or made known to the expert at or before the hearing. If of a type reasonably relied upon by experts in the particular field in forming opinions or inferences upon the subject, the facts or data need not be admissible in evidence.

Merrill v. Sprint Waste Services LP, 527 S.W.3d 663, 670 (Tex. App.—Houston [14th Dist.] 2017, no pet.) ("Rule of Evidence 704 ... abolished the common law rule that a witness cannot invade the province of the jury by offering an opinion on liability.").

Merrill v. Sprint Waste Services LP, 527 S.W.3d 663, 670 (Tex. App.—Houston [14th Dist.] 2017, no pet.) ("[A] lay opinion can establish causation when general experience and common sense will enable a layperson to determine, with reasonable probability, the causal relationship between the event and condition.").

Williams v. State, 417 S.W.3d 162, 182 (Tex. App.—Houston [1st Dist.] 2013, pet. ref'd) ("[O]pinion testimony that is otherwise admissible is not objectionable solely because it embraces an ultimate issue to be decided by the trier of fact.").

Fleming v. Kinney ex rel. Shelton, 395 S.W.3d 917, 928 (Tex. App.—Houston [14th Dist.] 2013, pet. denied) ("expert must testify before the jury has received the jury charge and before it has been instructed on specific elements and standards concerning specific claims.... In order for an expert to meaningfully apply legal terms to his understanding of the factual matters in issue in a way that assists the jury ... the expert must have some leeway to reference the controlling legal terms and related concepts while testifying. Otherwise, a jury would not be able to make sense of the expert's testimony or measure it against the charge's requirements, and the sponsoring litigant could not meet a motion for directed verdict.").

Fleming v. Kinney ex rel. Shelton, 395 S.W.3d 917, 928 (Tex. App.—Houston [14th Dist.] 2013, pet. denied) (standards governing admission of expert testimony do not automatically foreclose every reference to legal terms or the disciplinary rules in the course of expert testimony addressing an attorney's alleged breaches of the duties owed to a client).

Burke v. State, 371 S.W.3d 252, 258 (Tex. App.—Houston [1st Dist.] 2011, pet. ref'd, untimely filed) ("[O]pinion testimony that is otherwise admissible is not objectionable solely because it embraces an ultimate opinion to be decided by the trier of fact.").

Templeton v. Dreiss, 961 S.W.2d 645, 672 (Tex. App.—San Antonio 1998, pet. denied) (trial court did not err admitting lawyer's expert opinion on technical meaning of certain words in document).

Lyondell Petrochemical Co. v. Fluor Daniel, Inc., 888 S.W.2d 547, 555 (Tex. App.—Houston [1st Dist.] 1994, writ denied) (trial court should have allowed testimony that contractor violated OSHA).

Cohn v. State, 804 S.W.2d 572, 575 (Tex. App.—Houston [14th Dist.] 1991, writ granted), *aff'd,* 849 S.W.2d 817 (Tex. Crim. App. 1993) (expert testimony on behavioral symptoms victim of abuse exhibits and behavioral symptoms exhibited by victim in case not improper where did not cross line and tell jury how to decide case).

II. Sample Motions

A. Motion to Exclude Reference to Lost or Destroyed Evidence

NO. _____

	§	IN THE DISTRICT COURT
_____	§	
	§	
v.	§	_____ JUDICIAL COURT
	§	
_____	§	_____ COUNTY, TEXAS

Motion to Exclude Reference to Lost or Destroyed Evidence

Comes now _____, Defendant in this cause, and files this, his Motion to Exclude Reference to Lost or Destroyed Evidence, and in support thereof, Defendant would show the Court the following:

1.
FACTUAL BACKGROUND

This is an unfair competition case in which the Plaintiff alleges that the Defendant, a former employee, improperly utilized in-house software development information to advance his business interests. A key issue in this case relates to the content of the Plaintiff's network server ("server") during the two-week period prior to Defendant's departure from plaintiff's place of employment.

During discovery, the Defendant served a proper request to examine Plaintiff's backup data for this crucial time period. Initially, Plaintiff was cooperative, and a date was set for examination. Then, just twenty-four (24) hours before the scheduled examination date, Plaintiff's counsel advised that the backup data had been accidentally destroyed during the Plaintiff's analysis of this evidence. In follow-up discovery, the Plaintiff denied having any test results or other analysis relating to this data.

The Defendant moves herein for an order excluding any and all reference to the backup data and any tests or other analysis that Plaintiff or Plaintiff's expert or other agents may have conducted prior to the accidental destruction.

2.
THIS COURT MAY EXCLUDE PREJUDICIAL EVIDENCE
PURSUANT TO TEXAS RULE OF EVIDENCE 403

Texas Rule of Evidence 403 states: "[a]lthough relevant, evidence may be excluded if its probative value is substantially outweighed by the danger of unfair prejudice, confusion of the issues, or misleading the jury, or by considerations of undue delay, or needless presentation of cumulative evidence." *Brookshire Bros v. Aldridge*, 438 S.W.3d 9, 26 (Tex. 2014) (evidence that raises a risk of prejudice and confusion of the jury should be excluded); *Farmers Texas County Mutual Insurance Co. v. Pagan*, 453 S.W.3d 454, (Tex. App.—Houston [14th Dist.] 2014, no pet.) (evidence should have been excluded where its probative value was outweighed by danger of confusion of issues and misleading jury). In the case at bar, the Defendant would be severely prejudiced if the Plaintiff is able to introduce evidence about the backup data without the Defendant's having had the opportunity to review it.

3.
THE COURT MAY EXCLUDE REFERENCE TO EVIDENCE THAT IS DESTROYED BY A PARTY

The court may exclude references to evidence that is intentionally or accidentally destroyed by another party. *See Grossnickle v. Grossnickle*, 935 S.W.2d 830, 840 (Tex. App.—Texarkana 1996, writ denied) (trial court must exclude evidence when party fails to identify evidence in response to discovery request). See also Texas Rule of Civil Procedure 215.2.

The Plaintiff's willful or negligent failure to preserve the backup data has rendered it impossible for the Defendant to determine the stage of development of the disputed technology at a critically relevant time period in this case. The loss of this evidence has severely prejudiced the Defendant in that he has been unable to prepare a complete defense to Plaintiff's claim.

Therefore, if the Plaintiff is in possession of any test results or other data from the two-week period prior to Defendant's departure from Plaintiff's place of employment, said test results or other data must be excluded. Allowing the Plaintiff to present evidence or comment in any way on this data would unfairly prejudice the Defendant and simply should not be allowed.

4.
CONCLUSION

For all the reasons stated above, the defendant requests that this Court exclude any reference at the time of trial to the backup data and any tests or other analysis relating to such evidence.

Dated: _____ *(Date)* _____

By: _____

_____ *(Name of Counsel)* _____

Attorneys for Defendant,

_____ *(Name of Defendant)* _____

CHAPTER 10

Personal Injury Motions

I. Motion Authorities
   A. Motion to Exclude Evidence of Collateral Source Payments
      1. Suggested Motion Text
      2. Motion Summary
      3. Supporting Authorities
         a. Gratuitous Payments
         b. Medical or Liability Policy Payments
         c. Disability and Other Payments
         d. Workers' Compensation Payments
         e. Wage Payments
         f. Other Grounds
      4. Opposing Authorities
         a. Not Wholly Independent Source
         b. Relevant to Issues in Case
         c. Impeachment
   B. Motion to Exclude Evidence of Liability Insurance
      1. Suggested Motion Text
      2. Motion Summary
      3. Supporting Authorities
         a. Evidence of Defendant's Lack of Insurance
         b. Irrelevant
         c. Other Grounds
      4. Opposing Authorities
         a. Where Relevant to Issues or Otherwise Admissible
         b. Incidental Reference to Insurance
         c. Nonprejudicial References to Insurance
         d. Admissions
         e. To Prove Ownership or Employment
   C. Motion to Exclude Settlement Evidence
      1. Suggested Motion Text
      2. Motion Summary
      3. Supporting Authorities
         a. Prior Settlements
         b. Settlement Negotiations
         c. Settlement With Codefendants
         d. Where Offer Made Before Litigation
         e. Other Grounds

4. Opposing Authorities
   a. Bias or Prejudice
   b. Impeachment
   c. Settlement With Codefendant
   d. State of Mind
D. Motion to Exclude Evidence of Other Accidents
   1. Suggested Motion Text
   2. Motion Summary
   3. Supporting Authorities
      a. Prior Accident Evidence Used to Show Negligence
      b. Lack of Similarity—Dangerous Condition/Defective Products
      c. Irrelevant
      d. Exclusion of Subsequent Accident Evidence
      e. Other Grounds
   4. Opposing Authorities
      a. Similarity: Dangerous Condition/Defective Products
      b. Notice
      c. Evidence of Subsequent Accidents
E. Motion to Exclude Evidence of Subsequent Repairs
   1. Suggested Motion Text
   2. Motion Summary
   3. Supporting Authorities
      a. Other Grounds
   4. Opposing Authorities
      a. Relevant to Issues
      b. Strict Products Liability
F. Motion to Exclude Evidence of Statutory Violation
   1. Suggested Motion Text
   2. Motion Summary
   3. Supporting Authorities
      a. Not Proximate Cause
      b. Not Negligence Per Se
      c. Other Grounds
   4. Opposing Authorities
      a. Proximate Cause
         i. Negligence Per Se
G. Motion to Exclude Evidence of Driver's License Suspension
   1. Suggested Motion Text
   2. Motion Summary
   3. Supporting Authorities
      a. Other Grounds
   4. Opposing Authorities
H. Motion to Exclude Evidence of Failure to Wear Seatbelt
   1. Suggested Motion Text
   2. Motion Summary
   3. Supporting Authorities
      a. Other Grounds
   4. Opposing Authorities
      a. Where Use Would Have Reduced Injuries

PERSONAL INJURY MOTIONS 459

   b. Mandatory Seatbelt Laws
I. Motion to Exclude Evidence of Alcohol Consumption
 1. Suggested Motion Text
 2. Motion Summary
 3. Supporting Authorities
  a. Other Grounds
 4. Opposing Authorities
  a. Witness Perceptions
J. Motion to Exclude Evidence of Prior DWI
 1. Suggested Motion Text
 2. Motion Summary
 3. Supporting Authorities
  a. Exclusions of Arrests and Misdemeanor Convictions
  b. Exclusion of Convictions Where No Bearing on Credibility
  c. Where Probative Value Outweighed by Risk of Undue Prejudice
  d. Exclusion of DWI Evidence Where Used to Prove Improper Conduct
  e. Other Grounds
 4. Opposing Authorities
  a. Use of Felony Convictions Expressly Allowed for Impeachment
   i. DWI as a Felony
  b. Relevant to Issues
K. Motion to Exclude Evidence of Party's Health or Injuries Where Not at Issue
 1. Suggested Motion Text
 2. Motion Summary
 3. Supporting Authorities
  a. Other Grounds
 4. Opposing Authorities
L. Motion to Exclude Accident Reconstruction Evidence
 1. Suggested Motion Text
 2. Motion Summary
 3. Supporting Authorities
  a. Improper Foundation or Qualification
  b. Vehicle Speed Determinations
 4. Opposing Authorities
  a. Competent Facts/Foundation
  b. Vehicle Speed
  c. Skid Mark Analysis
  d. Stopping Distances
  e. Point of Impact
  f. Reaction Time
  g. Safer Alternative Design
  h. Cases Where Biomechanics Admitted
M. Motion to Exclude Evidence of Party's Financial Status
 1. Suggested Motion Text
 2. Motion Summary
 3. Supporting Authorities
  a. Punitive Damages Cases
  b. Other Grounds

            4. Opposing Authorities
                a. Necessary to Support Punitive Damages Claim
                b. Invited Error
        N. Motion to Exclude Tax Evidence
            1. Suggested Motion Text
            2. Motion Summary
            3. Supporting Authorities
                a. Improper Appeal to Jurors as Taxpayers
                b. Other Grounds
            4. Opposing Authorities
        O. Motion to Exclude Liability Evidence (Liability Not at Issue)
            1. Suggested Motion Text
            2. Motion Summary
            3. Supporting Authorities
                a. Other Grounds
            4. Opposing Authorities
        P. Motion to Exclude Improper Damage Evidence
            1. Suggested Motion Text
            2. Motion Summary
            3. Supporting Authorities
                a. Undisputed Matters
                b. Surprise Claims
                c. Amounts in Excess of Stated Damages
                d. Speculative Evidence
                    i. Exclusion of Evidence of Speculative Damages
                e. Statutory Limitations on Damages
            4. Opposing Authorities
                a. Reasonable Estimate of Damages
II. Sample Motions
    A. Motion to Exclude Evidence of Collateral Source Payments
    B. Motion to Exclude Evidence of Defendant's Liability
    C. Motion to Exclude Evidence of Computerized Valuations of Plaintiff's Business
    D. Motion to Exclude Surveillance Video
    E. Opposition to Motion for Destroyed or Missing Evidence Instruction

I. Motion Authorities

A. Motion to Exclude Evidence of Collateral Source Payments

1. Suggested Motion Text

The plaintiff hereby moves this Court for an order excluding any and all evidence, references to evidence, testimony, or argument relating to collateral payments to plaintiff arising from (*Describe Collateral Source Payments, e.g., Payments Under Medical Payments Policy*). The motion is based upon the grounds that the evidence is irrelevant, immaterial, confusing, prejudicial and is expressly prohibited by case law of this state.

2. *Motion Summary*

This motion is used to exclude evidence of collateral source payments, such as payments under a medical or disability insurance policy. The motion is based upon the court's authority to exclude evidence that is irrelevant [Texas Rule of Evidence 401] or prejudicial [Texas Rule of Evidence 403], and a long line of leading cases. *See Haygood v. De Escabedo*, 356 S.W.3d 390, 395 (Tex. 2011); *Jones v. Red Arrow Heavy Hauling, Inc.*, 816 S.W.2d 134, 136 (Tex. App.—Beaumont 1991, writ denied).

3. *Supporting Authorities*

Sky View at Las Palmas, LLC v. Mendez, 555 S.W.3d 101, 114 (Tex. 2018) ("The collateral source rule bars a wrongdoer from offsetting his liability by insurance benefits independently procured by the injured party.").

Sky View at Las Palmas, LLC v. Mendez, 555 S.W.3d 101, 114 (Tex. 2018) ("The theory behind the [collateral source] rule is that a wrongdoer should not have the benefit of insurance independently procured by the injured party, and to which the wrongdoer was not privy.").

Sky View at Las Palmas, LLC v. Mendez, 555 S.W.3d 101, 114 (Tex. 2018) ("[I]f a payment is within the collateral-source rule, the principle forbidding more than one recovery for the same loss is not applicable.").

Haygood v. De Escabedo, 356 S.W.3d 390, 395 (Tex. 2011) (collateral source rule precludes any reduction in a tortfeasor's liability because of benefits received by the plaintiff from someone else).

Haygood v. De Escabedo, 356 S.W.3d 390, 395 (Tex. 2011) (evidence of a claim of damages that are not compensable is inadmissible).

Brown v. Am. Transfer & Storage Co., 601 S.W.2d 931, 934 (Tex. 1980), *cert. denied*, 449 U.S. 1015 (1980) (collateral source rule prevented evidence of insurance payments made to plaintiff under policy plaintiff had obtained on his own).

McMillan v. Hearne, 584 S.W.3d 505, 519 (Tex. App.—Texarkana 2019, no pet.) ("The theory behind the collateral source rule is that a wrongdoer should not have the benefit of insurance independently procured by the injured party, and to which the wrongdoer was not privy.").

Rentech Steel, L.L.C. v. Teel, 299 S.W.3d 155, 162 (Tex. App.—Eastland 2009, pet. dism'd) ("The theory behind the collateral source rule is that a wrongdoer should not have the benefit of insurance independently procured by injured party and to which wrongdoer was not privy. . . . However, when the wrongdoer has provided for those damages, either by personal payment or insurance payment, the damages claim has been satisfied, and to permit the injured party in such circumstances to keep the insurance money and also collect from the wrongdoer would be a double recovery not sanctioned by law.").

Matbon, Inc. v. Gries, 288 S.W.3d 471, 481 n.5 (Tex. App.—Eastland 2009, no pet.) ("[The] collateral source rule is a rule of evidence that prevents testimony that the injured party has received payments from insurance or other sources.").

Tate v. Hernandez, 280 S.W.3d 534, 539 (Tex. App.—Amarillo 2009, no pet.) ("[The] collateral source rule is a common law rule that, in part, prevents a wrongdoer from benefiting from a collateral source of discharge of liability for medical expenses independently procured by a party, including the injured party, not in privity with the wrongdoer.").

Tate v. Hernandez, 280 S.W.3d 534, 539 (Tex. App.—Amarillo 2009, no pet.) ("[The] discharge of medical expenses through bankruptcy is akin to the discharge of an obligation by a collateral source.").

LMC Complete Auto., Inc. v. Burke, 229 S.W.3d 469, 480 (Tex. App.—Houston [1st Dist.] 2007, pet. denied) ("[The] collateral source rule is both a rule of evidence and damages.").

LMC Complete Auto., Inc. v. Burke, 229 S.W.3d 469, 480 (Tex. App.—Houston [1st Dist.] 2007, pet. denied) (under the collateral source rule, "a defendant is not entitled to present evidence of, or obtain an offset for, funds received by the plaintiff from a collateral source").

Triumph Trucking, Inc. v. S. Corporate Ins. Mgrs., Inc., 226 S.W.3d 466, 472 (Tex. App.—Houston [1st Dist.] 2006, pet. denied) (under the collateral source rule, "a defendant may not offer evidence of payment from a collateral source and may not take an offset for such payments").

Scottsdale Ins. Co. v. Nat'l Emergency Servs., Inc., 175 S.W.3d 284, 299 (Tex. App.—Houston [1st Dist.] 2004, pet. denied) (party precluded from using "pass-on" defense to mitigate damages where would violate collateral source rule).

Taylor v. Am. Fabritech, Inc., 132 S.W.3d 613, 626 (Tex. App.—Houston [14th Dist.] 2004, pet. denied) (offset for disability payments received by plaintiff improper under collateral source rule).

Kendrix v. S. Pac. Transp. Co., 907 S.W.2d 111, 112 (Tex. App.—Beaumont 1995, writ denied) (references to payments received from collateral source, including those from workers' compensation, are improper and prejudicial).

Lee-Wright, Inc. v. Hall, 840 S.W.2d 572, 582 (Tex. App.—Houston [1st Dist.] 1992, no writ) (evidence regarding workers' compensation benefits properly excluded under collateral source rule).

Jones v. Red Arrow Heavy Hauling, Inc., 816 S.W.2d 134, 136 (Tex. App.—Beaumont 1991, writ denied) (evidence that injured party received benefits from collateral source inadmissible under rules of relevancy).

a. Gratuitous Payments

Oil Country Haulers, Inc. v. Griffin, 668 S.W.2d 903, 904 (Tex. App.—Houston [14th Dist.] 1984, no writ) (plaintiff can recover amount of unpaid medical bills and can recover for medical services supplied gratuitously).

Greyhound Lines, Inc. v. Craig, 430 S.W.2d 573, 578 (Tex. Civ. App.—Houston [14th Dist.] 1968, writ ref'd n.r.e.) (trial court properly declined to allow offset for wage received by plaintiff regardless of whether gratuitous or earned).

Morgan v. Woodruff, 208 S.W.2d 628, 631 (Tex. Civ. App.—Galveston 1948, no writ) (plaintiff can recover amounts for lost wages and medical expenses even if paid by insurance, contract, or gratuitously).

Graves v. Poe, 118 S.W.2d 969, 970 (Tex. Civ. App.—El Paso 1938, writ dism'd) (plaintiff entitled to recover lost wages and cost of medical bills even though wages gratuitously covered by employer and medical bills gratuitously paid by employer's insurance carrier).

Houston Belt & Terminal Ry. Co. v. Johansen, 143 S.W. 1186, 1186 (Tex. Civ. App.—El Paso 1912), *aff'd*, 179 S.W. 853 (Tex. 1915) (plaintiff could recover lost wages despite employer's having gratuitously paid wages during period of injury).

b. *Medical or Liability Policy Payments*

Brown v. Am. Transfer & Storage Co., 601 S.W.2d 931, 934 (Tex. 1980), *cert. denied*, 449 U.S. 1015 (1980) (collateral source rule prevented evidence of insurance payments made to plaintiff due to policy plaintiff had obtained personally).

Taylor v. Am. Fabritech, Inc., 132 S.W.3d 613, 626 (Tex. App.—Houston [14th Dist.] 2004, pet. denied) (offset for disability payments received by plaintiff improper under collateral source rule).

Morgan v. Woodruff, 208 S.W.2d 628, 631 (Tex. Civ. App.—Galveston 1948, no writ) (plaintiff can recover amounts for lost wages and medical expenses even if paid by insurance, contract, or gratuitously).

Graves v. Poe, 118 S.W.2d 969, 970 (Tex. Civ. App.—El Paso 1938, writ dism'd) (plaintiff entitled to recover lost wages and cost of medical bills even though wages gratuitously covered by employer and medical bills gratuitously paid by employer's insurance carrier).

c. *Disability and Other Payments*

Taylor v. Am. Fabritech, Inc., 132 S.W.3d 613, 626 (Tex. App.—Houston [14th Dist.] 2004, pet. denied) (offset for disability payments received by plaintiff improper under collateral source rule).

Montandon v. Colehour, 469 S.W.2d 222, 229 (Tex. Civ. App.—Fort Worth 1971, no writ) (evidence of government benefits plaintiff received due to prior military service improper under collateral source rule).

Mo.-Pac. Ry. Co. v. Willingham, 348 S.W.2d 764, 766 (Tex. Civ. App.—Waco 1961, no writ) (evidence of pension benefits plaintiff would be able to receive if retired properly excluded).

d. Workers' Compensation Payments

Kendrix v. S. Pac. Transp. Co., 907 S.W.2d 111, 112 (Tex. App.—Beaumont 1995, writ denied) (references to payments received from collateral source, including those from workers' compensation, improper and prejudicial).

Lee-Wright, Inc. v. Hall, 840 S.W.2d 572, 582 (Tex. App.—Houston [1st Dist.] 1992, no writ) (evidence regarding workers' compensation benefits were properly excluded under the collateral source rule).

e. Wage Payments

Ryan v. Hardin, 495 S.W.2d 345, 350 (Tex. Civ. App.—Austin 1973, no writ) (plaintiff can recover for lost earning capacity where wages paid by employer; that wages are paid is irrelevant).

Greyhound Lines, Inc. v. Craig, 430 S.W.2d 573, 578 (Tex. Civ. App.—Houston [14th Dist.] 1968, writ ref'd n.r.e.) (trial court properly declined to allow an offset for wages received by the plaintiff regardless of whether they were gratuitous or earned).

Morgan v. Woodruff, 208 S.W.2d 628, 631 (Tex. Civ. App.—Galveston 1948, no writ) (plaintiff can recover amounts for lost wages and medical expenses even if paid by insurance, contract, or gratuitously).

Graves v. Poe, 118 S.W.2d 969, 970 (Tex. Civ. App.—El Paso 1938, writ dism'd) (plaintiff entitled to recover lost wages and cost of medical bills even though wages gratuitously covered by employer and medical bills gratuitously paid by employer's insurance carrier).

St. Louis & S.F. Ry. Co. v. Clifford, 148 S.W. 1163, 1165 (Tex. Civ. App.—Dallas 1912, writ ref'd) (plaintiff can recover lost wages even if received wages during period when injured).

Houston Belt & Terminal Ry. Co. v. Johansen, 143 S.W. 1186, 1186 (Tex. Civ. App.—El Paso 1912), *aff'd*, 179 S.W. 853 (Tex. 1915) (plaintiff could recover lost wages despite employer's having gratuitously paid wages during period of injury).

f. Other Grounds

Other possible grounds for excluding collateral source evidence include:

- Time-wasting;
- Confusing or misleading;
- Solely intended to create an emotional bias;
- Collateral to issues in case;
- Improper foundation;
- Inadmissible hearsay.

4. Opposing Authorities

Houston Chronicle Publ'g Co. v. McNair Trucklease, Inc., 519 S.W.2d 924, 930 (Tex. Civ. App.—Houston [1st Dist.] 1975, writ ref'd n.r.e.) (party entitled to show opposing party mitigated damages from party's breach of contract by leasing equipment to third party).

Garrett v. Brock, 144 S.W.2d 408, 414 (Tex. Civ. App.—Fort Worth 1940, writ dism'd, j. cor.) (evidence that repair bill paid by insurance company relevant to issue of damages).

a. Not Wholly Independent Source

Sky View at Las Palmas, LLC v. Mendez, 555 S.W.3d 101, 114 (Tex. 2018) ("[I]n cases where the defendant procures insurance for the benefit of the plaintiff, the plaintiff cannot then rely on the collateral-source rule for a double recovery.").

Publix Theatres Corp. v. Powell, 123 Tex. 304, 312, 71 S.W.2d 237 (Tex. 1934) (evidence of insurance payments received by plaintiff from policy provided by defendant was admissible).

Taylor v. Am. Fabritech, Inc., 132 S.W.3d 613, 626 (Tex. App.—Houston [14th Dist.] 2004, pet. denied) (offset for disability payments received by plaintiff improper under collateral source rule).

Tarrant County Waste Disposal, Inc. v. Doss, 737 S.W.2d 607, 610 (Tex. App.—Fort Worth 1987, writ denied) (employer entitled to offset for payments plaintiff received under policy purchased by employer to protect itself from cost of on-the-job injuries).

b. Relevant to Issues in Case

Gothard v. Marr, 581 S.W.2d 276, 281 (Tex. Civ. App.—Waco 1979, no pet.) (evidence of proof of loss for insurance benefits relevant for impeachment purposes).

Twin City Fire Ins. Co. v. Gibson, 488 S.W.2d 565, 573 (Tex. Civ. App.—Amarillo 1972, writ ref'd n.r.e.) (evidence of insurance claims for injury admissible as impeachment where evidence of prior inconsistent statements, even though also showed payment by collateral source).

Houston Chronicle Publ'g Co. v. McNair Trucklease, Inc., 519 S.W.2d 924, 930 (Tex. Civ. App.—Houston [1st Dist] 1975, writ ref'd n.r.e.) (party entitled to show opposing party mitigated damages from party's breach of contract by leasing equipment to third party).

Garrett v. Brock, 144 S.W.2d 408, 414 (Tex. Civ. App.—Fort Worth 1940, writ dism'd, j. cor.) (evidence that repair bill paid by insurance company relevant to damages).

c. Impeachment

LMC Complete Auto., Inc. v. Burke, 229 S.W.3d 469, 480 (Tex. App.—Houston [1st Dist.] 2007, pet. denied) ("[A] claim of financial hardship ... by the plaintiff may open the door to collateral source evidence to impeach the credibility of the witness.").

LMC Complete Auto., Inc. v. Burke, 229 S.W.3d 469, 480 (Tex. App.—Houston [1st Dist.] 2007, pet. denied) ("[B]efore the trial court allows impeachment [by collateral source] evidence, the witness must offer direct testimony inconsistent with the receipt of benefits.").

B. Motion to Exclude Evidence of Liability Insurance

1. Suggested Motion Text

Defendant hereby moves this Court for an order excluding any and all evidence, references to evidence, testimony, or argument relating to defendant's liability insurance coverage (*or Describe Name of Policy and Nature of Coverage*). The motion is based upon the grounds that the evidence is irrelevant, immaterial, prejudicial, and expressly inadmissible pursuant to Texas Rule of Evidence 411.

2. Motion Summary

This motion is used to exclude evidence of a defendant's liability insurance coverage. The motion is based upon the express authority of Texas Rule of Evidence 411 and the court's authority to exclude evidence that is irrelevant [Texas Rule of Evidence 402] or prejudicial [Texas Rule of Evidence 403]. *See Rojas v. Vuocolo*, 142 Tex. 152, 157, 177 S.W.2d 962 (Tex. 1944); *Kendrix v. S. Pac. Transp. Co.*, 907 S.W.2d 111, 112 (Tex. App.—Beaumont 1995, writ denied).

3. Supporting Authorities

Texas Rule of Evidence 411 states:

> Evidence that a person was or was not insured against liability is not admissible upon the issue whether the person acted negligently or otherwise wrongfully. This rule does not require the exclusion of evidence of insurance against liability when offered for another issue, such as proof of agency, ownership, or control, if disputed, or bias or prejudice of a witness.

Brown v. Am. Transfer & Storage Co., 601 S.W.2d 931, 934 (Tex. 1980), *cert. denied*, 449 U.S. 1015 (1980) (collateral source rule prevented evidence of insurance payments made to plaintiff due to policy plaintiff had obtained personally).

Rojas v. Vuocolo, 142 Tex. 152, 157, 177 S.W.2d 962 (Tex. 1944) (improper to let the jury know whether the defendant is insured).

Ex parte Wheeler, 146 S.W.3d 238, 247 (Tex. App.—Fort Worth 2004), *rev'd*, 203 S.W.3d 317 (Tex. Crim. App. 2006) (improper and prejudicial for prosecutor in criminal case to ask expert whether defendant's insurance company determined that defendant was at fault for incident).

Kendrix v. S. Pac. Transp. Co., 907 S.W.2d 111, 112 (Tex. App.—Beaumont 1995, writ denied) ("It is ordinarily error for plaintiff to mention the fact in the presence of the jury that the defendant is insured against the liability which he is seeking to establish, or that he has no protecting insurance. For the same reason it is error to refer to the fact that the plaintiff is protected by some form of insurance. It is improper in either case because such fact is irrelevant and immaterial, and is calculated to work injury.").

Eoff v. Hal & Charlie Peterson Found., 811 S.W.2d 187, 197 (Tex. App.—San Antonio 1991, no writ) (trial court correctly found that evidence defendant was charitable organization did not open door to questions regarding whether defendant was insured).

Meuth v. Hartgrove, 811 S.W.2d 626, 628 (Tex. App.—Austin 1990, writ denied) (although insurance certificate is admissible to demonstrate ownership or control, trial court properly redacted information regarding policy limits before admitting certificate).

Morgan v. Woodruff, 208 S.W.2d 628, 631 (Tex. Civ. App.—Galveston 1948, no writ) (plaintiff can recover amounts for lost wages and medical expenses, even if paid by insurance, contract, or gratuitously).

Graves v. Poe, 118 S.W.2d 969, 970 (Tex. Civ. App.—El Paso 1938, writ dism'd) (plaintiff entitled to recover lost wages and cost of medical bills even though wages gratuitously covered by employer and medical bills gratuitously paid by employer's insurance carrier).

a. *Evidence of Defendant's Lack of Insurance*

Rojas v. Vuocolo, 142 Tex. 152, 157, 177 S.W.2d 962 (Tex. 1944) (improper to let jury know whether defendant is insured).

b. *Irrelevant*

Kendrix v. S. Pac. Transp. Co., 907 S.W.2d 111, 112 (Tex. App.—Beaumont 1995, writ denied) (references to insurance generally irrelevant and prejudicial).

Meuth v. Hartgrove, 811 S.W.2d 626, 628 (Tex. App.—Austin 1990, writ denied) (evidence regarding policy limits irrelevant).

c. *Other Grounds*

Other possible grounds for excluding liability insurance evidence include:

- Time-wasting;
- Confusing or misleading;
- Solely intended to create an emotional bias;
- Collateral to issues in case;
- Collateral source rule.

4. *Opposing Authorities*

Gothard v. Marr, 581 S.W.2d 276, 281 (Tex. Civ. App.—Waco 1979, no pet.) (evidence of proof of loss for insurance benefits relevant for impeachment purposes).

a. Where Relevant to Issues or Otherwise Admissible

Texas Rule of Evidence 411 states:

> Evidence that a person was or was not insured against liability is not admissible upon the issue whether the person acted negligently or otherwise wrongfully. *This rule does not require the exclusion of evidence of insurance against liability when offered for another issue, such as proof of agency, ownership, or control, if disputed, or bias or prejudice of a witness.* (Emphasis added.)

Brownsville Pediatric Ass'n v. Reyes, 68 S.W.3d 184, 193 (Tex. App.—Corpus Christi 2002, no pet.) (trial court did not abuse discretion allowing party to mention insurance in discussing annuity where reference was not type of prejudicial reference that rule was designed to prohibit).

Meuth v. Hartgrove, 811 S.W.2d 626, 628 (Tex. App.—Austin 1990, writ denied) (although insurance certificate admissible to demonstrate ownership or control, trial court properly redacted information regarding policy limits before admitting certificate).

Gothard v. Marr, 581 S.W.2d 276, 281 (Tex. Civ. App.—Waco 1979, no pet.) (evidence of proof of loss for insurance benefits relevant for impeachment purposes).

b. Incidental Reference to Insurance

Brownsville Pediatric Ass'n v. Reyes, 68 S.W.3d 184, 193 (Tex. App.—Corpus Christi 2002, no pet.) (trial court did not abuse discretion allowing party to mention insurance in discussing annuity where reference was not type of prejudicial reference that rule was designed to prohibit).

Gothard v. Marr, 581 S.W.2d 276, 281 (Tex. Civ. App.—Waco 1979, no pet.) (evidence of proof of loss for insurance benefits relevant for impeachment purposes).

c. Nonprejudicial References to Insurance

Nguyen v. Myers, 442 S.W.3d 434, 440 (Tex. App.—Dallas 2013, no pet.) (mere mention of insurance not necessarily grounds for reversal; party complaining of ruling must show evidence of insurance was harmful).

Brownsville Pediatric Ass'n v. Reyes, 68 S.W.3d 184, 193 (Tex. App.—Corpus Christi 2002, no pet.) (trial court did not abuse discretion allowing party to mention insurance in discussing annuity where reference was not type of prejudicial reference that rule was designed to prohibit).

Beall v. Ditmore, 867 S.W.2d 791, 795 (Tex. App.—El Paso 1993, writ denied) (improper reference to insurance can be harmless error).

Univ. of Tex. at Austin v. Hinton, 822 S.W.2d 197, 201 (Tex. App.—Austin 1991, no writ) (trial court did not abuse discretion allowing party to clarify certain insurance coverage issues to prevent jury confusion regarding possible double recovery).

d. Admissions

Gothard v. Marr, 581 S.W.2d 276, 281 (Tex. Civ. App.—Waco 1979, no pet.) (evidence of proof of loss for insurance benefits relevant for impeachment purposes).

e. To Prove Ownership or Employment

Meuth v. Hartgrove, 811 S.W.2d 626, 628 (Tex. App.—Austin 1990, writ denied) (although insurance certificate admissible to demonstrate ownership or control, trial court properly redacted information regarding policy limits before admitting certificate).

Davis v. Stallones, 750 S.W.2d 235, 238 (Tex. App.—Houston [1st Dist.] 1987, no writ) (evidence of insurance coverage proper to demonstrate control).

Jacobini v. Hall, 719 S.W.2d 396, 401 (Tex. App.—Fort Worth 1986, writ ref'd n.r.e.) (insurance evidence properly admitted to show ownership).

C. Motion to Exclude Settlement Evidence

1. Suggested Motion Text

(*Name of Moving Party*) hereby moves this Court for an order excluding any and all evidence, references to evidence, testimony, or argument relating to prior settlements or settlement negotiations between parties to this action (*or Describe Parties and Specifics of Settlement or Negotiations*). The motion is based upon the grounds that the evidence is irrelevant, immaterial, prejudicial, and expressly inadmissible pursuant to Texas rule of Evidence 408.

2. Motion Summary

This motion is used to exclude evidence of settlements and settlement negotiations between parties and former parties to the action. The motion is based on the express authority of Texas Rule of Evidence 408 and the court's authority to exclude evidence that is irrelevant [Texas Rule of Evidence 402] or misleading, confusing, or unduly prejudicial [Texas Rule of Evidence 403], as well as leading cases. See *Martinez v. RV Tool, Inc.*, 737 S.W.2d 17, 18 (Tex. App.—El Paso 1987, writ denied).

3. Supporting Authorities

Texas Rule of Evidence 408 states:

> *Evidence of (1) furnishing or offering or promising to furnish or (2) accepting or offering or promising to accept, a valuable consideration in compromising or attempting to compromise a claim which was disputed as to either validity or amount is not admissible to prove liability for or invalidity of the claim or its amount. Evidence of conduct or statements made in compromise negotiations is likewise not admissible.*
> This rule does not require the exclusion of any evidence otherwise

discoverable merely because it is presented in the course of compromise negotiations. This rule also does not require exclusion when the evidence is offered for another purpose, such as proving bias or prejudice or interest of a witness or a party, negativing [sic] a contention of undue delay, or proving an effort to obstruct a criminal investigation or prosecution. (Emphasis added.)

Ford Motor Co. v. Leggat, 904 S.W.2d 643, 649 (Tex. 1995) (in considering certain discovery issues, settlement agreements not admissible to demonstrate liability).

In re Am. Nat. County Mut. Ins. Co., 384 S.W.3d 429, 435 (Tex. App.—Austin 2012, orig. proceeding) ("[E]xclusion of settlement offers promotes the settlement of claims and recognizes that such evidence does not represent a party's actual position, but is an amount he is willing to give or take to avoid the expense and annoyance of litigation.").

In re Foremost Ins. Co., 966 S.W.2d 770, 772 (Tex. App.—Corpus Christi 1998, no writ) (trial court should have severed bad faith claim against insurance company from personal injury claim where insurer had right to keep settlement negotiations and offers out of proceedings in personal injury matter).

Martinez v. RV Tool, Inc., 737 S.W.2d 17, 18 (Tex. App.—El Paso 1987, writ denied) (evidence of settlement inadmissible).

Osborne v. English, 458 S.W.2d 209, 213 (Tex. Civ. App.—Houston [1st Dist.] 1970, writ ref'd n.r.e.) (in personal injury claim, trial court properly excluded evidence of property settlement).

a. Prior Settlements

Ford Motor Co. v. Leggat, 904 S.W.2d 643, 649 (Tex. 1995) (prior settlement amounts irrelevant and properly protected from discovery).

Jones v. Red Arrow Heavy Hauling, Inc., 816 S.W.2d 134, 136 (Tex. App.—Beaumont 1991, writ denied) (evidence of settlement of claim against insurance company on unrelated contract not relevant).

Osborne v. English, 458 S.W.2d 209, 213 (Tex. Civ. App.—Houston [1st Dist.] 1970, writ ref'd n.r.e.) (in personal injury claim, trial court properly excluded evidence of property settlement).

b. Settlement Negotiations

In re Am. Nat. County Mut. Ins. Co., 384 S.W.3d 429, 435 (Tex. App.—Austin 2012, orig. proceeding) ("[W]hen an insurer has made an offer to settle a disputed contract claim, a conflict arises between the parties' right to introduce the settlement offer in trying the bad faith claim and the insurer's right to exclude the evidence in the defense of the contract claims; in such cases the claims should be severed.").

Vinson Minerals, Ltd. v. XTO Energy, Inc., 335 S.W.3d 344, 351 (Tex. App.—Fort Worth 2010, pet. denied) ("[I]n an offer of settlement or compromise, a party concedes some right to which that party believes he or she is entitled in order to bring about a mutual settlement.... But Rule 408 does not bar the admission of settlement offers when offered for another relevant purpose.").

Vinson Minerals, Ltd. v. XTO Energy, Inc., 335 S.W.3d 344, 351 (Tex. App.—Fort Worth 2010, pet. denied) (purpose of rule excluding evidence of offer to compromise a claim is to encourage settlement).

In re Foremost Ins. Co., 966 S.W.2d 770, 772 (Tex. App.—Corpus Christi 1998, no writ) (trial court should have severed bad faith claim against insurance company from personal injury claim where insurer had right to keep settlement negotiations and offers out of proceedings in personal injury matter).

Ochs v. Martinez, 789 S.W.2d 949, 959 (Tex. App.—San Antonio 1990, writ denied) (evidence of contradictory statements made by party during settlement negotiations properly excluded; bias and prejudice exception in rule is narrow and purpose is to show conflicts of interest in witness).

c. Settlement With Codefendants

Texas Civil Practice and Remedies Code § 33.015(d) states that "[n]o defendant has a right of contribution against any settling person."

Jordan v. Shields, 674 S.W.2d 464, 468 (Tex. App.—Beaumont 1984, no writ) (evidence of settlement between codefendants properly excluded).

Clayton v. Volkswagenwerk, A. G., 606 S.W.2d 15, 17 (Tex. Civ. App.—Houston [1st Dist.] 1980, writ ref'd n.r.e.) (trial court erred admitting evidence of settlement agreement between plaintiff and codefendants where codefendants did not assist plaintiff in obtaining verdict against remaining defendant).

d. Where Offer Made Before Litigation

Payne v. Edmonson, 712 S.W.2d 793 (Tex. App.—Houston [1st Dist.] 1986, writ ref'd n.r.e.) (settlement negotiations that occurred prior to filing suit inadmissible).

e. Other Grounds

Other possible grounds for excluding settlement evidence include:

- Time-wasting;
- Confusing or misleading;
- Solely intended to create an emotional bias;
- Collateral to issues in case;
- Inadmissible hearsay;
- Collateral source rule.

4. Opposing Authorities

Texas Rule of Evidence 408 states in relevant part:

> This rule does not require the exclusion of any evidence otherwise discoverable merely because it is presented in the course of compromise negotiations. This rule also does not require exclusion when the evidence is offered for another purpose, such as proving bias

or prejudice or interest of a witness or a party, negativing [sic] a contention of undue delay, or proving an effort to obstruct a criminal investigation or prosecution.

In re Am. Nat. County Mut. Ins. Co., 384 S.W.3d 429, 434 (Tex. App.—Austin 2012, orig. proceeding) ("[S]ettlement offers are not admissible to prove liability for, or invalidity of, the claim or its amount, but may be admissible for another purpose.").

Vinson Minerals, Ltd. v. XTO Energy, Inc., 335 S.W.3d 344, 351 (Tex. App.—Fort Worth 2010, pet. denied) (burden is on party objecting to evidence as an offer of settlement to show it was a part of settlement negotiations and not offered for another purpose).

Tatum v. Progressive Polymers, Inc., 881 S.W.2d 835, 837 (Tex. App.—Tyler 1994, no writ) (job offer made to plaintiff after lawsuit filed was not considered improper evidence of settlement offer where offer did not have conditions or benefits attached other than that which would attach to a normal job offer).

Portland Sav. & Loan Ass'n v. Bernstein, 716 S.W.2d 532, 537 (Tex. App.—Corpus Christi 1985, writ ref'd n.r.e.), *cert. denied*, 475 U.S. 1016 (1986), *overruled on other grounds, Dawson-Austin v. Austin*, 968 S.W.2d 319 (Tex. 1998) (settlement negotiations admissible to demonstrate alleged misrepresentations).

a. Bias or Prejudice

Texas Rule of Evidence 408 states in relevant part:

> This rule does not require the exclusion of any evidence otherwise discoverable merely because it is presented in the course of compromise negotiations. This rule also does not require exclusion when the evidence is offered for another purpose, such as proving bias or prejudice or interest of a witness or a party, negativing [sic] a contention of undue delay, or proving an effort to obstruct a criminal investigation or prosecution.

Vinson Minerals, Ltd. v. XTO Energy, Inc., 335 S.W.3d 344, 351 (Tex. App.—Fort Worth 2010, pet. denied) (offer of settlement or compromise is generally inadmissible, but settlement offers are admissible when offered for another relevant purpose such as to demonstrate bias or prejudice).

In re Univar USA, Inc., 311 S.W.3d 175, 179 (Tex. App.—Beaumont 2010, orig. proceeding) (settlement agreements and offers may be discoverable for purposes other than to establish liability, such as to demonstrate bias or prejudice of a party or witness, or, to establish the existence of a promise or agreement made by nonparties to the settled lawsuit).

L.M.W. v. State, 891 S.W.2d 754, 761 (Tex. App.—Fort Worth 1994, writ ref'd) (trial court erred excluding settlement evidence where showed that defendant's former husband offered to influence criminal proceedings in exchange for concessions in civil proceedings).

McAllen Kentucky Fried Chicken No. 1, Inc. v. Leal, 627 S.W.2d 480, 485 (Tex. App.—Corpus Christi 1981, writ ref'd n.r.e.) (where plaintiff settles with one defendant and gives that defendant stake in resulting verdict against another defendant, settlement agreement is admissible to prevent jury confusion and to suggest possible bias of settling defendant).

Robertson Tank Lines, Inc. v. Watson, 491 S.W.2d 706, 709 (Tex. Civ. App.—Beaumont 1973, writ ref'd n.r.e.) (evidence that defendant had voluntarily paid for damage to witness's property admissible to suggest witness's bias, prejudice, or motive to testify).

b. Impeachment

Texas Rule of Evidence 408 states in relevant part:

> This rule does not require the exclusion of any evidence otherwise discoverable merely because it is presented in the course of compromise negotiations. This rule also does not require exclusion when the evidence is offered for another purpose, such as proving bias or prejudice or interest of a witness or a party, negativing [sic] a contention of undue delay, or proving an effort to obstruct a criminal investigation or prosecution.

Gen. Motors Corp. v. Saenz, 829 S.W.2d 230, 242 (Tex. App.—Corpus Christi 1991), *rev'd on other grounds*, 873 S.W.2d 353 (Tex. 1993) (harmless error where settlement evidence should have been admissible for impeachment purposes).

McAllen Kentucky Fried Chicken No. 1, Inc. v. Leal, 627 S.W.2d 480, 485 (Tex. App.—Corpus Christi 1981, writ ref'd n.r.e.) (when plaintiff settles with one defendant and gives that defendant stake in resulting verdict against another defendant, settlement agreement admissible to prevent jury confusion and to suggest possible bias of settling defendant).

Robertson Tank Lines, Inc. v. Watson, 491 S.W.2d 706, 709 (Tex. Civ. App.—Beaumont 1973, writ ref'd n.r.e.) (evidence that defendant voluntarily paid for damage to witness's property admissible to suggest witness's bias, prejudice, or motive to testify).

c. Settlement With Codefendant

Mi-Jack Prods., Inc. v. Braneff, 827 S.W.2d 493, 497 (Tex. App.—Houston [1st Dist.] 1992, no writ) (court erred excluding evidence that settling defendants who also participated in trial had financial stake in outcome).

McAllen Kentucky Fried Chicken No. 1, Inc. v. Leal, 627 S.W.2d 480, 485 (Tex. App.—Corpus Christi 1981, writ ref'd n.r.e.) (when plaintiff settles with one defendant and gives that defendant stake in resulting verdict against another defendant, settlement agreement is admissible to prevent jury confusion and to suggest possible bias of settling defendant).

d. State of Mind

Texas Rule of Evidence 408 states in relevant part:

> This rule does not require the exclusion of any evidence otherwise discoverable merely because it is presented in the course of compromise negotiations. This rule also does not require exclusion when

the evidence is offered for another purpose, such as proving bias or prejudice or interest of a witness or a party, negativing [sic] a contention of undue delay, or proving an effort to obstruct a criminal investigation or prosecution.

Tarrant County v. English, 989 S.W.2d 368 (Tex. App.—Fort Worth 1998 pet. denied) (settlement letter admissible to demonstrate party's state of mind).

D. Motion to Exclude Evidence of Other Accidents

1. Suggested Motion Text

(*Name of Moving Party*) hereby moves this Court for an order excluding any and all evidence, references to evidence, testimony, or argument relating to (*Describe Date and Nature of Prior or Subsequent Accident, e.g., a Prior Automobile Accident Involving Plaintiff and an Unrelated Party That Occurred On or About January 31, 1999*). The motion is based upon the grounds that the evidence is irrelevant, immaterial, confusing and will create a substantial danger of undue prejudice to (*Name of Moving Party*).

2. Motion Summary

This motion is used to exclude evidence of prior and subsequent accidents and acts where irrelevant to the issues in the case. The motion is based upon the court's authority to exclude prejudicial evidence [Texas Rule of Evidence 403] and evidence that is irrelevant [Texas Rule of Evidence 402], and a line of leading cases. *See Felix v. Gonzalez*, 87 S.W.3d 574, 579 (Tex. App.—San Antonio 2002, pet. denied) [prior accidents]; *Buchanan v. Cent. Freight Lines, Inc.*, 462 S.W.2d 391, 398 (Tex. Civ. App.—Dallas 1971, writ ref'd n.r.e.) [prior good driving habits]; *Lovelace v. Sabine Consol., Inc.*, 733 S.W.2d 648, 654 (Tex. App.—Houston [14th Dist.] 1987, writ denied) [subsequent acts].

3. Supporting Authorities

Buchanan v. Cent. Freight Lines, Inc., 462 S.W.2d 391, 398 (Tex. Civ. App.—Dallas 1971, writ ref'd n.r.e.) (where eyewitness to accident, evidence of prior good driving habits properly excluded).

Lands v. York Oil Corp., 280 S.W.2d 628, 632 (Tex. Civ. App.—San Antonio 1955, writ ref'd n.r.e.) (where eyewitness testimony available, evidence of careful driving habits improper).

a. Prior Accident Evidence Used to Show Negligence

Felix v. Gonzalez, 87 S.W.3d 574, 579 (Tex. App.—San Antonio 2002, pet. denied) (trial court should not have admitted evidence of prior accident to suggest driver was negligent during incident in question).

Waldon v. City of Longview, 855 S.W.2d 875, 879 (Tex. App.—Tyler 1993, no writ) (evidence of past accidents or negligence properly excluded where offered to suggest conduct in conformity with past acts during events in question).

Port Terminal R.R. Ass'n v. Sims, 671 S.W.2d 575 (Tex. App.—Houston [1st Dist.] 1984, writ ref'd n.r.e.), *cert. denied*, 471 U.S. 1016 (1985) (evidence of prior accidents and prior acts of negligence properly excluded).

b. Lack of Similarity—Dangerous Condition/Defective Products

GB Tubulars, Inc. v. Union Gas Op. Co., 527 S.W.3d 563, 572 (Tex. App.—Houston [14th Dist.] 2017, pet. denied) (for evidence of other incidents in a product defect case, "the other incidents must have occurred under reasonably similar (though not necessarily identical) conditions.... To prove the proper predicate in a product defect case, the proponent of the evidence must offer evidence indicating that the defect that caused the other incidents was similar to the defect alleged in the case at hand.... Second, evidence of similar incidents is inadmissible if it creates undue prejudice, confusion or delay.... Prolonged proof of what happened in other accidents cannot be used to distract a jury's attention from what happened in the case at hand.... And third, the relevance of other accidents depends upon the purpose for offering them....").

Huckaby v. A.G. Perry & Son, Inc., 20 S.W.3d 194, 201 (Tex. App.—Texarkana 2000, pet. denied) (trial court erred admitting evidence of prior accidents where no proof accidents occurred under sufficiently similar conditions).

E-Z Mart Stores, Inc. v. Terry, 794 S.W.2d 63, 65 (Tex. App.—Texarkana 1990, writ denied) (trial court improperly allowed evidence of other injuries where there was an insufficient showing they occurred under similar conditions).

Klorer v. Block, 717 S.W.2d 754, 761 (Tex. App.—San Antonio 1986, writ ref'd n.r.e.) (evidence of prior accidents inadmissible where plaintiff failed to show other accidents sufficiently similar to incident in question).

Winkelmann v. Battle Island Ranch, 650 S.W.2d 543, 545 (Tex. App.—Houston [14th Dist.] 1983, no writ) (trial court properly excluded evidence of prior accident where conditions surrounding prior incident not sufficiently similar to conditions surrounding incident in question).

Davis v. Snider Indus., 604 S.W.2d 341, 344 (Tex. Civ. App.—Texarkana 1980, writ ref'd n.r.e.) (evidence of prior accident properly excluded where no evidence prior accident was sufficiently similar to accident in question).

Reynolds & Huff v. White, 378 S.W.2d 923, 930 (Tex. Civ. App.—Tyler 1964, no writ) (evidence of other accidents inadmissible unless foundation laid to show circumstances surrounding other incidents sufficiently similar to circumstances surrounding incident in question).

Acme Laundry Co. v. Ford, 284 S.W.2d 745, 746 (Tex. Civ. App.—El Paso 1955, writ ref'd n.r.e.) (evidence of other incidents irrelevant where there was no evidence of the circumstances of the other incidents).

Bonner v. Mercantile Nat'l Bank of Dallas, 203 S.W.2d 780, 782 (Tex. Civ. App.—Waco 1947, writ ref'd n.r.e.) (trial court properly excluded evidence of other locations as comparison to location in issue where no evidence of conditions of other locations).

c. Irrelevant

Kia Motors Corp. v. Ruiz, 432 S.W.3d 865, 882 (Tex. 2014) (spreadsheet detailing warranty claims regarding defects unrelated to a products liability claim were not relevant to because they were not substantially similar to the claims being made).

Serv. Corp. Int'l v. Guerra, 348 S.W.3d 221, 235 (Tex. 2011) ("Evidence of other wrongs or acts is not admissible to prove character in order to show action in conformity therewith.").

Klorer v. Block, 717 S.W.2d 754, 761 (Tex. App.—San Antonio 1986, writ ref'd n.r.e.) (evidence of prior accidents irrelevant where plaintiff failed to show other accidents sufficiently similar to incident in question).

Bell v. Buddies Super-Market, 516 S.W.2d 447, 450 (Tex. Civ. App.—Tyler 1974, writ ref'd n.r.e.) (testimony of other incidents properly excluded as irrelevant where no showing conditions surrounding other incidents sufficiently similar to conditions surrounding incident in question).

Acme Laundry Co. v. Ford, 284 S.W.2d 745, 746 (Tex. Civ. App.—El Paso 1955, writ ref'd n.r.e.) (evidence of other incidents irrelevant where no evidence of circumstances of other incidents).

d. Exclusion of Subsequent Accident Evidence

Lovelace v. Sabine Consol., Inc., 733 S.W.2d 648, 654 (Tex. App.—Houston [14th Dist.] 1987, writ denied) (evidence of subsequent acts not admissible to suggest negligence in incidents at issue).

e. Other Grounds

Other possible grounds for excluding evidence of other accidents include:

- Time-wasting;
- Confusing or misleading;
- Solely intended to create an emotional bias;
- Collateral to issues in case;
- Inadmissible hearsay.

4. Opposing Authorities

Tex. Dep't of Transp. v. Pate, 170 S.W.3d 840, 848 (Tex. App.—Texarkana 2005, pet. denied) (jury can consider whether there were prior accidents as factor in determining issue of foreseeability, but in this case, that factor not conclusive where other factors suggested foreseeability).

a. Similarity: Dangerous Condition/Defective Products

Texas Rule of Evidence 407 states in relevant part:

> (b) **Notification of Defect.** A written notification by a manufacturer of any defect in a product produced by such manufacturer to purchasers thereof is admissible against the manufacturer on the issue of existence of the defect to the extent that it is relevant.

UDR Texas Properties, L.P. v. Petrie, 517 S.W.3d 98, 101 (Tex. 2017) ("[Foreseeability] is a prerequisite to imposing a duty on a property owner to protect persons from third-party criminal acts.... For a landowner to foresee criminal conduct on property, there must be evidence that other crimes have occurred on the property or in its immediate vicinity.... Second, recency and frequency: Foreseeability also depends on how recently and how often criminal conduct has occurred in the past.... Third, similarity: The previous crimes must be sufficiently similar to the crime in question as to place the landowner on notice of the specific danger.... And fourth, publicity: The publicity surrounding the previous crimes helps determine whether a landowner knew or should have known of a foreseeable danger.... These factors—proximity, recency, frequency, similarity, and publicity—must be considered together in determining whether criminal conduct was foreseeable.").

Kia Motors Corp. v. Ruiz, 432 S.W.3d 865, 882 (Tex. 2014) (evidence of other incidents involving a product may be relevant in a products liability case if the incidents occurred under reasonably similar, though not necessarily identical, conditions).

Nissan Motor Co. Ltd. v. Armstrong, 145 S.W.3d 131, 138 (Tex. 2004) ("proof of other accidents may be introduced to show that a product is unreasonably dangerous).

Uniroyal Goodrich Tire Co. v. Martinez, 977 S.W.2d 328, 341 (Tex. 1998), *cert. denied,* 526 U.S. 1040 (1999) (evidence of lawsuits involving similar conditions admissible).

GB Tubulars, Inc. v. Union Gas Op. Co., 527 S.W.3d 563, 572 (Tex. App.—Houston [14th Dist.] 2017, pet. denied) (for evidence of other incidents in a product defect case, "the other incidents must have occurred under reasonably similar (though not necessarily identical) conditions.... To prove the proper predicate in a product defect case, the proponent of the evidence must offer evidence indicating that the defect that caused the other incidents was similar to the defect alleged in the case at hand.... Second, evidence of similar incidents is inadmissible if it creates undue prejudice, confusion or delay.... Prolonged proof of what happened in other accidents cannot be used to distract a jury's attention from what happened in the case at hand.... And third, the relevance of other accidents depends upon the purpose for offering them....").

Park v. Exxon Mobil Corp., 429 S.W.3d 142, 146 (Tex. App.—Dallas 2014, pet. filed) (foreseeability of potential criminal conduct in premises liability cases is established through evidence of specific previous crimes on or near the premises).

McEwen v. Wal-Mart Stores, Inc., 975 S.W.2d 25, 30 (Tex. App.—San Antonio 1998, pet. denied) (evidence of prior accidents should have been admitted to show dangerous condition and notice of same).

Rush v. Bucyrus-Erie Co., 646 S.W.2d 298, 301 (Tex. App.—Tyler 1983, writ ref'd n.r.e.) (trial court erred excluding evidence of prior similar accidents).

Henry v. Mrs. Baird's Bakeries, Inc., 475 S.W.2d 288, 294 (Tex. Civ. App.—Fort Worth 1972, writ ref'd n.r.e.) (evidence of prior incident admissible to suggest cause of occurrence and notice of defendant regarding condition).

Brockman v. J. Weingarten, Inc., 115 S.W.2d 753, 755 (Tex. Civ. App.—Galveston 1938), *aff'd*, 135 S.W.2d 698 (Tex. Crim. App. 1940) (evidence of prior similar accidents should have been admissible to demonstrate existence of dangerous condition and that defendant had notice of condition).

b. Notice

McEwen v. Wal-Mart Stores, Inc., 975 S.W.2d 25, 30 (Tex. App.—San Antonio 1998, pet. denied) (evidence of prior accidents should have been admitted to show dangerous condition and notice of same).

Rendleman v. Clarke, 909 S.W.2d 56, 58 (Tex. App.—Houston [14th Dist.] 1995, writ dism'd as moot, reh'g of writ overruled) (evidence of prior complaints on condition was evidence of defendant's notice of condition and refusal to correct it).

May v. Missouri-Kansas-Texas R.R. Co., 583 S.W.2d 694, 697 (Tex. Civ. App.—Waco 1979), *writ ref'd*, 600 S.W.2d 755 (Tex. 1980) (trial court erred excluding evidence of other prior incidents to show existence of dangerous condition and defendant's notice of condition).

Henry v. Mrs. Baird's Bakeries, Inc., 475 S.W.2d 288, 294 (Tex. Civ. App.—Fort Worth 1972, writ ref'd n.r.e.) (evidence of prior incident admissible to suggest cause of occurrence and notice of defendant regarding condition).

Safeway Stores Inc. v. Bozeman, 394 S.W.2d 532, 538 (Tex. Civ. App.—Tyler 1965, writ ref'd n.r.e.) (evidence of similar incidents admissible to show causation and knowledge of dangerous condition).

Brockman v. J. Weingarten, Inc., 115 S.W.2d 753, 755 (Tex. Civ. App.—Galveston 1938), *aff'd*, 135 S.W.2d 698 (Tex. Crim. App. 1940) (evidence of prior similar accidents should have been admissible to demonstrate dangerous condition and that defendant had notice of condition).

c. Evidence of Subsequent Accidents

May v. Missouri-Kansas-Texas R. Co., 583 S.W.2d 694, 697 (Tex. Civ. App.—Waco 1979), *writ ref'd*, 600 S.W.2d 755 (Tex. 1980) (trial court erred excluding evidence of subsequent incidents to show existence of dangerous condition and to reflect upon issue of exemplary damages).

E. Motion to Exclude Evidence of Subsequent Repairs

1. Suggested Motion Text

(<u>Name of Moving Party</u>) hereby moves this Court for an order excluding any and all evidence, references to evidence, testimony, or argument relating to subsequent repairs by (*Name of Party or Describe Subsequent Repair Evidence to Be Excluded*). The motion is based upon the grounds that the evidence is irrelevant, immaterial, confusing, prejudicial, and expressly precluded by law and public policy.

2. Motion Summary

This motion is used to exclude evidence of subsequent repairs where used to prove negligence or culpable conduct. The motion is based upon the express authority of Texas Rule of Evidence 407 and supporting cases, as well as the court's authority to exclude evidence that is irrelevant [Texas Rule of Evidence 402] or prejudicial [Texas Rule of Evidence 403]. Note that evidence of remedial measures may be admissible in strict products liability cases. *See Fed. Pac. Elec. Co. v. Woodend*, 735 S.W.2d 887, 892 (Tex. App.—Fort Worth 1987, no writ).

3. Supporting Authorities

Texas Rule of Evidence 407 states:

> **Subsequent Remedial Measures**. When, after an injury or harm allegedly caused by an event, measures are taken that, if taken previously, would have made the injury or harm less likely to occur, evidence of the subsequent remedial measures is not admissible to prove negligence, culpable conduct, a defect in a product, a defect in a product's design, or a need for a warning or instruction. This rule does not require the exclusion of evidence of subsequent remedial measures when offered for another purpose, such as proving ownership, control, or feasibility of precautionary measures, if controverted, or impeachment.
>
> **(a) Notification of Defect**. A written notification by a manufacturer of any defect in a product produced by such manufacturer to purchasers thereof is admissible against the manufacturer on the issue of existence of the defect to the extent that it is relevant.

Christus Health Southeast Tex. v. Wilson, 305 S.W.3d 392, 401 (Tex. App.—Eastland 2010, no pet.) (subsequent remedial measures are not admissible to establish liability for a prior accident).

Tex. Dep't of Transp. v. Pate, 170 S.W.3d 840, 848 (Tex. App.—Texarkana 2005, pet. denied) (evidence of remedial measures taken after an accident is ordinarily inadmissible, but such evidence need not be excluded if it is offered for another legitimate purpose).

Penley v. State, 2 S.W.3d 534, 541 (Tex. App.—Texarkana 1999, pet. ref'd), *cert. denied*, 530 U.S. 1243 (2000) (evidence that police department changed procedures for storing blood samples after defendant's first trial ended in mistrial was inadmissible where no issue regarding feasibility of new technique).

Brookshire Bros., Inc. v. Lewis, 911 S.W.2d 791, 796 (Tex. App.—Tyler 1995, writ denied) (trial court erred admitting evidence of subsequent remedial measures).

Pennington v. Brock, 841 S.W.2d 127, 132 (Tex. App.—Houston [14th Dist.] 1992, no pet.) (evidence of change in procedures after incident properly excluded as proof of subsequent remedial measures).

Eoff v. Hal & Charlie Peterson Found., 811 S.W.2d 187, 197 (Tex. App.—San Antonio 1991, no writ) (trial court properly excluded evidence of subsequent remedial measures).

Russell v. Dunn Equip., Inc., 712 S.W.2d 542, 546 (Tex. App.—Houston [14th Dist.] 1986, writ ref'd n.r.e.) (evidence of subsequent remedial measures used to suggest negligence was properly excluded).

a. Other Grounds

Other possible grounds for excluding subsequent repair evidence include:

- Time-wasting;
- Confusing or misleading;
- Solely intended to create an emotional bias;
- Collateral to issues in case;
- Inadmissible hearsay.

4. Opposing Authorities

Texas Rule of Evidence 407 states:

> (a) **Subsequent Remedial Measures**. When, after an injury or harm allegedly caused by an event, measures are taken that, if taken previously, would have made the injury or harm less likely to occur, evidence of the subsequent remedial measures is not admissible to prove negligence, culpable conduct, a defect in a product, a defect in a product's design, or a need for a warning or instruction. *This rule does not require the exclusion of evidence of subsequent remedial measures when offered for another purpose, such as proving ownership, control, or feasibility of precautionary measures, if controverted, or impeachment.* (Emphasis added.)

Keetch v. Kroger Co., 845 S.W.2d 276, 282 (Tex. App.—Dallas 1990), *aff'd*, 845 S.W.2d 262 (Tex. 1992) (subsequent remedial measures can be admissible as impeachment; case held evidence at issue properly excluded).

a. Relevant to Issues

Hagins v. E-Z Mart Stores, Inc., 128 S.W.3d 383, 392 (Tex. App.—Texarkana 2004, no pet.) (evidence of subsequent remedial measures properly admitted to show control over work being done at time of incident).

Tyson Foods, Inc. v. Guzman, 116 S.W.3d 233, 238 (Tex. App.—Tyler 2003, no pet.) (evidence of subsequent remedial measures properly admitted to show control where issue disputed).

Lee Lewis Const., Inc. v. Harrison, 64 S.W.3d 1, 13 (Tex. App.—Amarillo 1999), *aff'd*, 70 S.W.3d 778 (Tex. App.—Amarillo 1999) (evidence of subsequent remedial measures admissible on issue of control).

Exxon Corp. v. Roberts, 724 S.W.2d 863, 869 (Tex. App.—Texarkana 1986, writ ref'd n.r.e.) (evidence of subsequent remedial measures admissible to demonstrate control and feasibility of measures).

b. Strict Products Liability

Texas Rule of Evidence 407 states in relevant part:

> (a) **Notification of Defect.** A written notification by a manufacturer of any defect in a product produced by such manufacturer to purchasers thereof is admissible against the manufacturer on the issue of existence of the defect to the extent that it is relevant.

Uniroyal Goodrich Tire Co. v. Martinez, 977 S.W.2d 328, 341 (Tex. 1998), *cert. denied*, 526 U.S. 1040 (1999) (former Rule 407 does not apply to products liability cases based upon strict liability).

Fed. Pac. Elec. Co. v. Woodend, 735 S.W.2d 887, 892 (Tex. App.—Fort Worth 1987, no writ) ("The rule [former 407] does not prevent admissibility of such evidence in products liability cases based on strict liability. Nor, however, does the rule automatically render such evidence admissible. Other rules of evidence may apply to bar the admission of such evidence.").

> *Important Note: An amendment, effective in cases filed on or after July 1, 2003, re-wrote Texas Rule of Evidence 407(a). Prior to that amendment, it read:*
>
> *(a) Subsequent Remedial Measures. When, after an event, measures are taken which, if taken previously, would have made the event less likely to occur, evidence of the subsequent remedial measures is not admissible to prove negligence or culpable conduct in connection with the event. This rule does not require the exclusion of evidence of subsequent remedial measures when offered for another purpose, such as proving ownership, control or feasibility of precautionary measures, if controverted, or impeachment. Nothing in this rule shall preclude admissibility in products liability cases based on strict liability.*

F. Motion to Exclude Evidence of Statute Violation

1. Suggested Motion Text

(*Name of Moving Party*) hereby moves this Court for an order excluding any and all evidence, references to evidence, testimony, or argument relating to (*Describe Date and Nature of Violation*) by (*Name of Party*). The motion is based upon the grounds that the evidence is irrelevant, immaterial, confusing, and will create a substantial danger of undue prejudice to (*Name of Moving Party*).

2. Motion Summary

This motion is used to exclude evidence of the violation of a statute, ordinance, code, or other provision, where the violation was not the proximate cause of the subject incident and would therefore be highly prejudicial if admitted. The motion is based upon the court's authority to exclude evidence that is irrelevant [Texas Rule of Evidence 402] or misleading, confusing, or unduly prejudicial [Texas Rule of Evidence 403]. *See, e.g. Cody v. Mustang Oil Tool Co.*, 595 S.W.2d 214, 215 (Tex. Civ. App.—Eastland 1980, writ ref'd n.r.e.).

3. Supporting Authorities

Condra Funeral Home v. Rollin, 158 Tex. 478, 484, 314 S.W.2d 277 (Tex. 1958) (question on whether traffic ticket was given to one of drivers improper and constituted harmless error).

Cody v. Mustang Oil Tool Co., 595 S.W.2d 214, 215 (Tex. Civ. App.—Eastland 1980, writ ref'd n.r.e.) (trial court erred allowing officer to testify he had issued traffic ticket to one of parties resulting from incident).

a. Not Proximate Cause

Hudson v. Winn, 859 S.W.2d 504, 508 (Tex. App.—Houston [1st Dist.] 1993, writ denied) (where violation of statute was not proximate cause of injury in question, plaintiff could not obtain verdict on negligence per se theory).

Searcy v. Brown, 607 S.W.2d 937, 941 (Tex. Civ. App.—Houston [1st Dist.] 1980, no writ) (violation of ordinance at issue not proximate cause of incident in question).

b. Not Negligence Per Se

Perry v. S.N., 973 S.W.2d 301, 305 (Tex. 1998) (violation of child abuse reporting statutes did not constitute negligence per se).

Flutobo, Inc. v. Holloway, 419 S.W.3d 622, 633 (Tex. App.—Houston [14th Dist.] 2013, pet. denied) ("[T]he mere fact that an administrative agency promulgates a rule or regulation does not require the courts to accept it as a standard for civil liability.").

Discovery Operating, Inc. v. BP Am. Prod. Co., 311 S.W.3d 140, 162 (Tex. App.—Eastland 2010, pet. denied) ("[The] mere fact that the legislature adopts a criminal statute does not mean that the courts must accept it as a standard for civil liability in a negligence per se claim.").

Davis v. Jordan, 305 S.W.3d 895, 898 (Tex. App.—Amarillo 2010, no pet.) ("[I]f the verbiage in a statute is conditional or otherwise fails to impose an absolute restriction, the prohibition cannot be the fodder of negligence per se.").

Francis v. Coastal Oil & Gas Corp., 130 S.W.3d 76, 93 (Tex. App.—Houston [1st Dist.] 2003, no pet.) (regulations not penal in nature did not provide basis for negligence per se).

San Benito Bank & Trust Co. v. Landair Travels, 31 S.W.3d 312, 321 (Tex. App.—Corpus Christi 2000, no pet.) (not every violation of criminal code sufficient to demonstrate negligence per se; following factors, as set forth in *Perry v. S.N.*, 973 S.W.2d 301, 305 (Tex. 1998), guide court in determining whether imposing tort liability for violation of particular criminal statute is "fair, workable, and wise: (1) whether the statute is the sole source of any tort duty from the defendant to the plaintiff or merely supplies a standard of conduct for an existing common law duty; (2) whether the statute puts the public on notice by clearly defining the required conduct; (3) whether the statute would impose liability without fault; (4) whether negligence per se would result in ruinous damages disproportionate to the seriousness of the statutory violation, particularly if the liability would fall on a broad and wide range of collateral wrongdoers; and (5) whether the plaintiff's injury is a direct or indirect result of the violation of the statute.").

Cont'l Oil Co. v. Simpson, 604 S.W.2d 530, 534 (Tex. Civ. App.—Amarillo 1980, writ ref'd n.r.e.) (regulations of Railroad Commission insufficient to create duty for purposes of negligence per se where purpose not designed to protect against type of injury at issue).

c. Other Grounds

Other possible grounds for excluding evidence of traffic violations include:

- Time-wasting;
- Confusing or misleading;
- Solely intended to create an emotional bias;
- Collateral to issues in case;
- Inadmissible hearsay;
- Accident reports;
- Impermissible impeachment evidence.

4. Opposing Authorities

McIntire v. Sellers, 311 S.W.2d 886, 893 (Tex. Civ. App.—Austin 1958, writ ref'd n.r.e.) (evidence of traffic violations can be relevant in negligent entrustment cases).

a. Proximate Cause

Mo. Pac. R.R. Co. v. Am. Statesman, 552 S.W.2d 99, 103 (Tex. 1977) (violation of statute at issue was proximate cause of injury).

i. Negligence Per Se

Nixon v. Mr. Property Mgmt. Co., 690 S.W.2d 546, 549 (Tex. 1985) (violation of statute or ordinance can be negligence per se if injured person was within class of people law was designed to protect).

Murray v. O & A Express, Inc., 630 S.W.2d 633, 636 (Tex. 1982) (trial court properly instructed jury on issue of negligence per se where injured parties were among class of people statutes at issue were designed to protect).

Callahan v. Vitesse Aviation Services, LLC, 397 S.W.3d 342, 356 (Tex. App.—Dallas 2013, no pet.) ("[N]egligence per se is a common law tort concept in which a duty is based on a standard of conduct created by a statute rather than on the reasonably prudent person test used in "pure" negligence claims.").

Callahan v. Vitesse Aviation Services, LLC, 397 S.W.3d 342, 356 (Tex. App.—Dallas 2013, no pet.) ("[N]egligence per se is a tort concept whereby a legislatively imposed standard of conduct is adopted by the civil courts as defining the conduct of a reasonably prudent person, and in such a case the jury is not asked to judge whether the defendant acted as a reasonably prudent person would have acted under the same or similar circumstances because the statute itself states what a reasonably prudent person would have done.").

Callahan v. Vitesse Aviation Services, LLC, 397 S.W.3d 342, 356 (Tex. App.—Dallas 2013, no pet.) ("[I]n a negligence per se action, the trial court merely has the fact finder decide if the tortfeasor committed the act proscribed by the statute and if the act proximately caused injury.").

Lopez-Juarez v. Kelly, 348 S.W.3d 10, 27 (Tex. App.—Texarkana 2011, pet. denied) ("[N]egligence per se is a tort concept whereby the civil courts adopt a legislatively imposed standard of conduct as defining the conduct of a reasonably prudent person.").

Lopez-Juarez v. Kelly, 348 S.W.3d 10, 27 (Tex. App.—Texarkana 2011, pet. denied) ("[T]o establish negligence per se, a plaintiff must prove: (1) the defendant's act or omission is in violation of a statute or ordinance, (2) the injured person was within the class of persons which the ordinance was designed to protect, and (3) the defendant's act or omission proximately caused the injury.").

City of Dallas v. Patrick, 347 S.W.3d 452, 459 (Tex. App.—Dallas 2011, no pet.) ("[U]nexcused violation of a statute setting an applicable standard of care constitutes negligence per se if the statute is designed to prevent an injury to the class of persons to which the injured party belongs.").

Trujillo v. Carrasco, 318 S.W.3d 455, 458 (Tex. App.—El Paso 2010, no pet.) (to prove negligence per se, a plaintiff is required to show that a statute or ordinance was violated, that such violation was the proximate cause of plaintiff's damages, and that the statute was designed to prevent injury to a class of persons to which the plaintiff belongs).

Mathis v. Barnes, 316 S.W.3d 795, 804 (Tex. App.—Tyler 2010), *rev'd on other grounds*, 353 S.W.3d 760 (Tex. 2011) ("[O]rdinarily, if the duty imposed by a statute creates civil liability for its violation, the standard of care will be defined by the statute.... Thus, the jury would ordinarily be asked not whether the defendant acted reasonably, but only whether the defendant violated the statute.").

West v. SMG, 318 S.W.3d 430, 435 n.1 (Tex. App.—Houston [1st Dist.] 2010, no pet.) ("[N]egligence per se is a common-law doctrine that allows courts to rely on a penal statute to define a reasonably prudent person's standard of care.").

Discovery Operating, Inc. v. BP Am. Prod. Co., 311 S.W.3d 140, 162 (Tex. App.—Eastland 2010, pet. denied) ("[T]hreshold questions in every negligence per se case involving a penal statute are whether the plaintiff belongs to the class that the statute was intended to protect and whether the plaintiff's injury is of a type that the statute was designed to prevent.").

Discovery Operating, Inc. v. BP Am. Prod. Co., 311 S.W.3d 140, 162 (Tex. App.—Eastland 2010, pet. denied) ("[I]f a plaintiff satisfies the threshold questions for negligence per se liability, the court must determine whether it is appropriate to impose negligence per se liability for violations of the statute.").

Davis v. Jordan, 305 S.W.3d 895, 898 (Tex. App.—Amarillo 2010, no pet.) (negligence per se may be founded upon an administrative regulation).

Omega Contracting, Inc. v. Torres, 191 S.W.3d 828, 840 (Tex. App.—Fort Worth 2006, no pet.) (administrative regulation may form the basis of negligence per se; "threshold questions in every negligence per se case are whether the plaintiff belongs to the class that the statute was intended to protect and whether the plaintiff's injury is of a type that the statute was designed to prevent").

Mieth v. Ranchquest, 177 S.W.3d 296, 305 (Tex. App.—Houston [1st Dist.] 2005, no pet.) (in negligence per se case, "if an excuse is not raised, the only inquiry for the jury is whether the defendant violated the statute or regulation and, if so, whether the violation was a proximate cause of the accident").

Osti v. Saylors, 991 S.W.2d 322, 328 (Tex. App.—Houston [1st Dist.] 1999, pet. denied) (violations of municipal codes could form basis for negligence per se).

G. Motion to Exclude Evidence of Driver's License Suspension

1. Suggested Motion Text

(*Name of Moving Party*) hereby moves this Court for an order excluding any and all evidence, references to evidence, testimony, or argument relating to (*Describe Evidence, e.g., the Fact That Defendant's License Was Suspended at the Time of the Subject Incident*) (*or, Describe Date and Nature of Suspension*). The motion is based upon the grounds that the evidence is irrelevant, immaterial, confusing, and will create a substantial danger of undue prejudice to (*Name of Moving Party*).

2. Motion Summary

This motion is used to exclude evidence that a driver was unlicensed or had his or her license suspended or revoked. The motion is based upon the leading cases. *See Medina v. Salinas*, 736 S.W.2d 224, 225 (Tex. App.—Corpus Christi 1987, writ denied).

3. Supporting Authorities

Medina v. Salinas, 736 S.W.2d 224, 225 (Tex. App.—Corpus Christi 1987, writ denied) (evidence driver did not have driver's license is not evidence of negligence or causation in case that did not involve negligent entrustment claim).

Evans v. Jacobs, 228 S.W.2d 545, 547 (Tex. Civ. App.—Austin 1950, no writ) (evidence driver did not have permit to operate vehicle at issue improper and irrelevant and should not have been admitted as evidence of negligence or for impeachment).

a. Other Grounds

Other possible grounds for excluding license evidence include:

- Time-wasting;
- Confusing or misleading;
- Solely intended to create an emotional bias;
- Collateral to issues in case;
- Inadmissible impeachment evidence.

4. Opposing Authorities

Mundy v. Pirie-Slaughter Motor Co., 146 Tex. 314, 319, 206 S.W.2d 587 (Tex. 1948) (evidence regarding driver's lack of driver's license was relevant in negligent entrustment case and court should not have excluded it).

Williams v. Steves Indus., Inc., 678 S.W.2d 205, 211 (Tex. App.—Austin 1984, writ granted), *aff'd*, 699 S.W.2d 570 (Tex. 1985) (evidence regarding lack of driver's license can be relevant in negligent entrustment case; evidence may not be sufficient to prove negligence absent proof of actual prior incidents of bad driving by unlicensed driver).

Thomas v. Reed, 483 S.W.2d 61, 63 (Tex. Civ. App.—Dallas 1972, no writ) (lack of driver's license and knowledge of same can be relevant in negligent entrustment case).

H. Motion to Exclude Evidence of Failure to Wear Seatbelt

1. Suggested Motion Text

(*Name of Moving Party*) hereby moves this Court for an order excluding any and all evidence, references to evidence, testimony, or argument relating to (*Name of Party's or Witness's*) failure to wear a seat belt at the time of the subject accident in this case. The motion is based upon the grounds that the evidence is irrelevant, immaterial, confusing and will create a substantial danger of undue prejudice to (*Name of Moving Party*).

2. Motion Summary

This motion is used to exclude evidence of a plaintiff's failure to wear a seat belt or other restraining device at the time of the subject incident. *See Milbrand v. Daimler-Chrysler Corp.*, 105 F. Supp. 2d 601, 605 (E.D. Tex. 2000); *Carnation Co. v. Wong*, 516 S.W.2d 116 (Tex. 1974).

3. Supporting Authorities

Nabors Well Services, Ltd. v. Romero, 456 S.W.3d 553, 563 (Tex. 2015) ("As with any evidence, seat-belt evidence is admissible only if it is relevant.").

a. Other Grounds

Other possible grounds for excluding seatbelt evidence include:

- Time-wasting;
- Confusing or misleading;
- Solely intended to create an emotional bias;
- Collateral to issues in case;
- Inadmissible impeachment evidence.

4. Opposing Authorities

Nabors Well Services, Ltd. v. Romero, 456 S.W.3d 553, 563 (Tex. 2015) ("Under section 33.003(a), the fact-finder may consider relevant evidence of a plaintiff's failure to use a seat belt as a 'negligent act or omission' or as a violation of 'an applicable legal standard' in cases where the plaintiff was personally in violation of an applicable seat-belt law.").

Nabors Well Services, Ltd. v. Romero, 456 S.W.3d 553, 563 (Tex. 2015) ("[I]n cases in which an unrestrained plaintiff was not personally in violation of a seat-belt law, the fact-finder may consider whether the plaintiff was negligent under the applicable standard of reasonable care.").

Glyn-Jones v. Bridgestone/Firestone, Inc., 857 S.W.2d 640, 643 (Tex. App.—Dallas 1993, reh'g denied, writ granted), *aff'd*, 878 S.W.2d 132 (Tex. 1994) (despite statute precluding admission of evidence regarding seat belt use, plaintiff should have been allowed to raise issue in products liability action claiming seat belt was defective).

a. Where Use Would Have Reduced Injuries

Nabors Well Services, Ltd. v. Romero, 456 S.W.3d 553, 563 (Tex. 2015) ("The defendant can establish the relevance of seat-belt nonuse only with evidence that nonuse caused or contributed to cause the plaintiff's injuries.").

Vasquez v. Hyundai Motor Co., 119 S.W.3d 848, 851 (Tex. App.—San Antonio 2003), *rev'd on other grounds*, 189 S.W.3d 743 (Tex. 2006) (where manufacturer was going to raise claim that lack of seat belt contributed to child's death, parents of child killed when airbag deployed should have been allowed to ask jurors if they were prejudiced against people who did not use seat belts).

b. Mandatory Seatbelt Laws

Texas Transportation Code § 545.413 states in relevant part:

Safety Belts; Offense

    (a) A person commits an offense if the person:
        (1) is at least 15 years of age;
        (2) is riding in the front seat of a passenger vehicle while the vehicle is being operated;

(3) is occupying a seat that is equipped with a safety belt; and
(4) is not secured by a safety belt.
(b) A person commits an offense if the person:
  (1) operates a passenger vehicle that is equipped with safety belts; and
  (2) allows a child who is younger than 17 years of age and who is not required to be secured in a child passenger safety seat system under Section 545.412(a) to ride in the vehicle without requiring the child to be secured by a safety belt, provided the child is occupying a seat that is equipped with a safety belt.
(c) A passenger vehicle or a seat in a passenger vehicle is considered to be equipped with a safety belt if the vehicle is required under Section 547.601 to be equipped with safety belts.
(d) An offense under Subsection (a) is a misdemeanor punishable by a fine of not less than $25 or more than $50. An offense under Subsection (b) is a misdemeanor punishable by a fine of not less than $100 or more than $200.
(e) It is a defense to prosecution under this section that:
  (1) the person possesses a written statement from a licensed physician stating that for a medical reason the person should not wear a safety belt;
  (2) the person presents to the court, not later than the 10th day after the date of the offense, a statement from a licensed physician stating that for a medical reason the person should not wear a safety belt;
  (3) the person is employed by the United States Postal Service and performing a duty for that agency that requires the operator to service postal boxes from a vehicle or that requires frequent entry into and exit from a vehicle;
  (4) the person is engaged in the actual delivery of newspapers from a vehicle or is performing newspaper delivery duties that require frequent entry into and exit from a vehicle;
  (5) the person is employed by a public or private utility company and is engaged in the reading of meters or performing a similar duty for that company requiring the operator to frequently enter into and exit from a vehicle; or
  (6) The person is operating a commercial vehicle registered as a farm vehicle under the provisions of Section 502.163 that does not have a gross weight, registered weight, or gross weight rating of 48,000 pounds or more.
  (7) the person is the operator of or a passenger in a vehicle used exclusively to transport solid waste and performing duties that require frequent entry into and exit from the vehicle.
  . . .
(h) In this section, "passenger vehicle," "safety belt," and "secured" have the meanings assigned by Section 545.412.

Nabors Well Services, Ltd. v. Romero, 456 S.W.3d 553, 563 (Tex. 2015) ("Under section 33.003(a), the fact-finder may consider relevant evidence of a plaintiff's failure to use a seat belt as a 'negligent act or omission' or as a violation of 'an applicable legal standard' in cases where the plaintiff was personally in violation of an applicable seat-belt law.").

I. Motion to Exclude Evidence of Alcohol Consumption

1. Suggested Motion Text

(*Name of Moving Party*) hereby moves this Court for an order excluding any and all evidence, references to evidence, testimony, or argument relating to alcohol consumption by (*Name of Party or Witness or Describe Nature of Alcohol-Related Evidence to Be Excluded*). The motion is based upon the grounds that the evidence is irrelevant, immaterial, confusing and will create a substantial danger of undue prejudice to (*Name of Moving Party*).

2. Motion Summary

This motion is used to exclude evidence of a party's or witness's consumption of alcohol where unrelated to issues in the case. The motion is based upon the court's authority to exclude evidence that is irrelevant [Texas Rule of Evidence 402] and prejudicial [Texas Rule of Evidence 403], and leading cases that exclude alcohol evidence where there is no foundational showing of relevance or causation. *See Bituminous Cas. Corp. v. Martin*, 478 S.W.2d 206, 207 (Tex. Civ. App.—El Paso 1972, writ ref'd n.r.e.).

3. Supporting Authorities

Gibbs v. State, 385 S.W.2d 258, 259 (Tex. Crim. App. 1965) (impeachment evidence witness was terminated from employment for driving while intoxicated properly excluded where no evidence witness had been convicted for intoxicated driving and it did not represent crime of moral turpitude).

Holland v. State, 60 Tex.Crim. 117, 120, 131 S.W. 563 (Tex. Crim. App. 1910) (trial court improperly allowed impeachment of witness by evidence that someone had previously brought alcohol to her house and she drank it).

Bituminous Cas. Corp. v. Martin, 478 S.W.2d 206, 209 (Tex. Civ. App.—El Paso 1972, writ ref'd n.r.e.) (evidence regarding drinking habit properly excluded as impeachment evidence where no showing drinking related to incidents in question).

a. Other Grounds

Other possible grounds for excluding alcohol evidence include:

- Time-wasting;
- Confusing or misleading;

- Solely intended to create an emotional bias;
- Collateral to issues in case;
- Inadmissible impeachment evidence.

4. Opposing Authorities

Castaldo v. State, 78 S.W.3d 345, 349 (Tex. Crim. App. 2002) (evidence of passenger's and driver's intoxication relevant and admissible to prove issue of passenger's knowledge regarding marijuana in car).

Douthitt v. State, 127 S.W.3d 327, 335 (Tex. App.—Austin 2004, no pet.) (level of intoxication several hours after accident relevant to suggest level of intoxication at time of accident and admissible in trial for intoxication manslaughter).

Castaldo v. State, 78 S.W.3d 345, 349 (Tex. Crim. App. 2002) (evidence of passenger's and driver's intoxication relevant and admissible to prove issue of passenger's knowledge regarding marijuana in car).

a. Witness Perceptions

Lagrone v. State, 942 S.W.2d 602, 613 (Tex. Crim. App. 1997), *cert. denied*, 522 U.S. 917 (1997) ("We have held that a witness' credibility is only subject to attack on cross-examination when their perceptual capacity is physically impaired by the intoxicating effects of alcohol or drugs during their observation of pertinent events." (Citations omitted.)).

Bituminous Cas. Corp. v. Martin, 478 S.W.2d 206, 209 (Tex. Civ. App.—El Paso 1972, writ ref'd n.r.e.) (witness may be impeached by evidence that witness was drunk at time of events in question).

Russell v. State, 84 Tex.Crim. 245, 250, 209 S.W. 671 (Tex. Crim. App. 1919) (impeachment evidence that defendant was intoxicated at time of events held proper).

J. Motion to Exclude Evidence of Prior DWI

1. Suggested Motion Text

(*Name of Moving Party*) hereby moves this Court for an order excluding any and all evidence, references to evidence, testimony, or argument relating to prior criminal convictions for driving under the influence by (*Name of Party*) (*or, Describe Nature and Date of Violation*). The motion is based upon the grounds that the evidence is inadmissible to prove wrongful conduct or impeachment and is irrelevant, immaterial, confusing and will create a substantial danger of undue prejudice to (*Name of Moving Party*).

2. Motion Summary

This motion is used to exclude evidence of prior convictions for driving while under the influence of alcohol ("DWI") where used for impeachment or to prove wrongful conduct in civil cases. The motion is based upon statutory and case law authorities precluding the use of most misdemeanors and certain felony convictions. See Texas Rules of Evidence 609(a) and 404(b); *Arnold v. State*, 36 S.W.3d 542, 547 (Tex. App.—Tyler 2000, pet. ref'd) (prior misdemeanor evidence excluded where used to attack credibility); *Enriquez v. State*, 56 S.W.3d 596, 601 (Tex. App.—Corpus Christi 2001, pet. ref'd) (crimes evidence excluded where used to show disposition to commit similar act).

3. Supporting Authorities

Texas Rule of Evidence 608(a) states:

> The credibility of a witness may be attacked or supported by evidence in the form of opinion or reputation, but subject to these limitations: (1) the evidence may refer only to character for truthfulness or untruthfulness; and (2) evidence of truthful character is admissible only after the character of the witness for truthfulness has been attacked by opinion or reputation evidence or otherwise.

Texas Rule of Evidence 608(b) states:

> Specific instances of the conduct of a witness, for the purpose of attacking or supporting the witness' credibility, other than conviction of crime as provided in Rule 609, may not be inquired into on cross-examination of the witness nor proved by extrinsic evidence.

Texas Rule of Evidence 609 (a) states:

> General Rule. For the purpose of attacking the credibility of a witness, evidence that the witness has been convicted of a crime shall be admitted if elicited from the witness or established by public record *but only if the crime was a felony or involved moral turpitude, regardless of punishment, and the court determines that the probative value of admitting this evidence outweighs its prejudicial effect to a party.* (Emphasis added.)

Note: See also the exceptions in Texas Rule of Evidence 609(b) through (f).

Gibbs v. State, 385 S.W.2d 258, 259 (Tex. Crim. App. 1965) (impeachment evidence that witness was terminated from employment for driving while intoxicated properly excluded where no evidence that witness convicted for intoxicated driving and did not represent crime of moral turpitude).

Moore v. State, 143 S.W.3d 305, 314 (Tex. App.—Waco 2004, pet. ref'd) ("[P]rior DWI conviction is not relevant to [the victim's] truthful character because it is not a conviction for a crime involving moral turpitude").

Hilliard v. State, 881 S.W.2d 917, 922 (Tex. App.—Fort Worth 1994, no pet.) (trial court properly prevented defendant from cross examining witness about conviction for driving while intoxicated and alleged prior bad acts not resulting in conviction).

a. Exclusion of Arrests and Misdemeanor Convictions

Where the DWI evidence is a misdemeanor conviction, the motion may be based upon case law precluding the use of such evidence for impeachment.

Martinez v. State, 17 S.W.3d 677, 688 (Tex. Crim. App. 2000) (trial court properly excluded evidence of offenses not resulting in convictions where evidence offered to impeach witness).

Gibbs v. State, 385 S.W.2d 258, 259 (Tex. Crim. App. 1965) (impeachment evidence that witness was terminated from employment for driving while intoxicated properly excluded where no evidence that witness convicted for intoxicated driving and did not represent crime of moral turpitude).

Ortiz v. Furr's Supermarkets, 26 S.W.3d 646, 655 (Tex. App.—El Paso 2000, no pet.) (trial court did not abuse its discretion by determining that misdemeanor possession of marijuana was not a crime of moral turpitude and excluding impeachment evidence that a witness had been convicted of that offense).

Hilliard v. State, 881 S.W.2d 917, 922 (Tex. App.—Fort Worth 1994, no pet.) (trial court properly prevented defendant from cross examining witness about conviction for driving while intoxicated and alleged prior bad acts not resulting in conviction).

Hutson v. State, 843 S.W.2d 106, 107 (Tex. App.—Texarkana 1992, no pet.) (criminal trespass is not crime of moral turpitude for purposes of Texas Rule of Evidence 609).

Patterson v. State, 783 S.W.2d 268, 271 (Tex. App.—Houston [14th Dist.] 1989, pet. ref'd) (reckless conduct conviction not admissible as impeachment where not felony and did not involve moral turpitude).

b. Exclusion of Convictions Where No Bearing on Credibility

Texas Rule of Evidence 609(a) states:

> **General Rule.** For the purpose of attacking the credibility of a witness, evidence that the witness has been convicted of a crime shall be admitted if elicited from the witness or established by public record *but only if the crime was a felony or involved moral turpitude, regardless of punishment, and the court determines that the probative value of admitting this evidence outweighs its prejudicial effect to a party.* (Emphasis added.)

Note: see also the exceptions in Texas Rule of Evidence 609(b) through (f).

Moore v. State, 143 S.W.3d 305, 314 (Tex. App.—Waco 2004, pet. ref'd) ("[P]rior DWI conviction is not relevant to [the victim's] truthful character because it is not a conviction for a crime involving moral turpitude.").

c. Where Probative Value Outweighed by Risk of Undue Prejudice

Texas Rule of Evidence 609(a) states:

> **General Rule**. For the purpose of attacking the credibility of a witness, evidence that the witness has been convicted of a crime shall be admitted if elicited from the witness or established by public record but only if the crime was a felony or involved moral turpitude, regardless of punishment, *and the court determines that the probative value of admitting this evidence outweighs its prejudicial effect to a party.* (Emphasis added.)

Note: See also the exceptions in Texas Rule of Evidence 609(b) through (f).

Booker v. State, 103 S.W.3d 521, 530 (Tex. App.—Fort Worth 2003, pet. ref'd) (trial court did not abuse discretion determining that other offenses were sufficiently similar to demonstrate identity; appellate court held one of prior offenses should have been excluded under Rule 403 balancing test as unduly prejudicial, confusing, and time-consuming).

d. Exclusion of DWI Evidence Where Used to Prove Improper Conduct

Where the DWI evidence is used to prove a person's conduct in conformity with the prior conviction, it may be excludable under the authority of Texas Rule of Evidence 404(b), which states:

> *Evidence of other crimes, wrongs or acts is not admissible to prove the character of a person in order to show action in conformity therewith.* It may, however, be admissible for other purposes, such as proof of motive, opportunity, intent, preparation, plan, knowledge, identity, or absence of mistake or accident, provided that upon timely request by the accused in a criminal case, reasonable notice is given in advance of trial of intent to introduce in the State's case-in-chief such evidence other than that arising in the same transaction. (Emphasis added.)

Peters v. State, 93 S.W.3d 347, 352 (Tex. App.—Houston [14th Dist.] 2002, pet. denied) (in case involving possession of cocaine where only issue was consent to search, trial court committed harmless error admitting evidence of shotgun and marijuana found in room, where evidence represented improper character evidence).

e. Other Grounds

Other possible grounds for excluding D.U.I. evidence include:

- Time-wasting;
- Confusing or misleading;

- Solely intended to create an emotional bias;
- Collateral to issues in case;
- Improper impeachment evidence;
- Improper felony conviction;
- Inadmissible hearsay;
- Impermissible evidence of statute violation;
- Impermissible alcohol evidence.

4. Opposing Authorities

Bituminous Cas. Corp. v. Martin, 478 S.W.2d 206, 209 (Tex. Civ. App.—El Paso 1972, writ ref'd n.r.e.) (witness may be impeached by evidence that witness was drunk at time of events in question).

Russell v. State, 84 Tex.Crim. 245, 250, 209 S.W. 671 (Tex. Crim. App. 1919) (impeachment evidence defendant was intoxicated at time of events held proper).

a. Use of Felony Convictions Expressly Allowed for Impeachment

Texas Rule of Evidence 609 (a) states:

> **General Rule.** For the purpose of attacking the credibility of a witness, evidence that the witness has been convicted of a crime shall be admitted if elicited from the witness or established by public record but only if the crime was a felony or involved moral turpitude, regardless of punishment, and the court determines that the probative value of admitting this evidence outweighs its prejudicial effect to a party.

Note: See also the exceptions in Texas Rule of Evidence 609(b) through (f).

i. DWI as a Felony

Texas Penal Code § 49.09 states in pertinent part:

> **Enhanced Offenses and Penalties**
>
> (a) Except as provided by Subsection (b), an offense under Section 49.04, 49.05, 49.06 or 49.065 is a Class A misdemeanor, with a minimum term of confinement of 30 days, if it is shown on the trial of the offense that the person has previously been convicted one time of an offense relating to the operating of a motor vehicle while intoxicated, an offense of operating an aircraft while intoxicated, an offense of operating a watercraft while intoxicated, or an offense of operating or assembling an amusement ride while intoxicated.
>
> (b) An offense under 49.04, 49.05, 49.06 or 49.065 is a felony of the third degree if it is shown on the trial of the offense that the person has previously been convicted:

(1) one time of an offense under Section 49.08 or an offense under the laws of another state if the offense contains elements that are substantially similar to the elements of an offense under Section 49.08; or
(2) two times of any other offense relating to the operating of a motor vehicle while intoxicated, operating an aircraft while intoxicated, operating a watercraft while intoxicated, or operating or assembling an amusement ride while intoxicated.

Rice v. State, 163 Tex. Crim. 367, 292 S.W.2d 114 (Tex. Crim. App. 1956) (evidence showing defendant's prior conviction relevant and admissible to enhance sentence of current offense).

Blank v. State, 172 S.W.3d 673, 675 (Tex. App.—San Antonio 2005) (evidence of prior DWI can be used to enhance defendant's sentence; offered evidence found to be insufficient to prove prior conviction).

b. *Relevant to Issues*

Texas Rule of Evidence 404 states:

(a) **Character Evidence Generally.** Evidence of a person's character or character trait is not admissible for the purpose of proving action in conformity therewith on a particular occasion, except:
  (1) *Character of accused. Evidence of a pertinent character trait offered:*
    (A) *by an accused in a criminal case, or by the prosecution to rebut the same, or*
    (B) *by a party accused in a civil case of conduct involving moral turpitude, or by the accusing party to rebut the same;*
  (2) *Character of victim. In a criminal case and subject to Rule 412, evidence of a pertinent character trait of the victim of the crime offered by an accused, or by the prosecution to rebut the same, or evidence of peaceable character of the victim offered by the prosecution in a homicide case to rebut evidence that the victim was the first aggressor; or in a civil case, evidence of character for violence of the alleged victim of assaultive conduct offered on the issue of self-defense by a party accused of the assaultive conduct, or evidence of peaceable character to rebut the same;*
  (3) *Character of witness.* Evidence of the character of a witness, as provided in rules 607, 608 and 609.
(b) **Other Crimes, Wrongs or Acts.** Evidence of other crimes, wrongs or acts is not admissible to prove the character of a person in order to show action in conformity therewith. *It may, however, be admissible for other purposes, such as proof of motive,*

opportunity, intent, preparation, plan, knowledge, identity, or absence of mistake or accident, provided that upon timely request by the accused in a criminal case, reasonable notice is given in advance of trial of intent to introduce in the State's case-in-chief such evidence other than that arising in the same transaction. (Emphasis added.)

Booker v. State, 103 S.W.3d 521, 530 (Tex. App.—Fort Worth 2003, pet. ref'd) (trial court did not abuse its discretion determining other offenses were sufficiently similar to demonstrate identity; appellate court held one of prior offenses should have been excluded under Rule 403 balancing test).

Ludwig v. State, 969 S.W.2d 22, 30 (Tex. App.—Fort Worth 1998, pet. ref'd) (evidence of defendant's prior misdemeanor convictions for violating order of protection properly used to prove intent).

Murray v. State, 840 S.W.2d 675, 678 (Tex. App.—Tyler 1992, no writ) (evidence of drug paraphernalia relevant to rebut defendant's claim that he was intoxicated by accidentally inhaling gas fumes at time of offense).

Wade v. State, 803 S.W.2d 806, 808 (Tex. App.—Fort Worth 1991, no pet.) (defendant should have been allowed to introduce witness's testimony that he never saw defendant possess drugs where testimony represented evidence of pertinent trait for charged offense).

McIntire v. Sellers, 311 S.W.2d 886, 887 (Tex. Civ. App.—Austin 1958, writ ref'd n.r.e.) (evidence of prior DWI offenses can be relevant in negligent entrustment cases).

K. Motion to Exclude Evidence of Party's Health or Injuries Where Not at Issue

1. Suggested Motion Text

(*Name of Moving Party*) hereby moves this Court for an order excluding any and all evidence, references to evidence, testimony, or argument relating to the physical or mental health of (*Name of Party*) (*or, Describe Health or Physical Condition to Be Excluded*). The motion is based upon the grounds that the evidence is irrelevant, immaterial, confusing and will create a substantial danger of undue prejudice to (*Name of Moving Party*).

2. Motion Summary

This motion is used to exclude evidence of a party's health or injuries where not at issue or not disputed. The motion is based upon the court's authority under Texas Rule of Evidence 402 to exclude evidence that is irrelevant, as well as leading cases. *See generally Monk v. Cooper*, 454 S.W.2d 244, 247 (Tex. Civ. App.—Texarkana 1970, writ ref'd n.r.e.).

3. Supporting Authorities

New York Underwriters Ins. Co. v. Upshaw, 560 S.W.2d 433, 435 (Tex. Civ. App.—Beaumont 1977, no writ) (court found it proper in workers' compensation suit to exclude evidence of unrelated prior injuries).

Monk v. Cooper, 454 S.W.2d 244, 247 (Tex. Civ. App.—Texarkana 1970, writ ref'd n.r.e.) (trial court properly excluded evidence related to physical conditions not shown to be related to incident at issue).

Baltazar v. Neill, 364 S.W.2d 846, 848 (Tex. Civ. App.—Austin 1963, writ ref'd n.r.e.) (evidence of prior injuries properly excluded where no evidence they related to current injury).

a. Other Grounds

Other possible grounds for excluding evidence of unrelated injuries or health conditions include:

- Time-wasting;
- Confusing or misleading;
- Solely intended to create an emotional bias;
- Collateral to issues in case;
- Inadmissible hearsay;
- Improper foundation;
- Improper character evidence.

4. Opposing Authorities

Dallas Ry. & Terminal Co. v. Ector, 131 Tex. 505, 507, 116 S.W.2d 683 (1938) (evidence of prior injuries should have been allowed to negate or mitigate issue of causation of current injury for purposes of damages).

J. M. Dellinger, Inc. v. McMillon, 461 S.W.2d 471, 475 (Tex. Civ. App.—Corpus Christi 1970, writ ref'd n.r.e.) (evidence of prior injuries is allowed to negate or mitigate the issue of causation of the current injury for purposes of damages).

L. Motion to Exclude Accident Reconstruction Evidence

1. Suggested Motion Text

(*Name of Moving Party*) hereby moves this Court for an order excluding any and all evidence, references to evidence, testimony, or argument relating to (*Describe Nature of Test, Experiment, or Expected Testimony, e.g., "any tests or demonstrations comparing the impact forces in the subject accident with everyday activities such as plopping into a chair, stepping off a curb, etc."*) conducted or described by (*Name of Witness*). The motion is based upon the ground that the evidence is (*Describe Challenges to Evidence, e.g., "not generally accepted in the scientific community," "not made under substantially identical conditions to subject incident," "not reliable," etc.*) and therefore does not meet the standards required by *Cooper Tire & Rubber Co. v. Mendez*, 204 S.W.3d 797 (Tex. 2006), *Mack Trucks, Inc. v. Tamez*, 206 S.W.3d 572, 580 (Tex. 2006), and *Kelly v. State*, 824 S.W.2d 568 (Tex. Crim. App. 1992) and its progeny, and should be excluded.

2. Motion Summary

This motion is used to exclude inadmissible accident reconstruction and/or biomechanic evidence, typically arising in automobile accident litigation. The motion is based upon a series of authorities that have supported the exclusion of such evidence where it lacks sufficient foundation or reliability to be admissible.

In general, accident reconstruction evidence should be excluded where the evidence lacks sufficient evidentiary foundation [*Pilgrim's Pride Corp. v. Smoak*, 134 S.W.3d 880, 892 (Tex. App.—Texarkana 2004, pet. denied)] or lacks sufficient reliability [*Cooper Tire & Rubber Co. v. Mendez*, 204 S.W.3d 797, 800 (Tex. 2006); *Mack Trucks, Inc. v. Tamez*, 206 S.W.3d 572, 580 (Tex. 2006); *Kelly v. State*, 824 S.W.2d 568, 570 (Tex. Crim. App. 1992)]. Biomechanic evidence is typically challenged under reliability principles where the proposed test lacks sufficient reliability. *See Kelly v. State*, 824 S.W.2d 568, 570 (Tex. Crim. App. 1992).

This motion is typically presented at what is referred to as a *Robinson* hearing, named after the leading case of *E.I. du Pont de Nemours & Co. v. Robinson*, 923 S.W.2d 549 (Tex. 1995).

> *Important note: This section includes a detailed discussion on the exclusion of test evidence in low-impact automobile cases, which is an area of intense dispute in personal injury litigation. Since case law is scarce, the author has provided references to several commentators and provided analogous and out-of-state case support that may be of assistance in attempting to exclude questionable tests and experiments.*

3. Supporting Authorities

Volkswagen of Am., Inc. v. Ramirez, 159 S.W.3d 897, 904 (Tex. 2004) (accident reconstructionist's theory based on general "laws of physics" was not competent evidence where the expert conducted no tests nor cited to any tests to support his theory).

Damian v. Bell Helicopter Textron, Inc., 352 S.W.3d 124, 132 (Tex. App.—Fort Worth 2011, pet. denied) (testimony given by accident reconstruction expert was conclusory where expert did not explain or provide details supporting his theory).

Pilgrim's Pride Corp. v. Smoak, 134 S.W.3d 880, 892 (Tex. App.—Texarkana 2004, pet. denied) (accident reconstruction evidence based upon skid marks and vehicle damage must be given by someone qualified in science).

a. Improper Foundation or Qualification

Gen. Motors Corp. v. Iracheta, 161 S.W.3d 462, 472 (Tex. 2006) (testimony accident reconstruction expert was improper as witness was not qualified).

Lewis v. State, 402 S.W.3d 852, 864 (Tex. App.—Amarillo 2013), *aff'd,* 428 S.W.3d 860 (Tex. Crim. App. 2014) ("[A] computer animation reconstruction is merely a series of images generated by a computer that serves as demonstrative evidence, and may be authenticated by the witness's testimony that the computer animation presents a fair and accurate depiction of what it purports to represent; if it does not represent what it purports to represent, it will not be admissible.").

Lewis v. State, 402 S.W.3d 852, 864 (Tex. App.—Amarillo 2013), *aff'd,* 428 S.W.3d 860 (Tex. Crim. App. 2014) ("[A]ny staged, re-enacted criminal acts or defensive issues involving human beings are impossible to duplicate in every minute detail and are therefore inherently dangerous, offer little in substance, and the impact of re-enactments is too highly prejudicial to insure the State or the defendant a fair trial.").

Lewis v. State, 402 S.W.3d 852, 864 (Tex. App.—Amarillo 2013), *aff'd,* 428 S.W.3d 860 (Tex. Crim. App. 2014) ("[T]he artificial re-creation of an event may unduly accentuate certain phases of the happening, and because of the forceful impression made on the minds of the jurors by this kind of evidence, it should be received with caution.... This is particularly true where the event sought to be depicted is simple, the testimony adequate, and the animation adds nothing more than a one-sided, manipulated visual image to the mental picture already produced in the mind of the jurors by the oral testimony of an eyewitness who has been subjected to the crucible of cross-examination.").

Pilgrim's Pride Corp. v. Smoak, 134 S.W.3d 880, 892 (Tex. App.—Texarkana 2004, pet. denied) (harmless error to allow testimony of officer where not qualified to provide expert opinion on accident reconstruction).

Ford Motor Co. v. Bland, 517 S.W.2d 641, 644 (Tex. Civ. App.—Waco 1975, writ ref'd n.r.e.) (opinion regarding accident reconstruction based upon insufficient investigation properly excluded).

b. Vehicle Speed Determinations

Pena v. State, 155 S.W.3d 238, 250 (Tex. App.—El Paso 2004, no pet.) (harmless error where officer failed to demonstrate reliability of methodology he used to estimate speed of vehicles).

4. Opposing Authorities

TXI Transp. Co. v. Hughes, 306 S.W.3d 230, 238 (Tex. 2010) (testimony of accident reconstruction expert met standard for reliability).

Thomas v. Uzoka, 290 S.W.3d 437, 449 (Tex. App.—Houston [14th Dist.] 2009, pet. denied) (police officer's vehicle speed expert opinions were reliable).

Lincoln v. Clark Freight Lines, Inc., 285 S.W.3d 79, 87 (Tex. App.—Houston [1st Dist.] 2009, no pet.) (neutral expert's testimony in motor vehicle accident reconstruction was reliable, and admissible).

TXI Transp. Co. v. Hughes, 224 S.W.3d 870, 889 (Tex. App.—Fort Worth 2007), *rev'd on other grounds,* 306 S.W.3d 230 (Tex. 2010) (generally, accident reports prepared by investigating officers, possessing sufficient training in accident reconstruction, are admissible as an exception to the hearsay rule).

Gen. Motors Corp. v. Burry, 203 S.W.3d 514, 534 (Tex. App.—Fort Worth 2006, pet. denied) (expert testimonial evidence that included accident reconstruction and crash test video was admissible).

Gen. Motors Corp. v. Burry, 203 S.W.3d 514, 534 (Tex. App.—Fort Worth 2006, pet. denied) (biomechanical expert's testimony admissible).

Sosa By & Through Grant v. Koshy, 961 S.W.2d 420, 426 (Tex. App.—Houston [1st Dist.] 1997, pet. denied) (no error allowing an expert in accident reconstruction to testify regarding hearsay statements of eyewitness).

Sciarrilla v. Osborne, 946 S.W.2d 919, 920 (Tex. App.—Beaumont 1997, pet. denied) (police officer properly allowed to provide expert opinion regarding accident reconstruction).

Lovell v. DeHoney, 615 S.W.2d 276, 278 (Tex. Civ. App.—Dallas 1981, writ ref'd n.r.e.) (expert opinion regarding vehicle speed based upon reaction time, point of impact, photographs, and statements of witnesses was proper).

Kettle v. Smircich, 415 S.W.2d 935, 937 (Tex. Civ. App.—Corpus Christi 1967, no pet.) (no error allowing expert to rely upon photographs of scene and vehicles as basis for opinion regarding accident reconstruction).

a. *Competent Facts/Foundation*

DeLarue v. State, 102 S.W.3d 388, 396 (Tex. App.—Houston [14th Dist.] 2003, pet. ref'd) (police officer qualified to provide expert opinion regarding accident reconstruction).

Sciarrilla v. Osborne, 946 S.W.2d 919, 920 (Tex. App.—Beaumont 1997, pet. denied) (police officer properly allowed to provide expert opinion regarding accident reconstruction).

Pena v. State, 155 S.W.3d 238, 244 (Tex. App.—El Paso 2004, no pet.) (police officer qualified to give expert opinion regarding vehicle speed; officer failed to demonstrate reliability of methodology used to estimate speed).

Chavers v. State, 991 S.W.2d 457, 461 (Tex. App.—Houston [1st Dist.] 1999, reh'g overruled, pet. ref'd) (expert opinion of vehicle speed based upon "yaw marks" at scene proper).

Lovell v. DeHoney, 615 S.W.2d 276, 278 (Tex. Civ. App.—Dallas 1981, writ ref'd n.r.e.) (expert opinion regarding vehicle speed proper).

b. *Vehicle Speed*

Pena v. State, 155 S.W.3d 238, 244 (Tex. App.—El Paso 2004, no pet.) (police officer qualified to give expert opinion regarding vehicle speed; officer failed to demonstrate reliability of methodology used to estimate speed).

Chavers v. State, 991 S.W.2d 457, 461 (Tex. App.—Houston [1st Dist.] 1999, reh'g overruled, pet. ref'd) (expert opinion of vehicle speed based upon "yaw marks" at scene proper).

Lovell v. DeHoney, 615 S.W.2d 276, 278 (Tex. Civ. App.—Dallas 1981, writ ref'd n.r.e.) (expert opinion regarding vehicle speed proper).

c. Skid Mark Analysis

DeLarue v. State, 102 S.W.3d 388, 396 (Tex. App.—Houston [14th Dist.] 2003, pet. ref'd) (police officer permitted to provide expert opinion regarding accident reconstruction based, in part, upon skid marks).

Chavers v. State, 991 S.W.2d 457, 461 (Tex. App.—Houston [1st Dist.] 1999, reh'g overruled, pet. ref'd) (expert opinion of vehicle speed based upon "yaw marks" at scene proper).

Sciarrilla v. Osborne, 946 S.W.2d 919, 920 (Tex. App.—Beaumont 1997, pet. denied) (police officer properly allowed to provide expert opinion regarding accident reconstruction based upon physical evidence and marks at scene).

d. Stopping Distances

Waring v. Wommack, 945 S.W.2d 889, 892 (Tex. App.—Austin 1997, no writ) (expert opinion on stopping distances and point of impact proper).

Lovell v. DeHoney, 615 S.W.2d 276, 278 (Tex. Civ. App.—Dallas 1981, writ ref'd n.r.e.) (expert opinion regarding vehicle speed based upon reaction time, point of impact, photographs, and statements of witnesses proper).

e. Point of Impact

Waring v. Wommack, 945 S.W.2d 889, 892 (Tex. App.—Austin 1997, no writ) (expert opinion regarding stopping distances, reaction time, and point of impact proper).

Lovell v. DeHoney, 615 S.W.2d 276, 278 (Tex. Civ. App.—Dallas 1981, writ ref'd n.r.e.) (expert opinion regarding vehicle speed based upon reaction time, point of impact, photographs, and statements of witnesses proper).

f. Reaction Time

Waring v. Wommack, 945 S.W.2d 889, 892 (Tex. App.—Austin 1997, no writ) (expert opinion regarding stopping distances, reaction time, and point of impact proper).

Lovell v. DeHoney, 615 S.W.2d 276, 278 (Tex. Civ. App.—Dallas 1981, writ ref'd n.r.e.) (expert opinion regarding vehicle speed based upon reaction time, point of impact, photographs, and statements of witnesses proper).

g. Safer Alternative Design

Gen. Motors Corp. v. Burry, 203 S.W.3d 514, 534 (Tex. App.—Fort Worth 2006, pet. denied) (expert testimonial evidence that included accident reconstruction and crash test video was admissible).

h. Cases Where Biomechanics Admitted

Tanner v. Karnavas, 86 S.W.3d 737, 740 (Tex. App.—Dallas 2002, pet. denied) (if any error in admitting the biomechanical testimony, it was harmless).

Hurrelbrink v. State, 46 S.W.3d 350, 353 (Tex. App.—Amarillo 2001, pet. ref'd) (footprint analysis, based in part upon biomechanics principles, proper).

Gainsco County Mut. Ins. Co. v. Martinez, 27 S.W.3d 97, 105 (Tex. App.—San Antonio 2000, pet. dism'd by agr.) (biomechanical expert testified as to speed and force of impact, based in part upon amount of damage to vehicle).

Stanul v. State, 870 S.W.2d 329, 332 (Tex. App.—Austin 1994, pet. ref'd) (biomechanic testified as to amount of force required to cause certain injuries).

Quintanilla v. Tuma's Estate, 579 S.W.2d 531, 532 (Tex. Civ. App.—San Antonio 1979, writ ref'd n.r.e.) (court found party had properly disclosed expert's opinion was in area of biomechanics and verdict was supported by testimony).

M. Motion to Exclude Evidence of Party's Financial Status

1. Suggested Motion Text

(*Name of Moving Party*) hereby moves this Court for an order excluding any and all evidence, references to evidence, testimony or argument relating to the wealth or poverty of (*Name of Party*). The motion is based upon the grounds that the evidence is irrelevant, immaterial, confusing and will create a substantial danger of undue prejudice to (*Name of Moving Party*).

2. Motion Summary

This motion is used to prevent unfair prejudice where irrelevant evidence of a party's financial status is referenced at trial. The motion is based upon the court's authority to exclude irrelevant and prejudicial evidence and leading cases on this subject. *See, e.g., Carter v. Exxon Corp.*, 842 S.W.2d 393, 396 (Tex. App.—Eastland 1992, writ denied). Note that evidence of a defendant's financial status *is* relevant in punitive damages cases [*Lunsford v. Morris*, 746 S.W.2d 471, 472 (Tex. 1988)] but may not be admissible until a prima facie case of liability for punitive damages is established. *See Wal-Mart Stores, Inc. v. Cordova*, 856 S.W.2d 768, 773 (Tex. App.—El Paso 1993, pet. denied); and *Transp. Ins. Co. v. Moriel*, 879 S.W.2d 10, 30 (Tex. 1994).

3. Supporting Authorities

Transp. Ins. Co. v. Moriel, 879 S.W.2d 10, 30 (Tex. 1994) (evidence of party's net worth can be prejudicial and if requested, trial court should bifurcate issue of amount of punitive damages from issue of liability).

Knox v. Taylor, 992 S.W.2d 40, 65 (Tex. App.—Houston [14th Dist.] 1999, no pet.) (net worth of a party is not admissible during the liability phase of a bifurcated trial).

Wal-Mart Stores, Inc. v. Cordova, 856 S.W.2d 768, 773 (Tex. App.—El Paso 1993, pet. denied) (error to admit irrelevant testimony of defendant's net worth without first determining that evidence established prima facie case of gross negligence).

Carter v. Exxon Corp., 842 S.W.2d 393, 396 (Tex. App.—Eastland 1992, writ denied) (testimony on party's wealth or poverty ordinarily inadmissible in civil case as irrelevant and often prejudicial; opposing party here opened door to evidence regarding royalties).

Browning-Ferris Indus., Inc. v. Lieck, 845 S.W.2d 926, 944 (Tex. App.—Corpus Christi 1992), *rev'd on other grounds*, 881 S.W.2d 288 (Tex. 1994) ("In *Burnett*, the court held that evidence of cash flow indicating the number of stores Southland owned, and the gross sales for each store, was improperly admitted over a relevancy objection. There are relevancy problems with cash flow evidence if, without more, it is offered to prove the proper amount of punitive damages.").

Cooke v. Dykstra, 800 S.W.2d 556, 562 (Tex. App.—Houston [14th Dist.] 1990, no writ) (references to party's wealth are generally improper; in this case, the error was cured by the trial court's instructions).

Block v. Waters, 564 S.W.2d 113, 116 (Tex. Civ. App.—Beaumont 1978, no writ) (evidence of party's wealth or poverty inadmissible because immaterial and prejudicial).

a. Punitive Damages Cases

Transp. Ins. Co. v. Moriel, 879 S.W.2d 10, 30 (Tex. 1994) (evidence of party's net worth can be very prejudicial; therefore, if requested, trial court should bifurcate issue of amount of punitive damages from issue of liability).

Browning-Ferris Indus., Inc. v. Lieck, 845 S.W.2d 926, 944 (Tex. App.—Corpus Christi 1992), *rev'd on other grounds*, 881 S.W.2d 288 (Tex. 1994) ("In *Burnett*, the court held that evidence of cash flow indicating the number of stores Southland owned, and the gross sales for each store, was improperly admitted over a relevancy objection. There are relevancy problems with cash flow evidence if, without more, it is offered to prove the proper amount of punitive damages.").

b. Other Grounds

Other possible grounds for excluding financial evidence include:

- Time-wasting;
- Confusing or misleading;

- Solely intended to create an emotional bias;
- Collateral to issues in case;
- Inadmissible hearsay;
- Improper impeachment evidence;
- Improper tax evidence.

4. Opposing Authorities

Owens-Corning Fiberglas Corp. v. Malone, 972 S.W.2d 35, 40 (Tex. 1998) ("[E]vidence about the profitability of a defendant's misconduct and about any settlement amounts for punitive damages or prior punitive damages awards that the defendant has actually paid for the same course of conduct is admissible when the defendant offers it in mitigation of punitive damages.").

Birchfield v. Texarkana Mem'l Hosp., 747 S.W.2d 361, 366 (Tex. 1987) (evidence of the defendant's financial condition was relevant to its ability to provide proper hospital facilities).

Williams v. LifeCare Hosp. of N. Tex., L.P., 207 S.W.3d 828, 833 (Tex. App.—Fort Worth 2006, no pet.) (net worth evidence is admissible in second phase of bifurcated trial).

Durban v. Guajardo, 79 S.W.3d 198, 210 (Tex. App.—Dallas 2002, no pet.) ("[E]vidence of the defendant's net worth is [not] a necessary element for the plaintiff to recover any exemplary damages. Instead, it is merely a relevant issue, as relevant to the defendant to prove his low net worth as to the plaintiff to prove the defendant's high net worth.").

Burlington N. R. Co. v. Sw. Elec. Power Co., 925 S.W.2d 92, 100 (Tex. App.—Texarkana 1996), *aff'd*, 966 S.W.2d 467 (1998) (evidence of party's financial condition related to issues in case).

Mortgage Co. of Am. v. McCord, 466 S.W.2d 868, 872 (Tex. Civ. App.—Houston [14th Dist.] 1971, writ ref'd n.r.e.) (argument regarding party's business relevant to suggest that other party was entitled to rely upon that party's representations, even if argument also suggested relative wealth of parties).

Montgomery v. Gay, 222 S.W.2d 922, 925 (Tex. Civ. App.—Fort Worth 1949, writ dism'd) (evidence that party had participated in drilling eighteen oil wells proper because it demonstrated prior experience and knowledge, over objection that it also showed relative wealth of parties).

Walker v. Dickey, 44 Tex. Civ. App. 110, 123, 98 S.W. 658 (Tex. Civ. App. 1906, writ ref'd) (when party testified to cash payment, evidence that shortly before time of alleged payment, the party was unable to pay bills, was admissible to cast doubt on party's ability to make payment at issue).

a. Necessary to Support Punitive Damages Claim

Lunsford v. Morris, 746 S.W.2d 471, 472 (Tex. 1988) (the defendant's net worth is relevant in cases where punitive damages may be awarded).

Browning-Ferris Indus., Inc. v. Lieck, 845 S.W.2d 926, 944 (Tex. App.—Corpus Christi 1992), *rev'd on other grounds*, 881 S.W.2d 288 (Tex. 1994) ("However, like all other evidence, cash flow may be relevant, depending upon what it is offered to prove. In this case it was offered to prove the (short) period of time in which it would take for BFI to pay a damage award. This evidence was placed in the proper context by Dillman's testimony relating to BFI's net worth. We hold the evidence was properly admitted.").

b. Invited Error

Sw. Elec. Power Co. v. Burlington N. R.R Co., 966 S.W.2d 467, 472 (Tex. 1998, reh'g overruled) (party invited evidence regarding financial condition by admitting similar evidence).

N. Motion to Exclude Tax Evidence

1. Suggested Motion Text

(*Name of Moving Party*) hereby moves this Court for an order excluding any and all evidence, references to evidence, testimony or argument relating to (*Describe Tax Evidence to Be Excluded, e.g., the Fact That the Plaintiff Was Fined for Failing to Pay Taxes in 1999*). The motion is based upon the grounds that the evidence is irrelevant, immaterial, confusing and will create a substantial danger of undue prejudice to (*Name of Moving Party*).

2. Motion Summary

This motion is used to exclude irrelevant and prejudicial tax evidence. The motion is based upon the court's authority to exclude irrelevant and prejudicial evidence and leading cases in this area. *See, e.g.*, *Silberstein v. State*, 522 S.W.2d 562, 565 (Tex. Civ. App.—Austin 1975, no writ).

3. Supporting Authorities

Transp. Ins. Co. v. Moriel, 879 S.W.2d 10, 30 (Tex. 1994) (evidence of a party's net worth can be very prejudicial; therefore, if requested, the trial court should bifurcate the issue of the amount of punitive damages from the issue of liability).

Marsh v. Marsh, 949 S.W.2d 734, 745 (Tex. App.—Houston [14th Dist.] 1997, no writ) (evidence regarding a mistake regarding potential tax consequences of premarital agreement properly excluded).

Carter v. Exxon Corp., 842 S.W.2d 393, 396 (Tex. App.—Eastland 1992, writ denied) (testimony on party's wealth or poverty ordinarily inadmissible in civil case as irrelevant and often prejudicial; opposing party opened door to evidence regarding royalties).

Browning-Ferris Indus., Inc. v. Lieck, 845 S.W.2d 926, 944 (Tex. App.—Corpus Christi 1992), *rev'd on other grounds*, 881 S.W.2d 288 (Tex. 1994) ("In *Burnett*, the court held that evidence of cash flow indicating the number of stores Southland owned, and the gross sales for each store, was improperly admitted over a relevancy objection. There are relevancy problems with cash flow evidence if, without more, it is offered to prove the proper amount of punitive damages.").

a. Improper Appeal to Jurors as Taxpayers

Silberstein v. State, 522 S.W.2d 562, 565 (Tex. Civ. App.—Austin 1975, no writ) (attorney's argument to jury referencing "the people's money" was direct appeal to jury's self-interest and invited jurors to consider own self-interest in returning verdict).

Waddell v. Charter Oak Fire Ins. Co., 473 S.W.2d 660, 662 (Tex. Civ. App.—Fort Worth 1971, no writ) (error in insurance company's defense attorney's allusion to higher insurance premiums and cost of goods for general public if cases such as this are successful, allowed counsel to "figuratively craw[l] into the jury box and assum[e] the role of attorney representing each of the jurors.... Such argument was calculated to cause the jury to decide the case on the basis of their own financial well-being rather than on the basis of the evidence and the law.").

b. Other Grounds

Other possible grounds for excluding financial evidence include:

- Time-wasting;
- Confusing or misleading;
- Solely intended to create an emotional bias;
- Collateral to issues in case;
- Inadmissible hearsay;
- Improper impeachment evidence;
- Improper tax evidence.

4. Opposing Authorities

Lunsford v. Morris, 746 S.W.2d 471, 472 (Tex. 1988) (defendant's net worth relevant in cases where punitive damages may be awarded).

LSR Joint Venture No. 2 v. Callewart, 837 S.W.2d 693, 699 (Tex. App.—Dallas 1992, writ denied) (evidence of party's tax benefits should have been admitted to disprove causation).

City of San Antonio v. Fulcher, 749 S.W.2d 217, 220 (Tex. App.—San Antonio 1988) (tax returns should have been discoverable in workers' compensation case where evidence related to claimant's testimony on amount of income that came from "moonlighting").

Medrano v. City of El Paso, 231 S.W.2d 514, 515 (Tex. Civ. App.—El Paso 1950, writ ref'd n.r.e.) (evidence of tax renditions admissible in condemnation proceedings as admissions against interest).

O. Motion to Exclude Liability Evidence (Liability Not at Issue)

1. Suggested Motion Text

(*Name of Moving Party*) hereby moves this Court for an order excluding any and all evidence, references to evidence, testimony, or argument relating to defendant's liability in this action. The motion is based upon the grounds that the evidence is irrelevant, immaterial, confusing and will create a substantial danger of undue prejudice to (*Name of Moving Party*).

2. Motion Summary

This motion is used to exclude evidence of defendant's liability, where admitted or undisputed by defendant. The motion is based upon the court's authority to exclude irrelevant and prejudicial evidence and evidence of admitted matters. *See, e.g. Brown v. State*, 757 S.W.2d 739, 740 (Tex. Crim. App. 1988).

3. Supporting Authorities

Brown v. State, 757 S.W.2d 739, 740 (Tex. Crim. App. 1988) (evidence of victim's emotional trauma following rape irrelevant where only disputed issue was identity of rapist, not fact of rape).

Johnson v. State, 698 S.W.2d 154, 161 (Tex. Crim. App. 1985), *cert. denied*, 479 U.S. 871 (1986) ("[T]o be admissible, evidence must be relevant to a contested issue."). *But see Mayes v. State*, 816 S.W.2d 79, 84 (Tex. Crim. App. 1991, pet. denied) (relevant evidence need not pertain only to facts in dispute but includes any evidence that influences consequential facts).

Palomo v. State, 925 S.W.2d 329, 337 (Tex. App.—Corpus Christi 1996, no pet.) (evidence that defendant had tattoo suggesting gang membership irrelevant and should not have been admitted where defendant did not contest issue of gang membership).

Welex v. Broom, 806 S.W.2d 855, 869 (Tex. App.—San Antonio), *vacated on other grounds*, 816 S.W.2d 340 (Tex. 1991) (evidence of liability excluded where "death penalty" discovery sanction granted on that issue and allowed only evidence of damages; note: case later reversed based on finding that "death penalty" sanction was inappropriate).

Blackburn v. State, 820 S.W.2d 824, 829 (Tex. App.—Waco 1991, pet. ref'd) (photograph should have been excluded as irrelevant where defendant did not contest possession of controlled substance).

Fleming Mfg. Co. v. Capitol Brick, Inc., 734 S.W.2d 405, 409 (Tex. App.—Austin 1987, writ ref'd n.r.e.) (where liability admitted or established through default, trial should relate to issue of damages only).

a. Other Grounds

Other possible grounds for excluding liability evidence include:

- Time-wasting;
- Confusing or misleading;
- Solely intended to create an emotional bias;
- Collateral to issues in case;
- Inadmissible hearsay;
- Improper impeachment.

4. Opposing Authorities

Morgan v. Compugraphic Corp., 675 S.W.2d 729, 732 (Tex. 1984) (evidence of causal connection between events and injury at issue required to prove damages).

Mayes v. State, 816 S.W.2d 79, 84 (Tex. Crim. App. 1991, pet. denied) (relevant evidence need not pertain only to facts in dispute but includes any evidence that influences consequential facts).

Yates v. State, 941 S.W.2d 357, 365 (Tex. App.—Waco 1997, pet. ref'd) (evidence regarding circumstances surrounding offense relevant as context evidence).

Moreno v. State, 821 S.W.2d 344, 353 (Tex. App.—Waco 1991, pet. ref'd) (evidence regarding other offenses relevant as context evidence to demonstrate reasons why police stopped defendants for charged offense).

Callaway v. State, 818 S.W.2d 816, 826 (Tex. App.—Amarillo 1991, pet. ref'd) (evidence can be relevant as context evidence or to fully explain another matter that has already been introduced).

P. Motion to Exclude Improper Damage Evidence

1. Suggested Motion Text

(*Name of Moving Party*) hereby moves this Court for an order excluding any and all evidence, exhibits, testimony, references to testimony, or argument in any way relating to plaintiff's damages for (*State Specific Type(s) of Damage Evidence to Be Excluded, e.g., Lost Wages*). This motion is based upon the ground that the evidence is not at issue in this case, as (*State Reason(s) for Exclusion, e.g., the Plaintiff Has Denied Any Claim for Lost Wages in His Deposition and in Responses to Interrogatories, and Therefore Any Evidence on This Matter Will Create Unfair Surprise and Clear Prejudice to the Defendant Who, in Reliance Upon Plaintiff's Denials, Has Not Prepared Any Defense to Such Claims*).

2. Motion Summary

This motion is used to exclude evidence of damages, or portions of damages, based upon plaintiff's admissions, lack of foundational support, or other statutory authority. The motion is based upon a number of potentially applicable authorities, including exclusion of unpleaded issues [*Benson v. Weaver*, 250 S.W.2d 770, 772 (Tex. Civ. App.—Austin 1952), *aff'd*, 152 Tex. 50, 254 S.W.2d 95 (1952)]; limitations on claims not disclosed in discovery [*Capital Metro. Transp. Auth./Cent. of Tenn. Ry. & Navigation Co. v. Cent. of Tenn. Ry. & Navigation Co.*, 114 S.W.3d 573, 583 (Tex. App.—Austin 2003, pet. denied)]; preclusion of damages too uncertain or speculative [*Coble v. City of Mansfield*, 134 S.W.3d 449, 455 (Tex. App.—Fort Worth 2004, no pet.)]; and statutes limiting the amount of recovery [see, e.g., Texas Civil Practice and Remedies Code § 41.008].

Evidence on damages that are disallowed or denied prior to trial are collateral to issues in the case, and therefore subject to exclusion under established case law. *See generally Erisman v. Thompson*, 167 S.W.2d 731, 733 (Tex. 1943) ("[P]leadings determine the issues upon which parties go to trial, and it is not even proper to admit evidence unless it is addressed to or bears upon some issue raised by the pleadings."); *Miller-El v. State*, 782 S.W.2d 892, 895 (Tex. Crim. App. 1990, pet. ref'd) (evidence of future hardships suffered by victim irrelevant to issue of defendant's guilt).

3. Supporting Authorities

Erisman v. Thompson, 167 S.W.2d 731, 733 (Tex. 1943) ("[P]leadings determine the issues upon which parties go to trial, and it is not even proper to admit evidence unless it is addressed to or bears upon some issue raised by the pleadings.").

Miller-El v. State, 782 S.W.2d 892, 895 (Tex. Crim. App. 1990, pet. ref'd) (evidence of future hardships suffered by victim irrelevant to issue of defendant's guilt).

Martinez v. RV Tool, Inc., 737 S.W.2d 17, 18 (Tex. App.—El Paso 1987, writ denied) (existence of workers' compensation claim not material to issues in third-party suit).

Sherrod v. Bailey, 580 S.W.2d 24, 28 (Tex. Civ. App.—Houston [1st Dist.] 1979, writ ref'd n.r.e.) (damages awarded improper where not supported by allegations made in pleadings).

Weingartens, Inc. v. Price, 461 S.W.2d 260, 262 (Tex. Civ. App.—Houston [14th Dist.] 1970, writ ref'd n.r.e.) (damage award in excess of amount pled improper).

Benson v. Weaver, 250 S.W.2d 770, 772 (Tex. Civ. App.—Austin 1952), *aff'd*, 152 Tex. 50, 254 S.W.2d 95 (1952) (admissibility of evidence depends on whether relevant to issues made by pleadings and not error to exclude evidence on collateral issues).

Mo., K. & T. Ry. Co. v. Keaveney, 80 S.W. 387, 389 (Tex. Civ. App. 1904) (rules of evidence exclude all evidence of collateral facts, or those incapable of affording any reasonable presumption or inference as to principal fact or matter in dispute).

a. Undisputed Matters

Brown v. State, 757 S.W.2d 739, 740 (Tex. Crim. App. 1988) (evidence of victim's emotional trauma following rape irrelevant where only disputed issue was identity of rapist, not fact of rape).

Palomo v. State, 925 S.W.2d 329, 337 (Tex. App.—Corpus Christi 1996, no pet.) (evidence that defendant had tattoo suggesting gang membership irrelevant and should not have been admitted where defendant did not contest issue of gang membership).

b. Surprise Claims

Texas Rule of Civil Procedure 193.6 states in pertinent part:

> **Failing to Timely Respond—Effect on Trial**
>
> (a) *Exclusion of Evidence and Exceptions.* A party who fails to make, amend, or supplement a discovery response in a timely manner may not introduce in evidence the material or information

that was not timely disclosed, or offer the testimony of a witness (other than a named party) who was not timely identified, unless the court finds that:
(1) there was good cause for the failure to timely make, amend, or supplement the discovery response; or
(2) the failure to timely make, amend, or supplement the discovery response will not unfairly surprise or unfairly prejudice the other parties.

(b) *Burden of Establishing Exception.* The burden of establishing good cause or the lack of unfair surprise or unfair prejudice is on the party seeking to introduce the evidence or call the witness . . . .

Phan v. Addison Spectrum, L.P., 244 S.W.3d 892, 899 (Tex. App.—Dallas 2008, no pet.) (trial court did not abuse its discretion in precluding plaintiff's expert testimony on attorney's fees incurred, where plaintiff never responded to propounded discovery requests that she would be offering expert testimony on any issue, and, when asked by the trial court why she never supplemented her discovery responses, plaintiff gave no reason and made no showing that her failure to disclose any experts would not unfairly surprise or prejudice defendants).

Capital Metro. Transp. Auth./Cent. of Tenn. Ry. & Navigation Co. v. Cent. of Tenn. Ry. & Navigation Co., 114 S.W.3d 573, 583 (Tex. App.—Austin 2003, pet. denied) (trial court properly excluded evidence of damages for failure to disclose information until shortly before trial where court implicitly found unfair surprise from late disclosure).

Sherrod v. Bailey, 580 S.W.2d 24, 28 (Tex. Civ. App.—Houston [1st Dist.] 1979, writ ref'd n.r.e.) (damages awarded were improper where not supported by allegations made in pleadings).

c. *Amounts in Excess of Stated Damages*

Texas Rule of Civil Procedure 198.3 states in pertinent part, as follows:

> Any admission made by a party under this rule may be used solely in the pending action and not in any other proceeding. *A matter admitted under this rule is conclusively established as the party making the admission unless the court permits the party to withdraw or amend the admission.* (Emphasis added.)

Texas Rule of Civil Procedure 56 states:

> Special Damage. When items of special damage are claimed, they shall be specifically stated.

Capital Metro. Transp. Auth./Cent. of Tenn. Ry. & Navigation Co. v. Cent. of Tenn. Ry. & Navigation Co., 114 S.W.3d 573, 583 (Tex. App.—Austin 2003, pet. denied) (trial court properly excluded evidence of damages for failure to disclose information until shortly before trial where court implicitly found unfair surprise from late disclosure).

Picon Transp., Inc. v. Pomerantz, 814 S.W.2d 489, 491 (Tex. App.—Dallas 1991, writ denied) (damage award in excess of amount pled improper).

Sherrod v. Bailey, 580 S.W.2d 24, 28 (Tex. Civ. App.—Houston [1st Dist.] 1979, writ ref'd n.r.e.) (damages awarded improper where not supported by allegations made in pleadings).

Weingartens, Inc. v. Price, 461 S.W.2d 260, 262 (Tex. Civ. App.—Houston [14th Dist.] 1970, writ ref'd n.r.e.) (damage award in excess of amount pled improper).

d. Speculative Evidence

City of Pearland v. Alexander, 483 S.W.2d 244, 247 (Tex. 1972) ("[E]vidence based on possibilities rather than reasonable probabilities [is] incompetent.").

Lamont v. Vaquillas Energy Lopeno Ltd., LLP, 421 S.W.3d 198, 224 (Tex. App.—San Antonio 2013, pet. denied) (evidence must show that lost profit damages are not uncertain or speculative).

Lamont v. Vaquillas Energy Lopeno Ltd., LLP, 421 S.W.3d 198, 224 (Tex. App.—San Antonio 2013, pet. denied) ("[P]rofits that are largely speculative, as from an activity dependent on uncertain or changing market conditions, or on chancy business opportunities, or on promotion of untested products or entry into unknown or unviable markets, or on the success of a new and unproven enterprise, cannot be recovered; factors like these and others that make a business venture risky in prospect preclude recovery of lost profits in retrospect.").

Peterson Group, Inc. v. PLTQ Lotus Group, L.P, 417 S.W.3d 46, 66 (Tex. App.—Houston [1st Dist.] 2013, pet. denied) (a plaintiff may not recover breach-of-contract damages if those damages are remote, contingent, speculative, or conjectural).

Peterson Group, Inc. v. PLTQ Lotus Group, L.P, 417 S.W.3d 46, 66 (Tex. App.—Houston [1st Dist.] 2013, pet. denied) (lost profits cannot be based on pure speculation or wishful thinking).

Barton v. Resort Dev. Latin Am., Inc., 413 S.W.3d 232, 236 (Tex. App.—Dallas 2013, pet. denied) (profits are largely speculative, not reasonably certain, and cannot be recovered, if they result from an activity dependent on uncertain or changing market conditions).

U.S. Bank Nat'l Ass'n v. Stanley, 297 S.W.3d 815, 822 (Tex. App.—Houston [14th Dist.] 2009, no pet.) (there can be no recovery for damages that are speculative or conjectural).

In the Matter of V.M.D., 974 S.W.2d 332, 350 (Tex. App.—San Antonio 1998, no writ) (speculative and inconclusive nature of proffered evidence supported decision to exclude).

Sw. Pub. Serv. Co. v. Vanderburg, 526 S.W.2d 692, 695 (Tex. Civ. App.—Amarillo 1975, no writ) (speculative evidence should be excluded on question of value in condemnation case).

Cent. Mut. Ins. Co. v. D.&B., Inc., 340 S.W.2d 525, 526 (Tex. Civ. App.—Waco 1960, writ ref'd n.r.e.) (evidence was speculative and not proper subject of expert opinion testimony).

i. Exclusion of Evidence of Speculative Damages

Bedgood v. Madalin, 600 S.W.2d 773, 776 (Tex. 1980) (damage award was improperly based upon remote and speculative evidence).

Reid v. El Paso Const. Co., 498 S.W.2d 923, 925 (Tex. 1973) (verdict improper where based upon speculative evidence of damages).

Tex. Elec. Serv. Co. v. Campbell, 161 Tex. 77, 81, 336 S.W.2d 742 (Tex. 1960) (damage evidence remote, speculative, and conjectural should not have been allowed).

Coble v. City of Mansfield, 134 S.W.3d 449, 455 (Tex. App.—Fort Worth 2004, no pet.) (owner not entitled to remote, speculative, or conjectural damages in condemnation case).

DeFord Lumber Co. v. Roys, 615 S.W.2d 235, 237 (Tex. Civ. App.—Dallas 1981, no writ) (damage award improper where speculative, conjectural, and unsupported by evidence).

Spiritas v. Robinowitz, 544 S.W.2d 710, 720 (Tex. Civ. App.—Dallas 1976, writ ref'd n.r.e.) (case remanded for new trial where court determined breach of agreement had occurred, but damage issue remained speculative).

Sw. Pub. Serv. Co. v. Vanderburg, 526 S.W.2d 692, 695 (Tex. Civ. App.—Amarillo 1975, no writ) (speculative evidence should be excluded on question of value in condemnation case).

W. Hatcheries v. Byrd, 218 S.W.2d 342, 344 (Tex. Civ. App.—Dallas 1949, no writ) (damage award improper where based upon speculative evidence).

e. *Statutory Limitations on Damages*

Texas Rule of Civil Procedure 56 states:

> Special Damage. When items of special damage are claimed, they shall be specifically stated.

Texas Civil Practice and Remedies Code § 41.003 states as follows:

(a) Except as provided by Subsection (c), exemplary damages may be awarded only if the claimant proves by clear and convincing evidence that the harm with respect to which the claimant seeks recovery of exemplary damages results from:
  (1) fraud;
  (2) malice; or
  (3) gross negligence.
(b) The claimant must prove by clear and convincing evidence the elements of exemplary damages as provided by this section. This burden of proof may not be shifted to the defendant or satisfied by evidence of ordinary negligence, bad faith, or a deceptive trade practice.
(c) If the claimant relies on a statute establishing a cause of action and authorizing exemplary damages in specified circumstances

or in conjunction with a specified culpable mental state, exemplary damages may be awarded only if the claimant proves by clear and convincing evidence that the damages result from the specified circumstances or culpable mental state.
(d) Exemplary damages may be awarded only if the jury was unanimous in regard to finding liability for and the amount of exemplary damages.
(e) In all cases where the issue of exemplary damages is submitted to the jury, the following instruction shall be included in the charge of the court:

'You are instructed that, in order for you to find exemplary damages, your answer to the question regarding the amount of such damages must be unanimous.'

Texas Civil Practice and Remedies Code § 41.008 states in pertinent part:

Limitation on Amount of Recovery

(a) In an action in which a claimant seeks recovery of damages, the trier of fact shall determine the amount of economic damages separately from the amount of other compensatory damages.
(b) Exemplary damages awarded against a defendant may not exceed an amount equal to the greater of:
   (1) (A) two times the amount of economic damages; plus
       (B) an amount equal to any noneconomic damages found by the jury, not to exceed $750,000; or
   (2) $200,000.
(c) This section does not apply to a cause of action against a defendant from whom a plaintiff seeks recovery of exemplary damages based on conduct described as a felony in the following sections of the Penal Code if, except for Sections 49.07 and 49.08, the conduct was committed knowingly or intentionally:
   (1) Section 19.02 (murder);
   (2) Section 19.03 (capital murder);
   (3) Section 20.04 (aggravated kidnapping);
   (4) Section 22.02 (aggravated assault);
   (5) Section 22.011 (sexual assault);
   (6) Section 22.021 (aggravated sexual assault);
   (7) Section 22.04 (injury to a child, elderly individual, or disabled individual, but not if the conduct occurred while providing health care as defined by Section 74.001);
   (8) Section 32.21 (forgery);
   (9) Section 32.43 (commercial bribery);
   (10) Section 32.45 (misapplication of fiduciary property or property of financial institution);
   (11) Section 32.46 (securing execution of document by deception);
   (12) Section 32.47 (fraudulent destruction, removal, or concealment of writing);

(13) Chapter 31 (theft) the punishment level for which is a felony of the third degree or higher;
(14) Section 49.07 (intoxication assault); or
(15) Section 49.08 (intoxication manslaughter). Texas Civil Practice and Remedies Code § 41.004 states:

Factors Precluding Recovery

(a) Except as provided by Subsection (b), exemplary damages may be awarded only if damages other than nominal damages are awarded.
(b) Exemplary damages may not be awarded to a claimant who elects to have his recovery multiplied under another statute.

4. Opposing Authorities

Sharp v. Broadway Nat'l Bank, 784 S.W.2d 669, 671 (Tex. 1990) (absence of surprise alone does not satisfy good cause exception to sanction of automatic exclusion).

Miller v. Kennedy & Minshew Prof'l Corp., 142 S.W.3d 325, 349 (Tex. App.—Fort Worth 2003, pet. denied) (expert testimony from two witnesses not properly disclosed was proper where substance of testimony did not cause opposing party unfair surprise).

Bellino v. Comm'n for Lawyer Discipline, 124 S.W.3d 380, 384 (Tex. App.—Dallas 2003, reh'g overruled, pet. stricken) (witness not disclosed in timely fashion properly permitted to testify where opposing party not unfairly surprised).

Gutierrez v. Gutierrez, 86 S.W.3d 729, 736 (Tex. App.—El Paso 2002, no pet.) (witness properly allowed to testify as expert, even though only disclosed as fact witness, where opposing party not unfairly surprised).

a. Reasonable Estimate of Damages

Borden, Inc. v. Guerra, 860 S.W.2d 515, 524 (Tex. App.—Corpus Christi 1993, reh'g overruled, writ dism'd by agr.) (loss of future earnings usually uncertain and issue largely left to jury's discretion).

Baker v. Int'l Record Syndicate, Inc., 812 S.W.2d 53, 55 (Tex. App.—Dallas 1991, no pet.) (liquidated damages clause of contract proper if reasonable estimate of damages would be difficult to determine).

Tex. Steel Co. v. Douglas, 533 S.W.2d 111, 118 (Tex. Civ. App.—Fort Worth 1976, writ ref'd n.r.e.) (evidence sufficient to support verdict for lost future wages).

II. Sample Motions

A. Motion to Exclude Evidence of Collateral Source Payments

NO. _____

_____	§ §	IN THE DISTRICT COURT
v.	§ §	_____ JUDICIAL COURT
_____	§	_____ COUNTY, TEXAS

Motion to Exclude Evidence of Collateral Source Payments

Comes now _____, Plaintiff in this cause, and file this, his Motion to Exclude Evidence of Collateral Source Payments, and in support thereof, Plaintiff would show the Court the following:

1.
FACTUAL BACKGROUND

This action arises from an automobile accident that occurred on September 18, 2018, when the Defendant crashed his Ford Mustang into the rear of Plaintiff's Honda Civic. As a result of the accident, Plaintiff incurred severe neck and back injuries, property damage, and lost wages.

At the time of the accident, Plaintiff was insured with a "Medical Payments" policy by his automobile insurer. As of the date of this motion, Plaintiff has been reimbursed in the amount of $3,225 for medical expenses arising from the accident.

By this motion, Plaintiff seeks an order precluding the introduction of any evidence, or mention of evidence, relating to the insurance payments. This motion is based upon the grounds that evidence of payments by a collateral source, such as Plaintiff's medical insurance provider, is irrelevant, immaterial and clearly inadmissible under the laws of this State.

2.
THIS COURT MAY EXCLUDE PREJUDICIAL EVIDENCE
IN ADVANCE OF TRIAL BY WAY OF AN IN LIMINE MOTION

The Court has the inherent power to grant a motion in limine to exclude evidence which could be objected to at trial, either as irrelevant or subject to exclusion as unduly prejudicial. *Wackenhut Corp. v. Gutierrez*, 453 S.W.3d 917, 920 n.3 (Tex. 2016); *In re BCH Development, LLC*, 525 S.W.3d 920, 925 (Tex. App.—Dallas 2017, orig. proceeding). Texas Rule of Evidence 403 allows the court to exclude evidence where there is a substantial danger that the probative value will be outweighed by the danger of undue prejudice. *See Diamond Offshore*

Services Ltd. v. Williams, 542 S.W.3d 539, 549 (Tex. 2018); *Brookshire Bros. v. Aldridge*, 438 S.W.3d 9, 34 (Tex. 2014).

Moreover, the court may hear and determine the question of the admissibility of evidence outside the presence or hearing of the jury. *See Weidner v. Sanchez*, 14 S.W.3d 353, 363 (Tex. App.—Houston [14th Dist.] 2000, no pet.); *Kendrix v. S. Pac. Transp. Co.*, 907 S.W.2d 111, 113 (Tex. App.—Beaumont 1995, writ denied); Texas Rule of Civil Procedure 166; and Texas Rules of Evidence 103 and 104.

3.
THIS COURT SHOULD EXCLUDE ANY EVIDENCE OF MEDICAL PAYMENTS MADE TO PLAINTIFF BY A COLLATERAL SOURCE

A Defendant may not mitigate damages from collateral payments where the Plaintiff has been compensated by an independent source, such as insurance, pension, continued wages, or disability payments. *Taylor v. Am. Fabritech, Inc.*, 132 S.W.3d 613, 626 (Tex. App.—Houston [14th Dist.] 2004, pet. denied) (offset for disability payments received by Plaintiff improper under collateral source rule).

The principle espoused in the *Taylor* decision, known as the "collateral source rule," is well-recognized by the courts of this state. *See Haygood v. De Escabedo*, 356 S.W.3d 390, 395 (Tex. 2011); *Brown v. Am. Transfer & Storage Co.*, 601 S.W.2d 931, 934 (Tex. 1980), *cert. denied*, 449 U.S. 1015 (1980) (collateral source rule prevented evidence of insurance payments made to Plaintiff due to policy Plaintiff had obtained on own); *Kendrix v. S. Pac. Transp. Co.*, 907 S.W.2d 111, 112 (Tex. App.—Beaumont 1995, writ denied) (references to payments received from collateral source, including those from workers' compensation, improper and prejudicial); *Lee-Wright, Inc. v. Hall*, 840 S.W.2d 572, 582 (Tex. App.—Houston [1st Dist.] 1992, no writ) (evidence regarding workers' compensation benefits properly excluded under collateral source rule); and *Jones v. Red Arrow Heavy Hauling, Inc.*, 816 S.W.2d 134, 136 (Tex. App.—Beaumont 1991, writ denied) (evidence injured party received benefits from collateral source inadmissible under rules of relevancy).

Texas Rule of Evidence 402 states that "evidence which is not relevant is inadmissible." Relevant evidence is defined by Texas Rule of Evidence 401 as "having any tendency to make the existence of any fact that is of consequence to the determination of the action more probable or less probable than it would be without the evidence." *See Torrington v. Stutzman*, 46 S.W.3d 829, 845 n.13 (Tex. 2000). Irrelevant evidence is not admissible. *Morale v. State*, 557 S.W.3d 569, 573 (Tex. 2018); *Diamond Offshore Services Ltd. v. Williams*, 542 S.W.3d 539, 549 (Tex. 2018).

In the present case, Plaintiff received reimbursement for medical expenses incurred as a result of the subject accident, under a Medical Payments provision of his automobile policy. These facts are squarely on point with the decisions cited above. Allowing evidence of the insurance payments would be wholly inconsistent with the collateral source rule and would be prejudicial error. *See Kendrix v. S. Pac. Transp. Co.*, 907 S.W.2d 111, 112 (Tex. App.—Beaumont 1995, writ denied); *Jones v. Red Arrow Heavy Hauling, Inc.*, 816 S.W.2d 134, 136 (Tex. App.—Beaumont 1991, writ denied).

4.
CONCLUSION

Based on the foregoing, the Plaintiff respectfully requests that this Court exclude any and all evidence, or mention of evidence, regarding payments from Plaintiff's insurer for reimbursement of medical expenses arising from Plaintiff's injuries in this case.

Dated: _____ *(Date)* _____

By: _____

_____ *(Name of Counsel)* _____

Attorneys for Plaintiff,

_____ *(Name of Plaintiff)* _____

B. Motion to Exclude Evidence of Defendant's Liability

NO. _____

	§	IN THE DISTRICT COURT
_____	§	
	§	_____ JUDICIAL COURT
v.	§	
	§	
_____	§	_____ COUNTY, TEXAS

Motion to Exclude Evidence of Defendant's Liability

Comes now _____, Plaintiff in this cause, and file this, his Motion to Exclude Evidence of Defendant's Liability, and in support thereof, Plaintiff would show the Court the following:

1.
FACTUAL BACKGROUND

This action arises from a moderate speed automobile accident between the Plaintiff and Defendant that occurred on or about January 22, 2018, in Austin, Texas. In interrogatory responses, requests for admissions, and deposition statements, the Defendant repeatedly admitted to being the cause of the accident.

The only issue that remains in dispute is the nature and extent of the Plaintiff's injuries.

The Defendant anticipates that the Plaintiff will explore in great detail a number of liability issues at trial, including Defendant's conduct immediately prior to the accident, and the condition of the Defendant's brakes when the incident occurred. Defendant's belief is based upon a number of factors, including Plaintiff's proposed Exhibit List, the Plaintiff's designation of an automobile reconstruction expert, and statements of counsel to this effect.

Defendant contends that the introduction of any liability evidence is irrelevant, cumulative, and prejudicial, and therefore should be excluded.

2.
THIS COURT MAY EXCLUDE PREJUDICIAL EVIDENCE PURSUANT TO TEXAS RULE OF EVIDENCE 403

Texas Rule of Evidence 403 states: "[a]lthough relevant, evidence may be excluded if its probative value is substantially outweighed by the danger of unfair prejudice, confusion of the issues, or misleading the jury, or by considerations of undue delay, or needless presentation of cumulative evidence."

The Court may exclude marginally probative evidence that might easily confuse the jury. *See Brookshire Bros. v. Aldridge*, 438 S.W.3d 9, 26 (Tex. 2014) (evidence that raises a risk of prejudice and confusion of the jury should be excluded); *Farmers Texas County Mutual Insurance Co. v. Pagan*, 453 S.W.3d 454, (Tex. App.—Houston [14th Dist.] 2014, no pet.) (evidence should have been excluded where its probative value was outweighed by danger of confusion of issues and misleading jury).

In the present case, allowing evidence of Defendant's liability will unduly prejudice the Defendant without advancing even marginally probative evidence. Having admitted liability, the evidence is clearly not relevant or necessary to prove damages. Furthermore, there is a strong likelihood that the jurors will be confused by this evidence, which will have no bearing on material issues in this case.

If the evidence is allowed, the Defendant will be perceived as irresponsible, when in fact, the Defendant took immediate responsibility for the cause of the accident and has been cooperative and forthcoming in all aspects of this litigation and his dealings with the Plaintiff. The Defendant will be forced to present rebuttal evidence to correct this misperception, thereby wasting valuable time and resources of the Court, counsel, and parties on an issue that has no necessity being litigated.

3.
EVIDENCE OF DEFENDANT'S LIABILITY IS NOT AT ISSUE AND SHOULD THEREFORE BE EXCLUDED

Texas Rule of Evidence 402 states that "evidence which is not relevant is inadmissible." Relevant evidence is defined by Texas Rule of Evidence 401 as "having any tendency to make the existence of any fact that is of consequence to the determination of the action more probable or less probable than it would be without the evidence." *See Torrington v. Stutzman*, 46 S.W.3d 829, 845 n.13 (Tex. 2000). Irrelevant evidence is not admissible. *Morale v. State*, 557 S.W.3d 569, 573 (Tex. 2018); *Diamond Offshore Services Ltd. v. Williams*, 542 S.W.3d 539, 549 (Tex. 2018).

Matters that are admitted or uncontroverted may also be excluded. *Fleming Mfg. Co. v. Capitol Brick, Inc.*, 734 S.W.2d 405, 409 (Tex. App.—Austin 1987, writ ref'd n.r.e.) (when liability admitted or established through default, trial should relate to issue of damages only);

Palomo v. State, 925 S.W.2d 329, 337 (Tex. App.—Corpus Christi 1996, no pet.) (evidence that Defendant had tattoo suggesting gang membership irrelevant and should not have been admitted where Defendant did not contest gang membership).

In this case, the Defendant has admitted to liability. As such, any evidence relating to the nature of his liability and his actions leading up to the subject incident are irrelevant and should be excluded.

4.
EVIDENCE OF DEFENDANT'S LIABILITY IS NOT NECESSARY TO PROVE PLAINTIFF'S DAMAGES

Courts have held that evidence of Defendant's liability might be relevant if necessary to prove damages. *See Morgan v. Compugraphic Corp.*, 675 S.W.2d 729, 732 (Tex. 1984) (evidence of causal connection between events and injury at issue required to prove damages). However, in the present case, the facts surrounding the cause of the accident will in no way assist the jury in determining the nature and extent of the Plaintiff's injuries or damages.

In the present case, the circumstances of the occurrence do not provide probative value regarding the nature of the injuries. In addition, the nature of the injuries can be fully established through other competent evidence and therefore, admitting the liability evidence would be cumulative, even if it were probative. Any evidence of liability will only serve to prejudice the Defendant in the eyes of the jurors by focusing on Defendant's wrongdoing. This is not only improper, but as stated above, it is clearly prejudicial to the Defendant.

5.
CONCLUSION

For all the reasons stated above, the Defendant requests that this Court exclude any reference at trial, including physical evidence, witness testimony and attorney comments, relating to the Defendant's liability.

Dated: _____ *(Date)* _____

By: _____

_____ *(Name of Counsel)* _____

Attorneys for Defendant,

_____ *(Name of Defendant)* _____

C. Motion to Exclude Evidence of Computerized Valuations of Plaintiff's Business

NO. _____

	§	IN THE DISTRICT COURT
_____	§	
v.	§	_____ JUDICIAL COURT
	§	
_____	§	_____ COUNTY, TEXAS

Motion to Exclude Evidence of Computerized Valuations of Plaintiff's Business

Comes now _____, Defendant in this cause, and files this, his Motion to Exclude Evidence of Computerized Valuations of Plaintiff's Business, and in support thereof, Defendant would show the Court the following:

1. FACTUAL BACKGROUND

This action arises from an incident in August of 2018, when Plaintiff claims that Defendant removed certain trade secrets from Plaintiff's place of business and used them to benefit Defendant's business and as a result, diminish and devalue Plaintiff's business. Throughout the discovery in this matter, Plaintiff has repeatedly referred to and relied upon computer generated evidence to support his claims regarding the value of his business before August of 2018 and after August of 2018.

By this motion, Defendant seeks an order excluding evidence of computerized valuations of Plaintiff's business or, in the alternative, for a *Frye* hearing regarding the validity of the methodology underlying such computerized valuations.

2. THIS COURT MAY EXCLUDE PREJUDICIAL EVIDENCE IN ADVANCE OF TRIAL BY WAY OF AN IN LIMINE MOTION

The Court has the inherent power to grant a motion in limine to exclude evidence which could be objected to at trial, either as irrelevant or subject to exclusion as unduly prejudicial. *Wackenhut Corp. v. Gutierrez*, 453 S.W.3d 917, 920 n.3 (Tex. 2016); *In re BCH Development, LLC*, 525 S.W.3d 920, 925 (Tex. App.—Dallas 2017, orig. proceeding). Texas Rule of Evidence 403 allows the court to exclude evidence where there is a substantial danger that the probative value will be outweighed by the danger of undue prejudice. *See Diamond Offshore Services Ltd. v. Williams*, 542 S.W.3d 539, 549 (Tex. 2018); *Brookshire Bros. v. Aldridge*, 438 S.W.3d 9, 34 (Tex. 2014).

Moreover, the court may hear and determine the question of the admissibility of evidence outside the presence or hearing of the jury. *See Weidner v. Sanchez*, 14 S.W.3d 353, 363 (Tex. App.—Houston [14th Dist.] 2000, no pet.); *Kendrix v. S. Pac. Transp. Co.*, 907 S.W.2d 111,

113 (Tex. App.—Beaumont 1995, writ denied); Texas Rule of Civil Procedure 166; and Texas Rules of Evidence 103 and 104.

In the instant matter, the jury will be prejudiced merely by hearing any reference to the computerized valuations. Thus, the computerized valuations should be excluded from the trial in this matter.

3.
THIS COURT MAY EXCLUDE THE COMPUTERIZED VALUATIONS, AS IMPROPER SPECULATION

It is improper to provide an opinion to the jury that is based upon speculation or conjecture. *See Cooper Tire & Rubber Co. v. Mendez*, 204 S.W.3d 797, 800 (Tex. 2006); *Coastal Transp. Co. v. Crown Cent. Petroleum Corp.*, 136 S.W.3d 227 (Tex. 2004) (conclusory and speculative expert testimony irrelevant and insufficient to overcome directed verdict motion by opposing party).

Upon information and belief, in the case at bar, without establishing any foundation for the reliability of computerized valuations, Plaintiff will attempt to provide evidence of the valuations to the jury. The Plaintiff should be barred from offering evidence of the computerized valuations, because there is no evidence that they represent anything more than pure speculation. Without the proper foundation to establish the reliability and accuracy of the computerized valuations, they represent pure speculation and must be excluded.

4.
THIS COURT MAY EXCLUDE THE COMPUTERIZED VALUATIONS, AS HEARSAY

The computerized valuations should also be excluded as improper hearsay. Texas case law creates a distinction between computer-generated and computer-stored records. *See Ly v. State*, 908 S.W.2d 598, 599 (Tex. App.—Houston [1st Dist.] 1995, no pet.); *Murray v. State*, 804 S.W.2d 279, 283 (Tex. App.—Fort Worth 1991, pet. ref'd). Computer-generated records are records that are created solely by a computer's internal processing and are not hearsay. *Ly v. State*, 908 S.W.2d 598, 599 (Tex. App.—Houston [1st Dist.]1995, no pet.); *Murray v. State*, 804 S.W.2d 279, 283 (Tex. App.—Fort Worth 1991, pet. ref'd). In contrast, computer-stored records are defined as records that were purposefully and manually entered into a computer, through a human being's selection process, and are hearsay. *See Ly v. State*, 908 S.W.2d 598, 599 (Tex. App.—Houston [1st Dist.] 1995, no pet.); *Murray v. State*, 804 S.W.2d 279, 283 (Tex. App.—Fort Worth 1991, pet. ref'd). Moreover, even if an exception to the hearsay rule applies to the records at issue, they should not be admitted unless there is a foundation provided to indicate their reliability.

Expert testimony should be excluded if there is insufficient proof that the expert's methodology is generally accepted or if it is shown that the methodology is flawed. *Ford Motor Co. v. Ledesma*, 242 S.W.3d 32, 39 (Tex. 2007) (expert testimony is unreliable, and therefore inadmissible, if it is based on unreliable data, or if the expert draws conclusions from his underlying data based on flawed methodology). In addition, an expert cannot merely repeat hearsay statements made by another expert. *See Hooper v. Torres*, 790 S.W.2d 757, 760 (Tex. App.—El Paso 1990, writ denied) (portion of medical report representing summaries of findings by other physicians inadmissible).

Based upon the foregoing, the computerized valuations should be excluded from the trial in this matter, as hearsay.

5.
IN THE ALTERNATIVE, THIS COURT SHOULD HOLD A *FRYE* HEARING TO DETERMINE WHETHER THE COMPUTERIZED VALUATIONS ARE BASED UPON ACCEPTED METHODOLOGY

The authorities, described above, justify the preclusion of computerized valuation reports. In the alternative, this Court should conduct a *Frye* hearing, to determine the level of acceptance of such computerized valuations. *Frye v. United States*, 293 F. 1013 (D.C. Cir. 1923). In fact, an expert's opinion should be excluded if it is not shown to be reliable or to be based upon an acceptable method of proof. *Ford Motor Co. v. Ledesma*, 242 S.W.3d 32, 39 (Tex. 2007) (expert testimony is unreliable, and therefore inadmissible, if it is based on unreliable data, or if the expert draws conclusions from his underlying data based on lawed methodology); *State v. Cent. Expressway Sign Assocs.*, 302 S.W.3d 866, 870 (Tex. 2009) (to be relevant, the expert's opinion must be based on the facts; to be reliable, the expert's opinion must be based on sound reasoning and methodology).

For the foregoing reasons, if the Court declines to enter an order excluding evidence of computerized valuations of Plaintiff's business, then the Court should hold a *Frye* hearing regarding the validity of the methodology underlying such computerized valuations.

6.
CONCLUSION

Based on the foregoing, Defendant respectfully requests that this Court enter an order instructing Plaintiff and his counsel not to mention, refer to, interrogate concerning, or attempt to convey to the fact-finder, in any manner, either directly or indirectly, any of the above-mentioned facts or information, without first obtaining permission of this Court and further, to instruct Plaintiff and his counsel to warn and caution each and every one of his witnesses to follow these instructions. In the alternative, Defendant requests a *Frye* hearing, prior to the admission of any such evidence and prior to the use of any such evidence by counsel for the parties, the parties or the parties' witnesses.

Dated: _____*(Date)*_____

By: _____

_____*(Name of Counsel)*_____

Attorneys for Defendant,

_____*(Name of Defendant)*_____

D. Motion to Exclude Surveillance Video

NO. _____

_____ § IN THE DISTRICT COURT
                       §
v.   § _____ JUDICIAL COURT
                       §
_____ § _____ COUNTY, TEXAS

Motion to Exclude Surveillance Video

Comes now _____, Plaintiff in this cause, and files this, his Motion to Exclude Surveillance Video, and in support thereof, Plaintiff would show the Court the following:

1.
FACTUAL BACKGROUND

This action is based upon a rear end collision, wherein Plaintiff alleges that, on July 18, 2018, her vehicle was struck by Defendant's vehicle, causing her damages, pain, and suffering.

During the discovery of this matter, Defendant disclosed an alleged "surveillance video" of Plaintiff. The video contains five (5) hours of video of a person, purported to be Plaintiff, engaging in a variety of daily activities and tasks. By this motion, Plaintiff seeks an order excluding evidence of the alleged "surveillance video, as speculative, improper character evidence, irrelevant and unfairly prejudicial."

2.
THIS COURT MAY EXCLUDE PREJUDICIAL AND MISLEADING EVIDENCE
IN ADVANCE OF TRIAL BY WAY OF AN IN LIMINE MOTION

The Court has the inherent power to grant a motion in limine to exclude evidence which could be objected to at trial, either as irrelevant or subject to exclusion as unduly prejudicial. *Wackenhut Corp. v. Gutierrez*, 453 S.W.3d 917, 920 n.3 (Tex. 2016); *In re BCH Development, LLC*, 525 S.W.3d 920, 925 (Tex. App.—Dallas 2017, orig. proceeding). Texas Rule of Evidence 403 allows the court to exclude evidence where there is a substantial danger that the probative value will be outweighed by the danger of undue prejudice. *See Diamond Offshore Services Ltd. v. Williams*, 542 S.W.3d 539, 549 (Tex. 2018); *Brookshire Bros. v. Aldridge*, 438 S.W.3d 9, 34 (Tex. 2014).

Moreover, the court may hear and determine the question of the admissibility of evidence outside the presence or hearing of the jury. *See Weidner v. Sanchez*, 14 S.W.3d 353, 363 (Tex. App.—Houston [14th Dist.] 2000, no pet.); *Kendrix v. S. Pac. Transp. Co.*, 907 S.W.2d 111, 113 (Tex. App.—Beaumont 1995, writ denied); Texas Rule of Civil Procedure 166; and Texas Rules of Evidence 103 and 104.

A review of the video shows that there is no time and date stamp to reflect when the video was taken. In order to provide foundation for a surveillance videotape or photographs, without witness testimony, there must be sufficient proof of the reliability and accuracy of the process that produced the images. Tex. R. Evid. 901(b); *Huffman v. State*, 746 S.W.2d 212, 221 (Tex. Crim. App. 1988). Moreover, there is insufficient clarity in the video to determine who is depicted on the video during many portions of the video, making the images misleading and prejudicial. Furthermore, some of the images depict a person alleged to be Plaintiff drinking alcohol at a bar, which is prejudicial and irrelevant to this action and represents improper character evidence. *See, e.g., Nat'l Freight, Inc. v. Snyder*, 191 S.W.3d 416, 424 (Tex. App.—Eastland 2006, no pet.) (probative value of surveillance video showing personal injury Plaintiff in full range of motion with his injured arm simulating inappropriate act, was outweighed by its prejudicial effect; conduct depicted in video was inflammatory, many jurors likely would have been offended by it, and challenged portion of video was only small portion of much longer video showing Plaintiff working in his shop, and one remaining portion of video showed Plaintiff using both of his arms to pick up large object).

Based upon the forgoing facts and circumstances, this Court should enter an order excluding any and all evidence, references to evidence, opinions, testimony, or argument relating to the alleged "surveillance video."

3.
THE "SURVEILLANCE VIDEO" IS SPECULATIVE AND IRRELEVANT TO THIS ACTION

Texas Rule of Evidence 402 states that "evidence which is not relevant is inadmissible." Relevant evidence is defined by Texas Rule of Evidence 401 as "having any tendency to make the existence of any fact that is of consequence to the determination of the action more probable or less probable than it would be without the evidence." *See Torrington v. Stutzman*, 46 S.W.3d 829, 845 n.13 (Tex. 2000). Irrelevant evidence is not admissible. *Morale v. State*, 557 S.W.3d 569, 573 (Tex. 2018); *Diamond Offshore Services Ltd. v. Williams*, 542 S.W.3d 539, 549 (Tex. 2018).

The surveillance video at issue contains five (5) hours of video of a person, purported to be Plaintiff, engaging in a variety of daily activities and tasks. A review of the video shows that there is no time and date stamp to verify when the video was taken. Moreover, there is insufficient clarity in the video to determine who is depicted on the video during many portions of the video, making the images irrelevant and speculative. Furthermore, many of the images on the video have no relationship to any of the facts in issue in this case. Thus, the Court should exclude any and all evidence, references to evidence, opinions, testimony or argument relating to the alleged "surveillance video," as speculative and irrelevant.

4.
CONCLUSION

Based on the foregoing, Plaintiff respectfully requests that this Court enter an order excluding any and all evidence, references to evidence, opinions, testimony or argument relating to the alleged "surveillance video."

Dated: _____(Date)_____

By: _____

_____(Name of Counsel)_____

Attorneys for Plaintiff,

_____(Name of Plaintiff)_____

E. Opposition to Motion for Destroyed or Missing Evidence Instruction

NO. _____

	§	IN THE DISTRICT COURT
_____	§	
	§	
v.	§	_____ JUDICIAL COURT
	§	
_____	§	_____ COUNTY, TEXAS

Opposition to Motion for Destroyed or Missing Evidence Instruction

Comes now _____, Plaintiff in this cause, and files this, his Opposition to Defendant's Motion for Destroyed or Missing Evidence Instruction, and in support thereof, Plaintiff would show the Court the following:

1.
FACTUAL BACKGROUND

This is a tort case arising out of an automobile accident that occurred when Plaintiff's vehicle was struck by the Defendant's vehicle. On March 2, 2018, Plaintiff was driving down Main Street, when he began to cross the intersection at Main Street and Meadowview Drive. Defendant had also entered the intersection at the same time and struck Plaintiff's vehicle as Plaintiff was trying to cross against the traffic light.

Plaintiff instituted this action against Defendant for damages resulting from the accident, claiming that Defendant was negligent when his vehicle struck Plaintiff's vehicle and that his alleged negligence caused Plaintiff's injuries. Defendant's vehicle suffered minimal damage and Defendant was able to continue driving his vehicle. Shortly after the accident,

Defendant's vehicle was stolen. Plaintiff filed a motion for a missing evidence instruction, claiming that Defendant acted in bad faith in allowing his car to be stolen.

This opposition is based upon the grounds that the lost evidence was not the result of bad faith and, therefore, Plaintiff is not entitled to a missing evidence instruction.

2.
PLAINTIFF NOT ENTITLED TO A MISSING EVIDENCE INSTRUCTION

In the case of *Brookshire Bros. v. Aldridge*, 438 S.W.3d 9, 22 (Tex. 2014), the Court found that trial courts have discretion in assessing an appropriate remedy for the destruction or loss of evidence. In accordance with well-settled Texas precedent on remedying discovery abuse, however, the remedy must have a direct relationship to the act of spoliation and may not be excessive. *Brookshire Bros. v. Aldridge*, 438 S.W.3d 9, 22 (Tex. 2014). The submission of an instruction to the jury to presume that the missing evidence would have been unfavorable to the spoliator is "inherently a sanction," even though the purpose of a spoliation remedy is generally to be remedial rather than punitive. *Id.* The spoliation instruction is among the harshest sanctions a trial court may utilize to remedy an act of spoliation and is to be used cautiously. *Id.*

The Texas Supreme Court stated that a party must intentionally spoliate evidence in order for a spoliation instruction to constitute an appropriate remedy. *Id.* As specified by the Court, "a person who merely negligently destroys evidence lacks the state of mind of a 'wrongdoer,' and it makes little sense to infer that a party who only negligently lost or destroyed evidence did so because it was unfavorable to the party's case." *Id.* A court's finding of intentional spoliation is a necessary predicate to the proper submission of a spoliation instruction to the jury. *Id.*

The present case is not one in which the evidence was intentionally destroyed or lost. Defendant could not have foreseen that his car would be stolen, and Plaintiff has presented no evidence of bad faith. The circumstances of this case fall within those circumstances in which a missing evidence instruction should not be given.

3.
CONCLUSION

Based on the foregoing, Defendant respectfully requests that this Court deny Plaintiff's motion for a missing evidence instruction.

Dated: _____ *(Date of Motion)* _____

By: _____

_____ *(Name of Counsel)* _____

Attorneys for Defendant,

_____ *(Name of Defendant)* _____